THE ECONOMICS OF THE EUROPEAN UNION

The Economics of the European Union

Policy and Analysis

SECOND EDITION

EDITED BY

MIKE ARTIS and NORMAN LEE

Oxford University Press

Press, Great Clarendon Street, Oxford OX2 6DP
Oxford New York
nd Bangkok Bogota Bombay Buenos Aires
wn Dar es Salaam Delhi Florence Hong Kong
Kuala Lumpur Madras Madrid Melbourne
Mexico City Nairobi Paris Singapore Taipei Tokyo Toronto Warsaw
and associated companies in
Berlin Ibadan

Oxford is a trade mark of Oxford University Press

Published in the United States
by Oxford University Press Inc., New York

British Library Cataloguing in Publication Data
Data available

Library of Congress Cataloging in Publication Data
The economics of the European Union: policy and analysis / edited by
Mike Artis and Norman Lee.—2nd ed.
Includes bibliographical references (p.   ).
1. European Union.   2. European Union countries Economic policy.
I. Artis, Michael J.   II. Lee, Norman, 1936–   .
HC240.E288   1997   337.1'42—dc21   97–8966
ISBN 0–19–877561–X
ISBN 0–19–877560–1 (Pbk)

3 5 7 9 10 8 6 4 2

Printed in Great Britain
on acid-free paper by
Bookcraft (Bath) Ltd,
Midsomer Norton, Somerset

CONTENTS

Contents

Contents

12. The European Monetary System   330
ROBIN BLADEN-HOVELL

13. European Monetary Union   349
MIKE ARTIS

Contents

LIST OF FIGURES

List of Figures

LIST OF TABLES

List of Tables

LIST OF ABBREVIATIONS

AASM	Association of African States and Madagascar
ACARD	Advisory Council for Applied Research and Development
ACOST	Advisory Council on Science and Technology
ACP	African, Caribbean, and Pacific
AMS	aggregate measure of support
ASI	Agenzia Spatiale Italiana
ATM	Agreement on Textiles and Clothing
BAE	Bureau of Agricultural Economics
BMFT	Federal Ministry for Research and Technology
BTG	British Technology Group
CAD	computer-aided design
CAP	Common Agricultural Policy
CCIR	International Radio Consultative Committee
CEC	Commission of the European Communities
CEEC	Central and Eastern European Country
CEFTA	Central European Free Trade Association
CEPR	Centre for Economic Policy Research
CET	common external tariff
CFCs	chlorofluorocarbons
CFSP	Common Foreign and Security Policy
CI	Community Initiative
c.i.f.	cost, insurance, and freight
CMEA	Council for Mutual Economic Assistance
CNC	computer numerically controlled
CNR	Consiglio Nazionale delle Ricerche
CQS	Community Quota System
COAPRI	Official Association of Industrial Property Agents
CREST	Scientific and Technical Research Committee
CSF	Community Support Framework
CTP	Common Transport Policy
CV	commercial vehicle
DAC	Development Assistance Committee
DFG	German Research Association
DG	Directorate-General
DoT	Department of Transport
DPI	Department of Primary Industry
DRS	domestic rate of substitution
DRT	domestic rate of transformation

List of Abbreviations

EAGGF	European Agricultural Guidance and Guarantee Fund
EC	European Community
ECB	European Central Bank
ECE	Economic Commission for Europe
ECJ	European Court of Justice
Ecofin	Council of Economics and Finance Ministers
ECSC	European Coal and Steel Community
Ecu	European Currency Unit
EDC	European Defence Community
EDF	European Development Fund
EEA	European Economic Area
EEC	European Economic Community
EFTA	European Free Trade Association
EIB	European Investment Bank
ELDO	European Launcher Development Organization
EMCF	European Monetary Cooperation Fund
EMI	European Monetary Institute
EMS	European Monetary System
EMU	European Monetary Union
ENEA	Ente Nationale Energia Atomica
EP	European Parliament
EPO	European Patents Office
EPU	European Payments Union
ER	export refund
ERDF	European Regional Development Fund
ERM	Exchange Rate Mechanism
ERP	European Recovery Programme
ESA	Environmentally Sensitive Area
ESA	European Space Agency
ESCB	European System of Central Banks
ESF	European Social Fund
ESPRIT	European Strategic Programme for Research and Development in Information Technology
ESRO	European Space Research Organization
ETUC	European Trade Union Confederation
EU	European Union
Euratom	European Atomic Energy Community
EUREKA	European Research Coordination Agency
FAST	Forecasting and Assessment in Science and Technology
f.o.b.	free on board
FEOGA	Fonds Européen d'Orientation et de Garantie Agricole
FP1	Framework [programme] 1
FRT	Foreign Rate of Transformation
FTA	Foreign Trade Association
FTA	free trade area

GATT	General Agreement on Tariffs and Trade
GDP	Gross Domestic Product
GNP	Gross National Product
GSP	General System of Preference
HDTV	high-definition television
IATA	International Air Transport Association
ICP	International Comparison Project
IGC	intergovernmental conference
IICA	inter-institutional collaborative agreements
IMF	International Monetary Fund
INFN	Institute Nazionale di Fisica Nucleare
IPR	Intellectual Property Right
IPR	investment premium
IT	information technology
ITCB	International Textiles and Clothing Bureau
JHA	Justice and Home Affairs
JIT	just in time
JRC	Joint Research Centre
JNRC	Joint Nuclear Research Centre
LAC	long-run average cost
LDC	less-developed country
LTA	Long Term Arrangement
MCA	Monetary Compensatory Amount
MDS	Maximum Divergence Spread
MEP	Member of the European Parliament
METS	minimum efficient technical scale
MFA	Multi-Fibre Arrangement
m.f.n.	most favoured nation
MIP	minimum import price
MITI	Ministry of International Trade and Industry, Japan
MMC	Monopolies and Mergers Commission
MPTC	marginal pollution treatment cost
MPV	multi-purpose vehicle
MRD	marginal reduction in damage
MSC	marginal social cost
NACE	Nomenclature Générale des Activités Économiques des Communautés
NAFTA	North American Free Trade Agreement
NATO	North Atlantic Treaty Organization
NGO	non-governmental organization
NIEO	New International Economic Order
NIS	New Independent States
NRDC	National Research Development Corporation
NSI	national systems of innovation
NTB	non-tariff barrier
OCTs	overseas countries and territories

List of Abbreviations

ODA	Official Development Assistance
OECD	Organization for Economic Cooperation and Development
OEEC	Organization for European Economic Cooperation
OFT	Office of Fair Trading
OP	Operational Programme
OPT	outward-processing traffic
PAC	Pollution Abatement and Control
PEG	Production Entitlement Guarantees
PPP	purchasing power parity
PPS	Purchasing Power Standard
PSE	Producer Subsidy Equivalent
R&D	research and development
SDI	Strategic Defense Initiative
SEA	Single European Act
SEM	Single European Market
SME	small and medium-sized enterprise
SMU	Support Measurement Unit
SPD	Single Programming Document
SPRU	Science Policy Research Unit
Stabex	System for the Stabilization of Export Earnings
STU	Swedish Board for Technical Development
Sysmin	System for Safeguarding and Developing Mineral Production
TENS	trans-European networks
TEU	Treaty on European Union
TIP	Technology Integration Projects
TNO	Nederlandse Organisatie voor Toegepast-Natuurweten-Schappelijk Onderzock
UK	United Kingdom
UN	United Nations
UNDP	United Nations Development Programme
UNICE	Union of the Industries of the European Community
VC	Verkenningscommissie
VER	voluntary export restraint
VHSIC	very high speed integrated circuits
VIL	variable import levy
VLSI	very large scale integration
VSTF	very short term financing
WTO	World Trade Organization

LIST OF CONTRIBUTORS

Harvey Armstrong	Professor of Economic Geography, University of Sheffield
Mike Artis	Professor of Economic Policy, European University Institute, Florence
Robin Bladen–Hovell	Professor of Economics, University of Keele
Simon Bulmer	Professor of Government, University of Manchester
David Colman	Professor of Agricultural Economics, University of Manchester
Norman Lee	Senior Research Fellow, University of Manchester
Stan Metcalfe	Professor of Economics, University of Manchester
Lynden Moore	Senior Associate Member, St Antony's College, University of Oxford
Frederick Nixson	Professor of Economics, University of Manchester
David Purdy	Lecturer in Economics, University of Manchester
Deborah Roberts	Research Fellow, Arkleton Centre for Rural Development, University of Aberdeen
Peter Stubbs	Professor of Economics, University of Manchester
Elizabeth Symons	Lecturer in Economics, University of Keele
Jim Taylor	Professor of Economics, University of Lancaster
Nick Weaver	Research Assistant in Economics, University of Manchester
Allan Williams	Professor of Geography, University of Exeter
David Young	Lecturer in Economics, University of Manchester

Introduction

MIKE ARTIS and NORMAN LEE

The momentum towards 'ever closer union' in Europe—despite the setbacks associated with the upheavals in the currency markets in 1992 and 1993—has been little short of impressive. The development of the EC6 to the EC12, the adoption of the 1992 Single European Market (SEM) programme, the inauguration of the European Union (EU) in November 1993 and its subsequent enlargement to fifteen Member States are markers of that progress. As the economic significance and scope of policies decided at the level of the EU have increased and as the integration of the economies of the EU members has proceeded, so the need for sustained study of the development and impact of those policies has grown.

The basic aim of this book is to provide, for the intermediate-level student of economics, a comprehensive account of the economics of the EU. It contains a blend of theory, analysis, and application relating both to the EU as a whole and to a number of its constituent Member States. It is, therefore, intended to be of relevance and interest to university students in all the Member States of the Union.

The political context of the subject under study is of particular importance to its economic understanding and for this reason the first chapter in the book is devoted to a political analysis and history of the EU. The second chapter then sets out key statistical information relating to the economies of the EU and its Member States, together with comparative data for Japan and the USA to provide the broader economic context. The theory of customs unions and preferential trading areas—which is essential to the economic analysis of the European experiment—is laid out in the third chapter. This chapter not only covers classical theory but also takes a critical look at some more recent developments, notably the imperfect competition-based approach used by the European Commission to evaluate the benefits of the Single Market Programme. These three introductory chapters are succeeded by twelve individual chapters which are devoted to the description and analysis of particular policy areas.

Chapter 4 deals with the best-known and, in terms of money spent, much the largest economic policy area of the EU: the Common Agricultural Policy (CAP). It evaluates each of the main agricultural policy instruments which has been used, the reform process, and the future prospects for the CAP. Competition policy within the EU is reviewed in Chapter 5. It commences by examining the rationale for competition, then analyses the competition policies applied in three Member States (the UK, Germany, and France) and, finally, reviews the development of a Union-level competition policy.

Chapter 6 contains an analysis of science and technology policy within the EU. First, it examines the case for government support of science and technology, then it considers national policies for science and technology in Italy, the Netherlands, and Sweden, and, finally, it describes and evaluates the development of a Science and Technology Policy within the EU.

Regional Policy is the subject matter of Chapter 7. It analyses the regional economic disparities within the EU, the case for regional policy at national and Union levels, the policies pursued in different Member States (Netherlands, Germany, the UK, France, Italy, and Spain), and the development and operation of Union-level regional policies.

Chapter 8 deals with the Common Transport Policy (CTP). It examines the structure and growth of the Union and Member State transport sectors, the development of the CTP and its application to the major constituents of the transport sector (road transport, rail and inland waterways, maritime and air transport, and transport infrastructure), and concludes with an overall policy evaluation.

The environmental policy of the EU is reviewed in Chapter 9. It covers the evolution of a Union environmental policy, the economic character of the EU's environmental problems, to which it has to respond, the role of economic and regulatory instruments in dealing with these problems, and possible future developments in policy.

Chapter 10 is concerned with the role of social policy within the EU. To this end a typology of social-policy regimes is presented and explained (traditional, liberal, conservative, and social democratic), which is then used to explain the development of EU social policy and the forces which have constrained its scope.

The commercial policies of the EU *vis-à-vis* third countries are studied in Chapter 11. The discussion analyses the use of non-tariff barriers such as anti-dumping duties and voluntary export restraints (VERs) to limit competition from third countries in certain product areas and describes EU commitments, under the Uruguay Round, to phase out these restrictions. There is a detailed examination of the key areas of protection, ranging from steel and textiles to cars and electronic products.

Prior to the speculative crises of 1992–3, the development of the European Monetary System (EMS) and more particularly the operation of its Exchange Rate Mechanism (ERM) had been accounted without reservation as one of the most successful aspects of the European experiment. The nature of that achievement and the reasons for the collapse of the narrow-band ERM are analysed in Chapter 12. The success of the ERM had been great enough to foster the conception of European Monetary Union (EMU), which is analysed in Chapter 13. This chapter reviews the analytics of monetary union within a cost-benefit framework and goes on to discuss the criteria set out in the Maastricht Treaty for progression to EMU, the position of the Member States in relation to these criteria, and the provisions made in the Treaty for a European Central Bank.

Chapter 14 discusses the evolution of the EU budget, the development and refinement of the 'own-resources' principle for funding the budget, and the resolution of the problem of budgetary imbalance as it affected the UK and Germany. The possibility of introducing a stabilization role for the budget is also examined.

Chapter 15 examines the foreign aid and external assistance afforded by the Member States of the EU and the development of policy at the Union level through the Lomé Conventions.

A set of discussion questions and references appear at the end of each chapter, together with any suggestions for further reading and chapter notes.

It is clearly important that a book such as this should be as up to date as possible and for this reason we plan to issue revised editions every two or three years. In this, the second edition, we have endeavoured to ensure that the analysis and description are as accurate and as up to date as possible. The authors have sought to ensure that their accounts cover events up to at least the end of 1995. However, the ambition to be up to date can be only imperfectly realized in relation to the EU, where events can move very quickly. Indeed it is worth reflecting that, before the next edition of this book is due, the identity should be known of those Member States which have decided to opt for Monetary Union and the adoption of a single currency eventually to be used throughout the Union, a further huge step—if it is realized—in the process of ever-closer union.

Throughout this book, with the exception of Chapter 1, we have used the abbreviation 'EC' to refer to the European Community and 'EU' to refer to the European Union. Hence, historical accounts of the development of policy prior to the Treaty on European Union will refer mainly to the EC, whilst references to more recent and current policy will refer to the EU. (However, in Chapter 1 the abbreviation 'EC' is also used when referring to the economic 'pillar' of the EU.) A full list of the abbreviations used in this book can be found on pp. xv–xviii.

Postscript

As this book is going to press (March 1997) we have the occasion to add a little to the account of the progress of European integration that forms the core of this book.

The most important event not covered in the chapters is the European Summit held in Dublin in December 1996. At that Summit the member countries took the important further step of agreeing upon a 'Stability Pact' to govern the fiscal policies of those countries forming the membership of the European Monetary Union. According to this pact the prospective Member States committed themselves to maintaining a quite restrictive fiscal stance, agreeing to the payment of fines on deficits exceeding 3 per cent of GDP except where these could be shown to be incurred in exceptional circumstances. The significance of this pact is twofold: to begin with, it is the first occasion on which the coordination of fiscal policy among EU Member States has been clearly accepted at the macro-level, in this respect going much further than the previous agreements to harmonize certain taxes or to set the convergence criteria in the Treaty of European Union. Secondly, the restrictive nature of the pact—given the present circumstances in which countries are struggling to achieve the 3 per cent deficit/GDP requirement—provides Germany with another indication of the conversion to a 'stability orientation' in economic policies among her potential partners which may be seen as a requirement for Germany's acquiescence in a European Monetary Union which reaches a large size very quickly.

Paradoxically, though, the probability of European Monetary Union happening 'on time' (in January 1999) began to weaken shortly after the Dublin Summit, and for two reasons. The first reason was the evidence that Germany herself would find it difficult to reach a strict interpretation of the fiscal criteria by 1997; the second was that, by exceptional effort, Italy dramatically improved its own chances of meeting the fiscal deficit criterion. With this, the scenario under which a reason would easily be found to proceed to a two-stage monetary union with a small membership enforced at the first stage by a rigorous interpretation of the criteria, followed by a late entry of Italy and other countries in a second stage, began to crumble. The possibility of a postponement to the calendar for the establishment of EMU was aired in the press. Such a prospect seemed unnerving. It would threaten a massive loss of political momentum and, at worst, might undo the formula under which the EU had agreed to put deeper integration before wider enlargement.

All this goes to confirm once again that the process of integration is a difficult one, beset by all kinds of vicissitudes and set-backs.

CHAPTER 1

History and Institutions of the European Union

SIMON BULMER

1.1. Introduction

On 1 November 1993, after final ratification of the Treaty on European Union (TEU or, colloquially, the Maastricht Treaty), the European Union (EU) came into existence. No great transformation occurred at midnight on 31 October 1993: rather, a further step was taken in the lengthy evolution of post-war European integration. However, an important formal development did occur: the economic activities of the then twelve Member States in the European Community (EC) were subsumed within the wider political context of the EU. This formal change is particularly relevant to explaining the relationship between this chapter and the rest of the book. Over the years, the spotlight has been on the economic activities of the EC. But, increasingly since 1970, other joint activities have been developed, hidden away from public attention—for instance, activities on foreign policy and combating terrorism. The EU brings all the different activities together and places the economic activities of the EC in a wider context. The book is concerned with the economic activities. However, this chapter aims to show how a knowledge of the wider context—historical, political, and institutional—is essential to an understanding of the economic activities.

The peaceful integration of the European national economies has been a development specific to the post-1945 era. The integration of Europe was proposed as early as the fourteenth century, but it was not until the period of economic, political, and military reconstruction following the Second World War that it was put into practice. The form taken by integration was strongly influenced by the historical experiences of its founding fathers. Hence they sought to avoid the excesses of nationalism and of the nation–state system that had been demonstrated by the German Nazi regime. They also sought to open up the national economies as a means of avoiding the protectionism that had characterized inter-war Europe. Poor economic performance was widely perceived to have provided a climate of political instability conducive to the growth of Fascism in Europe.

Economic integration has also been rooted in a particular European geography. This, too, has a historical explanation, namely in the division of Europe through the Cold War. Thus the history of economic integration in the EC, until the 1990s at least, is *West* European history. Only with the collapse of Communism in Eastern and Central Europe at the end of the 1980s did the EC need substantively to develop economic relations with the other half of the Continent.

If the division of Europe has major contextual importance to economic integration, so in particular does the division of one state, Germany. After the Second World War France was concerned that the revival of the German coal and steel industries might trigger expansionism. The principal objective of the European Coal and Steel Community (ECSC) was to allay fears of a 'military–industrial complex' fuelling renascent German nationalism. The roots of economic integration through what we may call the 'Community method' (see below) thus lay in the need to find a political solution to the turbulent past of Franco-German relations.

There are many other ways in which historical circumstance has shaped the pattern of economic integration. In particular, it can explain the tortuous way in which the UK has come to grips with the integration process, as a reluctant participant seeking to come to terms with its 'descent from power'. Similarly, the persistence of non-democratic forms of government in Greece and on the Iberian peninsula isolated those states from the EC until their domestic political transformation permitted membership, as part of a second wave of enlargement in the 1980s.

Thus history has conditioned the process of economic integration. But what of the politics and institutional framework of economic integration? These, too, are important.

Economic integration has not evolved as the result of some functional logic. Nor has it developed as the result of some 'natural' economic law enforced by Adam Smith's 'invisible hand'. Functional and economic determinism fail to explain both the setbacks to integration and the relaunches; economic integration has not been a smooth process following some scientific logic. Rather, it has been dependent upon political and institutional dynamics.

At the level of the major integration developments—from the Schuman Plan creating the ECSC to the signature of the TEU in 1992—the need to create a package deal satisfying the participants' national interests has been paramount. Without satisfying all Member States, no deal can be achieved. However, where the agreement amounts to a new treaty or a treaty amendment, even consensus between the member governments may be insufficient. The French National Assembly's actions in August 1954 led to rejection of the European Defence Community Treaty and the collapse of that initiative. More recently, the Single European Act (SEA) was subject to referenda in both Denmark and the Irish Republic before it could be implemented from July 1987. The need to satisfy domestic political concerns was demonstrated most dramatically with the Maastricht Treaty—the TEU. The Danes' need to hold a second referendum following the Treaty's initial rejection by a narrow margin of voters in June 1992; the successful referenda in the Irish Republic and in France; and the tortuous ratification process during 1992–3 in the UK House of Commons: these all demonstrated the contingency of treaty amendments on domestic politics. Thus major integrative developments require not only agreement between the member governments but an ability on the part of the latter to ensure domestic approval.

On a more routine level, integration may be less publicly politicized. However, the political dynamics of policy-making are no less important. The EU is not like the many international organizations on the world stage. Uniquely amongst European and international organizations, it has supranational characteristics. These are concentrated overwhelmingly in the institutional arrangements concerning the economic 'pillar' of activity. It has its own body of law which has direct effect in the Member States, and takes precedence over national law. It has institutions with autonomy from the Member States. The most prominent of these are: the European Commission, which serves as an executive civil service: a parliamentary assembly which has been directly elected since 1979; a European Court of Justice (ECJ) which makes rulings on matters of law. Balanced against these three are two powerful institutions representing the interests of the member governments, namely the Council of Ministers and the European Council. The former is comprised of national ministers; the latter of heads of government or state. The EU is not like other international economic organizations in a further respect—namely, in the way that economic integration has been a continuing process of evolving goals from the first steps undertaken with the ECSC to the TEU and beyond.

Above all, however, it must be remembered that economic integration has never been an end in itself. It has always served as a means towards the end of political integration. The ECSC involved the integration of the coal and steel sectors as a means towards Franco-German reconciliation and towards creating a new system of post-war European relations. Similarly, an important motivating factor for some states, in particular France, in negotiating the TEU was to strengthen integration in the context of German unification in 1990. The French government feared that a more powerful Germany might become less predictable in European politics; it sought to pre-empt this through closer integration. These political objectives set the path towards the EU apart from the paths of more modest organizations, such as the European Free Trade Association (EFTA).

In reviewing the history of the EU, we explain the key developments summarized in Table 1.1. To do so, we need to commence with the situation in 1945, at the end of the Second World War.

Table 1.1. **Key stages in the development of the European Union**

Year	Key developments
1951	Treaty of Paris is signed, bringing the European Coal and Steel Community into effect from 23 July 1952. Membership comprised Belgium, the Federal Republic of Germany, France, Italy, Luxembourg, and the Netherlands.
1957	Treaty of Rome is signed, bringing into effect the European Economic Community and the European Atomic Energy Community from 1 January 1958.
1965	Merger Treaty is signed, with the effect of merging the principal institutions of the three communities from 1967. Henceforth the three communities are known collectively as the European Community.
1973	Denmark, the Irish Republic, and the UK join the EC on 1 January.
1981	Greece joins the EC on 1 January.
1986	Spain and Portugal join the EC on 1 January. The Single European Act is signed, coming into effect on 1 July 1987, and introduces the first systematic revisions to the founding treaties.
1992	Treaty on European Union is signed (following broad agreement in December 1991 at a meeting in Maastricht in the Netherlands). It entails systematic revisions to, and extension of, the existing treaties. Following ratification, the TEU comes into effect on 1 November 1993. Within the European Union, the EC represents one 'pillar' of activities: the others relate to foreign and security policy; and justice and home affairs.
1995	Austria, Finland, and Sweden join the EU on 1 January.

1.2. Economic integration in historical and political perspective

Why European cooperation and integration?

Although European integration was not an idea new to the post-1945 era, it was propelled initially by a distinctive 'mix' of circumstances and impulses. These comprised

- the defeat of Nazi Germany and of the Axis powers;
- the wish to avoid a repeat of the excesses of nationalism and of the nation-state system by creating a new system of European international relations;
- the economic dislocation caused by wartime destruction;
- the emergence of two global superpowers with competing political and economic ideologies;
- the division of Europe and the wish in the West for security from the Soviet threat;
- the need to base Western security and defence on economic reconstruction and well-being; and

- the desire for Franco-German reconciliation as the bedrock of stability within Western Europe.

In short, European integration was motivated by political, economic, and security considerations.

The protagonists of cooperation and integration were by no means of one view on how to address these issues. *Federalists* placed primary emphasis on the superseding of the nation state with a larger democratic structure. Their roots were frequently in the European resistance movements, and, in 1944, at a meeting in Geneva, they had already drawn up a plan for a federal European order based on a written constitution.

A second category of protagonists may be termed *functionalists*. Like the federalists, they were strongest in continental Europe, but they lacked the federalists' organization. They shared the federalists' objective of a united Europe but adopted a more pragmatic approach to its realization. They saw the need for economic cooperation as a starting-point for achieving their political goals. The Frenchman Jean Monnet was the most prominent figure in this camp. Other political figures, especially from the Low Countries, shared this approach. By 1944 the exiled governments had already agreed on the establishment of Benelux, a customs union to comprise Belgium, the Netherlands, and Luxembourg.

A third category may be termed the *nationalists*. Although they did not display nationalism in its negative sense, these figures did not see any need to participate in a new political order. The nationalists were strongest in those Member States which had either escaped invasion during the Second World War or had remained neutral, and fiercely retained national political traditions. Hence they were strongest in the UK, Scandinavia, the Irish Republic, and Switzerland.

For the UK, the allied victory was seen as the source of heightened pride in national institutions; it had, moreover, galvanized relations with the USA. The resultant 'special relationship', together with the Commonwealth, represented powerful alternative poles of attraction for post-war UK foreign policy. Both the main parties in the UK opposed participation in any integration schemes which would jeopardize national sovereignty.[1] Winston Churchill, regarded in continental Europe as one of the protagonists of a federal Europe, was most supportive of integration when out of power. Moreover, he saw the UK's relations with the strongest protagonists as 'with them but not of them'. The nationalists were prepared to participate in a number of European organizations, but these were characterized by cooperation between sovereign nation states. It was not until the 1960s that the position began to change, as nationalists came to realize that this approach offered very limited opportunities for joint policy action.

A final set of protagonists—and one which must not be forgotten—was comprised of *external actors*. Essentially this was the political élite of the USA. The US position was to support cooperation and integration, both through exhortation and through financial and political assistance. The European Recovery Programme (ERP), popularly known as the Marshall Plan, played a major role in facilitating economic reconstruction. US leadership within the North American Treaty Organization (NATO) provided the security framework within which economic integration could flourish.

By the early 1950s a small group of six Member States had emerged that had shared objectives and a willingness to sacrifice national sovereignty to achieve them. These were the states which launched the process of supranational integration (see Table 1.1). A wider group—which also included these six—was willing to cooperate on various economic, political, or security-policy goals. However, states in this group were unwilling to go further. It was the different response to post-war circumstances on the part of the six which led them to favour *supranational integration*, whereas the wider group was unwilling to go beyond *intergovernmental cooperation* between sovereign states. Accordingly, the European organizations established in the post-war period tended either to be limited to cooperation or to entail the formal transfer of sovereignty that characterizes supranational integration.

The international organization of the West European economies

The first attempt to organize the European economies in the post-war period was made with the establishment in 1947 of the Economic Commission for Europe (ECE), created under the auspices of the United Nations. However, its pan-European nature was to be its undoing, for the emergence of the Cold War rendered it unworkable as a body aimed at facilitating the reconstruction of Europe as a whole. From this point onwards we are concerned with Western European integration. The Eastern European economies were brought together in the Soviet-led Council for Mutual Economic Assistance (CMEA), which was set up in 1949.

The emergence of the Cold War overshadowed cooperation and integration at the end of the 1940s. In consequence, this was a period where the USA showed leadership in promoting West European developments. The scene was set when President Truman pledged US support for 'free peoples who are resisting attempted subjugation by armed minorities or by outside pressures'. The specific trigger for the 'Truman Doctrine' had been Communist destabilization in Greece, but the declaration was a broader commitment to contain Communism.

The Marshall Plan was announced in June 1947. The US Administration recognized that the objectives of the Truman Doctrine could best be attained if Europe's democracies were based on sound economies. Hence the initiative made by Secretary of State George Marshall was a response to the continued economic dislocation and food-rationing in Western Europe. Although notionally offered to all European states, Marshall aid was in fact accepted only by those in the West.

In defence policy the counterpart to the Marshall Plan was the signature, in April

1949, of the Atlantic Charter which created NATO as the principal organization for the defence of Western Europe. The USA was to play the leading role in NATO.

US leadership was not confined to the European arena. The principles of *international* monetary cooperation had already been established at the Bretton Woods conference of 1944 which led to the establishment of the International Monetary Fund (IMF) and the World Bank. In October 1947 the General Agreement on Tariffs and Trade (GATT) was created, providing the guiding principles of liberalization in the trade arena, namely through tariff reductions. The economic principles embodied in these organizations were to have an important impact on economic cooperation within Western Europe.

The first step towards economic integration came at the start of 1948 with the creation of the Benelux customs union, complete with the introduction of a common customs tariff. Benelux was to serve as a precursor to the European Economic Community (EEC).

Of wider geographical significance was the foundation, in April 1948, of the Organization for European Economic Cooperation (OEEC). This was the organization entrusted with implementing the Marshall Plan. Disbursement of US aid was very much a matter to be organized by the European states themselves through the OEEC and its key governing body, the Council of Ministers. The OEEC was essentially an intergovernmental organization, characterized by cooperation between states. It ensured fulfilment of the US condition that reconstruction should be coordinated, and that tariff reductions should be implemented. Its activities were concentrated on facilitating the reconstruction of the national economies, and reducing quotas on interstate trade and tariffs. Under its umbrella were established other, more specialized, bodies and arrangements such as the European Payments Union (EPU). Established in 1950, the EPU was designed to facilitate a multilateral system of payments for trade until initial liquidity problems were alleviated.

The OEEC, having overseen the task of reconstruction, was succeeded in 1961 by the Organization for Economic Cooperation and Development (OECD), an agency no longer confined to the West European economies. The OEEC and Marshall aid had facilitated the construction of an economic platform, upon which supranational integration could be founded.

For some states the OEEC was not enough. It neither took on ambitious tasks nor had any political component. The May 1950 Schuman Plan was an attempt by France to seize the reins of integration and take a different direction. Conceived as a Franco-German scheme, it was nevertheless open to other states to join. However, there was a condition: the principle of supranationalism, i.e. of relinquishing national power, had to be accepted. This precondition (and other factors) had the effect of ensuring that the UK did not participate in the negotiations.

The Schuman Plan, named after the French foreign minister, had in fact been elaborated by Jean Monnet. Its principal concern was with ensuring that reconstruction in the western part of Germany should not endanger peace. The heavy industries of the

Ruhr had been under allied control, but this could not continue indefinitely. The proposed arrangements were also welcomed from the German side, for they offered a route to its regaining control over its key industrial sectors, as well as to international rehabilitation.

Thus the Schuman Plan was an explicitly political proposal; it offered a breakthrough into supranationalism; and it followed a functional approach of sectoral integration but with wider objectives in view. These features have come to characterize the 'Community method' of integration. The plan was favourably received in Belgium, the Netherlands, Luxembourg, and Italy as well as in France and West Germany. These six states were to form the sole participants in the Community method until 1973 (see Table 1.1).

Before the ink was dry on the April 1951 Treaty of Paris, which established the ECSC, proposals had already been made for further integration in the shape of a European Defence Community (EDC). Conceived at the height of the Cold War, and with an eye upon the hostilities in Korea, the EDC proposal was designed to facilitate the rearmament of Germany through supranational control, since a German contribution was seen as indispensable to West European security. The French National Assembly's failure, in August 1954, to ratify the Treaty represented the first setback to supranational integration. Germany rearmament was achieved in May 1955, when the intergovernmental Western European Union commenced operations.

Those favouring further supranational integration were undeterred by this setback. The reasons for French non-ratification were varied but did not represent a rejection of supranationalism. Rather, there was a feeling that a supranational defence community was proceeding too far too fast. The death of Stalin and the end of the Korean War had also reduced the urgent need for the EDC. By 1955 new ideas were being floated for developing integration beyond the coal and steel sectors. Milward (1992: 120) points out that these proposals were not an attempt to relaunch integration *after* the failure of the EDC. Moves for a wider European customs union had already been mooted.

The forum for initial discussions on the proposals, which were advanced in particular by the Benelux countries, was to be the Messina conference of June 1955. This was attended by the foreign ministers of the EC6. The proposed areas for further integration comprised the creation of a common market (i.e. beyond the coal and steel sectors), a common transport policy, and integration in the energy sector. These ideas received broad support, and, in consequence, a committee of governmental representatives was set up, chaired by the Belgian Paul-Henri Spaak.

The UK was invited to participate in the negotiations; it accepted the invitation but then withdrew from the Sparak Committee, once again because of outright opposition to the proposed supranational form of integration. Negotiations between the EC6 were quite protracted, because of several thorny issues, and some matters were barely resolved by the time the EEC Treaty was finalized. Hence the Treaty contains quite limited indications as to the direction to be taken in the integration of agricultural policy and social policy. Nevertheless, negotiations during 1956 and early 1957 led to the two

Treaties of Rome: the EEC Treaty and the Treaty establishing the European Atomic Energy Community (Euratom). They were signed on 25 March 1957. Following ratification, they came into effect from the start of 1958.

One further development must be referred to before examining the three European Communities in more detail. Having withdrawn from the Spaak Committee, the UK government began to reappraise its policy. Following a UK initiative, a committee was set up in the framework of the OEEC to examine the creation of a European free trade area. Although the resultant report deemed such a development feasible, there was considerable suspicion on the part of the EC6 that the UK initiative was designed to undermine their much more ambitious plans for a common market and a supranational political system to supervise it. It was only once the Treaties of Rome had come into effect, and the EC6 had gone their own way, that the negotiations on a free trade area gained momentum. They culminated in the signing, on 4 January 1960, of the Stockholm Convention creating the European Free Trade Association (EFTA). The founding members were the UK, Norway, Denmark, Sweden, Austria, Portugal, and Switzerland.

EFTA was a classic intergovernmental forum for economic cooperation. There was no threat to national sovereignty. As such, it suited the instincts of UK politicians. EFTA was centred around trade in industrial goods; agriculture was largely excluded. As a free trade area, each Member State was free to set its own external tariff. This enabled the UK to continue its trading relations with the Commonwealth countries.

Until the 1970s the EC6 and the 'EFTAns' comprised two distinct camps within Western Europe. With the first EC enlargement of 1973, it was agreed to reduce tariff barriers on industrial trade between the two groupings. By the late 1980s a much closer relationship was proposed: the European Economic Area (see below).

The two camps corresponded quite neatly to the two different political approaches to integration that were identified earlier. The EC6 comprised those states which were prepared to transcend the nation state by means of supranational integration. By contrast, EFTA was composed of those states which preferred more limited arrangements and the maintenance of national sovereignty. How, then, did integration through the Community method shape the form of integration pursued by the EC6?

Integration through the community method

The ECSC

The ECSC, which commenced operations in July 1952, was the starting-point of the Community method of supranational integration. Its provisions were set out in the Treaty of Paris, which runs to 100 articles. The ECSC had three key features.

First, it proposed a degree of economic integration that went beyond anything developed in the other existing European organizations. It was not concerned with the lowest level of economic integration (a free trade area) but with the higher goal of a common market, albeit confined to the coal, steel, and related sectors. Nevertheless, given that these sectors were then regarded as the 'commanding heights' of the economy, the ECSC was concerned with core activities of the EC6. The ECSC's chief aims were to ensure security of supplies through the removal of quotas and customs duties over a five-year transitional period; the rational expansion and modernization of the industries; and the provision of mechanisms for managing serious shortages or gluts. The ECSC sought to restrict Member States' use of discriminatory state subsidies and it provided a common external commercial policy relating to the two sectors.

It is worth pointing out that the economic philosophy behind the Treaty of Paris was more interventionist than that behind the later EEC Treaty. This *dirigisme* owed much to the influence of the French; it was no coincidence that the author of the Schuman Plan, Jean Monnet, was head of the French Commission for Economic Planning. Moreover, the Treaty of Paris spelt out most of the detailed arrangements, thus reducing the need for secondary legislation. The ECSC's activities were financed by levies on coal and steel production.

The second key feature was that these detailed arrangements were subservient to the political goal of providing a framework for Franco-German reconciliation. One indicator of the success of this was the relatively smooth reintegration of the Saar into (West) Germany in 1956, after some ten years effectively under French control.

The third key feature, and central to the Community method, was the set of strong, supranational central institutions associated with the ECSC. These provided a model which was later employed for the EEC and Euratom.

The ECSC comprised five institutions:

- the executive, known as the High Authority (equivalent to the European Commission of today);
- the Council of Ministers, comprising representatives of the member governments;
- the Consultative Committee, consisting of representatives of employers/industry, trade unions, and consumers concerned with the ECSC's activities;
- the Assembly, composed of a total of sixty-eight delegates from the six national parliaments;
- the European Court of Justice (ECJ).

These institutions were all located in Luxembourg, thus explaining why some services of the EU are located there.

The High Authority had a considerable degree of autonomy in carrying out the tasks entrusted to the ECSC. It was headed by nine members who were appointed from the Member States but were to act independently in carrying out their duties. Fittingly, the first president of the High Authority was Jean Monnet. Beneath the 'members'—equivalent to present-day EU commissioners—the High Authority was staffed by an independent civil service. The independence of the High Authority and its staff from the national governments was a characteristic of the supranational approach to integration.

A Council of Ministers was created to allay the concerns of the Benelux countries. They were worried that the ECSC might be dominated by French and German interests. They were also concerned that the High Authority might pursue an excessively *dirigiste* form of economic policy. The Council of Ministers was thus a check against the realization of these worries. Although a check on supranationalism, the Council could not be compared with similar bodies in, for example, the OEEC. This was because the ECSC Council was able, under specified circumstances, to take decisions by qualified majority voting and simple majority, as well as by the conventional method of unanimity.[2]

The Consultative Committee and the Assembly were much less important institutions, confined to advisory roles. The ECJ, however, had a more important function. It was responsible for adjudicating on disputes relating to the ECSC's activities.

In operation, the ECSC was regarded initially as successful. Production and interstate trade in coal and steel increased markedly, although how much of this could be attributed to the ECSC's existence is open to question. The initial success was followed by a period of less progress. The coal crisis towards the end of the 1950s was caused by falling demand owing to cheap oil imports. The High Authority's attempt in 1959 to declare a 'manifest crisis' in the coal industry, so as to obtain powers of intervention in the market, failed because it could not obtain the necessary majority in the Council of Ministers. The ECSC was regarded as having failed its first real test. This was the first of numerous challenges by national interests to the supranational principles of the Community method. It indicated that the ECSC was not so supranational in practice as it was designed to be.

The ECSC retained its separate existence until implementation of the Merger Treaty in 1967. This resulted in the High Authority's absorption into the EC Commission. The Assembly and the ECJ had already been shared with the other Communities from 1958. The Consultative Committee continues to retain its separate identity.

Following the creation of the EEC and the merger of the three European Communities, activities based on the ECSC Treaty have tended to be overshadowed. In the coal sector activities have concentrated on combating the effects of declining demand. A more effective role has been hampered by the absence of clear provision for an EC energy policy. There has been greater prominence in the management of surplus capacity in the steel sector, where severe problems emerged in the 1980s.

Euratom

The Treaties of Rome expanded the area of joint activity considerably. Of the two, the Euratom Treaty was of much less significance. It was largely the product of French pressure. France had begun to develop a civilian nuclear programme and saw Euratom as a way of obtaining financial support for its extension and of developing a market for French technology.

In fact, Euratom was rather a failure. Differences between the Member States resulted in Euratom having little control over the development of the nuclear sector. Measures have been undertaken on health and safety in the nuclear industry, to promote joint research, and so on, but the core activities of civilian nuclear power have remained in the hands of the Member States.

The EEC

The establishment of the EEC was a most significant development in supranational integration. The ECSC's model of identifying functional bases for joint policy was continued. European integration retained a political objective, although no longer centrally concerned with fears of renascent German power; and the EEC Treaty followed the supranational model already established, albeit in a moderated form.

The activities and arrangements covered by the EEC Treaty can be seen from a summary of its structure (see Table 1.2). The EEC's policies are considered in detail in succeeding chapters. Remarks here are confined to general observations; an outline of the institutions of the EU is given later in the chapter.

The EEC Treaty was distinctly more market-oriented in ideology, compared to its rather *dirigiste* predecessor, the ECSC. Accordingly, the centrepiece of the Treaty was the creation of the common market. The deadline for removing interstate tariffs was set down in the Treaty as 31 December 1969, but this had already been achieved by 1 July

Table 1.2. **Contents of the EEC Treaty**

Contents		Articles
Preamble		
Part One.	Basic principles	1–8
Part Two.	Foundations of the Community	
Title I.	Free Movement of Goods, including creation of the customs union, elimination of quantitative restrictions	9–37
Title II.	Agriculture	38–47
Title III.	Free Movement of Persons, Services, and Capital	48–73
Title IV.	Transport	74–84
Part Three.	Policy of the Community	
Title I.	Common Rules, including on competition policy, state aids, tax provisions, and the harmonization of laws	85–102
Title II.	Economic Policy, principally the commercial policy	103–16
Title III.	Social Policy	117–28
Title IV.	The European Investment Bank	129–30
Part Four.	Association of Overseas Countries and Territories	131–36
Part Five.	Institutions of the Community	
Title I.	Provisions Governing the Institutions	137–98
Title II.	Financial Provisions (concerning the EEC budget)	199–209
Part Six.	General and Final Provisions	210–28

Note: The details relate to the 1957 EEC Treaty. They do not incorporate changes introduced by subsequent treaty amendments.

1968. The deeper economic integration associated with creating a common market is still being implemented in the 1990s. Only once all the Single European Market (SEM) legislation is fully in force—and this did not occur magically at midnight on 31 December 1992—will the goal of a common market have been achieved in full.

If the greater market orientation signalled a decline in French influence on negotiations, this was redressed by the EEC's Common Agricultural Policy (CAP). The French made agricultural provisions a prerequisite for agreement to the Treaty, although this was not their priority from the start, as conventional wisdom has it. It is also worth noting that the agricultural 'title' of the Treaty does not specify the highly regulated and protectionist policy which the CAP became. This was the product of secondary legislation—i.e. subsequent legal acts implementing the principles set down in the Treaty. A further area of the Treaty which particularly reflected French interests was Part Four, conferring associate status on colonies and former colonies of the EC6. The arrangement ensured minimal disruption to France's existing trading patterns.

One or two policy areas provided for in the EEC Treaty have not had the impact that one might assume from their presence in it (see Table 1.2). Transport-policy developments were minimal until the 1980s. Similarly, the social-policy provisions were of a very limited nature, and it was not until the end of the 1980s that attempts were made to extend their range. Finally, it is worth drawing attention to one of the final provisions of the Treaty, Article 235. This article states: 'If action by the Community should prove necessary to attain, in the course of the operation of the common market, one of the objectives of the Community and this Treaty has not provided the necessary powers, the Council shall, acting unanimously on a proposal from the Commission and after consulting the Assembly, take the appropriate measures.' The importance of Article 235 is that it has facilitated EC action beyond the immediate provisions of the Treaty. For example, the EC12 used Article 235 to agree four environmental-action programmes before they were given explicit constitutional authority to do so in the SEA (see Chapter 9)!

A final observation relating to the overall shape of the EEC Treaty is that it was principally concerned with setting policy principles. By contrast, the ECSC Treaty itself provided most of the detailed arrangements for the supranational governance of the coal and steel sectors. With the exception of the provisions relating to the establishment of the customs union and to the institutions, the EEC Treaty provided only a framework. Thus a vast amount of secondary legislation has been necessary in order to put into practice the Treaty's objectives.

The 1960s: consolidation and challenge

The period from 1958 to 1969 may be seen as one of consolidation and challenge. The consolidation derived from making progress in putting the EEC Treaty into operation. The challenge was provided by General de Gaulle. He became president of the Fifth

French Republic in 1958, in the first year of the EEC. Attempting to re-establish French credibility after the instability of the Fourth Republic, he sought to rebuild the prestige of the nation state. This put him on a collision course with the supranational EEC.

Putting the customs union into operation was achieved early, as already noted. The institutions were put into practice, although the (enlarged) Assembly and the ECJ were shared from 1958 with the ECSC and Euratom. The first president of the EEC Commission, Walter Hallstein, was a forceful individual and gave that institution activist leadership. In 1965 the first constitutional amendment was agreed: the Merger Treaty, which came into effect in 1967.[3] This merged the three Communities, with the creation of a single Commission being the principal result. The Treaties were not merged, however, and a few features remained distinct, such as the separate budgetary provisions for the ECSC.

A number of important legal developments occurred during the 1960s, also with a consolidating effect. These emerged in judgments on specific cases brought before the ECJ but that had wide-ranging implications and strengthened the EC's supranational character. Two cases were of particular importance. In its 1963 judgement on the *Van Gend en Loos* case, the ECJ established the principle of direct effect, i.e. that EC law confers both rights and duties on individuals that national courts must enforce. The effect of this was to make it possible for private individuals or companies to use the national courts to oblige governments to implement treaty provisions. Had this principle not been established, in what was an expansionist judgment on the part of the ECJ, progress towards the common market would have been much more difficult. The ECJ has made a number of major judgments facilitating the creation of the internal market. However, it cannot make these judgments until a case is referred.

A second important legal principle, that of the primacy of EC law over national law, was also established in the 1960s: a feature which had not been specified in the Treaty. This principle was enunciated in *Costa* v. *ENEL* (case 6/64) and in other ECJ judgments. The effect was to reinforce the supranationalism of the EEC. Added to the earlier case establishing the principle of direct effect, this facilitated a process of integration through law. So, whilst the 1960s are often characterized as a period of resurgence in national interests, as demonstrated by the 1965 crisis (see below), important legal developments were under way which had the opposite effect. They have also been of major importance in the realization of the economic objectives set out in the treaties.

Consolidation was also achieved through the translation of treaty objectives into secondary legislation. This was particularly necessary in the agricultural sector, for the whole regulatory structure of the CAP had to be introduced. Given the level of French interest in this policy area, it is not surprising that this was one of the principal battlefields for de Gaulle's assault on supranationalism.

De Gaulle's policy was based on a nation-state-centred view of world politics, and his particular wish was to strengthen French grandeur. His policy generated three specific flashpoints regarding the development of integration. The first resulted from his proposal for a 'Political Union'. Far from being an attempt to advance supranational integration, this was to be organized along traditional intergovernmental lines. The other Member States regarded it as a threat to the successful supranational Community method. His proposal failed. The second occurred as a result of a reconsideration by the United Kingdom of the merits of membership. The Conservative government of Harold Macmillan had already applied for membership in 1961. Applications were also made by Ireland, Denmark, and Norway. However, in a dramatic move, de Gaulle unilaterally rejected the UK application (and by extension the others) at a press conference in January 1963. De Gaulle clearly did not want competition from the UK for the leadership of the EEC. His actions irritated the other five governments both procedurally and substantively. In 1967 he vetoed the second UK application, this time made by the Labour government of Harold Wilson.

The third and most dramatic clash came with the 1965 crisis. Its immediate cause was the creation of the system for financing the CAP. Hallstein sought to link this provision with the creation of a self-financing, or 'own-resources', EEC budget. For de Gaulle, Hallstein was becoming too much like a government head. In addition, a step towards budgetary autonomy was a further (for de Gaulle, undesired) reinforcement of supranationalism. In the background, but at least as important, was the projected 1966 introduction of qualified majority voting in the EEC Council of Ministers. This was also regarded by de Gaulle as a major threat to national sovereignty, for that would mean that French interests could be overridden in the Council. The result was that in June 1965 France withdrew from the workings of the Council of Ministers. It was not until January 1966 that a solution was found in the so-called Luxembourg Compromise. While this had no status in EC law, it established the convention that, on matters of 'vital national interest' to one or more Member States, discussions would continue until consensus had been reached. The Luxembourg Compromise was important in practice, for it led to integration being dictated by the pace of the most reluctant Member State.

The result of the Luxembourg Compromise was a slowing-down of decision-making in the Council of Ministers. The need to satisfy all national interests contrasted with what was supposed to happen, namely decisions being taken by qualified majority vote. The Commission became less ambitious and the Community's supranationalism was in decline. This situation was not really reversed until the 1980s and the SEA. The Luxembourg Compromise is now considered to have been superseded in the economic domain of integration.

Revival through summitry

It was not until de Gaulle's resignation that the political will of the EC could be revived. Even so, Gaullist ideas continued to influence the policies of his successor as president, Georges Pompidou. Pompidou initiated a meeting with the heads of government of the other five states. Designed to give the EC new momentum, the summit initiated a number of developments:

- the opening of negotiations for enlargement of the EC;
- re-examination of the financing of the budget;
- the creation of a system of foreign-policy cooperation; and
- the drafting of proposals for an Economic and Monetary Union.

The enlargement negotiations were successful and, on 1 January 1973, the UK, the Irish Republic, and Denmark joined the EC. Norway, which had negotiated its terms of entry, rejected membership in a referendum held in September 1972. An 'own-resources' system was introduced for the EC budget through two treaty amendments (1970 and 1975). The new system was fully operational from 1980. A foreign-policy cooperation procedure was set up in 1970 and has developed considerably over the intervening period. Finally, the Economic and Monetary Union initiative was launched as a response to currency instability in the EC at the end of the 1960s. The proposals failed because of the collapse of the Bretton Woods international monetary system and the impact of the 1973 oil crisis.

Subsequent summits in 1972 and 1974 were less successful, although providing some initiatives. The 1972 Paris summit, for instance, placed environmental policy on the EC's agenda. The 1974 summit, again held in Paris, was more noteworthy. On the institutional front there were two key achievements. The first of these was agreement to the principle of holding direct elections to the European Parliament (EP). This distinctly supranational step, aimed at giving European parliamentarians their own source of democratic legitimacy, was first put into practice with elections in 1979. The second was the agreement to hold regular summit meetings, known as the European Council, at least twice each year. In the period since 1975 'most of the major political decisions in the EC have been taken in the European Council' (Bulmer and Wessels 1987: 2). The main policy decision was agreement on the establishment of the European Regional Development Fund (ERDF).

With two former finance ministers at the heart of the European Council—Chancellor Schmidt of Germany and President Giscard d'Estaing of France—it was scarcely surprising that international monetary affairs should feature strongly at its meetings. Thus in 1978 Schmidt launched the initiative for the European Monetary System (EMS) at the Copenhagen European Council. After elaboration of its operation by a group of three experts, it came into effect in March 1979. It was to be one of the main achievements of this period.

The period from 1979 to 1984 was dominated by the UK budgetary problem. Mrs Thatcher's Conservative government was intent upon achieving a lasting solution to what it perceived as an inequitable system. It had been anticipated from the outset of membership that the EC's own resources budget would not favour the UK (see Scott 1992). However, the economic recession induced by the oil crisis resulted in few of the predicted trade benefits of membership accruing to the UK. It was only after protracted negotiations that a settlement was reached at the Fontainebleau European Council in 1984.

This agreement was part of a typical 'package deal' of EC negotiations. Not only did the meeting provide a solution to the UK budgetary crisis, increase the size of the budget, and provide for limited CAP reform, it also decided to look at the institutional structure of the EC, the start of the process leading to the SEA. A further part of the package was to give approval in principle to Spanish and Portuguese enlargement. The two states joined on 1 January 1986; Greece had joined from the start of 1981. The southern enlargements were motivated essentially by political considerations—namely, the wish to strengthen these new democracies, for the three states' economies were at a relatively low level of development.

The SEA and renewed dynamism

The SEA was signed in February 1986 and came into effect on 1 July 1987. It had been negotiated within an intergovernmental conference (IGC) under the supervision of the European Council. The SEA's significance was that it amounted to the first comprehensive revision of the treaties. The motivations for it included:

- a recognition of the need to overcome the 'Eurosclerosis' that had characterized the EC economy compared with its global competitors;
- a wish to provide a stimulus to the European economy by means of the liberalization associated with completion of the internal market;
- a wish to bring the treaties into line with actual practice in the EC;
- a wish to relaunch supranational integration because of a realization that decisional weakness had impeded the collective interest; and
- a recognition of the need to make the EC more politically responsive if the Iberian enlargement were not to create political sclerosis.

The content of the SEA can be divided into two—namely, the policy and the institutional provisions. The policy developments took two broad forms. Some of the treaty revisions were largely concerned with formalizing the EC's competence—for example, in environmental policy, 'monetary capacity', and research and technology policy. In these cases the treaty revisions gave clearer competence for EC action. The codification of foreign-policy cooperation, including enhanced institutional provision, had a similar effect, but this development was contained in a separate part of the SEA. The main contribution of the SEA, arguably, was to making the single market programme achievable. Already agreed to in June 1985, this programme had been set out in a Commission White Paper, *Completing the Internal Market*, drawn up by the UK commissioner, Lord Cockfield. The White Paper was based on a threefold strategy:

- a relatively small legislative programme (under 300 items) aimed at setting the essential requirements, by the end of 1992, for completion of the internal market;
- reliance on the principle of mutual recognition of national product standards as established in ECJ landmark decisions, especially the 1979 *Cassis de Dijon* case; and
- the 'new approach' of devolving decisions on creating new European standards from the Council to standard-setting agencies.

To this programme the SEA contributed by including provision for increased use of qualified majority voting in the Council of Ministers, thereby limiting the obstacles to achieving the White Paper's legislative programme.

Other institutional changes comprised increased provision for qualified majority voting in other policy areas, increased powers for the EP, and the creation of the Court of First Instance as a means of alleviating the backlog of work facing the ECJ. Initially regarded as rather modest in nature, the SEA succeeded in developing renewed momentum for integration, not least by the establishment of the 'end-1992' deadline for completion of the SEM.

In the aftermath of the SEA, the European Council became concerned with various 'flanking measures', especially relating to economic and social cohesion. The first of these became important in the negotiations surrounding the 'Delors' package'—a set of measures designed to help the less-developed EC economies, and those regions suffering from industrial decline, to contend with the competitive challenges posed by the SEM. Agreement was finally reached at the 1988 Brussels summit to provide the finance for such measures, including through new restrictions on CAP spending. The wish to avoid the SEM being developed at the cost of declining social provision lay behind the so-called Social Charter. This whole area remains highly contested, as symbolized by the UK government's refusal to sign the charter at the December 1989 European Council in Strasbourg. Subsequently, in the negotiations leading to signature of the TEU in 1992, the UK secured an opt-out of the Social Protocol, an arrangement designed to put the Social Charter into practice.

The momentum for integration was maintained by a revival of interest in European Monetary Union (EMU), culminating in the June 1988 decision of the European Council to establish a committee under the chairmanship of Jacques Delors to report on its feasibility. The subsequent Delors Report, and the broad support to take discussion of EMU further (a position not shared by the UK government), contributed to the wish to engage in a further round of constitutional reform which culminated in the Maastricht negotiations and the TEU.[4]

The TEU

Whilst the initial momentum for reform was largely attributable to EMU, this was rapidly joined by other major political impulses. These derived from the collapse of

Communism in Eastern Europe and the new role expected of the EC in international relations after the Cold War. There was also a recognition that the number of applications for EC membership would consequently increase, and that work should commence on reforming the institutions to facilitate an effective political process within a Community of some twenty members. German unification in October 1990—creating the EC's first enlargement without formal accession—reawakened strong concerns about German power. For some states, especially France, the solution lay in containing this power through the deepening of European integration. Hence the support of its government and of President Mitterrand for the goal of EMU. Finally, there was a wish, as with the SEA, to tidy up constitutional provisions and make substantive policy changes beyond EMU.

The resultant Treaty, which was finalized at the Maastricht European Council in December 1991, had been prepared by two parallel IGCs. The structure of the Treaty is usually described as resembling a temple. Hence the 'roof' sets out various broad objectives in the so-called 'common provisions'. The roof is located on three pillars. The first pillar consists of the EC activities, i.e. comprising the three Communities as further enhanced by the TEU itself. The second pillar provides what is to be called a Common Foreign and Security Policy (CFSP). The third pillar covers Justice and Home Affairs (JHA), i.e. police cooperation, combating drug-trafficking and fraud, regulating immigration from third countries, and similar matters. The policies contained in the last two pillars are given greater prominence than before, and are strengthened but retain an intergovernmental basis under the TEU. Finally, the plinth of the 'temple' detailed relationships with the existing treaties, ratification arrangements, and so on. There are also eighteen protocols (e.g. the UK 'opt-outs' on EMU and the new social-policy provisions) and over thirty declarations.

The first of these pillars is of principal importance to economic integration. Once again the new provisions can be divided into policy provision and institutional provision. The most prominent policy development concerned the conditions and timetable set for achieving EMU by the end of the 1990s. In return for agreement to this, the economically weaker Member States insisted on the creation of a Cohesion Fund to enable resource transfers to their economies; this was also provided for. The EC12 had sought to give a treaty base to the substance of the Social Charter, but the situation was clouded by the UK opt-out. There were numerous other policy developments—for instance, on the EU's infrastructure, consumer protection, and industrial policy.

In order to put the institutional aspects of the TEU into context, attention is now turned to policy-making in the EC pillar.

1.3. **Economic integration and its policy-making context**

Economic integration is heavily dependent on legislation. Legislation takes one of two forms. *Regulations* are used chiefly to legislate on quite technical matters. They have direct effect in the Member States. *Directives* are used where there are different national traditions and it is felt more appropriate just to legislate on the objectives of policy. National legislation must then be enacted in order to translate these goals into national law. A third legal instrument is the *decision*. This is not so much a method of legislating as one of taking administrative decisions, such as on competition policy cases. A decision of this kind may be no less significant, especially if it imposes a substantial fine on a company in breach of European competition law. Resort to *recommendations* is another option to legislation but these do not have binding effect; they are not part of EC law.

To explain how legislation is developed, attention is first of all paid to the various EU institutions. Then brief attention is turned to other policy actors.

The EC's structure comprises three supranational institutions which are independent of the national governments—namely, the Commission, the European Parliament (EP), and the European Court of Justice (ECJ). As a counter-balance there are two powerful institutions comprising representatives of the national governments: the European Council and the Council of Ministers.

The *Commission* consists since the 1995 enlargement of twenty members (commissioners), with specific portfolios. The commissioners are appointed by the national governments but are then expected to detach themselves from national loyalty. Each commissioner has a group of political advisers to act as his or her 'eyes and ears'; they constitute the commissioner's 'cabinet'. One commissioner is appointed president and there are two vice-presidents. The five larger Member States (France, the UK, Germany, Spain, and Italy) have two commissioners each (see column three of Table 1.3). The Commission is divided into Directorates-General (DGs), which deal with specific policy areas. In 1996 there were twenty-three DGs as well as specific services, such as the legal and translation services. The overall staffing of the Commission exceeds 18,000 but only about 12,000 fulfil executive and policy functions, once translation and scientific research centre staff are discounted.

In the economic policy domain (the EC 'pillar' of the EU) the functions of the Commission are:

- the proposal of legislation;
- mediating between governments to achieve agreement on legislation;
- management of technical details of policy;
- representing the EU, particularly in commercial policy negotiations (for instance within GATT);
- acting as the defender of collective EU interests;
- acting as guardian of the treaties by ensuring that EC law is upheld.

Table 1.3. **The Member States' weightings in the EU institutions**

Member State	Qualified majority votes in Council	No. of Members of the European Parliament	Commissioners	Population (m.)
Austria	4	21	1	8.1
Belgium	5	25	1	10.1
Denmark	3	16	1	5.2
Finland	3	16	1	5.2
France	10	87	2	58.0
Germany	10	99	2	81.6
Greece	5	25	1	10.4
Ireland	3	15	1	3.6
Italy	10	87	2	57.1
Luxembourg	2	6	1	0.4
Netherlands	5	31	1	15.4
Portugal	5	25	1	9.4
Spain	8	64	2	39.2
Sweden	4	22	1	8.8
UK	10	87	2	58.2
TOTAL	87	626	20	370.7

The Commission's strength has varied over the years but achieved particular influence under the presidency of Jacques Delors (1985–94). The Commission's influence is challenged most when national interests are in the ascendant, and Delors's successor, Jacques Santer (1995–), has had to contend with just such ascendancy. Under the terms of the TEU, Santer and his team were subject to the approval of the EP. From 1995 commissioners have five-year terms, to coincide with the electoral periods of the EP.

The *European Parliament*, originally known as the Assembly, consists of members (MEPs) who, since 1979, have been directly elected by Member States on five-year mandates.[5] Following the 1995 enlargement, the number of MEPs was fixed at 626 (for the composition, see Table 1.3). Their election normally takes place at five-year intervals (most recently, June 1994). Turn-out for EP elections remains low by comparison with national elections. The EP plenary sessions are held in Strasbourg for twelve week-long sessions each year. Meetings of its committees, which generally 'shadow' one or more of the Commission's DGs, are held in Brussels.

The EP has ways of calling to account the Commission and, to a much lesser degree, the Council of Ministers. It has the power to dismiss the Commission but has never done so. Its chief contribution to EU policy-making is through the legislative process. However, its influence is dependent on the policy area, for the latter determines the extent of its procedural rights.

- Under the consultation procedure, which originally applied to all legislation, the EP merely gave its opinion and had no effective sanction over the real decision-making agency, the Council of Ministers.

- Under the 1970 and 1975 budget treaties the EP gained important powers in this policy area, including the power to reject the budget outright.

- Under the SEA the assent of the EP is needed in respect of the accession of new Member States and for Association Agreements with third countries. The TEU extended this procedure.

- The SEA also introduced the cooperation procedure, as a result of which certain legislation undergoes two readings in the EP. This allows the EP to propose amendments or even reject legislation but such decisions may be overruled by the Council of Ministers under specified circumstances. Ten treaty articles, including Article 100*a* relating to the SEM, afforded the EP these powers. Under the TEU this procedure now covers eighteen articles.

- Following the TEU the EP gained a new co-decision procedure (Article 189*b*, EC).[6] This is similar to the cooperation procedure except that the EP has the additional power to reject; thus it can kill legislation taking this route. It applies to fifteen areas but some of these, e.g. the internal market, were formerly subject to the cooperation procedure.

The picture, as will be gathered, is highly complex but reflects a gradual extension to the EP of new powers, which that institution uses to full effect (see Jacobs, Corbett, and Shackleton 1995).

The *European Court of Justice* consists of fifteen judges and nine advocates-general. The ECJ does not formulate policy but, in line with provisions in the treaties for referral, the ECJ's judgments on matters relating to the interpretation and application of EC law are cumulatively of great importance to the operation of the EU. The ECJ is assisted by a Court of First Instance.

The *Council of Ministers* consists of ministers of the Member States. It meets about 100 times per annum but in different guises according to the subject matter. Hence the Council of Agriculture Ministers deals with the CAP, the Council of Economics and Finance Ministers (Ecofin) with matters such as the EMS, EMU, and so on. These two Councils, along with the Council of Foreign Ministers, meet most frequently. Meetings are chaired by one of the Member States, which holds the 'presidency' of the Council for a six-month period. The UK last held this post July–December 1992. The presidency has become an important office facilitating the EU's operation. Meetings of the Council are prepared by the Committee of Permanent Representatives and an associated committee system. These meetings are attended by national civil servants and aim to pave the way for political agreement by the Council.

The Council is empowered to take decisions by qualified majority rather than unanimous vote in a number of policy areas. This was provided for in the original EEC Treaty but majority voting was rarely practised due to the Luxembourg Compromise.

The *practice* of majority voting increased first from the 1970s, following treaty changes relating to the budget, then following the SEA. The TEU has extended provisions still further but there remains a preference for decision-making with the consent of all governments. The dynamism of the Council of Ministers determines the effectiveness of the EU. The increased provision for majority voting assisted the EU's decision-making speed, particularly to meet the 1992 deadline for the SEM. Each Member State has to recognize that it will, on occasion, be in the minority, with a negative effect on its national sovereignty. The Council of Ministers is no longer a classic intergovernmental body owing to the departure from unanimous voting.

The exact weighting of the individual Member States is as set out in column one of Table 1.3. A vote by qualified majority requires at least sixty-two votes of the total of eighty-seven. As can be seen, the number of votes over-represents the small states, since Luxembourg receives one vote for approximately every 200,000 inhabitants, whereas Germany receives one vote for about every eight million of its population! Put another way: France, Germany, the UK, and Italy represent more than two-thirds of the EU's population but under half of the votes in the Council. This issue has become contentious in the 1990s, since recent and projected enlargements involve smaller states, so that the weighting of the larger ones is decreasing and may do so further unless reform of the voting system is agreed.

The *European Council* has, since its establishment in 1974, become a very powerful body. Comprised of the fifteen heads of state or government, the fifteen foreign ministers, the Commission president and a vice-president, it has had a hand in all the major EU decisions in the intervening period (the creation of the EMS, agreement on the single market, supervision of the SEA and TEU negotiations, decisions on enlargement, reform of the budget, and so on). The European Council meets at least twice a year. Its decisions are political; transposition into EC law is left to the Council of Ministers. The European Council is important to the strategic development of the EU and of other joint activities (i.e. the other two 'pillars' of the TEU). It is the principal institution of the EU, being common to all three pillars of activity. It has become a major 'media event', however, which can detract from its efficiency.

A number of additional institutions also exist. The Economic and Social Committee, a kind of parliament of interest groups, is consulted on most economic policy legislation but is overshadowed by the EP. The TEU created a Committee of the Regions. Its role reflects the increased involvement of subnational government in EU activities, most notably in regional policy. The Commission has sought to allay concerns that it is a centralizing agency by promoting links with regional authorities, some of which have important powers in their domestic context.

Surrounding the EU institutions are numerous lobby groups. There are thought to be some 500 such groups, which chiefly focus their activities on the Commission. The Commission is comparatively open to such lobbying, not least because it has no field agencies in the Member States; hence it needs information. Thus lobbies are an important part of the decision-making framework.

The result of all this is that policy-making consists of a dense network of contacts. The nature of the contacts depends on the precise form that policy-making takes in the area concerned (e.g. which procedure in the EP; what type of voting in the Council?), as well as on the efficiency of lobby groups (and there may be several in competition with each other). The increasing complexity of policy-making led to calls during the ratification of the TEU for greater openness and more decentralization of power following the so-called subsidiarity principle.[7]

Two characteristics of the EU's institutional structure unify the complex structure. First, the predominant style of policy-making is a regulatory one: it provides a *framework* for economic and political action that is largely left to the Member States themselves to enact and administer. The lack of large-scale supranational budgetary resources reinforces this regulatory approach at the expense of macro-economic or redistributive activities. A characteristic of regulatory politics is the conduct of policy-making in relatively closed groups of policy specialists. Thus, if decision-making at the more routine level has a relatively low profile, this does not mean that the political dynamic is absent; rather, it is present in discussions between specialist national civil servants, Commission officials, interest group representatives and committee members of the EP.

Secondly, national interests still loom large in these technical discussions. Thus behind an apparently technical debate about standardizing axle weights for heavy goods vehicles may stand national motor industries with different interests, governmental authorities faced with divergent financial implications for road improvement programmes, and so on. However, at the technical level individual national interests are often challenged. The increased utilization of qualified majority voting can mean that decisions can be reached against the wishes of a minority of governments, and enforced by EC law, which takes precedence over national law. What is important here, then, is that there are *supra*national interests challenging national ones. The supranational institutions - the Commission, the ECJ and the EP—have their own power resources and these often come into play at the technical level.

1.4. The EU in the 1990s

The EU has an extensive agenda for the 1990s. This agenda can be seen in terms of the issues of widening and deepening the EU.

The deepening of integration is a major task. The TEU embodied quite considerable plans for deepening: notably EMU, the strengthening of social policy (albeit excluding the UK), and some strengthening of budgetary transfers (the Cohesion Fund). Moreover, the TEU did not satisfy all Member States, so it contained a commitment to hold a further IGC in 1996 to consider additional treaty revisions. On the other hand, the ratification of the TEU revealed serious resistance to further integration in some

Member States, notably Denmark, the UK, and France. One common strand to this was a perceived remoteness of integration from the general public, engendered as a result of the essentially élite-driver route that integration has taken. The deepening of integration was also challenged by the speculative attacks against the EMS in 1992 and 1993. These developments raised serious questions about attaining the goal of EMU, which remains the key aspect of future deepening of the EU.

Despite these setbacks the EU pressed ahead with its reform programme and the 1996 IGC was opened in March of that year in Turin. Its objectives have been moderated considerably from what had originally been expected. It has now become concerned with institutional reform and improvements to the functioning of the CFSP and JHA pillars of the EU. Even the proposed institutional reforms were watered down, thus looking inadequate to accommodate a widened EU of perhaps twenty-seven Member States at the start of the next millennium.

Just as in the period leading to the 1973 enlargement, deepening has been linked to widening.[8] Already, Austria, Finland, and Sweden made up an EFTAn enlargement of the EU in 1995.[9] Originally these states had sought a closer economic relationship by negotiating, together with other EFTA members, an arrangement known as the European Economic Area (EEA). However, these states then opted for greater political involvement with the EU and eventually became full members. The EEA consequently has very limited importance, since it only comprises three states (Iceland, Liechtenstein, and Norway).

A Turkish application has been deemed problematic but negotiations are due to open with two 'micro-states', Cyprus and Malta, once the 1996 IGC is complete. A much greater challenge for the EU is presented by eastern enlargement. At the front of the queue are the Czech Republic, Hungary, and Poland. Other Central and Eastern European states have negotiated Europe Agreements which are designed to culminate in membership: Bulgaria, Estonia, Latvia, Lithuania, Romania, Slovakia. A further agreement with Slovenia is expected to be finalized during 1996. The Europe Agreements are designed to align the states with the EU's economic and legal practice but also entail dialogue on foreign-policy matters.

An eastward enlargement presents fundamental challenges for the EU. Not only are there major disparities in economic performance but some existing policies, notably the CAP, will require major surgery in order to be viable in a pan-European EU. It also remains to be seen how all the Central and East European states fare in economic restructuring (including with EU aid) and in developing a secure liberal-democratic underpinning. Further challenges lie ahead for the institutions. It is already problematic finding twenty portfolios for European Commissioners; the current system will require reform in order to facilitate enlargement. Similarly, with small and 'micro' states waiting in the wings, the qualified majority voting system must be reformed in order that larger states have sufficient weight in decision-making (see above).

The agenda of the 1990s thus provides the EU with a full workload. European integration has certainly not reached 'the end of history'. New political and economic challenges must be addressed. One development which looks likely is the emergence of differentiated integration: some states look likely to move ahead faster than others in certain policy areas, such as EMU. A uniformity of integration looks less likely in an EU of approaching thirty Member States.

Discussion questions

1. How far has economic integration within the EU been subordinated to the achievement of political objectives?

2. How far has the ceding of sovereignty to supranational institutions influenced the course of economic integration within Europe?

3. 'The shape of the EU's institutions reflects the need to harness national and common interests to the pursuit of specific policy goals.' Do you agree?

FURTHER READING

For accounts of the history of European integration, see Pryce (1987), Dinan (1994), and Urwin (1995). On the institutions, see Keohane and Hoffmann (1991), Sbragia (1992), and Nugent (1994). For an explanation of the treaties, see Church and Phinnemore (1994). Laffan (1992), Bulmer and Scott (1994), and Wallace and Wallace (1996) contain more thematic or theoretical discussion of particular areas of integrations. Bainbridge and Teasdale (1995) is a useful reference guide, whilst Duff *et al.* (1994) looks in detail at the 'Maastricht agenda' of the EU.

NOTES

1. The history of the UK's relationship to integration cannot be dealt with in detail here. For an account, see George (1994). For an interpretation, see Bulmer (1992).

2. Qualified majority voting is a system whereby the importance of larger countries in relation to smaller ones is reflected in voting through the assignment of a weighting. This system continues to operate: see the chapter on the Council of Ministers in Nugent (1994).

3. It is from this date onwards that one can refer to 'the EC', i.e. referring to the three Communities. However, where reference is made to the specific treaty provisions, it is necessary to refer to the community concerned.

4. For consideration of various aspects of the treaties, see the three articles by Artis (1992), Corbett (1992), and Nugent (1992).

5. When states join the EU between elections, they elect their MEPs at the earliest opportunity for terms of office expiring on the date of the next EU-wide elections.

6. Somewhat confusingly, the EEC Treaty was renamed the EC Treaty as part of the TEU reforms. Separate treaties remain for the ECSC and Euratom.

7. The subsidiarity principle calls for collective solutions within the EU only where the national level cannot provide them. However, some see subsidiarity as a call for power at the regional, sub-national level.

8. On the issue of enlargement, see Michalski and Wallace (1992).

9. Once again Norway had applied for membership but then its electorate voted against it in a referendum of November 1994.

REFERENCES

Artis, M. (1992), 'The Maastricht Road to Monetary Union', *Journal of Common Market Studies*, 30/3: 299–309.

Bainbridge, T., and Teasdale, A. (1995), *The Penguin Companion to European Union* (London: Penguin Books).

Bulmer, S. (1992), 'Britain and European Integration: of Sovereignty, Slow Adaptation and Semi-Detachment', in S. George (ed.), *Britain and the European Community* (Oxford: Oxford University Press), 1–29.

—— and Scott, A. (1994) (eds.), *Economic and Political Integration in Europe: Internal Dynamics and Global Context* (Oxford: Blackwell).

—— and Wessels, W. (1987), *The European Council: Decision-Making in European Politics* (Basingstoke: Macmillan).

Church, C., and Phinnemore, D. (1994), *European Union and European Community* (Hemel Hempstead: Harvester Wheatsheaf).

Corbett, R. (1992), 'The Intergovernmental Conference on Political Union', *Journal of Common Market Studies*, 30/3: 271–98.

Dinan, D. (1994), *Ever Closer Union: An Introduction to the European Community* (Basingstoke: Macmillan).

Duff, A., Pinder, J., and Pryce, R. (1994) (eds.), *Maastricht and Beyond: Building the European Union* (London: Routledge).

George, S. (1994), *An Awkward Partner: Britain in the European Community*, 2nd edn. (Oxford: Oxford University Press).

Jacobs, F., Corbett, R., and Shackleton, M. (1995), *The European Parliament* (London: Cartermill Publishing).

Keohane, R., and Hoffmann, S. (1991) (eds.), *The New European Community: Decisionmaking and Institutional Change* (Boulder, Colo.: Westview Press).

Laffan, B. (1992), *Integration and Cooperation in Europe* (London: Routledge).

Michalski, A., and Wallace, H. (1992), *The European Community and the Challenge of Enlargement*, 2nd edn (London: Royal Institute of International Affairs).

Milward, A. (1992), *The European Rescue of the Nation-State* (London: Routledge).

Nugent, N. (1992), 'The Deepening and Widening of the European Community', *Journal of Common Market Studies*, 30/3: 311–28.

—— (1994), *The Government and Politics of the European Union* (Basingstoke: Macmillan).

Pryce, R. (1987) (ed.), *The Dynamics of European Union* (London: Croom Helm).

Sbragia, A. (1992) (ed.), *Euro-Politics: Institutions and Policymaking in the 'New' European Community* (Washington, DC: The Brookings Institution).

Simon Bulmer

Scott, A. (1992), 'Fiscal Policy' in S. Bulmer, S. George, and A. Scott (eds.), *The United Kingdom and EC Membership Evaluated* (London: Pinter Publishers), 45–56.

Tsoukalis, L. (1993), *The New European Economy: The Politics and Economics of Integration*, 2nd edn. (Oxford: Oxford University Press).

Urwin, D. (1995), *The Community of Europe*, 2nd edn. (Harlow: Longman).

Wallace, H., and Wallace, W. (1996) (eds.), *Policy-Making in the European Union* (Oxford: Oxford University Press).

CHAPTER 2

The European Economy

MIKE ARTIS and NICK WEAVER

2.1. Introduction

The primary purpose of this chapter is to provide the reader with a statistical illustration of the basic economic features of the European Union (EU) and its constituent members. Some comparisons between the EU as whole and the USA and Japan and a brief examination of some possible future entrants to the EU are also made.

Whilst such a statistical picture of the European economy is useful, some discussion of economic policy is essential. Whatever problems there have been with the Treaty on European Union (TEU) (the 'Maastricht Treaty')—the 'No' vote in the Danish referendum, the refusal of the UK negotiators to accept the Social Chapter, the crisis in the Exchange Rate Mechanism (ERM), and the doubts over the single currency—the authors think it is likely that the approach adopted there will continue to dominate the European policy-making agenda over the next few years. To this end a discussion of the convergence criteria advanced in the TEU is presented in the final part of this chapter.

Statistics such as those presented in the first part of this chapter are often simply reproduced on the assumption that their meaning is unambiguous. This assumption is not always safe. An effort is, therefore, made to explain something about the nature of the statistics themselves as well as the information they convey about the world.

In producing a statistical picture it is always difficult to decide what to include and how it should be presented. Presenting data relating to all variables of interest, for all the countries, for all the years, could easily result in an information overload. The approach taken here is to present figures and tables illustrating the major economic indicators in the most recent years for which a complete and consistent data set is available and to look at the behaviour of some of the variables over a longer period.

2.2. Population

The populations of the EU15 and of the US and Japan for 1996 are shown in Fig. 2.1.

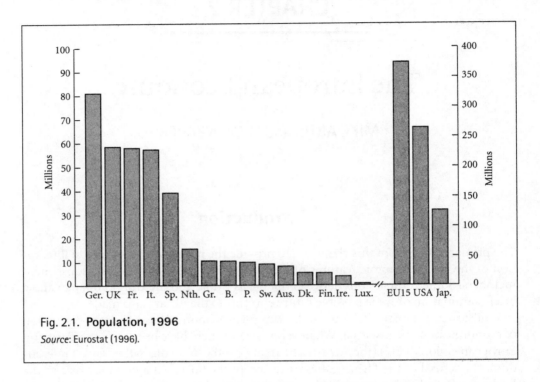

Fig. 2.1. **Population, 1996**
Source: Eurostat (1996).

The population of the EU, at over 375 million, is greater than that of either of the other major economies; the USA's population is 265 million and Japan's is only 125 million. The situation is, however, not static, with several Mediterranean, Central and Eastern European countries currently negotiating admittance to the EU, and the USA attempting to establish the North American Free Trade Agreement (NAFTA) with Canada and Mexico.

In terms of population the most notable feature of the EU's constituent members is that most of the population live in just a few big countries. Roughly 80 per cent of the people live in just five countries: Germany, France, Italy, the UK, and Spain. The remaining smaller countries—the Netherlands, Greece, Belgium, Portugal, Sweden, Austria, Denmark, Finland, Ireland, and Luxembourg—together account for less than 20 per cent.

It is difficult to make any broad statements about population densities, but it is possible to discern a London–Milan axis around which are areas of relatively high density (more than 100 inhabitants per square kilometre). In contrast, much of Spain and

Portugal, south and central France, the Irish Republic, Denmark, Sweden, Finland, and Greece outside the major urban centres, is relatively sparsely populated (less than 100 inhabitants per square kilometre).

2.3. **National Income and Expenditure**

There are various ways of measuring the size of an economy, with Gross Domestic Product (GDP) being the most commonly quoted. The GDP measure includes all goods and services for final consumption which are produced by the economic activity of producer units resident in an economy. It is a territorial measure. The other measure that is often used is Gross National Product (GNP). This measures the income earned by domestic citizens regardless of whether they earn their income at home or abroad. GNP equals GDP plus net property income from abroad. In fact there is only a small difference between GDP and GNP for most of the members of the EU and for both the USA and Japan.

A note of warning needs to be sounded about the use of either GDP or GNP as unqualified indicators of the size of an economy. Even in countries with advanced statistical services, a large part of human activity goes unrecorded. Accounting techniques are not available to measure the value of unmarketed production (such as housework or DIY activities) nor to provide estimates of the costs of pollution and environmental destruction. Tax evasion and moonlighting give rise to a substantial 'black economy'. In 1987 Italy, in response to evidence of the massive extent of under-reporting of economic activity, revised its GDP estimate upwards by 18 per cent and similar forthcoming adjustments to the figures for Belgium, Greece, and Portugal may add a similar amount to their economies. Despite the fact that the absence of broader measures has for a long time been recognized as a serious problem, progress in this area is only slowly being made and as yet there is no widely available alternative to GDP and GNP that is consistently reported.

In order to make international comparisons, GDP, which is initially calculated in terms of domestic currency, needs to be re-expressed in terms of some common or *numeraire* currency. Internationally this is usually done in terms of the US dollar, although any currency can be used. Increasingly within the EU the European Currency Unit (Ecu) is being used. The Ecu is a composite currency, based on a basket of the EU's currencies (see Chapter 12 for more details).

However, the use of market exchange rates when making international comparisons has been criticized on the grounds that it gives rise to a systematic bias (Gilbert and Kravis 1954). Market exchange rates do not necessarily reflect the amount of goods that can be bought with a currency—that is, the purchasing power of a currency in terms of a volume of goods. This is because the market exchange rate is the result of a whole variety of forces including not only the supply and demand for foreign exchange required to match the flows of real goods and services but also the speculative activities of for-eign-exchange dealers, capital flows, and so on. To the extent that these factors do not influence the purchasing power of the currency in a country, the market exchange rate will not be a good measure of the purchasing power of a currency in a country.

Various ways have been proposed to get around this problem. One simple method, proposed by *The Economist*, is the use of the 'Big Mac' index. This uses the relative prices of Big Macs in two countries to construct a new exchange rate. Big Macs are used because they are a standardized commodity whose price is widely known. However, price level differences between countries vary for different commodities and a more sophisticated measure, using a similar principle to the Big Mac index but taking into account a larger basket of goods, is required. Purchasing power parity (PPP) estimates attempt to do just this, their aim being to try to get rid of the difference in price levels to enable a comparison of the quantities or volumes that can be purchased.

The measures of PPP used in this chapter, Purchasing Power Standard (PPS), are produced by Eurostat (the EU's Statistical Office), which calculates them using meth-ods established by the International Comparison Project (ICP) of the United Nations. They are calculated on the basis of a list of products chosen for their representativeness and comparability. For each product a price ratio is established and a weighted average across all the products in the list can then be formed for each country. These weighted average price parities give an alternative (PPP) set of exchange rates which can be applied to the original national currency estimates of GDP to give PPP estimates of GDP. A scaling procedure ensures that the EU's total GDP in PPSs is the same as in Ecus.

Fig. 2.2 shows GDP at current market prices both in billions of Ecu and in PPS for each of the fifteen EU countries and offers a comparison of the EU and the USA and Japan. It can be clearly seen that a comparison of the relative sizes of the countries is influenced by whether market exchange rates or PPS measures are used.

In terms of GDP(PPS) the dominance of the five biggest EU economies—Germany, France, Italy, the UK, and Spain—is again clear. Together they account for roughly 80 per cent of the total GDP of the fifteen Member States.

GDP per capita

Scaling GDP by population gives us GDP per capita figures. Fig. 2.3 shows GDP per capita in both PPS and Ecus. Here the effect of adjusting the GDP figures for PPS is clear. All the countries having a below-EU-average per capita income (the UK, Italy, Ireland, Spain, Portugal, and Greece) are in real terms richer than would appear to be the case if market exchange rates, instead of some measure of PPPs, were used. This is the systematic bias that Gilbert and Kravis noted. The spread is still considerable, with the GDP(PPS) per capita in the richest country—Luxembourg—being roughly twice that in the poorest—Greece. In terms of the more populous countries, Germany, France, and Italy are above the EU average and the UK and Spain below it.

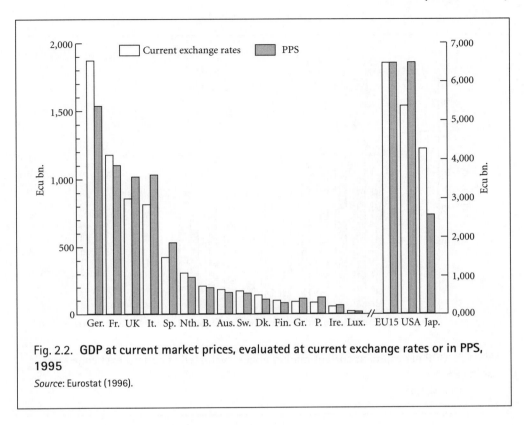

Fig. 2.2. GDP at current market prices, evaluated at current exchange rates or in PPS, 1995

Source: Eurostat (1996).

Economic growth

In addition to looking at the static picture that the statistics discussed above provide, it is interesting to look at how the economies have grown. To study the change over time it is again necessary to abstract from price changes so that comparisons in terms of volumes can be made. Volume measures of GDP, broadly constructed from volume indices of production, are the appropriate measure. The implicit GDP deflator is calculated as the ratio of the nominal measure of GDP to the volume measure.

Having constructed a series of figures for GDP in terms of constant prices, various methods may be used to calculate the growth rate of GDP over a period of years. Simple methods involve either comparing the first observation with the last or calculating a series of annual growth rates and then finding an average. Another popular method uses the continuous compounding formula. Both these methods have drawbacks, in particular their sensitivity to the choice of the period chosen.

A preferable method might be to find the slope of a trend line fitted through the data. This is done by regressing the natural logarithm of GDP on time and an intercept, $Ln\,GDP_t = \alpha + \beta t$. The coefficient, β, gives the trend annual growth rate. The advantage

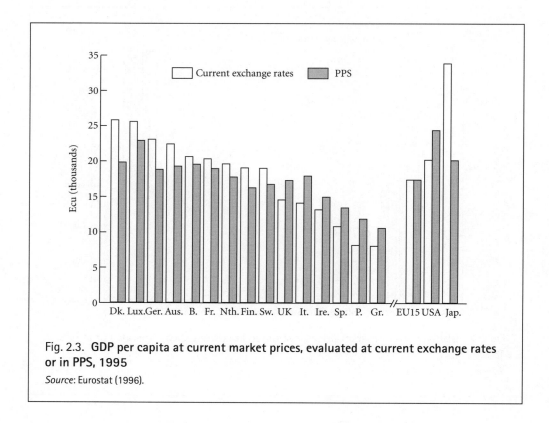

Fig. 2.3. **GDP per capita at current market prices, evaluated at current exchange rates or in PPS, 1995**

Source: Eurostat (1996).

of this method is that all the data are used in the calculation of the trend. This can be important when comparing countries which may have different business cycles and where slight differences in the choice of years over which to measure the rate of growth may have significant implications.

Fig. 2.4 shows growth rates of GDP and GDP per capita, measured using the regression method. It is noticeable that the four countries with the lowest GDP per capita—Greece, Portugal, Spain, and Ireland—all grew faster than the EU average. Luxembourg, the richest, also grew fast—a factor directly attributable to the growth of the EU institutions located there.

Since population growth in the EU countries has not been uniform, growth of GDP per capita tells a different story from GDP growth *per se*. Many of the faster growing economies have also been countries with faster growing populations.

Figures such as these enable us to examine the extent to which the GDP per capita of the EU economies are converging. Here we must be aware that convergence of levels may require divergence in growth rates. Thus for GDP per capita to converge across the economies of the EU, the poorest countries must grow faster than the richer ones.

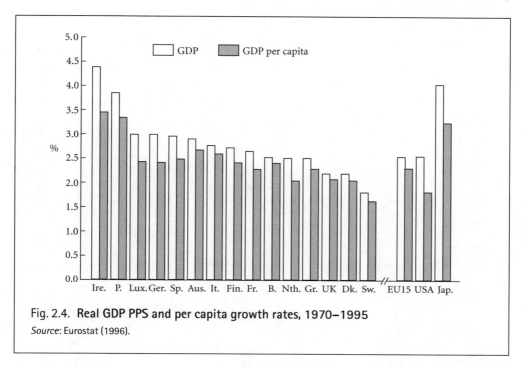

Fig. 2.4. Real GDP PPS and per capita growth rates, 1970–1995
Source: Eurostat (1996).

2.4. Regional GDP

In addition to the considerable differences in GDP per capita between countries there are even greater differences between regions across the EU as well as some quite marked differences between regions within particular countries. These differences in per capita GDP within countries associated with various historical factors have led to calls from groups within some regions for the EU to become a 'Europe of regions' rather than of nations.

Regional figures of GDP per capita are produced by Eurostat. They are based on estimates of the regional structure of gross value added and population. GDP per capita is a territorial measure of economic activity and not a direct measure of income. This leads to the very high per capita GDP in Hamburg, with its large number of non-residents working there, and in the oil-rich Grampian region in north-east Scotland.

The richest regions, when measured in terms of GDP(PPS) per capita, include some of the capital cities, Brussels, Île de France (including Paris), Vienna, Luxembourg, Greater London; several German regions—Darmstadt, Oberbayem, Stuttgart, Hamburg, Bremen; in Italy, Lombardia and the Valle d'Aosta; in Belgium, Antwerp; in the Netherlands, Groningen; and in Austria, Salzburg. Indeed a London–Milan axis linking highly populated regions with a high concentration of growth industries and intense business activity has been noticed.

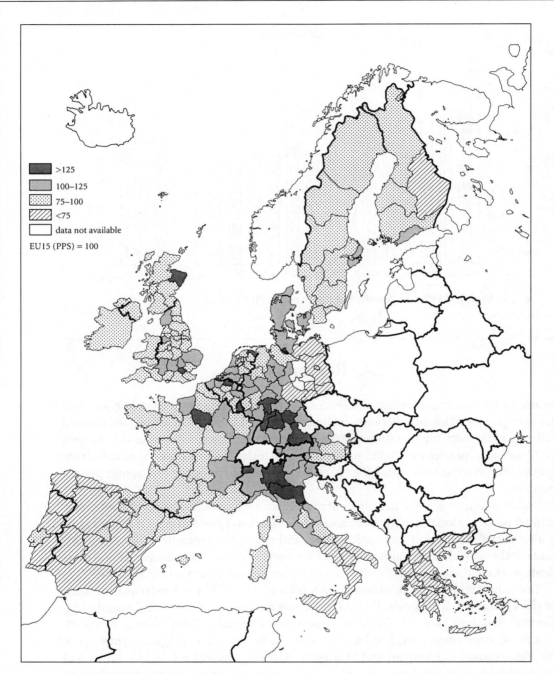

Fig. 2.5. Regional GDP per capita, 1993

Source: Eurostat (1996).

As can be seen from Fig. 2.5, the poorest regions are the regions of Greece, Portugal, Spain, and southern Italy—which are mainly agricultural regions far from the major centres—and the regions of east Germany where the structural changes following reunification have led to the collapse of industrial production. It needs to be noted that within regions themselves there are considerable disparities. Greater London, for example, the richest region in the UK, has within it areas where the level of poverty is as bad as in any in the EU.

2.5. **Disaggregation of GDP**

GDP can, in principle, be found as the sum of expenditures, the sum of sectoral value added or the sum of factor incomes in the economy. Correspondingly, there are three possible disaggregations of GDP. Figures are shown for a recent year illustrating each of the first two of these. Measurement of GDP by factor incomes is intrinsically more difficult than either by expenditure or by value added. Wages and salaries are fairly easily collected from taxation offices but distinguishing returns to the labour of the self-employed from returns to their capital and interest income from depreciation is difficult.

The disaggregation of GDP by expenditure

Total expenditure in an economy can be found by summing private consumption (C), government consumption (G), investment (I), changes in stocks by businesses (ΔS) and the balance of trade ($X - M$).

$$\text{GDP}_{\text{expenditure}} = C + I + \Delta S + G + (X - M).$$

Private consumption is made up of household expenditure on food, clothing, housing services, household goods, transport, and health. Government consumption consists of expenditure on health, education, defence, and social security payments. Investment includes expenditure on machinery, transport equipment, and building construction. Exports of goods and services minus imports give the balance of trade. Fig. 2.6 shows GDP disaggregated by expenditure for 1991.

As might be expected, the private consumption figures of most of the countries are close to the EU average. The noteworthy exceptions are Greece, where private consumption is considerably higher, and Denmark, where it is lower. Government expenditure is high in Denmark and Sweden and low in Germany and the Netherlands. Differences in the shares between private and government consumption are an indicator not only of what might be termed 'real' differences in the structure of the economy (for instance, how much is actually spent on health) but also of institutional differences

Mike Artis and Nick Weaver

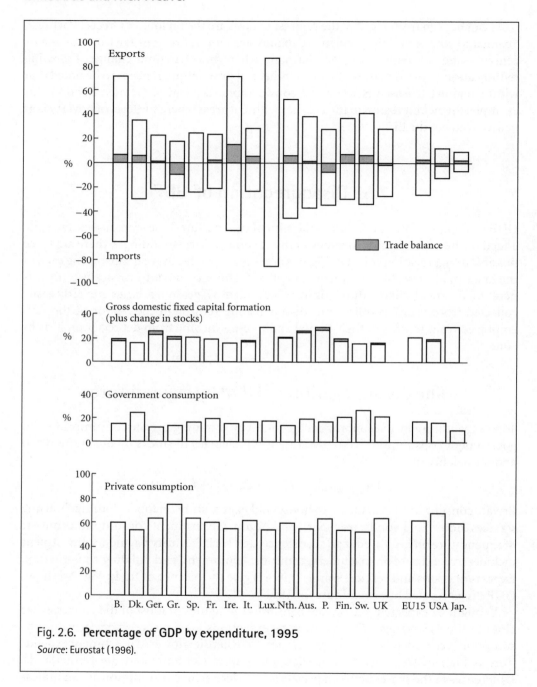

Fig. 2.6. **Percentage of GDP by expenditure, 1995**

Source: Eurostat (1996).

42

(for instance, health services may be almost entirely government run—as is the case in Denmark—and classified as government expenditure or there might be substantial private provision, in which case it would be classified in part as private consumption).

Expenditure on investment is relatively high in Luxembourg, Portugal, and Austria and low in the UK, Denmark, Sweden, and Ireland.

Exports plus imports are a good measure of the extent to which an economy is open to the rest of the world. By this measure the most open economies are Luxembourg, Belgium, Ireland, and the Netherlands, all of whose exports plus imports are greater than 100 per cent of GDP. Spain, Italy, France, and Germany are relatively more closed.

The disaggregation of GDP by sectoral value added

The total value added in an economy may be found by the summation of the value added by each economic sector.

$$\text{GDP}_{\text{value added}} = \text{VA Services} + \text{VA Industry} + \text{VA Agriculture}.$$

Fig. 2.7 shows GDP disaggregated by value added for 1995.

The share of GDP provided by the service sector in the EU (64.4 per cent) is greater than in Japan (55.7 per cent) but less than in the USA (68.8 per cent). Denmark (71.7 per cent) and the UK (69.2) are the only EU countries to exceed the US share. In all the EU countries services contribute a greater share to GDP than in Japan. The share of GDP provided by industry in the EU (32.7 per cent) is greater than in the USA (29.2 per cent) but less than in Japan (41.8 per cent). Germany (39.2 per cent) is the only EU country where industries' contribution approaches Japan's.

The share of GDP provided by manufacturing follows a similar pattern to that in industry. Manufacturing in the EU (23.3 per cent) is greater than in the USA (19.3 per cent) but less than in Japan (28.5 per cent). Germany (30.8 per cent) is the only EU country where manufacturing contributes a bigger share than Japan.

Agriculture provides a slightly higher percentage of GDP in the EU (2.9 per cent) than in either the USA (2.0 per cent) or Japan (2.5 per cent). For most of the fifteen Member states agriculture's share is less than 5 per cent. Only in the EU's three poorest countries (Greece, 13.8 per cent, Ireland, 9.6 per cent, and Portugal, 6.2 per cent) is it greater than this.

2.6. Income inequality

In addition to disaggregating income by factor of production it is desirable to analyse what is generally referred to as income inequality. The normal procedure is to rank households in terms of income received no matter what the source. The most complete

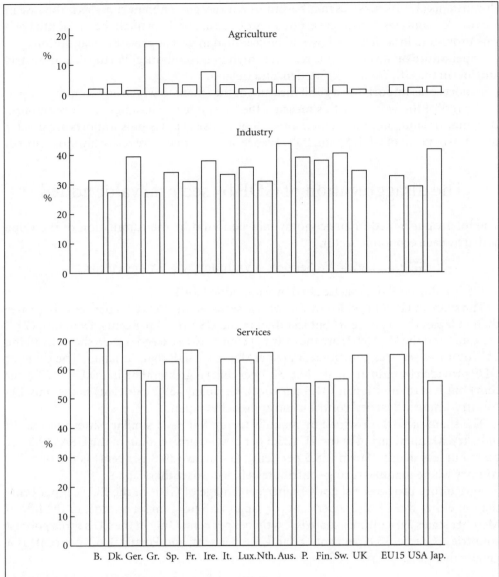

Fig. 2.7. Percentage of GDP by value added, 1995

Source: Eurostat (1996).

measure is a Lorenz curve which plots households ranked by income against the income they receive. Ideally one would be shown for each country. Data availability and space constraints preclude this. Rather Fig. 2.8 shows a simple statistic produced by the United Nations Development Programme (UNDP)—the share of total income accruing to the poorest 40 per cent of households—which aims to provide a summary measure of income inequality.

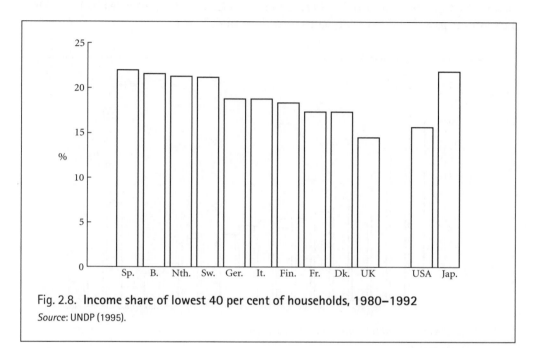

Fig. 2.8. Income share of lowest 40 per cent of households, 1980–1992
Source: UNDP (1995).

2.7. **Labour market**

The standard procedure, when analysing the basic features of the labour market, involves distinguishing the population of working age from the total population. The population of working age is then divided into three mutually exclusive and all-encompassing categories—the unemployed, persons in employment, and the inactive. The unemployed plus the employed together constitute the labour force. From these categories various measures such as employment–population ratios (employment as a percentage of the population of working age), activity rates (the labour force as a percentage of the population of working age), and unemployment rates (the number of unemployed as a percentage of the labour force) can be calculated. International comparability is again difficult because countries' statistical services tailor their own data to their national requirements and the political significance of the statistics renders them particularly vulnerable to interference. Eurostat, by adjusting national measures with the help of an EU-wide labour-force survey, aims to produce comparable standardized statistics.

The most commonly quoted of these measures is the unemployment rate. Fig. 2.9 shows that the standardized unemployment rate in the EU was higher in 1995 than that in either the USA or Japan. Unemployment rates vary widely between the EU countries. Spain (16.3 per cent) and Ireland (16.2 per cent) had the highest rates in 1995. Only Luxembourg, with 1.6 per cent, had a rate lower than Japan.

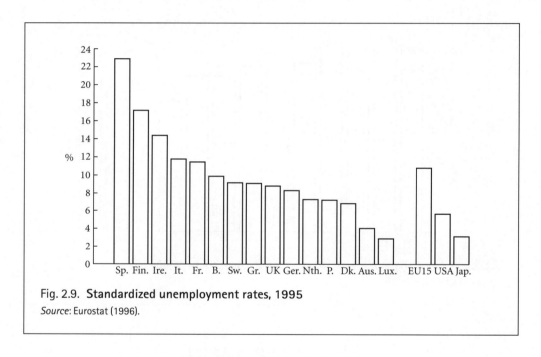

Fig. 2.9. **Standardized unemployment rates, 1995**
Source: Eurostat (1996).

Fig. 2.10 shows unemployment, disaggregated by gender and age. The unemployment rate is 50 per cent higher for females than for males in the EU, 10 per cent higher for females than for males in Japan, and 10 per cent less for females than for males in the USA. Again there are wide differences across countries. The differences are greatest in Greece, Italy, Portugal, and Belgium, where the female rate is more than 100 per cent greater than the male rate. The UK is the only EU country where the unemployment rate for females is less than that for males. The figure also shows how unemployment has particularly affected the young. Youth unemployment rates are generally far higher than the average. In Spain, Italy, Greece, and Ireland one in four of those aged less than 25 is unemployed. Only in Germany, with its exceptional training policy, is youth unemployment less than the national average.

It is also interesting to examine the sectoral structure of employment (Fig. 2.11). The

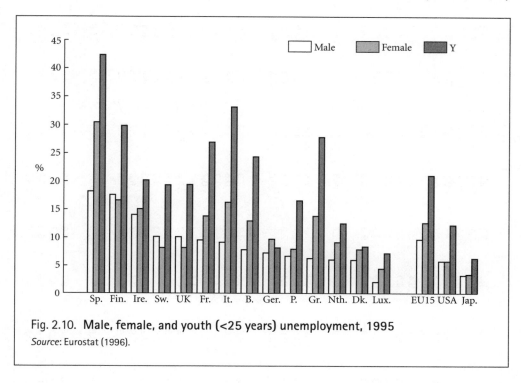

Fig. 2.10. Male, female, and youth (<25 years) unemployment, 1995
Source: Eurostat (1996).

small size of the agricultural sector is again noteworthy, despite the importance it takes on with regards to EU policy.

2.8. Trade

A major economic justification for the establishment and growth of the EU arises from the expansion of opportunities to exploit competitive advantages that result from the removal of barriers to trade. The beneficial effects of the removal of such barriers in theory are that high-cost sources of supply are replaced by lower-cost sources. Such a process is referred to as *trade creation*. Undoubtedly, the establishment of the EU has led to substantial trade creation. There are, however, other less beneficial effects associated with these aspects of the EU commercial policy which have led to high-cost sources of supply supplanting lower-cost sources—a process referred to as *trade diversion*. (Chapter 3 provides a thorough analysis of these concepts.)

Table 2.1 shows the direction of trade statistics for each of the EU12 countries and of the EU12 in total for 1958 and 1993 and illustrates a strong growth in the relative significance of intra-EU trade between the two years. Denmark and Ireland are the two exceptions.

Table 2.1. Direction of trade statistics for EU12, European OECD, USA, Japan and the rest of the world, 1958 and 1993

Year	B./Lux. Exports	B./Lux. Imports	Dk. Exports	Dk. Imports	D. Exports	D. Imports	Gr. Exports	Gr. Imports	S. Exports	S. Imports	F. Exports	F. Imports
1958												
B./Lux.	–	–	1.2	3.8	8.6	4.5	1.0	3.3	2.1	1.8	6.3	5.4
Dk.	1.6	0.5	–	–	3.0	3.4	0.2	0.7	1.7	1.3	0.7	0.6
Ger.	11.6	17.2	20.0	19.9	–	–	20.5	20.3	10.2	8.7	10.4	11.6
Gr.	0.8	0.1	0.3	0.0	1.3	0.7	–	–	0.1	0.2	0.8	0.6
Sp.	0.7	0.5	0.8	0.7	1.2	1.6	0.2	0.1	–	–	1.6	1.2
F.	10.6	11.6	3.0	3.4	7.6	7.6	12.8	5.4	10.1	6.8	–	–
Ire.	0.3	0.1	0.3	0.0	0.3	0.1	0.4	0.0	0.3	0.6	0.2	0.0
It.	2.3	2.1	5.3	1.7	5.0	5.5	6.0	8.8	2.7	1.8	3.4	2.4
Nth.	20.7	15.7	2.2	7.3	8.1	8.1	2.0	4.8	3.2	2.6	2.0	2.5
P.	1.1	0.4	0.3	0.3	0.9	0.4	0.3	0.3	0.4	0.3	0.8	0.4
UK	5.7	7.4	25.9	22.8	3.9	4.3	7.6	9.9	15.9	7.8	4.9	3.5
Total intra-EU12 trade	55.4	55.5	59.3	60.0	37.9	36.3	50.9	53.7	46.8	31.8	30.9	28.2
Other European OECD	8.7	7.7	16.6	18.8	22.7	15.2	10.3	11.5	12.4	8.4	9.0	6.7
USA	9.4	9.9	9.3	9.1	7.3	13.6	13.6	13.7	10.1	21.6	5.9	10.0
Japan	0.6	0.6	0.2	1.5	0.9	0.6	1.4	2.0	1.7	0.7	0.3	0.2
Rest of world	19.6	22.3	10.3	6.1	23.1	28.2	7.6	10.7	20.0	33.3	48.2	49.0
1993												
B./Lux.	–	–	2.0	3.7	6.6	6.5	1.5	3.3	2.9	3.8	8.2	10.0
Dk.	0.9	0.6	–	–	1.7	1.8	0.7	1.3	0.6	0.9	0.8	0.9
Ger.	21.1	20.9	24.0	22.8	–	–	23.7	16.8	13.7	16.1	18.6	20.6
Gr.	0.6	0.1	0.8	0.2	1.0	0.5	–	–	0.7	0.2	0.8	0.2
Sp.	2.8	1.6	1.7	1.1	3.1	2.5	1.6	2.7	–	–	6.3	5.3
F.	19.5	15.6	5.4	5.3	11.6	11.5	6.2	8.2	17.8	17.1	–	–
Ire.	0.4	0.7	0.5	0.6	0.4	1.0	0.2	0.8	0.4	0.8	0.4	1.3
It.	5.5	4.2	4.1	3.9	7.2	8.0	13.2	14.3	8.6	8.4	9.4	10.0
Nth.	13.1	15.8	4.3	6.4	7.3	10.2	2.5	6.6	3.2	4.3	4.6	6.5
P.	0.9	0.5	0.5	1.1	0.9	0.9	0.4	0.3	6.8	2.7	1.5	1.0
UK	8.3	9.2	8.9	7.5	7.7	6.0	5.7	6.0	7.5	7.6	9.2	8.0
Total intra-EU12 trade	73.1	69.2	52.2	52.6	47.5	48.9	55.7	60.3	62.2	61.9	59.8	63.8
Other European OECD	6.0	6.0	22.7	24.7	17.8	16.6	9.7	6.6	5.9	5.9	8.1	7.5
USA	4.7	5.6	7.3	4.5	7.7	6.3	4.5	3.7	4.5	6.3	7.0	7.5
Japan	1.1	3.0	0.9	3.1	2.6	5.4	0.9	6.8	0.8	3.2	1.9	2.8
Rest of world	15.2	16.1	16.3	15.0	24.3	22.8	29.1	22.6	26.7	22.5	23.2	18.3

Year	Ire. Exports	Ire. Imports	It. Exports	It. Imports	Nth. Exports	Nth. Imports	P. Exports	P. Imports	UK Exports	UK Imports	EU12 Exports	EU12 Imports
1958												
B./Lux.	0.8	1.8	2.2	2.0	15.0	17.8	3.7	7.3	1.9	1.6	4.8	4.4
Dk.	0.1	0.7	0.8	2.2	2.6	0.7	1.2	0.8	2.4	3.1	2.0	2
Ger.	2.2	4.0	14.1	12.0	19.0	19.5	7.7	17.6	4.2	3.6	7.6	8.7
Gr.	0.1	0.2	1.9	0.4	0.6	0.2	0.6	0.1	0.7	0.2	0.8	0.4
Sp.	0.8	0.4	0.7	0.4	0.8	0.4	0.7	0.4	0.8	1.0	1.0	0.9
F.	0.8	1.6	5.3	4.8	4.9	2.8	6.6	7.7	2.4	2.7	4.7	4.4
Ire.	–	–	0.1	0.0	0.4	0.0	0.3	0.1	3.5	2.9	1.1	0.9
It.	0.4	0.8	–	–	2.7	1.8	4.3	3.7	2.1	2.1	3.1	2.7
Nth.	0.5	2.9	2.0	2.6	–	–	2.5	2.9	3.2	4.2	5.3	5.2
P.	0.1	0.2	0.7	0.4	0.4	0.2	–	–	0.4	0.4	0.8	0.3
UK	76.8	56.3	6.8	5.5	11.9	7.4	11.3	12.9	–	–	5.9	5.4
Total intra–EU12 trade	82.6	88.9	34.5	30.2	58.3	50.7	38.9	53.4	21.7	21.8	37.2	35.2
Other European OECD	0.9	3.4	18.9	13.1	11.9	7.2	5.1	8.6	9.1	8.7	13.7	10.1
USA	5.7	7.0	9.9	16.4	5.6	11.3	8.3	7.0	8.8	9.4	7.9	11.4
Japan	0.0	1.1	0.3	0.4	0.4	0.8	0.5	0.0	0.6	0.9	0.6	0.7
Rest of world	2.4	13.5	28.2	33.9	19.1	26.0	44.0	29.0	46.6	48.3	32.1	35.7
1993												
B./Lux.	4.0	1.6	3.0	4.7	12.4	10.4	3.4	3.8	5.4	4.5	5.8	6
Dk.	0.9	0.8	0.7	1.0	1.4	1.1	2.1	0.8	1.2	1.4	1.2	1.2
Ger.	13.5	7.5	19.5	19.4	28.5	21.6	19.6	15.0	12.3	13.4	13.8	13.6
Gr.	0.6	0.1	1.8	0.8	1.0	0.2	0.5	0.1	0.7	0.2	0.9	0.3
Sp.	2.1	0.8	4.3	3.3	2.3	1.7	14.3	17.6	3.4	2.2	3.6	2.9
F.	9.3	3.9	13.1	13.6	10.2	6.9	15.0	12.9	9.4	9.1	10.3	9.4
Ire.	–	–	0.3	0.8	0.6	1.2	0.4	0.5	4.9	3.6	1.0	1.4
It.	3.6	1.8	–	–	5.1	3.5	3.0	8.6	4.6	4.5	5.9	6.1
Nth.	5.9	4.0	2.8	5.7	–	–	5.2	4.9	6.4	6.0	5.6	7.3
P.	0.4	0.2	1.3	0.3	0.8	0.5	–	–	1.1	0.8	1.3	0.8
UK	28.8	42.3	6.4	5.8	9.0	8.3	11.4	7.4	–	–	7.4	6.6
Total intra–EU12 trade	69.1	63.0	53.2	55.4	71.3	55.4	74.9	71.6	49.4	45.7	56.8	55.6
Other European OECD	5.7	4.7	11.6	11.4	7.4	8.2	8.6	6.4	8.3	11.3	11.2	11
USA	8.9	15.0	7.7	5.3	4.4	9.1	4.4	3.2	12.8	12.3	7.5	7.6
Japan	3.7	5.3	1.9	2.6	1.0	4.8	0.8	3.3	2.2	5.8	2.0	4.3
Rest of world	12.6	12.0	25.5	25.3	15.8	23.7	11.3	15.5	27.4	24.9	22.7	21.5

Source: Eurostat (1996).

49

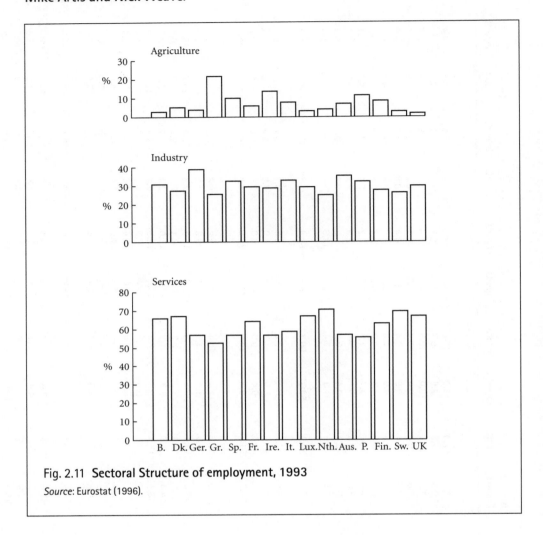

Fig. 2.11 **Sectoral Structure of employment, 1993**

Source: Eurostat (1996).

2.9. **Possible future entrants to the EU**

The number of countries in the EU has grown considerably since its foundation, and, despite many problems, a number of countries are queuing up to join.

At the time of writing all non-EU European countries are viewed as possible future entrants. They are often divided into three distinct groups on the basis of institutional and economic characteristics: the European Free Trade Association (EFTA) countries, the Central and East European Countries (CEECs) and the Mediterranean countries.

The EFTA countries—Norway, Iceland, Switzerland, and Liechtenstein—are all relatively rich stable countries with economies roughly similar to the richer of the existing members of the EU. Switzerland and Norway have decided against joining the EU; Iceland, because of fear for its fishing interests, and Liechtenstein are unlikely to apply.

However, these countries already have most of the benefits of access to the EU's market through their membership of the European Economic Area (EEA). This aims to reduce frontier barriers and to allow the free movement of services, capital, and workers. Agriculture, notably, is excluded.

Because of their small size, there is little for the EU to gain from bringing the EFTA countries into the single market of the EEA. There may be some gain in terms of its budget if EFTA countries were to become full members because their GDP per capita is something like 35 per cent higher than the EU average; they could expect to be net contributors and would be unlikely to receive structural funds allocated to poor regions.

A Centre for Economic Policy Research (CEPR) report estimated that increased competition would reduce costs and boost productivity, raising EFTA's GDP by up to 5 per cent. Full membership would entail adoption of the EU's Common Agricultural Policy (CAP) by the EFTA countries. This could cause problems for the EFTA countries, because their agriculture is even more heavily subsidized than the EU's (EU subsidies are roughly equal to 49 per cent of the value of farm output. EFTA countries' subsidies average 68 per cent of farm output and Swiss subsidies as much as 80 per cent).

Within the EEA, the EU's competition policy must be applied to cross-border trade in manufactured goods. Full membership requires competition policy to be applied to a much wider range of domestic activities. This would restrict much of the state aid to industry and restrictive business practices which are common in the EFTA countries.

The CEECs—Hungary, the Czech and Slovak Republics, Poland, Bulgaria, Romania, and Slovenia—are all former Communist countries, they are relatively poorer than the EU and have until recently had weak institutional links with the EU. All of them, except Bulgaria and Slovakia, have signed bilateral European Community (EC) association agreements.

Relative to the EU, the CEECs are all fairly poor. Agriculture employs a relatively high proportion of the workforce. These factors would make the CEECs eligible for large grants from both the Structural Fund and the CAP were they to become members.

The Mediterranean applicants—Turkey, Cyprus, and Malta—have for a long time had close links with the EU but for a variety of reasons have not yet come close to membership. The EU–Turkey Association agreement of 1963 specifically mentioned the possibility of Turkey's eventual accession to the Community after a twenty-two-year transitional period. Turkey now has a customs union agreement with the EU.

As things stand, both the EFTA countries and the CEECs seem to have pushed into the queue ahead of Turkey.

2.10. **Economic policy**

Unemployment

Fig. 2.12 shows the recent development of unemployment in the EU, the USA, and Japan. The unemployment rate in the EU now contrasts unfavourably not only with the past situation in Europe but also with the situation in the USA and Japan. Officially, unemployment is now regarded as Europe's foremost economic and social problem. The European Commission has issued a White Paper on the subject (CEC 1994) and European governments participated in the process, leading to the publication of the influential OECD Jobs Study (OECD 1993). A widespread view among economists is that the differences in the behaviour of unemployment in Europe and the USA can be related in large part to the relative lack of flexibility in the labour markets of Europe. Migration is low whilst wages legislation and social security arrangements put a floor under wages so that, in the face of a deflationary shock, unemployment bears the brunt of the adjustment. In particular, it has been argued that the introduction of new technology has undermined the position of the unskilled, for whom relative (and real) wages have fallen heavily in the USA and who feature disproportionately in the increase in unemployment in continental Europe, where wage inequality has not been touched. Fig. 2.13 provides some illustrative data on recent changes in wage dispersion in the

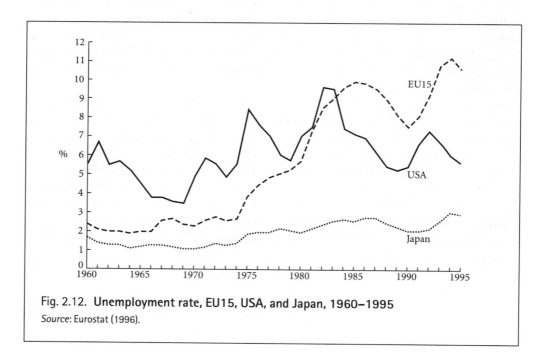

Fig. 2.12. Unemployment rate, EU15, USA, and Japan, 1960–1995
Source: Eurostat (1996).

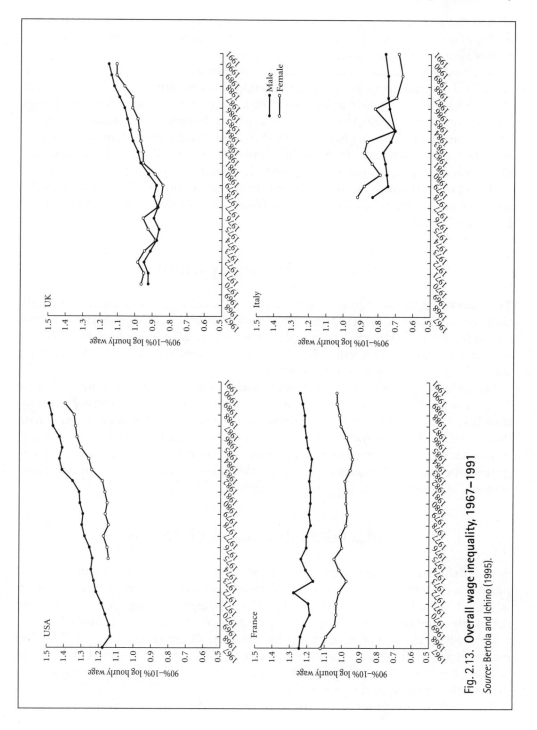

Fig. 2.13. Overall wage inequality, 1967–1991

Source: Bertola and Ichino (1995).

USA and in some of the major EU economies. The measure of wage dispersion used is the log of the ratio of average hourly wage rate of the nineteenth and tenth percentiles. As this measure increases, wage dispersion increases.

Despite the significance of the unemployment problem, however, it is apparent that, at the level of macroeconomic policy, the agenda has been captured by the rush to realize economic and monetary union. Even the most determined advocates of the view that the solution to unemployment lies in removing the obstacles to adjustment in the labour market would find it hard to deny that at least in the short term the fiscal consolidation enjoined by adherence to the Maastricht Treaty is likely to be deflationary. (The problem, in fact, is not so much with the Maastricht Treaty itself, which—as is explained in the following section—incorporates a degree of flexibility, but in the political pressure exercised by Germany in favour of a 'strict interpretation' of the Maastricht criteria.)

European Monetary Union

The Maastricht Treaty requires sufficient economic convergence to create the conditions for European Monetary Union (EMU) (see Chapter 13). It sets out criteria in relation to fiscal stance (budget deficits and debt burdens), inflation performance, interest rates, and exchange rate stability. Fig. 2.14 illustrates convergence criteria for the fiscal stance, inflation, and interest-rate performance.

Except in the case of the exchange-rate criterion, which is discussed fully in Chapter 13, the exact criteria are set out below, together with some relevant statistical information. It is important to note that the notion of economic convergence associated with these criteria refers essentially to 'nominal convergence', which should be distinguished from what might be referred to as 'real economic convergence'. Real economic convergence is the process of equalization of national/regional GDP per capita and the convergence of economic structures and institutions.

Budget deficits and debt burdens

Budget deficits are the difference between government expenditure (including interest payments on debt) and receipts. Such deficits are financed either by borrowing, which is usually done by selling bonds, or by selling foreign-exchange reserves or other nationally owned assets including the privatization of publicly owned enterprises.

Controlling the size of government has been the thrust of much policy. This has meant that, rather than just controlling deficits, policy has been aimed at trying to reduce government expenditure, partly because it has been thought that political expediency rules out increased taxation.

The protocol on convergence criteria in the TEU requires that 'at the time of the

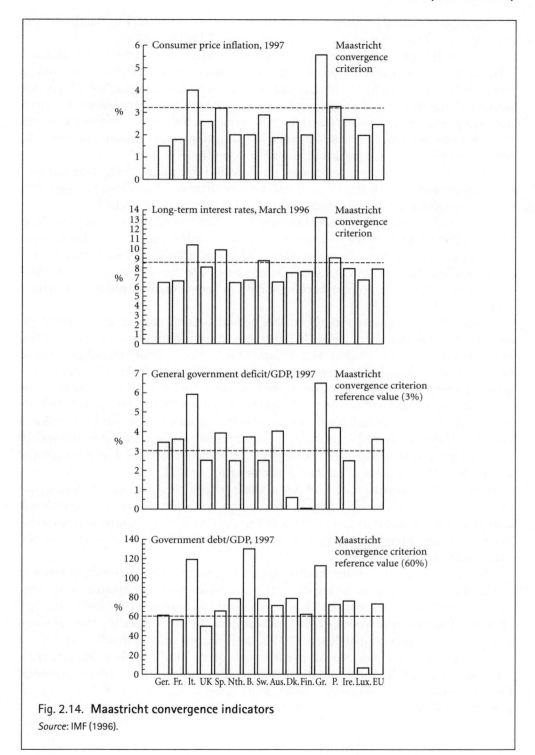

Fig. 2.14. **Maastricht convergence indicators**
Source: IMF (1996).

examination the Member State is not the subject of a Council decision under Article 104*c*(6) of this treaty that an excessive deficit exists' (CEC 1992: 185).

More specifically, an excessive deficit would be deemed to exist if the ratio of planned or actual government deficit to gross domestic product exceeds a reference value, unless either the ratio has declined substantially and continuously and reached a level that comes close to the reference value; or, alternatively, the excess over the reference value is only exceptional and temporary and the ratio remains close to the reference value (p. 27), where the reference value for the ratio of planned or actual government deficit to gross domestic product at market prices is 3 per cent (p. 183).

Asset-selling can only be a temporary measure and continuous budget deficits lead to the accumulation of debt. Accumulated debt becomes a problem in so far as government expenditure must be diverted towards paying interest on the debt.

The second consideration, under the excessive deficit procedure, pertains to the level of government debt. Here the criterion is 'whether the ratio of government debt to gross domestic product exceeds a reference value, unless the ratio is sufficiently diminishing or approaching the reference value at a satisfactory pace' (p. 27), where the reference value is '60% for the ratio of government debt to gross domestic product at market prices' (p. 183).

Article 104*c*(6), together with the further protocols, indicates that the fiscal criteria are subject to a degree of discretion. In particular, whilst minimum targets are specified by the reference values—a general government deficit of no more than 3 per cent of GDP and a gross government debt of no more than 60 per cent of GDP, caveats are provided. In respect of the deficit it appears that an excess can be 'forgiven' if 'the ratio has declined substantially and continuously and reached a level that comes close to the reference value . . . or, alternatively, the excess over the reference value is only exceptional and temporary and the ratio remains close to the reference value'. In respect of the debt ratio, it appears that an excess can be forgiven if 'the ratio is sufficiently diminishing or approaching the reference value at a satisfactory pace' (p. 27).

Should a Member State fail under one of these criteria, then the Commission would prepare a report which 'shall also take into account whether the government deficit exceeds the government investment expenditure and take into account all other relevant factors, including the medium term economic and budgetary position of the Member State' (p. 27).

The intellectual rationale for these fiscal convergence criteria, whilst not spelt out in the Treaty, is to be found in the argument that excessive debt is a temptation to governments to manipulate a surprise inflation as a means of wiping out its real value. The analysis of Sargent and Wallace (1981) was responsible for suggesting that, at some point, a large enough ratio of debt to GDP implies monetization and inflation.

Neither Sargent and Wallace nor the architects of the TEU are able to indicate critical magnitudes for this ratio, and the reference values quoted in the Treaty have been heavily criticized (see, particularly, Buiter and Kletzer 1992, Buiter *et al.* 1992 for their apparent arbitrariness).

There is an additional point that must be borne in mind, however, which is the critical need for fiscal flexibility. In a context where governments have eschewed any ability to cope with shocks by resort to independent monetary policy (which is what monetary union implies (see Chapter 13)), the fiscal convergence criteria appear to inhibit resort to a flexible fiscal policy as a substitute. There are some fundamental reasons why the 3 per cent and 60 per cent ratios are quite tough constraints aside from the incidence of below-average growth; public-services-sector productivity tends to grow less quickly than economy-wide productivity, implying that a greater expenditure is called for over time so as to maintain the same real level of provision (Leslie 1993); and taxes are always unpopular.

On the present (May 1996) trajectory (see Chapter 13) the Member States of the EU have determined to assess, during 1998 and on the basis of data available through 1997, which countries will be eligible to form a monetary union by 1 January 1999. Thus it is the latest available forecasts for the key convergence variables that are of greatest interest. Those used in Fig. 2.14 are taken from the forecasts of the International Monetary Fund (IMF) and take into account a realistically discounted version of the very substantial fiscal consolidation measures announced in a number of countries during the spring of 1996, most notably France and Germany.

Inflation

The criterion on price stability referred to in the first indent of Article 109*j*(1) of this treaty shall mean that a Member State has a price performance that is sustainable and an average rate of inflation, observed over a period of one year before the examination, that does not exceed by more than 1½ percentage points that of, at most, the three best performing Member States in terms of price stability. Inflation shall be measured by means of the consumer price index on a comparable basis, taking into account differences in national definitions. (p. 185)

Following Englander and Egebo (1992), we interpret the inflation-convergence criterion as implying that a country is convergent in this respect if its consumer price inflation is no more than 1½ points above the *average* of the three best-performing countries.

The lowest inflation economies, according to the IMF's predictions for 1997, are Germany (1.5 per cent), France (1.8 per cent) and Austria (1.9 per cent). The implied criterion is thus 3.2 per cent ((1.5 + 1.8 + 1.9)/3 plus 1½).

Interest rates

One of the major ways of financing a budget deficit is by the selling of government bonds. These bonds are one of the most secure forms of investment and in most EU countries the market for them is one of the largest sectors of the capital market. Other 'private' rates will tend to be higher, indicating the greater risks. Different governments sell different forms of bonds and comparison is again complicated and the rather loose description 'long-term interest rates' used in Fig 2.14 covers a whole range of different bond prices.

The criterion on the convergence of interest rates referred to in the fourth indent of Article 109*j*(1) of this Treaty shall mean that, observed over a period of one year before the examination, a Member State has had an average long-term interest rate that does not exceed by more than two percentage points that of, at most, the three best performing States in price stability. Interest rates shall be measured on the basis of long-term government bonds or comparable securities, taking into account differences in national definitions. (p. 186)

According to the normal interpretation of the convergence criteria, long-term interest rates must be within two percentage points of the average of the three lowest inflation rate states. More precisely, the convergence limit is the unweighted average of the interest rate in the three countries with the lowest inflation rate plus 2 per cent. These are, it must be emphasized, not necessarily the countries with the lowest interest rates, and this is a problem to the extent that, if the interest rates are being construed as an index of sustainable inflation performance, it might seem more appropriate to base the convergence limit on the countries' best interest rate performance.

The interest rates in the lowest inflation economies, according to the IMF's predictions for 1997, are Germany (6.5 per cent), France (6.7 per cent), and Austria (6.6 per cent). The implied criterion is thus 8.6 per cent ((6.5 + 6.7 + 6.6)/3 plus 2).

Discussion questions

1. What are the main problems involved in making international comparisons of countries' GDP? Illustrate with respect to the Member States of the EU.

2. Outline the Maastricht 'convergence criteria'. How closely do the EU countries appear to be meeting these?

3. Describe how you would assess the level of development and the economic strength of an economy. Illustrate your answer by reference to the Member States of the EU.

FURTHER READING

There are a variety of sources of data on the economies of the EU; noteworthy among these would be many of the publications of the OECD, the IMF, and several of the institutions of the UN. However, the statistics produced by Eurostat are incomparable as far as standardization and inter-country comparability are concerned. The institution, as well as producing a large number of annual, quarterly, or monthly reports, maintains a large statistical database. The most up-to-date source of information on these is the Eurostat home page on the Internet (*http://europa.eu.int/en/comm/eurostat*).

REFERENCES

Anderson, V. (1991), *Alternative Economic Indicators* (London: Routledge).

Barrell, R. (1992) (ed.), *Economic Convergence and Monetary Union in Europe* (Association for the Monetary Union of Europe and the National Institute of Economic and Social Research; London: Sage).

Bertola, G., and Ichino, A. (1995), 'Wage Inequality and Unemployed: United States vs. Europe', *NBER Macroeconomics Annual*, (Cambridge, Mass.: MIT Press), 13–66.

Buiter, W., and Kletzer, K. (1992), 'Reflections on the Fiscal Implications of a Common Currency', in A. Giovannini and C. Mayer (eds.), *European Financial Integration* (Cambridge: Cambridge University Press).

—— Corsetti, G., and Roubini, N. (1992), *Excessive Deficits: Sense and Nonsense in the Treaty of Maastricht* (Discussion Paper No. 750; London: Centre for Economic Policy and Research).

CEC (1992): Commission of the European Communities, *Treaty on European Union* (Luxembourg).

—— (1993), *European Economy*, Number 54.

—— (1994), *Growth, Competitiveness, Employment*, White Paper.

CEPR (1993): Centre for Economic Policy Research, *Is Bigger Better? The Economics of EC Enlargement* (Monitoring European Integration 3, Annual Report, 1992; London: CEPR).

Englander, A., and Egebo, T. (1992), 'Institutional Commitments and Policy Credibility: A Critical Survey and Empirical Evidence from the ERM', in Organization for Economic Cooperation and Development (OECD), *Economic Studies*, 18 (Spring), 45–84.

Eurostat (1985), *Purchasing Power Parities and Gross Domestic Product in Real Terms*, Results, 2 C.

—— (1988), *Labour Force Survey*, Methods and Definitions, 3 E.

—— (1989), *Labour Force Survey*, Results 3 C.

—— (1992), *Europe in Figures*.

—— (1993), *National Accounts ESA: Aggregates 1970–1991*, 2 C.

—— (1996), *Europe in Figures*.

Gilbert, M., and Kravis, I. B. (1954), *An International Comparison of National Products and the Purchasing Power of Currencies: A Study of the United States, the United Kingdom, France, Germany and Italy* (Paris: Organization for European Economic Cooperation).

IMF (1996): International Monetary Fund, *World Economic Outlook* (Washington: IMF), May.

Leslie, D. (1993) *Advanced Macroeconomics: Beyond IS/LM* (London: McGraw-Hill).

OECD (1993): Organization for Economic Cooperation and Development, *Economic Outlook, Historical Statistics 1960–1990* (Paris: OECD).

—— (1994) *The OECD Jobs Study* (Paris: OECD).

Sargent, T., and Wallace, N. (1981), 'Some Unpleasant Monetarist Arithmetic', *Federal Reserve Bank of Minneapolis Quarterly Review* (Autumn).

UN and CEC (1986): United Nations and Commission of the European Communities, *World Comparisons of Purchasing Powers and Real Product for 1980; Phase IV of the International Comparison Project: Part I: Summary Results for 60 Countries* (New York: UN).

UNDP (1996): United Nations Development Programme, *Human Development Report* (New York: UN).

CHAPTER 3

The Economic Analysis of Preferential Trading Areas

LYNDEN MOORE

3.1. Introduction

The European Community (EC) was established in 1957 as a *customs union*; all tariffs and quotas were abolished in stages on trade between member countries, and a common external tariff (CET) was imposed on imports from outside. By the end of 1992, with the establishment of the Single European Market (SEM), other non-tariff barriers with respect to standardization and public procurement, which enable governments to discriminate in favour of their own nationals, should have been removed.

In 1973 the EC also formed a *free trade area* (FTA) in manufactures with the remaining members of the European Free Trade Area (EFTA). This involved the removal of all barriers to trade in manufactures between member countries, but the EFTA members retained their own level of tariffs on imports from third countries (that is, those outside the EC and EFTA). In order to avoid imports into an FTA coming through the member country with the lowest external tariff, an FTA agreement limits free trade status to member countries' products. These are specified by its rules of origin.

In this chapter we will begin by considering an economic analysis of the effects of such preferential trading areas, and calculations as to their magnitude. First, we consider the effect of the imposition of a tariff, and then examine the situation in which the tariff is removed on imports from the partner country. We will assume that the market for the product is small enough for us not to have to consider the effect of changes in consumption and production on the total economy. Thus we will be able to use supply and demand curves in a partial equilibrium analysis.

3.2. **Partial equilibrium analysis of tariffs**

The effect of a tariff on imports can be seen in Fig. 3.1. The country is assumed to be 'small' and therefore faces an infinitely elastic supply schedule from the rest of the world S_W. The domestic supply schedule is shown as the upward-sloping supply line S_H and the demand schedule as the downward-sloping line D_H. Under free trade the price on the domestic market is the world price, P_W. Domestic consumption is Q_1 and domestic production is Q_2 with imports of $Q_1 Q_2$. If a tariff is imposed on imports of t in percentage terms or d in absolute terms with

$$t = P_W P'_W / OP_W \quad \text{and} \quad d = P_W P'_W$$

it appears to domestic consumers and producers that foreigners are now only willing to supply the domestic market at P'_W—that is, it looks as if the foreign supply schedule has shifted upwards to S'_W. Domestic consumers and producers respond by reducing consumption to Q_3 and increasing production to Q_4 respectively. Imports fall to $Q_3 Q_4$, *both* because production has increased by $Q_2 Q_4$ *and* because consumption has fallen by $Q_1 Q_3$. This involves a loss in consumer surplus of $P_W P'_W KL$. However, part of this represents a redistribution in favour of producers: there is a gain in producer surplus of $P_W P'_W JN$; and another part takes the form of a gain in tariff revenue (which could in principle be redistributed to consumers) of $JKVR$. The net result is an efficiency loss of the two triangles JRN, which is the additional cost of obtaining the extra output $Q_2 Q_4$

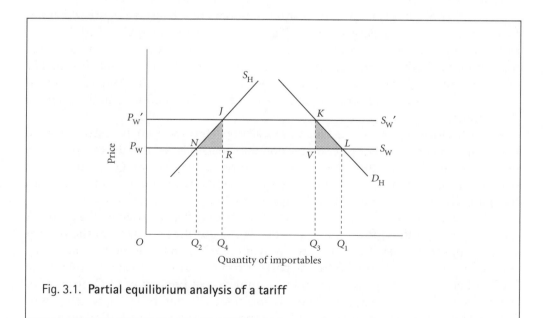

Fig. 3.1. **Partial equilibrium analysis of a tariff**

from domestic sources instead of from the international market, and *KLV*, which is the consumer surplus lost on the reduction in consumption Q_1Q_3.

Preferential trade agreements: partial equilibrium analysis

The formation of a customs union or FTA was initially regarded as a movement towards free trade. But Viner (1950) pointed out that it also included an element of greater discrimination between member countries and non-member countries. He distinguished two aspects of the situation, one in which production is transferred from a higher-cost to a lower-cost source of production, say from the home country to the partner country, because tariffs have been removed from the latter country's products, which he termed *trade creation*. The other occurs when production is transferred from a low-cost source to a higher-cost source of production—say, from a third country to a partner country because tariffs are no longer imposed on products from the latter; this he termed *trade diversion*. Trade creation he regarded as always beneficial, and trade diversion as detrimental (Viner 1950).

This is to look at benefits and costs entirely from the production point view—Viner assumed that the commodities were always consumed in the same proportion. It was left to Lipsey to point out that there was also a consumption angle. Indeed, the consumer benefits occurred in both cases and might even outweigh the losses in the case of trade diversion (Lipsey 1957).

To illustrate the effect on the market for a particular importable of a country becoming a member of a free trade area or customs union we may consult a figure which was first employed by Kindleberger (1973) (Fig. 3.2). The partner's supply schedule is also assumed infinitely elastic at S_P, but to lie above the rest of the world's supply schedule S_W; with a tariff, the partner's supply schedule is above S'_W and is not shown. The domestic supply schedule S_H is assumed to be upward sloping. The domestic demand schedule is D_H. Consumers are assumed not to differentiate according to the origin of the product.

Before the formation of the customs union, all imports come from the rest of the world as they appear cheapest. The price on the domestic market is equal to the world price P_1 plus the tariff P_1P_2 and is thus OP_2. Consumers purchase a quantity OQ_3 and the output of domestic producers is OQ_4. Q_4Q_3 is imported from the rest of the world, requiring a foreign-exchange expenditure of ADQ_3Q_4 and providing a tariff revenue of $BCDA$.

If a customs union or free trade area is formed, the tariff is removed on the partner's goods but not on those from the rest of the world and thus goods from the partner country appear cheaper at OP_3. If P_3 is less than P_2, prices on the domestic market fall. All imports are then acquired from the partner country and are greater in quantity at Q_6Q_5. There is, therefore, a diversion in the purchase of imports of Q_4Q_3 from non-members to the partner country. There is also trade creation of Q_6Q_4, which is now supplied by the partner country instead of domestic producers. In addition there is an

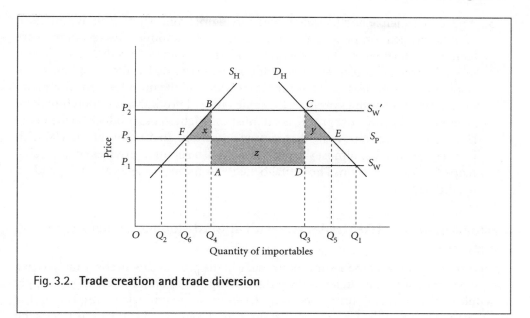

Fig. 3.2. **Trade creation and trade diversion**

increase in consumption of Q_3Q_5, which is supplied by the partner country. There is a gain in consumers' surplus of P_2CEP_3 and a loss in producers' surplus of P_2BFP_3 due to the lower price, and also a loss in tariff revenue of $ABCD$. In total this is equal to a net gain of $x + y - z$. z can be regarded as the cost of trade diversion—that is, of transferring purchases from a low-cost producer W to a higher-cost producer P. x and y are the familiar efficiency gains obtained from the reduction in tariffs.

Cooper and Massell (1965) challenged the assumptions underlying this particular argument. The comparison was being made between the pre- and post-customs unions position in order to assess whether it was beneficial. They argued that a comparison should be made between a discriminatory reduction of tariffs as in the formation of a customs union of free trade area, and a non-discriminatory removal of tariffs. A non-discriminatory removal of tariffs would always be superior and would avoid any trade diversion.

Nevertheless, most economists carrying out applied work have continued to use the original framework and have compared the situation of the country before and after it joined the preferential trading area. This then is a theory of 'second best'.

From this theory some general principles can be deduced:

1. The benefits are likely to be greater the higher the original level of the tariff—the larger will be x and y.

2. Losses due to trade diversion are likely to be lower, the smaller the differences in costs of production between the partner countries and third countries—in Fig. 3.2 the smaller P_3P_1 and therefore the smaller z.

3. A general principle not demonstrable from Fig. 3.2 concerns the relative merits of unions between competitive and complementary economies. Two economies are complementary when they produce a different range of products. Initially a union between complementary economics was regarded as the most beneficial. But it provides the least scope for trade creation and the most for trade diversion. Competitive economies produce the same range of products, and therefore there is scope for the low-cost producers to oust the higher-cost producers when barriers to trade are removed—that is, trade creation. So a union of the UK with Germany, which has almost the same industrial structure, provides considerable scope for trade creation. The actual benefits from this trade creation depend on the differences in cost.

Customs unions and free trade areas with upward-sloping partner supply schedules

Let us now drop some of the assumptions made in the previous theoretical analysis in a bid for greater realism. First, let us drop the assumption of an infinitely elastic supply schedule of the partner country. Secondly, let us drop the implicit assumption in the previous analysis that the CET of the customs union is imposed at the same rate as the previous tariff.

Let us analyse the situation for a preferential agreement between two countries, H for home, and P for partner. Let us assume that the marginal costs of production are greater in the home than in the partner country owing to the higher level of protection in the former. Thus the initial price T_H in country H is greater than that of the partner country T_P. Let us also make Robson's simplifying assumption that at the initial level of protection in the partner country it is just self-sufficient (Robson 1984). We will follow Robson's analysis and consider the final price and equilibrium that is established, the changes in welfare, and the effect on trade with the rest of the world (Robson 1984).

Free trade area

Each member country can retain its previous tariff on imports from outside the area. However, it is now possible for the high-priced home country H with a price level initially at OH_H (see Fig. 3.3b) to import goods duty free from the lower-priced partner country P with an initial price level $O_P T_P$ (see Fig. 3.3a). The maximum that the home country can import from the partner country will be the whole of the latter's *production*. The price in the country will come down to the world price plus the tariff in the partner country OT_P if the latter can supply all the home country's requirement at that price. This involves what is termed *trade deflection*. The partner exports its own output to the home country, and imports from the rest of the world to supply its own consumers.

The overall effect depends on the relationship between the supply schedule of the partner country S_P and the import schedule (demand minus supply) of the home

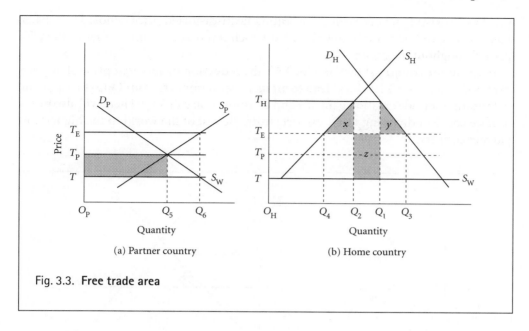

Fig. 3.3. **Free trade area**

country. If equilibrium can be achieved only at a price above that initially existing in the partner country such as T_E, then the partner producers will expand output from $O_P Q_5$ to $O_P Q_6$ and will gain from extra profits, and the partner country consumers will continue to purchase $O_P Q_5$ as before because they can import any amount at the world price plus tariff $O_P T_P$. Tariff revenue will be earned in the amount indicated by the shaded area owing to the switching of consumption from domestic to third-country sources.

The net effect in the home country is that it obtains the efficiency gains of x and y due to the trade creation and consumption effects respectively, but with the loss of z due to the trade diversion effect of obtaining $Q_2 Q_1$ imports from the partner country rather than from the rest of the world.

As the partner country now imports $O_P Q_5$, the imports of the free trade area as a whole from the rest of the world have increased by $O_P Q_5 - Q_2 Q_1$. There has been trade creation through the intermediation of the partner country.

Customs unions

To comply with the rules of the General Agreement on Tariffs and Trade (GATT), the level of protection in a customs union should be no greater than before. Thus, the EEC decided to set its CET at the arithmetic average or the previous tariffs of member countries. This, therefore, raised the level of protection against third countries in those members with liberal trade regimes and lowered it in the more protectionist ones.

Let us return to the analysis of two countries, assuming the CET is the average of previously existing tariffs, with the resulting tariff-distorted price denoted by CET in Fig. 3.4. The ceiling price becomes that at which imports can enter—that is, the CET price throughout the union.

In the home country shown in Fig. 3.4*b*, the reduction in apparent price of imports from OT_H to the CET level will lead to an increase in imports from Q_2Q_1 to Q_4Q_3 and to the familiar trade creation gain of *x* and consumption gain of *y*. There will also be the welfare cost *z* of diverting Q_2Q_1 imports from the rest of the world to the higher-cost partner country.

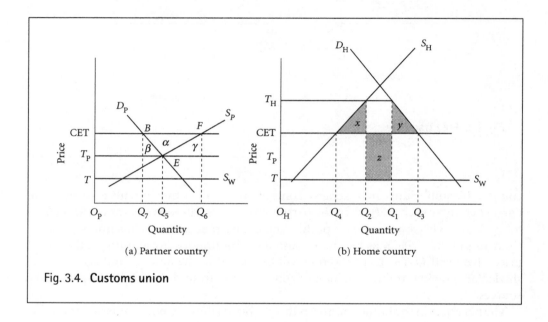

Fig. 3.4. **Customs union**

In the partner country (see Fig. 3.4*a*), prices will rise owing to increased protection. Thus, there will be a reduction in consumer surplus of $CETBET_P$, and a gain in producer surplus of $CETFET_P$ leading to a gain of α. This the partner country gains from her exports to the home country, which also compensates her for the marginal consumer loss β and producer loss γ. The ruling price will be at the ceiling if the partner country cannot supply, or can only just supply, the amount required by the home country, $Q_6Q_7 = Q_4Q_3$.

In the former case, there will be fewer imports from the rest of the world and in the latter none. However, the equilibrium price may be below the ceiling, with the partner country supplying all the imports of the home country and cutting out all imports from the rest of the world.

This analysis suggests that a customs union is inherently more likely to reduce trade with third countries than a free trade area. This is because of our assumption about the

CET, which, though it reduces protection in one country, raises it in another; by contrast, in a free trade area the trade deflection effect lowers the price in the highly protected market *without* increasing the prices to consumers in the other.

3.3. Applications of the theory

The above theoretical analysis identifies the effects that would be expected from the formation of a customs union, assuming everything else remained constant. However, to work out the effect of the formation of the EC in practice, allowance must be made for changes in other economic variables; for instance, demand and supply schedules may be expected to shift with changes in incomes and productivity. Herein lies the problem in calculating the economic effect of any institutional change—namely, that, in order to do so, an assumption has to be made about what would have happened in its absence. There are several approaches to that problem reflected in econometric exercises carried out to quantify the effect of the formation of the EEC and EFTA.

Balassa, in his investigation of the effect of the original EC6 (France, Germany, Italy, Belgium, Netherlands, and Luxembourg), assumed that the income elasticity of demand for imports would have remained the same in the absence of its formation (Balassa 1974). By income elasticity, he meant the ratio of the annual rate of change of imports to that of GNP, measured at constant prices. Thus, the effect of integration was assumed to be the residual. He thus calculated this income elasticity of imports for the period 1953–9 before any tariff cuts were instituted and compared it with periods afterwards, 1959–65 and 1959–70, for total imports of the EEC, intra-area imports, and extra-area imports (see Table 3.1).

A rise in the income elasticity of demand from the earlier to the later periods for intra-area imports would indicate gross trade creation (due to substitution for either domestic or third-country sources of supply). A rise in the import elasticity from all sources would indicate true trade creation. A fall in the import elasticity from third countries would indicate trade diversion. Comparing the period 1953–9 with 1959–70, Balassa calculated that the overall income elasticity of demand for imports from all countries had increased from 1.8 to 2.1—this suggests trade creation proper. The import elasticity of demand from non-member countries had stayed the same, suggesting no trade diversion.

However, the results for the individual categories of goods were very different. The union appeared to have had no appreciable effect on trade in raw materials. This was not surprising, as the initial tariffs on raw materials were zero or very low. There was a considerable amount of trade diversion in food, beverages, and tobacco. This was due to the Common Agricultural Policy (CAP). In fuels there was an increase in the import elasticity of demand from all sources. This was partly the result of the operation of the European Coal and Steel Community (ECSS) in the closing-down of high-cost

Table 3.1. **Ex-post income elasticities of import demand in the EC6**

Import Categories		Ex-post income elasticity of import demand		
		1953–9	1959–65	1959–70
Total imports				
0 + 1–07	Non-tropical food, beverages, tobacco	1.7	1.6	1.5
2 + 4	Raw materials	1.1	1.1	1.1
3	Fuels	1.6	2.3	2.0
5	Chemicals	3.0	3.3	3.2
71 + 72	Machinery	1.5	2.8	2.6
73	Transport equipment	2.6	3.4	3.2
6 + 8	Other manufactured goods	2.6	2.5	2.5
0 to 8–07	Total of above	1.8	2.1	2.0
Intra-area imports				
0 + 1–07	Non-tropical food, beverages, tobacco	2.5	2.4	2.5
2 + 4	Raw materials	1.9	1.9	1.8
3	Fuels	1.1	1.3	1.6
5	Chemicals	3.0	4.0	3.7
71 + 72	Machinery	2.1	3.1	2.8
73	Transport equipment	2.9	3.8	3.5
6 + 8	Other manufactured goods	2.8	2.9	2.7
0 to 8–07	Total of above	2.4	2.8	2.7
Extra-area imports				
0 + 1–07	Non-tropical food, beverages, tobacco	1.4	1.2	1.0
2 + 4	Raw materials	1.0	0.9	1.0
3	Fuels	1.8	2.5	2.1
5	Chemicals	3.0	2.7	2.6
71 + 72	Machinery	0.9	2.5	2.4
73	Transport equipment	2.2	2.4	2.5
6 + 8	Other manufactured goods	2.5	1.9	2.1
0 to 8–07	Total of above	1.6	1.7	1.6

Source: Balassa (1974: 97).

coalmines and the substitution of oil for coal. There was also an increase in the import elasticities of demand for machinery, and transport equipment, from all sources, in particular from non-members, which rose by respectively 1.5 and 0.3 from the earlier to the later period.

The reduction in the income elasticity of imports from non-member countries after 1953–9 in chemicals and other manufactured goods (clothing, travel goods, scientific instruments, etc.) indicated trade diversion.

Balassa at the time recognized that one of the problems with his approach was that some categories of goods were inputs into others. If, for instance, there was trade diversion in clothing (included in other manufactures) away from third countries, this would increase the relative demands for inputs into it, leading to trade creation in those categories. However, any approach through input–output tables appeared very complex.

He was also criticized by Winters for assuming that integration would lead to a change in an elasticity rather than a single (parametric) shift in trade between member countries (Winters 1984: app. 2).

EFTA

These problems were avoided by the EFTA Secretariat in its study of the effects of the formation of EFTA (EFTA 1969). In this case, imports were related to apparent consumption. The average annual change in the share of imports from 1954 to 1959 was extrapolated to the post-integration period 1959–65 and compared with the actual share of imports in apparent consumption, i.e. output minus exports plus imports. This comparison was carried out for imports from all areas, imports from other EFTA countries, and imports from non-EFTA countries.

In so far as imports from non-EFTA countries were lower than estimated by extrapolation from 1954 to 1959, this was regarded as trade diversion, and in so far as imports from EFTA countries were higher than the extrapolated estimate, this was regarded as trade creation. The results were that by 1965 the value of trade creation amounting to $US373 million was less than the value of trade diverted of $US457 million (EFTA 1969). This could be partly explained by the more complementary nature of the EFTA economies.

In both the Balassa and EFTA studies the whole of the difference between the estimate of what would otherwise have happened (the 'anti-monde') and what actually occurred is attributed to economic integration and thus is termed one of 'residual imputation'. This is generally regarded as producing rather high values.

Studies of the effect on the UK of its entry

The EFTA approach using shares in an export or import market has been used in assessing the effect on the UK of its entry into the EC, although some economists have just used total exports or imports. Most of these studies are of aggregate trade in manufactures. Winters (1987) criticizes those that used the residual imputation method and endeavoured to model the situation more directly by including dummy variables for the effect of UK entry in regression estimates.

The situation is complex because, while the UK by its entry gained free access to the EC market for its exports, it lost its preferential position in the markets of EFTA countries, the Irish Republic, and the Commonwealth. These countries also lost their preferential position in the UK home market, as imports from the other members of the EC could then enter freely. But, in addition, the EC's CET was lower for certain products than the UK's previous most-favoured-nation (m.f.n.) tariff.

The author has calculated that from 1970 to 1987 the real value of trade with the Commonwealth—that is, exports and imports—fell. Trade with EFTA increased, but that with the EC increased at a much faster rate, exports increasing by 172 per cent and imports by 250 per cent. For manufacturers there was a fivefold increase in imports from the EC (Moore 1989).

How much of this was due to integration? Winters investigates UK trade in manufactures with each of the main industrial countries (Winters 1987). He concludes that accession boosted exports to the EC by £4.5 billion but curtailed those elsewhere by £1.7 billion. More striking was the massive decline of £12 billion of sales by UK producers to their home market, i.e. trade creation. He qualifies this estimate by then saying that £4 billion of this reduction might reflect a long-term secular decline. This still leaves a reduction in home sales of £8 billion, which is only balanced by an increase in exports of £3 billion, leaving an increased manufacturing deficit of £5 billion. Even when modified to £3 billion, this still represents about 1.5 per cent of GNP. There is an increase in consumer surplus to set against this; the question is whether it is large enough to offset it.

Both in these exercises and in subsequent ones the implicit assumption is that an appropriate means of assessing any economic integration is to compare what would happen if there had been no reduction in tariffs with the effect of reducing trade barriers in the partner country. There is no comparison with the most efficient system of free trade.

Our exposition of the theory has been of the markets for individual products. The econometric work we have surveyed has made a similar approach, although the categories considered have been very much larger. Clearly, on joining a preferential trading area, the different markets within a country would be affected differently. If the resulting changes in trade do not balance out, some adjustment of the exchange rate has to take place. The overall effect on resource allocation has been considered in terms of whether trade creation outweighs trade diversion. The effects on consumer and producer surplus were also considered.

However, from the point of view of the individual country entering a customs union, there is also the effect on the rate at which exports are exchanged for imports—that is, its 'terms of trade'. An improvement in a country's terms of trade may balance out negative efficiency effects. For an individual product this is illustrated in Fig. 3.4a. However, to allow for the interconnection between markets we must employ a general equilibrium analysis.

3.4. A simplified exposition of the general equilibrium theory of customs unions

Let us now consider the general equilibrium approach to customs unions. Let us assume that there are only two products, manufactures and food. Perfect competition is assumed and increasing costs. Thus the country is operating on the outer boundary of its production possibilities, the production possibility curve (see Fig. 3.5). The slope of this curve at any point represents the domestic rate of transformation (DRT) between the two products—that is, the amount of food that would have to be given up at the margin in order to produce one more unit of manufactures. Equilibrium in production will be reached at the point where:

$$\text{DRT} = \frac{\text{price of manufactures}}{\text{price of food}}.$$

Demand is introduced into the picture by the use of community indifference curves. These are aggregates of the individuals' indifference curves and thus represent the contour lines of utility for the country as a whole. Here they are taken both to show the response of consumers to changes in price, and as levels of welfare; they are therefore

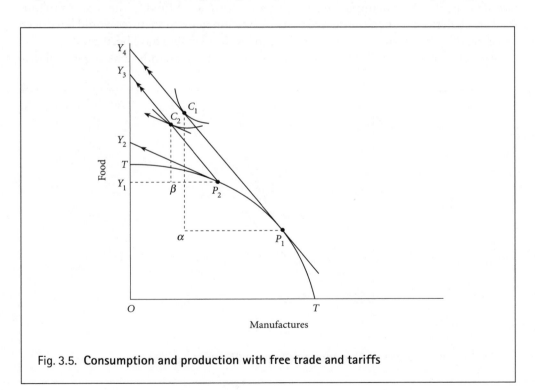

Fig. 3.5. **Consumption and production with free trade and tariffs**

71

assumed not to cross, and problems of the effects of the distribution of income on welfare are ignored.

If the country is closed to trade, the maximum welfare attainable will be where the production possibility curve just touches the highest possible community indifference curve, with domestic prices indicated by their slope at this point.

If the world price of manufactures in terms of food is greater than the domestic one (the price line is steeper), then, when the country is opened to trade, producers will have an incentive to increase their output of manufactures and reduce that of food. This will continue until the DRT is just equal to the international price as at point P_1, where the international price is given by the slope of Y_4P_1 equal to that of Y_3P_2 (see Fig. 3.5). On the other hand, the higher relative price of manufactures will induce consumers to switch purchases from them to food. However, the increase in real incomes resulting from the trade will tend to increase the consumption of both goods, assuming neither of them is inferior. The net result of changes in relative prices and incomes will be a change in consumption to point C_1, where the rate at which consumers are willing to substitute food for manufactures is just equal to the relative price of manufactures in relation to that of food, as indicated by the international price line.

Trade is the difference between production and consumption. The trade triangle $C_1\alpha P_1$ indicates that, at an international price given by the slope of Y_4P_1, the country would export αP_1 of manufactures in exchange for $C_1\alpha$ of food. If the price of manufactures had been higher, the degree of specialization in manufactures would have been greater still—that is, more manufactures and less food would have been produced.

An 'offer curve' showing the trade a country is willing to undertake at each relative

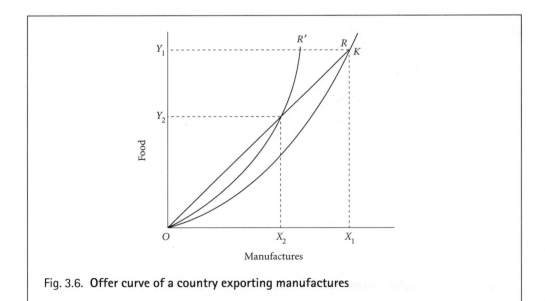

Fig. 3.6. **Offer curve of a country exporting manufactures**

price can be obtained by a plotting of the trade triangles, as in Fig. 3.6. OR represents a country's offer of manufactures for food. International equilibrium is reached when the country's offer curve intersects the offer curve of the rest of the world, assumed here to be infinitely elastic. At that equilibrium price OK, the country wants to export OX_1 of manufactures in exchange for OY_1 of food.

Tariffs and subsidies destroy the equality between domestic and international prices: see Fig. 3.5 again. If tariffs are imposed on imports of food, both consumers and producers face a higher price of food indicated by the slope of Y_2P_2. This induces an increase in the output of food at the expense of manufactures, and production shifts from P_1 to P_2. This reduction in efficiency lowers real income. But the country as a whole can still trade at the ruling international prices, and thus its consumption possibilities are along Y_3P_2. Consumers will equate their marginal rate of substitution indicated by the slope of their community indifference curve to the domestic tariff distorted price; this would suggest consumption along Y_2P_2. But if the tariff revenue is redistributed back to them, they will be able to consume along P_2Y_3 say, at C_2. $C_2\beta$ food will be imported, βP_2 of manufactures exported. The overall effect has been a contraction of trade, even though international prices remain the same.

Thus, a tariff has the effect of moving the offer curve depicted in Fig. 3.6 inwards to OR'. If, as we have assumed, the country is small, the international price, equivalent to the rest of the world's offer curve, remains the same. Thus the effect of the tariff is a clear efficiency loss in a general equilibrium, as in our previous partial equilibrium analysis.

However, a large country is by definition one with some monopoly power in world trade. With free trade

$$DRS = DRT = \text{international price}$$

but, unlike the situation of a small country, this is not equal to the *marginal* rate at which the large country can exchange manufactures for food on the world market, its foreign rate of transformation (FRT). A large country will face a less than infinitely elastic curve on the part of the rest of the world and will be able to improve its terms of trade by a tariff which leads to an inwards shift in its offer curve. The welfare of a country is always assumed to increase with an improvement in its terms of trade—that is, a rise in the price of its exports in relation to the price of its imports. Therefore, a large country can set the gain in its terms of trade against its efficiency loss.

Trade indifference curves

In order to consider the optimum tariff a large country can impose, it is necessary to introduce the concept of trade indifference curves, each one representing the combination of exports and imports between which the country would be indifferent. Each trade indifference curve of a country is uniquely associated with a community indifference curve, but the former includes the net result of changes in consumption and production on imports as relative price changes. At any point, the slope of a trade indifference curve is identical to that at the equivalent point on a community indifference curve.

Optimum tariff

The optimum tariff a large country can impose is one where at the margin the terms-of-trade gains just equal the efficiency losses. This is where the large country's trade indifference curve is tangential to the rest of the world's offer curve. At this point the tariff is inversely related to the elasticity of the other country's offer curve.

$$t^* = 1/(e_W - 1)$$

where e_W is the rest of the world's price elasticity of demand for imports, i.e.

$$e_W = \frac{\text{proportionate change in import volume demanded.}}{\text{proportionate decrease in real price of imports}}$$

Thus, when the rest of the world's offer curve is infinitely elastic, the optimum tariff is zero.

Customs unions

Now let us turn to the analysis of the formation of a customs union.

Let us simplify the analysis by assuming that there are three regions: A, the existing customs union or the country with whom membership is planned; B, the country whose interests we are considering; and W, the rest of the world. World efficiency will be maximized by free trade.

Calculations of the effect of the customs union will depend on the alternative scenario envisaged, i.e. the anti-monde. Are we, for instance, comparing the country in a customs union with its position under free trade, or with a tariff, maybe an optimum tariff? Given this point of comparison, the question is then whether membership of the customs union improves a country's terms of trade and who gains the tariff revenue; both will determine whether its consumers end up on a higher indifference curve than before.

Generally, it is assumed that both B and A specialize in the same products; in so far as the UK and the EU are taken as examples, let us assume that they both export manufactures in exchange for food. The situation is depicted in Fig. 3.7. OW is the rest of the world's offer curve, and $OA + B$ is the offer curve of $A + B$ with free trade. They can both be obtained by radial summation—that is, by adding the amount each country in the group would export and import at any given terms of trade.

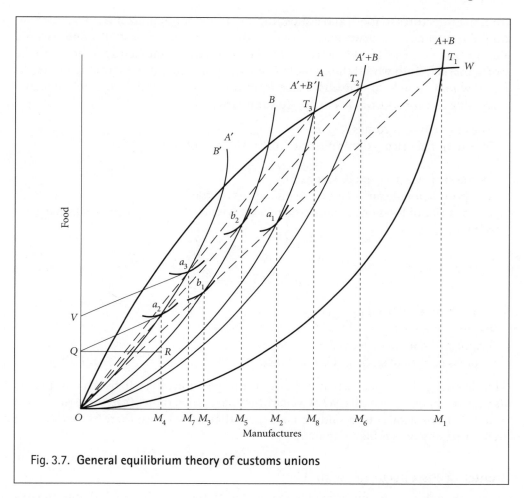

Fig. 3.7. **General equilibrium theory of customs unions**

Free trade

If A and B were to pursue a free-trade policy, the equilibrium position would be T_1 and the terms of trade OT_1. A's trade position would be at a_1 and B's would be at b_1. Exports of manufactures by A and B would be OM_2 and OM_3 respectively, summing to OM_1. Imports of food would be a_1M_2 and b_1M_3 respectively, summing to T_1M_1. Thus:

International price = domestic price = slope of OT_1.
Exports of $A + B = OM_2 + OM_3 = OM_1$.
Imports of $A + B = a_1M_2 + b_1M_3 = M_1T_1$.

Tariff imposed by A

If A, say the EU, then decided to impose a tariff on imports of food such that its internal domestic price is shown by the slope of Qa_2, this would induce a shift in its production

75

from manufactures to food, and a substitution of food for manufactures in consumption. The offer curve of A would shift to A' and the overall offer curve of A and B would shift to $OA' + B$. This would increase the relative price of manufactures to food on the world market. Both would thus benefit from an improvement in their terms of trade. But B would be able to take advantage from it by expanding its trade, in particular increasing its exports from M_3 to M_5. To summarize:

The offer curve becomes $A' + B$.
International price = domestic price of B = slope of $OT_2 = \dfrac{a_2 M_4}{OM_4}$.

Domestic price in A equals slope of Qa_2.
The proportionate tariff t is placed on imports of food.
$\therefore$ The price of food on A's domestic market is equal to $(1 + t) \times$ international price of food.

$$\frac{QR}{a_2 R} = \frac{OM_4}{a_2 R} = (1+t)\frac{OM_4}{a_2 M_4}$$

$$t = \frac{a_2 M_4 - a_2 R}{a_2 R} = \frac{RM_4}{a_2 R}.$$

Imports of A fall from $a_1 M_2$ to $a_2 M_4$.
Exports of A fall from OM_2 to OM_4.
Imports of B increase from $M_3 b_1$ to $M_5 b_2$.
Exports of B increase from OM_3 to OM_5.

Thus from Fig. 3.7 it appears that, although the imposition of a tariff by A has improved its terms of trade, its overall level of welfare may have fallen rather than increased—that is, a_2 may be on a lower trade indifference curve than a_1. Whereas there has been a clear welfare gain by B: b_2 is higher than b_1.

B enters a customs union with A

Let us apply this argument by analogy to the position of the UK in relation to the original EC6. The very high protection of agriculture within the EC6 improved its terms of trade but constricted its exports of manufactures abroad. The UK, outside the EC, benefited not only from the improvement in its terms of trade but also from being able to expand its exports of manufactures.

Clearly it is in the interests of the EC6 for the UK to join them and impose the same tariff on imports. Let us assume that the combined group maintains the same internal relative price of food to manufactures. Let us also assume for the sake of diagrammatic simplicity that the new offer curve for B, B', coincides with A'. Their overall offer curve shifts to $OA' + B'$ (assumed for diagrammatic simplicity to coincide with the previous offer curve OA). The relative price of manufactures on the world market rises still further to the slope of OT_3. Thus, we can see from Fig. 3.7 that:

The international price becomes OT_3.

The domestic price in A and B is assumed to be the same as A's previous price, i.e. Va_3 is parallel to Qa_2.

Both A and B are assumed to export OM_7 $\therefore$ $2\,OM_7 = OM_8$.

Both A and B are assumed to import a_3M_7 $\therefore$ $2\,a_3M_7 = T_3M_8$.

a_3 now represents the trade indifference point of both A and B; it is clearly higher than a_2 and may also be higher than a_1—if it is not higher than a_1, A has not been pursuing an optimum policy.

On the other hand, B may or may not be worse off, depending on the relative size of B in relation to A and the world market. Furthermore, the assumption so far made that the tariff revenue is redistributed back to the consumers of the country concerned does not apply to the EC where it is transferred to the Commission. (Thus, in Fig. 3.5, instead of reaching consumption point C_2, the country would be operating on the budget line Y_2P_2. Under these circumstances consumers are always worse off. The actual change in the offer curve also depends on how the Commission spends the revenue.)

There are clear limitations to this type of analysis. One is that both A and B are assumed to purchase all their imports of food from the world market.

However, Ghosh (1974) has considered customs unions of complementary economies. He evaluates the effect of union with respect to the prior tariff-ridden state of the constituent economies. He assumes that, with a union between two countries, one of them, described as passive, trades exclusively with the other. The active member trades its surplus with the rest of the world. The member that ends up with the more favourable terms of trade will gain and the other will lose. This situation most aptly reflects the entry of the smaller agricultural exporting countries into the EU, such as the Irish Republic, Portugal, and maybe Denmark, which have benefited greatly from an improvement in their terms of trade because of the CAP.

Thus, both partial and general equilibrium comparative static analyses show that entry to a customs union is not necessarily an improvement on a country's previous position. Furthermore, in both cases, from the point of view of the world as a whole, it is an inferior position to a non-discriminatory reduction of tariffs or the optimum of free trade. This applies also to a free trade area, except, as explained, because the prices to consumers are not raised, the cost of trade diversion is less.

This is why so much emphasis is placed on the other benefits that are alleged to arise from preferential trading areas, in particular, benefits arising from the greater exploitation of economies of scale, which it is is claimed that such arrangements encourage.

3.5. **The concept of economies of scale**

The concept of economies of scale has been carefully analysed by Silberston (1972), and discussed by Pelkmans (1984), whilst statistical evidence on the size of scale economies has been provided by Pratten and Dean (1965) and Pratten (1971). Scale economies exist if average costs fall when a firm increases its output by investing in greater productive capacity—that is, by increasing its scale of operations. It is shown by a fall in the long-run average cost curve, which is the envelope of the short-run average cost curves. Technological knowledge and the prices of factors of production, which include the rate of interest, are assumed constant for any given long-run average cost curve.

The economies are partly associated with the size of plant—that is, production at any given geographical location. They may occur because capital costs do not increase proportionally with output—machines producing twice as fast may not cost twice as much. There may also be a spreading of indivisibilities associated with operating at any particular location in the form of secretarial and administrative services. These will be called plant economies. The actual shape of the long-run average cost curve of a plant will depend on the relative factor prices of factors of production, and the way they are combined. For instance, with a given plant, a doubling of the number of hours it is worked per year with the same manning levels, say from 4,000 to 8,000, would halve the capital costs per unit of output. The minimum efficient technical size of a plant with these longer hours would be different from one in which the increase in output had been obtained by continuing to work 4,000 hours but building a larger size of plant. Thus, what are called 'engineering' estimates of economies of scale must include some assumption about the number of hours a plant is worked.

There may also be economies associated with the length of production run. Each time the specifications of a product are changed, turnround time is required for resetting machines. In so far as the production of a particular specification is carried out in only one plant, these are often regarded as contributing to plant economies.

However, the economies of scale may also be associated with the size of firm—that is, the unit of control and decision-making. In particular, for the high-technology industries, an increase in the total output of a product reduces the research-and-development (R&D) expenditure per unit.

These are all internal economies, the benefit of which may be appropriated by a firm. There are also external economies associated with the expansion of an industry which lead to the cost curves of firms within the industry falling as total output is increased. These may be due to the development of specialized services and the improvement in marketing facilities which may result from the expansion of industrial output.

The general approach in the theory is to assume that the firm discussed has only one plant and is the sole domestic producer of the product. Implicitly, the economies of both plant and firm are being considered.

Let us now consider how the formation of a customs union may lead to the greater exploitation of economies of scale, and the the benefits and losses that will accrue to the member countries. We will first consider this within a comparative static framework which is a development and extension of work by Mead (1968) and Corden (1972); this will be called Model T (for traditional). Then we will consider the imperfect competition model, termed Model M, which has been devised by Smith and Venables (1988a, 1988b).

Traditional analysis: Model T

In the traditional Model T, the product of the home industry is taken as indistinguishable from that of the foreign partner firms or the rest of the world. If the home producer is the sole seller in the domestic market, it might find it difficult to reach a profit-maximizing position, because, as the long-run marginal cost is below the long-run average cost curve, equating marginal cost with marginal revenue may lead to a firm making a loss unless the demand curve is relatively inelastic (although less than −1). A profit-maximizing firm would then either refrain from producing or produce the minimum possible. In order to avoid this, the government often regulates the price. The presumption in much theoretical work is that a policy of average cost pricing is pursued. This we will call assumption (i), which is assumed to be a possibility even with trade.

However, if the economy is open, the firm is faced with two exogenous prices—on the one hand, the world price, at which it can export the product, on the other hand, the tariff-distorted price, at which products can enter the market from abroad. These represent its minimum and maximum price respectively.

The general argument is that, if the country's cost curve is relatively low compared with that of the world as a whole, then it will expand production and export and will not need a preferential system to exploit economies of scale. No further mention will be made of this situation.

However, if the cost curve is high in comparison with the world price, it may be assumed (as in Corden 1972) that a firm will maximize its profits by charging the maximum price—that is, the price at which the product from abroad will just enter. If it can cover costs at this price, it will produce; otherwise it will not. This is taken as assumption (ii).

Therefore, in considering the outcome of a customs union formed between two countries whose long-run average cost curves exhibit economies of scale but lie above the world price, the important features are the pricing policies pursued, and whether the countries produce before and after the union.

For the sake of simplicity, we will assume that the level of protection existing in the members of the customs union prior to entry was the same level as the CET. To focus on the issues involved, the production function, shown by the long-run average cost (LAC) curve, is assumed to be the same in the home and partner country, and is implicitly assumed to be that of an industry, maybe consisting of only one firm, maybe consisting of only one plant.

Three situations can be distinguished, as shown in Fig. 3.8.

(a) No production prior to entry in either country (see Fig. 3.8a)

Prior to entry, imports will provide for all consumption in both countries, OQ_1 in H and OQ_2 in P. Home market prices will be P_W' and the tariff revenue will be $P_W P_W' \times OQ_1$ in H and $P_W P_W' \times OQ_2$ in P.

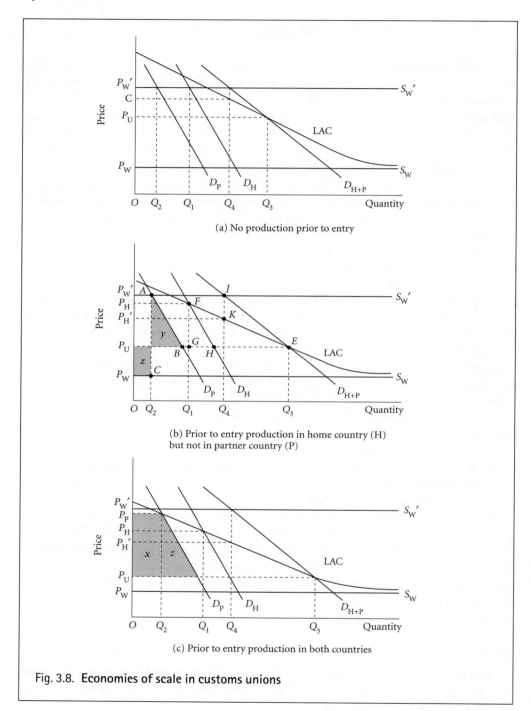

(a) No production prior to entry

(b) Prior to entry production in home country (H) but not in partner country (P)

(c) Prior to entry production in both countries

Fig. 3.8. **Economies of scale in customs unions**

After entry, if one country supplies the whole of the market, it can now produce at a lower average cost along LAC than P_W'. Let us assume that production is now carried out by H. There are two possibilities.

(i) If prices are equated with average cost, no producer surplus will be earned. The price within the customs union will fall to P_U with output OQ_3. There will be a gain in consumer surplus in both countries and a loss in tariff revenue. The net gain in each country will be the consumption effect—that is, the consumer surplus on the increase in consumption, minus the cost of trade diversion from the low-cost world producers to the higher-cost home-country producer, which will be $P_U P_W$ multiplied by the previous quantity of imports.

(ii) However, if prices remain at P_W', there will be no benefits to consumers. One country, assumed to be H, can now produce OQ_4 at a lower cost C than it can be be purchased from third countries with the CET. If the partner country P now obtains all its supplies from H, it suffers a loss of tariff revenue which represents its welfare loss; H also loses tariff revenue, but set against this it has profits of $P_W'C \times OQ_4$.

(b) Prior to entry production in home country H but not in partner country P (see Fig. 3.8b)

Prior to entry, the partner country will import all its supplies OQ_2 from third countries at a foreign-exchange price P_W, which with its tariff will appear as a price P_W'. Tariff revenue will be $P_W P_W' AC$. Again there are two possibilities.

(i) If average cost pricing is assumed prior to entry, country H will produce all its requirements OQ_1 at a price OP_H. On entry H will expand its output to OQ_3 at a price P_U—i.e. its costs of production will have fallen from P_H to P_U.

There will be a gain to consumers in both countries. The partner country will gain consumer surplus of $P_W'ABP_U$. This must be set against its loss of tariff revenue of $P_W'ACP_W$. Thus it shows a consumption gain of y and trade diversion loss of z.

The home country gains the benefit of a *cost reduction* due to the expansion of its industry. Thus, OQ_1 is now obtained at a lower cost—that is, P_U compared with a previous P_H—and the whole of this benefit is passed on to consumers. In addition, consumers gain a surplus of FHG on the expansion in their consumption. Thus, the home consumers have a clear gain and there are no trade diversion losses to set against them.

(ii) If prices remain at P_W', there are no benefits to consumers. If the partner country P transfers its purchases OQ_2 to the home country, it sustains a loss of tariff revenue and welfare of $P_W'ACP_W$. Country H will expand production to OQ_4. Its cost of production will now be P_H' and producers will make profits of $P_W'JKP_H'$.

(c) Prior to entry production in both countries (see Fig. 3.8c)

(i) If the prices in both countries are equal to their LAC, then prior to entry the price in the partner country will be P_P and quantity produced and purchased Q_2, and in the

Lynden Moore

home country the price will be P_H and quantity produced and consumed Q_1. There will be no imports into either country.

With the formation of the union, assuming that it is the firm in H which expands to supply the customs-union market, the price will fall to P_U. Country H will produce Q_3. Consumers in H will benefit from the *cost-reduction* effect $P_H P_U \times OQ_1$ on the amount H was originally supplying plus the additional consumer surplus on the increase in consumption that takes place because of the fall in price.

The industry of the partner country P completely disappears because of the expansion of it in H. There appears to be an efficiency gain due to trade creation equal to the shaded area x, and a gain in surplus on additional consumption z. Thus, country P appears to show gains without any losses.

(ii) If the prices charged are equal to P_W', then the initial production in both countries would be lower and so would the production after entry at OQ_4. The final cost of production would be P_H' and the difference between this and the price, $P_W' P_H'$ would represent a per-unit profit on the quantity OQ_4 which would go entirely to the producers in country H.

Conclusions

Consumers benefit only if prices are equated with average costs, or, if such an extreme assumption is modified, if they face lower prices which means that possibility (ii) examined above does not hold.

If a country is initially importing from third countries, entry into the customs union will always involve it in making a loss due to trade diversion. Thus, the only circumstances in which trade-diversion costs are not incurred is when both countries are initially dependent on home production. In that case, expansion of production in one country leads to the disappearance of the industry in the other. This is not regarded as a loss in this type of marginal welfare analysis. But clearly, if this involved a number of industries in P or was important to country P's economy, some adjustment to exchange rates would be required.

Because of the assumption that the LAC curves are the same in both countries, the direction of trade is inherently indeterminate, although the country that can produce in the larger market will appear to have lower costs of production.

In all cases shown, the countries would be better off if they imported from the rest of the world.

Imperfect competition: Model M

The Emerson Report on the benefits the EC would obtain by removing their non-tariff barriers to trade by the end of 1992 approached the problem in an entirely different way

(CEC : 1988) using an imperfect competition model, Model M, developed and applied by Smith and Venables (1988*a*, 1988*b*).

In the Smith and Venables model each EC firm is assumed to produce in only one EC country, and, as in the previous analysis, implicitly in one plant. Each firm may produce several varieties of product, but the varieties are peculiar to it and cannot be produced by any other firm. The products of different firms within the same industry are imperfect substitutes.

Each firm can produce for its home market or can export its product; it will receive the consumer price in the former, but only $(1 - t)$ multiplied by the consumer price in the latter, where t represents the selling costs associated with exporting. It is assumed that because of the selling cost the firms will account for a smaller proportion of their export than home markets. A reduction in the selling costs, such as those associated with the removal of non-tariff barriers to intra-EC trade, will lead to greater exports and thus induce greater competition and lower prices in all markets. This will expand consumption and allow firms further to exploit their economies of scale.

The empirical basis of this Emerson Report was a series of studies, in particular Pratten (1988). Much of the data referred to the 1960s. Pratten identified various factors which contributed to economies of scale and then listed the 'engineering' estimates. Most of these were associated with the size of plant or production runs, but some were also attributed to the spreading of R&D expenditure over more units. The minimum efficient technical scale (METS) of plant is defined where costs cease to fall rapidly. The measurement of economies of scale is the percentage increase in costs at half or a third of the METS.

Smith and Venables initially propose a cost function with an initial fixed cost and a constant marginal cost. This then becomes modified by averaging it with another function with a declining marginal cost. They regard this as approximating Pratten's empirical findings on economies of scale.

Each producer is assumed to maximize profits by equating marginal cost with marginal revenue. This is achievable because there are a number of producers which each individually face an elasticity very much greater than the elasticity of demand for the product itself. Smith and Venables considered the firms to be making either the 'Cournot' assumption, in which each firm regards the sales of other firms as fixed, or the 'Bertrand' assumption, in which each firm regards the prices of other firms as fixed. In both cases, the elasticity of demand that the firm faces in its export market is assumed to be greater than that in the home market and therefore marginal revenue is a greater proportion of price in the former.

As sales expand, so does output, and therefore there is a greater exploitation of economies of scale. If the less efficient firms are forced out by the increased competition, this will enable those remaining to exploit their economies of scale still further.

Smith and Venables take production and consumption data for ten industries as follows:

242 cement, lime, and plaster
257 pharmaceutical products
260 artificial and synthetic fibres
322 machine tools
330 office machinery
342 electrical motors, generators, transformers
346 electrical household appliances
351 motor vehicles and engines
438 carpets, carpeting, oilcloth, linoleum
451 footwear

In some cases these industries were divided up into a number of equal-sized sub-industries—for instance, office machinery was broken down into two sub-industries, electric motors into three, and domestic electrical appliances and pharmaceuticals each into five. Each of these industries or sub-industries is treated as one market.

In order to apply this model, Smith and Venables divided the world into six 'countries'—France, Germany, Italy, the UK, the rest of the EC, and the rest of the world. For each industry a matrix of production and consumption for the six 'countries' was obtained for 1982. The elasticities of demand for the products of the industries were available, but, in order to obtain the elasticities of demand facing the individual firms, information on concentration was required. This was constructed from the Eurostat data on the size distribution of firms using the Herfindahl index of concentration from which was 'calculated the number of "representative" firms in each country. This is the number of equal-sized firms which would give rise to the same effective degree of market concentration as the observed distribution of unequal-sized firms . . . The minimum efficient scale [was] taken to be the size of the average "representative" firm in the EC' (Smith and Venables 1988a: 5.9).

The removal of non-tariff barriers was regarded as being equal to a tariff equivalent reduction of between 2.5 and 13.5 per cent. This was then regarded as a reduction in the selling cost of exporting to other EC countries.

Using these calculations, the Emerson Report shows the percentage reduction in cost from exploiting economies of scale and from restructuring—that is, the disappearance of the less efficient firms. The greatest welfare gains were expected from the chemical industry (Ecu 7.7 billion), electrical goods (Ecu 5.4 billion), motor vehicles (Ecu 4.7 billion), and mechanical engineering (Ecu 4.6 billion) (CEC 1988: table A.7).

Comparison of Model M and Model T

Clearly, the assumptions underlying the two analyses of economies of scale, Model T and Model M, are entirely different. In Model T one industry or firm is assumed for each country, the production functions for different firms are the same (although this assumption could be modified), and the benefits and costs from the formation of a customs union depend on the reduction in the average cost obtained, and the pricing policy pursued. The absolute height of the tariff (or tariff equivalent of non-tariff barriers) determines the maximum exploitation of economies of scale that can occur because of the customs union, because at the tariff-distorted world price imports could enter and at the world price the country could export.

However, in Model M, because of the heterogeneity of product, there is no 'world price'. Model M allows for several firms in each country and for differentiation of products. But these advantages of approximation to reality are thrown away by substituting a number of representative firms for the actual number and size distribution of firms. There is also a very limited concept of differentiation.

From the point of view of trade, the question is whether in the long run the initial advantages of a country or firm are sufficient to determine trade flows. Thus although, in Model T, H is assumed to have the lowest average cost and therefore to increase its output, in the very long run P would be just as cheap a location. The direction of trade flows is therefore indeterminate. In Model M, where individual firms appear to have advantages specific to themselves, if these are specific to the firm as distinct from the country, it is not clear why the firm should not relocate its production to the cheapest location within the EC or maybe abroad. This is precisely what worries trade unionists in the countries with higher wages and higher social-security contributions.

Another aspect of the situation is the identification of the economies of scale. The implicit assumption in both models appears to be that a one-plant firm is being considered; in particular, the Emerson Report is perpetually slithering from a discussion of the METS and economies of scale of plant to that of a firm without distinguishing the two. However, Smith and Venables discount economies of scale associated with plant size by assuming that their representative firms are at the METS; it is not clear whether their cost function, which appears to allow for the further spreading of fixed cost, which they discuss in terms of R&D, is therefore only an economy of scale of a firm. If it is specific to the firm, then the argument in the previous paragraph applies.

The greatest contrast between these models is in their treatment of trade with the external world. In Model T it is assumed that, if, by exploiting its economies of scale, a firm could produce at the world price, it would already have expanded sufficiently to export. However, in the Emerson Report, one of the advantages that is said to accrue from further exploitation of economies of scale is that, as costs fall, European firms will become more competitive and their exports to the outside world will increase. But in this case the argument used in Model T—that they will already be exporting—appears just as applicable to imperfect competition. Furthermore, there are considerable exports to non-member countries of all the products considered by Smith and Venables. This suggests that economies of scale of the most efficient firms are already being exploited.

Both models assume that the removal of barriers to trade between members of preferential-trading-area countries is likely to lead to trade diversion from non-member countries.

Neither of the models allows for the multinational nature of the firms operating in the industry. In so far as these producers straddle national boundaries, the assumptions about the bases of the competing firms do not hold. For instance, the choice is not so much whether the French and Germans buy French or German cars, but where the Germans wish to produce their cars. The concept of differentiation being associated with a firm producing in a particular country which then determines trade collapses. The location of production becomes determined by costs.

This situation, in which a firm looks at the rest of the world before deciding where to locate production to supply a particular market, is called 'globalization'. Clearly the fewer the barriers to trade the easier it is to move production around. Thus, although Germany is still the largest EU exporter of cars, it has not responded to the Single European Market or the reduction in trade barriers with Eastern Europe by expanding output and thereby further exploiting economies of scale. On the contrary, as it is now a high-cost producer, it expects to lose 100,000 jobs in the cars and components sector by the end of the decade. This is due partly to the relocation of production to Eastern Europe (Done 1996), and partly to the takeover of Austin Rover, the British champion, by BMW in 1994 and subsequent rationalization. In 1995 there were thirty takeovers of EU automotive component manufacturers. However, only sixteen were by other EU firms, ten were by US firms, and the others were by firms from Japan, Canada, and Korea (Simonian 1996). (In addition, one UK firm, Automotive Products, was a management buyout.) This illustrates that multinationals from outside the EU can also take advantage of the free market.

3.6. Conclusion

The traditional analysis of the exploitation of economies of scale in a customs union has been in terms of a homogeneous product. In this case, a firm may benefit and expand its output if its potential long-run average cost of production lies somewhere between the international price at which it could export and the tariff-distorted price at which imports can enter the union. The actual distribution of costs and benefits depends on which firms produce before and after the formation of the union, and the price policy being pursued.

The imperfect competition approach pursued by Smith and Venables for the Emerson Report eschews all consideration of the level of protection. It is solely concerned with firms within the customs union. Each is assumed to be based in its home country producing and exporting from it. In the Emerson Report the economies of scale of plant are not distinguished from those of the firm. The more efficient firms are regarded as expanding at the expense of the less efficient.

However, both models exclude the possibility of firms choosing to shift production to lower-cost locations, which has occurred. The great incentive to inward direct investment which is provided by high levels of protection is also ignored.

Discussion questions

1. Define a customs union and a free trading area. With the aid of diagrams explain how their formation results in trade creation and trade diversion, and the effect of these on the welfare of member countries.
2. Under what circumstances is a country likely to benefit from the greater exploitation of economies of scale by joining a customs union?

REFERENCES

Balassa, B. (1974), 'Trade Creation and Trade Diversion in the European Common Market', *Manchester School*, 62/2: 93–135.

CEC (1988): Commission of the European Communities, 'The Economics of 1992: An Assessment of the Potential Economic Effects of Completing the Internal Market of the European Community' (the Emerson Report), *European Economy*, 35 (Mar.).

Cooper, C. A., and Massell, B. F. (1965), 'A New Look at Customs Union Theory', *Economic Journal*, 75: 742–7.

Corden, W. M. (1972), 'Economies of Scale and Customs Union Theory', *Journal of Political Economy*, 80: 465–75.

Done, K. (1996), 'A Drive in the Fast Lane', *Financial Times* (28 Feb.), 17.

EFTA (1969): European Free Trade Association, *The Effects of EFTA on the Economies of Member States* (Geneva: EFTA).

Ghosh, S. K. (1974), 'Towards a Theory of Multiple Customs Unions', *American Economic Review*, 64/1: 91–101.

Kindleberger, C. P. (1973), *International Economics*, 5th edn. (Homewood, Ill.: Richard D. Irwin).

Krugman, P. R. (1979), 'Increasing Returns, Monopolistic Competition, and International Trade', *Journal of International Economics*, 9: 469–79.

Lipsey, R. G. (1957), 'The Theory of Customs Unions: Trade Diversion and Welfare', *Economica*, 24: 40–6.

Mead, D. C. (1968), 'The Distribution of Gains in Customs Unions between Developing Countries', *Kyklos*, 21: 713–34; repr. in P. Robson (ed.), *International Economic Integration* (Harmondsworth: Penguin, 1972), 278–303.

Moore, L. (1989), 'Changes in British Trade Analysed in a Pure Trade Theory Framework', in D. Cobham, R. Harrington, and G. Zis (eds.), *Money, Trade and Payments: Essays in Honour of D. J. Coppock* (Manchester: Manchester University Press), 153–75.

Pelkmans, J. (1984), *Market Integration in the European Community* (The Hague: Martinus Nijhoff).

Pratten, C. (1971), *Economies of Scale in Manufacturing Industry* (Department of Applied Economics, Occasional Papers, No. 28; Cambridge: Cambridge University Press).

—— (1988), 'A Survey of the Economies of Scale', in Commission of the European Communities, *Research on the 'Cost of Non-Europe'—Basic Findings*, ii. *Studies on the Economics of Integration* (Luxembourg: Office for Official Publications of the European Communities).

—— and Dean, R. M. (1965), *The Economies of Large-Scale Production in British Industry* (Department of Applied Economics, Occasional Papers, No. 3, Cambridge: Cambridge University Press).

Robson, P. (1984), *The Economics of International Integration*, 2nd edn. (London: Allen & Unwin).

Silberston, A. (1972), 'Economies of Scale in Theory and Practice', *Economic Journal*, 82: 369–91.

Simonian, H. (1996), 'Parts and the Big Story', *Financial Times*, 2, Automotive Components (21 May).

Smith, A., and Venables, A. J. (1988*a*), 'The Costs of Non-Europe: An Assessment Based on a Formal Model of Imperfect Competition and Economies of Scale', in Commission of the European Communities, *Research on the 'Cost of Non-Europe'—Basic Findings*, ii. *Studies on the Economics of Integration* (Luxembourg: Office for Official Publications of the European Communities).

—— —— (1988*b*), 'Completing the Internal Market in the European Community', *European Economic Review*, 32: 1501–25.

—— —— (1991), 'Economic Integration and Market Access', *European Economic Review*, 35.

Viner, J. (1950), *The Customs Union Issue* (Carnegie Endowment for International Peace), 41–55.

Winters, L. A. (1984), 'British Imports of Manufacturers and the Common Market', *Oxford Economic Papers*, 36: 103–18.

—— (1987), 'Britain in Europe: A Survey of Quantitative Trade Studies', *Journal of Common Market Studies*, 25/4: 315–25.

CHAPTER 4

Economics of the CAP in Transition

DAVID COLMAN and DEBORAH ROBERTS

4.1. Introduction

The Common Agricultural Policy (CAP) of the EU (European Union, as the enlarged Community is now named) is a remarkably complex assembly of instruments and regulations covering trade controls, price support measures, income transfers, production subsidies, investment grants, conservation policies, health regulations, labelling standards, etc. It has its own monetary unit—the 'green Ecu' (European Currency Unit) and a huge bureaucracy to manage and oversee its operations. Additional complexity continually emerges as the policy as a whole adjusts to the quadruple pressures of (1) budgetary and consumer costs, (2) anguished responses by non-Member States whose trade interests are damaged, (3) concerns for the environmental damage caused by modern farming methods, and (4) protests about falling farm incomes despite the high costs of the policy.

In response to these pressures the CAP underwent a major change in 1992/3 which added to its complexity. These reforms, named after the then Agriculture Commissioner Ray MacSharry, involved a large reduction (phased until 1995/6) in the commodity price support levels, and the introduction of a system of compensation for these price cuts for those farmers prepared to reduce and limit input use (essentially in respect to area planted and number of livestock). In the wake of these changes, it is now necessary to explain both elements of this system, the 'old' system of price support, which continues but with diminished importance, and the 'new' system of compensation or income support which has been grafted on.

There is no doubt that the shape of the reformed policy was greatly influenced by the negotiations on agriculture in the Uruguay Round of the General Agreement on Tariffs and Trade (GATT), which commenced in 1986 and were finally ratified in 1994.[1] A significant contribution to achieving the final settlement was the negotiation by

MacSharry in November 1992 of a bilateral agreement with the USA, the so-called Blair House accord. He and the Commission claimed that the EU could comply with the agricultural commitments in the Uruguay Round of GATT up to the year 2000 without breaking the bounds of the 1992/3 CAP reform package, a position which appears to be substantially correct (Tangermann 1996).

In reflection of the situation sketched above, the chapter continues by exploring the economics of the main agricultural policy instruments which have endured since the founding of the European Economic Community (EEC) in 1957. This is followed in Section 4.3 by a brief review of the pressures which have helped to bring about the reform of the CAP. Sections 4.4 and 4.5 deal with the reforms themselves, starting first with reforms prior to 1992 and then proceeding to examine the 'MacSharry reform package'. This is followed by a summary plus a brief discussion of possible future changes to the CAP.

4.2. The original system of CAP

The establishment of an integrated common market for agriculture by its original six Member States was a pivotal task in the formation of the EEC, and is the one which has persistently made the largest demands on its budgetary resources. Article 39 of the Treaty of Rome sets out a number of objectives, including ensuring supplies to consumers at reasonable prices, but the consistent emphasis of the CAP until the mid-1980s was 'to increase agricultural productivity by promoting technical progress' and 'to ensure a fair standard of living for the agricultural community'.

In the post-war period, when the memory of food shortages was relatively fresh, the productivist emphasis of the founding member countries was understandable. The dominant method of agricultural support had been import tariffs, which were effective means of raising agricultural prices, since, in the early 1960s, the six Member States were net importers of cereals and oilseeds and only just self-sufficient in livestock products. With this background of external protection, the movement to a common external tariff (CET) for agriculture, as required by the Treaty of Rome, was a politically acceptable step towards the creation of a common market when accompanied by the abolition of customs duties on internal trade within the ring-fence of the CET. Importantly, for agriculture, instead of fixed tariffs, the EEC adopted a variable import tariff or levy system (which persisted until July 1995, when fixed tariffs were, in principle, introduced—see below). This entailed setting minimum import prices (MIPs) with variable import levies (VILs) equal to the difference between the minimum import price and the *lowest* c.i.f. price offered by importers at the Community's borders. In the case of cereals, the MIP is called the *threshold price*, for beef, it is the *guide price*.

Because the MIP for all major products was (with minor exceptions in 1974 and

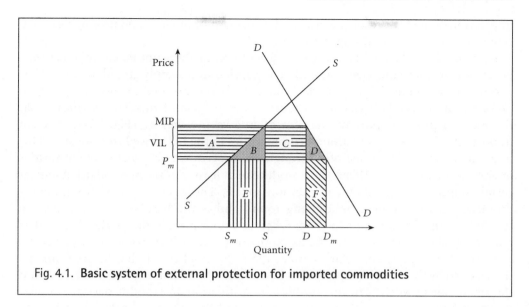

Fig. 4.1. Basic system of external protection for imported commodities

1978) consistently maintained above the c.i.f. international prices (P_m), at which imports were available, EU market prices of imported commodities have been forced upwards. Fig. 4.1 shows the theoretical effects of this. EU supply is increased from S_m to S and demand is depressed from D_m to D. Thus the imported quantity falls from ($D_m - S_m$) to ($D - S$). This trade-distorting feature of the policy was, however, exacerbated from the standpoint of agricultural exporting countries by two attendant facts. One is that import demand ($D - S$) became completely inelastic to changes in world prices. As P_m fell, the VIL increased to ensure that no imports entered the EU at below the MIP; the EU market was completely insulated from all movements in international prices unless they rose above the MIP. The second is that international market prices are forced downwards; they would rise if EU price support and trade distortion was reduced and EU import demand was higher.

The increase in internal EU prices causes *producer surplus to rise* by the value of area A, as shown in Fig. 4.1. *Budgetary revenues* equal in value to C accrue to the EU from import levies/tariffs and may be counted as a gain (less some cost for collection). These gains are, however, more than offset by the *loss in consumer surplus* equivalent to areas $A + B + C + D$.[2] In fact, using this neo-classical economic calculus shows an overall *economic welfare loss* to the EU from the policy of $B + D$, reflecting a basic result of comparative static economic theory that free trade is optimal and that trade interventions result in a loss of economic welfare.

This last result can be confirmed by a dual calculation based on Fig. 4.1. *Extra resource costs* of $B + E$ are stimulated by the price support to generate output which could be *imported at a cost* of E, thus registering a *welfare loss B*. Consumers have also reduced consumption which they value at $F + D$, but which cost them only F before the imposition of the MIP, resulting in an additional *welfare loss* of D and producing a total economic welfare or 'deadweight loss' of $B + D$.

Because of rapid technical change in agriculture, further stimulated by prices supported above international levels, underlying agricultural supply growth in the EU has continuously exceeded domestic demand growth and resulted in the emergence of excess supply in cereals, beef, dairy products, wine, and some fruits. This has meant that the internal price support mechanism of *intervention buying* (Fig. 4.2) played an important role when production of commodities in the EU moved into surplus. This internal support system operates through the process whereby national authorities operating the EU policy offer to buy produce of at least minimum standard quality at certain times of the year at the intervention price P_i. The latter is set in Ecus at the community-level EU's annual price-fixing round and is the basis of common pricing throughout the Community. In effect P_i acts as a floor price in the market,[3] and it has been consistently set above the f.o.b. export price, P_x, which could be obtained by exporting the surplus. This form of price support has not been applied to all commodities covered by the CAP, but applies to wheat, barley, to milk in the forms of butter and skimmed milk powder, beef, and to wine after distillation. In a modified form it applies to certain fruits and vegetables and fish, surpluses of which cannot be stored but have to be destroyed.

The effects of the internal price support policy are broadly as shown in Fig. 4.2. The higher price and additional output stimulated (from S_x to S_i) results in *increased* producer surplus of $H + I + J$. *Consumer surplus* is reduced by $H + I$, as demand is cut from D_x to D_i. The amount by which supply exceeds consumer demand, $S_i - D_i$, is purchased

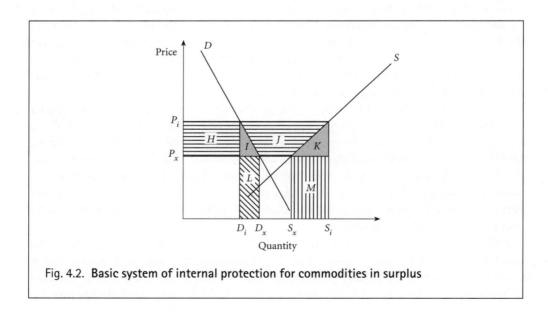

Fig. 4.2. **Basic system of internal protection for commodities in surplus**

into intervention stores, where it develops into the beef and butter mountains, and wine lakes, as they are often referred to in the media. It is conventional to explain the *budgetary costs* which arise from these intervention surpluses as being equivalent to areas $I + J + K$ in the figure. This is the cost which would arise if all the surplus $(S_i - D_i)$ is disposed of as exports with the aid of an *export refund* (ER), or export subsidy, equal to $P_i - P_x$; alternatively it is the loss made by the intervention authority from buying the surplus at P_i and selling at P_x. In reality $I + J + K$ underestimates the budgetary cost of surplus management, since it does not allow for the storage costs or for the deterioration and wastage of product while stored. If, however, we accept this measure of budgetary cost and add the consumer surplus loss of $H + I$, it transpires that the producer surplus gain of $H + I + J$ only partially offsets it, and leaves an economic welfare loss of $I + K$. The same result is obtained by setting the increased export revenue $(L + M)$ against the resource cost $(K + M)$ plus the reduction in consumption value $(I + L)$.

A point which should be emphasized is that the system of intervention buying (Fig. 4.2) cannot be operated without a minimum import price policy (as in Fig. 4.1) if P_i exceeds P_m, which is how the CAP has been operated. Without an MIP in excess of P_i it would be profitable to import at price P_m in order to sell into intervention, which would be a completely unstable and untenable state of affairs. Thus, even though in the 1980s and early 1990s the primary instrument of agricultural price support has been intervention buying, the import-levy/minimum-import-price system has been necessary to protect its operation.[4]

The agrimonetary system

The minimum import prices, intervention prices, import levies, and export refunds described above are all fixed in terms of Ecus and converted into each of the Member States' national currencies, using so-called *green rates* of exchange. Such agricultural green rates are essential because it is not administratively feasible to change, say, sterling- or franc-denominated intervention prices on a daily basis, as market-exchange rates to the Ecu continuously change. Rather, they and other agricultural support prices and payments are reviewed only on a periodic basis during which a Member State's green rate of exchange and its market rate of exchange may have diverged. If the EU had a single currency, the need for green rates would not exist and there would be 'common agricultural policy prices' throughout the EU. However, as it stands, agricultural policy has its own agrimonetary system of exchange rates, which has the capacity differentially to influence returns to producers in different countries or of different products.

If green exchange rates had been adjusted at periodic intervals in a simple way to realign with currency market rates so that *monetary gaps*[5] were always small, the agrimonetary system would have been of minor significance. However, because Member States have, on occasions, resisted adjustments in policy prices set in their own currency which should follow either currency appreciation or depreciation, monetary gaps have at times been large, so that reforming and adjusting the agrimonetary system has been a continuous and significant process. This has been complicated by the continuing enlargement of EU membership.

It was the large Deutschmark revaluation and franc devaluation of 1969 which first led to major divergence of green exchange rates from commercial market rates. Revaluation of the Deutschmark against the Ecu should have meant a decline in Deutschmark denominated intervention and minimum import prices, which would have caused agricultural prices (and farm incomes) to fall, even though prices of other German-produced goods and services would not have fallen. This was politically unacceptable in Germany, so that agrimoney green rates were not revalued and a (positive) monetary gap emerged. On its own, this monetary gap meant that agricultural imports from other Member States would have become cheaper than German produce, and German agricultural exports would have become less competitive.[6] This problem was exacerbated by devaluation of the French franc because France did not wish immediately to devalue its green rate as that would have pushed up agricultural prices and intensified inflationary pressures. A negative monetary gap therefore emerged for the franc, which, if no other measures had been taken, could have led to a major flood of agricultural exports to Germany and other Member States. To prevent this 'artificial trade' arising from the monetary gaps a system of Monetary Compensatory Amounts (MCAs) was introduced. These were intra-Community measures applied as import taxes and export subsidies for countries with positive monetary gaps (e.g. Germany) and as export taxes and import subsidies to those with negative gaps (e.g. France in 1969 and later the UK almost persistently). The MCAs were set to correspond approximately to the monetary gaps with the intention of neutralizing trade distortions arising from failure to adjust green exchange rates. Instead of being a temporary accommodation to the conditions of 1969, MCAs persisted until 1 January 1993, when the move to completion of the 'single market' required elimination of all internal trade barriers such as tariffs and subsidies.

A persistent factor influencing reform of the agrimonetary system has been the reluctance of the strong currency countries (principally Germany) to accept the price-reducing consequences of green-rate revaluation. In 1984 the agrimonetary system was modified, using the so-called *switchover coefficient* to create a *green central rate* of exchange such that the positive MCAs of Germany (and the other currencies maintaining parity with the Deutschmark in the European Exchange Rate Mechanism (ERM)) were to be eliminated by tying the green central rate to the Ecu exchange rate in the European Monetary System (EMS). Consequently only negative MCAs of weakening currencies were supposed to exist and these had to be reduced to less than a set rate (see below). This switchover system had the effect of increasing agricultural support prices expressed in domestic currencies, since every time the Deutschmark revalued the switchover coefficient increased to ensure that EU support prices did not fall in Germany.

The move to the 'single market' in January 1993 had been preceded by the 15 per cent devaluation of sterling in September 1992, followed by the lira, both of which dropped out of the European ERM. This led to relaxation of the exchange-rate bands for currencies remaining in the ERM, which, together with the fact that sterling and the lira were floating, meant continuous movement in market exchange rates. To accommodate this, a revised agrimonetary system has been operating to limit the maximum monetary gap between any pair of currencies to 5 per cent, the so-called 'floating franchise'. Adjustment of a green rate is supposed to be initiated at the end of each ten-day review period if its monetary gap has either exceeded +3 per cent or fallen below –2 per cent.

In fact, negative monetary gaps are dealt with more quickly than positive ones. The positive franchise is allowed to 'float up' to +5 per cent, and a breach of that bound has to be 'confirmed' before the correcting green-rate revaluation takes place. Furthermore, when revaluations do occur, countries are allowed to pay compensatory aid to farmers for price reductions, with 50 per cent of the cost met by the EU. Strong-currency countries' farmers are also protected from the effects of revaluation on direct payments (see below), since up to 1999 these are transformed from Ecu levels at green exchange rates prevailing at the end of 1995.

The removal of MCAs under the new agrimonetary system has moved the EU closer to common agricultural prices, but the operation of the 'franchise' still enables national prices persistently to differ slightly from those which would be dictated by market exchange rates.

4.3. The pressures for CAP reform

Budgetary pressure

The budgetary costs of the CAP provided a persistent source of pressure leading to the MacSharry reforms of 1992 (see below). They contributed significantly to the need to increase the total tax transfer from 0.77 per cent of the GDP of the nine members in 1980 to 1.03 per cent of the GDP of the twelve members in 1989. This permitted the expansion of spending on regional and social policy and for the percentage of total EC budgetary expenditure on the CAP to drop from 73 per cent in 1980 to 66 per cent in 1989. This modest change was only achieved by a combination of a stream of patching, *ad hoc* measures, as described in Section 4.4 below, to contain agricultural spending, and the periodic effects of a stronger US dollar which reduced the subsidy cost of exporting EC surpluses. The reforms which subsequently occurred have reduced CAP expenditure since 1993 to under 55 per cent of the total EU budget.

It is the costs of agricultural surplus management which dominate the budgetary expenditure of the European Agricultural Guidance and Guarantee Fund (EAGGF).[7] This is apparent from Table 4.1, which shows export restitution costs alone regularly accounting for over 30 per cent of total EAGGF, with the bulk of the 'other expenditure'

David Colman and Deborah Roberts

Table 4.1. **EAGGF expenditure on the CAP, selected years (Ecu m.)**

Year	Guarantee section expenditure			Guidance Section expenditure
	Export restitutions	Other[a]	Total	
EC6				
1971	879	1,129	2,008	—[b]
1972	1,186	1,514	2,700	376
EC9				
1973	1,026	2,807	3,833	182
1977	2,191	4,794	6,585	157
1980	5,441	5,850	11,291	479
EC10				
1982	4,739	7,632	12,371	563
1984	6,202	12,128	18,330	702
1985	6,587	13,141	19,728	243
EC12				
1987	9,147	13,802	22,950	895
1989	9,708	16,164	25,872	1,348
1991	10,029	22,306	32,335	2,128
1993	10,159	24,589	34,748	3,386
1994[c]	8,161	25,296	33,457	2,619

[a] Includes storage, withdrawals from the market, price subsidies (including aids to producers, processors, and marketeers), and guidance premiums.
[b] Not available in Ecu.
[c] Provisional.
Source: CEC, *Official Journal* (various issues).

being on costs for surplus storage and subsidized market disposal within the EU. As can be seen, Guidance Section expenditure on improving the farm structure of agriculture has (despite increases) remained small, with the vast bulk of budgetary resource diverted to market support.

Some of the patching measures to contain budgetary costs and surpluses prior to the 1992 reform package were quite significant, such as the milk quotas and co-responsibility levies which are discussed below. These measures failed to halt the relentless rise in the budget required for the CAP, and the reforms of 1992 became inexorable.

It must be recognized that budgetary costs are *transfers*. Funds are paid as taxes by certain groups in society and paid out or transferred to others. In economic welfare terms, such transfers are not a complete loss of resource; this is evident from the analysis based on Figs. 4.1 and 4.2 above, where the triangular areas of deadweight loss are much smaller than the budgetary and consumer cost transfers. In the case of the budgetary transfers, revenue is raised as a VAT levy at the country level, through direct national budgetary contributions and through import and sugar production levies; these are transferred to the EU in support of the principle of common financing of the Union's costs. These revenues are then used to finance storage and subsidized disposal of surplus products, and also the new forms of agricultural support detailed below. It follows that countries which import more agricultural products tend to contribute more and that there is a net transfer to countries with greater surpluses to store and export. For example, in 1992 the largest net contributors to the CAP budget were (in billions of Ecus) Germany (9.7) and the UK (2.4), while the main net gainers were Greece (3.6), Spain (2.7), Ireland (2.1), and Portugal (2.1).[8] Inevitably it has been the case that some countries have pressed for budgetary reform of the CAP with less enthusiasm than others, and that those which have pushed hardest, such as the UK, have sometimes been accused of lacking 'Community spirit'.

Consumer pressure

All the estimates of the costs of the original CAP system have demonstrated (unsurprisingly, given the assumption that any change in agricultural prices in the EU would be fully transmitted to food consumers) that the estimated transfer costs from consumers exceed the budgetary or taxpayer transfer by a significant margin. This is shown in the estimates for the EC by Roningen and Dixit (1989) in Table 4.2.[9] These are that in 1986 the cost to consumers in terms of higher food costs was over twice the budgetary cost of supporting agriculture and was almost equal to the net benefits to producers.

Various estimates have been made of the average cost imposed on EU non-farm families through higher prices and taxes to support the CAP. For 1984 the Department of Primary Industry (DPI)-Australia (1986, p. 1) estimated this at $US900 per family per year. This estimate of £600 (at an exchange rate of $US1.5 : £1), or £11.54 per week per family, compares with other estimates which range up to £16 per week per family of

Table 4.2. **Benefits and costs of agricultural support, 1986/7**

Countries	Producer benefits ($USbn.)	Consumer costs ($USbn.)	Taxpayer costs ($USbn.)	Net economic costs[a] ($USbn.)	Transfer ratio[b]
USA	26.3	6.0	30.0	9.2	1.4
EC	33.3	32.6	15.6	14.9	1.5
Japan	22.6	27.7	5.7	8.6	1.5

[a] Consumer costs + taxpayer costs – producer benefits.
[b] (Taxpayer + consumer costs)/producer benefits.

Source: Roningen and Dixit (1989).

four depending upon the year considered. Since even non-taxpayers, the poorest members of society, may have to bear perhaps 60 per cent of this cost, and since larger farms and generally wealthier farmers benefit most, the CAP can be legitimately criticized for transferring funds from the poorest members of society (since all must eat) to some who are relatively well off—there are also poor farmers in the EU. While this fact has been well recognized, the political lobby for consumers' interests has not developed the same weight of influence as the farm and agro-industry lobbies which have a specified central place in agricultural policy negotiations. Thus it has been largely left to academics, and particularly economists, to argue for CAP reform on the grounds of excessive cost to non-farm families as consumers and taxpayers (e.g. Josling and Hamway 1972, BAE (1985: ch. 6), and Brown 1989).

External pressure—the Uruguay Round of GATT

The CAP gave rise to progressive increases in trade distortion up to 1990. This was not even disguised by the incorporation of new Member States, which, by a process of trade diversion, switched a significant proportion of their agricultural imports from non-member to Member States. (This was particularly true of the accession to the EC of Eire, the UK, Spain, and Portugal). Table 4.3 confirms this general picture, showing, for several major commodities, either a substantial increase in EC net exports between 1973 and 1990 or, even more strikingly, a switch from being a net importer to a major net exporter. From the standpoint of non-member exporters of temperate zone agricultural products, not only have they suffered a severe contraction of their EU market as a consequence of the principle of community preference, but they have had to face intensified competition in other markets from the EU's subsidized exports. Australia and New Zealand were particularly badly affected when the UK joined the EC, and the USA, as the world's largest agricultural exporter, suffered particularly in the early 1980s prior to the inauguration of the Uruguay Round of negotiations on GATT in 1986. As an indication of this, Table 4.4 displays the dramatic changes in EC and US agricultural export volume in this period.

The USA's concern about the CAP and about protective policies in Japan and elsewhere can be gauged from the fact that, although it was at the USA's insistence that agricultural policy was excluded from earlier rounds of GATT negotiations and agreements, it was made the centrepiece of the Uruguay Round. Although agriculture was only one of fifteen negotiating heads, the USA stated that without a satisfactory solution on agriculture it would not sign an agreement. In seeking drastically to reduce agricultural support policies, the USA was backed by the so-called Cairns Group of agricultural exporting countries, which includes Australia and New Zealand.

In order to explain how the GATT negotiations influenced the 1992 reform of the CAP it is helpful to give a simplified account of the negotiating position of the USA and

Table 4.3. **Net external trade in selected agricultural products, 1973–1993**

Year	Product					
	Wheat[a] (million tonnes)	Other cereals[a] (excl. rice) (million tonnes)	Sugar[a] (million tonnes)	Butter (thousand tonnes)	Cheese (thousand tonnes)	Beef and veal[b] (thousand tonnes)
EC9						
1973	–	−10.8	−1.1	+204	+41	−913
1977	+0.9	−20.8	+0.1	+140	+84	−210
EC10						
1981	+10.7	−3.4	+3.3	+373	+213	+389
1983	+11.5	+0.5	+2.6	+250	+292	+165
1986	+11.9	+5.5	+2.6	+220	+269	+714
EC12						
1989	+18.3	+7.6	+3.3	+332	+324	+589
1991	+21.9	+7.4	+2.9	+275	+374	+804
1992	+23.5	+9.8	+3.6	+176	+355	+759
1992	n.a.	n.a.	n.a.	+120	+414	+666

Notes: Net imports are denoted by a minus (–) sign, and net exports by a plus (+) sign. n.a. = not available.

 [a] Wheat, other cereals, and sugar data are for harvest years 1973/4–1992/3; other commodities data are for calendar years.
 [b] Estimated: includes the carcass weight equivalent of trade in live animals.

Sources: CEC, *The Agricultural Situation in the Community*; *Official Journal of the Commission of the European Communities* (various issues).

Table 4.4. **Export volume indices of agricultural products, 1980–1986 (1980 = 100)**

Countries	1980	1981	1982	1983	1984	1985	1986
EC10	100	109	109	116	124	132	136
USA	100	100	93	89	90	73	67
Other developed countries	100	110	108	106	111	113	119

Source: GATT (1988: i, app., table III).

EU. (These and the positions of other groups are more fully summarized in Rayner *et al.* 1993). At the outset, in 1987–8 the USA demanded (i) elimination of all trade-distorting subsidies within ten years, (ii) elimination of all import barriers, including all health and non-health non-tariff barriers (NTBs), (iii) changes to policies for individual commodities to permit the agreed phasing-out of government support, and (iv) use of an aggregate measure of support (AMS), to establish initial levels of protection and to monitor progress with their elimination.

The importance of the last condition is apparent. In order to obtain a multinational agreement covering many commodities on reforming agricultural policy, there has first to be a common consent to use a particular measure of the distortion to be reduced or eliminated, and agreement as to its size for each commodity and each country. Then it is possible to negotiate timetables for reducing this distortion. The USA proposed a version of a measure called a Producer Subsidy Equivalent (PSE).

From the outset the EU accepted the need for an AMS but championed its own version, the Support Measurement Unit (SMU), which could reflect the impact of supply and support control measures taken in the second half of the 1980s. The EU, however, did not accept the objective of eliminating all agricultural support, proposing instead the notion of a short-term agreement on international market sharing and prices, with a long-term strategy of achieving more balanced support through reciprocal agreements.

In the process of negotiation which ensued some key ideas emerged, two of which, *tariffication* and *decoupling*, deserve mention. One aspect of EU policy which was particularly abhorrent to other exporting countries was the variable import levies and export subsidies, since (as noted above) these insulated the EU market almost completely from short-term fluctuations in world prices. The key to tariffication was the expression of non-tariff barriers as tariff equivalents and the combining of these with specific import tariffs to create single, bound (i.e. fixed maximum) tariffs. This placed an upper limit on protection against imports and paved the way for fixed (as opposed to variable) tariffs and their reduction according to a negotiated schedule. In implementing the GATT Agreement, however, special conditions affect the way tariff reduction is applied for individual commodities. Tariffs do still change and are not completely fixed.

Given that the central issue is trade distortion, it can reasonably be argued that there is no fundamental cause for international dispute if a country chooses to support its farmers in ways which do not cause supply to exceed competitive free trade levels (S_m and S_x in Figs. 4.1 and 4.2). Such payments might be said to be *decoupled* from supply response and not to be trade distorting. Academically the hunt has been on to identify forms of support which might be sufficiently decoupled. One proposal (Blandford *et al.* 1989) was for the introduction of Production Entitlement Guarantees (PEGs) whereby, for each commodity, farmers would be eligible for fixed payments on a quantity of output less than S_m and S_x in Figs. 4.1 and 4.2. In that way, it can be argued, supply at the margin would be influenced only by the free market price and would not be affected by the support payment offered.

Over the course of the Uruguay Round, the USA relaxed its position and agreed to accept that certain types of support, modelled very much on its own policy at that time, were sufficiently decoupled to be exempt from the reductions in support levels required by GATT. These are support payments for which farmers can qualify only by adopting certain supply-restricting measures such as *setting aside* (taking out of production) a proportion of previously farmed arable land. The acceptance of these and other environmentally related support payments proved critical in bridging the gap between the US position and that of the EU and led, in November 1992, to the signing of the so-called Blair House Accord, a bilateral agreement between the two negotiating parties.

The Blair House Accord contained four critical elements to be phased into the CAP over the period 1993–9. These are, first, a commitment to *tariffy* all existing border measures and reduce tariff levels by 36 per cent (although an element of Community preference has been maintained by the EU via the so-called 'special safeguard clause'); secondly, an agreement to reduce internal support measures by 20 per cent from 1986–8 levels (with new compensation payments exempt for the reasons outlined above); thirdly, a commitment to reduce the value of export subsidies by 36 per cent and subsidized export volume by 21 per cent, and, finally, the acceptance of a 'Peace Clause' which lasts until 2000 and effectively limits either the EU or the USA from taking unilateral trade action against each other's farm policies. This Accord, which formed the basis of the final GATT Agreement, paved the way for the European Council of Ministers to approve the MacSharry reforms of the CAP in 1992, before the Uruguay GATT Round was concluded, in a way which reduced the impression that the EU had been forced into reform by external international pressure.

Environmental pressure

As agricultural production has intensified since 1960, particularly in the northern EU countries, concern about its adverse environmental impacts has grown. Increased use of inorganic fertilizer has resulted in high nitrate and phosphate levels in rivers and lakes with consequent problems of eutrophication. Field sizes have been increased by eliminating hedgerows and removing small woodlands and trees, with a consequent loss of wildlife. Wildlife has also been adversely affected by the use of pesticides and herbicides, some of which cause a damaging build-up of toxic compounds in the food chain. Draining of wetlands and improvement of permanent pasture have caused serious habitat loss to birds, plants, insects, and amphibians. While these changes have occurred in areas of higher agricultural potential, more remote disadvantaged areas have been struggling to maintain farming systems held to have high landscape value. There, the underlying problems are agricultural neglect and depopulation of some areas.

To the extent that most of the environmental concerns are the consequence of intensification of production, itself stimulated by EU price support, diverse strong environmental pressure groups have emerged arguing for agricultural policy reform. The Commission's 1984 Green Paper 'Perspectives for the Common Agricultural Policy' explicitly recognized that there was a 'need for agricultural policy to take more account of environmental policy, both as regards the control of harmful practices, and the promotion of practices friendly to the environment' (von Meyer 1990). However, despite this recognition, environmental measures introduced as part of the CAP prior to the 1992 reforms were limited.

The agricultural structures policy Regulation 797/85 permitted the designation of Environmentally Sensitive Areas (ESAs) within which contractual payments were allowed to be paid to farmers to compensate them for profitability loss as a result of agreeing to deintensify production and take measures to conserve traditional methods, features, and habitats. Limited to special protection areas and depending on voluntary recruitment of farmers into the scheme, this policy initiative did little to alleviate the mounting environmental concerns. Moreover, the scheme violated the 'polluter-pays principle' adopted by EU environmental policy; instead, it provided compensation for not polluting and created a new form of agricultural support. Up to 1990, ESAs were implemented in only four Member States with a cost to the EC budget in 1989/90 of Ecu 10 million out of the total CAP budget of some Ecu 30 billion. However, as described in Section 4.5 below, the Agri-Environmental Programme which accompanied the 1992 CAP reforms has subsequently enhanced the role of environmental policies within the CAP.

4.4. The start of the reform process: the introduction of supply control mechanisms

Throughout the existence of the CAP, its policy instruments and regulations have been adapted to meet the changing economic and political circumstances of the Community. For example, during the 1970s, in response to the growing surpluses of some commodities, the EC introduced several new measures to the CAP designed to encourage domestic consumption including subsidies to certain categories of final consumers, subsidies to industrial users of food products and even 'denaturing premiums' (whereby product was dyed and in other ways made unfit for human consumption) to encourage the use of grain in livestock feed. Alternatively, the EC attempted to decrease the budgetary cost of an existing policy instrument, intervention buying, by manipulating its rules of operation; for many commodities supported by this policy instrument, the period of availability of intervention buying has been shortened and the quality standards for acceptance have been raised, whilst the price received for sales to intervention has been reduced to a so-called *buying-in price*, set some percentage points below the relevant intervention price. However, few, if any, of these patching measures did anything substantial to alleviate the mounting pressures for more radical reform of the CAP.

It was not until the early 1980s that more significant changes to the CAP were initiated with the introduction of three new supply control mechanisms—*marketing quotas, co-responsibility levies,* and *budgetary stabilizers.* The introduction of these supply control mechanisms essentially marked the end of unlimited price guarantees, with each incorporating what has become known as the 'fourth principle' of the CAP, *producer co-responsibility* for surplus production. For commodities covered by such policy instruments, if production exceeded a certain fixed level (known as the guarantee threshold), action was triggered which ensured that at least part of the cost of the additional surplus disposal was borne by producers. The discussion below focuses on one mechanism which was retained in the May 1992 CAP reform package—marketing quotas.

The economics of marketing quotas

Marketing quotas were first imposed on EC dairy producers in spring 1984 against a background of long-term structural surpluses of dairy products, an extremely depressed world market, and escalating budgetary costs of milk support. Throughout the 1970s and early 1980s the milk regime accounted for the largest proportion of total guarantee expenditure of the CAP, although this fell from 29.7 per cent of EAGGF expenditure in 1984 to 18.2 per cent in 1992.

Prior to the introduction of quotas, in 1981 the EC had introduced a system of maximum guaranteed thresholds intended to operate in such a way that, should milk deliveries in any year exceed the (pre-fixed) quantitative threshold, action would be triggered to offset the additional costs of the regime caused by the excess production. As early as 1983 the guarantee threshold was exceeded by 6.5 per cent. The reduction in intervention price for dairy products which should have been triggered by this surplus was estimated by the Commission to have been in the order of 12 per cent—too large to be politically feasible. Instead, the EC chose to maintain the level of price support at its existing level and adopt a system of marketing quotas made effective by charging a very high tax, or *super-levy,* on excess deliveries beyond the quota.

Initially, each Member State was allocated a national quota or 'reference quantity' set equal to their 1981 milk delivery levels plus 1 per cent (apart from Italy and Ireland, whose initial reference quantities were based on the quantity of milk delivered during 1983). Quotas were then allocated to individual farmers, again on the basis of their historical production levels.

The welfare implications of quotas as compared to those arising from a straight price support reduction for dairy products are shown in Fig. 4.3. Importantly, both sets of welfare effects are measured relative to a base scenario of surplus production and of the EU maintaining a support price at a level significantly above the world price for dairy products. In other words, the base scenario is intended to reflect the situation in the EC dairy industry at the beginning of the 1980s.

A straight reduction in the level of intervention price for dairy products from P_i to P_i' would cause consumers to increase their consumption from D_i to D_i' and farmers to

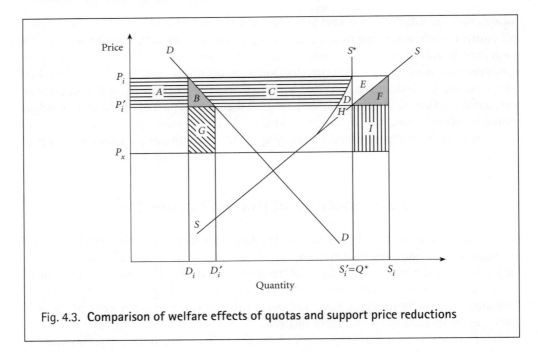

Fig. 4.3. Comparison of welfare effects of quotas and support price reductions

decrease their production from S_i to S_i' by moving down the supply function SS. Consequently, the level of surplus production decreases from $(S_i - D_i)$ to $(S_i' - D_i')$, and the budgetary cost of disposing of the surplus through export refunds falls. A cut in the level of price support would *increase consumer surplus* by area $A + B$, *reduce producer surplus* by the area $A + B + C + D + E$, and *reduce the budgetary cost* of support by $B + C + D + E + F + G + I$, causing overall a net welfare gain relative to the base scenario of $B + G + F + I$.

In comparison, the imposition of a total quota at Q^* (which, for ease of comparison, is set equal to S_i') shifts the supply curve to SS^*. At output level Q^*, the supply curve is perfectly inelastic, implying that the penalty for surplus production is severe enough to discourage any farmers from exceeding the production threshold and thus incurring the super-levy. Consumers are unaffected by the implementation of the new policy instrument—they continue to purchase the same level of output, D_i, at prices significantly above the world price of the commodity, P_x; thus *the change in consumer surplus is zero*. The figure suggests that farmers lose producer surplus equal to area $E + D + H$. Whilst area E *is* an unavoidable loss of surplus due to the output-restricting nature of the policy instrument, area $D + H$ is lost because of the manner in which quotas are allocated between individual producers. Distributing quotas purely on the basis of historical production levels rather than efficiency criteria means that some low-cost, efficient production is lost from the industry whilst some high-cost, inefficient production is maintained. If, following the initial allocation, transfer of quota is permitted, then it can be shown that low-cost producers would be willing to purchase or lease quota from high-cost producers and the area $D + H$ can be restored as surplus (Burrell 1989). Assuming that such trade takes place, total *producer surplus loss* to the dairy industry can be reduced to E.[10] The reduction in surplus production by $(S_i - Q^*)$ results in *budgetary savings* relative to the base scenario of $E + F + I$. Thus, overall, Fig. 4.3 suggests that the implementation of quotas results in a net welfare gain of only $F + I$ which is less than that of a price cut to P_i by $B + G$.

The preceding analysis begs the question; if a straight cut in support prices offered the greatest potential net welfare gains, why did the EC choose instead to implement milk quotas? The answer seems to be that quotas, whilst restraining the budgetary cost of milk support, minimized the dislocation caused to the farm sector. Analysis of previous CAP policy changes has suggested that the weight given to farmers' interests in the decision-making process is far higher than that afforded to consumers or taxpayers (MacLaren 1992) and, in this sense, the choice of milk quotas simply conformed with past precedent. However, quotas also helped nullify a widely held belief amongst CAP decision-makers—that in the short run reducing the support price of a commodity might not lead to a reduction in output of that commodity but may even cause output levels to increase. Whilst little empirical evidence has been found to support this idea of 'perverse' supply response, it is interesting to contrast the two alternative policy options from a producer's perspective. A straight reduction in price support levels would keep the marginal revenue and average revenue of output perfectly elastic at the new (lower) price and retain the open-ended nature of support. Thus, it can be argued that it would offer individual producers an incentive to reduce costs per unit output but not necessarily their total output level. Surplus production has long been considered by the European Commission as the central problem of the CAP and it was consequently keen to introduce a policy instrument which gave it direct control over aggregate output levels.

The total quota for milk has been periodically reduced from 103.7mt in 1984 to 96mt in 1991/2 for the EC10, although, with the inclusion of Spain, Portugal, and East Germany, the total has increased to 109.6mt. The system, as noted above, has been fairly successful at reducing the budgetary cost of the milk regime, but its success has only been possible because of the system of milk marketing. Virtually all milk is sold from farms to a relatively small number of processing plants. This bottleneck in the marketing chain allows the output of each producer to be monitored and, if necessary, permits enforcement of the quota by charging appropriate individuals the super-levy on excess production. The same policy instrument would be ineffective if applied to the cereals regime, because no equivalent bottleneck in the marketing chain of cereals exists. Instead, during the 1980s, the EC adopted the other two types of supply control methods mentioned above—*co-responsibility levies* and *budgetary stabilizers*—to control the output level and budgetary cost of the cereals regime. Whilst both these mechanisms share the basic characteristics of quotas in that they penalize production in excess of some threshold quantity by imposing some kind of pricing penalty, they offer far less of an incentive to an individual producer to reduce output levels. As explained by Burrell (1987), a rational individual producer will respond to a quantitative threshold on output only if that threshold has been imposed directly on his own production levels. 'Otherwise he is a price-taker, and in spite of the threshold for aggregate output, he perceives the demand for his own output as perfectly elastic at the going price.'

The introduction and gradual increased reliance on supply control mechanisms in the 1980s failed to stifle calls for yet more fundamental reform of the CAP. Thus, in May 1992, the CAP entered into a second stage of reform marked by the Council of Ministers' acceptance of the MacSharry reform package.

4.5. **The MacSharry reform package**

As intimated above, the MacSharry reform package owed much to the multinational trade negotiations and the pressure from agricultural trading partners to reduce the level of trade distortion caused by the CAP. Whilst the basic price support mechanisms described in Section 4.2 above have been retained, reductions in the level of support prices will significantly weaken their effectiveness. The impact of such price cuts for commodities in surplus can be ascertained by referring back to Fig. 4.2—consumers should benefit (assuming that reductions in the support price of raw agricultural products is passed on in the form of lower food prices), the budgetary cost of disposing of any remaining surplus production should decrease, whilst the farm sector, in the absence of any countervailing policy action, should suffer a loss in producer surplus. However, to compensate farmers for their potential loss in income, the EU has decided to give direct income payments to farmers provided they adhere to certain restraints on input use. For livestock producers, compensation payments will be limited to a fixed number of animals based on historical herd sizes and contingent upon a maximum stocking density; whilst for arable producers, compensation will be paid only if a farmer agrees to set aside (take out of production) a proportion of his/her arable land, the exact proportion being determined by the Council of Ministers each year.

By partly replacing price support with direct income payments, the correlation between the amount of support received and the amount of output produced has been weakened. In the jargon of the GATT negotiations, the MacSharry reform package marks a move towards 'decoupled' farm income support.[11] The main changes to the commodity regimes of the CAP following the reform agreement are summarized in Table 4.5.

In addition to the changes in the various commodity regimes, a set of 'accompanying measures' were introduced as part of the CAP reforms to encourage farm forestry and farmer retirement and to generalize and enhance existing agro-environmental policies. Previously, these types of measures were funded under the Agricultural Structures Policy, and they received little budgetary support. However, as part of the reform

Table 4.5. **Summary of the MacSharry CAP reforms**

Commodity	Cuts in support	Compensation and other gains	Production control
Cereals	• Target price cut by 29% from 1991/2 buying-in price. • Price reduction phased in over three years from 1993/4.	• Per hectare compensation payments available provided set-aside is implemented. • Producers of less than 92 tonnes of cereals are exempted from set-aside. • Compensation payments based on historical yield levels for regions of the EU. • Co-responsibility levy abolished from 1992/3.	• Annual set-aside required for producers to receive compensation payments. • The minimum % of base arable area to be set aside varies from year to year. • Controls over which land can be set aside.
Oilseeds and pulses	• No price support 1993/4 onwards.	• Per hectare area payments available but cut from 1992/3 levels. • Linseed added to list of eligible crops.	• Controlled by same set-aside scheme as cereal production.
Sheep	• Payment of ewe premium restricted by producer quota. • Producer quotas based on number of ewe premiums paid in 1991.	• Quota has market value. • Special extensification premiums for reduced stock levels. • Lower feed grain costs.	• If quota sold without land, 15% of quota taxed to national reserve. • No transfer of quota outside existing Less Favoured Areas.
Beef	• Intervention price cut by 15% from 1993/4. • 350,000t. limit set on intervention purchases by 1997.	• Beef and suckler cow premium increased but made contingent on stocking levels. • An extra extensification premium available if stocking rates below minimum level. • Suckler cow quota has marketable value. • Lower feed grain costs.	• Beef premium limited by regional ceiling equal to number of premiums paid in 1991. If exceeded, producer payments reduced pro rata. • Suckler cow premiums restricted by producer quota. • Beef and suckler cow premium payments subject to stocking-rate restrictions.
Dairy	• 5% cut in butter intervention price by 1994/5.	• Milk quota and associated value to last at least to 2000. • Co-responsibility levy abolished from 1992/3.	• Cuts in quota may be made.

package, financial support was switched to the Guarantee Section of the CAP's budget and Ecu 6.2 billion, or 5 per cent of the total guarantee budget, was targeted at these issues. In particular, over half was earmarked for policies under the Agri-Environment Programme.

The introduction of the Agri-Environment Programme was significant in that it allows the implementation of policies at the national level to be flexible, with such policies being co-financed by Member States' governments. By the end of 1994, about 190 programmes, 12 national and 165 regional, had been approved. The changes suggest that more emphasis is being given to the long-recognized role of the CAP in securing environmental goals. This will have been consolidated by the subsequent 1993 Treaty on European Union (TEU) requiring all Union policies, including the CAP, to take environmental impacts into account. However, some Member States are concerned that the reforms do not go far enough and are keen to see a more widespread introduction of *cross-compliance* within the CAP whereby the payment of all farm support subsidies is conditional on farmers complying with some pre-agreed environmental conditions. To some extent, some of the 1992 reforms do introduce an element of cross-compliance—for example, the limits on stocking rates associated with livestock subsidies. However, the degree to which the reformed CAP has embraced environmental concerns remains far from complete.

The economics of the new arable regime

The changes to the arable regime of the CAP are particularly significant, not just because of the introduction of land set-aside,[12] but because of the importance of cereals within the agricultural industry. Under the new arrangements, each cereal farmer in the EU producing more than 92 tonnes faces a decision of whether (a) to use the whole of his arable acreage and receive the new (lower) market price for cereal output, or (b) to comply with the set-aside requirements and thus be eligible for compensation payments in addition to his market returns for output from land remaining in production.

For those who adopt the latter strategy and opt into the set-aside scheme, two types of compensation payments can be distinguished—price compensation on land farmed (the so-called arable area payment) and set-aside compensation. The planned levels of both payments over the transitionary period are shown in Table 4.6. The level of price compensation was intended to increase gradually throughout the transitional period, as the gap between the old buying-in price and new target price widened. Importantly, price compensation is converted from a tonnage to an area basis by applying a fixed yield factor. The yield factor has been calculated from historical data and varies between regions of the community. The table shows that, for England, the yield factor was *initially* set at 5.93t./ha., thus implying that by the end of the three-year period, every farmer who choses to participate in the set-aside scheme was to receive a payment of Ecu 266.85 for each hectare remaining in production. In addition, participating

Table 4.6. **Compensatory payments for the reformed CAP cereals regime, 1993/4–1995/6**

	Marketing year		
	1993/4	1994/5	1995/6
A. 1991/2 Buying-in price (Ecu/t.)	155	155	155
B. Target price (Ecu/t.)	130	120	110
C. Price compensation [A − B] (Ecu/t.)	25	35	45(54)[a]
D. Yield factor (England) (t./ha.)	5.93	5.93(5.89)[b]	5.93(5.89)[b]
E. Price compensation (England) [C × D]	148.25	207.55	266.85(320)[c]
F. Set-aside compensation (Ecu/ha.) (England)	266.85	266.85(338)[a]	266.85(405)[c]

Note: Figures in parentheses represent adjustments to the original planned scheme.

[a] Adjusted upwards as a result of political pressure. [b] Technical adjustment.
[c] Adjusted upwards to adjust for abolition of switchover.

farmers receive a compensation payment for land left idle. The level of this set-aside compensation was intended to be fixed during the transition period and was initially set equal to the level of price compensation in 1995/6. However, political pressures caused the set-aside payment to be raised in 1994/5 to 338 Ecu/ha., and both the set-aside and arable area payments were raised in 1994/5 by around 20 per cent to adjust for the abolition of the agrimonetary switchover mechanism in 1995 (though green exchange rates were simultaneously altered to neutralize the effects in domestic currency terms).

The decision of whether or not to participate in the set-aside scheme depends on the market price of cereals and farms' actual yields. In particular, the decision depends on the value of compensation payments relative to the revenue from planting the area which would be set aside. When cereal prices are high, the opportunity cost of leaving land to stand idle is also high and a farmer is less likely to participate in the scheme. As the market price for cereals falls, the opportunity cost of idling land also falls. At some point, the value of the compensation payments from participating in set-aside will exactly equal the profit that could be earned from planting the additional set-aside area. The price of cereals which gives rise to this equivalence can be called the 'indifference price', since at this price the farmer is indifferent as to whether he opts out of production and into set-aside—either way his total profit level is the same. If the market price of cereals exceeds the indifference price, a rational producer would choose to plant his full area. Alternatively, if the market price for cereals is less than the indifference price, a rational producer would participate in the set-aside scheme in order to be eligible for the compensation payments.

Because farms are not identical, indifference prices will vary between cereal producers. One would expect inefficient, high-cost producers to have a low opportunity cost of idling land and thus a relatively high indifference price. Conversely, one would expect efficient, low-cost producers to have a high opportunity cost of leaving land fallow and thus a relatively low indifference price. Taking such variability into account and aggregating across all producers in the industry, the supply curve for cereals under the new voluntary set-aside scheme would shift from its original competitive level, SS to the kinked curve $S'S$, as shown in Fig. 4.4.

In Fig. 4.4, P_{ih} and P_{il} represent the highest and lowest indifference price in the industry respectively. At any price above P_{ih}, the market return for cereals is sufficient to deter *all* farmers from participating in set-aside. Therefore, the total arable area would be utilized and the supply curve would coincide with the competitive supply curve, SS. However, once the price of cereals falls below P_{ih}, the least efficient, high-cost producers would chose to opt out of full production and into set-aside, idling the required proportion of their land and thus causing the supply curve to rotate to the left. As the price falls further, more and more farmers would opt into set-aside and more and more land would be withdrawn from production. Once the price has fallen to P_{il}, *all* farmers would choose to idle the necessary portion of their land in order to be eligible for compensation payments.

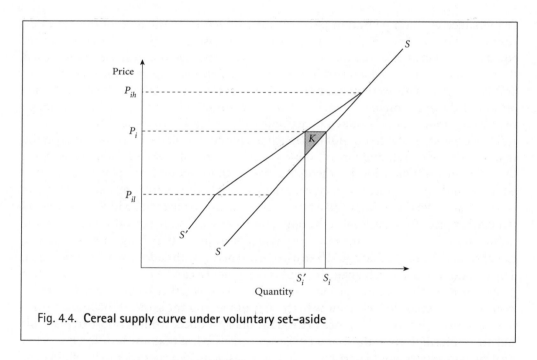

Fig. 4.4. **Cereal supply curve under voluntary set–aside**

The shift in supply curve shown in Fig. 4.4 allows us to identify the minimum value of set-aside compensation payments necessary to induce a certain reduction of cereal output. For example, if the EU had decided to implement a voluntary set-aside scheme with a fixed compensation payment per hectare *without* reducing the level of price support for cereals from its original level, P_i, Fig. 4.4 suggests that enough farmers would opt into the scheme to cause output levels to fall from S_i to S_i'. It can be assumed, since the scheme is voluntary, that this would occur only if there were no overall reduction in producer surplus. In other words, the value of set-aside compensation payments must be at least equal to area K in the figure, which represents the amount of surplus lost from production.

The new supply curve with set-aside, $S'S$, is replicated in Fig. 4.5, where the changes in welfare and transfer effects between the old and new cereals regime are investigated.

From an initial buying-in price of P_i, the support price for cereals once the scheme is fully implemented falls to P_i'. Additionally, by the time the full reduction of 29 per cent in support price has been phased in, the world market price for cereals is shown to have increased from P_x to P_x', owing to the reduction in volume of subsidized exports from the EU. These changes in prices suggest that, relative to the free-trade scenario, the *change in consumer surplus loss* is given by $(A + B) - (A' + B')$, implying that, in principle, EU consumers should benefit from the change in the CAP.

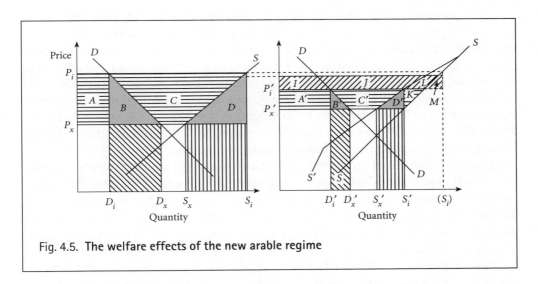

Fig. 4.5. **The welfare effects of the new arable regime**

The welfare effect for producers is less clear-cut. From a starting position of producer surplus gain of $(A + B + C)$ under the old regime, their surplus from cereal production is reduced to $(A' + B' + C')$. However, in addition, they receive direct compensation payments. Since, as drawn, the new (lower) support price P_i', corresponds to the lowest indifference price of the industry, we can assume that every eligible cereal producer is participating in the set-aside scheme.[13] Given the actual yield obtained in any region or country, the total amount of the arable area and set-aside payments can be shown as area $I + J + K + L$ in Fig. 4.5. In other words, one can express the area and set-aside payments as a payment per unit of output that would have been produced in the absence of the policy. Thus the *change in producer surplus gain* is given by $(A + B + C) - (A' + B' + C' + I + J + L + M)$. Whether or not this is positive or negative depends on whether the value of compensation payments is larger or smaller than the loss in producer surplus from reducing output level to S_i'.

The impact of the new regime on the budgetary cost of cereal support is also not easily predicted. Whether or not the total budgetary cost of supporting cereal farmers decreases or increases depends upon whether the saving in terms of the disposal of surplus production $(B + C + D) - (B' + C' + D')$ is larger or smaller than the value of compensation payments $I + J + L + M$. As drawn, the figure suggests a fall in the budgetary cost of support. However, in practice, this will depend upon the change in the world price for cereals and the extent of participation in the set-aside scheme. The reduction in net welfare loss caused by the policy reform is less ambiguous. Taking into account the preceding analysis, the change in net welfare loss is represented by area $(B + D) - (B' + D')$. Importantly, as drawn, the MacSharry reforms reduce but do not eliminate the trade distortion caused by CAP support for cereal producers with the level of exports falling from $(S_i - D_i)$ to $(S_i' - D_i')$.

Whilst useful as an indication of the general welfare effects of the new CAP arable regime, the preceding analysis has ignored the more detailed aspects of the regime which will be critical in governing its effectiveness. For instance, no mention has been made of the problem of *slippage*, which is associated with any policy requiring that farmers set aside land. Slippage can be most easily described as the phenomenon whereby a certain reduction in cereal area does not necessarily lead to the same percentage reduction in cereal output. In terms of Figs. 4.4 and 4.5, slippage would result in a smaller rotation in the supply curve for cereals to the left. There are many different reasons for slippage, including farmers using inputs more intensively on the land remaining in production, the setting-aside of less productive land, and increased fertility of land left to stand fallow, which would result in increased yields once that land is brought back into production. Alternatively, slippage may occur simply because of ineffective policing of set-aside, allowing farmers to plant more hectares than intended under the rules of the new regime. In addition, producers of less than 92 tonnes of cereals (equivalent to around 15 hectares) do not have to participate in set-aside to qualify for area compensation. The analysis has also ignored the fact that the rules of the regime are such that the base arable area of each individual farmer is defined to include land previously sown with oilseeds and protein crops as well as cereals. Thus there will not be a direct correspondence between the change in cereal area and the area of land removed from production under set-aside, even before considering the complications of slippage. Again, the rotation in cereal supply curve shown in Figs. 4.4 and 4.5 may be less pronounced than initially implied.[14]

In early 1996, the Commission proposed certain modifications to the arable regime described in Table 4.5. As well as adjusting the proportion of arable land to be set aside and hence the value of compensation payments, it also proposed to make the scheme more flexible. Whilst such modifications look set to continue, it is clear that the period of reliance of the CAP primarily on market price support is well and truly over.

4.6. **Summary and outlook**

The 1992 CAP reform package represents an uneasy compromise between continuing the traditional policies of protecting agriculture through price supports and income aids and the various pressures for reform discussed in Section 4.3. By compensating for commodity price reductions through the introduction of direct income payments to farmers, the reform has allowed a transfer of some of the cost of support from food consumers to taxpayers, which is socially progressive in reducing food costs to poor non-taxpayers. It also means that the costs of the CAP will be increasingly transparent, being revealed in budgetary accounts rather than being hidden away in the mass of consumer spending. Nevertheless, by retaining some price support and adding the new compensation payments, the operation of the CAP has been made even more complex. This is because the compensation payments are conditional upon compliance with a variety of qualifying actions, all of which have to be checked before payment is authorized. Inevitably, this raises administrative costs and increases the size of the bureaucracy while at the same time increasing the incentives and possibilities for fraud which are already a well-established consequence of the CAP.

Adding new supply controls in the form of arable land set aside and animal stocking rates to the existing marketing quotas for milk and sugar has been necessary to achieve an approximation to the decoupling of agricultural support and to help control budgetary costs. However, these actions reflect continued unwillingness to subject EU agriculture to the rigours of free trade and open competition, and indicate that the solution of managed markets is still politically preferred.

Several important factors mean that further reforms of the CAP cannot be delayed for long. There is a commitment under the Uruguay Agreement to begin new multilateral negotiations in 1999. Significantly, the USA passed a new Farm Bill in April 1996 which makes major changes to its system of agricultural policy and sets new reform challenges to the EU. In particular, the Bill ends the use of acreage controls within the USA and completely severs the link between production levels and government payments.

A combination of high world commodity prices, along with skilful negotiation and manipulation of the basic measures for implementing the Uruguay Round agreements, has meant that no further reductions in CAP support are likely to be necessary before 2000 to meet agreed targets for reducing aggregate support (Tangermann 1996). There may be some difficulties in meeting the requirements to reduce subsidized export quantities for beef (particularly following the BSE scare), pigmeat, and dairy products, but the EU has many instruments at its disposal to try to deal with these.

However, the biggest challenge to the CAP arises from the possibilities of enlarging the EU15 to include Central and East European Countries (CEECs) and the Baltic States. Ten countries currently have Europe Agreements with the EU. These are the so-called Visegrad countries (Poland, Hungary, the Czech Republic, and Slovakia) plus Slovenia, which are the countries more likely to join in the first wave; Estonia, Latvia and Lithuania, which are in a second wave; and Bulgaria and Rumania, which are currently at the end of the queue. Agriculture is a markedly bigger contributor to employment and GDP in many of these countries than in the EU15 as a whole. The levels of agricultural price support are well below those in the EU. Yield levels in most of these countries are comparatively low and have declined since the break-up of the Soviet bloc and the switch to becoming market economies. Thus there is a large latent capacity for agricultural output to increase substantially in these countries.

From the narrow agricultural perspective of the potential members, incorporation into the EU holds out the prospect of major investment and foreign-company involvement in their agricultural systems, better access to the markets of current Member States, and perhaps a massive increase in price support and subsidies for agriculture.

To extend the current CAP support system to these countries would cause great problems, and is basically not feasible. For example, it would make no sense to raise their support prices, and simultaneously to force farmers to set aside arable land, and to introduce to them arable payments currently designed to compensate EU12 producers for reductions in price support. Also there is the danger that rapid increases in yields to EU levels would result in disruptive surplus disposal problems. There are various ways in which the problem could be handled. One is to try to preserve the status quo by maintaining and strengthening supply controls for the EU15 and by establishing a second tier CAP for new Member States at lower levels of price support and entitlements to direct payments; but this would violate the whole spirit of having a *Common* Agricultural Policy. Another is to go for radical reform of the CAP by slashing support prices, abolishing marketing quotas and supply management measures, reducing compensatory payments, and switching to direct income support and environmental management measures; this would ease the problems of assimilating new Member States, provided new members were not eligible for income support designed for farmers in current Member States. In its Agricultural Strategy Paper of 29 November 1995, the Commission rejects the two above options in favour of a third, which is to develop the 1992 MacSharry approach. This would entail further reductions in price support (but with some compensation through direct payments and a move to greater international competitiveness), while switching emphasis from agricultural policy to an 'integrated rural policy'. There would be attempts to 'simplify' the policy and possibly greater emphasis would be given to *subsidiarity*, in which a higher proportion of CAP expenditure was self-financed by Member States, leading to greater flexibility in patterns and levels of expenditure in Member States. This is a feature of agri-environmental programmes introduced in the 1992 reforms, and extending the principle might ease the problems of admitting new members but at a cost of weakening the 'commonness' of the CAP.[15] What is clear is that further reform of the CAP is inevitable, and that this will involve further reductions in price protection and support.

Discussion questions

1. To what extent have the reforms of the CAP been driven by political and economic pressures within the expanding EU rather than by the external trade liberalization agenda set by the USA and the Cairns Group?
2. Why has the EU persistently favoured supply control and market regulation methods to free trade and uncontrolled price determination in agricultural markets?
3. What additional pressures are created by the potential expansion of the EU to include countries of Eastern and Central Europe?
4. Despite the costs to consumers and taxpayers, are there any justifications for continuing a policy of price support for agriculture?

FURTHER READING

Readers wishing to explore issues related to the EU's agricultural policy further might wish to consult the book by Michael Tracy (1993), which provides an excellent overview, the new edition of the Common Agricultural Policy edited by Ritson and Harvey (1997), which provides up-to-date coverage, and the paper by Tangermann (1996) evaluating the implementation of the Uruguay Round of the GATT.

NOTES

1. For a review of these negotiations and their substance, readers are referred to Rayner *et al.* (1993).
2. This assumes that all increases in the price of agricultural commodities such as wheat are passed through to the retail prices of bread, cakes, flour, etc.
3. For a whole series of reasons (see Colman 1985), the floor is not as rigid as portrayed in Fig. 4.2, but it is an acceptable approximation for much analysis.
4. It may be noted that the position is more complex than this. For example, although the EU is a large exporter of soft wheat, it still has to import more expensive hard wheats for bread-making. Import levies/tariffs calculated with respect to soft wheats result in hard wheats entering the EU at prices very much higher than the MIP.
5. A monetary gap is defined as the difference between a currency's agricultural conversion rate (green rate) and its representative market rate, and is expressed as a percentage of its agricultural conversion rate.
6. These are precisely the outcomes that revaluing a currency should cause, but they were intensified by refusal automatically to revalue the Deutschmark green rate.

7. This is also known by its French initials FEOGA, which stand for Funds Européen d'Orientation et de Garantie Agricole.
8. For a fuller analysis of distribution of budgetary and trade gains and losses from the CAP, see Ackrill *et al.* (1994).
9. The numbers in this table are generated by a computable model, and reflect *estimates* of the *reductions in cost* which would arise if agricultural policy was reformed in a specific way. This is the standard approach to calculating the effects of any price support system which exists. The current position, with support, is known; the question is 'what would the position be if it was reduced or eliminated?'
10. This assumes that there are no inefficiencies in the quota market.
11. Under 'truly' decoupled income support, a farmer's decisions on levels of output would be based on the free price equivalents of commodities. Since, under the new CAP arable regime, the decision of whether or not to set aside land depends on the relative size of compensation payments *vis-à-vis* the new lower *support* price for cereals, the move towards decoupled farm income support is far from complete.
12. The option allowing EU farmers voluntarily to set aside arable land in return for compensation strictly dates from 1988. However, the impact of the initial set-aside scheme was extremely limited, with very low uptake levels in almost all Member States.
13. If this were not the case, it would be impossible to show the value of compensation payments in price/output space, as in Fig. 4.5.
14. Yet another complication to measuring the effects of the new arable regime has been caused by farmers planting set-aside land with crops intended for industrial usage (e.g. linseed) or, alternatively, choosing to plant set-aside area with forage crops which has implications for other commodity regimes.
15. For comment on the Agricultural Strategy Paper, see Tracy (1995).

REFERENCES

Ackrill, R. W., Suardi, M., Hine, R. C., and Rayner, A. J. (1994), *The Distributional Effects of the Common Agricultural Policy between Member States: Budget and Trade Effects* (CREDIT Research Paper, 94/1; University of Nottingham).

BAE (1985): Bureau of Agricultural Economics, *Agricultural Policies in the European Community* (Policy Monograph, No. 2; Canberra, Australia: BAE).

Blandford, D., de Gorter, H., and Harvey, D. R. (1989), 'Farm Income Support with Minimal Trade Distortions', *Food Policy* (Aug.), 268–73.

Brown, C. (1989), *Distribution of CAP Price Support* (Statens Jordbrugsokonomiske Institut, Report 45; Copenhagen).

Burrell, A. (1987), 'EC Agricultural Surpluses and Budget Control', *Journal of Agricultural Economics, 38/1*: 1–14.

—— (1989) (ed.), *Milk Quotas in the European Community* (Wallingford: CAB International), ch. 8.

Colman, D. (1985), 'Imperfect Rransmission of Policy Prices', *European Review of Agricultural Economics, 12/3*: 171–86.

DPI-Australia (1986), *The Political Economy of Agricultural Policy Reform* (Canberra, Australia: DPI).

GATT (1988): General Agreement on Tariffs and Trade, *GATT International Trade 87–88* (Geneva: GATT).

Greenaway, D. (1991), 'The Uruguay Round of Multilateral Trade Negotiations: Last Chance for GATT?', *Journal of Agricultural Economics*, 42/3: 365–79.

Josling, T. E., and Hamway, D. (1972), *Burdens and Benefits of Farm Support Policies* (London: Trade Policy Research Centre).

MacLaren, D. (1992), 'The Political Economy of Agricultural Policy Reform in the European Community and Australia', *Journal of Agricultural Economics*, 43/3.

Rayner, A. J., Ingersent, K. A., and Hine, R. C. (1993), 'Agricultural Trade and the GATT', in A. J. Rayner and D. Colman (eds.), *Current Issues in Agricultural Economics* (Basingstoke: Macmillan), ch. 4.

Ritson, C., and Harvey, D. (1997) (eds.), *The Common Agricultural Policy* (Wallingford: CAB International).

Roningen, V. O., and Dixit, P. M. (1989), *How Level is the Playing Field: An Economic Analysis of Agricultural Policy Reforms in Industrial Market Economies* (United States Department of Agriculture, ERS, FAE Report 239; Washington).

Tangermann, S. (1996), 'Implementation of the Uruguay Round Agreement on Agriculture: Issues and Prospects', *Journal of Agricultural Economics*, 47/3: 315–37.

Tracy, M. (1993), *Food and Agriculture in a Market Economy: An Introduction to Theory, Practice and Policy* (La Hutte, Belgium: Agricultural Policy Studies).

—— (1995), 'The Commission's "Agricultural Strategy Paper": A Commentary' (paper presented to One-Day Agricultural Economics Society Conference, London, 13 December, 1995).

Von Meyer, H. (1991), 'From Agricultural to Rural Policy in the EC', in M. Tracy (ed.), *Europe 1993: Implications for Rural Areas* (Aberdeen: Arkleton Trust).

CHAPTER 5

Competition Policy

DAVID YOUNG and STAN METCALFE

5.1. **The rationale for competition policy**

Competition policy is concerned with maintaining competition between firms in all sections of the economy in an attempt to promote the efficient working of the market. The fundamental rationale for such policy is that the market does not, by itself, function perfectly or that there are certain necessary conditions for the proper functioning of markets which the state can attempt to create. Competitive markets are normally viewed as having a number of inherent advantages, such as the efficient allocation of resources, the maintenance of consumer choice, the promotion of technological innovation, and the autonomy of industrial enterprises, which it is believed is important for long-run economic progress. Mainstream economics has long emphasized the possible imperfections which may arise and that monopoly power, public goods, externalities, and such like provide grounds for a degree of state intervention on public policy in order to attempt to alleviate such problems.

It is not surprising, therefore, that individual countries within the European Union (EU) have long pursued some type of competition policy. Similarly it is a matter of considerable importance for the development of the EU. A report of the Commission (CEC 1992) emphasized the increasing importance of competition policy within the context of the internal market. The need for 'improved monitoring of Member States' anticompetitive behaviour' (CEC 1992: 9) was noted as a crucial aspect of the move towards a single internal European market. There is, however, a variety of opinions as to the exact nature of competition and the extent to which state intervention is required. Moreover, it is also the case that any view as to the desirability of any type of competition policy is founded on a particular view of the nature of the competition process and the workings of a market economy.

5.2. **The nature of the competitive process**

In order to develop effective competition policy it is necessary to have a clear view of the meaning of competition. Competition policy is often seen as being necessary or helpful in aiding the competitive process and to correct any inadequacies or distortions existing in product (or less often factor) markets. But this view is based on a specific notion of the competitive process. Although there is a dominant theory of competition in economics, there are, in fact, a number of different theories or views of the nature of competition, and the dominant view sometimes draws on ideas from these alternative approaches. Before we can discuss and evaluate competition policy, we must explore the meaning of competition itself.

The mainstream view of competition is founded on the neoclassical notion of perfect competition. Although there are many dissenters from the application of such a strict condition, perfect competition still forms the theoretical basis of modern mainstream analysis of competition and hence competition policy. Perfect competition provides a bench-mark against which all and any actual form of competition may be judged. It defines a position of equilibrium which represents an optimal allocation of resources. This specifies a situation involving zero super-normal profits and free entry and exit. A deviation from this state is definitionally sub-optimal (although there may be dynamic gains which offset such static inefficiencies). Firms which possess a degree of market power, that are able to influence the market price, are regarded as distorting the allocation of resources from the socially optimal position. The conception of monopoly/market power as a distortion or imperfection is particularly important and is associated with the view that the market process is basically competitive but that at any point in time there may be a number of reasons why this is not so. The role of competition policy, therefore, is to correct these distortions and restore the market process to its correct competitive path.

However, some economists have been dissatisfied with such an abstract and static notion of the welfare bench-mark and in response have tried to develop a more suitable description of a baseline from which actual competition may be judged. In particular, the idea of 'workable' competition has been proposed. This does not involve any fundamentally different conception of what competition is, but rather is concerned with defining a state which relates more clearly to 'real-world' competitive conditions. It involves a neoclassical view of competition but eschews perfect competition as a realistic objective. Unfortunately, there are a number of different views and definitions of what workable competition actually is (see, for example, Devine *et al.* 1985). All, however, may be regarded as an attempt to describe a market which has an 'acceptable' set of competitive conditions from a policy perspective. Indeed, it is from a policy, rather than a theoretical, perspective that workable competition has been mainly thought to be a useful notion. Early attempts to define the term have focused on conditions where there are large numbers of sellers of similar products who do not collude, and where entry is not seriously restricted.

More radically different views of the nature of competition are offered by alternative schools of economic thought, such as the Austrian school, which emphasizes the 'process' character of competition. This view has enjoyed something of a revival in recent years (see, for example, Reid 1987) and has arguably been influential in determining changes in government policy on monopolies (since the early 1980s). The essence of the Austrian view is that competition is an ongoing *process* and that the neoclassical conception of competition, being essentially static, does not provide an appropriate basis for assessing actual markets. Competition according to this view is a continual process of entrepreneurial rivalry. Entrepreneurs are alert to profit opportunities and it is their purposeful pursuit of profit which is the driving force of the economy. This Austrian view, therefore, regards profit as necessary for motivating agents and also forms the basis of coordination and market order in the economy. Given that it is argued that perfect competition is not an appropriate baseline, this argument applies to profits generally and may include profits which neoclassical analysis would regard as super-normal profits. Therefore the argument that super-normal profits necessarily result from firms' monopoly power and that this should be a concern of state competition policy is denied. Rather, in the Austrian view, profits reflect superior firm-specific competence. Another significant dimension of the Austrian approach is the emphasis it places on innovation. This is particularly so in Schumpeterian theories, which develop the idea that the efficiency gains from innovations over time may outweigh any short-term inefficiencies resulting from market imperfections. For example, a degree of monopoly power may result in an inefficient use of resources at a particular point in time, but if the profits generated by such market power generate greater innovation then there will be offsetting advantages in the longer term.

Another important alternative view of competition is propounded by radical or Marxian theorists. Though these views have had less impact on mainstream economics in general and competition policy in particular, some of the policy implications to which these approaches give rise represent important alternative perspectives on policy options. There are, in fact, two lines of thought (at least) in radical views on competition. One is based on the notion that market structure has an important influence on market performance, which is clearly similar in certain respects to the neoclassical view; the other is based on a radically different conception of competition as involving competing 'blocks' of capital. According to this latter view, the process of accumulation which drives the economic system involves each block of capital attempting to expand into, and therefore to invade, the domain of other blocks of capital; and it is this process of different capitals expanding and competing with each other which describes the nature of the competitive process. The alternative view accepts the concept of market structure proposed by neoclassical theory, but argues that the market system has a natural tendency towards monopoly. The process of competition involves the gradual monopolization of product markets by large corporations. Oligopoly and market power are seen as the norm. This contrasts with the standard neoclassical view of market power as an imperfection or deviation from a competitive state. Rather, competition is fundamentally about market power and more generally the exercise of economic and political power.

5.3. The theoretical basis of competition policy: impediments to competition

Having outlined the different views of competition, we are now able to consider the principal sources of departure from a competitive state which might provide the basis for the main issues of concern in competition policy. It should be emphasized at the outset that posing the problem in terms of a departure from an optimal state does in itself form the question in a neoclassical/mainstream way. But, given that it is the most familiar and influential approach, this seems acceptable in the present context.

The most obvious obstacle to competitive behaviour in a market is the presence of monopoly. The standard theoretical approach to monopoly defines it as a situation in which there is a single seller of a given product, where there are no close substitutes for this product, and where entry into the market is blocked. It is normally further assumed that the firm's (industry) demand curve is downward sloping.

The profit maximizing firm, as always, equates marginal cost with marginal revenue and, under perfect competition, this implies producing where $MC = P(=AR)$. The difference between the equilibrium price and output positions, in monopoly and perfect competition, can therefore be compared (see Fig. 5.1).

Under perfect competition, consumer surplus is given by the total area $DP_c B$. After the monopolization of the industry (assuming demand and cost conditions remain unchanged), this is reduced to area $DP_m A$. Part of the difference between consumer surplus under perfect competition and under monopoly now becomes producer surplus—namely, the area $P_m P_c CA$. The remainder is the area ACB. This is the 'cost' due to the contraction in output from Q_c to Q_m; hence the triangle ABC represents the 'deadweight' loss to society.

There have been numerous attempts to estimate the social costs of monopoly power. Obviously some idea of the magnitude of welfare losses is of great importance, in as much as this can provide some basis for assessing the need for a competition policy. (It might also be noted that it may also be important in assessing the competing claims regarding the inherent tendency of the system towards competition or monopoly.) Early estimates, produced for the USA (such as Harberger 1954), tended to suggest that welfare losses were very low, leading to a 'conventional' view that the social costs of monopoly are in fact rather trivial. However, in the last twenty years there have been a number of studies which have produced quite different estimates, suggesting that the cost of monopoly, associated with the reduction in gross output, is quite significant. For example, Cowling and Mueller (1978) and Sawyer (1980) have published estimates for

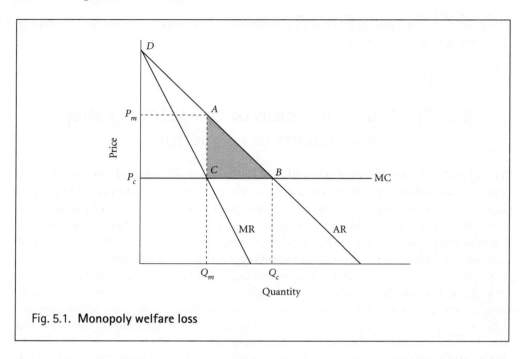

Fig. 5.1. Monopoly welfare loss

the UK which suggest that welfare losses might be as high as 9 per cent of gross output. Similarly, significant 'high' estimates have been produced for France by Jenny and Weber (1983). There are a variety of reasons for the differences between these estimates, but the principal factors which have led to the higher estimates include attempts to include the costs of attempting to acquire and maintain monopoly positions (by including advertising expenditures in some form) and different assumptions regarding demand elasticities.

Other assessments of the magnitude of social costs arising from monopoly power have produced an even more diverse set of estimates. Littlechild (1981), in criticizing the Cowling and Mueller (1978) estimates, adopted an Austrian position, arguing that welfare losses were considerably smaller than Cowling and Mueller suggested. This was due, in his view, to the positive role of profits as the reward for risk-taking and the necessity of profits for encouraging innovation, as well as a number of other factors, such as alleged aggregation bias and price discrimination. At the other end of the spectrum, Baran and Sweezy (1966) report estimates of surplus value for the US economy which suggest that more the 50 per cent of total US national product may take the form of surplus value produced by the monopolistic character of modern capitalism.

Although basic monopoly theory does provide some basis for identifying the social costs of non-competitive outcomes, it would be helpful if this theory provided an analysis of the consequences of monopoly power and not only of monopoly pricing. However, at present, a full theoretical explanation of monopoly power does not exist.

Attempts to remedy this situation may arise out of developments in oligopoly theory, which is now firmly based on game-theoretic models. Although it is not possible or appropriate to discuss these developments here, it is important to consider the principal dimensions of oligopoly as they relate to the state of industrial competitiveness and therefore the formation of competition policy.

A particularly important factor is the notion of dominance. This is of specific concern from a policy perspective, because much legislative action has been concerned with dominant positions. The theoretical basis for this begins with the idea that a particular firm, or group of firms, may, by virtue of its relatively high share of industry/market output, be in a position to exert a degree of dominance over that market. The basic theoretical model which attempts to represent such a situation is referred to as the dominant firm or dominant firm-price leadership model (see, for example, Hay and Morris 1991). Such a model embodies the assumption that the dominant firm or dominant group acts as the price leader by setting the price for the market in accordance with maximizing its own profits subject to a demand constraint. This demand constraint (i.e. the dominant firm's demand curve) is obtained by deducting the total supply of all other producers in the industry from total industry demand, which is exogenously given. The other producers in the industry are assumed to be a competitive 'fringe', each firm being a price-taker. All of these firms take the dominant firm's (group's) price as given and produce the output which maximizes their profit given this price. This model has been criticized for a number of reasons, including its essentially static nature and its assumption that the dominant firm knows the supply of the 'fringe'; the conception of dominance involved is also rather narrow. In particular, the fact that the 'fringe' treats prices as given, but is important in determining the residual demand curve facing the dominant firm, limits the nature of the leading firm's dominance.

A broader view of dominance often involves the idea that a firm can restrict other firms' choices via strategic behaviour. (See, for example, Geroski's and Jacquemin's (1984) discussion of the persistence of dominant firms.) There are potentially many aspects to such behaviour, such as a firm's attempt to secure market share through advertising and attempts to establish a 'reputation' with regard to pricing or output strategies. Another crucial dimension of the interaction between firms which is particularly important is the degree of collusion. Overt collusion is normally the direct concern of competition policy and in many countries is effectively outlawed. There are various forms which collusion may take, but the main examples may be categorized as either some form of price-setting or some type of explicit agreement concerning outputs. (This is often analysed in terms of cartel behaviour. A cartel is the most formal and explicit form of collusion and normally involves a common price structure and some agreement over the output of the firms within the cartel.)

Although there is a wide variety of issues which must be evaluated when considering a firm's dominance, it should be noted that its relative size in terms of market share is still seen as a singularly important indicator of its potential dominance. This is clearly

David Young and Stan Metcalfe

reflected in a number of previous European competition policy decisions. For example, the well-known *Continental Can* case in the early 1970s invoked the company's substantial market share in establishing its abuse of a dominant position. (For a discussion of this and other cases, see Jacquemin and de Jong 1977 and Utton 1995). Further, examples of the importance of market share are provided by various competition policies within the EU, which we shall discuss later.

Another source of restriction on competition is merger activity. Mergers are normally categorized under three main types: horizontal, vertical, and conglomerate. Each, at least potentially, has welfare implications arising from a variety of effects on the degree of competition. Perhaps the simplest case is that of horizontal merger, which at certain times in the past, such as the famous merger boom of the late 1960s, has been the dominant type of merger. Definitionally horizontal mergers involve the merging of firms at the same stage of the production process. This can result in direct changes in the level of concentration in a given industry and this may result in increased market power and higher price-cost margins. For example, two firms merging within a particular industry will clearly reduce the number of firms and increase size inequalities between firms, hence leading to an increase in concentration (as measured by, for instance, the Herfindahl index). The newly formed firm (resulting from the merger) will have a higher market share and greater market power than either of the previous firms. This market power might be used to increase profit margins, leading to decreases in the level of consumer surplus.

Cases involving vertical mergers—i.e. mergers between firms at different stages of the production process—also have welfare implications. Usually, the principal concern here is the restrictions placed on the suppliers of the vertical outlets for the particular products concerned. For example, if a firm at an intermediate stage of the production process merges with a firm at a later stage (retail), then there might be some welfare concern with regard to the restriction of supplies to other retail outlets supplied by the old intermediate firm, now part of the 'new' merged firm.

Conglomerate mergers have in recent years become the most important type of merger and their welfare implications are potentially very significant. These involve firms merging across different markets (i.e. mergers in which there are no vertical or horizontal relations). The analysis of the effects of mergers of this type, however, is the most complex, as by their very nature they involve activities in a number of different markets, and therefore it is impossible easily to assess their effects in terms of changes in concentration or vertical constraints. However, the overall effect on the economy may be indicated by changes in aggregate concentration, and specific pricing and/or output effects may be identified. The case of conglomerate merger also raises broader aspects concerning firms' 'power', and this may be of great importance from a policy perspective. For example, Jacquemin and de Jong (1977) have stated that the eventual goals of competition policy in Europe should include 'the diffusion of economic power' and the protection of the 'economic freedom of market participants'. However, these are much more difficult aspects of economic life to regulate, partly because there are quite different interpretations of what constitutes 'economic freedom' and 'economic power'. An important point to note, however, is that such consideration of such policy issues broadens our conception of competition to include the Austrian and radical viewpoints outlined previously. For example, Austrians might argue that maintaining the freedom of economic agents is of primary importance, whilst a radical approach might suggest that competition policy should take greater steps to contain the economic (and political) power attained by large corporations.

Having outlined some of the main theoretical issues, we may now turn to actual policy. Before doing so, however, it is worth emphasizing that, although the insights of economic theory are important in determining the nature of competition policy, there are many other influences. The perception of the problems arising from monopoly power, for example, are much influenced by political ideas and are not necessarily closely related to particular elements of economic theory. This said, the economic theories of the day are a critical ingredient in determining actual competition policies.

5.4. Competition policy in different EU countries

In order to illustrate how the principles of competition policy are applied in practice and to describe the different interpretations and methods of application which exist, it is useful to consider some examples of competition policy in some of the member states of the EU. In particular, we shall consider the basic legislation and policy measures which have been developed in the UK, Germany, and France, before proceeding to discuss policy at the EU level, which is our main concern. It is important, however, to consider briefly individual countries' policies, not only to illustrate the different approaches to competition policy but also as an illustration of issues which may arise at the interface between domestic and European competition policy.

There are a number of critical problems which arise when considering competitive policies in an international context. For example, there may be difficulties in deciding on the relevant jurisdiction of a particular policy or piece of legislation. Similarly, problems arising from price discrimination across different national markets ('dumping') have also raised difficult economic and legal questions. However, it is first necessary to consider individual national policies.

The United Kingdom

The main piece of legislation underpinning much of modern competition policy in the UK is the 1973 Fair Trading Act. This extended previous legislation concerning monopolies and mergers and established the Office of Fair Trading (OFT), which has the task of monitoring competition. The OFT is under the headship of the Director-General of

Fair Trading, who has the legal power to refer any cases of anti-competitive behaviour to the Monopolies and Mergers Commission (MMC). Such anti-competitive behaviour concerns cases which involve the exploitation of a 'monopoly situation' which exists in relation to the acquisition or supply of goods within the UK. The definition of monopoly was amended in the 1973 Act to apply to a firm holding a 25 per cent market share or more (the previous definition specified a one-third market share); a 'complex monopoly', where two or more firms account for at least a 25 per cent share of the market and are deemed to act in such a way as to restrict competition, may also be referred. The definition of the relevant market is, of course, crucial in making such definitions meaningful. This is decided on the basis of a specific range of products and is determined by the Secretary of State for Trade and Industry on the advice of the Director-General.

Once a reference has been made, it is then incumbent upon the MMC to decide whether a monopoly situation exists (in accordance with the Act) and whether or not it operates against the 'public interest'. What is or is not against the public interest involves a balancing of the possible efficiency gains (such as scale economies) against the restriction of competition (as caused by the abuse of market power), and this has normally been considered on a case-by-case basis. The criteria used to decide this include the maintenance of effective competition for supply within the UK; promoting competition through cost reduction by the use of new techniques and products, and facilitating entry into existing markets; maintaining/promoting a balanced distribution of industry and employment throughout the UK; and the maintenance of competitive activities outside the UK by UK suppliers and producers. If a firm (or firms) is found to be acting against the public interest, then it will normally be required by law to agree to refrain from the activities identified by the MMC as anti-competitive and harmful to the public interest. The decision on this rests with the Secretary of State.

Two other pieces of legislation of significance for contemporary policy are the Resale Prices Act 1976 and the Restrictive Trade Practices Act 1976. These build on previous Acts in 1964 and 1956 respectively. The 1976 Restrictive Trade Practices Act broadened the information which firms are required to register, which was established in the 1956 Act and requires the Director-General to act against agreements which significantly restrict competition. This usually attempts to prohibit collusion and price-fixing agreements.

Much of the legislative basis of competition policy was altered in the Competition Act of 1980, which widened the investigating power of the Director-General. It also provided for the recommendation that a firm's activities were against the public interest on the grounds of only one outstanding effect (such as higher future prices) rather than having to weigh all possible pros and cons. Associated with this principle was the introduction of the concept of an 'anti-competitive practice', which has been interpreted to include refusal to supply 'tie-ins' and discounts, predatory pricing, and forcing retailers to stock a whole range of products ('full-line forcing').

The 1980 Act also provided for the investigation, by the MMC, of public enterprise 'monopolies', which was strongly associated with the government's drive towards privatization and was perhaps inspired in part by the Austrian notion that most (if not all) impediments to competition have their origins in state intervention. The subsequent privatization of many utilities has, of course, greatly reduced the number of references made on these grounds.

The continued development of the EU internal market has created new pressures for further revision of the UK legislative framework. A series of White and Green papers, from 1989 onwards, culminated in a government statement of policy in April 1993. In brief, reform will involve the replacement of the 1976 Restrictive Practices Act with a prohibition of cartels, anti-competitive arguments, and concerted practices, and a strengthening of the powers of the Director-General of Fair Trading in relation to investigation, the importance of interim measures, and abuses of market power. The model for this policy framework is Article 85 of the Treaty on European Union (TEU). It certainly makes sense to bring regulatory consistency and certainty to the appraisal of the activities of those UK located companies which involve cross-border trade, while, at the same time, not losing sight of subsidiarity considerations in relation to competitive issues which are purely national in character. The central features of the new framework will include the *prohibition* of anti-competitive practices, the definition of *exemptions and exclusions*, and provisions for *penalties* and an *institutional framework* including rights of appeal. It is also the intention to extend competition law to the exercise of certain property rights—e.g. access to land—where there is the potential to damage competition.

Germany

German competition policy is based on the 1957 Act against Restraints on Competition. This Act prohibits actions/agreements to restrain competition, production, or market conditions with regard to trade in goods and commercial services. This includes any form of cartel arrangement, price-fixing, resale price maintenance, exclusive deals, and 'buying' arrangements. The distinguishing feature of German competition policy embodied in this Act is the emphasis on market dominance by large corporations. The Act has been amended several times since its inception, specifically in 1965, 1973, 1976, 1980, and 1989. The 1973 amendments established merger controls and notification requirements for proposed mergers, expanded the legal definition of market dominance, and extended the exemptions of small firms, which was the main amendment introduced by the previous alteration in 1965. The 1980 amendments were particularly significant in clarifying the definitions of abuse of dominant positions by illustrating the principal characteristics of dominant firms, and in specifying the criteria for control of vertical and conglomerate mergers.

The most recent amendment, in 1989, extended the dominance issue to 'powerful' buyers (in addition to sellers) and to situations involving smaller trading partners rather than the hitherto exclusive concern with large firms. This introduced a new dimension to German anti-trust policy, which has, generally speaking, always been primarily concerned with the abuse of dominant market positions, typically by large single suppliers. The system of law supporting this, which is in contra-distinction to US legislation, has been adopted by a number of other anti-trust systems, including those in Japan and the EU itself, which we shall discuss later. The actual size of firm is crucial, in that the law is formulated to protect the interest of small firms against the exercise of market power/dominant positions by large firms. Activities of small firms are allowed which would be illegal if they were carried out by large firms, which are regarded as having a natural market advantage. This allows small firms, for example, to attempt to exploit economies of scale without fear of contravening competition policy. This exemption clause is important in simplifying the enforcement of anti-trust law, which, in comparison with the UK (and also the USA), is generally simpler, as it does not require the balancing of anti-competitive behaviour with efficiency. Under German law, conduct which is found severely to restrict competition is generally illegal. Efficiency is treated under grounds for exception rather than by the case-by-case evaluation typified by the UK, as discussed in the previous section.

France

Modern competition policy in France also has its legislative roots in the early post-Second World War years. Anti-trust policies of some type, however, are significantly older and represent one of the oldest systems of anti-monopoly legislation in the world. Most current legislation and policy is based on the post-war system, which was substantially revised in 1977. This included a much tougher policy on mergers, which in the 1950s and 1960s had been broadly encouraged in an attempt to strengthen domestic companies in order to make them better able to compete with foreign/international rivals. (This was also an important view prevailing in the UK during this time, and was, in part, responsible for the merger 'boom' of the late 1960s.) The new policy on mergers required post-merger notice, and provided for the prohibition of mergers, including firms with large (domestic) market shares. This Act also established the Commission de la Concurrence, which is empowered to investigate anti-trust violations and to recommend corrective measures. These changes, though altering the underlying laws very little, significantly expanded the means of enforcing anti-trust legislation.

Further changes in 1985 and 1986 strengthened merger policy by subjecting more mergers to the controls established in 1977, and the applicability of competition and anti-trust norms was broadened. This seems to have resulted in a significant increase in enforcement activity in France. The 1986 amendment also replaced the Commission by the Conseil de la Concurrence, which, unlike the Commission, is independent from the Ministry of Economics. Most significantly, this coincided with the separation of the administration from the interpretation and enforcement of anti-trust law. The interpretation of the law became the responsibility of the judiciary. This was an important change, which essentially shifted the onus of anti-trust enforcement from political discretion to judicial assessment. This is in contradistinction to the UK, where control of implementation rests with the Secretary of State, as noted previously. Merger control, on the other hand, has remained the subject of political review, and in this area recommendations by the Conseil require the authorization of the Minister of Economics.

Finally, it should be noted that these amendments (particularly the 1986 amendment) have drawn heavily on Articles 85 and 86 of the Treaty of Rome in formulating a view on competition. This illustrates, as do other national policies, the increasing influence and importance of EU competition policy, to which we now turn.

5.5. **EU competition policy**

The development of competition policy

An essential element in the concept of a common market is the unfettered mobility of goods, services, and factors of production so as to ensure the greatest efficiency in resource allocation. This was an essential theme throughout the development of the European Community, culminating in the establishment of the Single European Market (SEM) in 1992. Naturally, the first concern of the founders of the EC was the free mobility of goods, and, since it would have been pointless to eliminate national tariff barriers to trade if private firms could construct their own countervailing barriers, the whole question of competition policy was central to its progress. As with so many areas of EC activity, competition policy evolved steadily from the founding guidelines established in the Treaty of Rome. The advent of the single market is bound to result in further developments, as the experience of trading in different markets identifies new areas of anti-competitive practice previously sheltering in national backwaters. The production of services is one likely focus of attention, as is the enduring question of subsidiarity and the respective domains of national and EU competition authorities. Among the factors shaping the evolution of policy, in addition to the guidance provided by economic theory, are the diverse traditions of different countries, the extension of the EU to include other nations, and the changing role of public monopoly in the member states. Of some relevance here are the differing Anglo-Saxon and continental approaches to competition. The Anglo-Saxon viewpoint is best exemplified by the US anti-trust practice, of which the UK legislation is a loose imitation based on a case-by-case approach. In the USA, firms are subject to stringent scrutiny and fierce compliance regulations, including provision for triple damages to be awarded to injured third parties. In contrast, the continental view has always been more relaxed, accepting social dimensions to competition, close links between suppliers and customers, and the establishment of group interests to the detriment of outsiders. Agreements not to compete have traditionally been part of a European business mentality. It is not surprising, therefore, that, from the outset, the Commission has faced difficulties in imposing a competition policy on the Member States. At one extreme were Germany, and subsequently the UK, with well-developed frameworks for dealing with monopoly and restrictive practices, and, at the other, states such as Italy and Belgium, where a competition policy tradition scarcely existed. Out of this diversity a clear European dimension has emerged, and our purpose now is to sketch its main features in the light of the previous discussion of economic principle.

Some history

The central feature of EU policy is the belief in the static and dynamic benefits of competition, and the origins of this view can be traced back to the Treaty of Paris in 1951 and the subsequent establishment of the European Coal and Steel Community (ECSC) in May 1953. Given its concern with these strategic commodities, it is not surprising that the Treaty identified certain business practices and state aids as being incompatible with the foundation of an integrated market in coal and steel. Thus the High Authority of the ECSC was empowered to identify and rule on cases of anti-competitive behaviour. From this foundation, the next step was the Messina conference of May 1955 and the subsequent Spaak Report, which laid the foundations for the Treaty of Rome. By then it was well recognized, within the Commission and more generally, that static considerations relating to the abuse of market power had to be weighed in the balance against the more dynamic considerations relating to technological and organizational innovation. The Treaty of Rome established the Commission as the authority in all matters of competition policy, with DG IV being established as the appropriate branch of the Commission. To this branch fell the complex task of turning the guidelines of the treaty into a workable policy. The relevant Articles of the Treaty are 85, which deals with anti-competitive practices, and 86, which deals with dominant market practices and their abuse. In addition we should note that Articles 37 and 90 cover the conduct of public enterprises and Article 91 covers dumping of goods across national boundaries. However, our prime concern here is with Articles 85 and 86. The former has certainly been the more actively used of the two. Between 1964 and 1990 a total of 284 formal Commission decisions were made with respect to Article 85 and only twenty-one with respect to Article 86. Indeed, the first referral under the latter did not occur until 1971, an index of the jealousy with which national governments viewed this matter.

Article 85

This article sets out the practices deemed to be incompatible with a common market: all agreements between undertakings which may affect trade between Member States and have as their object or effect the prevention, reduction, or distortion of competition within the common market. It covers horizontal and vertical distortions of all kinds, price-fixing, price discrimination, agreements to predetermine market shares, and any controls on production, investment, or technical development. All such practices are declared void and unenforceable. However, it is also recognized that such agreements may, in clearly specified circumstances, be in the public interest and on these grounds exempt from the provisions of this article. The general rule here permits agreements if they promote efficiency in production and distribution, promote technical progress, and provide consumers with a fair share of the benefits. Provided an agreement is essential to the provision of these beneficial effects, it could be approved. The immediate consequence of these negative (85/1) and positive sides (85/3) to Article 85 is that each situation has to be treated on its own merits, and so DG IV's principal task has been to build the appropriate body of case law. To assist in this process, regulations have had to be drafted which translate the general principles of Article 85 into clear-cut practice.

We should first note that the Commission has very substantial powers of investigation, supported by the relevant national authorities (in the UK case, the OFT) and bolstered by a system of fines for failure to cooperate with an investigation. Investigations can be prompted by the Commission or by the complaints of third parties. These matters are codified in Regulation 17/62, which was the practical response to the experience of the early years gained in DG IV. This regulation empowered the Commission to enforce the rules of competition on a uniform basis throughout the Community and to exempt small firms with less than a 5 per cent market share from the provisions of Article 85, and instituted a system of fines for breaches of the competition rules. In principle, the fine could amount to up to 10 per cent of a company's world-wide turnover. Pressure of work on the Commission soon led to further regulations defining a category of group exemptions to Article 85—that is, a class of practices which by their generic nature are considered not to have anti-competition effects. Thus Regulation 19/65 proposed exemption for resale agreements within the EC and restriction on the acquisition and use of industrial property rights. Group exemptions of this nature are typically granted for a period of ten to fifteen years. Not only do they limit the Commission's workload; they also save firms legal and other costs incurred in seeking an individual exemption. In the light of the Schumpeterian conflict between the static and dynamic aspects of innovation-based competition, it is particularly interesting to note the group exemptions which have been developed to accommodate firms' arrangements jointly to develop new technology. Thus, Council Regulation 2821/71 established that Article 85(1) does not apply to agreements between undertakings which have, as their objective, the application of standards or the joint undertaking of an R&D programme up to the stage of industrial exploitation, provided the results are shared between the partners in relation to their contributions. The increasing importance of high-technology competition to the perceived success of the EC *vis-à-vis* the rest of the world, led, in the 1980s, to further refinements. Commission Regulation

418/85 extended the group exemptions to cover the joint exploitation of a joint R&D programme. In this context, joint exploitation covers production and marketing, the assignment of licences and other intellectual property, and the commercial know-how required for manufacture. One could hardly find a better example of the continually evolving nature of the Commission's competition policy.

Once a case has been dealt with by the Commission, a number of outcomes are possible. At one extreme is a negative clearance: that is, a declaration that the practice does not violate the conditions of Article 85(1). At the other extreme, a violation is found and fines may be imposed. The policy on fines has grown bolder with the acquisition of experience. The first case occurred in 1969, when a quinine cartel involving Dutch, German, and French firms was decreed in violation of 85(1), and was duly fined by the Commission. Relatively small beer one might think, but large firms in major sectors have not been exempt. Then a market-sharing agreement between ICI and Solvay for the production of soda ash was considered a violation in 1990 and fines of Ecu 17 million and Ecu 30 million were imposed on the respective companies. Nor were non-EC companies exempt: in 1991, Toshiba was fined Ecu 2 million for illegal arrangements with its European distribution companies. In between these extremes are the many cases where the partners involved voluntarily abandon their restrictive agreement or agree to modify it in a way in which the Commission considers is compatible with Article 85(3).

It would be a mistake to imagine that all the cases dealt with by the Commission relate to industrial markets. An interesting illustration of this is provided by the case of the Official Association of Industrial Property Agents (COAPRI), the Spanish trade association, which fixed scales of charges in relation to services provided for the acquisition of patent rights and trade marks in Spain and externally. Reporting in January 1995, the Commission found that, in determining categories of activity and setting the related charges, the Articles of COAPRI restricted the freedom of competitive action of agents and constituted an entry barrier to aspiring agents. Such collective action was deemed to be a serious restriction on competition that could not be justified on the grounds that the ensuing market stability resulted in a higher quality of service. COAPRI was obliged to cease these practices.

Some examples of the grounds on which the Commission has granted negative clearance may prove helpful at this stage. An early example was provided in 1965 concerning a German manufacturer of mechanical cultivators (Hummel) and its Belgian distribution company (Isbecque). The exclusive nature of the agreement was considered to bring it within the scope of Article 85(1), but, none the less, negative clearance was granted on the grounds that the arrangement led to superior customer services without any adverse pricing effects. Two more recent examples indicate the complexities of a case-by-case approach. In 1988 an arrangement between AEI and Reyroll Parsons to set up a joint manufacturing company (Vacuum Interrupters Limited) was granted exemption in spite of being the sole European supplier, entirely on the grounds that the associated product innovations would benefit consumers. A further example of the

Commission's attitude to the dynamics of the competitive process is provided by the decision in 1990 to exempt a joint venture to develop and produce electronic components for satellites (Alcatel Esaci/ANT Nachrichten technik). Notwithstanding the fact that this agreement was judged to affect competition adversely within the Community, it was allowed on the grounds that it strengthened European industry relative to the foreign competition.

A final, and very interesting, example is provided by the clearance in December 1992 of the joint venture agreement between Ford and Volkswagen to develop, engineer, and manufacture a multi-purpose vehicle (MPV). The proposal was to build one plant (in Portugal) and produce two products, one for each partner, distinguished by their engines and body-design details. In reaching its decision to clear this venture, the Commission noted that the venture related to a new market segment (MPVs) and that the venture would influence competition in a number of dimensions, including cross-border trade and the sharing of technical know-how. However, the agreement did not raise any issues of market dominance and fulfilled all the criteria for exemption noted above. It is worth noting that clearance was granted subject to a number of important conditions, including a request to ring-fence commercially sensitive information from the parent companies and to seek the approval of the Commission should either partner seek not to market its model in a Member State.

Article 86

Article 86 prohibits the abuse by one or more undertakings of a dominant position within the single market or a substantial part of it, but only in so far as the abuse may affect trade between Member States. It would cover, for example, restrictions on supply or technical development and unfair pricing. Unlike Article 85, there is no provision for granting an exemption, but like that Article the system of fines is used to penalize abuses of dominance. One example is the heavy fine imposed on Tetrapak (a Swiss company): this was fined Ecu 75 million in 1991 on a turnover of Ecu 3.6 billion for engaging in discriminatory pricing and other practices, including unfair charges for early termination of contracts by its customers. Tetrapack held 90 per cent of the EC market in one market segment and 50 per cent in the other relevant segment, and not only set limits on cross-border competition as a basis for discrimination but also set some limitations on the use of the machinery it supplied to certain manufacturers. One interesting aspect of this case was that, although the abuses were EC-wide, the complaint came from a competitor in the Italian market, who claimed that Tetrapack was selling at predatory prices and excluding it from certain advertising media. Although the complaint was in a national context, the Commission judgement applied to abuse of market power in all the EC markets. As with decisions reached under Article 85, the European Court of Justice stands as the court of appeal in all cases.

We have already pointed to the relatively infrequent use of Article 86, in part due to the hostility of national authorities. More telling though is the failure of this Article to provide clear guidance on the treatment of mergers and acquisitions within the EU. At best it gives grounds for a decision *ex post* once a merger has been carried out and is judged to lead to adverse dominant behaviour. What it does not do is to provide guidance *ex ante* as to whether a merger is permissible. Equally, it becomes clear that mergers created a loophole in Article 85 in that two independent parties to an anti-competitive arrangement could merge and thereby avoid scrutiny—the Commission having no jurisdiction over the internal practices of companies.

The merger boom of the 1980s created very real concerns that a policy on mergers consistent with the principles of the Treaty of Rome was conspicuously absent. The outcome of this debate was the European Commission Merger Regulation, introduced in 1990.

The European Commission Merger Regulation

To understand the current position some history is again useful. In 1971 the Commission deployed Article 86 to judge a takeover by the Continental Can Company of New York of a West German and a Dutch company. It found against Continental Can on the grounds that its acquisitions had created a monopoly position for metal cans and bottle tops within the Community. The case went to appeal and the Court of Justice overturned the Commission's judgment. However, in its judgment it ruled that Articles 85 and 86, while they did not mention mergers, possessed a unity of purpose to protect competition and that, on these grounds, Article 86 applied on principle to merger situations. The period of drafting and consultation which followed led finally to Regulation 4064/89, the merger regulation which came into force in September 1990. This outlines the procedure for assessing whether cross-member State mergers create a dominant position which may have abusive effects, and it may also be applied to mergers between EU and non-EU companies. Authority to judge is again vested in DG IV, which has established a Merger Task Force to handle these cases. The essence of the EU position is that a merger falls within the regulation's scope if it leads to concentration and passes three tests. First, the aggregate world-wide turnover of all the undertakings involved (including parent companies of merging subsidiaries) must exceed Ecu 5 million. Secondly, the aggregate EU turnover of each of at least two of the firms involved must exceed Ecu 250 million. Finally, the regulation does not apply if each of the firms involved has two-thirds of its EU-wide turnover within one Member State. In these calculations, turnover is to be calculated net of all sales taxes. It is apparent that the identification of turnover will be a crucial and contentious aspect of the application of this regulation, although it is not obviously the most relevant measure of market dominance. It remains the responsibility of the merging parties to notify the Commission of their intention to merge, and the relevant national authorities lose jurisdiction whenever a merger has the identified EU dimension. We should also note that the merger provisions also apply to cooperative agreements between firms if that agreement is judged to be concentrative rather than cooperative—that is, creates a lasting economic unit to produce a product or develop a technology. The latter remains subject to the provisions of Articles 85 and 86.

As to its procedures, the Merger Task Force has one month from notification to decide whether to proceed with a case, and a further four months to reach a final decision. Having defined the appropriate market, the emphasis of the investigation is on the maintenance of competitive conditions. Perhaps the most pressing issues concerning the merger regulation relate to the relationship between the Commission and national authorities. National authorities are kept informed of the progress of an investigation, and they can, under Article 9 of the Regulation, request the referral of the merger back to themselves—a procedure which had happened only once, in response to a UK request. Also important here is the requirement further to limit the operation of the Regulation in 1993 with a view to reducing the turnover criteria which provide the tests for potential dominance. The Commission has proposed a reduction of the aggregate turnover threshold to Ecu 2 billion, and this is certain to meet with opposition from those members with well established merger policies (the UK, Germany, and France). Not surprisingly, this has become entangled with post-Maastricht Treaty sensitivities about subsidiarity and the relative roles of national and European-level authorities. Finally, we note that some commentators are in favour of a European Central Office as the focus for merger policy at EU level.

5.6. Overview

It will be apparent from the above that competition policy at the European level has evolved considerably since 1958 and must continue to evolve as the EU grows in membership and the internal market develops. Central to this development will be its relationship with competition policies at national level within the EU and increasingly outside the EU as global competition plays an increasing role in EU thinking.

The extent to which national governments will be willing to forego the adjudication of monopoly, merger, and anti-competitive practices remains the great practical conundrum for the future of EU policy. But deeper issues are also at work, reflecting the contrasting perspectives on competition outlined in the opening section of this chapter. Broadly speaking, these views may be typified in terms of competition as a state of equilibrium versus competition as a process of change. According to the first view, a firm is more competitive to the extent that it has less power to charge a price in excess of marginal costs (itself a vague concept depending on whether a short-run or long-run view is taken) and to control entry into its specific markets. According to the second view, a firm is more competitive to the extent that it has cost and product advantages relative to its rivals and can turn these advantages into gains in market share. Thus competition implies change in the relative market position of the different rivals, a situation of stable market shares indicating a neutral balance of competitive forces. Whichever view one takes of these contrasting positions, the openness of markets to entry by new firms, new products, and new methods of production is a central feature of a competitive environment. Thus policy to limit entry barriers, deregulate markets, and stimulate innovation through technology policy is immediately recognizable as a pro-competitive policy. Whenever entry entails the outlay of irrevocably sunk costs, it is clear that competition cannot be too fierce: as Downie (1956) pointed out, the effective operation of competition requires a modicum of grit in the market mechanism. The obvious example here is when entry is premised on product or process innovations, which require a firm to sink outlays in research, design, and development programmes. If imitation is too easy or the market too competitive, the incentive to undertake those innovation expenditures can be undermined to the detriment of the dynamics of competition. Within the EU, an obvious case is provided by the regulation of the pharmaceutical industry, which will be one important test bed for competitive policy. Pressure to cut health-service costs and open markets to generic producers will have to be weighed carefully against the need for sufficient profitability to fund the science and technology base of the major drug companies. An important policy issue here relates to the question of the optimum length of life of a patent under European law, and the associated regulatory limitations placed on drug developers. In short, firms have to be given sufficient monopoly power to induce the development of beneficial pharmaceutical products, the dynamic gains from product improvement taking precedence over any static losses from granting these companies an element of patent-protected market power.

While open-entry conditions are common to all views of competition, the interpretation of market power and the profits so generated are not. In all practical cases, it is very difficult to decide the extent to which reported profits are the result of market power or the result of the superior competence of the firm in generating lower costs or better service to consumers. The great danger always lies in penalizing the successful for their very success and thus constraining the long-run development of the economic system. None of this, of course, is a recipe for turning a blind eye to anti-competitive practices intended to rig markets and offset the dynamic effects of customers' choice on the relative position of competing firms. Rather, it is a case for careful treatment of each situation on its merits, and an awareness that the competitive process generates losers as well as winners. As with so much in economic theory, the powerful general insights which it provides must always be qualified by the details of the specific circumstances of the individual case. Since these circumstances transcend national boundaries, it is clear that much will be learned (and need to be learned) by the practitioners of competition policy at both EU and national level.

Discussion questions

1. Outline the main objectives of EU competition policy. What are the main problems facing the EU in developing a more effective competition policy?

2. What is meant by a 'dominant market position'? What are the main economic problems likely to arise from the exercise of market power by dominant firms within the EU? How might these problems be best resolved?

FURTHER READING

Much of the theoretical background concerning the various impediments to competition can be found in Devine *et al.* (1985) or, at a more advanced level, in Hay and Morris (1991) and Reid (1987). The latter includes some material relating to Austrian views. For a 'radical' perspective, Cowling (1982) is an important source. In addition, Downie (1956) is a classic reference on the control of monopoly. On EU competition policy *per se*, Jacquemin and de Jong (1977) contains a useful introductory chapter. For recent analysis and discussion, Sapir, Buigues, and Jacquemin (1992) is valuable, as is much of Comanor *et al.* (1990).

REFERENCES

Baran, P., and Sweezy, P. (1966), *Monopoly Capital* (New York: Monthly Review Press).

CEC (1992): Commission of the European Communities, *Seventh Report of the Commission to the Council and the European Parliament*, COM (92), 383 final (Brussels: CEC).

Comanor, W. S., George, K. and Jacquemin, A. (1990), *Competition Policy in Europe and North America: Issues and Institutions* (Chur: Harwood Academic).

Cowling, K., and Mueller, D. (1978), 'The Social Costs of Monopoly Power', *Economic Journal*, 88/4: 727–48.

—— (1982), *Monopoly Capitalism* (London: Macmillan).

Devine, P. J., Lee, N., Jones, R. M., and Tyson, W. J. (1985), *An Introduction to Industrial Economics*, 4th edn. (London: Unwin Hyman).

Downie, J. (1956), 'How should We Control Monopoly?', *Economic Journal*, 66/2: 573–7.

Geroski, P., and Jacquemin, A. (1984), 'Dominant Firms and their Alleged Decline', *International Journal of Industrial Organization*, 2/1: 1–27.

Harberger, A. (1954), 'Monopoly and Resource Allocation', *American Economic Review Proceedings*, 44/2: 77–87.

Hay, D., and Morris, D. (1991), *Industrial Economics and Organization: Theory and Evidence* (Oxford: Oxford University Press).

—— and Vickers, J. (1988), 'The Reform of UK Competition Policy', *National Institute Economic Review* (Aug.), 56–67.

Jacquemin, A., and de Jong, H. (1977), *European Industrial Organisation* (London: Macmillan).

Jacquemin, A., and Sapir, A. (1989) (eds.), *The European Internal Market: Trade and Competition* (Oxford: Oxford University Press).

Jenny, F., and Weber, A. P. (1983), 'Aggregate Welfare Loss due to Monopoly Power in the French Economy', *Journal of Industrial Economics*, 32/2: 113–30.

Littlechild, S. (1981), 'Misleading Calculations of the Social Costs of Monopoly Power', *Economic Journal*, 91/2: 348–63.

Reid, G. (1987), *Theories of Industrial Organisation* (Oxford: Blackwell).

Sapir, A., Buigues, P., and Jacquemin, A. (1992), 'European Competitive Policy in Manufacturing and Services: A Two-Speed Approach', *Oxford Review of Economic Policy*, 9: 113–32.

Sawyer, M. (1980), 'Monopoly Welfare Losses in the U.K.', *Manchester School*, 48/4: 331–54.

Schumpeter, J. (1944), *Capitalism, Socialism and Democracy* (London: Allen & Unwin).

Utton, M. (1995), *Market Dominance and Antitrust Policy* (Aldershot: Edward Elgar).

CHAPTER 6

Science and Technology Policy

PETER STUBBS

6.1. Introduction

The first and most fundamental issue to address in considering EU Science and Technology Policy is why nation states and collectivities of nation states should have a science and technology policy at all. Could we not leave the production and distribution of scientific and technological knowledge to the market mechanism, which, after all, ranges from the humblest individual worker to the largest international firm?

Not surprisingly, scientists and technologists tend to oppose such a proposition. Since Bernard Shaw vilified all professions as conspiracies against the laity, we might suspect self-interest in that opposition; governmental support means more jobs, more prestige, and more money for scientists and technologists. Yet even hard-headed economists have agreed that, objectively, the scientists have a tenable and intellectually respectable case. The most powerful economic support was offered by Kenneth Arrow (1962), who was to become a Nobel laureate in economics in 1972. He observed that there are three categories of economic problems which make it inadvisable to leave the allocation of resources for invention (and, by implication, technological progress) to the market mechanism. They are uncertainty, indivisibility, and inappropriability, and they require some elaboration.

6.2. Reasons for the support of science and technology

Arrow advocated government financial support for basic research. Basic research is the bedrock of technological progress: its accepted definition is provided by the 'Frascati Manual' as 'experimental or theoretical work undertaken primarily to acquire new knowledge of the underlying foundations of phenomena and observable facts, without any particular application or use in view' (OECD 1981: 19). Clearly, work of this sort is likely to be far removed from the market place, yet it has the potential to yield immensely important advances such as the microchip or genetic engineering. For most private investors, including even large corporations, the uncertainty of such research disqualifies it as an acceptable pursuit of financial gain. The risks of failure are high, both because the research might lead to a dead end and because there is a risk that, even if it were fruitful, a speedier rival might beat them to the harvest. It also takes many years to recoup the investment, because basic scientific advances usually take much time and money to translate into saleable products or processes. Applying a typical commercial discount rate to compute a net present value for the speculative benefits of long-term basic research tends to disadvantage it when compared with less radical development work with a quicker pay-off.

Governments can pool these risks, since they are bigger than their national companies and may be able to consider longer-term benefits from the social rather than the private point of view: it does not matter to the government whether company A or company Z exploits the research findings, as long as they are exploited; but, if A contemplated doing the research itself, any prospect that Z, or B, or C could exploit it at the expense of A would be a disincentive. Notwithstanding, even nation states can find basic research risky; but the funding of much basic research in most countries is a government responsibility.

There is a further benefit from public funding of basic research. Where a private research body would want to maintain its property rights—that is, 'keep hold' of its research results to cover its costs and make private profits—the public source can be more open. Basic research findings may be more likely to be translated into useful innovations if they can 'spill over' and be adopted and developed by a wide range of innovators. The prevailing ethic among basic researchers is for wide publication and circulation of their findings among their peer group, and this is most likely to be realized where there is no corporate restraint due to secrecy.

Indivisibilities present problems. Where markets are indivisible, there are problems both in assessing demand and in securing payment. A public-health research programme, analogous to a public-health investment such as urban drainage, can benefit a whole community, but, given the choice of whether to contribute to its costs, some people could become free riders, enjoying the benefits without making any contribution to the costs. In this case it is better to fund and operate the project at community level.

There may also be indivisibilities in the process of research itself. Where an industry is atomistic, with many small producers, no single member may be able to afford a worthwhile research-and-development (R&D) facility. In agriculture a multitude of competing farmers is most unlikely to do systematic R&D; individually they lack the assets, the expertise, and the incentive. Centralized R&D, supported by a levy on users, can overcome this problem; this solution can be applied to specific industrial processes or other small-scale industries by establishing research associations. Governments have subsidized these bodies permanently, or temporarily as a pump-priming exercise, until they becoming self-financing.

Inappropriability is a problem because the originator of the invention or technology may be unable to gain due reward, unless he or she can appropriate the returns to the effort. Ideas are easily stolen. If much of the originator's benefit is dissipated through copying and illicit application by others, there is no immediate social loss—indeed there may seemingly be social gain if the innovation is diffused more widely and more cheaply, as happens notoriously in the case of pirated computer software, which has been estimated to cost the industry £400m. a year in the UK alone (*The Times*, 22 Oct. 1993, p. 33). But, quite apart from the issue of legality, the loss to the innovator may prove a serious disincentive to the inspiration and hard work which R&D entails: short-run opportunistic gains would then compromise long-run technological progress. Most nation states, therefore, protect the intellectual property of inventors through patents and copyrights granted upon original works.

A related issue concerns the benefits which accrue to users, as distinct from the innovator. Support for innovation may be given by governments on the grounds that there are social benefits from innovation beyond the private benefits which accrue through payments to the innovator. Empirical studies of specific innovations by Mansfield *et al.* (1976) show that the social rate of return to innovation is usually higher than the private rate, sometimes helped by the spill-over effect noted above. The argument can be pressed further, in suggesting that there are second-order effects in enhancing industrial development and national competitiveness. If so, and the support improves dynamic resource allocation and the responsiveness of the economy, the effects can be subtle, profound, and long-lasting. However, it is very problematic to verify these effects in ways rigorous enough to persuade national treasuries to provide funding in the face of other less speculative and more populist claims for finance.

Beyond these central issues of uncertainty, indivisibility, and inappropriability, there are other motives for government support of technology. It is often asserted that imperfect private capital markets restrict the funds available for R&D, that bankers are unappreciative of the full value of technological opportunities. In response to this view, governments have from time to time established mechanisms targeted at the provision of funds for technology, such as the National Research Development Corporation (NRDC) and its eventual successor, the British Technology Group (BTG), which was later privatized.

Government may also act as a disseminator of scientific and technological information, and finance arbitration where there are conflicts arising from the use of new technology. Many governments have given support for communications technology in recent years, and there are well-known cases where they have funded inquiries into technological matters of public concern, such as the Sizewell B nuclear power station in the UK.

Finally, the view may be expressed that economic rationale alone should not rule the allocation of funds for science (in particular) and technology. This view rests on the belief that scientific investigation is a manifestation of advanced civilization with a justifiable ethic of its own, rendering it just as eligible for state support as the arts are—this latter support perhaps being more generously provided in certain EU states other than the UK. In this context, allocation to science is not simply to be regarded as an investment decision but also involves elements of desirable consumption. Indeed, some of the allocations to basic research face such high degrees of uncertainty and long gestation that it is difficult to apply to them any risk criteria where risk is understood in Frank Knight's sense of 'measurable uncertainty' (Knight 1921). However, even if this viewpoint is given some credit, there are problems of adjudicating between open-ended claims from the science lobby, and of deciding on the total allocation to the science sector.

6.3. National policies for science and technology

Before the advent of the EC, national policies for science and technology were inevitably separate. Though they shared a common focus of correcting market failures and enhancing scientific and technological performance in the search for improved economic performance and enhanced scientific prestige, there were evident differences among the nations of the Community in their priorities and methods of support. Since the doctrine of subsidiarity applies today and still admits a wide degree of independence to national policies, it is relevant in both a historic and a contemporary context to examine very briefly the national innovation systems and government policies that have developed. In the first edition of this book, we examined Germany, France, and the UK, as the three biggest performers of R&D in the EU. In this edition we examine another major economy, Italy; a small economy with a long tradition of government science policy, the Netherlands; and a new entrant to the EU with a small, advanced economy, Sweden.

In aggregate, Member State expenditures on science and technology dwarf EU-level expenditures. The distribution of some national technological expenditures is tabulated at the end of this section.

Italy

The Italian economy has performed well in the past half century, growing to become a member of the G7, and enlarging its share of world exports from 3.2 per cent in 1960 to 5.2 per cent in 1986. The industrial sector is unusually polarized, including a small number of major multinational corporations such as Fiat, Olivetti, and Pirelli, but also a vast array of small family firms in northern Italy engaged in a wide range of industries.

The proportion of employment in firms with less than 100 workers is exceeded among the major industrialized countries only by Japan. Compared with other EU states with similar populations—France and the UK—Italy has a much lower level of R&D, reflecting this unique industrial structure.

Italy was slow to develop its R&D capacity. In the 1950s and 1960s it had low R&D intensity, spent very little on defence R&D, and was a technological follower, making extensive use of licensed know-how well into the 1970s (Malerba 1993). However, there was an impressive growth of R&D expenditure across the 1980s, averaging 9.9 per cent annual growth between 1980 and 1987, which was well above the OECD average. As a percentage of GDP, it rose from 0.8 in 1970 to 1.4 in 1992 (Dottorini 1995).

An important source of strength in Italian industry has been the clusters of small family firms, which do not conduct formal R&D yet display remarkable adaptability for learning by doing, developing engineering skills and product know-how, and paying keen attention to specialist customer needs. Italy is in the forefront of world exporters of textiles and apparel, household goods, personal products, and food and beverages; moreover, this eminence is emphasized by the clustering of industries in compact geographic areas, so that supplier functions such as specialist machinery manufacturing and custom-design capacity flourish in the same locality, offering feedback loops and valuable externalities to the industries concerned. Porter (1990) suggests that certain disadvantages have provoked positive reactions among Italian firms: inefficient state bureaucracy has led firms to develop pragmatic extemporization, and the upward spiral of higher wages and social benefit costs which began in 1969 obliged firms to enter more expensive and sophisticated market segments, to their ultimate benefit.

Despite the strength of the sector of small and medium-sized enterprises (SMEs), there are identifiable weaknesses in Italy's industrial capacity, manifested in limited R&D intensity and weak international performance in R&D intensive industries. Porter (1990: 447–8) said that Italian government at national level had created far more disadvantages than advantages, neglecting support for R&D, indulging large firms, and failing to encourage a competitive industrial environment, though local government had been more constructive. He advocated improvements in the general technological competence of industry, national infrastructure, capital markets, and universities, as well as a reduction in the state industrial sector and greater emphasis on competition. Malerba (1993: 244–51) identified six factors inhibiting the full development of national R&D potential: limited indigenous generation of technological opportunities; weak demand conditions; a small oligopolistic core; few small high-technology firms; an undeveloped interface between industry, universities, and research organizations; and a limited degree of internalization.

Italy has a number of public research agencies, with the National Research Council (Consiglio Nazionale delle Ricerche (CNR)) covering a broad range of activities, and other specialist agencies covering energy, new technology and the environment (ENEA), nuclear physics (INFN), and space (ASI), with seven-eighths of the budget of the last-named devoted, somewhat controversially, to the European Space Agency.

Other functional national agencies include their own research institutions. The Triennial Research Plan for 1994–6 was designed to support traditional areas of Italian industrial eminence as well as emphasizing Information Technology, and to monitor programmes which have potential for inter-sectoral applications (Dottorini 1995). Science parks are being encouraged, often in economically disadvantaged regions, as well as so-called Relay Centres, financed by the EU to encourage innovation. Though the general trend of Italian R&D has been quite strongly upwards in recent years, in 1992 it appeared to suffer a setback in real terms of about 6 per cent, and scientific research in universities has been under pressure for a decade, suggesting that improvements have still some way to go before the fears can be allayed of the critics of Italy's technology.

The Netherlands

The Netherlands is a traditionally prosperous economy, with a higher income per head than the UK, though lower than some of its other northern neighbour countries. Its prosperity rests on manufacturing industry, natural gas, intensive agriculture, and trade, with over half of GDP concerning exports and imports. Economic growth has been led by chemicals, rubber, paper, and food and drink industries, accompanied by growth in service industries. The industrial sector includes some high-profile multinational corporations such as Royal Dutch Shell, Philips, and Unilever NV. In the 1980s economic growth lagged behind the EU average, and the social welfare system, which was one of the most ambitious in Europe and cost about 7 per cent of GDP, came under pressure. During the 1990s austerity measures were introduced by government and reforms were applied to the welfare system. The Netherlands government was early in the application of science policy with a view to enhancing technological innovation. In 1930 it set up the Nederlandse Organisatie voor Toegepast-Natuurweten-Schappeljik Onderzock, the Netherlands Organization for Applied Scientific Research, popularly known as the TNO. The scope of science and technology policy was enlarged, and in 1978 the role of the Ministry of Science Policy was extended from a largely coordinating function to one which included the disbursal of modest funding, closer and earlier involvement in individual ministries' R&D budgets, and the creation of long-term investment plans for research equipment and buildings fully financed by central government (Tisdell 1981: 163–5). Sector councils and programming committees, comprising researchers, user-group representatives, and government officials, were set up to advise on research themes. Increasing emphasis was placed in the 1980s on the expansion of R&D, especially the development of new technologies which could improve Dutch industrial competitiveness, including measures to improve the quality, efficiency, and economic relevance of university research and of research institutes. Innovation-oriented research programmes were launched with major inputs from industry in their specification, beginning with biotechnology in 1982. So-called

'Spearhead' programmes were set up as temporary supports for urgent issues, such as the SPIN programme for IT research across 1984–8. Exploratory Commissions, known as VCs or Verkenningscommissies, were employed in the 1980s to evaluate the quality and effectiveness of research, consider future policy including state support for the field of research, and make recommendations about its development (Garrett-Jones 1989).

In the late 1980s, gross expenditure on R&D exceeded 2 per cent, putting the Netherlands on a proportional par with the UK. Industrial R&D accounted for over half of gross national expenditure on R&D, and was dominated by five large companies which gave the Netherlands a relatively high research-and-technology profile. However, there has not always been the fullest exploitation of technological potential; while the electronics giant, Philips, has pioneered many new products such as the standard compact sound cassettes, domestic VCRs, and videodiscs, Japanese rivals have exploited these advances and vastly overshadow Philips in world markets. However, in another less obvious area, technology has brought major benefit (Porter 1990: 95): the Netherlands is the world's largest exporter of cut flowers, with a value exceeding $US1 billion by the late 1980s. Improved glasshouse growing techniques, new strains of flower, efficient handling and airfreight, and efficient energy conservation in the use of natural gas-fired heating all benefited from specialized research organizations.

By the mid-1990s, however, pressures bore heavily on Dutch industry, some of whose famous industrial names were humbled. Philips made serious losses, and the air-craft company Fokker, which had earlier been taken under the wing of the the German Daimler Benz group, effectively went bankrupt in March 1996, and the administrator, having failed to find a buyer, began proceedings to wind the company up in December 1996. The pressures for economy in public funding affected the government's capacity for R&D support, just as industry itself was facing competitive pressures on its funding. Total spending on R&D by industry fell from 1.3 per cent to less than 1 per cent of GDP between 1987 and 1993, partly because some major Dutch R&D performing companies transferred part of their programmes abroad. Total spending on science and techno-logy by government and industry declined from 2.3 per cent of GDP in 1989 to 1.8 per cent in 1994. Of government support in that year, 1.8 billion guilders went to uni-versities, 500 million to TNO, and 2.5 billion to other leading research institutes, while participation in international research organizations totalled about 600 million guilders.

In summary, the major problems for science and technology policy in the Netherlands in the late 1990s are the perennial requirement for prioritization (which is usually more problematic for small economies) and pressure on public funds for sup-port. In June 1995 the White Paper *Knowledge in Action* addressed these problems by proposing generic R&D tax incentives, measures to stimulate ineraction between high-tech companies and public-research institutions, an 'information highway', improved vocational training, five centres of excellence in specific technological areas, and a measure to attract foreign R&D performing companies, as a partial counterweight to the outward migration of Dutch R&D. However, many of the proposals are seen as modifications and adaptations of existing policy, and it remains to be seen whether they will succeed in reversing the unwelcome trends of recent years, given the government's expressed need to save 500 million guilders of research expenditure over the period 1995–8.

Sweden

Sweden has a population of less than 9 millions, and thus feels the restrictions of small size even more acutely than the Netherlands, with its population of 15 millions. Like the Netherlands it developed an extensive system of social welfare, which similarly came into question when a centre-right coalition government in 1991 succeeded the Social Democrats, who had been in power for six decades.

Following its emphasis on farm and forest products in the nineteenth century, Sweden was an industrial latecomer, but several individual innovations within the Swedish engineering industries around the turn of the century contributed to the success of firms such as Ericsson, SKF, ASEA, and Alfa Laval and established a tradition of cumulative technological competence. Porter (1990) noted that Sweden's exports were unusually concentrated in large firms, with twenty large multinationals accounting for over 40 per cent of total exports, including, in addition to those already mentioned, Volvo, SAAB-Scania, Atlas Copco, and Electrolux. Its specialization is characterized by Porter as deep but narrow, with heavy concentration in a range of manufactured products, many of which originally derived from her natural resource base but now exist quite independently from it.

In their search for markets, successful Swedish firms have had to employ an overseas focus which has made them adept in the use of licensed technology, helped by government policy which has encouraged overseas R&D links (Tisdell 1981: 175). At the same time, they have developed their own technological expertise and a substantial R&D capability, absorbing 2.8 per cent of GDP in the mid-1980s, with business enterprise expenditure on R&D exceeding 3 per cent of the domestic product of industry. Only about one-third of Swedish R&D was state financed, helping to ensure that it had a keen focus on commercial potential. In 1985 Sweden took out in the USA more patents per head of its population than did Japan, and more than double that of the UK (Edquist and Lundvall 1993). About a quarter of Swedish R&D work is performed within the higher education sector. Public support for techological R&D often follows initiatives by firms and is channelled by agencies such as STU (the Swedish Board for Technical Development).

Some apparent disadvantages have been turned to good account: high wages and the other burdens upon employers of an advanced welfare system have stimulated extensive automation in Swedish industry, such that it is second only to Japan in the use of industrial robots, equal first in computer numerically controlled (CNC) machine tools, and has the highest usage of computer-aided design (CAD). High internal and external transport costs have stimulated logistic innovations and the establishment of sub-sidiaries overseas.

Despite the impressive performance described above, the Swedish economy has a number of problems (Porter 1990; Edquist and Lundvall 1993). Demand for its raw material and semi-manufactured products may be vulnerable, which could threaten exports and the stability of the economy. There is a heavy emphasis on engineering, but a low proportion of exports emanating from industries with high R&D intensity. SMEs have not featured strongly in the Swedish industrial structure, yet they are thought to be important to technological flexibility and the development of new industries; con-cern has also been expressed about the tendency for Swedish firms to shift production abroad, possibly in response to high domestic costs of employment, and the Swedish Royal Academy of Sciences has emphasized the need to alleviate the shortage of science and technology students in higher education (*Outlook on Science Policy* 1994: 124).

The new government introduced a number of reforms. In 1993 it dissolved the Wage Earners' Funds, and introduced a more securely funded pensions system. Budgetary savings were used to fund eighteen research foundations, to boost higher education in technology and sciences and its links with industry, and to finance a range of measures encouraging SMEs. With the country's entry into the EU in 1995, the government has also emphasized the importance of integrating into the EU research effort.

Table 6.1 shows the national pattern of expenditure on R&D by selected nation states, as percentages of GDP. Since some of the countries, notably USA, Japan, and Germany, have a much larger GDP than the UK, it is evident that in absolute terms their R&D expenditure is very much higher than that of the UK. UK expenditure on R&D has failed over the years to keep pace with its major competitors, and the positive technolo-gical balance of payments of 1986 was significantly negative by 1990, became positive in the early 1990s, but seems likely to suffer in the latter part of the decade as industrial R&D declined in 1995. The USA, alone of the countries shown in the table, has a strongly positive balance of payments on technology account, partly though not wholly because the US Revenue Service is assiduous in requiring US companies to declare every conceivable element of their technology earnings.

6.4. The history of the development of the EU science and technology policy

The original Treaty of Rome in 1957, signed by Belgium, France, Italy, Luxembourg, the Netherlands, and Germany, concentrated on the abolition of customs between the EC6 and on the adoption of a common external tariff (CET) on goods entering from other countries. Matters such as competition policy, freedom of movement for labour and

Peter Stubbs

Table 6.1. **Statistics of national science and technology performance, 1994**

R&D category	Expenditure on R&D as percentage of GDP					
	USA	Japan	UK	Germany	France	Italy
Gross R&D	2.5	2.7[a]	2.2	2.4	2.4	1.2
Civil R&D	2	2.8[b]	1.9	n.a.	2.0[b]	n.a.
Government-funded civil R&D	0.46	0.47	0.43	0.88	0.84	0.57
Defence R&D	0.5	0	0.3	0	0.4	0
Government-funded defence objectives	0.57	0.03	0.35	0.08	0.43	0.06
Business R&D	1.80	1.94	1.43	1.56	1.46	0.70
In-government R&D	0.27	0.27	0.30	0.35	0.52	0.26
Higher-education R&D	0.38	0.38	0.38	0.44	0.39	0.25

Indicator	Indicators of national size and growth					
	USA	Japan	UK	Germany	France	Italy
GDP (£bn. at ppp[c])	4,253	1,629	666	981	719	674
GDP growth rate, 1986–94 (% p.a.)	7.8	8.4	7.1	9.4	7.2	7.1
Domestic product of industry 1993 (£bn. at ppp)	3,165[b]	1,439[b]	460	748	519	520
Gross expenditure on R&D 1994 (£bn. at ppp)	108	44.0[a]	14.6	23.2	17.1	8.2
GERD growth rate 1986–94 (% p.a.)	6.1	n.a.	6.6	7.5	8.0	8.1

Notes: Definitional anomalies and rounding can cause seeming inconsistency within national figures.
   n.a. = not available.
   [a] Data for 1992.
   [b] Data for 1993.
   [c] ppp = purchasing power parity.
Source: DTI (1996).

capital, customs unions, state aid, and the harmonization of national laws fell within the Treaty's area of competence, so that one could say that there were components of an industrial policy but no overall framework, though there was a limited precedent in the experience gained in running the European Coal and Steel Community (ECSC), which had operated since 1951. However, there was no provision in the Treaty for science and technology in the then European Economic Community (EEC), or for the adoption of policy towards them.

This state of affairs fell short of the hopes of the founding fathers of Europe, as Jean Monnet and the Action Committee for a United States of Europe had earlier included plans for a 'European Technological Community' among their proposals. However, there was some recognition of a technological issue, albeit very narrow, in respect of civilian atomic energy. At that time, atomic energy was perceived as one of the most dazzling and important frontiers of science. It was scientifically challenging and exciting. It was expected, in time, to provide very cheap power, and potentially could release Europe from its heavy dependence on deep-mined coal and imported oil. It was an area where there ought to be economies in conducting R&D collectively. And there was an obvious European dimension, in that the USA and the Soviet Union were committed to nuclear energy programmes, but would probably be secretive about their knowledge because of its military implications. Against this background, the European Atomic Energy Community (Euratom) Treaty was also signed in 1957.

Under the Treaty it was intended that the Euratom Supplies Agency would own and control the supply of all fissile materials in the EC and the Commission would control the distribution of patent rights and the production licences for nuclear reactor designs and fuel technologies, which were expected to arise from the work of the Joint Nuclear Research Centre (JRNC) which was set up to conduct a five-year research and training programme. Inspired by the examples of Los Alamos and Oak Ridge in the USA and Harwell in the UK, JRNC was to be established on several sites. As Peterson notes (1991: 269), some commentators at the time foresaw a more influential future for Euratom than for the EEC. Harsh realities soon intruded upon these visionary intentions (Ford and Lake 1991). Rivalry occurred between the German and French nuclear industries, in the early climate of buoyant demand for nuclear power stations. The JRNC's reactor design, described as 'somewhat eccentric', was unsuccessful. Across the 1960s, oil provided increasing rather than shrinking competition under the efficient organization of the multinational oil majors. The JRNC was left with nuclear scientists but little or no nuclear work to do. Gradually it mutated to become the Joint Research Centre (JRC), with a main base at Ispra in northern Italy, with others at Karlsruhe in Germany, Petten in the Netherlands, and Geel in Belgium. The Ispra Operation has long been criticized for its inefficiency, with one account reporting that only thirty or forty people from a total staff of 1,600 were qualified and scientifically active (Linkohr 1987). The JRC operation has been described as characterized by 'listlessness, apathy, lack of direction, and lack of conviction' (Ford and Lake 1991: 40). The failure of Euratom was a critical one: what should have been the exemplary flagship for European technology seemed to have run seriously aground. In 1993 its mandate was extended to conduct non-nuclear research, and Ecu 900 million was earmarked for it in the fourth Framework programme, as part of a strategy to make it more market-oriented and competitive.

The failure of this role model for successful collective international research coincided in the 1960s with strongly interventionist national industrial policies in Europe, particularly in France and the UK (though the UK did not enter the EEC until 1972). The publication of an influential book by a French journalist, *Le Défi Américain* or *The American Challenge* (Servan Schreiber 1967), added to the pressures on European governments to boost the capacity of the industries to counter the competition of powerful foreign concerns, typified by IBM, the burgeoning US computer giant. The key weapons were mergers and subsidies, which were intended to afford the necessary resource and scale to match foreign competition. There were also several European collaborative initiatives, such as the Anglo–French Concorde airliner project, and the European Space Agency (ESA), but these occurred independently of the EEC. Concorde was a technical success but a commercial disaster and one commentator has noted 'the advanced technologies of the 1960s provided suitable objects on to which the fantasies of European unity could be projected, while in reality they did not have any substantial long-term significance in contributing to a process of European integration' (Barry 1990, cited by Ford and Lake 1991).

Potentially more successful was the Airbus commercial airliner project, in which the consortium partners were France (38 per cent), Germany (38 per cent), the UK (20 per cent), and Spain (4 per cent). This has developed a family of airliners which has gained a significant market share from the USA, though it has yet to become profitable and has prompted bitter complaints from US manufacturers that it has been unfairly subsidized, as described in Chapter 11. In the mid-1990s there was growing pressure, in the interests of internal efficiency and transparency of its accounting procedures, for the consortium to set up a public company, which it announced in July 1996. However, it has shown that European manufacturers can collaborate successfully in a high-technology area and compete with world leaders such as Boeing and McDonnell–Douglas.

Another technologically successful example in the space sector was not specifically an EC initiative. In 1962 two organizations were established to foster collaboration in space technology: the European Launcher Development Organization (ELDO) and the European Space Research Organization (ESRO). ELDO became a Franco-German initiative after the UK withdrew, but, with the merger of the two bodies in 1973 to form the ESA, a more pan-European stance was evident. ESA fared better than its predecessors, partly because of some specific features of its programme. First, inter-institutional collaboration was easier because governments and public agencies were the prime contractors; secondly, the specialized character of the technology led to a closely knit community of policy-makers, engineers, scientists, and industrialists; and, thirdly, its programme was designed so that all the Member States would share formally in the contracts let by the agency. Its thirteen members are Austria, Belgium, Denmark, France, Germany, Ireland, Italy, the Netherlands, Norway, Spain, Sweden, Switzerland, and the UK, plus Finland as an associate member.

The European Patent Office (EPO), which was founded in 1977 following the European Patent Convention of 1973, was another significant extra-EC development. The EPO provides a single application process for the grant of a 'European patent', which is valid in all the signatory states for twenty years, and saves the administration and expense of applying individually to them. By 1993 membership comprised Switzerland, Austria, Finland, Sweden, and Norway from outside the EC, plus twelve members from within it. Patents issued grew from 1,500 a month in 1980 to over 4,000 a month in 1990. It has headquarters in Munich and the Hague, and sub-offices in

Berlin and Vienna. The EPO also distributes patent information, which is an important function of any worthwhile patent system, and represents Europe in the World Intellectual Property Organization.

Thus by the beginning of the 1980s it seemed rather ironic that the most successful examples of international collaboration were those deriving not from the EC, but from narrower combinations, like the Airbus, or wider ones, like ESA.

The shift of support from firms to generic technologies

Generally, the interventionist policies of support by national governments were not successful. They tended to focus on big firms in industries, which the governments perceived as strategically important to the nation (in terms of employment or expected future role or both). By the mid-1970s, after the UK had joined the EC, it was apparent that this policy of 'picking winners' was beyond the capacity of governments: the phrase was heard increasingly that 'the business of government is not the government of business' (Lawson 1992: 211). One of the most difficult problems was that, if a government selected a firm (sometimes by the merger of former competitors) to be the national champion in an area of technological promise and to endow it with the size and subsidy to compete with the champion of rival states, the most immediate effect was to remove its domestic competition and give it a comfortable, if temporary, feather bed on which it might as readily relax as take up the bruising cudgels of foreign competition. However, there is much evidence that a competitive domestic market tends to be an important precondition of the vigour required to compete internationally (Porter 1990: ch. 3).

In the 1970s the trend moved from the selectiveness outlined in the previous paragraph towards the identification and support of selected or 'generic' technologies, which might be expected to impact on a wide range of industries: electronics and biotechnology were probably the foremost examples. Again, it was national governments rather than the EC which were prime movers in the new trend, but the first signs appeared of an EC policy towards science and technology.

On 14 January 1974 the Council decided on the progressive development of 'a common policy in the field of science and technology'. The scope of the policy was twofold: to coordinate the policies of the Member States and to implement research programmes and projects of EC interest. This sounds simple but is difficult in practice, since the finance available to the EC for implementation was between 1 and 2 per cent of the public funds spent by the Member States on R&D support. Three years later, the Commission produced guidelines for the period 1977–80 (CEC 1977). They set out four prime objectives:

1. securing the long-term supply of resources—namely, raw materials, energy, agriculture, and water;

151

Peter Stubbs

2. the promotion of internationally competitive economic development;
3. improvement of living and working conditions; and
4. protection of the environment and nature.

These pious if worthy aims posed a number of problems of implementation, apart from modesty of financial resources already noted. How would Member States cooperate, given the record of national divergence discussed earlier in this chapter? Could EC policy be reconciled with the problems which the states themselves faced in their national science and technology policies? How should science and technology relate to other EC policies?

Several criteria for EC support were itemized, four 'general' and eleven 'specific'. The general ones emphasized the need for rationalization and efficiency at EC level, the need for transnational action which would involve several countries, the economic need to spread development costs over several national markets, and the need to meet common national requirements. Specific selection criteria included cases where costs or required R&D capacity would be too high for a single nation to bear them, or where there would be savings through joint efforts; cases where R&D was in an initial phase, where an EC programme would stand a good chance of competing internationally, as in new transport systems; cases where potential is real, such as new sources of energy, and where there is long-term potential, such as nuclear fusion. The need for standardization of measures and information systems was also noted. The distribution of effort for the period 1977–80 is shown in Table 6.2.

The Scientific and Technical Research Committee (CREST) was responsible for the development of Community R&D policy and coordination at policy level with Member

Table 6.2. **Distribution of Direct Action projects, 1977–1980**

Sectoral policies	Expenditure on Direct Action projects (m. units of account)	Total expenditure (m. units of account)	Percentage of total expenditure
Energy	188	566	58.8
Industrial	–	137	14.2
Environment	28	42	4.3
Resources and raw materials	7	28	2.9
Transport	–	19	1.9
Agriculture	–	14	1.5
Social	–	9	0.9
Development aid	–	4	0.5
Public service and other	127	144	15.0
TOTAL	350	962	100.0

Note: Direct Action projects were carried out by the JRC. Indirect Action projects were 50% funded by the EC.
Source: CEC (1977).

States, and included within its membership senior officials from the member countries as well as Commission officials. The Commission established an internally staffed pilot programme of Forecasting and Assessment in Science and Technology (FAST), to collaborate with outside bodies such the Science Policy Research Unit (SPRU) at the University of Sussex, and DATAR in France. The FAST programme helped to highlight shortcomings in Europe's capacity in capitalizing on basic research, which too seldom produced successful final products. The Commission also acknowledged the importance of evaluating the effectiveness of its research activities and programmes, which we examine later.

Thus by the late 1970s the Commission had begun to address some of the key issues concerning science and technology and establish tentative proposals for action, but these bore the stamp of a hesitant bureaucracy rather than the confidence which marked the execution of policy by the Ministry of International Trade and Industry (MITI) in Japan.

The primacy of US and Japanese technology

Evidence accumulated in the 1980s that the 'technology gap' noted between US and European industry in the 1960s was widening, and that Japan was also outstripping Europe in many critical industries. One of the most visible industries was electronics, because its products could be seen to pervade industrial and domestic use, including the fashionable information technology (IT) sector. The national governments of France, Germany, and the UK had all supported their IT industries across the period from the mid-1960s to the early 1980s through subsidy, merger, and procurement preference in government purchases, to little effect (Sandholtz 1992). In 1975 the EC had a positive balance of payments in information technology, but it was in deficit by 1982. Europe's shares of world production in semiconductors and in integrated circuits were declining, foreign penetration of the European market was increasing, and European semiconductor manufacturing was unprofitable. Over four-fifths of the European computer market was held by US firms. Worse still, perhaps, was the fact that the USA and Japan were both pursuing ambitious research programmes in search of future IT supremacy, the former on very high speed integrated circuits (VHSIC), while the latter, after its successful very large scale integration (VLSI) programme which had launched Japanese industry into the manufacture of mainstream memory chips in the 1970s, announced an initiative on fifth-generation computers intended, in popular parlance, 'to think for themselves'. Faced with this mounting challenge, a number of leading European IT firms had, with EC encouragement, already begun to collaborate in the late 1970s on 'pre-competitive' research—that is, research on innovations in principle rather than at the level of products for imminent commercial launch.

The emergence of Community programmes

In 1979–80, the Commissioner of DG III, the Directorate-General of Internal Market and Industrial Affairs, Viscount Étienne Davignon of Belgium, invited the heads of Europe's leading IT firms to form a 'Big 12 Round Table', including ICL, GEC, and Plessey from the UK; AEG, Nixdorf, and Siemens from Germany; Thomson, Bull, and CGE from France; Olivetti and STET from Italy; and Philips from the Netherlands. As heads, they commanded more authority than more junior personnel who had attended earlier, less fruitful, discussions. And they were well aware of the gravity of their industrial and collective circumstances. Sandholtz (1992) has suggested that 'in general, states will attempt unilateral strategies first and surrender the goal of autonomy only when unilateral means have proved to be impossible or too costly'. The participant national firms knew that unilateralism had failed, and this recognition gave a climate favourable to cooperation, and Davignon played the key role as the champion of new policies, as described by Sharp (1993). Two years of talks failed to fulfil the early hopes of establishing joint manufacturing companies along the lines of the Airbus consortium, but instead they did establish a consensus for collaborative research. Moral support for such collaboration also followed from the Gyllenhammer group, which was an informal gathering of twenty leading European industrialists, representing Gyllenhammer's Volvo, as well as Pilkington and Philips, and which urged an end to national subsidies, intra-European trade barriers, and divided R&D programmes (Pearce and Sutton 1985: 53–4).

There was, however, a potential conflict with EC competition policy, which forbids collaboration at the stage of developing products for an immediate market. However, Articles 85 and 86 allow collaboration for 'pre-competitive research'. Davignon's alliance of the EC and heavyweight industrialists, supported by the work of 550 industrial, scientific, and university experts (Sandholtz 1992: 14–15), was powerful enough to overcome the doubts of national government officials, and establish the European Strategic Programme for Research and Development in Information Technology (ESPRIT). The first outline proposal of September 1980 led to a formal proposal, to establish a strategic collaborative IT research programme between the major European companies, together with smaller companies, research institutes, and universities, which was presented in May 1982, and approved by the EC Commission in December, with funding of Ecu 11.5 million (£8.5 million). Contracts under the pilot programme were invited in February and first signed in May with thirty-eight projects, chosen from our 200 proposals involving 600 companies and institutes, under way by September 1983. The twelve round-table companies won about 70 per cent of the funds. Davignon's gambit of pilot projects with a streamlined application and vetting procedure paid off in overcoming Member State reservations and led to a ten-year Ecu 1.5 billion (£1 billion) programme for 1984–93.

The first five-year phase, ESPRIT I, 1984–8, was to concentrate on pre-competitive research in microelectronics, advanced information processing, and software techno-logy, as well as applications in computer-integrated manufacturing and office systems. Approval was delayed until February 1984 because of German and UK government concerns about the costs of the programme. There was an enormous response to the first call for proposals in March 1984, with only about one proposal in four winning acceptance. The 227 projects in Phase I involved about 3,000 researchers from 240 com-panies (of which about 55 per cent were 'small', employing less than 500 workers apiece) and 180 universities and research institutes. Three-quarters of the projects involved firms and academic centres in collaborative work. Of the ten-year budget of Ecu 1.5 bil-lion, Ecu 1.3 billion had been committed by January 1987. The EC funded up to half of the project expenditure, and firms from at least two Member States had to participate.

The successful reception of ESPRIT I was heartening to Europeans, and the conse-quences were positive.

(a) It created a useful European IT network of researchers, and allowed companies to economize on scarce technological personnel. They could commit one or two researchers to an ESPRIT project, and have their efforts geared up by the joint participation of other institutions' workers, with both short- and long-term benefits of collaboration and familiarity.

(b) Because the research was pre-competitive, collaboration was more open than if it had been near-market, when corporate secrecy would have created inhibitions between the partners.

(c) Collaboration across national boundaries, required intentionally, meant that the narrow horizons of 'national champions' had to widen.

(d) In cases of industrial participation, industry met 50 per cent of the costs, thus enjoying an effective subsidy from the EC.

(e) Although the Commission identified priorities and broad areas of research, actual research projects were nominated by the applicants. Thus, within the restriction that they could not be too near-market, projects became more demand-driven.

(f) Once agreed, each project was subject to a tight timetable and monitored through a system of programme management.

ESPRIT generated a new awareness of Europe's technological strengths, and provided a model for initiatives in other areas of technology. Indeed it helped establish the climate for the 'Framework' programmes, and produced a tribe of acronyms—RACE, BRITE, BRIDGE, BAP, ECLAIR, FLAIR, COMETT, and others—which we detail later.

Another consequence of the success of ESPRIT I was the need to find funds for the remainder of the programme's decade. The Commission brought forward the second phase, ESPRIT II, from 1989 to 1987. The 'Big 12 Round Table' wanted to triple the budget and scope of ESPRIT II, but the proposal fell foul of UK and German govern-ment feelings that the EC R&D budget was too high. Compromises were struck over the

Framework programme, and in April 1988 ESPRIT II was formally approved for 1988–92 with a budget of Ecu 1.6 billion (£1.07 billion), which was less than originally proposed but more than double the allocation for ESPRIT I. The Commission received about 1,000 proposals and agreed to fund about half of them. Three principal areas of research were emphasized: microelectronics, IT processing systems, and applications technologies. The emphasis on pre-competitive research, however, still left the difficulty of how to capitalize at market level, and ESPRIT II went some way to address this issue by emphasizing 'demand driven aspects of the programme' (Sharp 1993)—for example, Application Specific Integrated Circuit Technology, and Technology Integration Projects (TIP), which were intended to meld different elements of separate work and show how they linked together. Funds for ESPRIT II were all earmarked by the end of 1990, and the Commission launched ESPRIT III with Ecu 1.35 billion (£645 million) for 1990–4, to exploit seven areas—microelectronics, advanced business and home systems peripherals, high-performance computing and networking, technology for software intensive systems, computer integrated manufacturing and engineering, open microprocessor systems, and basic research to 'contribute to the programme's main objectives from an upstream position' (DTI 1993: 9).

A further development in the 1980s deserves attention. This is the European Research Coordination Agency, or EUREKA initiative, which was initiated by France and founded in 1985 as a European response to President Reagan's announcement of the Strategic Defense Initiative (SDI, or 'Star Wars' as it became popularly known) in the USA. It extended beyond the EC Member States to include the seven countries of the European Free Trade Association (EFTA), Turkey, and, latterly, Hungary; but it was managed and coordinated by the EC Commission. It was intended to help industry-led, market-driven projects involving collaboration of at least two organizations from at least two EUREKA member countries. By March 1993 there were 623 projects involving Ecu 8.8 billion (£6.2 billion). No priority areas were specified but the project had to involve technical innovation, and to that extent was closer to the market and more concerned with commercial applications than ESPRIT was allowed to be. In practice, most current projects fell into the following areas: communications, energy, environment, IT, lasers, medical and biotechnology, new materials, robotics and automated production, and transport. Specific concerns included high definition television (HDTV), which has also been the subject of much Japanese R&D, the Prometheus initiative for automatic car navigation systems, and JESSI, the Joint European Structure on Silicon Initiative.

EUREKA has no central funding, simply acting as an umbrella mechanism for encouraging inter-firm collaboration: public funding is granted at the discretion of national governments, which usually follows any approval by the EUREKA programme. Thus EUREKA has a large nominal budget but no actual resource: the figures in Table 6.3 reflect a commitment to expenditure by Member States rather than effective expenditure. The partners negotiate the sharing of Intellectual Property Rights (IPRs), for which there are no general rules. Unlike ESPRIT there is no central monitoring or evaluative role within EUREKA.

Table 6.3. **EUREKA funding commitments, September 1992**

Technology	Number of active projects	Cost (Ecu m.)	Percentage of total expenditure
Medical and biotechnology	102	830	9.4
Communications	28	1,452	16.4
Energy	22	490	5.5
Environment	117	881	9.9
IT	77	2,067	23.4
Lasers	14	405	4.6
New materials	53	317	3.6
Robotics and automation	104	1,291	14.6
Transport	22	1,110	12.6
TOTAL	539	8,843	100.0

Source: EUREKA (1992).

EUREKA was conceived as a rival to ESPRIT and other Commission programmes; but, despite occasional overlaps it has become more complementary, partly because its projects can be more applied than the pre-competitive ESPRIT projects. The two programmes, together with others listed in Table 6.2, raised the profile for research in the EC by the mid-1980s. Perceptions were also concentrated by the EC-wide acknowledgment of the technology gap, and of problems of the environment, and by a growing appreciation, through experience, of the benefits of inter-firm and inter-institutional collaboration. Peterson (1991: 270–1) has argued that 'the interests of public and private actors in promoting new collaborative R&D programmes converged as the Framework programme and EUREKA were launched in 1985'.

The instrument which allowed this fuller development of collaborative research was the Single European Act (SEA).

6.5. The SEA of 1987

The 1987 Act contained an additional section, called Title VI—Research and Technological Development, in which it set out in Article 130*f* the following credo:

The Community's aim shall be to strengthen the scientific and technological base of Europe's industry and to encourage it to become more competitive at international level.

In order to achieve this, it shall encourage undertakings including small and medium-undertakings, research centres and universities in their research and technological development activities; it shall support their efforts to cooperate with one another, aiming notably at enabling undertakings to exploit the Community's internal market potential to the full, in particular through the opening up of national public contracts, the definition of common standards and the removal of legal and fiscal barriers to that cooperation.

In the achievement of these aims, special account shall be taken of the connection between the common research and technological development effort, the establishment of the internal market and the implementation of common policies, particularly as regards competition and trade.

The next Articles, 130g to 130l, spelled out the means. Research, technological development and demonstration programmes would promote cooperation between businesses, research centres, and universities. Cooperation would also be promoted with third countries and international organizations, as would the 'dissemination and optimization of results'. Training and mobility would also be stimulated. Member States undertook to coordinate amongst themselves policies and programmes carried out at national level, in liaison with the Commission.

The key provision was the adoption of a multiannual Framework programme setting out all the EC's proposed activities over a five-year period: it would lay down scientific and technical objectives, prioritize them, set out the main lines of activity and the amount deemed necessary, including detailed rules for EC participation, and its distribution across the appropriate activities. The Framework would comprise specific programmes of fixed duration within each activity. An implementation mechanism worked at two levels: the Framework as a whole had to secure unanimous agreement among the Member States; and sub-programmes were to be adopted by the Council by qualified majority voting after consultation with the European Parliament (EP) and the Economic and Social Committee. Programmes subsidiary to the Framework were permissible involving certain Member States only, which could finance them subject to possible EC participation; and cooperation with third states and international organizations was also feasible.

This was a dramatic advance upon the 1956 Treaty of Rome, since it legitimized EC technology policy—as it did industry policy elsewhere in the Act.

In fact, the Framework system had already been subject to discussions for two years when it was launched in 1987, in the hope of an earlier introduction. The motive of both the Commission and the EP was to break out of the stop–start cycle of *ad hoc* decision-taking and wrangling over funding of research proposals. The first Framework programme, now commonly labelled Framework 1, or FP1, was scheduled to run from 1987 to 1991. It was followed by others, with successive increases in funding, as shown in Table 6.4: the proportionate distributions of activity with the Framework programmes are shown in Fig. 6.1. In the event, the take-up of funds for programmes was faster than expected; for example, the most important member programme, ESPRIT, over-ran its budget by Ecu 200 million in 1988, in the face of 'the high quality of the proposals, the industrial commitment underlying them and the urgency of the work proposed' (Peterson 1991: 282–3). A second Framework programme had been introduced to run across 1987–91, and by December 1989 the Research Council in Brussels agreed with the new Research Commissioner Pandolfi to establish

Table 6.4. Framework programmes of European activities in research and technological development, 1987–1998

Framework programme	Period	Budget (Ecu m.)
FP 1	1984–8	3,750
FP 2	1987–91	5,396
FP 3	1990–4	6,600
FP 4	1994–8	12,300

Source: CEC, various.

a third-generation Framework programme: its funds were topped up in December 1992 from Ecu 5.7 billion to Ecu 6.6 billion.

The total extent of the European programmes for new technology is wide, and Table 6.5 lists some of the key examples. Often programmes continued through successive generations of Framework, as in the cases of ESPRIT, COMETT, and SPRINT.

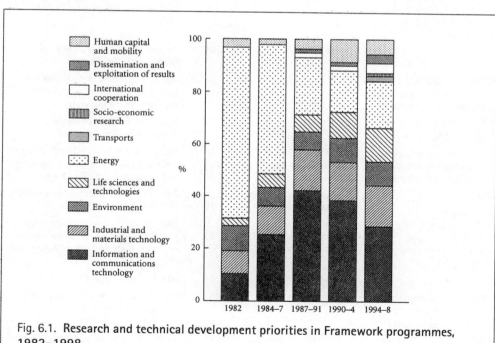

Fig. 6.1. Research and technical development priorities in Framework programmes, 1982–1998

Source: CEC (1994).

Table 6.5. **Major European programmes promoting new technology**

Acronym and full name	Period	Budget[a] (Ecu m.)	Prime objectives
ESPRIT: European Strategic Programme for R&D in IT	I 1984–8 II 1988–92 III 1992–4	750 1,600 1,350	To promote EC capabilities and competitiveness in IT, especially micro-electronics systems
RACE: R&D in Advanced Communications Technologies for Europe	Definition 1985–7 RACE I 1990–4 RACE II 1992–4	21 460 489	Help EC competence in broadband communications equipment, standards and technology
TELEMATICS	1990–4	380	Develop telematics in e.g. health, transport, public administration

BRITE/EURAM:
Basic Research in Industrial Technologies/Advanced Materials for Europe
	BRITE I 1985–8
	EURAM I 1986–8
	BRITE/EURAM I
	  1989–92
	BRITE/EURAM II
	  1992–6
	BRITE/EURAM III
	  1996–
		100
		
		450
		
		663
		
		402
			Support for R&D which upgrades technological or materials base of production

BAP: Biotechnology Action Programme	1985–9	75	Develop infrastructure in biotechnology, esp. research and training
BRIDGE: Biotechnological Research for Innovation, Development and Growth in Europe	1990–3	100	As BAP, but for large projects, e.g. molecular modelling, advanced cell culture
BIOTECH	1992–6	164	Prenormative research, more basic than BRIDGE, includes safety
ECLAIR: European Collaborative Linkage of Agriculture and Industry through Research	1989–94	80	Applying advanced biotechnology in agro-industrial sector, esp. using raw materials from agriculture
FLAIR: Food Linked Agro-Industrial Research	1989–94	25	As ECLAIR, but food oriented, in manufacture and processing
COMETT: Community Action Programme for Education and Training for Technology	COMETT I 1987–9 COMETT II 1990–4	30 200 + 30	Training programmes between university and industry, via enterprise partnerships and international staff exchange
VALUE	VALUE I VALUE II 1992–4	66	Disseminate and exploit research results of Community programmes
SPRING: Strategic Programme for Innovation and Technology Transfer	SPRINT I experiment SPRINT II 1986–9 SPRINT III 1989–94	9 90	Promote innovation and technology transfer, esp. among small and medium enterprises internationally. Merged with VALUE 1994
EURET	1990–3	27	Rail, sea, air transport research
STRIDE: Science and Technology for Regional Innovation and Development in Europe	1990–3	400	DG XVI programme to promote R&D in assisted regions
MONITOR	1989–3	22	Identify R&D policy priorities

[a] The figures shown as budgeted do not include industrial contributions to ESPRIT and other shared cost programmes: in those cases actual expenditure involved in the programmes will approximate twice the budget figure shown above.
Sources: CEC (various publications).

6.6. Evaluations of policy effectiveness

EU-sponsored research is important in both quantity and quality: some system of accountability is, therefore, necessary. Technically the Commission is accountable to the Council, which is made up of national ministers, and to the EP, which scrutinizes legislation and the drafting and execution of budgets. However, science and technology require expert examination of their effectiveness, as to both their scientific and their economic worth, to judge whether the work is worth doing in the first place and whether, once authorized, it has been well accomplished.

One possibility was to employ FAST in evaluations. But there seemed little enthusiasm at the top of the Commission to involve FAST: its resources were small for such a vast job, and independent outside judgement was deemed desirable (Holdsworth and Lake 1988: 424).

When the third Framework programme was adopted, the Council required the Commission to undertake an evaluation of all programmes which operated under the second programme, formally to provide 'an overall appreciation of the current state of execution and achievements of the specific programmes adopted under the second Framework . . . and to set out the principal lessons that have been learned from the execution of these programmes'. The main source of information was the reports of the independent evaluation panels commissioned to examine the operations of specific programmes. In addition there were reports from consultants commissioned to examine particular questions, internal Commission reviews drawing on the reports of panels or outside experts, reviews and reports of programme committees, plus findings from specially commissioned studies of the horizontal aspects of the effects of Community R&D programmes. An example of commissioned work was a study of the impact of EC policies for R&D on science and technology in the UK, which was prepared for the UK Office of Science and Technology and the Commission (HMSO 1993a).

The findings of these studies are generally positive; they chronicle good work and effective international and inter-institutional collaboration. A report from CREST was submitted to the Council in September 1992, giving an evaluation of the second Framework programme (CREST 1992). It addressed three major issues—the quality of programme results and their impact on competitiveness; management and cost-effectiveness of research; and consistency with EC policy and principles. It noted a substantial amount of state-of-the-art research, with a fair balance between incremental and more ambitious research, but intellectual property rights problems were an inhibition on dissemination and exploitation, for which there was, implicitly, more scope. While there were cases of R&D conferring significant technological advantage over international rivals, the most significant impact was felt to be in promoting the idea of collaboration across industry, academia, and the nations of the EC. There remained much scope for developing the harmonization of standards across the EC. Though there was general satisfaction over programme management; sometimes project assessment needed more attention, as did the lags between calling for proposals and beginning the research. Programme objectives could be more clearly defined and there was scope for closer and more transparent links with other DGs responsible for policy in areas such as transport, environment, energy, health, and agriculture. According to Pownall (1995), ESPRIT I raised 'European awareness' but brought less evidence of tangible and marketable results because of the pre-competitive nature of the work, but business and market factors were better considered in ESPRIT II.

With nearly 18,000 collaborative links in Framework 2, the UK was its most active participant. In fact, the UK fared well in the early Framework provisions, as Table 6.6 reveals, though the shares need to be viewed in the light of Member State contributions to the EU budget, shown in Chapter 14. UK views on Framework 2 were analysed by questionnaire and interviews among participants in academia and industry (Georghiou *et al.* 1993). Academics were more positive, but two-thirds of industrial firms involved considered the benefits outweighed the costs, against 21 per cent who did not; and over three-quarters intended to reapply for future participation. It was estimated that about half of EC R&D spending in the UK was 'additional'—that is, adding to the total of publicly financed R&D, and not just funding what would have been undertaken without EC monies. Moreover, EC programmes had a bigger impact than the 6 per cent of publicly funded R&D that they constituted, because they were

Table 6.6. **Major recipient countries of Framework funding, 1987–1991**

Programme area	Percentage granted to			
	UK	Germany	France	Italy
IT	18	22	25	11
Communication technology	20	25	22	8
Telematics	20	17	18	9
Industrial and materials	19	20	22	12
Measurement and testing	22	23	15	7
Environment	21	19	19	9
Marine sciences	22	15	18	9
Biotechnology	17	18	14	7
Agri and agro–industrial	20	4	22	7
Biomedicine	24	10	16	7
STD	18	10	25	5
Non–nuclear energy	14	19	21	11
Fission	21	25	22	5
Human capital	25	15	25	7
TOTAL (weighted average)	19	21	23	9

Note: Data exclude Fusion Programme and JRC funding.

Source: Cabinet Office (1992).

approved by senior staff, they concentrated on recently established priorities, eased research-funding scarcities, and were geared up by EC participation. However, UK industrial participation in Framework 3 has been disappointing in comparison with German and French industry. There were also complaints that project approval rates were low in the third programme and that there was not enough continuity, which is vital to long-term research work (*Research Fortnight*, 30 Nov. 1994, p. 12).

An independent panel of experts also found in favour of EUREKA's benefits (*Outlook on Science Policy*, 1993: 73–4). Most partnerships were vertical, between firms, customers, and suppliers, rather than horizontal. Collaboration worked best between partners of similar size, with smaller firms more product-oriented than large ones, which focused on longer-term research projects. Over 40 per cent of participants were found to expect substantial sales increases within three years, reflecting the near-market emphasis of EUREKA compared to Framework.

In the discussions leading to the fourth Framework programme, numerous lessons were drawn from earlier experience. The UK government submitted a policy paper in February 1992 (Cabinet Office 1992) drawing together the views of the UK science and technology community. It stressed the need for evaluation of Framework 2, for planning of annual commitments, for emphasis on generic technologies and dissemination of technology from research projects, as well as the need for consultation between DGs. Some of these views were accepted in CREST (1992), but the fourth Framework proposal was controversially received (Hill 1993: 16). Its anatomy is shown in Table 6.7.

The programme proposed Ecu 13.1 billion of expenditure, but its adoption required a unanimous decision from the twelve member states. However, the three biggest con-

Table 6.7. **Fourth Framework programme, 1994–1998**

Programme area	Budget (Ecu m.)	% R&D
Information and communications technology	3,405	27.7
Industrial technologies	1,995	16.2
Environment	1,080	8.8
Life sciences and technologies	1,572	12.8
Clean and efficient energy sources	1,002	8.1
Nuclear safety and security	414	3.4
Controlled thermo–nuclear fusion	840	6.8
Research for European transport policy	240	2.0
Socio–economic research	138	1.1
Cooperation with third countries and international organizations	540	4.4
Dissemination and utilization of results	330	2.7
Stimulation of training and mobility of researchers	744	6.0
TOTAL	12,300	100.0

Source: CEC (1994).

tributors to the EU, Germany, the UK, and France, sought against the wishes of the other nine to reduce the Framework budget by at least Ecu 1 billion. One of the difficulties has been that the pay-off to Framework R&D is singularly problematic to assess in financial terms. Since it is not near-market research, it will take time to see clear financial benefit, and the advantages so far ascribed to it by expert analysts are inevitably qualitative rather than measurable in money terms. A cynic might observe that of course firms will welcome, and laud, Framework programmes if they bring handsome subsidies with them. The EU still seems to be lagging behind its US and Japanese technological competitors in many industries, but this can hardly be laid at the door of the EU programmes, which account for only a very small part of *total* R&D effort across the companies and countries of the EU. While Framework 4 remains directed, like its predecessors, at pre-competitive research, it is designed to complement national research efforts, and projects are expected to offer practical longer-term advances.

In 1995 the Research Commissioner, Mme Edith Cresson, proposed several task forces to operate under Framework 4, focusing on the car of the future; educational multimedia; next-generation civil aircraft; the train of the future; vaccines for viral illnesses; clean technology; and socially useful applications of IT. Each task force is to consult with industry to set research priorities, to foster coordination, and to help garner resources. However, this ambitious approach raises potential problems for competition policy.

There is now debate about the policy to be followed in a proposed Framework 5, but some countries face pressures over its funding. Germany is conscious of the need for restraint over public expenditure if it is to satisfy the financial criteria set out in the TEU, and seeks concentration on a small number of strategic industries, flexible funding to make programmes more adaptable in the face of emerging needs, as well as 'variable geometry' which would allow Member States to opt in or out of individual programmes. Pressure on research funds may well intensify. The UK capped its contribution to ESA in 1995, and the present policy, under which the receipt of EU research by UK companies is balanced by a cutback of national government funds, is a considerable disincentive to the effort required to bid for them.

Indeed, there are a number of fundamental problems which face the EU in the light of changing international relationships and corporate practices.

6.7. Technology, industrial, and trade policies: tensions and contradictions

Industrial policy is traditionally concerned with matters such as influencing industrial and market structure and competitiveness, and encouraging the modernization of capital stock. It shares an uncertain border with technology and trade policies. For example, the structure of output cannot be decided independently of trade policies. If a country wishes to develop a new industrial sector in which other countries already have capabilities and experience, it may have to invoke the infant industry argument and offer its industry a period of protection from unrestricted foreign competition. Subsidies to indigenous R&D may also be considered necessary. Technology, industrial, and trade policies clearly overlap here; perhaps the simplest theoretical discriminator is that industry policy emphasizes physical capital, whereas technology policy emphasizes the creation and utilization of knowledge.

However, it is a practical and not just a theoretical dilemma. Technology policy seeks to create productive capability, which often requires public sponsorship of R&D. Such support is only compatible with competition (which is a common goal of industrial policy) if the R&D is pre-competitive; but the boundary between pre-competitive and near-market R&D is fuzzy, at best. The tension between protectionism and enhancing capability is exemplified by European attitudes towards microelectronics and IT. European firms have persistently failed to compete satisfactorily in these sectors in spite of varied forms of protectionism, which are detailed in Chapter 11. How long, and by how much, is it necessary to support the development of European potential, before an infant industry can be weaned? Yet is it possible for the EU to achieve adequate economic performance and prospects for the future if these strategic industries are allowed to wither?

The tension between a protectionist *Fortress Europa* and an open, competitive EU of the sort which Porter (1990) would consider a prerequisite for efficiency is reinforced by the institutional division of labour which assigns industrial, technology, and trade policies to different DGs. Each DG develops its own routines, traditions, and power structure. Programmes once initiated are difficult to terminate and attitudes harden. Thus the rigidities and contradictions can persist if they are inherent in the priorities of different interest groups. It will take time to reconcile these conflicting forces and establish an acceptable balance of competition, protection, and capability enhancement. Further, one of the goals of EU policy is to enhance the science and technology capacities of Member States presently less capable in these areas. Resource is transferred via taxation from the advanced, efficient Member States to the disadvantaged. This may be acceptable in times of general prosperity and growth, but can create tensions if the advanced states face competitive pressures from non-Member States.

Interfirm collaboration and its implications for EU technology policies

As we have seen, EU technology policy has concentrated on sponsoring different forms of collaboration between European countries. Such forms of collaboration are not generally those which participants would choose spontaneously, otherwise the EU initiatives would have been redundant, having been implemented already by the market. Part of the motive for the policy is political, to accelerate European integration. In this context one should note the rise across the late 1970s and 1980s of inter-institutional collaborative agreements or IICAs (Chesnais 1991; Mytelka 1991). They can be of very different scope, varying from licensing agreements, joint R&D, joint development of new products, joint ventures in marketing and distribution, with or without joint equity. The Airbus consortium is just one of many possible manifestations.

The growth of IICAs poses a considerable theoretical and practical problem. From a theoretical standpoint, firms are not expected to collaborate. As they grow in size, we might expect them to integrate vertically and develop internal hierarchical organizational forms. Chandler (1962, 1977) has ably charted the progression of firms from small unstructured enterprises to U- (unitary) and M- (multi-divisional) forms of company. Given the realities of market imperfection, firms tend to internalize functions (Coase 1937; Williamson 1975, 1985). Industrial R&D in particular is a function often internalized, because of the difficulties of establishing satisfactory markets in technology, given the complexities of valuation and the need for secrecy to ensure appropriability of returns to technological effort. The development of internalized R&D has been one of the most striking insitutional changes of this century (Schumpeter 1943; Freeman, 1982). In this context, inter-institutional collaboration might be considered the exception rather than the rule.

Why then do IICAs happen and why have they proliferated? Several authors have suggested contributory factors. One is the growing importance of knowledge in production, revealed by the growth of R&D in GDP and as a proportion of corporate turnover in many industries, and by the growing percentage of non-material investment (Mytelka 1991). Most IICAs are in relatively high-technology industries, such as IT, biotechnology, aerospace, or new materials. Other possible contributing factors are the productivity slowdown of the late 1960s and 1970s, and the observed shortening of product life cycles, which implies more frequent innovation with its attendant costs and uncertainties. The decline of traditional mass production ('Fordism') and the rise of flexible manufacturing systems also place a premium on technological capability. Collaborative agreements can reduce the heavy fixed costs of entry, as well as facilitating exit by providing a partner to whom an interest might be sold. So long as technology continues to grow in complexity and expense, IICAs are likely to figure prominently in the corporate landscape.

Collaborative agreements impinge upon technology policies. It might seem that they are in tune with the collaborative tenor of current EU technology policy; but IICAs are driven in opportunistic directions, not those favoured by state or community governments. Thus Rover chose to collaborate with Honda, rather than an EC firm, although it was later taken over by BMW of Germany. Possibly the EU programmes may facilitate intra-EU IICAs; but collaboration outside the EU makes it more difficult to evaluate the pay-off to EU technology policy, and Sachwald (1993) has shown that major European firms tend to adopt a global rather than a Eurocentric view of their markets. In this context, it can make more sense for a European firm aspiring to a global presence to seek global, rather than European, partnerships.

National systems of innovation and EU technology policy

The concept of national systems of innovation (NSI) has recently gained much attention among leading scholars of technology (Freeman, 1987, 1988; Lundvall 1988, 1993; Nelson, 1988, 1990, 1993) to interpret the persistence or areas of industrial and technological strength in national economies, and of very specific institutional configurations for very long periods of time. Such areas of industrial strength are chemicals, luxury cars, and machine tools in Germany; cars and consumer electronics in Japan; electronics, aircraft, and biotechnology in the USA. Furthermore, the institutions which control the generation and adoption of innovations in each country show a high degree of national specificity. Thus, not only do the degree of centralization and of state intervention, and the organization of universities and research institutes (to mention just a few factors), differ widely across countries, but these differences persist over time. Finally, what contributes still more to the specifically national character of the innovation system is the pattern of interactions between different institutions. There are powerful networks formed by research laboratories, government departments, and firms which are extremely important and, again, very specific.

Pronounced differences exist at the level of national institutions; Lundvall (1988, 1993) laid particular emphasis on user–producer relations. These create institutional networks which communicate and interact, and define a system which may be highly country- or even region-specific, as Porter (1990) has noted widely. The role of MITI has been profoundly influential in defining industrial and technological priorities and coordinating firms' actions, stressing the role of forecasting and horizontal flows in organizations as significant elements of the Japanese national system of innovation (Freeman, 1987, 1988). In particular, information flows in enterprises improve the relationship between R&D and production, in which the Japanese system has been singularly successful.

However, the observations of Sharp and Holmes (1989: 220–1) are apposite:

The degree to which a nation state seeks to carve out for itself an area of 'industrial space' which it can dominate is now minimal. The growing interdependence of the economic and industrial systems of the nations of Western Europe means that actions pursued in one country spill over rapidly into others . . . the degree of autonomy available to the individual nation state for the pursuit of industrial objectives is severely constrained. . . . It is technology as much as political dogma that has put paid to the era of national champions.

In this context, EU-sponsored forms of inter-institutional collaboration across national boundaries may establish a new network, with links across the entire Union.

This prospect prompts several questions. Will it be a stable network? How will it benefit the EU and Member States? Will there be conflicts between the EU and national systems of innovation? And there is the question of opportunity costs: will the resources allocated to the EU system of innovation impair the performance of NSIs? In essence, this poses the question of subsidiarity on a technological plane. Disquiet is also appearing among some Member States about the tendency of EU Science and Technology programmes to grow when national programmes are under budgetary pressures, as they have been in the mid-1990s. In Italy, questions have arisen about the dominance of the EU in its space research, while in the UK there has been criticism of the practice of cutting back national research support when applicants are successful in winning EU research funds, as well as misgivings about allegedly over-ambitious and unduly *dirigiste* policies for Frameworks 4 and 5 under the Cresson regime.

6.8. Summary and conclusions

EU science and technology policy seeks to create new inter-institutional links and forms of collaboration, as well as establishing capabilities in specific sectors. Any such attempt is problematic, because the spontaneous development of the system would be unlikely to replicate those links. However, it can be argued that the EU level of aggregation is the only possible locus at which adequate technological capacity can be established in certain industries or sectors. We began by looking at some national differences of Member States, resources, capabilities and national systems of innovation, followed by an examination of the emergence of EC collaborative programmes. It will take time to assess the true efficacy of the EU system of innovation; there will probably be continued haggling over its budget; there remain thorny problems of reconciling industrial and trade policies; and the principle of subsidiarity still appears to leave a great deal of autonomy in national hands; but it is highly significant that there seems to be no pressure to abandon the Framework system, and revert to a combination of market place and nation state. However, the precise role of the EU system of innovation remains to be defined and appraised fully; and it will require a continuous scrutiny, both because the interaction of profit-seeking companies will always generate new forms of organization and collaboration, transcending the boundaries of nations and of blocs, and because the growth of EU-directed science and technology activity may be perceived as a threat to national autonomy.

Discussion questions

1. What sorts of activities in science and technology do you think national governments should support, and why? Illustrate, using specific examples.
2. Why have industrial policies for supporting 'national champions' proved disappointing in Europe? What lessons can be drawn from such experiences?
3. Why might there be conflicts between the scientific and technological policies of Member States and those of the Union?

FURTHER READING

Arrow (1962) is the classic reference justifying the role of government in supporting science and technology. Freeman (1982) is a valuable introduction to innovation in the real world, while G. Dosi *et al.* (1988) put innovation in a theoretical framework. CEC (1994) is an invaluable source of EU data. Porter (1990) is an intriguing, if long, analysis of the basis of national competitiveness, and Nelson (1993) examines the importance of national characteristics and policies which underlie performance.

REFERENCES

Arrow, K. J. (1962), 'Economic Welfare and the Allocation of Resources to Invention', in *The Rate and Direction of Inventive Activity* (Princeton: Princeton University Press), 609–25.

Barry, A. (1990), 'Community and Diversity in European Technology', paper at the Science Museum.

Cabinet Office (1992), *United Kingdom Paper on the Fourth Framework Programme* (London: Office of Science and Technology).

CEC (1977): Commission of the European Communities, 'Common Policy for Science and Technology', *Bulletin of the European Communities*, supplement (Mar.).

—— (1993), Working Document on the Fourth Framework Programme, 22 Apr.

—— (1994), *The European Report on Science and Technology Indicators 1994* (Brussels: CEC).

Chandler, A. D., jun. (1962), *Strategy and Structure; Chapters in the History of Industrial Enterprise* (Cambridge, Mass: MIT Press).

—— (1977), *The Visible Hand: The Managerial Revolution in American Business* (Cambridge, Mass: Harvard University Press).

Chesnais, F. (1991), 'Technical Cooperation Agreements between Independent Firms: Novel Issues for Economic Analysis and the Formulation of National Technological Policies', *STI Review*, 4: 51–120.

Coase, R. H. (1937), 'The Nature of the Firm', *Economica*, 4: 386–405.

Dosi, G., Freeman, C., Nelson, R., Silverberg, G., and Soete, L. (1988) (eds.), *Technical Change and Economic Theory* (London: Pinter).

Dottorini, S. (1995), *Italian Science and Technology Handbook* (Canberra: Italian Embassy).

Peter Stubbs

DTI (1993): Department of Trade and Industry, *Innovation: A Guide to European Community R&D Programmes* (London: DTI).

—— (1996), Office of Science and Technology, *Forward Look of Government-Financed Science, Engineering and Technology*, Cm 3257 (London: HMSO).

Edquist, C., and Lundvall, B. A. (1993), 'Comparing Danish and Swedish Systems of Innovation', in R. R. Nelson (ed.), *National Innovation Systems: A Comparative Analysis* (Oxford: Oxford University Press).

EUREKA (1992): EUREKA Secretariat, Annual Progress Report.

Ford, G., and Lake, G. (1991), 'Evolution of European Science and Technology Policy', *Science and Public Policy*, 18: 38–50.

Freeman, C. (1982), *The Economics of Industrial Innovation*, 2nd edn. (London: Pinter).

—— (1987), *Technology Policy and Economic Performance: Lessons from Japan* (London: Pinter).

—— (1988), 'Japan: A New National System of Innovation?' in G. Dosi *et al.* (eds.), *Technical Change and Economic Theory* (London: Pinter), 330–48.

Garrett-Jones, S. (1989), *Public Policies for the Exploitable Areas of Science: A Comparison of the United Kingdom, Japan, the Netherlands and Sweden* (Canberra: Australian Science and Technology Council).

Georghiou, L., Cameron, H., Stein, J. A., Nederva, M., Janes, M., Yates, J., Pifer, M., Boden, M., and Senker, J. (1993), Cabinet Office, *The Impact of European Community Policies for Research and Technological Development upon Science and Technology in the United Kingdom* (London: HMSO).

Hill, A. (1993) 'R&D in a Tussle over EC Funding', *Financial Times*, 26 Oct., p. 16.

Holdsworth, D., and Lake, G. (1988), 'Integrating Europe: The New R&D Calculus', *Science and Public Policy*, 15: 411–25.

Lawson, N. (1992), *The View from Number Eleven* (London: Bantam).

Linkohr, E. (1987), European Parliament document A-2 174/87, p. 18.

Lundvall, B.-Å. (1988), 'Innovation as an Interactive Process: From User-Producer Interaction to the National System of Innovation', in G. Dosi *et al.* (eds.), *Technical Change and Economic Theory* (London: Pinter).

—— (1993) (ed.), *National Systems of Innovation: Towards a Theory of Innovation and Interactive Learning* (London: Pinter).

Malerba, F. (1993), 'The National System of Innovation: Italy', in R. R. Nelson (ed.), *National Innovation Systems: A Comparative Analysis* (Oxford: Oxford University Press).

Mansfield, E., Rapoport, J., Romeo, A., Wagner, S., and Beardsley, G. (1976), 'Social and Private Rates of Return Form Industrial Innovations', *Quarterly Journal of Economics*, 91: 221–40.

Mytelka, L. K. (1991) (ed.), *Strategic Partnerships and the World Economy* (London: Pinter).

Nelson, R. R. (1988), 'Institutions Supporting Technical Change in the US', in G. Dosi *et al.* (eds.), *Technical Change and Economic Theory* (London: Pinter).

—— (1990), 'Capitalism as an engine of progress', *Research Policy*, 19: 193–214.

—— (1993) (ed.), *National Innovation Systems: A Comparative Analysis* (Oxford: Oxford University Press).

OECD (1976): Organization for Economic Cooperation and Development, *The Measurement of Scientific and Technological Activities* (Frascati Manual) (Paris: OECD).

Outlook on Science Policy (1993), 15 (July–Aug.).

Pavitt, K., and Patel, P. (1988), 'The International Distribution and Determinants of Technological Activities', *Oxford Review of Economic Policy*, 4: 35–55.

Pearce, J., and Sutton, J. (1985), *Protection and Industrial Policy in Europe* (London: Routlege & Kegan Paul).

Peterson, J. (1991), 'Technology Policy in Europe: Explaining the Framework Programme and Eureka in Theory and Practice', *Journal of Common Market Studies*, 29: 269–90.

Porter, M. E. (1990), *The Competitive Advantage of Nations* (London: Macmillan).

Pownall, I. (1995), 'The Capture of Internalisation as a Policy Tool: The Case of ESPRIT', *Science and Public Policy*, 22: 39–49.

Sachwald, F. (1993), *L'Europe et la globalisation: Acquisitions et accords dans l'industrie* (Paris: Masson Éditeur; English edn., *European Integration and Competitiveness: Alliances and Acquisitions in Industry*, Aldershot: Edward Elgar, 1994).

Sandholtz, W. (1992), 'ESPRIT and the Politics of International Collective Action', *Journal of Common Market Studies*, 30: 1–24.

Saunders, C. T., Matthews, M., and Patel, P. (1991), 'Structural Change and Patterns of Production and Trade', in C. Freeman, M. Sharp, and W. Walker (eds.), *Technology and the Future of Europe* (London: Pinter).

Servan Schreiber, J. J. (1967), *Le Défi Américain* (Paris: de Noel; English edn., *The American Challenge*, Harmondsworth: Penguin Books, 1968).

Sharp, M. (1993) 'The Community and the New Technologies', in J. Lodge (ed.), *The EC and the Challenge of the Future*, 2nd edn. (London: Pinter), 200–23.

—— and Holmes, P. (1989) (eds.), *Strategies for New Technologies: Case Studies from Britain and France* (London: Philip Allan).

—— and Pavitt, K. (1993), 'Technology Policy in the 1990s: Old Trends and New Realities', *Journal of Common Market Studies*, 31: 129–51.

—— and Shearman, C. (1987), *European Technological Collaboration* (London: Routledge & Kegan Paul).

Tisdell, C. A. (1981), *Science and Technology Policy: Priorities of Governments* (London: Chapman & Hall).

Williamson, O. E. (1975), *Markets and Hierarchies* (New York: Free Press).

—— (1985), *The Economic Institutions of Capitalism* (New York: Free Press).

CHAPTER 7

Regional Policy

HARVEY ARMSTRONG, JIM TAYLOR, and ALLAN WILLIAMS

7.1. Introduction

Since 1989 regional policy in the EU has undergone a remarkable change. Whilst always a popular policy among the individual Member States, regional policy at the Union level was for many years something of a poor relation among EU common policies. This is no longer the case. While serious weaknesses still remain, regional policy has now moved from the wings to centre stage. It is seen as a central part of the EU's efforts to take economic integration forward. This has been achieved, moreover, without eliminating the regional policy efforts of the individual Member States. Any examination of regional policy in the EU must, therefore, consider both the regional policies of the Member States and the policy constructed by the EU itself.

This chapter considers the structure of existing regional policy in the EU, together with possible future developments. It begins, in Section 7.2, with an examination of regional disparities within the EU. These are wide when compared with economic entities of a similar size such as the USA, and are a cause of considerable concern. Section 7.3 explains why governments choose to have a regional policy. This is followed in Section 7.4 by a description of the broad alternative strategies available to regional policy-makers. Section 7.5 considers the regional policies of a number of EU Member States: the Netherlands, Germany, the UK, France, Italy, and Spain. Space constraints prevent the examination of regional policies for all the EU15; those chosen comprise the larger Member States and also encompass a wide range of different types of regional policies. This is followed in Section 7.6 by a review of the EU's own regional policy. The conclusion points the way forward to regional policy issues in the period following the ending of the current EU regional policy budget period in 1999.

7.2. Regional economic disparities in the EU

Two economic variables are widely used to indicate an economy's current level of economic welfare: output per capita and the unemployment rate. These two variables can be used to provide an indication of national and regional disparities in economic welfare among the Member States of the EU. The immensity of the spatial disparities in economic welfare in the EU is clear from Table 7.1. This shows that output per capita was around one-third of the EU average in Greece and Portugal, compared to 44 per cent above the EU average in Sweden and around 30 per cent above in Denmark. These huge differences in output per capita between Member States conceal equally huge differences within Member States. Output per capita in Germany, for example, varies from over twice the EU average in Hamburg to around one half the EU average in the regions of East Germany (see Table 7.1). Regional disparities in output per capita in the EU as a whole are, therefore, very large indeed, varying from 213 per cent of the EU average in Hamburg to around 20–25 per cent in the poorest regions of Portugal and Greece.

Regional disparities in output per capita will diminish only if those regions with the lowest levels of output per capita grow faster than the regions with the highest levels. Although there is some evidence that this has been occurring since 1950 (Barro and Sala-i-Martin 1991, 1992), the process of convergence is extremely slow and there is no indication that regional disparities in output per capita will narrow significantly in the foreseeable future (Armstrong 1995).

The second measure of economic welfare, the unemployment rate, also varies substantially both among regions *within* countries as well as among the Member States themselves. Unemployment disparities are particularly large in Spain, Italy, Belgium, and Germany (see Table 7.1). Spain, for example, with an unemployment rate at the depressingly high level of nearly 24 per cent has regional rates varying from 14 per cent (in Navarre) to an astronomical 34 per cent (in the Balearic Islands).

A further determinant of economic welfare is a region's participation rate. This is the proportion of the population which is in the labour force. Other things being equal, the higher the participation rate, the higher the level of output per capita. Regions with a low participation rate can, therefore, be expected to be less well off than regions with a high participation rate (see Table 7.1). Furthermore, regions with a low participation rate also tend to have a high unemployment rate, which suggests that potential workers are discouraged from joining the labour force when unemployment is high.

7.3. The case for regional policy

Regional economic disparities within the EU are not only substantial; they also show remarkable persistence over long periods of time. Poor regions tend to stay poor and

Table 7.1. Regional economic disparities in the EU

Member State	Output per capita, 1994 (EU = 100)			Unemployment 1994 (%)			Participation rate 1994 (%)		
	National average	Regional maximum	Regional minimum	National average	Regional maximum	Regional minimum	National average	Regional maximum	Regional minimum
Germany	113.2	212.9	55.8	10.5	19.8	5.8	47.2	54.5	41.0
France	116.2	178.5	79.3	12.8	17.4	8.6	43.9	50.0	34.8
Italy	96.7	123.4	54.0	12.5	24.5	4.0	39.7	45.4	32.9
Netherlands	104.3	150.8	70.3	9.0	12.4	6.7	47.8	51.2	43.3
Belgium	101.8	163.8	73.8	12.9	25.7	7.4	42.3	45.0	37.4
Luxembourg	121.9	–	–	2.7	–	–	45.2	–	–
UK	103.7	135.9	77.1	9.8	15.0	5.0	48.2	60.0	39.4
Irish Republic	81.3	–	–	15.6	–	–	39.2	–	–
Denmark	129.4	131.7	118.2	11.5	13.7	11.2	56.0	56.7	54.3
Greece	37.8	49.6	25.6	9.6	11.9	3.8	40.3	45.4	29.3
Spain	62.4	83.6	44.1	23.6	34.2	13.8	40.3	43.7	34.6
Portugal	31.6	45.6	18.8	7.1	11.3	4.1	48.5	49.9	39.8
Austria	112.6	159.5	72.0	6.7	8.5	4.2	40.9	53.1	29.9
Sweden	144.0	173.4	119.3	8.0	11.3	5.7	48.4	52.2	44.7
Finland	116.0	148.0	93.8	19.9	26.7	15.6	48.6	52.6	44.4

Note: The regional maximum and minimum values were calculated from NUTS2 level data using the EU's standard system of Nomenclature des Unités Territoriales Statistiques. Output per capita is measured by gross value added (GVA), since this provides the most up-to-date measure of output per capita at regional level. GVA is measured in purchasing power parities (PPPs) and is defined as gross domestic product plus value added tax plus import taxes.

Source: European Regional Database, Apr. 1996, Cambridge Econometrics.

rich regions tend to stay rich. As would be expected, the residents of poor regions are keen to emulate the residents of rich regions, and this is one of the driving forces behind the development of regional policy both within individual Member States and at the supra-national EU level. The urge for greater prosperity in less prosperous regions, however, is only one of several reasons for the existence of regional policy, which can be justified on economic efficiency grounds as well as for social and political reasons. The purely economic arguments used to support regional policy stem from the harmful consequences which regional economic disparities can have on the efficiency of the national economy (Taylor 1991; Martin 1992). These harmful effects are as follows:

1. Regional economic disparities lead to a higher *national* unemployment rate than would occur if regional disparities were less severe.
2. Inflationary pressures increase as regional economic disparities increase.
3. Regional economic disparities lead to a sub-optimal use of the nation's economic infrastructure.

Although we concentrate here upon the economic gains from regional policy, it is important not to underestimate the social and political gains which a reduction in regional disparities in living standards may bring. Persistent disparities in living standards between regions can lead to dissatisfaction and resentment with the political process, thereby fuelling the call for devolution. The cohesion of the nation state may therefore require national governments to pay careful attention to regional economic disparities. A similar argument applies to the EU as a whole, as will be explained below.

The argument that a reduction in regional economic disparities would result in economic gains for the economy as a whole stems from the mismatch between labour demand and labour supply. This mismatch takes two forms: a geographical mismatch occurs when unemployed workers are located in the wrong place to fill vacant jobs; and a skill mismatch occurs when unemployed workers have the wrong skills to fill vacant jobs. Both types of mismatch unemployment help to explain why unemployment has a tendency to remain permanently higher in some regions than in others. Reducing the geographical or skill mismatch (through regional policy and training policy) could lead to significant reductions in the national unemployment rate. This would occur if the unemployed could fill job vacancies more quickly, especially during periods of economic expansion. If unemployment could be permanently reduced in the traditionally high unemployment regions without this leading to a loss of jobs in the areas of low unemployment, the whole nation would be better off. Those previously unemployed would be producing output and earning a wage instead of being supported by the taxpayer. Lower unemployment could also be expected to reduce crime rates as well as alleviating economic hardship for a large number of people.

The second way in which a reduction in regional economic disparities can provide economic gains to the national economy is related to the first, since it stems from the regional disparities in the balance between labour demand and labour supply. Persistent disparities in the unemployment rate between regions mean that inflationary pressures build up very quickly in low unemployment regions whenever there is a significant business upturn. As the national demand for goods and services begins to grow more quickly, this puts more pressure on the supply of skilled labour in low unemployment areas. The consequence is an increase in wage inflation as firms raise wages to attract more labour (and to discourage their existing workers from looking for jobs elsewhere). These wage increases are then transmitted to other regions, one of the main reasons being that firms with plants in several regions have to maintain pay relativities for workers in different parts of the same organization.

Regional policy could help to reduce inflationary pressures by reducing regional differences in labour scarcity during upturns. This could be achieved either by reducing the barriers to labour migration so that labour shortages could be relieved more quickly; or alternatively by diverting the demand for labour from labour-scarce to labour-abundant regions, so that any expansion of the national economy would not hit supply bottlenecks as quickly.

Thirdly, regional disparities in economic growth can inflict severe economic costs on rapidly growing urban areas through the over-utilization of social overhead capital. Exactly the opposite occurs in areas suffering from slow growth: social overhead capital may be under-utilized as workers and their families migrate to more prosperous regions. Roads, rail networks, airports, and housing are often severely over-utilized in rapidly expanding regions. Congestion and pollution are the consequences of over-rapid growth, especially in major cities.

Greater London provides an excellent example of a city-region which has suffered from excessive expansion of economic activity. The popularity of Heathrow with the major airlines means that this airport is persistently short of capacity. The same is true of the motorway system around Greater London. The M25 orbital motorway was expected to relieve road traffic congestion, yet within three years of its opening (in 1987) it became apparent that three lanes each way were grossly inadequate to meet traffic needs. No sooner does supply expand to accommodate demand than the whole cycle begins again; demand increases as supply constraints are relieved and the vicious circle continues.

The classic response by governments to congestion is invariably to relieve it by expanding capacity. There is a great reluctance of governments to tackle congestion by introducing policies to reduce the demand for road space. It is politically more expedient to increase the supply of social overhead capital than it is to reduce demand. The result is a never-ending spiral whereby demand and supply are forever chasing each other. A longer-term solution is offered by regional policy, since the major aim of such policy is to increase economic growth in less prosperous regions so that the migration of workers and their families to the more rapidly growing regions is stifled. Congested regions would benefit from not having to take in more people and the less prosperous regions would benefit by not losing their most productive workers (since the latter are the most likely to migrate to the rapidly growing regions).

The fundamental aim of regional policy is, therefore, to reduce regional disparities in variables such as output per capita and the unemployment rate in order to increase *national* output and to achieve a more equitable distribution of income. The next section discusses the alternative approaches which are available to policy-makers for achieving these two primary objectives.

7.4. Regional policy: some alternative approaches

Regional policy exists because of market failure. The stability and persistence of regional disparities in unemployment rates and in output per capita over long periods of time indicate that market forces are unable to remove these disparities. Governments throughout the EU have, therefore, opted for interventionist policies. These take three main forms:

1. inducing inward investment into designated assisted areas;
2. stimulating indigenous growth in designated assisted areas;
3. regeneration through investment in the economic and social infrastructure of designated assisted areas.

Inducing inward investment into designated assisted areas through offering investment grants and other subsidies to incoming firms typifies the interventionist approach. The policy need not always consist solely of inducements and subsidies. This type of policy, for example, was supplemented in the UK during 1947–81 by the imposition of location controls on manufacturing firms located in the non-designated areas (especially the south-east region). The primary purpose of this carrot-and-stick policy was to achieve a better geographical balance between the demand for labour and the supply of labour, so that unemployment would fall in areas of high unemployment while inflationary pressures would be lessened in labour-scarce areas (Armstrong and Taylor 1993).

Traditional regional policy, based upon offering subsidies to firms locating their new plant and equipment in designated assisted areas, became less popular in many Member States in the 1980s. The emphasis swung towards stimulating indigenous growth rather than relying on inward investment. This indigenous-growth approach gained popularity because policy-makers became more interested in the growth of small firms and in the birth of entirely new firms. Moreover, this fitted with the policy shift away from 'state capitalism' towards privatization, deregulation, and the enterprise economy. This does not, however, mean that inward investment is unimportant for the assisted areas. Foreign multinational companies are continuously being courted by regional development agencies in an attempt to induce them to locate their new plant in their regions. The success of several assisted areas in the UK in inducing Japanese manufacturing firms to locate in these areas indicates the continued importance of foreign direct investment to job creation in the UK's assisted areas (Taylor 1993; Hill and Munday 1994). Similar policies have been pursued in other EU countries (Morriss 1991).

The third arm of regional policy is the improvement of the economic and social infrastructure of the less prosperous regions. Investment in the infrastructure includes redeveloping derelict areas, provision of industrial and commercial premises, improving the transport network, providing better recreational facilities, enhancing the stock of housing, and improving health and educational facilities. Public investment in an area's infrastructure is important, since it acts as a signal to the private sector that the government is committed to the long-term future of the less prosperous regions. It acts as a confidence booster to private-sector investors while simultaneously helping the less prosperous regions to retain their most highly skilled workers.

7.5. Regional policies in EU Member States

The origin of regional policy in Europe goes back to the global economic crisis of the late 1920s and 1930s. Initially, regional policy emerged as a matter of contingency, but, as the immediate crisis passed, regional policy evolved into a genuine policy for structural change in the economy rather than for 'fire-fighting' (Bleitrach and Chenu 1982). In the very early days of regional policy, before the existence of the EC, individual Member States pursued their own individual policies.

In practice, the development of regional policy in the European Member States appears to have passed through three stages (Nicoll and Yuill 1980). In the first stage, the emphasis of policy was on *national* economic growth, and meaningful regional policy was both weak and confined to only two Member States: Italy with its *Cassa per il Mezzogiorno*, and the UK with its programme of incentives and controls to assist the Development Areas. Elsewhere there was little in the way of regional policy. The UK case is interesting, in that the initial 'fire-fighting' phase was quickly superseded by a switch to longer-term policies designed to engineer structural change. UK regional policy began in the late 1920s when financial help was made available to induce unemployed coal-miners (and later other unemployed persons) to move to areas where jobs were in more plentiful supply. Although over 200,000 workers received financial assistance under this scheme during the 1930s, the direct targeting of the visible symptom of the problem (i.e. the unemployed themselves) made little impression on regional unemployment disparities. In the immediate post-war years, therefore, the UK government turned to the opposite strategy of 'taking work to the workers' (i.e. enlarging the industrial base and changing the structure of the economies of the disadvantaged regions) as a means of reducing regional unemployment disparities.

The second phase in the development of regional policy in Europe—the 1950s to the early 1970s—saw most West European governments follow the lead of Italy and the UK and develop some form of regional policy, especially in the face of persistent unemployment and inflationary pressures. Finally, in the third phase—after the mid-1970s—regional policy was given a much lower priority by most Member States in the face of a deepening recession, budgetary constraints, and reductions in the pool of potentially mobile firms that had traditionally been the target of regional policy. Ironically, the period since the mid-1970s, during which Member State regional policies have been cut back, was also the period of rapid expansion of the EC's own regional policy. The retrenchment of the third phase after the mid-1970s was not the result of diminishing pressures for intervention, for, as Albrechts *et al.* (1989: 4) argue, 'the crisis that erupted in the mid-seventies has triggered a range of corporate, social and policy responses'. These responses have included an array of local and urban policies (e.g. waterfront redevelopment and inner-city regeneration), but they have become less likely, especially in southern Member States of the EU, to include specifically regional policies. There is, generally, less emphasis on financial incentives, whilst more attention is paid to increasing competitiveness and to providing an attractive regional environment for businesses.

Comparing the rationale for different Member State regional policies

Within the broad framework of the case for regional policy set out in Section 7.3, there are differences among the Member States in the reasons for the development of regional policy. This section considers the cases of the Netherlands, Germany, the UK, France, Italy, and Spain. These case studies underline the similarities as well as the differences in regional policy within the EU, and also the ways in which the underlying economic rationale of policy is interlinked with social and political considerations.

The Netherlands

The Netherlands has one of the more all-embracing approaches to regional policy to be found within the EU. There is a long tradition of physical planning in the Netherlands dating from the early 1950s. This tradition is the result of intense pressures on factors of production—especially land—in a relatively small country with Europe's highest population density. The earliest regional planning focused on the reorganization of the war-damaged Rotterdam economy, and the rehabilitation of its economic infrastructure. By the 1950s attention had shifted to the border regions, where there were persistently high levels of unemployment (Gay 1987). Over time, regional policy has become increasingly sophisticated as it has tried to take into account the interrelated requirements of regions in a small and increasingly complex economy. By the 1970s there were distinct policies for three different types of regions: stimulation areas in the north, which still had persistent unemployment difficulties; old coal-mining and textiles communities, which required major restructuring; and the highly developed Randstadt, where production costs were rising as a result of the demands on a relatively inelastic supply of economic infrastructure. Since the 1980s the scale of regional incentives, and the areas they apply to, have been sharply reduced. For example, the proportion of the population living in investment-premium (IPR) areas was reduced from 20 per cent to 10 per cent in 1993, and the value of grants was also reduced.

Germany

Germany shares many of the structural features of the Netherlands, in that regional policy has been developed to diffuse inflationary pressures and maximize national economic potential in an economy experiencing strong economic growth, but where there are also persistently weak regions. There are, however, important differences stemming from both the *Länder* federal structure and the economic and political shock of the sudden unification of East and West Germany. Unification brought into the most powerful European economy a region which is one of the weakest in the EU. German regional policy faced a pressing need to develop the economy of the Eastern region in a manner which would maximize local job opportunities. The rationale behind this was that, if this was not quickly achieved, labour migration would add to the difficulties of all the German regions at a time of slackening economic growth in the national economy.

Despite the distinctive features brought on by reunification, the evolution of German regional policy in the past has broadly followed trends prevalent in northern Europe. There appear to have been four main periods in this evolution in Germany (Blacksell 1987). In the first, in the 1950s, the main concern was with post-war reconstruction. In the 1960s the principal interest was in regional policy as a means of securing a more equitable distribution of the fruits of Germany's economic success. In the third phase there was greater attention to coordinating Federal and *Länder* policies. Finally, in common with other north European Member States, there was some withdrawal from regional policy as part of the budget restructuring of the 1980s; for example, aid ceilings were reduced in 1988 and investment allowances were abolished in 1989. In general terms, it must be noted that regional policy in Germany has lacked the urgency it has attracted in some of the other Member States with more severe problems.

The United Kingdom

The UK's regional policy has developed against the background of a weaker national economic performance than that of either the Netherlands or Germany, but with a set of problem regions more typical of northern Europe than the south. The overwhelming majority of the UK's problem regions in the period since the institution of regional policy in the late 1920s have been declining *industrial* areas. The UK was considered to have very few disadvantaged rural regions of the type found in France and in southern Europe. As has already been noted, after an initial attempt to persuade the unemployed to move away from their home areas, UK regional policy rapidly settled, from the mid-1930s onwards, into a policy based on 'taking work to the workers' by restructuring the economies of regions suffering industrial decline. The major phases of UK regional policy since the 1930s have coincided with differing degrees of commitment by successive governments, rather than variations in the fundamental nature of the policies operated. Labour governments have, on the whole, tended to pursue more active regional policies than have Conservative governments. The lack of regional governments in the UK and the weakness of local government have meant that for most of the post-war period the attitude of the national government has been all-important. Regional policy was most actively operated during 1945–51 and 1963–75 (Martin and Tyler 1992). Throughout the post-war period up until 1975 the policy concentrated on inward investment. Given the predominance of regions in industrial decline, it is not surprising that particular effort was placed on attracting manufacturing firms to the disadvantaged regions.

From the mid-1970s onwards, UK regional policy, like those in other EU Member States, experienced severe problems associated with deepening economic crises. This had the twofold effect of reducing the number of potential manufacturing projects available for inward investment in the disadvantaged regions, and also led to cuts in regional policy funding. The retrenchment in UK regional policy in the 1980s, while similar in kind to that experienced elsewhere in the EU, was accelerated by successive governments' ideological commitment to free markets and the 'rolling back of the state'. The 1980s also witnessed the first fundamental change in the *nature* of regional policy in the UK since the 1930s. Supporting inward investment was partially supplanted by policies designed to encourage indigenous development—renewal 'from within'. The main exception to this process has been the use of regional inducements to attract foreign investment seeking a foothold within the EU (particularly Japanese car manufacturers and electronics firms). Policies designed to help new firm formation, the growth of small businesses, the encouragement of innovation, and the creation of an 'enterprise culture' gradually made their entrance in the 1980s against a background of a diminishing regional policy budget.

France

France represents a very different context for regional policy in the EU. While it has become one of the more prosperous European economies, and in Paris it has one of the most powerful metropolitan areas in the EU, in the immediate aftermath of the Second World War it also possessed large rural regions whose economic potential had been very little developed. The contrast between the rural regions and the Paris region was highlighted in Gravier's influential book (Gravier 1947). This and other contemporary reports set in train what was to become one of Europe's most comprehensive systems of regional policy. The process was one of four main phases (Clout 1987). In the first, the main aim was to iron out some of the more glaring regional imbalances in the country, primarily as a social goal. Then, in the second phase in the 1960s, there was greater emphasis on comprehensive spatial economic management as part of a programme to maximize national economic growth. In the 1970s economic recession weakened regional policy. Finally, this was exacerbated in the 1980s, when, according to Clout (1987: 171), 'in the present bleak economic climate the chances of effective territorial management have become slim'. The overall result is that regional development policy has evolved incrementally and in an *ad hoc* fashion during recent years (Flockton and Kofman 1989); for example, a new regional incentive for smaller projects in rural areas was introduced in 1991.

Italy

In Italy, regional policies developed differently from France and were dominated by the specific needs of the South. This region continued to experience economic difficulties even during the 'economic miracle' of the late 1950s and early 1960s when the national economy experienced rapid growth. The *Cassa per il Mezzogiorno* was established in 1950 and devoted much of its early attention to land reform, agricultural improvements, and basic infrastructure. These were considered to be essential prerequisites for the integration of the South into the market economy. This emphasis on what can best be described as regional modernization later gave way to more conventional regional policies concerned with the relocation of industry. In the face of strong barriers to development in the *Mezzogiorno*, it was not surprising that regional policy in the 1960s was guided by the concentration of resources into growth centres. The rationale for regional policy in Italy was based on several goals. Initially it aimed to provide the minimum infrastructure necessary for the development of the region's economic potential. A cynical view, however, would suggest that regional policy was only weakly pursued in this period, given the priority allocated to promoting national growth. The latter was premised on the leading role of the North, which in turn relied on the availability of labour supply from the South. However, by the 1960s the North was experiencing increasing inflationary pressures, which were epitomized by the wage inflation which followed the 'Hot Autumn' of 1969 (Williams 1987). Thereafter, there existed a stronger case for a strategy of balanced economic development typical of other EU Member States.

Spain

Spain's economy in the 1940s bore many striking resemblances to that of the *Mezzogiorno*: large numbers were employed in relatively unproductive agriculture, regional infrastructures were poorly developed, and there was a strong geographical polarization concentrated on Madrid, Catalonia, and the Basque Country. There was the additional dimension, however, of the highly centralized dictatorial government of Franco. Regional policy, such as it was, was not responsive to local needs, was carried out through the poorly coordinated actions of individual ministries, and was consistently subordinated to the priority allocated by Madrid to the national economic performance. Regional policy objectives were inserted into the National Plans as much to please international agencies, such as the World Bank, as to commit the central government to a more equitable distribution of jobs and income. As a result, while Spain did experience an 'economic miracle' in the 1960s, this was accompanied by wide regional income differentials (Naylon 1987). The restoration of democracy after 1975 changed the accountability of regional policy, but occurred at a time of recessionary constraints and was followed in the 1980s by the transfer of powers to the autonomous regions. Membership of the EC, and the need to conform to the rules of the European Regional Development Fund (ERDF), led to the redefinition of regional assistance areas and incentives in 1986 and 1987.

Comparing regional policy instruments in the different Member States

The individual Member States of the EU operate regional policies which differ significantly in their rationale, but which also display considerable operational similarities. This is the case when the policy instruments used to implement regional policy are considered. While considerable variation still exists from country to country, 'the multiple ideas on tools of regional policy development in the Member States of the European Community are settling in a kind of pattern, and some consensus is gradually crystallising out' (Molle 1990: 424). The various instruments can be disaggregated into those aimed at labour, those aimed at industries, and those involving improvements in infrastructure. While most states have one or more of these types of policies, only rarely have they been linked in integrated programmes, as in France, for example, with its *aménagement du territoire*.

There are few examples of policies to promote labour mobility, even though the reduction of regional unemployment differentials has been one of the primary objectives of regional strategies. In part, the reluctance to employ such measures is political, stemming from the unwillingness of governments to be seen to promote the break-up of communities and the 'abandonment' of regional economies. There is also the economic argument that interregional transfers of labour on a large scale would add to inflationary pressures in the more dynamic regions. Nevertheless, there have been some examples of labour-transfer policies, including the UK's Employment Transfer Scheme in the 1970s, which provided grants to help offset the costs of workers moving to other regions to obtain jobs. This was, however, only a minor component in UK regional policy. The depth and persistence of the economic crisis in recent years—leading to the more generalized distribution of high unemployment rates across all regions—has further eroded the economic rationale for labour-transfer policy instruments. The speed of technological change and the pace of economic restructuring have also meant that labour-market policies have focused more on general training programmes than on specific regional measures.

Instruments aimed at particular industries have usually sought to influence the location of new investment and the relocation of existing capacity. There have been two types of measures: restrictions on investment in the more prosperous regions, and incentives to attract investment projects to the poorer regions. These are commonly known as 'stick-and-carrot' policies. Locational constraints are less widely used than financial incentives. Examples of locational constraints used in the past have included the UK's Industrial Development Certificate scheme, which restricted investment projects in the south and the Midlands between 1947 and 1981. In France a system of *agréments* was introduced in 1955 to regulate new and existing developments in the Paris region. At first the *agréments* applied only to manufacturing but later they were extended to services. Italy also developed a system of location controls for the Milan and Turin areas in 1971 in response to the inflationary pressures which followed the 'Hot Autumn' of 1969. In the Netherlands, a Selective Investment Levy was introduced for new office construction in the prosperous and congested Randstadt area in the mid-1970s, supplementing earlier controls on the location of manufacturing industry investment in this region. In all of the countries which experimented with locational constraints, the policies lost favour during the persistent economic crises of the 1970s and 1980s. These crises led governments to reduce constraints—locational or otherwise—on economic activity and expansion. In France, for example, locational controls on new office developments in Paris were relaxed in the late 1980s in response to fears that jobs could be lost to other European capital cities.

While locational controls aimed at the private sector have had only a limited impact, they have been important in the public sector. King (1987), for example, argues that the Italian regional policy instrument which was most effective in bringing industry to the South was that which compelled nationalized and state-holding industries to locate at least 60 per cent of all their new investment in the *Mezzogiorno*. In contrast, it is symptomatic of the neglect of regional policy in Spain that the Franco government never required the Instituto Nacional de Industria, the industrially dominant state-holding company, to locate activities in the poorer regions.

Financial incentives have been more important than controls amongst the policy instruments which have been used to redirect industries from richer to poorer regions. The precise form of incentives is variable but may include grants, loans at below market rates of interest, tax concessions, and transport subsidies. Under the 1957 Industrial Areas Law, Italy was able to bring all of these financial incentives to bear on the relocation of private-sector investment to the South. In France, the main emphasis was on a system of grants and subsidized loans to encourage firms to relocate from Paris. These instruments were most effective in the economically buoyant early 1960s, when more than 250 relocations a year took place from Paris (Clout 1987). The Netherlands also employed financial incentives to encourage private-sector relocations, especially to border regions and to Limburg, a coal-mining centre experiencing decline.

In the UK, for most of the post-war period, the main type of incentive has taken the form of investment grants to businesses. The nature of UK investment incentives has changed several times, however, since 1945. Up until the mid-1970s *automatic* investment grants tended to predominate. From the mid-1970s onwards this instrument was supplemented by more *selective* investment assistance. Since 1988, and the abolition of regional development grants, UK regional investment incentives have been almost entirely discretionary; the amount of assistance provided to individual firms is now determined mainly by government officials (after negotiation with each individual applicant for financial aid). UK investment incentives, such as regional enterprise grants introduced in 1988, have become more closely focused on indigenous firms than on inward investment.

The switch from automatic to discretionary incentives in the UK has not been followed by all Member States of the EU. Differences remain in the balance between discretionary and automatic financial assistance. The latter is usually preferred by industry, as automatic assistance is simpler and more transparent. However, many governments prefer discretionary assistance, since it is more flexible and less costly. With discretionary assistance, judgements can be made concerning the contributions of individual projects to the regional economy and also on whether an investment would occur anyway irrespective of the availability of financial assistance (a phenomenon known as 'deadweight' spending). There is some evidence from research in the UK (Wren 1987, 1989) that 'deadweight' spending can occur when automatic incentives are used. The problem with discretionary incentives, however, is that the associated spending cuts tend to reduce the overall volume of investment in the disadvantaged regions. The Netherlands has attempted to get the best of both worlds by combining the two types of investment incentive. The rate of award of the Netherlands Investment Premium scheme is automatic up to a fixed limit, and thereafter it is discretionary. The general trend, however, has been away from automatic incentives towards discretionary incentives, particularly in response to budgetary constraints (Allen, Yuill, and Bachtler 1989). For example, the Netherlands abolished its automatic regional allowance scheme in 1983, and Germany abolished automatic investment allowances in 1989. The pattern of financial incentives is set out in Table 7.2.

Financial incentives differ in a variety of other ways amongst the Member States of the EU. Incentives can be either capital-related (usually expressed as a proportion of project costs), or labour-related (according to the number of jobs created by the investment). Traditionally most incentives have been capital-based. With growing unemployment, however, there has been a shift to labour-related schemes. Other differences among Member States are a function of whether the financial incentives are available over large areas of the national economy (e.g. Italy) or are highly spatially selective (e.g. the Netherlands). If the overall level of resources available for regional policy is limited, then there is an economic argument for concentration so as to optimize the external economies of scale realized by such investments. A combination of budgetary constraints and the EU's competition-policy requirements is leading to reductions in the spatial coverage of Member States' regional policies, particularly in northern Europe (see Table 7.3). The most significant reductions, 1980–92, were in the Netherlands and

Table 7.2. **Selected features of the regional policies of EC Member States, 1990**

Member State	Type of regional policy incentive	Automatic (A), or discretionary (D)	Labour-related (L)	Eligible services
France	Regional policy grant	D	L	Research
	Business tax concessions	A	—	Non-local markets
Germany	Investment grant	D	—	Export-based
	Special depreciation allowance	A	—	All
	Regional soft loans	A	—	Export-based
UK	Regional selective assistance	D	—	Non-local consumer
	Regional enterprise grant	A	—	Non-local and non-financial
	N. Ireland selective assistance	D	L	Export-based
Italy	Capital grant	A	—	Consultancy and producer
	National fund scheme	A	—	Consultancy and producer
	Social security concession	A	L	Tourism, R&D, transport, producer
	Tax concession	A	—	R&D, data-processing.
Spain	Regional incentives grant	D	—	Tourism, producer

Source: Yuill et al. (1991).

Germany. In contrast, there has been little change in spatial coverage in southern Europe.

Finally, there is considerable variation between Member States in the sectors included within the regional policy remit. Traditionally, manufacturing was favoured on the grounds that it was more likely to be export orientated and to be locationally mobile. Tourism has also been included in the regional policies of some countries for the same reasons. In contrast, other countries, such as Germany and the Netherlands, have long recognized the potential contribution of the service sector to regional development, particularly as many service industries are labour intensive. The general trend has been for the regional policies of EU Member States to become more inclusive of the service sector (see Table 7.2). Financial incentives have also become more focused on certain *types* of establishments, such as small firms and high-technology firms (Mason and Harrison 1990; Thwaites and Alderman 1990).

The third main arm of regional policy in Europe has been state investment in economic infrastructure as a means of changing the comparative advantage of poorer regions. A considerable variety of options is available, but of particular importance has been the provision of transport infrastructure and serviced (usually subsidized) industrial land and buildings. Industrial estates were one of the mainstays of regional policy in the 1950s and 1960s, but, given the crisis facing the traditional manufacturing sectors in the 1970s and 1980s, this policy has given way to an increasing emphasis on office

Table 7.3. **Regional policy in the Member States, 1980–1990/1992**

Member State	Population coverage to assisted regions (% national population)		Regional incentive expenditure per head of population in assisted regions (Ecu 1990 prices)	
	1980	1992	1980	1990
Belgium	39.5	33.1	38.2	44.7
Denmark	27.0	19.9	9.8	5.4
France	38.2	40.0	16.9	7.6
Germany	36.0	27.0	30.1	33.2
Greece	65.0	58.0	7.1	52.5
Ireland	28.0	28.0	117.0	58.1
Italy	35.6	35.6	185.2	404.6
Luxembourg	100.0	79.7	64.0	70.1
Netherlands	27.4	19.9	58.5	33.1
Portugal	100.0[a]	100.0	–	27.4
Spain	58.6	58.6	–	31.9
UK	49.5	38.6	70.6	36.9

[a] 1986 data.

Source: CEC (1994a).

parks and science parks. The Tecnopolis Novus Ortis near Bari in southern Italy is an outstanding example of the latter, as is the Cambridge Science Park in the UK. The creation of enterprise and incubation units is also important, signifying the greater emphasis on endogenous growth.

One of the most popular forms of infrastructure investment has been the growth centre, representing the concentration of state investment in particular locations with the aim of building up interlinked industrial complexes which, it is argued, will diffuse growth outward into the surrounding region. The idea has its origins in the theoretical work of Perroux in the early 1950s on growth poles in economic space. This work emphasizes the growth potential of clusters of interlinked, innovative firms. Growth centres have extended this concept to the notion that *spatial* concentrations of industry can realize these growth advantages and achieve self-sustaining growth. It can be argued, however, that the real attraction of growth centres to policy-makers has been the economies of scale offered in terms of urbanization costs.

It is symbolic of the internationalization of regional policy that growth centres have been essential policy instruments in five of the six countries considered here (the exception being the UK). France has had a particularly well-developed strategy, including both industrial poles and *métropoles d'équilibre* for tertiary activities. Growth centres also provided one of the main arms of Italian regional policy under the landmark 1957

187

Industrial Areas Law, with incentives initially concentrated on twelve growth areas and thirty growth nuclei. As a result of political pressures (King 1987), they encompassed more than 50 per cent of the total population of the *Mezzogiorno*, a far higher proportion than would be expected in terms of the economic rationale of concentration. Growth centres are also to be found in the Netherlands and Germany, where there have been attempts to channel growth into, respectively, 18 and 312 development centres. The wide differences from country to country in the number of growth centres reflect the lack of theoretical and empirical guidance on the most effective means of implementing a growth-centre strategy. Finally, Spain, too, has had a growth-centre strategy which dates back to the first National Development Plan (1964–7). The policy in Spain has been weakly implemented in practice (Naylon 1987), with the result that little employment has been generated and overall costs have been high.

The differences in policy trends have meant that there have been divergences in Member States' experiences, although these have been set in a framework of overall reduced regional incentive expenditures (Table 7.3). The reductions have been greatest in northern Europe, particularly in Denmark, the Netherlands, and the UK. Reductions in Germany in the early 1980s have been reversed since unification. Regional incentive expenditure has actually increased in some southern Member States, notably Italy.

Evaluating the effectiveness of Member State regional policies

After fifty years of regional policy in the Member States of the EU, there is considerable evidence of the relative strengths and weaknesses of the various instruments. Nevertheless, there are difficulties involved in any such evaluation. Not least, there is the critical question of whether some plant relocations would have occurred anyway, even in the absence of regional policy, perhaps as a consequence of the reorganization of production linked to technological change (Massey 1979). Both econometric and survey techniques can be used to investigate the impact of regional policy, but neither approach has proved to be entirely satisfactory. The EU has undertaken one of the few cross-Member State surveys of the effectiveness of regional policy. Firms in declining/lagging regions and in control regions were asked to rank the importance of regional incentives as positive or negative factors in regional competitiveness. The results are set out in Table 7.4 and show that regional policy was considered to be a negative rather than a positive influence by firms in lagging or declining regions in France, Spain, and Germany, while in Italy firms in the control regions viewed it more favourably than did those in the lagging regions. Even where it is ranked positively, as in the declining regions of France and Spain, and in the lagging regions of Italy, it receives a relatively low priority compared to other competitive factors.

Table 7.4. The ranking of regional incentives by firms as a factor affecting a region's competitiveness

Member State	Type of region	Rank of regional policy as a factor affecting a region's competitiveness for the location of firms	
		Positive factor	Negative factor
France	Control	15 of 19	
	Declining	15 of 19	
	Lagging		7 of 19
Germany	Control		6 of 8
	Declining		3 of 5
UK	Control		2 of 2
	Declining	12 of 22	
	Lagging	3 of 18	
Italy	Control	10 of 21	
	Lagging	7 of 8	
Netherlands	Control		3 of 3
	Declining	18 of 21	
Spain	Control	18 of 19	
	Declining	11 of 16	
	Lagging		6 of 9

Note: Terms such as '15 of 19' mean that regional policy is ranked as 15th of 19 factors affecting the competitiveness of the region.

Source: CEC (1990a: 86).

A number of criticisms have been levelled at regional policies, and these are remarkably consistent across the Member States. First, the location controls have been criticized for being one-sided. While they restrict investment in the more prosperous regions, they cannot influence the destination of the diverted production capacity. Thus in France manufacturing decentralization from Paris in the 1960s seems mainly to have benefited the outer Paris region rather than poorer regions such as Brittany or Limousin. Secondly, there has been criticism of the kinds of plants established by industrial relocations from richer to poorer regions. The classic criticism is that branch plants are established which are externally controlled, have few intra-regional linkages, lack R&D content, specialize in less skilled assembly work, and are vulnerable to closure in times of recession. Thirdly, the policies of growth centres have been criticized for polarizing growth intra-regionally. In Italy this has been labelled the 'cathedrals-in-the-desert' effect, reflecting the lack of linkages between the capital-intensive industries of the growth centres and their surrounding hinterlands (King 1987). Hermansen (1971) explains this in terms of a lack of complementarities between the economic structures of the growth centres and their hinterlands. Fourthly, the switch to promoting small firms as part of the emphasis on indigenous development has been criticized because of the limited number of jobs created, the low quality of jobs in small firms, and the limited innovation potential of small firms (Mason and Harrison 1990). Regional incentive schemes also tend to be too complicated for most small firms (Allen, Yuill, and Bachtler 1989). Fifthly, infrastructure investments are criticized as being permissive. If they fail to generate additional economic activity, then regions may simply be endowed with expensive but under-utilized fixed capital in the form of roads or airports. Nevertheless, evidence does exist that there is a strong correlation between infrastructure endowment and levels of regional income, employment, and productivity (CEC 1986).

Member State regional policies have diminished in importance since the mid-1970s for several reasons. The EU is seeking to reduce the level of assistance as part of a general programme of removing barriers to competition. At the same time, economic crises and budgetary constraints have limited the amount of discretionary expenditure available to governments. Finally, there is constant tension between policy objectives and the means of policy implementation. For the most part, the objectives are set by the government, but the majority of the means of implementation rest with the private sector, which regional policy can seek to influence but cannot control.

7.6. EU regional policy

As we have seen, most of the individual Member States of the EU operate their own regional policies. These Member State regional policies coexist alongside a central EU regional policy, which in the period since 1989 has been greatly strengthened. The individual Member State policies differ substantially from one another in both the size of the resources devoted to them and the types of policies utilized. It is clear, therefore, that the principle of subsidiarity is alive and well in the field of regional policy. No attempt has been made to bring about the complete central control of EU regional policy. Indeed, in the 1980s and 1990s the role of regional and local governments in regional industrial regeneration has, if anything, been strengthened in most of the Member States.

The continued vitality of the Member States in the operation of regional policy raises an obvious but key question: what is the justification for an EU regional policy running alongside those of the Member States? In the aftermath of the debate on the Treaty on European Union (TEU) in 1992, the issue of subsidiarity has been given greater prominence and there have even been one or two calls for regional policy to be wholly 're-patriated' to the Member States. With the looming enlargement of the EU to incorporate a number of very poor East and Central European countries some time after 1999, the extra pressure on EU finances may lead to further calls for repatriation. The arguments advanced for a central EU regional policy are crucial, not only to justify its continued existence, but also to determine what the nature of the EU's role in regional policy should be.

A number of different reasons can be advanced in support of a separate central EU role in regional policy. The first is concerned with the concept of 'cohesion'. This concept is most clearly defined in the TEU, which states that: 'In order to promote its overall harmonious development, the Community shall develop and pursue its action leading to the strengthening of its economic and social cohesion. In particular the Community shall aim at reducing the disparities between the various regions and the backwardness of the less favoured regions, including the rural areas' (Article 130a).

The importance of cohesion, and the key role to be played by regional policy in achieving it, are the result of the quickening pace of integration. The Single European Market (SEM) legislation introduced during 1989–92, the entry of Finland, Austria, and Sweden in 1995, the prospect of European Monetary Union (EMU) in the years ahead, together with the likelihood of a wave of new entrants from Eastern and Central Europe after 1999, have all combined to raise concern on the issue of cohesion. In principle, the integration process does not necessarily threaten cohesion by widening regional disparities. As was shown earlier, there is some evidence (particularly from the USA) that highly integrated economies experience a gradual narrowing of regional disparities (Barro and Sala-i-Martin 1991, 1992). These are, however, very long-term effects. Indeed, since the mid-1970s there is almost no evidence that convergence has continued, and some researchers have found that a certain amount of widening of disparities may have been occurring in the 1980s and 1990s (Dunford 1994). Moreover, in the short and medium term there is no doubt that the effects of the full implementation of the SEM and of the creation of EMU will be profound. EU regional disparities are already wide by international standards (OECD 1989; CEC 1991). Further EU integration may well lead to a further widening of disparities (Camagni 1992; Steinle 1992). Even on the most optimistic scenarios, the integration processes set in motion by the SEM and EMU will cause profound structural changes among the regions of the EU. In order to reap the static and dynamic gains from integration, most of the industries of the EU must rationalize their production processes. The effect of this will be felt in every region of the EU, in some more than others.

The regional effects of further integration have been widely used to justify the existence of an EU regional policy and its post-1989 strengthening. There are two aspects to this argument. First, a strong EU regional policy is necessary because the EU is itself the *cause* of part of the regional problem as a side effect of the integration process it has set in motion. Secondly, a strong EU regional policy is vital if the full benefits of the SEM and EMU are to be *achieved*. Wide differences in the performance of the different regional economies pose a threat to the attainment of integration, just as the lack of convergence between Member State economies does.

In addition to the link between EU regional policy and the integration process, supporters of EU regional policy point to additional arguments in its favour. First, the more prosperous Member States tend to have fewer regional problems but also have the greater financial resources. Without EU intervention, the outcome would be that richer Member States could spend more on their problem regions than could the poorer Member States (CEC 1990b). Indeed, some Member States such as the Irish Republic and Greece are virtually disadvantaged regions in their own right and face severe financial constraints in trying to fund an active regional policy. An EU regional policy is vital if resources are to be concentrated in those regions of the EU in greatest need.

The need for an EU regional policy as a means of targeting help where it is most needed is really part of a broader *coordination* case for an EU regional policy. Money, however, is only part of the solution to the regional problems of Europe. The efficiency with which regional policy is operated is also important. The EU has a crucial role to play in coordinating the activities of the EU15. At one level this involves simple but effective actions, such as ensuring that Member States sharing a common frontier tackle regional problems on either side of the frontier in a sensible coordinated manner, or in ensuring that cross-EU transport and other links are highly integrated. At another level, coordination involves bringing the Member States, regional, and local organizations together, so that a common integrated strategy for tackling the EU's regional problems can be hammered out. Coordination is also necessary as part of EU competition policy to prevent Member States from using their domestic regional policy subsidies to bid against one another for 'mobile' investment projects.

Finally, it is important not to lose sight of a fundamental reason for regional policy: that regional disparities are socially inequitable. To be an EU citizen means being part of a community of interest in which equity is just as important as economic efficiency. Regional policy at the EU level can, therefore, be seen as a way of expressing the desire to help fellow EU citizens in poorer regions to realize their potential. As such, it is part of the EU's more general target of trying to overcome 'social-exclusion' problems. In addition, the presence of low-income and high-unemployment regions with depressed spending power is not in the interests of the more prosperous parts of the EU.

EU regional policy since 1989

The current EU regional policy was moulded by a set of major reforms introduced in 1989 as part of the SEM process (CEC 1989) and subsequently fine-tuned in 1993 (CEC 1993a). The current budget period for regional policy runs from 1994 to 1999, at which point a full review of the policy will take place. The 1989 reforms were by far the most radical, since the creation of the original ERDF in 1975 (CEC 1975; Armstrong 1978).

The 1989 reforms were designed as a complete revamp of the EU's three *structural funds*. The three structural funds are the ERDF, the European Social Fund (ESF), and the Guidance Section of the European Agricultural Guidance and Guarantee Fund (EAGGF). All three funds had been in existence for many years prior to the 1989 reforms. The gradual introduction of the SEM legislation between 1988 and 1992 proved to be the catalyst for the design of a coordinated framework for administering these three structural funds. The new framework, in addition to attempting to coordinate the activities of the structural funds, also sought to integrate the actions of two other EU financial instruments providing help to the disadvantaged regions: the European Investment Bank (EIB) and the European Coal and Steel Community (ECSC).

The 1989 reforms established a set of common objectives for the structural funds. As a result of the 1993 fine-tuning exercise and the entry of Sweden, Finland, and Austria in 1995, there are now six common objectives, four of which are explicitly 'regional' (Objectives 1, 2, 5B, and 6):

1. *The economic adjustment of regions whose development is lagging behind.* These are structurally backward regions with GDP per capita under (approximately) 75 per cent of the EU average (see Fig. 7.1). They comprise the most disadvantaged of the EU's problem regions and are dominated by the Mediterranean South together with East Germany and Ireland. Within the UK the regions of Northern Ireland, Merseyside, and the Scottish Highlands and Islands are eligible for Objective 1 help between 1994 and 1999. All three structural funds, together with the EIB, are charged with the redevelopment of the Objective 1 areas.

2. *The economic conversion of declining industrial areas.* The ERDF and ESF, together with the EIB and, where appropriate, the ECSC, are charged with helping these regions. Although the Objective 2 areas shown on Fig. 7.1 were initially designated only for the period 1994–6, their designations have now been extended through to the year 1999.

3. *The combating of long-term unemployment and the facilitation of the integration into working life of young persons and those exposed to exclusion from the labour market.* This objective, and Objective 4 below, are not explicitly 'regional' objectives and hence do not appear on Fig. 7.1. They are only supported by the activities of the ESF.

4. *The facilitation of the adaptation of workers to industrial changes and to changes in production systems.*

5. This objective is in two parts. Objective 5A (*the adjustment of agricultural structures in the framework of the reform of the common agriculture policy*) is a non-regional objective for which the EAGGF has prime responsibility. Objective 5B (*facilitating the development and structural adjustment of rural areas*), however, is a regional objective. Eligible areas are shown in Fig. 7.1. All three structural funds, including the ERDF, are charged with attaining Objective 5B.

6. *The promotion of the development and structural adjustment of regions with an extremely low population density.* This objective, as Fig. 7.1 shows, is designed to provide help for the remote arctic and sub-arctic regions of northern Finland and Sweden.

The 1989 reforms led to a doubling (*in real terms*) of EC assistance to the disadvantaged regions between 1989 and 1993. This reflected the determination of the EC to

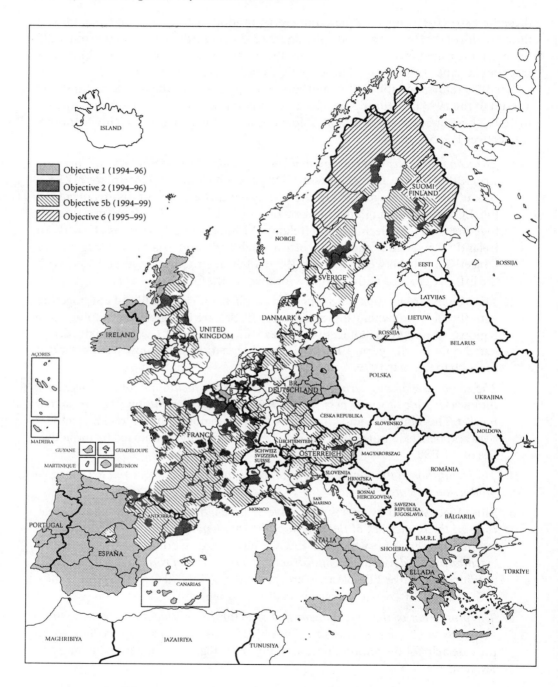

Fig. 7.1. **Areas eligible for the EU structural funds, 1994–1999**
Source: Artis (1996).

develop a powerful and effective regional policy of its own. It also reflected fears that the SEM (and EMU eventually) might exacerbate regional disparities unless remedial measure were put in place. During the subsequent 1994–9 budget period the resources devoted to regional policy have again been doubled in real terms (from the 1989 baseline). The two-phase expansion of resources has been accompanied by measures designed to ensure that EU funding is *concentrated* on those objectives and those regions which are in greatest need. As was shown earlier, one of the main arguments in favour of an EU-level regional policy is its inherent ability to direct resources to the regions in greatest distress. It is the Objective 1 regions which are by far the most disadvantaged.

By 1999 the structural funds of the EU will command some Ecu 25.939 billion at 1995 prices (35.6 per cent of the complete EU budget). A good idea of how far regional policy has come in the EU can be gained by considering that in the 1980s regional policy rarely attained 5 per cent of the EC annual budget. It is anticipated that between 1994 and 1999 the Objective 1 regions will be allocated 70 per cent of the total structural funds' budget, reflecting the commitment to concentration of help. This help will be reinforced by some Ecu 14.5 billion from a new fund, the Cohesion Fund, set up in 1994, which is restricted to Greece, Spain, Portugal, and Ireland (i.e. four of the countries with the most Objective 1 areas).

The ERDF (and the other structural funds) are essentially grant-giving financial instruments. Other types of financial assistance, such as loans, are the province of agencies such as the EIB and the ECSC. Before 1989 most of the assistance provided by the ERDF was in the form of project-by-project grants, given mainly to large infrastructure projects and with lesser amounts going to industrial projects. This approach tended to draw the EC into detailed work requiring expertise and information not available in Brussels. The 1989 reforms sought to bring about a fundamental change in the manner in which EU regional policy is administered and these changes have been carried forward into the 1994–9 period. The key features of this post-1989 system are *planning*, *partnership*, *subsidiarity*, and *additionality*.

Since 1989 a comprehensive system of regional economic planning has effectively been created. The process is designed to be a collaborative one, drawing the Member States together (increasingly) with regional and local organizations (hence the terms 'partnership' and 'subsidiarity'). The planning process represents the most determined attempt yet by the EU to capitalize upon its key role as a policy coordinator. The planning process has several distinct phases. At the first stage the Member States (after drawing in lower-level authorities) draw up plans for each Objective 1, 2, 5B, and 6 region and submit them to the Commission. After detailed discussions between the Member State and the Commission, Single Programming Documents (SPDs—sometimes called Community Support Frameworks) are produced by the Commission. These SPDs set out, for the 1994–9 budget period, the contribution which the EU's structural funds will make to the attainment of the regional plan, and also indicate the role which the Member States' own regional policy will play and the inputs of the various other regional and local partners to be involved. Once the SPD and the regional plan have been agreed, the next stage is implementation. This is undertaken partially via assistance to individual projects (particularly large infrastructure projects), but principally through *programmes* of assistance. Programmes are carefully coordinated packages of help, in which the EU is only one partner. A programme is designed to run for several years (usually for the budget period, but many stretch over longer periods than this), have a clear and precise set of goals, comprise a variety of individual projects and other initiatives (e.g. help for small firms), and will involve the Member States and regional and local organizations. The EU provides partial funding for the various SPDs and programmes but does not directly implement them; this is left to the Member States.

The SPDs are carefully evaluated both before and after implementation and are also subject to regular monitoring. The programming approach to regional policy is not new. Prior to 1989 the EC had developed a range of Community Programmes such as STAR (improvement of telecommunications in disadvantaged regions). These Community-level programmes (now called Community Initiatives (CIs)), encompassing several Member States, have been retained and expanded to comprise around 9 per cent of the structural funds' budget (see Table 7.5). The bulk of ERDF money, however, is channelled through the various programmes grouped together within the individual region SPDs and, as such, is specific to individual Member States.

Once the budget period has ended and the SPDs have been evaluated, the whole process is repeated, with new plans being agreed and new SPDs and programmes being developed. At no stage does the EU act on its own. The key principle, therefore, is that of partnership between the EU, the Member States, and regional and local organizations. The expectation is that, in return for close EU involvement, the Member States

Table 7.5. **Community initiatives, 1994–1999**

Initiative	Description	ECU million 1994–1999
Interreg II	Border regions	3,520.40
Leader II	Rural development	1,758.70
Regis II	Remote regions	608.20
Employment/Adapt	Labour market change	3,478.50
Rechar II; Resider II; Konver; Retex	Sectoral: coal, iron/steel, defence sector, textiles.	2,368.70
SMEs	Small firms	1,077.00
Urban	Inner cities	816.90
Pesca	Fishing communities	296.40
Peace	Northern Ireland	300.00
TOTAL		14,275.50

Note: Excludes a reserve of Ecu 50.7 million not subdivided by Initiative.

Source: CEC (1995: 3).

will commit money of their own in an 'additional' manner (i.e. as a complement to the structural funds and not as a substitute). Whether the system genuinely results in 'additionality' in the use of Member States' money has been the subject of fierce controversy, with some countries being accused of reducing their domestic regional policy spending as the EU structural funds have grown. The past record of some of the Member States in this respect has been very poor.

The initial implementation of the 1989 reforms stimulated considerable discussion (EP 1991; CEC 1992a). The rapid pace of change in the EU subsequently in the 1990s has meant that there has been continuing questioning of the role of the structural funds. With the signing of the TEU in 1992 it became apparent that EMU was a realistic possibility. Economic and monetary union would have very important implications for the EU's disadvantaged regions. The major increase in the size of the structural funds for the 1994–9 period and the reform package of 1993 (CEC 1993a, 1993b) were both designed to try to help the regions to meet the challenges of EMU. The 1993 reform package, though minor when compared to the 1989 reforms, did include a number of significant changes: (*a*) an additional new objective for the structural funds (the reintegration of workers affected by industrial change), (*b*) additional help for fishing communities, (*c*) simplified procedures for drawing up programmes of assistance, and (*d*) a strengthened role for regional and local-level partners. As we have seen, the accession of Sweden, Austria, and Finland in 1995 also led to a further new Objective (number 6) and revised structural funds' budgets for the new entrants.

7.7. Conclusion

Regional policy has become one of the key policies within the EU. The 1992 Edinburgh Summit which established the 1994–9 budget for the structural funds, together with the 1993 reform package, consolidated the whole policy. The rapid growth of EU regional policy since 1989 is welcome in that it has occurred at a time when the regional policies of the individual Member States have been under increasingly tight financial constraints as they have struggled to meet the Maastricht convergence criteria for monetary union. The EU, however, has not supplanted the Member States. Individual Member States continue to operate strong regional policies of their own. A situation of considerable complexity has, therefore, emerged, particularly as the policy of concentrating help on small firms and other types of 'indigenous development' has given a great boost to regional and local development organizations.

The EU now plays a crucial role in regional policy, both through the sheer scale of its budget and through the planning mechanisms into which it has drawn the Member States, and the regional and local organizations. A number of key issues are likely to dominate regional policy in the EU as the end of the 1994–9 budget period draws closer. The first will be the issue of the size of the regional policy budget. Existing regional disparities are proving to be strongly resistant to attempts to eliminate them. Further EU integration (e.g. EMU), combined with the gradual coming to fruition of the SEM, will place further strains on the economies of the weakest regions. Most pressing of all, however, is the looming issue of how to finance the proposed enlargement to incorporate the Visegrad countries of Eastern and Central Europe (Poland, Hungary, the Czech Republic, Slovakia, Bulgaria, and Rumania). Even on the most optimistic assumptions, regions in all six of these countries would be eligible for Objective 1 status under current structural funds arrangements (Baldwin 1994). The threat to the existing EU budget is a clear one, with implications for the existing Member States' receipts too. A second issue of looming importance is that of the effectiveness of the existing policies funded by the structural funds. Indigenous development policies are proving to be extremely slow in bring about regional regeneration. Moreover, the evaluation procedures for the structural funds leave a lot to be desired. It is, therefore, by no means clear that the structural funds are being efficiently used.

Other issues likely to be important in the years ahead are subsidiarity and additionality. The final division of regional policy powers between the EU and the Member States and the precise role for regional and local governments (subsidiarity) has yet to be decided, and further evolution of the situation is bound to occur. Additionality will be important because the drive towards monetary union and the need to get within the TEU convergence criteria is forcing Member States to seek ways of cutting back on domestic spending programmes such as regional policy. This invariably results in subtle attempts by Member States to use EU regional policy spending as a substitute for their own.

Discussion questions

1. What are the strengths and weaknesses in the case advanced for having an EU regional policy? To what extent do you think existing regional policy is capable of achieving the aims set for it?

2. Why would enlargement of the EU to include Central and East European countries cause concern for existing EU regional policy? How can the EU respond to the challenges enlargement would pose?

3. Are the great differences among the regional policies operated by the individual Member States a source of weakness or of strength for regional policy in the EU? Should diversity be encouraged by the EU or restricted?

FURTHER READING

A more detailed exposition of current EU regional policy can be found in CEC (1996). A good discussion of how recent trends have affected the pattern of regional disparities in the EU can be found in Dunford (1994). The threat to existing regional policy posed by the possible entry of East and Central European countries is carefully examined by Centre for Economic Policy Research, *Is Bigger Better? The Economics of EC Enlargement*, CEPR, London, 1992. A wide-ranging discussion of EU regional policy and its implications for jobs can be found in Harrop (1996). The role of regional planning and future prospects for the European system of regions are examined in CEC (1994*b*).

REFERENCES

Albrechts, L., Moulaert, F., Roberts, P., and Swyngedouw, E. (1989), 'New Perspectives for Regional Policy and Development in the 1990s', in L. Albrechts, F. Moulaert, P. Roberts, and E. Swyngedouw (eds.), *Regional Policy at the Crossroads* (London: Jessica Kingsley).

Allen, K., Yuill, D., and Bachtler, J. (1989), 'Requirements for an Effective Regional Policy', in L. Albrechts, F. Moulaert, P. Roberts, and E. Swyngedouw (eds.), *Regional Policy at the Crossroads* (London: Jessica Kingsley).

Armstrong, H. W. (1978), 'Community Regional Policy: Survey and Critique', *Regional Studies*, 12: 511–18.

—— (1995), 'An Appraisal of the Evidence from Cross-Sectional Analysis of the Regional Growth Process within the European Union', in H. W. Armstrong and R. W. Vickerman (eds), *Convergence and Divergence within European Regions* (London: Pion), 40–65.

—— and Taylor, J. (1993), *Regional Economics and Policy*, 2nd edn. (Hemel Hempstead: Harvester Wheatsheaf).

Artis, M. (1996) (ed.), *The UK Economy: Prest and Coppock's Manual of Applied Economics*, 14th edn. (Oxford: Oxford University Press).

Baldwin, R. E. (1994), *Towards an Integrated Europe* (London: Centre for Economic Policy Research).

Barro, R. J., and Sala-i-Martin, X. (1991), 'Convergence across States and Regions', *Brookings Papers*, 1: 107–82.

—— (1992), 'Convergence', *Journal of Political Economy*, 100: 223–51.

Blacksell, M. (1987), 'West Germany', in H. Clout (ed), *Regional Development in Western Europe*, 3rd edn. (London: Fulton), 229–56.

Bleitrach, D., and Chenu, A. (1982), 'Regional Planning: Regulation or Deepening of Social Contradictions?', in R. Hudson and J. R. Lewis (eds.), *Regional Planning in Europe* (London: Pion).

Camagni, R. P. (1992), 'Development Scenarios and Policy Guidelines for the Lagging Regions in the 1990s', *Regional Studies*, 26: 361–74.

Clout, H. (1987), 'France', in H. Clout (ed.), *Regional Development in Western Europe*, 3rd edn. (London: Fulton).

CEC (1975): Commission of the European Communities, 'Regulation Establishing a Community Regional Policy', *Official Journal of the European Communities*, L73 (21 Mar.).

—— (1986), *The Contribution of Infrastructure to Regional Development* (Brussels: CEC).

—— (1989), *Guide to the Reform of the Community's Structural Funds* (Brussels: CEC).

—— (1990*a*), *An Empirical Assessment of the Factors Shaping Regional Competitiveness in Problem Regions* (Brussels–Luxembourg: CEC).

Harvey Armstrong, Jim Taylor, and Allan Williams

CEC (1990*b*), *Second Survey on State Aids in the European Community in Manufacturing and Other Sectors* (Brussels: CEC).

—— (1991), *The Regions in the 1990s: Fourth Report on the Social and Economic Situation and Development of the Regions of the Community* (Brussels: CEC).

—— (1992*a*), *The ERDF in 1990* (Brussels–Luxembourg: CEC).

—— (1992*b*), *Community Structural Policies: Mid-Term Assessment and Outlook* (Brussels: CEC).

—— (1993*a*), *Community Structural Funds 1994–1999* (Brussels: CEC).

—— (1993*b*), *The Community's Structural Fund Operations 1994–1999*, COM (93) 67 final-SYN 455 (Brussels: CEC).

—— (1994*a*) *Competitiveness and Cohesion: Trends in the Regions* (Brussels: CEC).

—— (1994*b*), *Europe 2000+ Cooperation for European Territorial Development* (Brussels–Luxembourg: CEC).

—— (1995), *Newsletter No. 23: December 1995* (Brussels: DGXVI, CEC).

—— (1996), *Structural Funds and Cohesion Fund 1949–99: Regulations and Commentary* (Brussels–Luxembourg: CEC).

Council of Ministers (1992), *Treaty on European Union* (Brussels: CEC).

Dignan, T. (1995), 'Regional Disparities and Regional Policy in the European Union', *Oxford Review of Economic Policy*, 11: 64–95.

Dunford, M. (1994), 'Winners and Losers: The New Map of Economic Inequality in the European Union', *European Urban and Regional Studies*, 1: 95–114.

EP (1991): European Parliament, *A New Strategy for Social and Economic Cohesion after 1992*, study by the National Institute for Economic and Social Research for European Parliament (Brussels–Luxembourg: EP).

Flockton, C., and Kofman, E. (1989), *France* (London: Harper & Row).

Gay, F. J. (1987), 'Benelux', in H. Clout (ed.), *Regional Development in Western Europe*, 3rd edn. (London: Fulton).

Gravier, J. (1947), *Paris et le désert français* (Paris: Plaminiarian).

Harrop, J. (1996), *Structural Funding and Employment in the European Union* (Cheltenham: Edward Elgar).

Hermansen, T. (1971), 'Development Poles and Development Centres in National and Regional Development', in United Nations (ed.), *Growth Poles and Growth Centres in Regional Policies and Planning* (Geneva: United Nations).

Hill, S., and Munday, M. (1994), *The Regional Distribution of Foreign Manufacturing Investment in the UK* (London: Macmillan).

Keeble, D., and Wever, E. (1986), 'Introduction', in D. Keeble and E. Wever (eds.), *New Firms and Regional Development in Europe* (London: Croom Helm), 1–34.

King, R. (1987), *Italy* (London: Harper & Row).

Lewis, J. R. (1984), 'Regional Policy and Planning', in S. Bornstein, D. Held, and J. Krieger (eds.), *The State in Capitalist Europe* (London: George Allen & Unwin), 138–55.

Martin, R. (1992), 'Reviving the Case for Regional Policy', in M. Hart and R. Harrison (eds.), *Spatial Policy in a Divided Nation* (London: Jessica Kingsley), 270–90.

—— and Tyler, P. (1992), 'The Regional Legacy', in J. Michie (ed.), *The Economic Legacy 1979–92* (London: Academic Press), 140–67.

Mason, C. M., and Harrison, R. T. (1990), 'Small Firms: Phoenix from the Ashes', in D. Pinter (ed.), *Western Europe: Challenge and Change* (London: Belhaven), 72–90.

Massey, D. (1979), 'In What Sense a Regional Problem?', *Regional Studies*, 13: 233–44.

Molle, W. (1990), *The Economics of European Integration: Theory, Practice, Policy* (Aldershot: Dartmouth Publishing Co.).

Morriss, J. (1991), 'Japanese Foreign Manufacturing Investment in the EC: An Overview', in J. Morriss (ed.), *Japan and the Global Economy* (London: Routledge).

Naylon, J. (1987), 'Iberia', in H. Clout (ed.), *Regional Development in Western Europe*, 3rd edn. (London: Fulton), 383–418.

Nicoll, W. R., and Yuill, D. (1980), *Regional Problems and Policies in Europe: The Post-War Experience* (Studies in Public Policy, No. 53; Glasgow: University of Strathclyde).

OECD (1989): Organization for Economic Cooperation and Development, *Economic Outlook, July* (Paris: OECD).

Perroux, F. (1950), 'Economic Space: Theory and Applications', *Quarterly Journal of Economics*, 64.

Steinle, W. J. (1992), 'Regional Competitiveness and the Single Market', *Regional Studies*, 26: 307–18.

Taylor, J. (1991), *Reviving the Regions* (Fabian Society Pamphlet, No. 551; London).

—— (1993), 'An Analysis of the Factors Determining the Geographical Distribution of Japanese Manufacturing Investment in the UK, 1984–91', *Urban Studies*, 30: 1209–224.

Thwaites, A. T., and Alderman, N. (1990), 'Technological Change and Regional Economic Advance', in D. Pinter (ed.), *Western Europe: Challenge and Change* (London: Belhaven), 91–107.

Williams, A. M. (1987), *The Western European Economy: A Geography of Post-war Development* (London: Hutchinson).

Wren, C. (1987), 'The Relative Effects of Local Authority Financial Assistance Policies', *Urban Studies*, 24: 268–78.

—— (1989), 'The Revised Regional Development Grant Scheme: A Case Study in Cleveland County of a Marginal Employment Subsidy', *Regional Studies*, 23: 127–38.

Yuill, D., Allen, K., Bachtler, J., Clement, K., and Wishlade, F. (1991), *European Regional Incentives 1991* (London: Bowker Saur).

CHAPTER 8

Transport Policy

NORMAN LEE

8.1. Introduction

Transport is an important sector in the economies of all Member States of the European Union (EU) (with approximately 7–8 per cent of GNP being spent each year on transport activities). Traditionally, it has been expected to serve a variety of different, sometimes conflicting, objectives—economic, social, and environmental. Given this, it became one of the most regulated sectors in most European economies, although the nature and extent of such regulations varied greatly between them. Therefore, it was not surprising that, when it was first established, attempts were made to develop a common transport policy for the European Community (EC) as a whole.

This chapter contains a review and evaluation of the Common Transport Policy (CTP). The next section describes its origins and subsequent development. There is then a brief review of the main characteristics of the EU transport sector and the problems that transport policies need to address. This is followed by an economic analysis of certain efficiency and equity issues raised by such problems and policies. Thereafter, EU transport policy and its effects are analysed in each of a number of policy areas—road freight and passenger transport, rail and inland waterways transport, maritime and air transport, and transport infrastructures. The chapter concludes with an overall evaluation of the CTP and its future development.

8.2. Origins and development of the CTP

The Treaty of Rome (1957) established, in Articles 3e and 74–84, the legal basis for a CTP within the EC. This is one of only three common policies specifically mentioned in the original Treaty—the others being agriculture and external commerce.

Prior to this, the European Coal and Steel Community (ECSC), established by the Treaty of Paris (1951), had been developing its own common transport policy (Erdmenger 1983). This was because discrimination in transport rates and related practices by Member States were being used to favour domestic exporters and to penalize imports, and this was considered harmful to the establishment of a common market in coal and steel within the ECSC.

Continuing concern over similar issues resulted in provision for a CTP within the Treaty of Rome. The following features are worth noting:

1. Article 84 restricts the automatic application of the CTP to road, rail, and waterway transport, whilst giving the Council of Ministers powers to add marine and aviation transport if they unanimously agree (eventually this was agreed in 1974).

2. Article 74 established the fundamental objectives of the CTP as being the overall objectives of the Treaty itself (see Article 2). These objectives are broadly defined and leave considerable discretion in interpretation to the Commission and Council of Ministers. They have also been subsequently amended, as discussed later, through the Single European Act (SEA) (1987) and the Treaty on European Union (TEU) (1992).

3. Articles 75–84 contain a mixture of more specific requirements of the CTP which relate to the elimination of discriminatory practices but also permit state subsidies for transport activities under certain circumstances.

The principles and guidelines to be followed by the CTP were set down in the Schaus Memorandum of 1961 and the types of measures to be introduced in implementing these were listed in the Commission's first Action Programme of 1962 (Despicht 1969). These proposed measures were of the following main kinds:

- *Anti-discrimination* measures: these were intended to eliminate discrimination between Member States and between different modes of transport.
- *Liberalization* measures: carriers were to be given additional opportunities to supply services across national frontiers within the EC.
- *Harmonization* measures: these proposed standardization of provisions, across Member States, relating to such matters as the weights and dimensions of road vehicles, conditions of work in road transport, and the taxation of vehicles.

Additionally, the Commission proposed an EC role in coordinating transport investment relating to 'trunk routes of Community importance'.

However, progress in implementing many of these measures was very slow. Then, the enlargement of the EC in 1973 led the Commission to review the future development of the CTP and, *inter alia*, it proposed the establishment of an EC transport system (Erdmenger 1983)—but progress continued to be limited.

There were many reasons for slow progress, but a principal factor has been conflicts of interest between different Member States and between those providing different forms of transport. Some interests, for example, favoured 'harmonization' measures which might protect or strengthen their own competitive and financial position; others favoured 'liberalization' measures, because they believed they would benefit from greater access to other Member State markets. The different attitudes of Member States in the early 1980s can be seen from the following statement by the then Director of Transport in the Commission:

The Benelux countries and the peripheral Member States—the United Kingdom, Denmark, Greece and Ireland—primarily seek freedom of movement in the Community for their road haulage and inland waterway companies in order to open up a large economic area for their transport operations. The Federal Republic of Germany and Italy, however, stress the need for harmonising the conditions of competition. This has the twin aim of protecting their own road haulage companies and their national railways . . . The United Kingdom, Denmark and Greece are the strongest advocates of the traditional freedom of navigation (in sea transport). Belgium, France, the Federal Republic of Germany and Italy are inclined to allow their own fleet to benefit from the fact that their industries have a high level of imports and exports . . . The traditional air transport policy of the Member States is mainly directed at gaining a share of traffic for their national airline . . . The Member States are reluctant therefore to make any promises in Brussels. However, the United Kingdom, which has a policy of admitting several airlines—and, to a certain extent, the Netherlands as well—advocates specific European solutions. (Erdmenger 1983: 7–8)

However, the pace of change in the CTP has accelerated considerably since the mid-1980s. This has been mainly for two reasons:

1. The Judgment of the European Court of Justice (ECJ) in May 1985, which, *inter alia*, required the Council of Transport Ministers to adopt 'within a reasonable time' measures to liberalize transport services. This was in response to an action brought by the European Parliament (EP) against the Council of Ministers for failing to introduce and implement a common transport policy (DG for Research 1991).
2. The political initiative to establish, by an 1993, a single market in Europe. 'The abolition of frontiers and the concrete implementation of the freedom of move-ment for people, goods and capital could not, in fact, be conceived without an internal market for transport' (DG for Research 1991: 21).

In effect, these two changes, supported by an international trend towards deregulation (Button and Pitfield 1991), broadened the political support for the liberalization and anti-discrimination measures which had previously been lacking. In November 1985 the Council of Transport Ministers agreed a work programme comprising

- the creation of a free transport market, without quantitative restrictions, no later than 1992; and
- a progressive liberalization of transport services and elimination of distortions to competition within the EC transport market, in the intervening period.

The progress made in implementing this work programme is reviewed, for each main policy area, later in the chapter. Measured according to the scope and number of new regulations and directives approved at EC level, the overall progress has been impressive. However, account has to be taken of provisions for exemptions and delays in implementation which occur at the Member State level. In most cases it is only since the late 1980s that certain of these measures have begun to have significant, practical consequences, and their full effects have not yet been fully experienced.

Also, from the mid-1980s, the Commission has made further efforts to strengthen the infrastructure investment component of the CTP. In 1986 it identified its medium-term policy objectives as

- improvement of transport communications in land–sea corridors;
- reduction in the transport costs incurred within 'transit' countries;
- integration of the peripheral regions within the EC's network; and
- construction of links offering a high level of service between major Member State cities, particularly high-speed rail links (Lee 1992).

However, some Member States, including the UK, did not support the development of a substantial EC transport fund for these purposes, and its impact has been fairly limited. Much larger financial support for transport infrastructure has been available through the European Regional Development Fund (ERDF).

The future role and operations of EC/EU transport policy are also affected by the provisions of the SEA (1987) and the TEU (the 'Maastricht Treaty'). *Inter alia*, they provide for

- the introduction of majority voting on certain transport-policy issues;
- the need to respect the subsidiarity principle within the CTP;
- the need to reflect the new statement of EC objectives (in Article 2 of the Treaty) following the Maastricht agreement—that is, of promoting throughout the EC: a harmonious and balanced development of economic activities; sustainable and non-inflationary growth respecting the environment; a high degree of convergence of economic performance; a high level of employment and of social protection; the raising of the standard of living and quality of life, and economic and social cohesion and solidarity among Member States;
- the need to include, within the CTP, measures to improve transport safety; and
- the development of trans-European networks in the areas of transport, telecommunications and energy.

It is clear that the existence of multiple objectives for a Common Transport Policy will continue, and the need to reconcile these, where they conflict, will remain. The Commission has indicated how the CTP might evolve in the future, in its report on *The Future Development of the Common Transport Policy* (CEC 1992). This identified three main goals:

1. the removal of any remaining restrictions or distortions in the single market;
2. the proper functioning of EC transport systems; and
3. the integration of environmental objectives within the CTP.

Subsequently, it published its *Common Transport Policy Action Programme 1995–2000* to promote the attainment of these goals and the transport objectives of the TEU (CEC 1995*a*). This will be examined further in the final section of the chapter.

8.3. EC and Member State transport sectors

Between 1970 and 1990, passenger transport within the EC (measured by total passenger kilometres travelled) increased by 3.1 per cent per annum and goods transport (measured by tonne kilometres moved) by 2.3 per cent per annum. This compares with an annual growth rate in GDP, in real terms, of 2.6 per cent (CEC 1992). In the absence of major policy changes, these kinds of growth rates are likely to continue in the future.

The relative shares of the different modes in the EC transport market changed considerably over the period, as illustrated in Figs. 8.1 and 8.2. In the case of *inland freight* movements, the dominance of road transport increased. Its share of the total market rose from 50 to 70 per cent, whilst the shares of the other three modes declined—rail transport from 28 to 15 per cent, inland waterways from 14 to 9 per cent, and pipelines from 8 to 6 per cent. Comparable data are not available for *sea transport*, but it has been estimated that this accounted for at least 30 per cent of all freight transported between Member States, though for only 2–3 per cent, on average, of all domestic transport within Member States (CEC 1992).

In the case of the EC *passenger transport* market, private car transport was already dominant in 1970 and this increased further over the period (from 76 to 79 per cent). The modal share of air transport also rose from 2 to 6 per cent. In contrast, the bus and coach share declined from 12 to 9 per cent and the rail transport share from 10 to 7 per cent.

The relative shares of the different transport modes vary considerably between the Member States. In the case of freight movements, for example, road haulage is of much greater relative importance in Spain than in the Netherlands. In contrast, inland waterways are of major significance in the Netherlands but are insignificant in the UK. In the case of passenger transport, the differences are less pronounced, but, for example, the private road transport shares of the northern, higher-income, countries are greater and those of bus and coach transport considerably lower than in the southern, lower-income Member States. Other examples of these differences (in 1988) are shown in Table 8.1.

The trends within certain transport modes have also differed between Member States (DoT 1991). The growth in 1968–85 in both freight and passenger transport by road in many of the southern countries was considerably above the EC average. Some

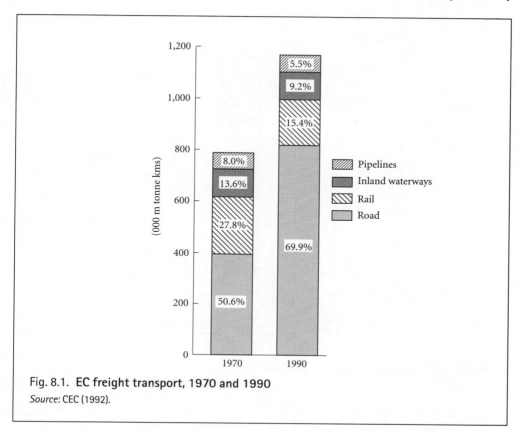

Fig. 8.1. EC freight transport, 1970 and 1990
Source: CEC (1992).

Member States experiences a significant absolute increase in rail freight traffic (e.g. Portugal, Italy, the Netherlands), whilst others (e.g. the UK) experienced an absolute decline.

These differences help to explain why the transport problems and policy interests of different Member States do not always coincide. Additionally, they may adopt different policies because their transport philosophies are different. Some adopt more narrowly defined economic objectives for transport policy, whilst others emphasize its broader social and environmental role.

Despite such differences, there are a number of common problems which face most Member States or are likely to do so in the near future. These include:

- Increasing pressure on the transport infrastructure, especially roads, as traffic continues to increase. This is reflected in a number of different policy issues: growing concern over the financing of new infrastructure, increasing congestion and road-safety problems, problems of pollution and resource conservation, and growing interest in traffic constraint by regulatory or fiscal measures.

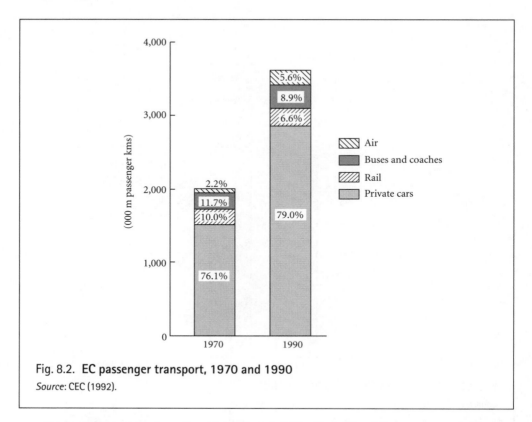

Fig. 8.2. **EC passenger transport, 1970 and 1990**
Source: CEC (1992).

- Increasing pressure on the provision and funding of public passenger transport facilities as car-ownership levels continue to rise. This is reflected in a growing preoccupation with the mobility of lower-income groups and the use of state subsidies to support this.

These transport trends and concerns, although manifest in individual Member States to different degrees and in somewhat different ways, provide the context within which the CTP has to operate in pursuit of the objectives described at the end of the previous section. The Commission's proposals for addressing these, according to its *Programme for Sustainable Mobility* (CEC 1992) were to

- promote the proper functioning of the internal market by facilitating the free movement of goods and persons within the EC;
- remove distortions and inefficiencies within the transport market;
- assist, through investment in new transport infrastructure, in reducing regional disparities in economic and social development;
- ensure that the development of transport systems contributes to a sustainable pattern of development by respecting the environment; and

Table 8.1. **Range of variation in the relative importance of different transport modes between the Member States, 1988**

Freight movements		Passenger movements	
Mode	% of total movements in Member States	Mode	% of total passenger traffic in Member States
Road	34.1 (Netherlands) −75.5 (Spain)	Cars and taxis	73.2 (Spain) −87.3 (UK)
Rail	6.8 (Netherlands) −24.5 (Germany)	Buses and coaches	6.6 (France) −18.4 (Spain)
Inland waterway	0.1 (UK) −54.4 (Netherlands)	Rail (excluding metro)	5.8 (UK) −9.7 (France)
Sea-going	0.2 (Germany −27.1 (UK)		
Pipeline	2.2 (Spain) −10.8 (Denmark)		

Source: DoT (1991).

- improve transport safety.

The next section examines, at a general and more theoretical level, how these different types of goals might be simultaneously achieved.

8.4. Economic analysis of transport policies

The transport-policy goals listed at the end of the previous section can be regrouped into three categories for the purpose of economic analysis:

1. those relating to an efficient allocation of resources within the transport sector and between that sector and other economic sectors (the *allocative-efficiency* objective);

2. those concerned with meeting individual transport market requirements at least resource cost (*marketing* and *productive-efficiency* objectives); and

3. those relating to an equitable distribution of benefits and costs from transport and other economic activities (*equity* objectives—interpersonal, inter-generation, and geographic).

A CTP which meets these three sets of objectives should satisfy the CTP goals which were previously listed. The types of policy measures which, within the framework of a single, internal market, are likely to achieve these objectives, are now considered. This provides an analytical basis for evaluating developments in a number of more specific policy areas in the following sections of the chapter. Allocative-efficiency and equity objectives are discussed first of all, followed by marketing and productive-efficiency objectives.

Allocative-efficiency and equity objectives

Welfare economics demonstrates, on certain market assumptions, that welfare will be maximized, for any given distribution of income, if prices are set equal to the marginal social costs of production (Laidler and Estrin 1989). This is automatically achieved in perfectly competitive markets, but not in the imperfect markets which are typically found in real-world situations. Inefficiencies result from 'market failures', and it is part of the purpose of transport (and other) policies to address these.

Traditionally, many transport markets have been very imperfectly competitive. In some cases, this is because the available transport technology has favoured large, relatively indivisible, infrastructure systems (e.g. railways, ports), which have led to high seller concentration. In other cases, it has been consciously fostered through agreements between operators (e.g. shipping conferences). Additionally, competition within the transport market has been restricted by governments nationalizing transport undertakings and regulating transport activities in the belief that this would better serve a wider range of economic and social objectives. In the event, it is questionable whether the forms that these interventions took actually achieved their goals. Therefore, today, a CTP has to address both 'market-failure' and 'regulatory-failure' problems.

One kind of policy response to this situation is to try to make transport markets more 'workable' or 'contestable'—that is, 'more competitive' (Clark 1940; Baumol 1982). This approach is examined later when reviewing the role that deregulation and anti-discriminatory measures might play within a CTP. A second approach, which under certain circumstances may be complementary to the first, is to improve transport-pricing and investment decision-making so that they are more consistent with allocative-efficiency objectives.

The transport-pricing principle which is often advocated to achieve allocative efficiency is the marginal social cost (MSC) rule of pricing. According to this, the transport user is expected to pay a price equal to the social-opportunity cost of the service with which he is provided.

This is illustrated, in a simple form, in Fig. 8.3. The transport operator is assumed to produce under conditions of constant returns to scale—that is, long-run marginal costs and long-run average costs are equal. Therefore, in long-run equilibrium, if there are no external costs for which he is responsible and given the market-demand conditions (DD), he should supply OY services at a price of OX.

However, the provision of transport services often causes additional costs to fall on other members of society—for example, road accidents to pedestrians, delays to other

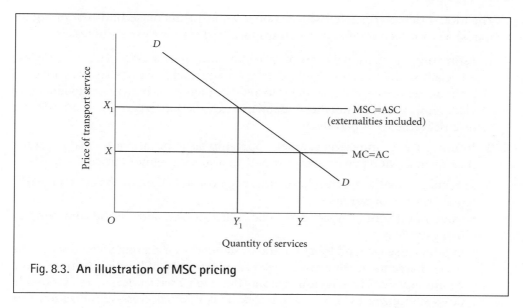

Fig. 8.3. **An illustration of MSC pricing**

road users, noise and air pollution impacts on nearby residents. These external costs should also be taken into account and, in Fig. 8.3, would justify raising the transport price to OX_1 and reducing the supply of services to OY_1.

Where competing transport services are not charged according to their MSCs, there may be a case for departing from strict MSC pricing on 'second-best' grounds (Lipsey and Lancaster 1956). For example, it has been argued that, if motorists pay less than their MSCs on congested roads, bus and coach operators should charge their customers less than their MSC by a similar proportion. If this applied in Fig. 8.3, there would be a case for lowering price below OX_1 *by a specified amount.*

A second type of justification for departing from MSC pricing may be on equity grounds. In this case, it is argued that those with low incomes cannot adequately reflect the strength of their demand for certain transport services in the market and that they should be compensated for this by paying lower fares than strict MSC pricing would imply. Given the case for assisting low-income consumers, the issues to be considered are twofold:

1. Is the subsidization of transport services the best way of providing assistance? An alternative (such as redistributive direct taxation) may be preferable, since it may be difficult, in practice, to confine the benefits of subsidized transport to low-income householders, who, in any case, may prefer to use the financial assistance provided to meet other, more urgent, requirements.

2. If transport subsidization is the most effective form of financial assistance, what should be its extent? As in the case of the 'second-best' arguments, it is necessary to justify the *extent* to which departures from MSC pricing are to take place.

The MSC-pricing principle (with reasoned adjustments on second-best or equity grounds) has not been widely used, in transport markets, for a variety of reasons.

1. Estimating the marginal costs of providing transport services can be complex, especially where transport facilities (e.g. railway track, roads, ports, etc.) are used by many services and it is difficult to allocate their costs between individual services. However, this is not the fundamental explanation, especially as some degree of 'cost averaging' is permissible.

2. In unregulated, imperfect markets, operators have been free to charge profit-maximizing (MC (marginal cost) = MR (marginal revenue)) prices.

3. In regulated markets, prices have often been controlled on the basis of quite different criteria, for example:
   - some rail freight charges used to be related to the value of the commodities being carried;
   - in both passenger and freight markets, standardized charging schemes (i.e. the same charge made for a given distance, irrespective of location or time) were commonplace. The consequence was that high-cost services were commonly cross-subsidized by low-cost services. This internal cross-subsidization was often regarded as part of a 'public-service obligation' to help in providing 'necessary', but unremunerative, services; and
   - sometimes, minimum charges were established to ensure the long-run viability of the operators and the continued provision of their services.

4. In the case of roads, the charges payable for their use (mainly vehicle-licence duties and fuel duties) have often been determined by general fiscal requirements rather than by the marginal social costs incurred by different categories of road users.

5. Externalities have not, in most cases, been internalized in operators' costs and charging schemes.

6. Grants and subsidies have been paid to transport producers and users without sufficient attention to their justification on efficiency or equity grounds.

In principle, transport investment schemes should be justified by the same efficiency and equity criteria as apply to transport pricing. All costs and benefits (including externalities) should be taken into account in a scheme's appraisal. Also, any costs or benefits in the more distant future should be given a sufficient weighting to reflect society's views on inter-generational equity. Similarly, if the benefits and costs affecting particular income groups or regions are considered to be of particular importance, this should be consciously reflected in the weighting they receive in the project's appraisal.

In practice, though formal social cost-benefit appraisal studies have been carried out on a number of occasions, they are not yet widely used in reaching decisions on new scheme proposals. The reasons for this are often similar to those for the limited use of MSC pricing:

- it is often difficulty to place reliable monetary measures on all costs and benefits, especially externalities;
- financial criteria (such as the ability of the investment to be self-financing) may be used instead of the economic criteria described above:
- the availability of grants, rather than the justification upon which their payment is based, may have the stronger influence upon whether a scheme proceeds; and
- broad equity considerations may have a strong influence on scheme approval, but not necessarily within a systematic, well-justified project appraisal.

In summary, the economic logic relating to transport-pricing and investment appraisal which has been described above has not had a strong influence on transport policy. As a result, both market and regulatory failures have continued, and in some cases they have been intensified. However, there is some indication that this economic logic *may* influence the CTP to a greater degree in the future. For example, the Commission has suggested, in its report on the future development of the CTP, that

- the strong shift to the use of roads by both passenger and freight transport may be partly due to the underpricing of road use and proposes 'incorporating, into the transport prices, the infrastructure and external costs which are presently not taken into account' (CEC 1992: para. 97);
- internalizing external costs (especially environmental costs) will be necessary to ensure the development of a sustainable transport system:

  Such a policy will influence the demand for all modes by increasing the price of individual modes to the extent that they impose costs on society which are presently not paid for by the respective transport users. As the external costs associated with various modes differ significantly . . . the price increases will also vary across transport modes leading transport users to adjust their demand, in particular, to favour those forms of transport that impose fewer external costs or even to reduce or avoid unnecessary movements. (CEC 1992: para. 95)

Marketing and productive-efficiency objectives

Marketing and productive-efficiency objectives are concerned with ensuring that:

- the transport services provided, in terms of their combined attributes of price and quality, are those most preferred by consumers in the market (market efficiency); and
- services are produced at least source cost (productive efficiency).

Other things being equal, improvements in market efficiency are reflected in increases in demand, and improvements in productive efficiency in a reduction in the marginal and average costs of production. An illustration of the benefits of a simultaneous improvement in the marketing and productive efficiency of a transport service is given in Fig. 8.4.

In the past there have been two contrasting views of how marketing and productive-efficiency improvements might be best achieved. One favoured the establishment of larger integrated transport undertakings through which it was hoped to achieve more technical harmonization between different parts of the transport system, greater economics of scale in production, and more effective marketing of transport services. The second favoured the removal of restrictions on the competitive process (sometimes loosely described as deregulation, but also including anti-discrimination measures), believing that increased consumer choice would raise marketing efficiency, and greater rivalry between operators would result in increased productive efficiency and cost reductions.

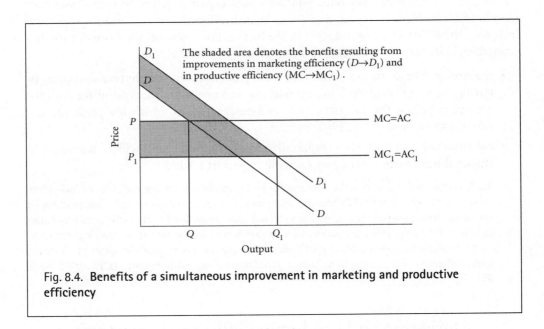

The shaded area denotes the benefits resulting from improvements in marketing efficiency ($D \rightarrow D_1$) and in productive efficiency ($MC \rightarrow MC_1$).

Fig. 8.4. Benefits of a simultaneous improvement in marketing and productive efficiency

The former viewpoint tended to dominate transport policy thinking in most Member States until the 1980s. However, there has been a shift of opinion, starting in the late 1960s, towards the latter view. This has probably been most evident in the UK, which liberalized its own road-haulage industry in the late 1960s, its bus and coach services in the 1980s, and has extended a similar approach to its railways in the mid-1990s. However, many other Member States have changed the orientation of their transport policies both later and to a more limited extent. Inevitably, therefore, changes in the CTP, which, until recently, required the unanimous support of all Member States, were very slow to occur.

The economic consequences of deregulation are fairly straightforward to predict if it is assumed that this will result in a perfectly competitive or perfectly contestable transport market (Baumol 1982). In these circumstances, the welfare gains from improvements in marketing and productive efficiency are unambiguous and are additional to those resulting from improved allocative efficiency, as described previously. However, deregulation is unlikely completely to realize either of the above market forms in practice, and, therefore, the market outcomes are less certain.

For example, following deregulation there may still be a small number of sellers within the market, new entry may still be difficult, and consumers may have imperfect knowledge of the services being supplied. In the more oligopolistic, rather than perfectly competitive, transport markets that result, anti-competitive practices may continue and mergers may further limit the effectiveness of the competitive process over the longer term. Marketing and productive-efficiency benefits may be reduced—as may allocative-efficiency benefits, if operators have commercial freedom to price and make investments as they choose. Without some form of intervention, broader equity objectives may also be unfulfilled. Evaluations of the effects of transport deregulation in the UK and the USA (which have the greatest experience of deregulation to date) tend to support the conclusion that these have been of a mixed nature (Kahn 1988; Gwilliam 1989; McGowan and Seabright 1989; Doganis 1991).

Harmonization measures

Harmonization measures have traditionally formed an important part of the CTP and therefore it is worth analysing how they relate to the efficiency and equity objectives described earlier. Their economic consequences can differ considerably as illustrated below.

- *Technical harmonization.* Member States may agree to common technical specifications for specific types of transport equipment because of the potential benefits from economies of scale in production which this can bring. However, if the market is not satisfied with the supply of standard equipment, there will be some loss of marketing efficiency. There may also be a case for technical harmonization to promote the interconnection of transport systems and operation of rolling stock between Member States. However, if existing systems and rolling stock are not to be retired prematurely, this type of technical harmonization may be achieved only gradually over a considerable period of time.

- *Charge and tax harmonization.* There are good reasons to base transport charges and taxes on the same pricing principles (e.g. an agreed form of MSC pricing). However, this does not support the establishment of uniform levels of charges and taxes in all Member States, if their MSC levels vary. Similarly, there are good reasons for applying the same principles to the payment of transport grants and subsidies (e.g. in accordance with MSC pricing, with agreed adjustments for 'second-best' and equity reasons). Again, however, this does not imply that the same level of grants and subsidies must apply throughout the Member States.

- *Harmonization of conditions of employment.* To the extent that the EU accepts minimum conditions of employment for all workers, as one of its social objectives, this should be reflected in its CTP. However, the opportunity costs of labour do vary between Member States. To go beyond the basic social objective and harmonize actual conditions of employment of all transport workers could provide unjustified protection to the Member State transport industry with the highest per capita incomes and conditions of employment.

Thus, proposals for harmonization measures across Members States need to be carefully evaluated to check their consistency with efficiency and equity objectives.

In summary, economic analysis provides useful criteria and guidelines to evaluate both existing and new CTP measures. However, it cannot be expected to supply simple transport-policy solutions, because the context in which the CTP has to operate is itself inherently complex:

- the objectives it is expected to pursue are multiple—economic, social, and environmental—and, from time to time, will conflict;
- the Member States, whose support for new CTP measures is needed, have different sectional interests and their transport-policy philosophies may also conflict; and
- the CTP is not being designed for an idealized, perfectly competitive, market system but for one in which market and regulatory failures are endemic.

8.5. Road freight and passenger transport

Road freight transport

Road transport is the major means of moving freight within the EU (see Fig. 8.1). The haulage industry contains a large number of operators, many of whom are relatively small scale. Some carry only materials and goods belonging to their own business ('own-account' operators), whilst others are commercial hauliers (carrying for 'hire and reward'). Many operate only at a local or, at most, national market level. Others engage in international transport between Member States and/or with non-EU countries.

At the time when the EC was first established, most Member States tightly regulated their road-haulage activities, for two reasons.

1. To reduce competition between road haulage and their national railway systems. The railways were already subject to considerable regulation and their financial

performance had previously been undermined by the growth of the road-haulage industry.

2. To reduce competition within the road-haulage industry. The unregulated industry was characterized by a large number of sellers and relative ease of entry by new operators. It was felt that these conditions had led to excessive cost and rate cutting, neglect of road safety, high rates of bankruptcy, and undesirable instability within the industry.

The regulations which existed were of two main kinds: those intended to preserve the quality and safety of the services provided (qualitative controls), and those controlling their quantity and price (quantitative controls). The latter took somewhat different forms in different countries (Button 1984) but included

- preventing own-account operators from obtaining 'hire-and-reward' work;
- restricting the geographic area within which a commercial operator might operate, or the types of goods he might carry;
- restrictions on the charges that might be levied;
- restrictions on the numbers of vehicles licensed to engage in hire and reward work; and
- restrictions on the transport of goods to or from other countries and on 'cabotage'—i.e. undertaking road-haulage business *within* other countries on the return journey.

Many of these practices were considered to conflict with the objectives of the CTP, as established in the Treaty of Rome, but, for many years, there was resistance to major changes. Slowly, attitudes began to alter. In 1968 the UK removed the quantitative restrictions on its own road-haulage industry and, when it entered the EC in 1973, it began to support similar changes within the Community. However, a number of other Member States (notably France, Germany, Italy, and, later, Spain) continued to resist radical changes. After the mid-1980s, for reasons that have been previously described, the pace of change accelerated, especially as 1992 approached. The potential benefits of greater productive efficiency, according to Emerson (CEC 1988), were considerable—he suggested that the removal of any remaining regulatory restrictions in the road-haulage industry could be equivalent to a 5 per cent reduction in road-haulage costs and charges. The main changes that have been made to road-haulage operations, through the CTP, are summarized below.

1. *Harmonization measures*. Typically, these measures were justified on the grounds that they prevented distortions of competition between carriers from different Member States operating within the internal market. In many cases the measures have been relatively non-controversial, but in others the standardization they sought may have created rather than removed distortions in competition. The harmonization measures fall into three categories—technical, social, and fiscal—

and most measures have fallen within the first two categories. The first relates to vehicle standards and to such matters as brakes, lighting, windscreens, noise, emissions, weights and measures, road-worthiness tests, etc. Of all of these measures, the most controversial (at least from a UK viewpoint) have related to the maximum size of lorries. Social harmonization measures have been of two kinds. The first relates to maximum driving-hours per day, installation of tachographs, training and certification of drivers, etc. The second relates to the requirements for obtaining operator licences, which have become increasingly important as the liberalization of the internal market has taken place (see below). Fiscal harmonization measures, for example, designed to reduce disparities between fuel taxes and licence duties for lorries, have been little evident until the 1990s. This issue is discussed more fully in the later section dealing with transport infrastructure investment and pricing.

2. *Controls over haulage charges.* When the EC was first formed, some Member States operated a fixed-freight-charges system (e.g. Germany) whilst others had a relatively free-market system (e.g. Netherlands). The EC initially responded to this by establishing a system of maximum and minimum rates for traffic between Member States. From 1977 onwards, pairs of Member States could continue with this system or with a reference rate system in which the reference rate only had the status of a recommendation. From 1983 onwards, the system of recommended prices became the norm. Then, from 1 January 1990 (according to Council Regulation 4058/89), it was decided that all rates should be set by free negotiation between the parties to the haulage contract. Thus, all price regulation should have ceased.

3. *Licensing, quotas, and cabotage.* As previously explained, the EC inherited a situation in which road-haulage transport between Member States was regulated by a series of bilateral agreements, most Member States applied fairly restrictive arrangements in their own domestic markets, and opportunities for cabotage were limited.

   In 1968 (under Regulation 1018/68) the Council agreed, initially on an experimental basis, to introduce a Community Quota System (CQS) which provided for a specified number of vehicle permits to be allocated between the Member States, which allowed their holders to carry goods within the EC without the need to negotiate bilateral agreements (Button 1984). This became a permanent system, and the number of CQS permits was progressively increased over the years, but, even by the early 1980s, they accounted for only around 5 per cent of total intra-EC road haulage (Whitelegg 1988). The slow rate of liberalizing the EC road-haulage market was severely criticized in the 1985 Judgement of the European Court of Justice (ECJ). Since then the process has been considerably accelerated.
   • According to Regulation 1841/88, all quantitative restrictions on inter-Member

State road-haulage operations, for hire and reward, were to be terminated by the end of 1992. This was later confirmed in Regulation 881/92. In the intervening period, the number of CQS permits issued was to be substantially increased each year. As from 1 January 1993, all Member State hauliers may engage in inter-Member State haulage activities provided they have the appropriate authorization. This is granted automatically provided certain 'quality' requirements (professional competence, financial probity, etc.) are met. There is, however, provision for a surveillance system (Regulation 3916/90), which would, in the event of chronic over-supply, enable the Commission to intervene.

- The removal of cabotage restrictions has been more recent. In 1990 a limited number of EC cabotage permits were made available. According to an agreement reached in 1993, cabotage will be fully liberalized within the EU by July 1998. This will, in effect, allow qualified EU carriers in one Member State to engage (whilst undertaking inter-Member State haulage work) in temporary domestic road-haulage operations in another Member State.

Whilst the overall pace of policy change in the EU haulage market has greatly accelerated, the Commission still has 'unfinished business', additional to the complete liberalization of cabotage. This includes extending the opportunities for 'own-account' operators to engage in 'hire-and-reward' operations between and within Member States, and facilitating road-haulage operations with non-EU countries. Crucially, the differences between Member States in road-user charging systems still need to be addressed.

Road passenger transport

The CTP has, until recently, paid much less attention to road passenger transport operations than it has to road haulage. This is partly because a high proportion of bus and coach travel is of a local or regional nature, which, except in order areas, does not pass from one Member State to another.

The bus and coach market has experienced considerable competition from increased car-ownership. Typically, it has been highly regulated, particularly for local services (Tyson 1991), although in the UK there has been a considerable degree of deregulation through, for example, the Transport Acts of 1980 and 1985 (Gwilliam 1989). Again, typically, local passenger transport undertakings have been expected to meet a range of 'public-service' obligations, rather than simply act commercially. As a consequence they have often required subsidization on a considerable scale (see Table 8.2).

The inter-Member State market is of a somewhat different character, since it contains a significant proportion of tourist and scheduled long-distance coach services. Here, also, few significant policy changes have been implemented until very recently.

Since the mid-1980s the main thrust of policy has been to liberalize the coach mar-

Norman Lee

Table 8.2. Cost recovery rates of selected
urban public transport systems, 1985
and 1993 (% of operating costs recovered from fares)

City	1985	1993
Amsterdam	25	25
Athens	21	27
Copenhagen	54	52
Dublin	80	96
Frankfurt	44	45
Helsinki	44	44
Lisbon	70	62
London[a]	57	79
Madrid	68	75
Paris	36	33
Rome	16	10

[a] After depreciation costs are also taken into account.

Source: CEC (1996a).

ket, though it was never regulated to the degree existing in local transport markets. Regulation 684/92 removed the requirement for authorizations for certain inter-Member State coach services (principally, package-holiday tourist services). Authorizations were still required for other types of services, but the grounds on which these could be refused were curtailed. Additionally, Regulation 2454/92 made provision for a limited form of cabotage to be practised by international coach operators and the scope of its application is being extended in 1996. These two measures increase the freedom to operate between Member States and, on a temporary basis, within the domestic market of another Member State, but stop well short of full, immediate liberalization.

The Commission has recently signalled its increasing interest in policy relating to all forms of public passenger transport through the publication of its consultative document on *The Citizens Network* (CEC 1996a). This envisages the promotion of integrated public passenger transport systems through, *inter alia*, tendering concessions which increase the opportunities for competition within passenger transport markets. However, they stop short of complete deregulation and envisage some measure of financial support to 'safeguard fulfilment of public service requirements' (para. 89).

8.6. **Rail and inland waterway transport**

Rail transport

As Figs. 8.1 and 8.2 show, in 1970–90 railways accounted for a significant but declining share of EC freight and passenger transport markets. Rail systems have been predominantly in public ownership and expected to shoulder a wide range of 'public-service' obligations which have been a major source of their unprofitability. Typically, Member State rail systems have made operating financial losses (though to varying degrees) and have been dependent on substantial state aids (Whitelegg 1988; CEC 1995b).

One of the principal objectives of the CTP, since its inception, has been to enable the railway systems to compete more effectively with other modes of transport, particularly in the freight market. With this in mind, efforts have been made to:

- eliminate distortions of competition which arose from state intervention in railway operations; and

- achieve better transparency of state financial contributions to railway undertakings (Erdmenger 1983). An intermediate aim was to segregate the public-service element from the commercial-service element and to reflect this in the system of railway accounting and state subsidization that was adopted. A series of Regulations was passed to this end in the late 1960s and early 1970s (1191/69, 1192/69, 1107/70). This was reinforced by a Council Decision in 1975 that railway management should become more independent of state governments and develop more effective business and financial planning.

Despite these measures, progress in their practical implementation has been slow, because of resistance from the Member States. The situation at the beginning of the 1990s was described in the following terms:

The practical application of these principles has left something to be desired. The public service obligations, with the characteristics specific to each individual country, have been changed very little or not at all and the public service charges are, in most countries, still not identifiably shown in the accounts of the companies; and the system of state aids which eliminates the financial imbalances of the railways is still not entirely clear and has yet to be resolved. (DG for Research 1991: 14)

However, in 1989 the Commission issued a new set of proposals relating to the future development of rail services within the single market (CEC 1990). These addressed a number of long-standing issues and contained a mixture of familiar and new suggestions whose purpose was to strengthen the management of the railway systems by increasing the degree of their independence from the state. *Inter alia*, it proposed:

- separating, into two distinct units, the management of the rail infrastructure (e.g. track and signalling systems) from the management of the rail services operating on that infrastructure;

- operating railway services according to commercial criteria, with the state becoming 'a mere customer of railway companies [which] would have to pay for the services required in order to meet public needs, in a proper, open and fair manner' (DG for Research 1991: 15);

- free access to the use of all rail systems within the EC by international groupings operating rail services between Member States; and

- responsibility for the provision of the rail infrastructure remaining with the Member State, which would have a choice between retaining it in the public sector or privatizing its management and investment. However, whichever was adopted, there should be a clear separation of the accounts and management between the provision of infrastructure and rail-service operations.

These proposals were broadly agreed and then incorporated into Directive 91/440/EEC. Subsequently, in 1995, the Commission reported on the progress made in its implementation (CEC 1995b). It indicated that implementation was incomplete in many Member States in each of the main areas it covered—i.e. in giving railway systems legal independence and managerial autonomy, in separating infrastructure management from operations, in securing access rights to use of the infrastructure, and in strengthening the financial situation. On the last of these, the Commission reported 'the financial situation has not generally improved since 1991 . . . Many railways appear to have experienced a cycle of new development programmes, increased loans, higher financial charges to service the loans and, in due course, greater deficits' (p. 5). This situation has led the Commission to propose further measures to assist in achieving the 1991 Directive's objectives (CEC 1995b).

Additionally, within the framework of an EC investment programme in transport infrastructures, the Council of Ministers agreed, in 1990, to provide some financial assistance for the development of a European high-speed rail network (Regulation 3359/90). Provision was also made for measures to develop a combined transport network (i.e. to facilitate trans-shipment of freight between transport modes, such as road to rail). Further, as part of the EC's regional policy (see Chapter 7), assistance was provided for investments in rail and other transport infrastructures in the poorer (mainly southern) Member States. Transport infrastructure investment and pricing are reviewed in Section 8.8.

Inland waterways

As previously explained, inland waterways are of limited significance as a means of freight transport in such countries as the UK but are of considerable importance in the

Netherlands, Belgium, and Germany. For these Member States in particular, the Rhine is the backbone of the European inland navigation system. However, the Rhine is also recognized as an international river regime in which certain non-EU members also have navigation rights. This has both complicated and delayed policy actions relating to EU inland waterways as a whole.

Since 1970 and earlier, the share of inland waterways in the EU market has declined and Member State carriers have experienced a prolonged period of overcapacity. By the late 1980s it was urgently necessary for the CTP to address this issue as well as the creation of a single market by 1992.

A programme for the reorganization of inland waterway transport was approved in 1989 (Regulations 1101/89 and 1102/89). It provided for each Member State to establish a dismantling fund to reduce total carrying capacity which was to be mainly financed by vessel owners but with some assistance from EC funds. The programme also provided for some restrictions to be imposed on bringing new vessels into the market.

A number of preparatory measures for the single market were also approved, notably relating to the elimination of border controls. However, a number of other 'single-market' issues requiring attention, were also identified. These included restrictions on captains sailing the waterways of certain Member States because their qualifications were not recognized, certain market-sharing arrangements which restrict competition, the operation of mandatory scales of charges for certain national waterway carriers, and the existence of some restrictions on cabotage (DG for Research 1991). Regulation 3921/91 partially addressed certain of these issues and provided for the removal of cabotage restrictions on inland waterways from the beginning of 1993, but with certain exemptions applying in France and Germany until the beginning of 1995.

The Commission reviewed the overall situation in 1994, and, in 1995, proposed a further liberalization of the inland waterway market (to be fully implemented by the year 2000) and additional measures to reduce overcapacity through scrapping programmes and to encourage investment in inland waterway terminals (CEC 1995c).

8.7. Maritime and air transport

Maritime transport

Around 95 per cent of the tonnage of EU trade with non-EU states and some 30 per cent of intra-EU traffic is carried by sea (Kreis 1992). EU-based shippers have experienced increasing international competition since 1965 at least from non-EU fleets, which have benefited from lower costs partly resulting from their non-EU registration and financial assistance from their own governments. The consequences for EU-based shipping operations have been overcapacity in the industry, a pronounced decline in the shipping tonnage registered under EU Member State flags, as EU shippers switched to 'off-shore' registration, and pressures on Member States to continue and/or extend state aids to shipping and to continue certain restrictive measures to protect 'home' fleets (Brooks and Button 1992). Certain of these pressures potentially conflict with the objective of liberalizing maritime shipping operations within the single market.

As previously explained, maritime shipping was not included in the provisions relating to the CTP within the Treaty of Rome. This, combined with the lesser interest of the original EC members in intra-Community sea transport, helps to explain the limited progress in developing a Community shipping policy until the mid-1970s. However, action was precipitated in 1974 by the finding of the European Court of Justice (ECJ) that the UN Code of Conduct for Liner Conferences, which the Member States were prepared to accept, was in violation of the competition rules of the Treaty of Rome. This was subsequently resolved by granting a block exemption for liner conferences from compliance with these rules provided they met with certain conditions—but the potential conflict between traditional shipping policies (of which restrictive agreements between operators within liner conferences is one example) and the EC's competition policies was apparent.

It was not until 1986 that the Council agreed a package of measures, comprising four regulations (Regulations 4055/86–4058/86), which established the legal foundations of an EC maritime policy. In brief, the package

- established the principle of freedom to provide maritime services, without discrimination, for intra-EC traffic and traffic between Member States and third countries (but not for domestic traffic within a Member State);
- provided for the application of the Treaty of Rome's competition rules to liner shipping, but with a conditional exemption for liner cargo conferences, as described above; and
- provided for measures to be taken to deal with unfair pricing and other practices by non-EC shipowners and third countries (Erdmenger and Stasinopoulos 1988).

However, the flight from registering ships under Member State flags continued, and the Commission became increasingly concerned that differences in fiscal and employment conditions between different flags of registration were distorting competitive conditions within the EC. This led it to propose the establishment of an EC shipping register (EUROS) which aimed to offer some economic attractions to encourage EC-based fleets to register but was also intended to harmonize registration conditions within the EC. However, successive forms of this proposal were not found acceptable (Brooks and Button 1992) and the Commission decided, in 1996, not to proceed with the proposal (CEC 1996b).

Another area of concern has been the role of subsidies, tax exemptions, and other forms of fiscal assistance within the maritime market. State aids of different kinds have for many years been provided by virtually all Member States as well as by third countries (Brooks and Button 1992). The EC's response was to try to encourage a more consistent approach between Member States by issuing guidelines which listed seven categories of aid which are permissible under the Treaty and the detailed criteria to be applied in their calculation. The seven categories covered aids to reduce manning levels, reimbursement of costs of repatriating seafarers, assistance with training costs, special tax treatment of shipping earnings, operating aids, investment aids, and aids through public authority holdings (CEC 1989).

When reviewing the situation in 1996, the Commission acknowledged that consistency in state aid policy within the EU had not been achieved and announced its intention to revise the state aid guidelines.

EC Governments have different national priorities and perceptions of the need and best means to support their shipping industry. Some have vigorously sought to maintain their flag fleets, some have preferred a more laissez-faire approach. . . . These different priorities have determined the structure of support measures given by national governments. They include special fiscal regimes, generous accounting provisions to reduce taxation, aid to bridge the cost gap, capital injections linked with restructuring, and special ship registers. (CEC 1996b: 29)

A long-standing problem has been the continuation of restrictions on cabotage in maritime shipping within the EU. These restrictions were not removed by the First Package of regulations in 1986, and, though their partial removal was proposed in 1989, this was not formally approved until 1992. According to Regulation 3577/92, cabotage rights could be exercised by all EC shipowners registered with EUROS. This was due to come into operation for coastal trade at the beginning of 1993 (or as soon as EUROS was approved by the Council of Ministers) but inter-island and mainland-island cabotage would operate only from 1999 (2004 in the case of Greece).

Another continuing issue has been whether agreements between shipping consortia should comply with EC/EU competition law or, like liner conference agreements, should have a block exemption. The issue is a complex one, both because of the variety of activities in which consortia may engage but also because they may yield some economic benefits in the process of reducing competition between their members. These benefits are discussed in Kreis (1992). Regulation 479/92 permitted, subject to certain safeguards, the exclusion of particular categories of agreements by consortia from the general prohibition of cartels contained in the Treaty and this was later updated by Regulation 870/95.

In summary, whilst some steps have been taken towards the establishment of a single, liberalized market in maritime transport, there are a number of ways in which competition is still restricted and where state aids continue to have a distorting influence on market conditions.

Air transport

Air transport accounts for a small but increasing share of intra-EU traffic. Until the mid-1980s scheduled air-transport services were tightly regulated, although there was greater freedom in the provision of charter-flight services (Van de Voorde 1992). Regulation originally arose as a consequence of nations being granted sovereignty over their own airspace at the Chicago conference of 1944. The exercise of this sovereignty led to a form of regulation comprising the following elements:

- Each state had its own flag-carrying airline, which was usually in public ownership. It was often expected to serve some non-commercial objectives, as part of its general remit, and was accustomed to receive state aids to assist in this.
- States made bilateral agreements with each other about landing rights and flight routes between their two countries. Typically, scheduled services were shared on a 50 : 50 basis between the two flag carriers. In this way, capacity was controlled and arrangements for revenue-sharing made.
- Negotiations about fares were held within the framework of the International Air Transport Association (IATA). However, government approval was needed once these fares had been negotiated (Button 1992).

Though this regulatory system had certain attractions to Member State governments, it was also seen to have some undesirable features (Van de Voorde 1992), for example:

- fare levels were likely to be higher than in a more competitive market environment;
- cost levels were likely to be higher (because of lower productive efficiency and higher 'rental' payments to factors of production) than would otherwise have been the case; and
- consumer choice was more limited, and the absence of price competition led to an over-stimulus of quality of service competition (e.g. 'in-flight' refreshments).

These matters received little attention from the EC until the ECJ ruling in 1974 that air and maritime transport within the EC was subject to the Treaty of Rome's general rules. Even then, little substantive action was taken until the mid-1980s. This was triggered by a number of developments, including

- the recommendations of the Cockfield Report (CEC 1985) relating to the measures necessary to complete the single market and, more specifically, proposing changes to the system for setting and approving tariffs, and limiting the rights of governments to restrict capacity and access to the market;
- the ECJ ruling in the *Nouvelles Frontières* case (1986), which stimulated investigation of the application of the Treaty's competition rules to the aviation sector; and
- growing international interest in the deregulation of air transport, in part stimulated by deregulation experience in the USA (McGowan and Seabright 1989; Doganis 1991).

This led to the first Liberalization Package for air transport, approved in December 1987.

First Package (1987). The Package consisted of two Council Decisions (601/87 and 602/87) and two regulations which came into force on 1 January 1988 (Vincent and Stasinopoulos 1990). It applied only to scheduled services between Member States and contained some block exemptions, for certain traffic categories, until 1991. However, it did provide for

- greater fares flexibility, by making provision for discount fares;
- greater capacity flexibility by allowing limited variations in the 50 : 50 traffic sharing rule; and
- some easing of market access.

Its overall impact was fairly limited because some of these changes had already been incorporated into earlier bilateral agreements. Its main significance, according to Stasinopoulos (1992), was that it set up a mechanism through which gradual liberalization could be realized.

Second Package (1990). A further package of measures (Regulations 82/91–84/91) was agreed in June 1990 (Stasinopoulos 1992). This provided for more extensive fares-discounting, greater variations in the 50 : 50 rule, and greater market access, including some limited provision for cabotage. Block exemptions were to continue to January 1993, but it was envisaged that full liberalization would be achieved by that date.

Third Package (1992). This package of measures comprised three regulations (2407/92–2409/92), covering scheduled, non-scheduled, and cargo services, and came into force on 1 January 1993 (CEC 1993; Stasinopoulos 1993; Aviation Group 1995). It made the following provisions:

- Any carrier satisfying safety, financial fitness, and EU nationality tests is entitled to an EU operator's licence.
- Virtually all intra-EU air routes are open to recognized EU operators. Cabotage restrictions are further reduced, with full cabotage rights being established by April 1997 (but with a delay of ten years in the case of the Greek Islands and the Azores).
- Airlines are free to determine their own scheduled passenger fares, subject to certain safeguards. All restrictions on charter fares are removed and cargo rates continue to be unregulated.

Regulations were also approved, in 1992 and 1993, and brought into force relating to competition rules, block exemptions, and allocation of slots at EU airports.

The extent to which the EU's aviation market has been liberalized since 1987 has been substantial. The pace of change has almost certainly been greater than in any other sector of the transport market, yet:

- certain exemptions still apply and their effects (e.g. in the allocation of landing/take-off slots) are difficult to gauge;

- cabotage restrictions are not due to be fully removed for a few years;
- state aids continue; and
- as experience elsewhere has shown (Kahn 1988; Doganis 1991), not all of the outcomes of a deregulated air-transport market may be desirable. In particular, the effects of mergers between airline operators, stimulated by deregulation, are uncertain (Van de Voorde 1992).

8.8. Transport infrastructure

Each of the transport modes reviewed makes use of a different form of transport infrastructure—the road system, railway track and signalling system, waterways, ports, and/or airports. Transport policy has to consider in each case:

- how to make best use of *existing* infrastructure facilities, and the role of user charges in achieving this (*infrastructure pricing*); and
- how best to develop *future* infrastructure facilities (*infrastructure investment*).

The problems which exist in these two areas, and the attempts to address these through EU-level transport policy, are reviewed below.

Infrastructure pricing

The charging systems which exist for the use of transport infrastructures vary considerably. Users pay tolls on some roads in certain Member States (e.g. France and Italy) but, more generally, pay road-user taxes (e.g. annual vehicle licence and fuel duties). Airlines pay landing charges for the use of airports and shippers pay berthing charges for port facilities. Railway undertakings have typically owned the rail track and not paid separately for its use (although, as mentioned in Section 8.6, this situation is changing in some Member States).

The principles upon which charges schemes have been based are also highly variable. In some cases, commercial criteria ('what the market will bear') apply; in others, the objective is cost recovery (in some cases, after deduction of any state aids received); in other cases (e.g. certain road-user tax systems), the level of charges depends upon the general fiscal requirements of the government.

From at least the mid-1960s, the Commission has been concerned about the distortions to competition which could result from different approaches to infrastructure pricing in the Member States (Whitelegg 1988). In 1971 it proposed the introduction of a system of infrastructure pricing for all inland transport modes, based on the MSCs of using the infrastructure. However, it was not implemented and only limited progress has been made in achieving this subsequently, as illustrated below in the case of road-user pricing.

The first task, in applying the MSC pricing principle to road use, is to estimate the marginal social costs incurred by the main categories of road user. The UK probably has the greatest experience in attempting to calculate these costs, which are published annually (see e.g. DoT 1993a). However, these calculations do not cover all cost items (notably they exclude road congestion and environmental costs), and the methods used to calculate certain cost items that are included have been criticized (DoT 1993b: annex A). Fowkes, Nash, and Tweddle (1992) have suggested that UK road cost estimates might need to be increased, on average, by 50 per cent to cover the excluded cost items.

Fowkes, Nash, and Tweddle (1992) also compared the annual road-track costs of a 'reference' vehicle (38 tonnes gross weight averaging 74,000 kilometres per year), as estimated by the Department of Transport in the mid-1980s, with the total road-user taxes (from licence and fuel duties) that would have been paid in a number of different European countries (see Table 8.3). Assuming the road-track costs for the reference vehicle were broadly similar in all of these countries, it would seem that, in all of them, heavy lorries were charged less than their MSCs, and in certain countries (e.g. Italy, Netherlands) charges were substantially below these MSCs. The inclusion of tolls revenue in the calculations would not substantially alter the conclusion.

The movement to establish the SEM by the end of 1992 provided a new impetus to harmonize excise and other duties relating to vehicle use. Two Council Directives (92/81 and 92/82) provided for the adoption, by the beginning of 1993, of common minimum rates of excise duty on petrol and diesel oil in all Member States. However, they also permitted a number of important delays and exemptions in their application. Table 8.4 shows that, by 1993, there were still considerable differences in the levels of the major road-user charges, particularly in the case of annual vehicle licence duties.

An additional problem, in the case of inter-Member State road transport, is that the

Table 8.3. **Highway revenue/cost ratios for selected EC countries, mid–1980s**

Member State	Fuel and annual licence duty revenues as % of highway costs (excluding externalities)
Denmark	41
Germany	96
France	60
Italy	27
Netherlands	38
UK	119

Source: Fowkes, Nash, and Tweddle (1992).

229

Table 8.4. **Variations in road-user charges between Member States, 1993**

Type of charge	Lowest charge	Highest charge
Four-star petrol duty (pence per litre)	32 (Luxembourg)	52 (Netherlands)
Diesel duty (pence per litre)	20 (Luxembourg)	34 (Italy)
Annual car licence duty or equivalent (£)	15 (Spain)	270 (Denmark)
Annual heavy goods vehicle (38t.) licence duty (£)	318 (Greece)	3,900 (Germany)

Source: DoT 1993b.

revenue from road-user charges does not necessarily accrue to the Member State which incurs the road-track costs. Various devices have been proposed to satisfy the so-called 'territoriality' principle, including the transfer of payments between Member States to settle any net imbalances (Crowley 1992).

For its part, the Commission has indicated the importance it attaches to the development of an overall EU framework for charging users according to the infrastructure costs and externalities they incur (CEC 1995c). However, because of the complexities involved, this is likely to be attempted in phases—developing a satisfactory costing system for allocating capital and maintenance costs to main user groups, reviewing and revising taxes and charges on heavy goods vehicles, and later devising satisfactory systems for reflecting infrastructure costs and externalities in charges systems for the different modes of transport. The Commission concludes:

The evidence . . . suggests that in transport—as a general rule—the relation between prices and costs is weak at the level of individual transport users. Some costs—related to infrastructure, environmental pollution, noise, accidents and congestion—are only partly covered or not at all. Some transport users seem to pay too much, others too little. The situation is both unfair and inefficient. (CEC 1995d: 49)

Infrastructure investment

Community-level investment in transport infrastructure did not become a CTP issue until the late 1970s (Whitelegg 1988). Once it did, the extent to which EC-level institutions should become involved in transport investment planning, financing, and decision-making become a subject of some debate.

The main reasons advanced for Community-level involvement were

- the absence of adequate interconnections between national transport networks because of missing links, bottlenecks, and technical incompatibilities between systems; and
- unbalanced economic development within the EC, because of previous under-investment in transport infrastructure in the (mainly) peripheral regions.

The policy goal continues to be 'the integration of the Community's transport system through the completion and combination of its networks, taking particular account of the needs of its more geographically isolated regions' (CEC 1993: para. 140). The first type of deficiency is being mainly addressed through the CTP itself and is examined immediately below; the second is being mainly tackled through the EU's regional policy (see Chapter 7) and is briefly discussed at the end of this section.

The first deficiency is essentially due to a 'market-failure' problem. The economic case for EU-level intervention is that it may be able to assist by taking account of cross-border spillovers of costs and benefits and through access to the geographically, broader-based information needed for infrastructure planning and investment appraisal. Whether this necessitates EU-level involvement in decision-making and the financing of new transport infrastructures, or engaging in a more limited role in facilitating transport planning by the Member States themselves, remains an unresolved issue.

In 1979 the Commission outlined its overall transport infrastructure policy, stating that 'the CTP will not achieve the objectives defined for it in the Treaty and play its part in the economy as a whole unless it relates more and more to transport infrastructure' (CEC 1979). It defined the types of investment that it considered necessary and later provided lists of projects that it believed met these criteria. However, the Council of Ministers agreed to allocate only relatively small amounts of investment finance for this purpose. In 1986 the Commission published its medium-term transport infrastructure policy, which restated its earlier objectives but added support for 'the general Community objective of completing the internal market and strengthening its economic and social cohesion' (Crowley 1992). It also proposed support for the construction of links in a European high-speed rail network (see Section 8.6 for further details). However, the Council was reluctant to accept this policy statement or a five-year plan identifying infrastructure programmes that might be financed by the EC. As a result, prior to 1990, financial support for such measures was largely provided, on a case-by-case basis, by the EP (DG for Research 1991).

In 1990, the Council approved some modest proposals for financing certain transport infrastructure schemes between 1990 and 1992 (Regulation 3359/90). Similar kinds of provisions were subsequently made for 1993 and 1994. However, the situation changed once the TEU (1992) came into force, since it made explicit provision for 'the development of trans-European networks in the area of transport, telecommunications and energy'. To this end, it required the establishment of guidelines 'covering the objectives, priorities and broad lines of measures envisaged in the sphere of trans-European networks [TENS]' and made provision for EU financial support of projects of common interest on those networks.

The TENS Financial Regulation was adopted in 1995 (Regulation 2236/95), whilst a Decision on the Community Guidelines for the Development of the trans-European network was due to be reached during 1996. These should identify, on a series of maps, the transport projects (mainly, but not exclusively, rail projects) eligible for financial assistance. The annual EU funding of TENS is planned to grow from less than Ecu 200 million in the early 1990s to nearly Ecu 500 million by the turn of the century (CEC 1995*a*).

Additional to the above arrangements within the framework of the CTP, there has been much more substantial EU-level financial assistance for investments in transport infrastructure in the Member States through the Structural Funds (especially the ERDF). According to Commission estimates in 1993, since 1975 approximately Ecu 16,000 million had been invested in transport infrastructures through the ERDF. Additionally, the European Investment Bank (EIB) loaned approximately Ecu 14,000 million for financing transport infrastructures between 1982 and 1991, whilst the ECSC has contributed a further Ecu 1,200 million approximately since 1987 (CEC 1992: para. 137). Financial support for these types of transport infrastructure investments continues to be provided through the Cohesion and Regional Development Funds.

8.9. Overall evaluation

The progress made in implementing a CTP within the EC was very limited during the first thirty years of its existence. The measures that were introduced largely related to particular aspects of harmonization and reduction in discriminatory practices in the provision of transport services between Member States. Community-level investments in transport infrastructures were mainly undertaken as part of regional, rather than transport, policy. Little progress was made in realizing the kinds of efficiency and equity objectives specified in Section 8.4.

Since the mid-1980s the pace of change in policy formation and implementation has accelerated and its focus has changed, placing greater emphasis on liberalization than harmonization (CEC 1993). This was initially stimulated by the ECJ judgment in 1985, which criticized the lack of progress with the CTP, and by the political drive to establish a single European market.

The principal measures which have been brought into force since the mid-1980s, in each of the main transport sectors, have been reviewed in the preceding sections of this chapter. Given the relatively short time period over which they have been introduced, the aggregate level of activity has been substantial—especially in such sectors as air transport and road haulage. However, in evaluating their likely effects, it is important to note that:

- a significant proportion of these measures has been brought into force only since 1990;
- in a number of cases, they provide for exemptions and/or delayed application until later in the decade;

- their practical effects depend to a large degree on the speed and extent of their implementation by the individual Member States. In the past, examples of delayed and/or incomplete compliance have been quite common; and

- not all of the measures that were envisaged have yet been agreed—there is still some 'unfinished business' (CEC 1993; 1995a).

The Emerson Report concluded that the economic benefits of transport liberalization could be substantial. For example, it indicated that the removal of regulatory restrictions in the road-haulage and air-transport markets could cause road-haulage and air-transport costs and prices within the single market to fall by 5 and 10 per cent respectively (CEC 1988). It also suggested that there could be significant transport-cost savings through the simplification and/or removal of customs procedures. However, it is still too early to assess the actual scale of the economic effects of the measures that have been implemented, although some initial evaluations have been undertaken (e.g. Bayliss and Millington 1995).

There are, however, a number of issues which remain unresolved and need to be addressed in any future development of the CTP:

- The liberalization of the single market will not establish a perfectly competitive, or perfectly contestable, market. Therefore, it will be necessary to continue to address those types of transport problems which can occur in liberalized imperfect markets, such as arise from increased merger activity (e.g. among airlines) or the neglect of environmental externalities.

- Public-service obligations (i.e. commitments to non-commercial objectives, such as certain equity objectives) will remain. Cost-effective means of achieving these within liberalized markets will have to be devised, and existing systems of state aid for transport services will need to be restructured in the light of these.

- Given the differences in transport arrangements between Member States, some conflicts of interest will continue. More effective ways of resolving these will need to be found whilst, at the same time, respecting the subsidiarity principle.

- So far, the main focus of the CTP has been on inter-Member State transport policy. In the future it will be necessary to clarify its relationship to the regulatory systems for intra (domestic) Member State transport and, particularly, for transport with non-EU countries. 'Member States continue to maintain a network of traditional, reciprocity-based transport agreements with third countries. This situation implies continued existence of discriminations along nationality lines creating potentially considerable distorting effects' (CEC 1995a: 6).

- In the light of each of the above, the role of EU transport policy in planning and financing investments in the EU transport infrastructure will also have to be more clearly defined.

In summary, the significant increase in EU transport-policy activities, since the mid-1980s, has not dealt with all of the deficiencies that previously existed. Careful evaluation of the economic consequences of those measures that have been introduced, and of the deficiencies that remain, should be used to guide the future development of the CTP.

Discussion questions

1. Explain why the pace of change in the Common Transport Policy was much slower prior to the mid-1980s than it has been subsequently.

2. What have been the main economic consequences which have resulted from the harmonization measures within the Common Transport Policy? To what extent are such measures consistent with the achievement of efficiency and equity objectives?

3. What are the main problems which remain to be addressed through a Common Transport Policy, and by what means should their solution be sought?

FURTHER READING

Comparative data on trends within the EU and Member State transport sectors can be found in Eurostat (annual) *Europe in Figures*. The early history of the CTP is reviewed in Erdmenger (1983). More recent and prospective policy developments are covered in CEC 1995*a* (general), 1995*b* (railways), 1995*d* (transport pricing), 1996*c* (public passenger transport), and Aviation Group 1995 (air transport). The *Journal of Transport Economics and Policy* also contains periodic reviews and evaluations of recent EU transport policy developments (e.g. Bayliss and Millington 1995).

REFERENCES

Aviation Group (1995), *EC Aviation Liberalisation Information Pack* (London: Aviation Group, Department of Transport).

Bayliss, B.T. and Millington, A.I. (1995), 'De-regulation and Logistics Systems in a Single European Market', *Journal of Transport Economics and Policy* 29/3: 305–16.

Baumol, W. J. (1982), 'Contestable Markets: An Uprising in the Theory of Industry Structure', *American Economic Review*, 72/1: 1–15.

Brooks, M. R., and Button, K. J. (1992), 'Shipping within the Framework of a Single European Market', *Transport Reviews*, 12/3: 237–51.

Button, K. J. (1984), *Road Haulage Licensing and EC Transport Policy* (Aldershot: Gower).

—— (1992), 'The Liberalisation of Transport Services', in D. Swann (ed.), *The Single European Market and Beyond* (London: Routledge), 146–61.

—— and Pitfield, D. (1991) (eds.), *Transport De-regulation: An International Movement* (London: Macmillan).

Clark, J. M. (1940), 'Towards a Concept of Workable Competition', *American Economic Review*, 30: 241–56.

CEC (1979): Commission of the European Communities, *A Transport Network for Europe: Outline of a Policy* (Brussels: CEC).

—— (1985), *Completing the Internal Market*, COM (85) 310 final (Brussels: CEC).

—— (1988), 'The Economics of 1992: An Assessment of the Potential Economical Effects of Completing the Internal Market of the European Community' (the Emerson Report), *European Economy*, 35 (Mar.).

—— (1989), *Financial and Fiscal Measures Concerning Shipping Operations with Ships Registered in the Community*, SEC (89) 921 (Brussels: CEC).

—— (1990), *Communication on a Community Railway Policy*, COM (89) 564 (Brussels: CEC).

—— (1991), *Council Directive of 29 July 1991 on the Development of the Community's Railways* (91/440/EEC), *Official Journal of the European Communities*, L237/25 (24 Aug.).

—— (1992), *The Future Development of the Common Transport Policy* (Brussels: CEC).

—— (1993), *A Common Market for Services: Current Status 1 January 1993* (Brussels: CEC).

—— (1995*a*), *The Common Transport Policy Action Programme 1995– 2000*, COM (95) 302 (Brussels: CEC).

—— (1995*b*), *Communication from the Commission on the Development of the Community's Railways*, COM (95) 337 (Brussels: CEC).

—— (1995*c*), *Communication on a Common Policy on the Organisation of the Inland Waterway Market and other Supporting Measures*, COM (95) 199 (Brussels: CEC).

—— (1995*d*), *Towards Fair and Efficient Pricing in Transport*, COM (95) 691 (Brussels: CEC).

—— (1996*a*), *The Citizen's Network: Fulfilling the Potential of Public Passenger Transport in Europe* (Luxembourg: Office for Official Publications).

—— (1996*b*), *Towards a New Maritime Strategy*, COM (96) 81 (Brussels: CEC).

Council of the European Communities (1990), Council Regulation 3359/90/EEC for an *Action Programme in the Field of Transport Infrastructure with a view to the Completion of an Integrated Transport Market in 1992* (Brussels).

Crowley, J. A. (1992), 'Inland Transport in the European Community following 1992', *Antitrust Bulletin*, 37/1: 453–80.

Despicht, N. (1969), *The Transport Policy of the European Communities* (European Series, No. 12 (PEP); London: Chatham House).

DG for Research (1991): Directorate-General for Research, *The Judgement of the Court of Justice of the European Communities in Case 13/83 and the Development of the Common Transport Policy* (Regional Policy and Transport Series 21; Luxembourg: CEC).

Doganis, R. (1991), *Flying Off Course: The Economics of International Airlines* (London: Harper Collins Academic).

DoT (1991): Department of Transport, *International Comparisons of Transport Statistics 1970–88* (London: HMSO).

—— (1993*a*), 'The Allocation of Road Track Costs', *Statistical Bulletin*, 3/31 (London: DoT).

—— (1993*b*), *Paying for Better Motorways* (London: HMSO).

Erdmenger, J. (1983), *The European Community Transport Policy—Towards a Common Transport Policy* (Aldershot: Gower).

—— and Stasinopoulos, D. (1988), 'The Shipping Policy of the European Community', *Journal of Transport Economics and Policy*, 22/3: 355–60.

Eurostat (annual), *Europe in Figures* (Luxembourg: CEC).

Fowkes, A. S., Nash, C. A., and Tweddle, G. (1992), 'Harmonizing Heavy Goods Vehicle Taxes in Europe: A British View', *Transport Reviews*, 12/3: 199–217.

Gwilliam, K. M. (1989), 'Setting the Market Free—Deregulation of the Bus Industry', *Journal of Transport Economics and Policy*, 23/1: 29–43.

Kahn, A. E. (1988), 'Surprises of Airline Deregulation, *American Economic Review*, Papers and Proceedings, 78: 316–22.

Kreis, H. W. R. (1992), 'EC Competition Law and Maritime Transport', *Antitrust Bulletin*, 37/1 (Summer), 481–505.

Laidler, D., and Estrin, S. (1989), *An Introduction to Microeconomics*, 3rd edn. (Deddington: Philip Allan).

Lee, N. (1992), 'Transport Policy', in S. Bulmer, S. George, and A. Scott (eds.), *The United Kingdom and EC Membership Evaluated* (London: Pinter), 83–8.

Lipsey, R., and Lancaster, K. (1956), 'The General Theory of Second Best', *Review of Economic Studies*, 24: 11–32.

McGowan, F., and Seabright, P. (1989), 'Deregulating European Airlines', *Economic Policy*, 9 Oct. 283–344.

Stasinopoulos, D. (1992), 'The Second Aviation Package of the European Community', *Journal of Transport Economics and Policy*, 26/1: 83–7.

Stasinopoulos, D. (1993), 'The Third Phase of Liberalization in Community Aviation and the Need for Supplementary Measures', *Journal of Transport Economics and Policy*, 27/3: 323–7.

Tyson, W. J. (1991), 'Analysis of the Organisation of Local Public Transport in the European Community', in International Union of Public Transport, *Public Service and Competition* (Brussels: UITP).

Van de Voorde, E. E. (1992), 'European Air Transport after 1992: De-regulation or Re-regulation?', *Antitrust Bulletin*, 37/1: 507–28.

Vincent, D., and Stasinopoulos, D. (1990), 'The Aviation Policy of the European Community', *Journal of Transport Economics and Policy*, 24/1: 95–100.

Whitelegg, J. (1988), *Transport Policy in the EEC* (London: Routledge).

CHAPTER 9

Environmental Policy

NORMAN LEE

9.1. Introduction

Environmental problems have traditionally been viewed as unwanted side effects of economic activities which should be controlled by a range of regulatory measures. A less widely held view is that environmental problems stem from market failures within economies—and, therefore, market-based measures are needed to resolve them. Though the former approach has dominated EU and Member State environmental policies so far, the balance of view is changing.

The next section of this chapter surveys the historical development of EU environmental policy, which has enlarged in scope and changed its emphasis over the years—from a reactive to a more anticipatory approach and from reliance on control and command (regulatory) instruments towards greater use of economic (market-based) measures. The following three sections (9.3–9.5) examine the essentially economic nature of environmental problems within the EU and the logical case for using economic instruments to help in dealing with them. They also identify the weaknesses inherent in both regulatory and economic instruments, as practical tools of environmental policy, and the need to use different types of instruments in a complementary manner. Section 9.6 contains a review and evaluation of the practical use made of economic instruments within the European Union (EU) and some other member countries of the Organization for Economic Cooperation and Development (OECD), which further demonstrates their particular strengths and limitations. Section 9.7 reviews a proposal for an EU energy/carbon tax to help in reducing the risks of global warming. Section 9.8 analyses the attempts that have been made to assess, in economic terms, the benefits and costs of environmental policies and their likely consequential effects on Member States within the EU. The chapter concludes, in Section 9.9, with a review of possible future developments in EU environmental policy.

9.2. **Evolution of EU environmental policy**

The Treaty of Rome (1957), which led to the establishment of the European Community (EC), contained no reference to environmental protection. Indeed, it was only through the enactment of the Single European Act (SEA) (1987) that the EC explicitly adopted environmental objectives, namely:

   (i) to preserve, protect and improve the quality of the environment;
   (ii) to contribute towards protecting human health;
   (iii) to ensure a prudent and rational utilization of natural resources.

(Article 130R)

More recently, the Treaty on European Union (TEU) (1992) extended the environmental-policy objectives of the EU to include the goals of 'sustainable and non-inflationary growth respecting the environment' (Article 2) and of promoting measures to help resolve global environmental problems (Article 130R).

Despite the absence of an explicit legal basis, the Heads of the Member States, meeting shortly after the UN Stockholm Conference on the Environment in 1972, invited the European Commission to prepare the first Environmental Action Programme. To date, the Commission has prepared five Action Programmes for approval by the Council of Ministers (1973–6, 1977–81, 1982–6, 1987–92, 1993–2000 (with a review in 1995)).

These Programmes contain the environmental-policy intentions of the Commission and the Council of Ministers. To varying degrees, and often after a considerable period of negotiation with Member State governments, these result in Council Decisions in the form of regulations, directives, recommendations, and non-binding opinions. In turn, after a further interval and to varying degrees, these are transposed into Member States' laws and practice. The delayed and incomplete implementation of EU-level actions is, in effect, one of the important mechanisms by which EU-level and individual Member State interests are reconciled. Such mechanisms need to be taken into consideration when assessing the actual costs and benefits to individual Member States which result from EU-level actions.

Since the preparation of the first 1995 Environmental Action Programme, the EC/EU had approved, by the end of 1995, over 200 legally binding acts as well as a considerable number of non-binding measures relating to the protection of the environment (CEC 1992a; CEC 1996a). These related, *inter alia*, to:

- water quality: the quality of drinking water, surface waters in rivers and the sea, bathing waters, ground waters, and discharges of pollutants into water;
- air quality: the concentration of pollutants in the atmosphere and emissions from stationary and mobile (transport) sources of pollution;
- wastes: the collection, treatment, and disposal of solid and semi-solid wastes;
- chemicals and other dangerous substances: the testing, marketing, and use of

dangerous substances, and the regulation of major accident hazards and of chloro-fluorocarbons (CFCs);

- noise: maximum noise levels from stationary and mobile sources;
- wildlife and countryside protection: the protection of wildlife, their habitats, and environmentally sensitive areas, and the regulation of trade in endangered species; and
- the 'polluter-pays' principle: originally formulated as an EC Recommendation in 1975 (and based on an earlier OECD Recommendation of 1972). It establishes the general principle, subject to certain possible exemptions, that polluters should pay for the full costs of their pollution.

These actions have taken place within a policy framework which has changed in emphasis over time, as the EU's approach to environmental policy has itself developed. In the early 1970s its policies primarily emphasized the need for corrective measures to 'clean up' specific pollution problems through the use of regulatory instruments. By contrast, its latest action programme, whilst not abandoning the more traditional types of corrective measures, gives a new emphasis to

- anticipatory measures (i.e. planning and related actions designed to prevent new environmental problems being created, e.g. environmental assessment of new development projects; testing, before use, of new chemicals; etc.);
- multi-media measures (which recognize that pollution problems in one environmental medium cannot be satisfactorily resolved, in many cases, without considering possible repercussions on other environmental media);
- integrative measures (the integration of environmental-protection measures into the policies and programmes of development for the main economic sectors);
- sustainable development measures (the complementary use of resource-conservation and pollution-control measures to promote sustainable development both within the EU and in other parts of the world); and
- market-based measures (i.e. financial/economic instruments to encourage environmental costs being fully taken into account in all decisions relating to the allocation and use of resources).

The most recent (Fifth) Action Programme, which covers the period 1992–2000, emphasizes the long-term objective of sustainable development (CEC 1992a). It states that the main environmental policy issues facing the EU—of climate change, acidification and air pollution, depletion of natural resources and biodiversity, pollution of water resources, deterioration of the urban environment and coastal zones—are themselves symptoms of more fundamental resource-management problems. To address these, the Commission proposes to broaden the range of policy instruments which are applied. In particular, it recommends the greater use of *market-based* instruments 'designed to sensitise both producers and consumers towards responsible use of natural resources [and] avoidance of pollution and waste by internalising of external costs' (CEC 1992*a*: 8).

Thus, the intention is to integrate environmental policy considerations into the future development and operation of those sectors (notably industry, energy, transport, agriculture, and tourism) which are considered to be the main contributors to current environmental problems, and, at EU level, into those of its own policies and programmes (relating to agriculture and fisheries, energy and transport, regional development and overseas aid, etc.) which, in the past, may themselves have been environmentally damaging on a considerable scale.

The progress made in implementing the Fifth Action Programme was reviewed, in 1995, by the Commission, which also proposed a set of further actions for implementation by the year 2000 (CEC 1996*a*, 1996*b*). These matters are examined further in subsequent sections of the chapter.

9.3. Linkages between environmental and economic systems

Environmental problems are essentially economic in nature. Therefore, not surprisingly, economic-policy instruments have a role to play in their resolution. The purpose of this and the following two sections is to explore the economic nature of environmental problems and the theoretical justification for using economic instruments, as well as regulatory instruments, to deal with these.

Environmental and economic systems are inextricably linked (see Fig. 9.1). Production entails the *abstraction* of natural resources (water, minerals, forest products, etc.), which, depending upon the rate of abstraction, renewability, etc., may result in a resource-conservation problem. Production and consumption involve the

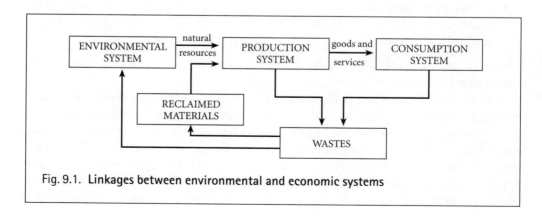

Fig. 9.1. Linkages between environmental and economic systems

transformation and *use* of materials which create wastes (gaseous, aqueous, solid, etc.) which, when returned to the environmental system, may result in an environmental pollution problem.

Other things being equal (notably resource/output and waste/output ratios remaining constant), economic growth results in faster rates of natural-resource depletion and higher levels of waste disposal. On these assumptions, and given limits to the stock of natural resources and the capacity of the environment to assimilate increased wastes, continuing economic growth eventually ceases to be sustainable. In other words, the environmental system is no longer able to sustain the levels and quality of production and consumption which have previously been achieved within the economic system.

This type of reasoning underlines the approach of the 'limits-to-growth' school which was presented in the late 1960s and, in a modified form, more recently (Meadows *et al.* 1970; Meadows, Meadows, and Randers 1992). It was used to suggest that there was an inherent conflict between economic growth and the maintenance of environmental quality—hence the arguments in favouring of 'limiting growth'.

However, in market systems, these simplifying assumptions rarely hold, and the resulting relationships between economic growth and environmental quality are more complex than the above analysis implies (Pearce, Markandya, and Barbier 1989; Pearce and Warford 1993). Under certain circumstances, especially where markets work efficiently, a number of the above effects may be reduced, delayed, or not occur at all. For example:

- The increased scarcity of particular natural resources will lead to increases in their prices. This may encourage greater economy in their use, higher rates of reclamation and re-use, and the development of substitute materials.

- Increased difficulties in finding suitable waste-disposal sites are associated with increased disposal costs. This provides a financial incentive to reduce wastes at source, and to increase waste reclamation and recycling.

- Products which use the scarcest natural resources or cause the greatest waste-disposal problems become relatively more expensive, causing production and consumption patterns to alter in favour of more 'environmentally friendly' activities.

However, in practice, the conditions necessary for markets to work efficiently may not apply. For example:

- The prices charged for the use of natural resources should fully reflect their social opportunity costs. Yet, in practice, prices may be substantially below these levels because of price regulation (e.g. for the use of water), neglect of long-term social opportunity costs (e.g. costs of forest clearance to future generations), or the absence of markets (e.g. for nature reserves or natural landscapes).

- The costs of environmental pollution should be fully borne by those responsible (i.e. the producers or consumers of the goods and services concerned). Yet, in practice, the 'polluter-pays' principle may not operate, either because the law does not so provide or because of its unsatisfactory implementation.

- Governmental interventions for other policy purposes, in the absence of satisfactory resource and pollution charging, may intensity environmental problems. For example, fertilizer subsidies originally designed to increase agricultural production have encouraged excessive fertilizer use leading to increased water-pollution problems. Similarly, policies designed to encourage the provision of 'cheap' energy and transport have contributed to increased consumption and adverse environmental effects in both sectors.

Thus, the underpricing of natural resources and the failure to internalize environmental externalities reduce the capacity to resolve resource conservation and environmental problems—and certain forms of market intervention inadvertently increase these problems.

9.4. Role of regulatory instruments in environmental policy

The traditional approach to problems of over-use of natural resources and of excessive pollution has been to curb these excesses by regulation. These regulations take a variety of forms which include:

- prohibiting the abstraction, use, or disposal of particular substances, products, processes, etc., which are considered to be environmentally damaging (e.g. hunting wildlife, use of prescribed chemicals, discharge of particular radio-active substances);
- setting of maximum limits for the abstraction of particular natural resources (e.g. water abstraction, minerals extraction, fish catches);
- setting of maximum limits (i.e. emission standards) for discharges of pollutants to air, water, or land;
- prescribing the technology which may be used for particular processes of production or the materials which may be used in particular processes (e.g. cement manufacturing processes, sulphur content of fuels used in certain industrial boilers); and
- establishing ambient quality standards (e.g. minimum water quality standards to be achieved in a river receiving polluting discharges).

The achievements of this traditional approach have been considerable, as comparisons between the environmental quality in countries within the EU which have effective environmental regulations, and those in parts of Central and Eastern Europe which have not, amply demonstrate (see European Environmental Agency 1995 for data on the state of the environment within the EU).

However, the regulatory approach is not without its problems, for example:

- The criteria by which environmental standards have been set are often unclear or are insufficiently justified in terms of their benefits and costs.
- Standards may not be enforced: problems of non-compliance are pervasive in some countries.
- Uniform emission standards are not the most cost-effective methods of achieving environmental quality standards.
- At best, regulations provide only limited incentives to cost-reducing innovations in pollution-control technology.

More fundamentally, the regulatory approach tends to be directed at the *symptoms* of the environmental problem (i.e. observed pollution and resource-use levels) rather than at its underlying socio-economic *causes* (i.e. failure of those engaging in environmentally damaging activities to take the externalities for which they are responsible into account in their own decision-making). Given this, exclusive reliance on regulations to control a specific pollution or conservation problem is likely to result in its eventual re-emergence in another form or location rather than provide a comprehensive solution.

9.5. Role of economic instruments in environmental policy

Economic instruments aim to achieve environmental objectives by using financial incentives and disincentives to encourage more 'environmentally friendly' behaviour by producers and consumers. This section contains a theoretical analysis of economic instruments, whilst the two following sections examine their use in practice.

The environmental objectives which economic instruments serve should be consistent with the broader socio-economic objectives of society. These are often characterized by economists as *efficiency* and *equity* objectives, where

- the efficiency objective is to promote the efficient allocation and use of resources within society; and
- the equity objective is to promote an equitable distribution of goods and services both between different sectors of society and between different generations of society (intra- and inter-generational equity, respectively).

In order to use these two objectives, it is necessary to have an operational definition of such terms as '*efficient* allocation of resources' and '*equitable* distribution of goods and services'. In the former case, this has typically been based on the use of market prices as expressions of value and the application of the Pareto criterion or potential Pareto criterion. Thus, an efficient allocation of resources exists where it is not possible to make one member of society better off without making another worse off or, in the case of the potential Pareto criterion, to do so after allowance for those made better off compensating those made worse off.

Within a market system, efficiency is to be achieved through the price mechanism, with governments intervening to correct for imperfections in the market system and/or in the operations of the price mechanism. Central to this approach is the notion that prices for environmental services or the use of natural resources should reflect their full social opportunity costs. For example, in the case of abstracting a mineral from land or sea, these should cover

- the marginal private opportunity cost of its abstraction;
- the marginal external cost of the environmental damage that its abstraction causes; and
- the future net benefit of the consumption forgone by its earlier exhaustion (if it is a non-renewable resource).

This implies a fairly broad definition of the 'polluter-pays' principle contained in the 1975 EC Recommendation. As will be seen later, narrower interpretations of this principle are often adopted in practice.

The objective of an 'equitable distribution of goods and services' does not have a widely accepted operational definition. Typically, it is not interpreted to imply strict equality in the distribution of income and wealth. Frequently it is expressed in a weaker and broader form, such that policy instruments which increase income and wealth inequalities tend to be regarded as undesirable. The *extent* to which any distributional changes are desirable or undesirable is usually considered to be a matter of value judgement, on which economists can provide little professional guidance.

Bargaining, based on environmental rights

If the legal rights to use all natural resources (including air, water, land, etc.) are well defined, then the efficient allocation of those resources should be automatically achieved (*without* government intervention) *in a perfectly competitive market system*. This is illustrated, in simple form, in Figs. 9.2–9.5 below.

Fig. 9.2 illustrates the case where industrialists, producing a given level of output, negotiate with fishermen (who own the water rights) to accept the discharge of their waste-water into the river. The payments acceptable to the fishermen depend upon the damage which the waste-water will cause to their fishing activities; the higher the level of waste-water treatment by the industrialist prior to its disposal, the more the damage

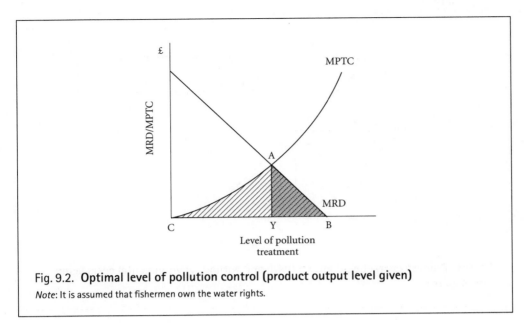

Fig. 9.2. **Optimal level of pollution control (product output level given)**

Note: It is assumed that fishermen own the water rights.

will fall (this being reflected in the shape of the marginal reduction in damage (MRD) function in Fig. 9.2). Thus profit-maximizing industrialists will be prepared, on a voluntary basis, to treat their waste-water to a higher level so long as the reduction in damage to fishing activities (which is reflected in a reduction in compensation payable to fishermen) exceeds the increase in their waste-water treatment costs (shown in the marginal pollution treatment cost (MPTC) function in Fig. 9.2). Thus, the outcome of the negotiations between industrialists and fishermen is that the industrialists are permitted to discharge into the river provided the waste-water is treated to a level of *CY* and that compensation is paid by them equal to the area *YAB*.

At this level, the combined total pollution-damage and pollution-control costs are at a minimum, which is consistent with the efficiency objective. In this situation, also, the 'polluter pays' in two senses: industrialists are paying all of their pollution-treatment costs (area *YAC* in Fig. 9.2) and are paying full compensation for any remaining pollution damage (*YAB*) which is caused. In effect, what is happening is that the environmental costs are being fully internalized within the costing and decision-making systems of the industrialists. This, as shown in Fig. 9.3, will tend also to reduce total output of their (polluting) products and raise their prices.

Fig. 9.4 illustrates the same case as Fig. 9.2, except that it is assumed that the water rights are held by the industrialists. As a consequence, the fishermen have to make payments to the industrialists to persuade them to treat their waste-waters before discharging them to the river. The maximum payments that fishermen are prepared to pay are based on the marginal damage to them that would be avoided by waste-water treat-

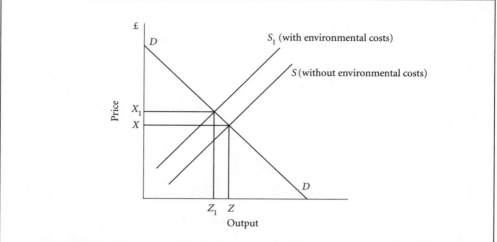

Fig. 9.3. **Product–market equilibrium (with and without environmental costs being internalized)**

ment. For their part, the industrialists will treat the waste-waters so long as the extra payments (based on the marginal damage avoided) exceed their marginal pollution-treatment costs. The outcome, in terms of the mutually agreed level of treatment, is the same (i.e. CY) as in Fig. 9.2. However, the distributional consequences are different

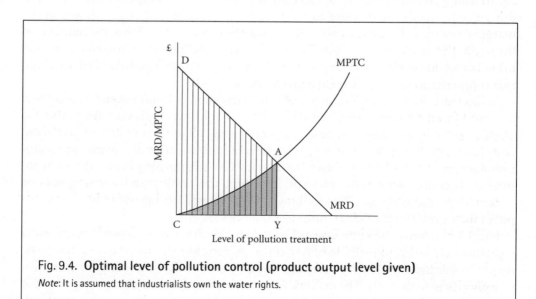

Fig. 9.4. **Optimal level of pollution control (product output level given)**
Note: It is assumed that industrialists own the water rights.

(reflecting the different distribution of property rights). In this latter case, the polluter is 'bribed' to pollute less than he would have done. Also, the output effects are different—polluters produce more output than in the 'no-bargaining' situation (see Fig. 9.5).

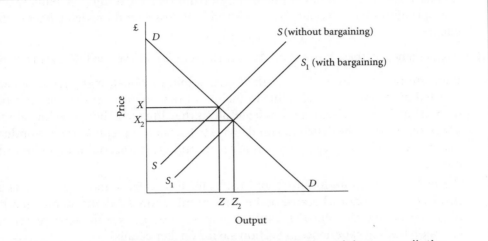

Fig. 9.5. Product–market equilibrium (with and without bargaining over pollution treatment)

Note: It is assumed that industrialists own the water rights.

The above analysis is used to show how markets might respond, in the absence of government intervention, to the presence of environmental pollution. However, its practical value is limited, given that real markets are often imperfect and legal rights to the use of the environment are often inadequately or unsatisfactorily (from an equity viewpoint) defined.

One possible type of policy response to this situation would be to define legal rights to the environment more clearly and, from an equity viewpoint, more satisfactorily and to improve the functioning of the relevant markets so that the bargaining process works more efficiently. In this context, various measures might be considered; for example:

- clearer specification of rights relating to natural resources, especially common property natural resources;
- transfer of certain rights (e.g. to discharge into air and water) from private to public ownership;
- improvements to the judicial system, including provisions relating to strict liability for environmental damage (i.e. onus of proof placed on the polluter), legal aid

to finance environmental protection cases, and reductions in the transactions costs and uncertainties of outcome within the judicial system;

- improvements to the knowledge about pollution damage held by those involved in the bargaining process; and

- institutional strengthening to support the development of markets for environmental resources. The development of emission permit trading systems is one example of this kind of policy initiative and is discussed in more detail later in the chapter.

However, reliance on these types of market instruments is still likely to be limited where:

- there are many sources of a pollutant (e.g. sulphur oxides), many receptors are affected by it, and the legal rights to the use of the environment are in multiple ownership. In these circumstances it will always be difficult, in both a technical and a legal sense, to establish liability for damage to particular receptors and to conduct negotiations without high transactions costs and great uncertainties about outcomes;

- the pollutant is more localized and there are few sources and affected parties involved. In such cases, because of the small numbers involved, the market may be oligopolistic and the efficient solution may not emerge (see the later review of emission trading experience in Section 9.6 for further details).

Therefore, other types of economic instrument, involving some form of government intervention, are likely to be needed. These are examined below.

Charging systems

Suppose that legal rights to the environment are vested in a public authority which is empowered to charge for their use. Assume further that these charges should reflect the efficiency and equity objectives identified earlier. So far as efficiency is concerned, this implies that users should be charged the marginal social costs (MSCs) incurred from their use of the environment (it is assumed, for expository purposes, that there are no 'second-best' or other market distortions which justify departures, on efficiency grounds, from the MSC pricing rule (see Laidler and Estrin 1989 for further details). This implies, in the case of a waste discharge, that the user should be charged according to the estimated damage his discharge causes to the environment in addition to covering any costs incurred by the public authority in providing disposal services for him.

So far as the first component of the charge is concerned, this will vary according to the degree of pre-treatment by the user and the resulting reduction in damage caused. Faced by a schedule of charges, reflecting different levels of environmental damage, the profit-maximizing user will choose the level of pre-treatment where the marginal reduction in the charges bill (which reflects the marginal reduction in pollution damage) is just equal to the marginal cost of pre-treatment.

This is, seemingly, the same response as in the bargaining solution in Fig. 9.2. At first sight, this charging system appears to offer the same efficiency benefits as the bargaining solution, without the difficulties highlighted above. However, there are some differences between the two approaches and this type of charging system also has its own drawbacks.

1. Unlike in the bargaining case shown in Fig. 9.2, those damaged by the residual pollution do not necessarily receive compensation and therefore its distributional consequences also need to be considered.

2. The public authority has to assess the likely damage, at each level of treatment, and express this in monetary terms in order to construct its charges schedule. To do this, in a way that is generally acceptable to all of the parties involved, is a very difficult task. In many cases, scientific knowledge on the environmental effects of pollutants is incomplete or subject to considerable uncertainty. Additionally, many types of environmental resources (e.g. air, sea water, nature reserves, archaeological sites) have no market price, or, if there is a price, it is fixed at a level unrelated to its social value. Therefore, other methods have to be used in an attempt to derive suitable market values. A number of such methods exist, which are briefly reviewed in a later section of this chapter (see Section 9.8), but there is a continuing debate over their validity, and examples of their practical application, although increasing, are still relatively limited.

In the absence of sufficiently reliable monetary measures of damage on which to base charges schedules which will 'steer' polluters to apply optimal (i.e. efficient) levels of pollution control, charges systems may still be used to serve a more modest objective. This is to curtail, in a cost-effective manner, the use of, or damage to, a particular environmental resource, to a target level which is predetermined by the environmental control authority. This is illustrated in Fig. 9.6, where a charge of OX per unit of waste is imposed on each of two dischargers, A and B, as a means of achieving a combined target waste reduction of OY_{A+B} waste units. Each finds it profitable to reduce the wastes it discharges so long as the savings in charges (OX per unit) are greater than its MPTC. Since Firm B is more cost efficient in waste reduction than Firm A, it finds it profitable to abate its wastes to a greater extent and therefore it makes a greater contribution to the overall waste-reduction target.

This type of charging system has certain advantages over a regulatory system which, for example, may achieve its overall waste reduction target by requiring all dischargers to achieve the same waste reduction (e.g. $\frac{1}{2}OY_{A+B}$ in Fig. 9.6):

• the target is achieved at the lowest total treatment cost (note that total cost minimization is achieved where the MPTC for the last unit of waste reduction achieved is the same for all dischargers); and

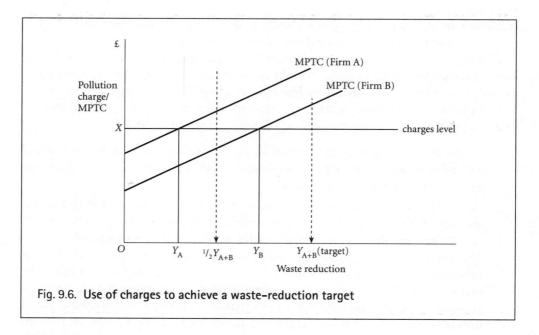

Fig. 9.6. Use of charges to achieve a waste-reduction target

- it provides a stronger financial incentive to all dischargers to reduce their MPTCs (thereby further reducing the total resource cost of achieving any waste target) in the future.

However, even this more modest charging system has its problems.

- If the public authority does not have accurate information on the individual MPTCs, it cannot correctly identify the level of charge needed to achieve the overall target waste reduction. If, because of this, the charge level is set too high, the target will be exceeded; if it is too low, the target will not be reached. If the latter situation is of concern (e.g. where there is a risk of irreversible damage if a target is not met), then individual maximum discharge levels may initially need to be set until practical experience with different levels of charging has revealed the most appropriate charge level.

- The use of charges will place a greater financial cost on certain dischargers (and, indirectly, on their customers) than a regulation designed to achieve the same waste-reduction target. For this reason, it is likely to be less popular than an equivalent regulation among dischargers and customers. However, the use to be made of the charges revenue also needs to be taken into consideration. Assuming, for example, that pollution charges systems are intended to be fiscally neutral, the charge revenue could be used to reduce other charges or taxes on the dischargers and their customers (provided this does not undermine the original purpose of the charges scheme) or to reduce taxes elsewhere in the economy. The notion of environmental charges providing a 'double dividend'—improving the quality of the environment and enabling other tax rates to be reduced—can help to reduce their unpopularity in some quarters.

Marketable permits

An alternative approach to achieve a target level of total discharges is to introduce a system of marketable permits. In this case, the public authority provides a fixed quantity of permits, each of which contains an authorization to discharge a given quantity of wastes. The owner of such a permit (or permits) may freely sell it to others. Thus, in principle, a market for discharge permits is established. A number of benefits are claimed for such a system, for example:

- The total number of permits issued is controlled by the authorities, who can then ensure that any target for total authorized discharges is respected.
- The authorities do not need to know the marginal damage or MPTC functions of the individual dischargers.
- The establishment of an effective market for permits would lead to those dischargers who value the permits most highly (because, for example, of their high MPTCs) acquiring them by offering the highest prices. Those with low MPTCs would find it more profitable to sell some of their permits and reduce their own discharges through higher levels of treatment. In this way, the total costs incurred in reaching the target for total discharges are minimized.
- If permits have a market price, this provides a financial incentive to all dischargers to reduce their MPTCs in order to lower their future permit requirements. This should stimulate further cost savings in pollution control over the longer term.

However, there are a number of concerns about marketable permit systems:

- There is concern over how the initial allocation of permits by the authorities should be undertaken. Some favour the use of an auction, others support their allocation, free of charge, to the existing holders of waste-disposal authorizations. Clearly, the distributional consequences of the two approaches are quite different.
- The transfer of permits between dischargers at different locations within a market can result in serious environmental problems where environmental impacts are very location-specific.
- Markets work well only if there are a sufficient number of buyers and sellers and there is reasonable freedom of market entry and exit. In most, small area, permit markets there will be very few buyers and sellers. Also, those who possess permits may prefer to retain them (either to hold back opportunities for expansion by their rivals or because they are uncertain whether they could buy them back should they

need them again in the future) rather than sell them, even when they are surplus to their current requirements.

A fuller treatment of these, and related issues, is to be found in OECD (1992c).

Grants and subsidies

Grants and subsidies are often provided in support of pollution-control activities, despite concerns that this might conflict with the 'polluter-pays' principle. Therefore, it is necessary to clarify the circumstances in which different forms of financial assistance for environmental protection may be acceptable, on efficiency or equity grounds, and where they are not.

Figs. 9.4 and 9.5, earlier in the chapter, establish that the optimal level of pollution can, in principle, be achieved by those who are damaged by pollution making payments to the polluters to induce them to treat or abate their wastes to the desired level. Alternatively, this could be achieved by a public authority offering payments to polluters up to the value of the marginal damage reduction they are prepared to achieve. Or, such payments to polluters may be fixed at a level which provides sufficient incentive to achieve the target reduction in wastes set by the authorities.

Thus, in addition to economic instruments which involve payments *by* polluters to achieve environmental goals in an efficient or cost-effective manner, one can envisage instruments which involve payments *to* polluters to achieve the same objectives. However, the effects of the two types of economic investments are not identical in all respects, notably:

- their *output* effects are different, charges being output-contracting and grants/subsidies output-expanding (compare Figs. 9.4 and 9.6);
- their *distributional* effects are different, charges being imposed upon polluters and grants/subsidies being received by them.

Other reasons have also been given to justify grants or subsidies, such as:

- where developments give rise to external environmental benefits—for example, where a river-bank improvement scheme leads to environmental benefits which are not reflected in financial benefits to the developer. The maximum grant justified in this case would correspond to the value placed on the external environmental benefit; and
- transitional assistance to polluters where environmental quality standards are raised substantially and at relatively short notice. This may be justified, as a temporary measure, where the short-term adjustment costs are high; however, there is a danger that such financial assistance schemes will continue where the original justification no longer applies.

OECD (1996*a*, 1996*b*) contain a fuller analysis of the effects of different types of subsidies on environmental quality.

Summary

Environmental policy-makers within the EU and its Member States have a potentially wide range of instruments—regulatory and economic—available to them. However, there is a need for careful selection and specification of the instruments to be used. The types of criteria by which this might be carried out are listed below:

- *economic efficiency*: is the instrument likely to assist in achieving 'optimal' environmental quality (i.e. minimize the sum of environmental damage and treatment costs)?
- *environmental effectiveness*: is the instrument likely to be effective in achieving and preserving the prescribed level of environmental quality?
- *cost effectiveness*: is the instrument likely to assist in achieving the required environmental quality at least resource cost, both at present and in the future?
- *equity*: is the distributional effect of the instrument likely to be broadly acceptable?
- *administrative feasibility*: is the use of the instrument feasible in terms of its information requirements, administrative demands, and political acceptability?
- *institutional compatibility*: is the instrument compatible with the approach to environmental policy and the existing administrative framework in the countries in which it would operate?

It is evident from the above review that both of the types of instruments that have been examined—regulatory and economic—are likely to have some deficiencies when measured against one or more of these criteria. However, the strengths and weaknesses of each do not always coincide. Regulatory instruments tend to perform relatively better in terms of their administrative feasibility, institutional compatibility, and, in certain cases, their environmental effectiveness. In contrast, economic instruments have greater potential in terms of cost effectiveness and, in certain cases, economic efficiency. Because of this it has been argued that the use of 'hybrid' systems, which combine regulatory and economic instruments, is preferable to realize the principal benefits of each. Finally, in the case of all instruments, their merits and limitations vary according to how well or poorly they are designed and used in practice. This becomes more evident in the review of the uses made of economic instruments in the next section.

9.6. Use of economic instruments in practice

A number of surveys of the use of economic instruments in developed economies, including certain EU countries, have been carried out by OECD and others (Opschoor and Vans 1989; Huppes *et al.* 1992; OECD 1992*a*, 1992*b*, 1993, 1994*a*, 1995*a*). The following review is largely based upon these studies, supplemented by more recent OECD data. It highlights their use within EU countries but also includes some data relating to other OECD countries for comparative purposes. The next section (9.7) examines one specific economic instrument proposal—for an energy-carbon tax to reduce carbon dioxide (CO_2) emissions.

The economic instruments in use may be classified as follows:

- *charges and taxes*: these include effluent charges, user charges, product charges and taxes, and administrative charges. They may be used to reduce consumption of specific natural resources, to discourage polluting activities, and/or to provide financial assistance to achieve reductions in pollution by other technical means;

- *grants and subsidies*: these include grants, soft loans, and tax allowances which may be used to encourage less polluting, or more 'environmentally friendly', forms of behaviour;

- *deposit-refund schemes*: for example, on beverage containers, to encourage re-use and/or more environmentally acceptable means of their disposal;

- *market-creation arrangements*: for example, emission permit trading arrangements, to encourage more efficient and cost-effective use of emission permits; and

- *financial enforcement incentives*: for example, non-compliance fees and performance bonds, which provide a financial inducement to comply with existing environmental regulations.

A survey of OECD member countries, undertaken in 1987, identified 153 economic instruments in use, of which eighty-one took the form of charges and taxes, forty-one consisted of some type of subsidy, and thirty-one fell within the other three categories mentioned above (Opschoor and Vans 1989). More recent OECD data suggest that the number of economic instruments in use may have increased by 25–50 per cent over the following five years. However, these are very approximate estimates which reveal little about the comprehensiveness of their coverage or of the extent to which they conform with the efficiency and equity principles described in the previous section. Some indication of this is provided below, where each main type of economic instrument is discussed in greater detail.

Charges

Table 9.1 summarizes the types of charges in force in 1987, with some updating from more recent sources. It shows that each of the five types of charges which are listed are in use but their extent is highly variable.

Table 9.1. **Types of charges in use in selected EC and OECD countries, 1987 updated**

Country	Types of charges Effluent				User	Produce	Administrative	Tax differentiation
	Air	Water	Waste	Noise				
Canada					X	X		X
USA				X	X	X	X	
Australia		X	X		X		X	
Japan	X			X				
Austria		X			X			X
Belgium		X	X		X		X	X
Denmark			X		X	X	X	X
Finland					X	X	X	X
France	X	X		X	X	X		
Germany		X	(X)	X	X	X	X	(X)
Greece	X				X		X	X
Italy		X			X	X		
Netherlands		X	X	X	X	X	X	X
Norway					X	X	X	X
Portugal		X					X	
Spain		X			X		X	
Sweden	X				X	X	X	X
Switzerland	(X)			X	X	(X)		X
Turkey			X					
UK		X		X	X		X	X

Note: X = applied, (X) = under consideration.

Source: OECD (1991).

Effluent charges

These are charges related to the size and/or composition of the polluting discharge to the environment. They are applied only to a limited extent to atmospheric emissions within EU countries but are more commonly used in the case of aqueous waste discharges (e.g. in France, Germany, Italy, and the Netherlands). Noise charges are common in many EU countries but are mainly confined to aircraft landing charges. Overall, effluent charges are set at relatively low levels and their incentive effect in reducing discharges is weak. Also, the motivation of these charges may vary; for example, water effluent charges in France are more closely linked to revenue-raising to finance investment in pollution control facilities than directly internalizing externalities.

User charges

These are charges for the use of natural resources (e.g. water) or for the use of waste treatment and disposal facilities. According to the efficiency principle, these should cover at least the private opportunity cost of the resource or facility provided and, if not covered by an effluent or similar charge, any external costs incurred.

Water use and effluent disposal charges (in some cases combined within a single charger) are commonly applied within the EU and elsewhere. However, in a number of cases the charges appear to be below the marginal social costs incurred. User charges are also frequently applied for the collection and treatment of municipal solid wastes but are often fixed charges based on covering the overall accounting costs of the service.

Product charges and taxes

These are charges imposed on products that are considered polluting in their manufacturing or consuming phase. They include charges on fuels (reflecting the presence of pollutants such as sulphur or carbon) and on non-returnable containers. So far, these charges are confined to a limited range of products and, with the possible exception of the Netherlands, the level of the charges has been too small to have a significant environmental effect. A variation on the product charge is the use of differential rates in taxes to favour the purchase of 'environmentally friendly' products—notably 'clean' cars and unleaded petrol (International Energy Agency 1993). More recent reviews of environmental taxes are to be found in OECD (1995a).

Administrative charges

These are charges used in a number of EU countries, principally in the form of licence and registration fees. Their intended purpose is often to help in financing the administrative costs of pollution regulation activities. However, they are frequently too low for this purpose and this results either in their implicit subsidization or in under-funding leading to ineffective administration of the pollution regulations.

Grants and subsidies

According to OECD surveys, the majority of member countries for which data are available provide some financial assistance for their pollution control activities. In certain cases, these payments are linked to charges schemes where revenues are then used to help finance investment in pollution control equipment. In other cases, subsidies appear to be hidden in 'below-cost' charges for environmental services or take the form of grants, soft loans, or special tax allowances.

For a number of years, OECD has operated a procedure for the 'Notification of Financial Assistance Systems for Pollution Prevention and Control'. Taken at face value, the amounts of financial assistance provided may not suggest significant departures from the 'polluter-pays' principle, especially as, in some cases, they are justified as 'transitional' arrangements. However, not all member countries comply with the notification procedure, nor do the data necessarily cover all forms of pollution control expenditure. For these reasons the extent to which pollution control activities are subsidized on a continuing basis within the EU, and the environmental consequences this has, remains in some doubt (OECD 1996b).

Deposit-refund schemes

These are quite widely used for beer and soft-drink bottles in a number of EU countries and especially in Scandinavia. Up to a certain level, companies find such schemes commercially viable and require no financial assistance unless governments wish to raise the proportion of bottles returned above the commercial level. The range of containers to which these schemes relate is limited and, though they have a useful demonstration value, their overall contribution to environmental protection is probably fairly small.

Market-creation arrangements

Practical experience in tradable permit systems is, to date, mainly confined to the USA (OECD 1992c, 1994). This system provides for internal trading within the same plants (through 'bubble' and 'offset' arrangements) and external trading between different enterprises (through the buying and selling of emission licences). The former has introduced a welcome degree of internal flexibility into the US regulatory framework, which, to a varying degree, already existed in other European countries. However, external trading has occurred to a much less extent and no effective market for emissions trading has yet been established. In contrast, stronger provisions for strict liability (i.e. where the onus of proof, relating to liability for environmental damage, resides with the polluter) are being reflected in higher insurance claims and higher insurance for polluters or those who acquire their liabilities when they purchase contaminated land. In this way, the insurance market, both in North America and Europe, is beginning to internalize these environmental damage costs and secure greater adherence to the 'polluter-pays' principle (OECD 1992b).

Enforcement incentives

The main form of enforcement incentives used within Europe are non-compliance charges when polluters' emissions exceed those permitted by regulations. In the past, these charges have been set at very low levels and this, combined with low rates of detection and action for non-compliance, has meant that the financial incentive to comply has been very weak. The situation is gradually changing as some countries (e.g. Norway, the USA, the UK) begin to raise the level of these charges.

Overall assessment of current practice

The numbers and types of economic instruments of environmental policy in use within the EU appear to have grown considerably over recent years. However, closer examination suggests that they play a limited, if expanding, role in environmental protection. Charges schemes, though relatively numerous, are still confined to a small range of polluting activities and products and are mainly set at too low a level to have a major incentive effect. Grants and subsidies are still used—and their full extent may be underestimated—but the environmental rationale for their use is not always clear and, in some cases, their consistency with the 'polluter-pays' principle is in doubt. Deposit-refund schemes play a limited, but useful, role in pollution control. Market-creation schemes are still in their infancy in Europe. Financial enforcement incentives have been very weak in the past but, in some EU countries at least, are getting stronger.

The Fifth Action Programme (CEC 1992a) indicated the intention to make greater use of economic instruments within the EU in the future. However, the Progress Report on the implementation of this programme (CEC 1996a: 93) concluded that 'the interest in and use of economic instruments has increased, but they have proved to be more difficult to introduce than was envisaged when the Fifth Programme was prepared'. This is confirmed by attempts to introduce environmental taxes to control CO_2 emissions and reduce the risks of global warming, as illustrated below.

9.7. Reducing CO_2 emissions

Among recent environmental policy issues facing the EU and the international community, one of the most widely publicized has been the threat of global warming from increased emissions to the atmosphere. The precise causes, likely extent, and consequences of global warming continue to be debated. However, it is clear that, if the more pessimistic 'do-nothing' scenarios were to be realized, the resulting environmental and economic consequences would be of enormous scale. In these circumstances, the precautionary policy response has been to set target levels which should not be exceeded for the main emissions believed to contribute to global warming, and then to determine, and hopefully reach political agreement on, the best ways of achieving these.

The major type of emission believed to contribute to global warming is CO_2. In October 1990 the Council of Ministers undertook to stabilize CO_2 emissions in the EC at 1990 levels by the year 2000. In the absence of any specific measures to curb emissions, total energy use has been predicted to grow by more than 12 per cent, and CO_2 emissions by more than 11 per cent, over this period.

In order to achieve these targets, the Commission proposed a package of measures which included:

- voluntary, regulatory, and other related measures to encourage energy conservation and switching to lower carbon fuels;
- a combined energy and carbon tax whose level would be progressively raised between 1993 (the originally assumed start date) and 2000 (with provision for certain exemptions and tax reductions);
- increases in annual vehicle licence duties; and
- a redistribution of the tax revenue through reductions in other taxes so as to achieve tax neutrality.

It was envisaged that approximately one-third of the target reductions in energy use and CO_2 emissions would be achieved by the non-tax measures, leaving the remainder to be achieved by the energy-carbon tax and the increased vehicle licence duties. The tax and licence duty levels needed to achieve the required reductions are considerable and would be reflected in substantial increases in the prices of particular fuels (by year 2000, over 60 per cent for coal and 40 per cent for heavy fuel oil used by industry, and 10–20 per cent for residential/commercial fuel prices). However, it was envisaged that certain of the high energy industrial users would benefit from exemptions or tax-rate reductions, and, most importantly, the very considerable tax revenues generated would be used to reduce other tax rates (e.g. personal income taxes, social security charges, etc.).

The likely economic consequences of this package of measures were assessed using a linked set of energy industry, and macroeconomic models (DRI 1992). The results were sensitive to the precise form of the package, the technical properties of the particular models used, and the assumptions made about the levels of energy-carbon taxes that would be adopted by non-EC countries over this period. For the EC as a whole, the average rate of inflation was estimated to rise by 0.25 per cent per annum more, and GDP to increase by 0.07 per cent per annum less, than if the package was not introduced. These small, but not insignificant, economic consequences would be more limited if other OECD countries adopted similar packages. However, the averages conceal considerable variations in impacts between Member States and regions, economic sectors, and different socio-economic groups. For example, carbon taxes tend to be regressive, and, on equity grounds, careful attention would need to be given to the income distribution effects of any tax reductions introduced to achieve tax neutrality (Pearson 1992).

In June 1992 the EC presented a proposal for a Council Directive to introduce an energy-carbon tax along the lines described above (CEC 1992b). However, this proposal encountered considerable opposition, partly because of sensitivities over the subsidiarity issue but also due to concern over the likely public reaction to substantial increases in energy prices. There have been considerable delays in reaching agreement and the latest Commission proposal (March 1995) is a much diluted version of the original proposal which would grant Member States considerable discretion, over a lengthy transitional period, in the levels of taxes on CO_2 emissions and energy use which they apply.

Debate over the future use of economic instruments has led to greater attention to their likely distributive effects and to the need for compensating fiscal measures in specific cases (OECD 1994b, 1995b).

9.8. Benefits and costs of environmental policies: an overview

This section examines how the benefits and costs of environmental policies might be assessed and compared and reviews the limited estimates which are available.

Measuring environmental benefits

Conceptually, the measurement of environmental benefits is relatively straightforward. It involves calculating the *welfare gain* from the environmental improvement to which the policy gives rise. *In practice*, measuring the size of this gain is often difficult. In part, this stems from incomplete *scientific* knowledge about the bio-physical effects of the policy. However, even where these are reasonably well known, problems remain in placing an *economic value* upon them.

Where improvements in environmental quality result in increased yields of commercial crops, forests, or fisheries, then market prices may be used in their economic valuation, provided these prices are competitively determined. This is illustrated in Fig. 9.7. However, many environmental benefits and dis-benefits relate to receptors and natural resources which do not have a market value—for example, human life and well-being, nature conservation sites, famous landscapes, etc. In these cases, alternative, more indirect, methods of economic valuation have to be used. Over recent years a number of these methods have been developed, as illustrated in Table 9.2. However, outside the USA, their practical application (although growing) has been quite limited

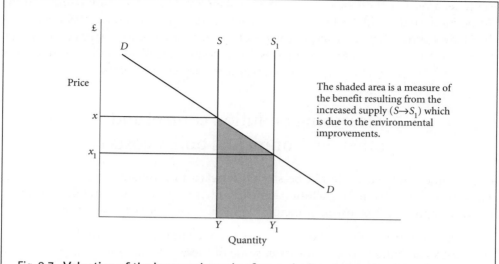

The shaded area is a measure of the benefit resulting from the increased supply $(S \rightarrow S_1)$ which is due to the environmental improvements.

Fig. 9.7. **Valuation of the increased supply of an agricultural crop, due to environmental improvements**

and their usefulness continues to be debated (OECD 1989; Winpenny 1991; Kuik *et al.* 1992; OECD 1992*a*; Dixon *et al.* 1994; OECD *et al.* 1994*c*; Winpenny 1996).

The available estimates of the country-wide benefits of existing environmental policies, and of the potential benefits of new policies, are very approximate and incomplete. However, they do suggest that both types of benefits are considerable. For

Table 9.2. **Examples of economic valuation methods for assessing environmental benefits**

Environmental benefits	Economic valuation methods
Reductions in crop losses	Quantity of crop loss is valued at its mean market price (see Fig. 9.7).
Savings in expenditure	Reductions in costs associated with materials, corrosion, cleaning of structures, sound-proofing, etc., due to reduction in pollution and noise are estimated.
Increases in property prices	Increases in property prices (and numbers of properties affected) due to reductions in air and road traffic noise, improvements in air quality, etc., are estimated.
Wage–risk studies	Wage differentials, reflecting risk premiums in dangerous occupations, are used to value reductions in the probability of accidents from pollution.
Travel cost approaches	Increased visit rates, combined with travel cost data, are used to value improvements to natural amenities and associated recreational facilities.
Contingent valuation studies	Questionnaire and survey techniques are used to deduce how much respondents would be willing to pay for specified environmental improvements or how much they would need to accept if agreeing to particular environmental benefits being withdrawn.

example, a very incomplete estimate of annual air and water pollution damage in the Netherlands in the mid-1980s calculated that this was equivalent to 0.5–0.9 per cent of the Netherlands GNP. A corresponding, but more broadly based, estimate of annual pollution damage costs in Germany was found to be equivalent to 6 per cent of that country's GNP (OECD 1989; Pearce, Markandya, and Barbier 1989).

Measuring pollution control and other environmental policy costs

In principle, these costs should be straightforward to estimate—they are the costs which would be saved if the pollution control and other policy measures did not apply. However, applying this costing principle in practice is problematic, because

- many enterprises and authorities do not keep separate cost data for their pollution control activities, and, in any case, some of these costs are jointly incurred with other activities;
- cost-accounting methods are not standardized and this creates problems of comparability, especially in the treatment of capital expenditures on pollution control; and
- some pollution control costs are 'hidden' in higher process design costs.

OECD collects and periodically publishes Pollution Abatement and Control (PAC) annual expenditures for its member countries (OECD, various years). The data are incomplete and very approximate but indicate, at least on the basis of early-1990s data, that PAC expenditures in the higher income EU countries were in the region of 1.5 per cent of GDP. These percentages are considerably lower in the poorer, southern regions of the EU. The trend in PAC expenditures is probably rising in absolute terms, but, relative to GDP, any increase since the mid-1980s has probably been modest (OECD 1996c). The incidence of PAC expenditures does, however, vary considerably between sectors and, for this reason, is considerably higher than the percentages quoted above in parts of the electricity, mining and quarrying, chemicals, petroleum, and other polluting industries.

Economic impacts of environmental control

Considerable concern is expressed, especially in times of recession, about the likely economic consequences of stricter environmental controls. In broad terms, the fear is that, in the Member State concerned, increased expenditure on such controls will raise the general level of production costs and prices, lower the competitiveness of exports, reduce the overall growth rate of the economy, and raise the level of unemployment. In contrast, others have argued that, in addition to the environmental benefits it may bring, increased investment in pollution controls may be a useful, counter-cyclical measure in periods of unemployment.

Attempts have been made to model the macroeconomic consequences of particular policy measures (such as the energy-carbon tax described previously), and of entire pollution control programmes in a number of OECD countries. An OECD survey, mainly based on six OECD countries (including France and the Netherlands within the EC), examined the macroeconomic consequences of the PAC expenditures in place or projected in the late 1970s and early 1980s (OECD 1985). At the aggregate level, in all cases, the economic consequences were assessed to be very small and to be an insignificant factor in the overall performance of the countries concerned. The effects on output and unemployment were both extremely limited and in a mixed direction—typically having limited positive effects in the initial years of implementation followed by equally limited negative effects in the following years. A task force of the Commission used the HERMES macroeconomic model to predict the likely effects, over a five-year period, of increased expenditure on environmental controls, equivalent to 1 per cent of GDP, in each of five Member States—Belgium, Germany, France, Greece, and the UK—based upon alternative assumptions about the method of financing to be used (Task Force 1990). On the basis of a 'combined' scenario (which was believed to be the most realistic scenario), GDP was predicted to change, by the end of the five-year period, between –0.10 per cent (in the UK) and +0.14 per cent (in France). Similarly, unemployment was predicted to fall by approximately 14,000 in Germany and increase by approximately 13,000 in the UK.

More recently, a modelling study was completed which predicts the likely environmental and economic consequences of different environmental policy scenarios within the framework of the Fifth Action Programme. One of these scenarios, which assumes integration of environmental objectives into economic and sectoral policies using market-based instruments to internalize major externalities, was predicted to result in both environmental improvements *and* slightly higher GDP and employment levels compared with the 'current trends' reference scenario (DRI 1994).

Though the *overall* changes appear to be relatively small, it should be noted that

- the impacts on individual economic sectors, geographic areas, and socio-economic groups *within* countries may differ considerably from the average changes described above; and
- beyond a certain point the marginal costs of achieving stricter environmental controls can rise sharply. Therefore, the economic consequences of further substantial increases in PAC expenditures on a country, especially if it pursues such a policy unilaterally, could be very considerable.

This implies that all major *new* policy initiatives should be carefully examined to ensure that their likely benefits, costs, and economic consequences (including their distributional effects) are properly assessed before they are approved.

9.9. **Future developments**

The status and scale of EU environmental policy activities have increased substantially since 1973 when the first Action Programme was approved. However, the new long-term goal of promoting sustainable development, within and outside the EU, is extremely ambitious and is unlikely to be achieved, in any meaningful sense, if existing policy measures are not strengthened.

The Commission's 1995 Progress Report on the implementation of the Fifth Action Programme (CEC 1996*a*) is accompanied by a call for renewed political commitment to the following priorities for action (CEC 1996*b*):

- strengthening measures to integrate environmental considerations into policy developments in five key sectors: agriculture, transport, energy, industry and tourism;
- broadening the range of instruments used to promote sustainable development, including:
  - greater use of market-based instruments, including environmental charges and fiscal reforms;
  - strengthening the application of such horizontal instruments as environmental assessment of plans and programmes and environmental management and auditing schemes;
  - use of the EU's own financial support mechanisms (notably the Structural and Cohesion Funds) better to integrate environmental considerations into the planning of EU-level activities;
- increasing the effectiveness of EU environmental legislation by measures aimed at improving its implementation and enforcement;
- raising awareness of sustainable development issues, and the means by which it may be brought about, through the provision of more effective communication, information, education, and training;
- reinforcing EU's role in international action to promote sustainable development through:
  - greater cooperation in environmental improvements with Central and Eastern European countries and with countries in the Mediterranean basin;
  - strengthening the sustainable development dimension in the EU's development assistance programmes and in implementing Agenda 21 requirements arising from the United Nations Rio Summit;
  - facilitating the integration of environmental requirements into multilateral trade agreements.

Almost certainly, the goals of the Fifth Action Programme will not be fully realized by the year 2000, but, with the necessary political commitment, significant progress is achievable during the intervening period.

Discussion questions

1. What are the respective advantages and disadvantages of regulatory instruments and economic instruments when used to achieve environmental policy objectives within the EU?

2. Explain why monetary measures of environmental benefits and disbenefits could be useful in environmental policy formulation within the EU. Why is it so difficult to obtain reliable measures in practice?

3. How might future EU environmental policies best contribute to the attainment of sustainable development?

FURTHER READING

Further information on the EU's Fifth Action Programme and its review can be obtained from CEC (1992a, 1996a). Reviews of the use of different economic instruments of environmental policy are to be found in OECD (1994a, 1995a, 1996a, 1996b). Studies and reviews relating to the economic valuation of environmental costs and benefits are contained in Dixon *et al.* (1994), OECD (1994c), and Winpenny (1991, 1996).

REFERENCES

CEC (1992a): Commission of the European Communities, *Towards Sustainability: A European Community Programme of Policy and Action in relation to the Environment and Sustainable Development*, 2 vols., COM 23 (Brussels: CEC).

—— (1992b), *Proposal for a Council Directive Introducing a Tax on Carbon Dioxide Emissions and Energy*, COM 226 final (Brussels: CEC).

—— (1996a), *Progress Report from the Commission: On the Implementation of the European Community Programme 'Towards Sustainability'*, COM 95 (Brussels: CEC).

—— (1996b), *Proposal for a European Parliament and Council Decision on the Review of the Fifth Action Programme*, COM 647 (Brussels: CEC).

Dixon, J. A., Scura, L. F., Carpenter, R. A., and Sherman, P. B. (1994), *Economic Analysis of Environmental Impacts*, 2nd edn. (London: Earthscan).

DRI (1992): European Industry Service, *Impact of a Package of EC Measures to Control CO_2 Emissions on European Industry*, DG XI (Brussels: CEC).

—— (1994), *Potential Benefits of Integration of Environmental and Economic Policies: An Incentive-Based Approach to Policy Integration* (London: Graham & Trotman/CEC).

European Environment Agency (1995), *Environment in the European Union, 1995* (Copenhagen: EEA).

Haigh, N. (1989), *EEC Environmental Policy and Britain* (Harlow: Longman).

Huppes, G., van der Voet, E., Van der Naald, W. G. H., Vonkeman, G. H., and Maxson, P. (1992) (eds.), *New Market-Oriented Instruments for Environmental Policy* (London: Graham & Trotman).

Norman Lee

International Energy Agency (1993), *Cars and Climate Change* (Paris: Organization for Economic Cooperation and Development/International Energy Agency).

Kuik, O. J., Oosterhuis, F. H., Jansen, H. M. A., Holm, K., and Ewers, H. J. (1992) (eds.), *Assessment of Benefits of Environmental Measures* (London: Graham & Trotman).

Laidler, D., and Estrin, S. (1989), *An Introduction to Microeconomics*, 3rd edn. (Deddington: Philip Allan).

Meadows, D. H., Meadows, D. L., Randers, J., and Behrens, W. W. (1970), *The Limits to Growth* (London: Earth Island).

Meadows, D. L., Meadows, D. H., and Randers, J. (1992), *Beyond the Limits: Global Collapse or a Sustainable Future* (London: Earthscan).

OECD (1985): Organization for Economic Cooperation and Development, *Macroeconomic Impact of Environmental Expenditure* (Paris: OECD).

—— (1989), *Environmental Policy Benefits: Monetary Valuation* (Paris: OECD).

—— (1991), *The State of the Environment* (Paris: OECD).

—— (1992a), *Benefit Estimates and Environmental Decision-Making* (Paris: OECD).

—— (1992b), *Pollution Insurance in OECD Countries* (Environmental Monograph; Paris: OECD).

—— (1992c), *Climate Change—Designing a Tradeable Permit System* (Paris: OECD).

—— (1992d), *Agricultural and Environmental Policy Integration-Implementation* (Paris: OECD).

—— (1992e), *Market and Government Failures in Environmental Management: The Case of Transport* (Paris: OECD).

—— (1993), *Taxation and the Environment: Complementary Policies* (Paris: OECD).

—— (1994a), *Managing the Environment: the Role of Economic Instruments* (Paris: OECD).

—— (1994b), *The Distributive Effects of Economic Instruments for Environmental Policy* (Paris: OECD).

—— (1994c), *Project and Planning Appraisal: Integrating Economics and Environment* (Paris: OECD).

—— (1995a), *Environmental Taxes in OECD Countries* (Paris: OECD).

—— (1995b), *Climate Change, Economic Instruments and Income Distribution* (Paris: OECD).

—— (1996a), *Integrating Environment and Economy: Progress in the 1990s* (Paris: OECD).

—— (1996b), *Subsidies and Environment: Exploring the Linkages* (Paris: OECD).

—— (1996c), *Pollution Abatement and Control Expenditure in OECD Countries* (Paris: OECD).

Opschoor, J. B., and Vans, H. B. (1989), *Economic Instruments for Environmental Protection* (Paris: OECD).

Pearce, D. W., Markandya, A., and Barbier, E. B. (1989), *Blueprint for a Green Economy* (London: Earthscan).

—— and Warford, J. J. (1993), *World Without End: Economics, Environment and Sustainable Development* (Oxford: Oxford University Press).

Pearson, M. (1992), 'Equity Issues and Carbon Taxes', in OECD, *Climate Change—Designing a Practical Tax System* (Paris), 213–40.

Task Force on the Environment and the Internal Market (1990), *1992: The Environmental Dimension*, DG XI (Brussels: CEC).

Winpenny, J. T. (1991), *Values for the Environment: A Guide to Economic Appraisal* (London: HMSO).

—— (1996), 'Economic Valuation of Environmental Impacts: The Temptations of EVE', *Project Appraisal*, 11/4.

CHAPTER 10

Social Policy

DAVID PURDY

10.1. Introduction

A social dimension has been present within the EU since its foundation, broadly shaped by the process of economic integration, but continually evolving and always contested. One reason why the EU's social policy arrangements have remained unsettled is that the policy regimes of its Member States continue to diverge. Moreover, although the very existence of the EU imposes *some* degree of commonality, the possibility that initial divergences might eventually wither away has so far been blocked by fundamental disagreements, both about the 'proper' scope and objects of social policy, and about the 'proper' division of responsibility and power between the Union and its Member States. One of the main aims of this chapter is to clarify these differences of policy regime and policy paradigm.

To set the scene, Section 10.2 examines the general remit of social policy in the world (or worlds) of welfare capitalism. The perspective adopted invokes the now familiar distinction, first formulated by Marshall (1950), between three aspects of citizenship—civil, political, and social—and encompasses both the sphere of work, whether paid or unpaid, and the various branches of the welfare state.

Section 10.3 draws on recent comparative literature to propose a typology of social policy regimes in contemporary Western Europe. Four 'ideal types' are distinguished: traditional, liberal, conservative, and social democratic. Actual states, it is emphasized, usually combine the characterististics of more than one type. Hence, what varies from one state to another is the mix between alternative principles of social organization. The resulting amalgam may be stable or unstable. In the latter case, the regime in question will be in a state of flux or transition.

I am indebted to Pat Devine, who co-authored the chapter on Social Policy in the first edition of this book, on which the present chapter is largely based.

Analogous points apply to a union of states: the character of its policy arrangements depends on the balance between the regimes of its Member States and on the way in which issues requiring union-wide coordination are handled. At one extreme, for example, if national regimes were all clustered around a single centre of gravity, the role of union institutions would be confined to removing or correcting for minor discrepancies. Alternatively, national regimes may pull in different directions. In this case, the Member States must either forge a new, union-wide social settlement or, failing that, acquiesce in whatever arrangement is thrown up by spontaneous social evolution. Of course, without an agreed design for their union, Member States will be reluctant to cede sovereignty over social policy. Indeed, if the tensions and discords are strong enough, the union itself may dissolve.

In the final two sections of the chapter, this general scheme is applied to the institutional framework and historical development of EU social policy. Section 10.4 focuses on the factors which have constrained its role, looking first at disparities of economic condition and differences of social regime among Member States, and then at the policy-making institutions of the EU itself. Section 10.5 seeks to explain why periods of policy activism have alternated with periods of stagnation, and briefly speculates about the shape of things to come as Europe responds to the pressures of global competition, mass unemployment, and the fiscal crisis of the welfare state.

10.2. The remit of social policy

In very general terms, *social policy* may be defined as that branch of public policy which deals with the institutions and activities of *social reproduction*. The relevant institutions include the family, the labour market, and the state; the relevant activities include the various formative, supportive, and regenerative processes, from child rearing and health care to retraining and risk management, which help to provide people with the resources and capacities they need in order to participate in social life, and which, in the process, help to keep society going.

The scope and character of social policy, thus defined, vary from one society and era to another. In the advanced capitalist democracies since the Second World War, the primary goal of social policy has been to enhance *social welfare*. It is hard to say exactly what is meant by 'welfare', but a *welfare state* may be defined as one which seeks to promote some morally grounded and popularly accepted conception of individual and collective well-being. While this definition is compatible with a wide variety of arrangements, there is clearly a difference between having a social policy and being a welfare state. All modern governments, even in the most underdeveloped societies, operate social policies of some kind, but welfare states have emerged only in the twenty or so countries that belong to the Organization for Economic Cooperation and Development (OECD). Conversely, even if the welfare state as we know it becomes a thing of the past, students of social policy are unlikely to find themselves redundant.

Table 10.1 sets out the general remit of social policy in the world of welfare capitalism under two broad headings: 'labour market' and 'welfare state'. The distinction made here reflects the institutional separation of social life into distinct spheres—work, leisure, family, politics, and so on—which is characteristic of modernity. It is, however, important not to equate work with employment: social reproduction also depends on the unpaid care that people (mostly women) bestow on their children and other family dependants, and on the efforts of the myriad voluntary bodies, from mountain-rescue teams to parent–teacher associations, which are neither profit-seeking enterprises nor agencies of the state.

Table 10.1. **The remit of social policy in the world(s) of welfare capitalism**

Labour market	Welfare state
Macroeconomic management	*Social services*
fiscal, monetary, exchange rate,	primary and secondary education
and commercial policy	public health care
wages and prices policies	personal social services
Active labour-market policy	housing policy
and human-resource development	*Social transfers*
job-market services	*explicit*
regional policy	social insurance
tertiary education, vocational	social assistance
training, and work experience	categorical transfers
Industrial relations	*implicit*
collective bargaining	tax expenditures
industrial democracy	some producer subsidies
social dialogue	*Family policy*
Terms and conditions of employment	pre-school education and other
health and safety at work	caring services
minimum wages and non-wage	social transfers for caregivers
employment rights	maternity/paternity and parental leave
hours of work	
Economic discrimination and social exclusion	
anti-discrimination and equal opportunity policies	
regulation of atypical employment	
community development and social action programmes	

In practice, labour market and welfare state are inseparably intertwined. Schools, for example, help to develop people's capacities before they start their working lives, and pension schemes help to sustain them in retirement, but both kinds of provision necessarily rest on certain presumptions about what people will or should be doing in between. Similarly, the division of responsibility for paid and unpaid work between men and women depends, in part, on how far public policies towards pre-school

David Purdy

childcare, transfer payments, and patterns of working time enable and encourage parents to share the roles of caregiver and breadwinner. Indeed, most social policies are just as much concerned with regulating or otherwise influencing what happens in the labour market as they are with providing services and redistributing income.

Not every state makes provision for every item in Table 10.1. Since 1979, for example, successive UK governments have taken a minimalist view of social policy. However, in a context where other states actively intervene in certain areas, a policy of 'leaving it to the market' may itself be considered a form of regulation. It is certainly quite specious to suggest that a concerted drive to deregulate the labour market, privatize retirement pensions, and encourage commercial child-minding is anything other than a radical exercise in social engineering.

In thinking about the role of social policy under welfare capitalism, it is instructive to ask: what is the basis of citizenship in a state of this kind? And what does the status of citizenship entail? Nowadays, as a rule, the sole qualification for becoming a citizen is permanent (legal) residence within the jurisdiction of the state concerned, though some states continue to discriminate against 'resident aliens' by restricting citizenship to those with appropriate ancestry, as laid down in nationality law. In modern democracies, the rights (and correlative duties) of citizens fall into three broad groups: *civil rights*, comprising the liberal freedoms of thought, expression, worship, assembly, association and movement, together with the rights of property and contract which are indispensable for market transactions; *political rights* to vote in elections for central and local government and to hold public office; and *social rights* to enjoy certain guaranteed standards of material and cultural well-being. Being more recent in origin than civil and political rights, the social rights of citizens are correspondingly less secure. They are also more limited in scope and uneven in coverage. Indeed, to the extent that people who belong to the same political community hold *unequal* social rights, we are dealing not with citizenship, but with privilege. The citizens of a given state may all be privileged by comparison with outsiders, and their natural abilities and acquired assets may be highly unequal. But their common status as citizens is inherently egalitarian.

The substantive content of social citizenship has an important bearing on the distribution of income, work, and power under welfare capitalism. Given that only a few people own more than modest amounts of income-yielding property, most depend for their livelihood on continuous access to paid work, whether in their own right or as dependants of others who are continuously willing, or legally obliged, to support them. Regular employment also confers access to other social advantages besides money: experience and skills, friendship and contacts, self-esteem, social identity, public recognition, and political weight. In addition, regular jobholders are covered by *social insurance*. Employers, employees and self-employed persons are all required to pay 'contributions' (or 'social security taxes') into one or more earmarked insurance funds. People who meet the requisite contribution conditions are more or less adequately protected both against *temporary* disruptions of earning power due to unemployment, sickness, or maternity, and against *permanent* loss of earnings due to chronic invalidity, industrial disablement, and old age; and protection normally extends to their dependants and survivors too. Conversely, people who are *not* in stable, full-time employment throughout their working lives are less well served by social insurance, and may not be covered at all. The main groups at risk are the long-term unemployed, women who take time out of the labour market to care for children or elderly relatives, and workers of either sex engaged in part-time, temporary, and other forms of atypical employment.

Most welfare states provide some kind of 'safety net' outside the framework of social insurance. But *social assistance*—to use a generic name for schemes which vary widely in operational detail—is almost always means-tested, and able-bodied claimants of conventional working age are normally expected to satisfy some kind of work test. They may simply be required to show that they are 'available for' or 'actively seeking' (paid) work. Alternatively, they may be required to participate in some approved programme of work, education, or training organized or financed by the government. 'Workfare' schemes of this kind have developed apace in recent years, particularly in response to the problem of youth unemployment, and are variously intended to serve the community, deter benefit fraud, uphold the work ethic, prevent social exclusion, and reassure taxpayers that public funds are not being squandered.

Contributory social insurance is designed to replace lost or interrupted earnings; means-tested social assistance offers a safeguard against poverty. In addition, most welfare states also provide *categorical transfers* to meet the extra costs or special needs of designated sections of the population. The best known example is *Child Benefit*—a grant payable to all parents and guardians in respect of every child in their care from the moment the child is born until he or she leaves school. No state has yet introduced a *Citizens' Income*—a recurrent transfer payable to every individual citizen, each in his or her own right, with no means test and no work requirement. There has, however, been a lively debate in recent years about the idea of redesigning social-security arrangements on this basis. Van Parijs (1992) and Purdy (1994) survey the relevant literature.

Besides using earmarked social security contributions and general tax revenues to pay for *explicit* social transfers, modern governments also dispense *implicit* transfers in the form of tax expenditures, sometimes known as 'the hidden welfare state'. The effect of personal tax allowances and tax reliefs is to drive a wedge between *gross* income and *taxable* income, thereby raising the *disposable* incomes of eligible taxpayers, just as cash transfers enhance the disposable incomes of eligible claimants. Certain quasi-permanent producer subsidies also help to sustain personal incomes in particular sectors of the economy. Agricultural price support and deficiency payment schemes furnish the main examples.

Since the 'golden age' of welfare-capitalism came to an end in the mid-1970s, all welfare states have faced tight fiscal constraints and all have undergone internal reform. In the name of efficiency and choice, governments have sought to separate the *finance* of social services from their *provision*, and to replace public bureaucracies by quasi-markets in which service-providers compete for public contracts and service-users enjoy greater freedom of choice. It is, however, premature to proclaim the death of the welfare state. By and large, the core welfare programmes which were introduced or extended during the 'golden age'—social security, public education, and public health care—remain in place, not least because they remain popular with electorates. Relevant opinion-poll evidence from various countries is reviewed by Pierson (1991: 168–71).

More generally, certain core tasks are still recognized as public reponsibilities, though different governments may discharge them in different ways. Thus, with varying degrees of commitment and varying records of achievement, governments everywhere continue to frame their macroeconomic policies with a view to raising or lowering the overall level of employment, and hence, at one remove, but in the opposite direction and with less certainty of effect, the overall level of unemployment. 'Macroeconomic policy' must here be broadly understood as including not just fiscal, monetary, exchange rate, and commercial policy, but also the various instruments that governments may bring to bear on the movement of wages, prices, and non-wage incomes, from 'hands-on' incomes policies to cash limits on public expenditure and other methods of influence by remote control.

The mere existence of a unitary state with a common currency and a centralized fiscal system automatically affects the spatial distribution of production, employment, and income within its borders. In addition, most governments make some effort to pursue 'active labour-market policies' and 'strategies for human-resource development'. These too are umbrella terms. They include information and coordination services designed to improve the allocative efficiency of the job market; regional policies intended to affect the geographical distribution of jobs and/or workers; and public provision for tertiary education, vocational training, and work experience, whether to relieve specific skill shortages, upgrade the general quality of the labour force, reintegrate the long-term unemployed into the mainstream of society, or reinforce the work ethic.

Whilst none of these matters is uncontroversial, their *presence* on the agenda of public policy is not. Nowadays, whatever their ideological complexion, all governments operate some more or less coherent policy for the labour market. The same applies to certain other tasks which are generally acknowledged—by economic liberals no less than social collectivists—to require positive public action: notably, the regulation of health and safety at work and the prohibition of discrimination by sex, race, and other morally irrelevant criteria in pay and conditions, hiring and firing, training and promotion, and tax and social-security law. The status of other employment issues is more contentious. Economic liberals argue that the broader the remit of social policy, the greater the threat to individual freedom (conceived as the freedom to seek out and choose between market options), and the greater the damage to social welfare (likewise evaluated by reference to market outcomes). The implication is that, apart from a small number of essential public goods, including a minimally intrusive framework of contract law, governments should leave employers and employees to work out their own salvation subject to the 'impersonal' discipline of the market.

Opponents of this view variously stress the need for public action to prevent social exclusion, preserve social cohesion, or promote social justice. There are many kinds of social collectivist, each with different views about family policy, social citizenship, and the appropriate 'welfare mix' between market, state, and voluntary provision. But collectivist liberals, social democrats, Christian Democrats, one-nation conservatives, Marxists, feminists, and Greens all emphasize the interdependence of human individuals and the interconnectedness of social activities, and all favour a correspondingly vigorous and wide-ranging role for social policy. Under welfare capitalism, this has typically included a commitment to some form of enterprise democracy and some form of social dialogue between government, trade unions, and employers' associations; the enactment of minimum wage laws and other statutory employment rights; the regulation of hours of work; and the pursuit of community development and social-action programmes to protect or rescue threatened localities and vulnerable minorities from impoverishment and marginalization.

Disputes about the 'proper' remit of social policy are rooted in theoretical, as well as ethical, disagreements. Economic liberals treat markets as free-standing, self-adjusting institutions, whereas social collectivists adopt a more sociological approach to the economy, arguing that market phenomena cannot be understood in isolation from the legal, cultural, political, and historical contexts in which they are embedded. It is this moral and intellectual divide, as much as national sentiment and antipathy to 'federalism', that explains why successive Conservative governments in the UK have been so adamant in opposing all proposals to extend and strengthen the social dimension of the EU.

10.3. Social policy regimes

If the remit of social policy is much the same in all EU countries, the way it is handled is not. Transnational differences in social provision range from minor variations in official definitions of 'industrial accidents' to deep-seated and long-lasting contrasts of historical formation, social philosophy, and institutional design. To mark this latter, *systemic* source of diversity, social policy analysts have developed the concept of a *social policy regime*.

Even under the most liberal dispensation, state and economy are bound together by a complex of legal, organizational, and cultural links, and in order to understand social policy arrangements, one must study this complex. Neither the mere presence of a given programme in a given state, nor the scale or growth of expenditure devoted to it, is likely to tell us much, if anything, about its significance for the citizens of that state and their mutual relations. Nor is it any use generalizing from the experience of one country or sticking to one academic discipline: the study of policy regimes must be comparative and cross-disciplinary. Whilst the eventual aim is to understand *why* states have different regimes and what causes them to change, an essential intermediate step is to classify states in ways that clarify *how* they differ and change. For this reason, researchers have concentrated on delineating certain models or 'ideal-types', to which actual states approximate more or less closely, it being understood that in reality all regimes are mixed.

In a path-breaking study, Esping-Andersen (1990 and 1992) distinguishes three welfare regimes—the liberal, the conservative, and the social democratic—taking the USA, Germany, and Sweden as their respective exemplars. This schema is not beyond criticism. Esping-Andersen is concerned with the interface between employment policy, social transfers, and social stratification. But it is doubtful whether the same 'regime clusters' would emerge from a comparison of other social programmes such as health services or housing policies. Leibfried (1993) questions whether Esping-Andersen's typology reflects the experience of specific countries, while Langan and Ostner (1991) and Lewis (1993) contend that it is gender-blind and fails to accommodate the role of public policy in reinforcing or modifying the sexual division of labour. These are all valid points. Yet it is important to stress that, without *some* overarching comparative and historical framework, more localized or specialized studies remain at best incomplete and potentially misleading.

If the 'three worlds of welfare capitalism' differ markedly from each other, they all stand apart from what may be called the *traditional* model of social policy. In contemporary Western Europe, this model is largely obsolete, even in those countries and regions which are sometimes cited as examplars: Greece, Spain, Portugal, and the Italian *Mezzogiorno*, which in this, as in other respects, is unlike the northern and central regions of Italy. In traditional or premodern societies, the state does little to regulate the economy or redistribute income. This abstentionist stance should not, however, be confused with that favoured by economic liberals: the ambient culture is quite different. A single, dominant religion permeates both state and civil society; kinship, loyalty, honour, and community count for more than commerce, citizenship, and the rule of law; agriculture remains the mainstay of the economy and domestic 'subsistence' production is common; the extended family caters for children and old people, absorbs social distress, and perpetuates the subjection of women; and against the background of a thriving underground economy, politics is 'clientelist' and government corrupt—a pattern which, as the case of Italy shows, may well survive the 'late' arrival of modernity.

By contrast, *liberal* welfare regimes celebrate markets, property, and the work ethic. Their basic presumption is that all who are not incapacitated by age, disability, or illness have a duty to support themselves and their dependants. Accordingly, the aim of social policy is to encourage those with no private means of support to participate in the labour market. The state provides a safety net for market casualties and social misfits, ensuring that cash benefits are strictly targeted, means-tested, and stigmatizing. Social services are similarly residual and the better-off are encouraged to opt out of state welfare, not least through the provision of tax relief on the costs of private pensions and health insurance. Thus, far from counteracting social inequality, liberal regimes impose a clear line of division between self-reliant citizens and a dependent underclass. Note, however, that, while the former outnumber the latter, they are unlikely to form a *contented* majority, as Galbraith (1992) assumes, if their economic security is jeopardized by corporate employment strategies and deregulated labour markets.

In the past, liberal welfare states treated unpaid care-giving as a free service that women performed for the benefit of society as whole. This has changed with the growth of female employment, marital instability, and one-parent families, and nowadays 'neo-liberal' governments encourage working mothers to buy childcare on the market by offering tax relief or issuing redeemable vouchers. They are also zealous in pursuing absentee fathers who fail to maintain their children, and in exerting pressure on unmarried mothers to maintain some connection with the labour market. Even so, public provision for mothers and children in these states remains scanty, whether in cash or in kind. Women *may* benefit from the deregulation of working hours to the extent that their gendered need to juggle commitments coincides with employers' competitive need for greater flexibility. In recent years, a variety of new working-time patterns has been introduced, including flexitime, annualized hours contracts, the compressed working week and weekend working, and supplementing traditional arrangements such as part-time work, shiftwork, and homework. It is noteworthy that in the UK, where these developments have gone farthest, women have consistently experienced lower rates of unemployment than men, in contrast to the pattern found elsewhere in Europe.

Nevertheless, although the old breadwinner–homemaker version of the sexual division of labour has virtually disappeared, women still do far more unpaid work than men. (See Gershuny *et al.* 1994 for comparative evidence.) As a result, relatively few women are financially independent, either in the absolute sense that their personal income from all sources—earnings, property, and social transfers—exceeds the official poverty line, or in the relative sense that they and their partners contribute approximately equally to family income (Lister 1992). Where governments are committed to 'non-intervention', and 'new men' are thin on the ground, this basic situation seems unlikely to change.

Conservative regimes are less enamoured of the market. Nor are they hostile to social rights. Indeed, it was Germany, Esping-Andersen's exemplar country, which invented social insurance. The German model, however, is hierarchical. Instead of a comprehensive insurance scheme covering all employees and all risks, a multiplicity of schemes caters for different occupations and sectors, and health insurance is funded and administered separately from retirement pensions and unemployment compensation. Each scheme is self-governing, though supervised by the state. Both for this reason, and because benefits are earnings-related rather than flat-rate, the system provides income security without disturbing established hierarchies of income and status. It also attracts middle-class support and fosters a *corporatist* approach to social policy.

Historically, the conservative model originated in the efforts of Bismarck to preempt the appeal of socialism by securing the allegiance of the German working class to the newly unified German state. The influence of Catholic social thought is also evident: in the provision of 'family-wage' supplements for (male) breadwinners; in the principle of *subsidiarity*, whereby the role of the state is limited to issues which cannot be handled by voluntary agencies—notably, the Church; and in a system of industrial relations designed to affirm the dignity of labour, prevent class conflict, and incorporate employee representatives in both enterprise management and national policy-making.

The continuing importance of these formative influences may be gauged by comparing responses to deindustrialization. Whereas the USA, the UK, and New Zealand sought to deregulate the labour market, the core EU countries adopted a strategy of labour-supply management, encouraging women to stay at home, older men to take early retirement, and foreign workers (*Gastarbeiter*) to return to their countries of origin. By lowering resistance to redundancies, this policy helped domestic firms to regain competitiveness through higher productivity rather than lower wages (Esping-Andersen 1994). Its viability depended critically on the willingness of employers and their remaining employees to continue to meet the cost of extended periods of pension entitlement, and this was sorely tried by the 'solidarity' taxes and high interest rates that were required to pay for German reunification. Nevertheless, when Italian, French, and German workers took to the streets in 1995 and 1996 to protest against planned cuts in welfare spending, it was they, not their governments, who were defending the conservative tradition.

Social democratic regimes are also committed to social insurance and social partnership, but as elements in an egalitarian scheme of social citizenship. In this model, the state is not a second or last resort, but plays a primary role in ensuring that every citizen benefits from the highest attainable degree of income security and a wide range of social services. Esping-Andersen (1990) argues that such arrangements *decommodify* the labour market in the sense that they protect people's livelihoods from market contingency. This is true, but should not be taken to imply antipathy to the wages system or commodity production. The social democratic model remains firmly wedded to traditional forms of employment and, indeed, helps to *promote* market relations to the extent that the state becomes a major provider or purchaser of services that were formerly provided by unpaid care-givers.

Social insurance plays a key part in mitigating market insecurity. As in conservative regimes, contributions and benefits are earnings-related. But everyone belongs to a common, unified scheme. Apart from its symbolic value, this inclusive arrangement pre-empts the growth of private pensions and insurance. It also raises the ceiling of tax tolerance, making it easier to raise the ratio of benefits to earnings. Thus, income is redistributed not only over each worker's lifecycle, but also from incumbent jobholders to those who are unemployed or 'economically inactive'.

The viability of a system that guarantees paid work or generous transfer incomes from cradle to grave depends on the maintenance of full employment, not just as a state of equilibrium between labour supply and demand, but in the more vital sense that numbers in employment are maximized. It is, therefore, essential for the government to pursue an active labour-market policy, absorbing labour that is surplus to the requirements of private industry and drawing women out of the home by creating jobs in the public sector. In the process, childcare is partially socialized and provision for paid parental leave makes it easier to combine parenthood with employment. This said, to the extent that the state is simply paying some women to look after other women's children, the underlying sexual division of labour remains intact.

Full employment in an open economy cannot be sustained without some form of wages policy. Otherwise, uncoordinated wage bargaining may lead to a damaging wage-price spiral. Government cannot avert this risk single-handed: it needs the active collaboration of trade unions and employers' associations which are in a position to speak with authority and act with discipline. And, having established a permanent process of policy negotiation, government must endeavour to reconcile conflicts of interest between workers and employers, not only over wages, but also over questions of power. This may not prove easy, even in a country like Sweden where there is a strong commitment to consensus politics and social democratic governments have held office for all but nine of the years since 1932. Tensions were already apparent in the early 1980s when Swedish employers rejected trade-union demands for greater industrial democracy. As the decade wore on, the high cost of the active labour-market policy gave rise to further strains. Finally, in the early 1990s, budgetary pressures forced the government to make deep cuts in public expenditure and to accept a sharp rise in unemployment.

Caution is needed, however, before writing off the Swedish model. Unlike its liberal and conservative counterparts, this model contains many of the elements favoured by proponents of *productivist* welfare reforms—lifelong learning, 'welfare-to-work' programmes, and a commitment to 'stakeholder capitalism'. Indeed, these ideas were pioneered in Sweden. The problem is that, in order to free resources for further investment in human capital, it may be necessary to make further cuts in social transfers, and this may undermine the consensus politics and corporatist policy-making on which the model depends.

10.4. **The framework of EU social policy**

So far, the argument has focused on social policy in one state. It is now time to consider the EU as a whole. In this section, I examine the constraints which continue to inhibit EU action in the social field: economic disparities and regime differences *between* Member States; and the policy-making arrangements of the EU itself. In the next section, I review the history of EU social policy and speculate about the future. It must be said at once that the social policy of the EU is not comparable with that of an individual nation state, even if the comparison is limited to *federal* states such as Germany and Canada. It does not even resemble the more ambitious policies of the EU itself such as the Common Agricultural Policy (CAP). Of course, a social dimension has been present in the EU since its inception. But the role of the EU as a social policy actor in its own right has always been limited. Moreover, although social issues have become more prominent as the EU has evolved, there is still no prospect of a lasting social settlement.

Disparities and differences between Member States

Because of differences in demographic and social structure, Member States generate different *demands* for social expenditure. Because of uneven levels of economic development and unequal standards of economic performance, they differ in their *capacity* to respond to these demands. And, as we have seen, the *form* of each state's response depends on the nature of its policy regime.

Tables 10.2 and 10.3 illustrate the resulting disparities and highlight recent trends. As Table 10.2 shows, the populations of EU countries are growing at very different rates: between 1982 and 1992 those of Luxembourg and the Netherlands rose by 6 per cent, whereas those of Portugal and Italy were virtually static. Similarly, the number of chil-

Table 10.2. **EU selected demographic and labour-market indicators, 1982–1992**

Member State	Population	Children	Labour Force		Unemployment	Employment
	% growth	Nos below age 15 as % of total population	Participation rate		Average % rate	% growth
			Total	Female		
	1982–92	1992	1992	1992	1982–92	1982–92
Austria	4.1	17.5	69.4	58.0	3.3	11.3
Belgium	1.9	18.1	63.4	54.0	11.0	5.2
Denmark	1.0	17.0	83.5	78.9	8.2	10.1
Finland	4.4	19.1	74.6	70.7	5.7	−1.7
France	5.3	20.0	66.7	58.7	9.6	3.4
Germany	5.2	15.3	70.7	61.3	7.3	9.0
Greece	5.2	18.3	57.8	42.7	7.5	5.2
Ireland	1.9	26.8[a]	61.2[a]	39.9[a]	15.5[b]	−2.0[b]
Italy	0.4	15.7[c]	62.8	46.5	10.7	4.5
Luxembourg	6.6	17.7	61.5[a]	44.8[a]	1.4	3.2
Netherlands	6.1	18.3	68.4	55.5	9.5	30.0
Portugal	−0.2	19.1	72.2	61.8	6.4	14.0
Spain	3.0	18.4	58.4	42.0	17.3	9.4
Sweden	4.2	19.0	81.2	79.1	2.7	−0.5
UK	2.9	19.3	74.7	64.8	9.4	6.5
EU15	3.4	19.0	67.3	55.9	10.0	3.6

[a] 1991.
[b] 1982–91.
[c] Below age 14.

Source: OECD (1995a).

dren below the age of 15 as a percentage of the total population ranged from just below 27 per cent in Ireland to just over 15 per cent in Germany. In the same year, the labour-force participation rate—the proportion of the population aged 15 to 64 which is 'economically active'—ranged from 83 per cent in Denmark to 57 per cent in Greece. *Female* participation rates were even more diverse, ranging from nearly 80 per cent in Denmark and Sweden to only 40 per cent in Ireland, Greece, and Spain.

Unemployment rates were also uneven: between 1982 and 1992, the averages recorded by the EU's 'star performers'—Austria and Sweden—were only a fifth of those prevailing in the EU's unemployment blackspots—Ireland and Spain—while employment growth ranged from a remarkable 30 per cent in the Netherlands to minus 2 per cent in Ireland and Finland. Table 10.3 shows the proportions of GDP devoted to health, education, and social security in those EU states for which fully comparable data are available. Between 1985 and 1990 there was some convergence in expenditure on health and education, as Spain caught up with other EU states and France took steps to curb its health bill. Social security budgets, by contrast, varied widely, with poverty-averting Denmark well ahead of the rest and the poverty-ridden UK well behind.

Table 10.3. **EU social expenditure, 1985–1990**

| Member State | Total government outlays as % of GDP at current market prices | | | | | |
| | Education | | Health | | Social security and welfare | |
	1985	1990	1985	1990	1985	1990
Denmark	6.7	7.2	5.2	5.3	21.3	23.6
France	5.6	5.3	9.9	7.3	18.1	19.5
Germany	4.7	4.1	6.4	5.9	19.1	17.8
Italy	5.1	5.4	5.4	6.3	16.0	16.6
Spain	3.7	4.2	4.7	5.1	14.8	14.8
UK	4.8	4.8	5.0	5.0	14.7	13.0

Source: OECD (1995b).

The period covered by Table 10.3 was one of general prosperity. In the early 1990s rising unemployment added significantly to the cost of social security everywhere. In this connection, it is worth noting that the convergence criteria for monetary union make no reference to any of the factors likely to affect either the demand for social expenditure or the capacity to sustain it. Since social policy has played a secondary role in the development of the EU, this is hardly surprising, but it is, on the face of it, perverse. The deflationary policies which several EU governments have adopted in order to meet the convergence criteria have undoubtedly contributed to high unemployment and low growth rates, thereby increasing the demand for social transfer spending, while making it harder for governments to finance it. Since joining the EU, Sweden has pressed for a relaxation of the convergence criteria to take account of conditions in the 'real economy', but so far other EU governments have resisted this proposal. One 'technical' problem is that the furious pace of economic and social change has made it more than normally difficult to distinguish between 'cyclical' and 'structural' budget deficits. In addition, even left-wing governments have now become fiscal conservatives.

Even if Europe's economies were less divergent and its governments less cautious, differences of policy regime would still be a powerful obstacle to an EU-wide social policy. Whilst some resolution of these differences cannot be ruled out—indeed, *some* convergence is already evident—the process is bound to be uneven and protracted. The issues involved are explored in the final section of this chapter.

The institutions of the EU

The legal basis of EU social policy is set out in the Treaty of Rome (1957), as modified by the Single European Act (SEA) (1986) and the Treaty on European Union (TEU) (1992). The relevant legal instruments consist of Regulations, Directives, and Decisions. The principal agency responsible for formulating and implementing social policy is the Commission's Directorate-General (DG) V, which deals with Employment, Industrial Relations, and Social Affairs. Technical issues arising from the need to reconcile diverse social-security systems with the free movement of labour are handled by the Administrative Commission for Social Security. The DG V is also assisted by a large number of standing advisory committees made up of government, trade-union, and employer representatives from each Member State. The most important of these is the Economic and Social Committee.

The provisions of the Treaty of Rome relating to social issues are contained mainly in Articles 117–28, though relevant matters are also referred to elsewhere. Articles 117 and 118 record the agreement of Member States to promote improved standards of living and working conditions. They also charge the Commission with the task of promoting cooperation in the social field. This is defined as covering vocational training, employment, working conditions, occupational health and safety, labour law, the rights of association and collective bargaining, and social security. The scope of social policy is thus explicitly confined to matters affecting *employees* rather than *citizens*. Furthermore, on matters covered by these two Articles, the role of the Commission is restricted to conducting research and offering opinions.

Articles 119–22 proclaim the objectives of equal pay for equal work and equal provisions for paid holidays; establish links with Articles 48–51 which seek to facilitate labour migration—*between* Member States, that is; and empower the Commission to report on social conditions in the Union. Articles 123–28 provide the legal basis for establishing a European Social Fund (ESF) with a view to promoting employment opportunities and facilitating both geographical and occupational mobility within the

EU. They also authorize the Council of Ministers to develop a common vocational training policy.

The operational design of the ESF has changed several times in the course of its history. In its most recent guise, the Fund supports a variety of projects, some organized centrally by the Commission, but most sponsored by public- and private-sector organizations at national, regional, and local levels. Eligible projects must be directed towards reducing unemployment, either in designated areas of rural underdevelopment or industrial decline, or among specified groups exposed to social exclusion—young people, the long-term unemployed, women seeking to re-enter employment, disabled people, and ethnic minority groups. The scale of the Fund, however, remains small and applications for support have consistently outstripped appropriations, despite a fourfold expansion in its budget since 1988. Indeed, the resources allocated to *all* EU Structural Funds, including the European Regional Development Fund (ERDF) and the European Agricultural Guidance and Guarantee Fund (EAGGF), currently represent not much more than 0.3 per cent of Union GDP. The White Paper on European Social Policy (CEC 1994) announced that Structural Funds were to have a budget of Ecu 141 billion for the period 1994–9, with Ecu 40 billion going to the ESF, but this still falls a long way short of what would be needed to make an impact on regional and social deprivation. The introduction of a Single European Currency would provide a historic opportunity, as well as a pressing reason, to increase regional and social expenditure by several orders of magnitude, but whether national governments and electorates would be prepared to accept the requisite redistribution of power and resources is another matter.

The reason social policy was assigned a minor role by the Treaty of Rome is that the EC was originally envisaged as a strictly *economic* union: issues which had no direct bearing on this project were ignored or discounted. Accordingly, except in the special case of agriculture, the EC lacked the attributes of a federal state, processing demands, allocating resources, and securing legitimacy. Rather, the emphasis was on standardizing access to the market through law. While this might be seen as adding a European layer to the *civil* rights of citizenship, the *political*, and still more the *social* rights of citizenship remained at a pre-European, national level. This state of affairs did not really change until the mid-1980s, when the Commission's newly appointed President, Jacques Delors, seized the opportunity presented by the Single Market programme to propound the idea that social cohesion was just as important as market integration. Even then, the preoccupation with *employment* remained, and the concept of a European 'social space' was fiercely contested by Delors's opponents, who were by no means confined to the UK.

Articles 100*a* and 118*a* of the SEA commit the EU to improving and harmonizing national standards of health and safety and of environmental and consumer protection. Article 118*b* gives the Commission responsibility for promoting a social dialogue between management and labour at the European level. Articles 130*a* and 130*b* seek to strengthen 'economic and social cohesion' through the use of reformed Structural Funds.

These additions to the EU's remit were accompanied by significant changes of legislative procedure. Except for certain reserved issues, the SEA introduced qualified majority voting in the Council of Ministers and strengthened the powers of the European Parliament (EP) in relation to the Council. Proposals concerning taxation and social security, the free movement of people, and the rights of employees still require unanimity and can, therefore, be blocked if a Member State chooses to exercise its veto. There is also a grey area in which it is open to argument which procedure should be used. This has been actively exploited both by the Commission, which argues that the protection of health and safety overlaps with the regulation of working time, and by the UK government, which sees no need for *any* restrictions on hours of work. Nevertheless, as Springer (1992) shows convincingly, the introduction of qualified majority voting has facilitated some important new initiatives in the social field by helping to expedite action in the Council, expand the scope for coalition-building between Commission, Parliament, and Council, and reduce the scope for obstructionism.

The fall-out from the SEA both reflected and reinforced a wider shift among opinion-makers. Political, business, and labour leaders were all keen to relaunch the project of European union and revitalize Europe's economies, and were all happy to embrace an activist conception of EU social policy. Statesmen and industrialists, impressed by the economic dynamism of the East Asian 'tigers' and by the striking success of the USA in creating new jobs, sought antidotes to 'Eurosclerosis'. The labour movement, devastated by mass unemployment and political defeat, was desperate for new jobs and new horizons. The high point of this new mood was reached at the Strasbourg Summit in December 1989, which, with the dissent of the UK, adopted the 'Social Charter' or, to give it its full title, the Community Charter of Fundamental Social Rights.

The significance of this event was largely symbolic. Despite the controversy it aroused, the Charter was purely declaratory and had no legal force. Its final version had, in any case, been diluted for the sake of consensus. Moreover, the Charter's Preamble includes a pointed reference to the principle of subsidiarity. This was a coded way of acknowledging limitations on the EU's authority to enact and enforce social legislation. Even so, the importance of symbols should not be underrated. The immediate reason for treating the 'social dimension' as a second pillar of the Single Europe project was to alleviate dislocations due to economic restructuring and to reassure workers that existing, nationally guaranteed rights and standards would not be undermined by intensified competition. Beyond this, however, lay a wider, political purpose. Supporters of the social dimension saw it as a building block in the creation of a 'People's Europe', which would, in time, come to rival the older nation states as a focus of social identity. From this standpoint, the Charter was less a statement of legislative intent and more the proclamation of a social ideal to stand alongside the market economy and parliamentary democracy as an emblem of European civilization.

The Social Charter formed the basis of the Social Chapter of the Maastricht Treaty, agreed in December 1991, signed in 1992, and ratified by all Member States in 1993. At the UK's insistence, the Social Chapter was formally excluded from the main body of the Treaty. But a Protocol was adopted by all Treaty signatories referring to an Agreement among the eleven Member States other than the UK to comply with the terms of the Social Chapter and to use the institutions and machinery of the Union to put this Agreement into effect. Thus, on matters covered by the original Treaty of Rome, as amended by the SEA, and on occasions when the UK wishes to participate in discussions arising from the Social Chapter, decision-making proceeds in the normal way. When the UK does *not* wish to participate in such discussions, decisions are made by the other Member States only, acting under the terms of the Protocol.

The Social Chapter adds three new objectives to Article 117 of the Treaty of Rome: 'proper social protection', dialogue between management and labour, and 'the development of human resources to achieve lasting employment'. The EU is empowered by Article 118 to legislate by qualified majority voting on questions of health and safety, working conditions, sex equality at work, and the integration of excluded groups into the labour force. Unanimity is still required for legislation on social security, redundancy procedures, the funding of job creation, the working conditions of third-country nationals, and worker representation. In all these areas, the Commission is obliged to consult representatives of management and labour before bringing proposals to the Council of Ministers. Note, however, that questions concerning pay, the right of association, and the right to resort to strikes or lock-outs are expressly excluded from Article 118. Note also that, under the terms of the new Article 3*b* on subsidiarity, the EU is authorized to act only in cases where action by Member States would be ineffective, or less effective, in achieving jointly agreed objectives.

10.5. **The development of EU social policy**

Besides being tightly circumscribed, EU social policy has developed in fits and starts. Sometimes it has been assigned a minor role, either by general consent or because any other course was blocked by an adverse balance of forces. But there have also been spurts of activism as those who favoured a collectivist, Union-wide approach to social issues—whether in the conservative or the social-democratic mould—temporarily gained ground over the supporters of economic liberalism and national autonomy, groups which often, though not invariably, coincide. In general, the policy activists have included the Commission, the majority groupings within the EP, and the European Trade Union Confederation (ETUC). They have been opposed by the Union of the Industries of the European Community (UNICE), which speaks for European employers and normally favours an internal market as free as possible from physical, technical, fiscal, and social 'distortions'. The UK government has also taken this view, sometimes gaining the backing of other Member States which objected to specific proposals and were happy to form an alliance of convenience. In the end, the fate of social

David Purdy

policy has depended on the Council of Ministers. But the Council is the focus of efforts by the Member States to uphold what they take to be their national interests. It is, therefore, the least 'European' of the EU's policy-making bodies.

Given this line-up of forces, raising the profile of social policy has usually required the assistance of one or both of two conditions: an easing of the institutional constraints—as with the introduction of qualified majority voting—or a change in the political complexion of the Council. Suitable conjunctures have arisen, either at times when the EU is being enlarged through new accessions, or when it is about to embark on some wider policy initiative such as closer monetary union or the Single Market project, the success of which can plausibly be shown to depend on stronger supranational social regulation.

Modest beginnings: from the Treaty of Rome to the late 1960s

EU social policy was originally envisaged as a minor adjunct to economic integration, focused almost exclusively on the labour market and concerned mainly with labour mobility and the impact of internal free trade on working conditions, wages, and social insurance. Policy-makers assumed that aspirations for higher wages and social expenditure would be met from the economies of scale and rapid economic growth that were expected to result from market liberalization. Since the 1960s were, indeed, years of unprecedented economic growth in the founding Member States, there was little pressure for anything more.

Nor, it could be argued, was there much *need* for policy harmonization among the original EC6. Leibfried (1993) notes that, apart from the Italian *Mezzogiorno*, these states formed a relatively homogeneous bloc. Taking into account *all* the relevant factors—economic structure, technological proficiency, wage levels, social insurance levies, labour productivity, transport costs, and exchange rates—they were evenly matched in competitive strength. Also, their welfare regimes formed a relatively tight cluster approximating to the conservative model. This homogeneity was disrupted by the successive enlargements of the EC in the 1970s and 1980s, which introduced a new pole of liberalism to the west, along with vestiges of traditionalism to the south. Once the EC's original equilibrium had been disturbed in this way, it could be regained, if at all, only by deliberate negotiation.

During the 1960s, then, EC social policy was modest both in intention and in achievement. Some progress was made in redeploying redundant workers, especially in unskilled occupations, with the ESF being used to support national retraining and resettlement schemes. But hopes that the Fund would benefit the less-developed regions of the EC proved unfounded. The total size of the Fund was left unspecified, but the proportions in which Member States contributed were predetermined, with France and Germany providing 32 per cent each and Italy 20 per cent. The assumption was that France and Germany, with lower unemployment rates, would be net losers. However, since the Fund operated by reimbursing Member States for 50 per cent of approved national expenditure, the amount which each state received depended critically on the scale of its own training efforts. As a result, Germany became a net beneficiary, receiving over 40 per cent of Fund expenditure during this period.

Ideas for harmonizing social insurance systems proved equally unrealistic. In part, this was because initial variations in coverage, scope, standards, costs, methods of finance, and eligibility rules were too wide to permit any easy or rapid convergence. But a more serious problem was that any uniform, Community-wide scheme would have entailed inter-state transfers on a scale that Germany, as the principal prospective net loser, was unwilling to countenance. The only concession to supporters of harmonization was an agreement to introduce equal pay for equal work throughout the EC. This move was instigated by France, where the law already prohibited sex discrimination with respect to rates of pay. The motive was strictly commercial: French employers were anxious not to be saddled with a competitive handicap. It was, nevertheless, an important precedent. Over the next thirty years both the Commission and the European Court of Justice (ECJ) exerted consistent pressure on Member States to equalize the terms on which women participate in the labour market. This said, it is pertinent to point out that legislation against sex discrimination does not in itself change the underlying sexual division of labour. Indeed, the law on its own *cannot* do much to change social practices which are rooted in everyday life and sustained by powerful ideologies. The achievements and limitations of EU legislation with special relevance for women are discussed by Hoskyns (1985), Mazey (1988), Springer (1992: ch. 6), and Meehan (1993).

Hopes and disappointments: the Social Action Programme of the 1970s

At the end of the 1960s, several developments stimulated a reassessment of the EC's low-key approach to social issues. The deliberations of the Werner Committee on Monetary Union prompted the realization that a system of 'irrevocably' fixed exchange rates would lead to regional imbalance and political tension if it were not accompanied by an adequately funded and centrally directed programme of regional aid. At the same time, the EC was about to undergo its first enlargement, and an economic framework which the original EC6 had been able to take for granted now required explicit attention. The political scene, too, had changed. After the explosion of working-class militancy and youth revolt in the late 1960s, political élites could no longer disregard either the social costs of economic growth or the popular image of the 'Common Market' as a 'rich man's club'. On both counts, the EC needed a 'human face'.

David Purdy

The new initiative was launched at the 1972 Paris Summit after several years of preparation. The Heads of State undertook to establish a Community regional policy, complete with its own Commissioner and a Regional Development Fund (discussed in Chapter 7). They also instructed the Commission to draw up a Social Action Programme. The Commission's proposals, unveiled in 1974, spawned a stream of new Directives. Two of these conferred rights of information and consultation on employees in firms which were proposing to institute redundancies or were involved in a change of ownership as a result of mergers, takeovers, or acquisitions. Other Directives required Member States to guarantee women equal access to vocational training and social security, and imposed tougher standards of workplace health and safety. In addition, the ESF was given a larger budget and a new, more tightly specified list of priorities. However, by the time these measures were implemented, the economic and political context had changed radically, and in the end the high hopes which had been vested in the Social Action Programme were largely disappointed.

The recession which hit the advanced capitalist world in the mid-1970s marked the end of the long post-war boom and transformed both the nature and the scale of the social problems facing the EC. Member States responded by seeking national rather than Community solutions. In the social sphere, the Commission had always favoured a levelling-up approach to the development of common rights and standards. At the best of times, this was hard to achieve: the richer states were unwilling to pay for EC policies that would mainly benefit the poorer states, and the poorer states were unwilling to agree to EC policies that they were unable to pay for themselves. In conditions of recession, what had previously been difficult became well-nigh impossible.

The least successful parts of the Social Action Programme were those concerned with industrial democracy. The idea that trade unions had a right to participate in policy-making at every level, from workplace and boardroom to nation and Community, was deeply rooted in the social policy regimes of the EC's core states and was strongly supported by the Commission. But policy regimes are organic formations and cannot easily be transplanted from one state to another. The UK, in particular, was steeped in the tradition of 'free collective bargaining'. British trade unions, which at this time were opposed to UK membership of the EC, showed little enthusiasm for 'foreign' notions of industrial democracy, while British employers flatly rejected proposals which they perceived as threat to the 'prerogatives' of management.

Throughout the 1970s the Commission laboured to find an acceptable way of securing a common commitment to workers' participation. But even though it abandoned its preference for the German model and was prepared to allow for several alternative systems from which governments could choose according to their national traditions, this effort failed. The final act in the cycle of social legislation that had begun a decade earlier was the proposed 'Vredeling' Directive of 1980. This sought to extend the EC's disclosure laws to transnational companies, obliging them to inform and consult their employees on a regular basis and with respect to their global operations, not just those in the EC. The proposal aroused strong opposition from UNICE and was thrown out by the Council of Ministers after orchestrated resistance led by the UK. It was to be another six years before any major new employment laws were enacted.

The 1980s: the SEA and the Social Charter

After drifting into the doldrums in the late 1970s, social policy received a new impetus in the early 1980s, following the electoral victory of the French Socialists in 1981. The turning-point was the Fontainebleau Summit in 1984 and the appointment of Jacques Delors as President of the Commission. Building on the decisions of the Summit, the Commission proposed a new Action Programme with four major themes: (i) completion of the Single European Market (SEM) by the end of 1992; (ii) extension of the EC's legal competence in the social sphere to include the working environment; (iii) a package of reforms covering the CAP, the EC's finances, and the three Structural Funds; and (iv) revival of the practice of social dialogue.

From 1985 onwards, all shades of opinion paid greater heed than before to what became known as the 'social dimension' of European integration. The rationale and significance of this development were briefly touched on in the previous section. Social policy did not, however, suddenly cease to be a battleground. For economic liberals, the 'social dimension' meant removing obstacles to the free movement of labour by improving information about job prospects and establishing uniform professional standards and job qualifications. Pragmatists, more alert to the negative consequences of closer economic union, stressed the need to compensate those regions and social groups which stood to lose from economic restructuring, and urged that action be taken to prevent 'social dumping'—the levelling *down* of established wages, standards and rights which, it was feared, would result from the removal of barriers to pan-European competition. Finally, as noted earlier, European idealists saw the social dimension as a means of winning popular support for the goal of closer political union.

By the end of the 1980s, the Social Charter had emerged as the central focus of conflict. Mrs Thatcher denounced it as 'Marxist interventionism'. Yet the Charter was non-binding and most of its specific principles, such as the right to belong or not to belong to a trade union, had long been observed in most Member States or, as in the case of equal treatment for women at work, had actually been enshrined in Community law. What the Charter's opponents chiefly disliked was its underlying philosophy. In so far as they had specific, practical objections, these centred on commitments which would, or might, add to employers' costs or limit their room for manœuvre: notably, the requirement that the wages of 'atypical' employees should be set by reference to an equitable bench-mark; the potential extension of disclosure rights through the establishment of works councils; and the Commission's well-known and long-standing desire to establish Community-wide collective bargaining in transnational companies. Critics were also unhappy that the Commission was empowered to compile an annual report on the application of the Charter throughout the EC. Of course, there is little point in having a statement of principles without some way of monitoring outcomes. But recurrent monitoring would enable the Commission and its allies in the EP to keep social regulation permanently on the agenda.

In fact, with one exception discussed below, the Commission tended to soft pedal the implementation of the Charter: there was no flurry of new Directives on the pattern of the 1970s. The Directive is, in any case, of limited value as an instrument of social policy. The latitude given to Member States in deciding how to set about achieving specified targets necessarily complicates the Commission's responsibility for ensuring that different technical means really are equivalent—the more so when the targets in question are difficult, if not impossible, to quantify.

Steps were, however, taken to regulate the working environment, broadly construed to include working time. Standards of workplace health and safety proved relatively uncontroversial, partly because of the technical nature of the issues at stake and partly because even economic liberals have no wish to seem careless of human life. But the same could not be said of working time. The Working Time Directive, adopted in 1993 and due to be implemented in Member States by November 1996, was bitterly contested by the UK, which challenged its legality and applied unsuccessfully to the ECJ to have it annulled. It provides for a maximum working week of forty-eight hours on average, including overtime, and confers employee rights to minimum rest breaks during working hours and to four weeks' annual paid holiday. The Directive is significant not only because it curtails the very long working hours which have been traditional in certain industries and occupations, and recognizes that workers have family and other responsibilities, but also because several of its provisions are subject to *derogation* and may be implemented by collective agreements between the two sides of industry at the appropriate level. This could mark the emergence of a form of European labour law in which collective bargaining plays a key role. Ironically, such a pattern is familiar in the UK, but less so in other Member States, where legislation has traditionally been the principal method of labour regulation.

After Maastricht

By the time the ratification of the Maastricht Treaty had been completed in 1993, the Exchange Rate Mechanism (ERM) had effectively broken down and progress towards monetary union was stalled. In the early 1990s, the anxieties which had been displaced by enthusiasm for the Single Market programme re-emerged. The special dispensations obtained by the UK and Denmark interacted with a shift in public opinion to create a general reluctance, even in those Member States most committed to the European ideal, to cede further sovereignty to the Union. In this uncertain setting, one can only speculate about the future.

Hitherto, conceptions of a 'common' EU social policy have veered between two extremes. Ardent 'Europeans' have sought to achieve *positive harmonization*, a dynamic process in which diverse national systems gradually converge as the ground they share in common is continually enlarged. At times of perceptible progress towards closer union, this has seemed a plausible goal, but whenever momentum has been lost, pessimism has set in and sights have been lowered towards the more modest objective of *negative coordination*. On this view, there is little scope for a distinctively *European* social policy beyond removing inconsistencies between otherwise autonomous national systems by organizing the area of overlap between them—for example, through mutual recognition of professional standards and job qualifications. The Social Charter and its successor, the Social Chapter, attempted to strike a balance between these two views by formulating a common set of general norms, based on an agreed 'European' view about the role of labour in society, whilst at the same time accommodating economic disparities and national traditions. That the attempt failed, in the end, to satisfy economic liberals testifies to the severity of the twin conflicts which have bedevilled EU social policy: between competing ideologies and between divergent conceptions of European unity.

Because of the way the EU has evolved, debate about EU social policy has focused on the *labour market*. Yet it has never made much sense to treat paid work in isolation from unpaid work, and it makes even less at a time when the institutions of employment and family life are being transformed. In the labour market, mass unemployment and work flexibilization are undermining personal security and unravelling social cohesion. In domestic life, the demise of the male breadwinner and the partial convergence of gender roles have highlighted the distinction between work and employment and have challenged the sexual division of labour as a whole. Moreover, these changes are unfolding against the backdrop of wider social upheaval. The nation state, historically the focus of efforts to extend and enhance the various elements of citizenship, has lost some of its potency as a source of social identity, not to mention its capacity to manage the economy. At the same time, the welfare state is being steadily redesigned in response to financial and competitive pressures.

In these circumstances, it is worth considering a third approach to European social policy, involving what might be called 'European social citizenship' as an integral part of a federal European state. The aim would be to create a supranational social space with common rights extended to all citizens of the EU, regardless of their economic status. Hitherto, in the eyes of most ordinary people, the EU has seemed remote and irrelevant or labyrinthine and sinister: either way, they had little reason to love or trust it. If its policies impinged on them at all, it was as the outcome of multi-levelled bargaining between sectional interest groups, national governments, and EU agencies over the allocation of Structural Funds or the application of EU law. By contrast, the links between European social citizenship and an emergent federal state would be direct and transparent. This would require a separate EU tier of taxes and transfers, over and above those which continued to be levied and dispensed by each national state. And Eurofiscal policy would, in turn, need to be coordinated with macroeconomic and active labour-market policies, similarly framed on a Union-wide scale. It would also need to be endorsed by a federal EP, equipped with the requisite powers of initiative, amendment, supervision, and inquiry.

In the prevailing climate of disillusion, cynicism, and foreboding, it is easy to dismiss this vision as utopian. And, indeed, it *is* utopian, but none the worse for that. Invective apart, utopias are *thought experiments*—deliberately 'unrealistic', but internally coherent attempts to visualize what the world would be like if some taken-for-granted feature of the social landscape could somehow be removed, replaced, or reshaped. As long as one bears in mind that such an exercise is not the same as devising a *political programme* which must, perforce, take account of cultural inertia, political reaction, and historical contingency, it can be a useful tool of intellectual enquiry, helping to fix ideas and explore possibilities. In any case, in contemplating the future, it is unwise to consider only the pieces which are currently on the board and to think only a few moves ahead. History provides no warrant for the view that attempts to refashion social institutions and reorder international relations are doomed to failure. Consider, for example, the role of creative statesmanship in overcoming global dislocation after the Second World War. The lesson to be drawn is that Europe's current social problems *can* be tackled, but it is going to require the same combination of social vision, political courage, and practical wisdom that gave its peoples a new lease of life half a century ago.

Discussion questions

1. Does the EU have a role to play in social policy? If so, what is it? If not, what degree of social diversity can the EU tolerate and still survive?

2. For what reasons, in what ways, and with what success did the EC seek to enhance the role of social policy during the period from the mid-1980s to the ratification of the TEU?

3. Analyse the challenges facing contemporary welfare states. How, if at all, can and should the EU help Member States to respond to these challenges?

FURTHER READING

Hantrais (1995) reviews the historical development and current state of EU social policy. Meehan (1993) discusses the geometry of social citizenship in the context of the changing division of power and responsibility between the EU and its Member States. Esping-Andersen (1990) remains the *locus classicus* for students of social policy regimes, while Leibfried (1993) offers critical comments on Esping-Andersen's schema, discusses the role of the EU as a social policy actor in its own right, and compares alternative conceptions of European integration.

REFERENCES

Anderson, M., Bechofer, F., and Gershuny, J. (1994) (eds.), *The Social and Political Economy of the Household* (Oxford: Oxford University Press).

CEC (1994): Commission of the European Communities, *European Social Policy—A White Paper* (Brussels: CEC).

Esping-Andersen, G. (1990), *The Three Worlds of Welfare Capitalism* (Cambridge: Polity Press).

—— (1992), 'The Three Political Economies of the Welfare State' in Kolberg (1992), 92–123.

—— (1994), 'Welfare States and the Economy', in Smelser and Swedberg (1994), 711–32.

Galbraith, J. K. (1992), *The Contented Society* (Harmondsworth: Penguin).

Gershuny, J., Godwin, M., and Jones, S. (1994), 'The Domestic Division of Labour', in Anderson *et al.* (1994), 151–97.

Hantrais, L. (1995), *Social Policy in the European Union* (Basingstoke: Macmillan).

Hoskyns, C. (1985), 'Women's Equality and the European Community', *Feminist Review*, 20 (June), 71–88.

Jones, C. (1993) (ed.), *New Perspectives on the Welfare State in Europe* (London: Routledge).

Kolberg, J. E. (1992) (ed.), *The Study of Welfare State Regimes* (New York: M. E. Sharpe).

Langan, M., and Ostner, I. (1991), 'Gender and Welfare: Towards a Comparative Framework' in Room (1991), 127–50.

Leibfried, S. (1993), 'Towards a European Welfare State?' in Jones (1993), 133–56.

Lewis, J. (1993) (ed.), *Women and Social Policies in Europe: Work, Family and the State* (Aldershot: Edward Elgar).

Lister, R. (1992), *Women's Economic Dependency and Social Security* (Manchester: Equal Opportunities Commission).

Marshall, T. H. (1950), *Citizenship and Social Class and Other Essays* (Cambridge: Cambridge University Press).

Mazey, S. (1988), 'European Community Action on Behalf of Women: The Limits of Legislation', *Journal of Common Market Studies*, 27: 63–84.

Meehan, E. (1993), *Citizenship and the European Community* (London: Sage).

OECD (1995a): Organization for Economic Cooperation and Development, *Labour Force Statistics 1973–93* (Paris: OECD).

—— (1995b): *National Accounts 1981–93* (Paris: OECD).

Pierson, C. (1991), *Beyond the Welfare State* (Cambridge: Polity Press).

Purdy, D. (1994), 'Citizenship, Basic Income and the State', *New Left Review*, 208 (Nov.–Dec.), 30–48.

Room, G. (1991) (ed.), *Towards a European Welfare State* (Bristol: School for Advanced Urban Studies Publications).

Smelser, N. J., and Swedberg, R. (1994) (eds.), *The Handbook of Economic Sociology* (Princeton: Princeton University Press).

Springer, B. (1992), *The Social Dimension of 1992: Europe Faces a New EC* (New York: Praeger).

Van Parijs, P (1992) (ed.), *Arguing for Basic Income* (London: Verso).

CHAPTER 11

Developments in Trade and Trade Policy

LYNDEN MOORE

11.1. Introduction

The trade policy of the EU should be considered within the international context because, although much of the CEC efforts have been devoted to removing impediments to trade within the EU, there have also been parallel developments in the international market. At both levels, provisions have been extended to encompass trade in services as well as goods. Policies of privatization in most countries of the world have also opened markets to international competition, most significantly in telecommunications. Even in areas where these have not been introduced, there have been agreements to open up government procurement to international competition.

11.2. The international context

The EU is a member of the World Trade Organization (WTO), which, at the beginning of 1995, took over the role of the General Agreement on Tariffs and Trade (GATT). Set up in 1948, GATT was based on the principle of non-discrimination and the progressive reduction of barriers to trade. Most West European countries belonged to it. On becoming a member, each nation had extended to it the most-favoured-nation (m.f.n.) tariff—that is, the lowest tariff—of every other member, and vice versa.

Although custom unions and free trade areas (FTAs) appeared to conflict with this principle of non-discrimination, they were favourably regarded as leading on to greater liberalization in trade. But under Article XXIV they were required to comply with certain provisions; they should cover 'substantially all the trade between constituent territories', 'the (external) duties . . . shall not on the whole be higher or more restrictive than . . . prior to the formation of such a union' and they 'shall include a plan and schedule for [their] . . . formation within a reasonable length of time' (GATT 1986: Article XXIV).

The Treaty of Rome of 1957 was drafted with these provisions in mind. The EC was set up as a customs union with provision for the removal of all impediments to trade in goods and the establishment of a common external tariff (CET) for manufactures. None the less, there was criticism of the setting of the CET at the simple unweighted arithmetic average of the tariffs applied by each of the six EC Member States on 1 January 1957. Inevitably it raised tariffs on extra-EC imports into EC countries with previously low levels of tariffs (WTO, 1995a), but then these tariffs were lowered by the GATT's subsequent rounds of tariff negotiations.

However, as tariffs were reduced, the developed countries had frequent recourse to non-tariff barriers to trade, which were quite inconsistent with the ethos and legal requirements of GATT. Prominent among these devices was the 'voluntary' export restraint (VER) by which the importing country negotiates a physical limit on exports from a particular country. The VER is, in effect, a bilateral quota. It has a similar effect to a tariff in raising the price of the product on the market of the importing country. But no tariff revenue is gained. Instead, there is an 'economic rent' associated with the quota, due to the fact that the product is sold on the domestic market at a much higher price than it can command on the international market. Who gains the economic rent depends on how the quota is allocated. When VERs are imposed on developing countries, those countries are generally given the entitlement to export and are therefore generally regarded as acquiring the rent from the quota.

In addition there has been a widespread use by both the EU and the USA of countervailing and anti-dumping duties. Dumping is defined as the situation in which a product is sold in a market at less than its 'normal' value, which is regarded as either being 'the comparable price . . . when destined for consumption in the exporting country, or, in the absence of such domestic price is less than either the highest comparable price . . . (of the) product for export to any third country . . . or, the cost of production of the product in the country of origin plus a reasonable addition for selling cost and profit' (GATT 1986: Article VI). The importing firm country can levy an anti-dumping duty not greater than the margin of dumping on the exports of the firm. Alternatively, if the difference is due to a government subsidy, a countervailing duty may be imposed to offset it. Sometimes firms avoid anti-dumping duties by accepting a 'price undertaking'— that is, a minimum import price, by which the exporting firms lose their competitive advantage but gain a higher price. In the year to June 1995 the EU led the field initiating thirty-seven anti-dumping actions, but EU companies themselves were the targets for eight started by other countries (Williams 1995).

The problem with these non-tariff barriers is their arbitrary nature, the way they discriminate not only between countries but, also, in the case of anti-dumping duties between firms, penalizing the most efficient producers. In calculating the size of anti-dumping duties, the EU is also accused of the dubious use of statistics.

11.3. The recent trading position

The trading position in the early 1990s is shown in Tables 11.1 and 11.2. It is somewhat difficult to relate the trade to the production classification. None the less, this has been done for some of the major categories. Table 11.1 shows the production, value added, and imports and exports of manufactures in total and 'extra'—that is, from trade with non-EU countries. The last column shows the degree of import penetration—that is, imports as a percentage of consumption (production minus exports plus imports). The highest degree of import penetration, at 47 per cent, appears to be in instrument engineering; it is also high in office and DP equipment, leather and leather goods, footwear and clothing. The last three categories are ones in which the newly industrialized countries of Asia are major suppliers.

Table 11.2 shows how, in 1994, EU exports of the different categories were distributed between other members of the EU, other countries in Western Europe, and the rest of the world. Overall, 58 per cent of exports of manufactures went to other members of the EU, but the proportion varied considerably as between products. In automotive products 66 per cent went to other members of the EU and therefore automotive producers appear the most dependent on the EU market. As will be described later, this appears to be due to the quotas erected against imports from Japan. At the other extreme, only 35 per cent of power-generating equipment went to other members of the EU; 57 per cent went to the rest of the world. The latter was also an important destination for exports of other non-electric machinery, and other transport equipment—that is, aircraft.

11.4. The Uruguay Round, 1986–94

The Uruguay Round was the latest and most extensive of the GATT tariff negotiations. Quantitative restrictions are due to be phased out, as will be discussed later. More explicit provisions have been accepted for the imposition and calculation of anti-dumping duties.

With respect to tariffs, the overall result for manufactures will be a reduction in the EU's unweighted average CET from 6 per cent in 1995 to 3.7 per cent in 2000. But there will still be a considerable variation in the degree of tariff protection for different product categories, as can be seen from Fig. 11.1. The tariffs on construction equipment, agricultural equipment, medical equipment, pharmaceuticals, most steel categories,

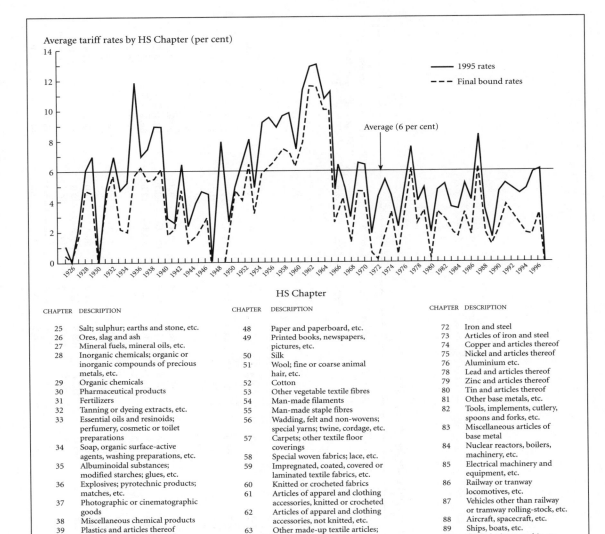

Average tariff rates by HS Chapter (per cent)

—— 1995 rates

- - - Final bound rates

Average (6 per cent)

HS Chapter

CHAPTER	DESCRIPTION	CHAPTER	DESCRIPTION	CHAPTER	DESCRIPTION
25	Salt; sulphur; earths and stone, etc.	48	Paper and paperboard, etc.	72	Iron and steel
26	Ores, slag and ash	49	Printed books, newspapers, pictures, etc.	73	Articles of iron and steel
27	Mineral fuels, mineral oils, etc.			74	Copper and articles thereof
28	Inorganic chemicals; organic or inorganic compounds of precious metals, etc.	50	Silk	75	Nickel and articles thereof
		51	Wool; fine or coarse animal hair, etc.	76	Aluminium etc.
29	Organic chemicals	52	Cotton	78	Lead and articles thereof
30	Pharmaceutical products	53	Other vegetable textile fibres	79	Zinc and articles thereof
31	Fertilizers	54	Man-made filaments	80	Tin and articles thereof
32	Tanning or dyeing extracts, etc.	55	Man-made staple fibres	81	Other base metals, etc.
33	Essential oils and resinoids; perfumery, cosmetic or toilet preparations	56	Wadding, felt and non-wovens; special yarns; twine, cordage, etc.	82	Tools, implements, cutlery, spoons and forks, etc.
		57	Carpets; other textile floor coverings	83	Miscellaneous articles of base metal
34	Soap, organic surface-active agents, washing preparations, etc.	58	Special woven fabrics; lace, etc.	84	Nuclear reactors, boilers, machinery, etc.
35	Albuminoidal substances; modified starches; glues, etc.	59	Impregnated, coated, covered or laminated textile fabrics, etc.	85	Electrical machinery and equipment, etc.
36	Explosives; pyrotechnic products; matches, etc.	60	Knitted or crocheted fabrics	86	Railway or tranway locomotives, etc.
37	Photographic or cinematographic goods	61	Articles of apparel and clothing accessories, knitted or crocheted	87	Vehicles other than railway or tramway rolling-stock, etc.
38	Miscellaneous chemical products	62	Articles of apparel and clothing accessories, not knitted, etc.	88	Aircraft, spacecraft, etc.
39	Plastics and articles thereof			89	Ships, boats, etc.
40	Rubber and articles thereof	63	Other made-up textile articles; sets, worn clothing, etc.	90	Optical, photographic, etc. apparatus
41	Raw hides and skins and leather	64	Footwear, gaiters, etc.		
42	Articles of leather, etc.	65	Headgear and parts thereof	91	Clocks and watches, etc.
43	Furskins and artificial fur; manufactures thereof	66	Umbrellas, walking-sticks, etc.	92	Musical instruments, etc.
		67	Prepared feathers and down, etc.	93	Arms and ammunition, etc.
44	Wood and articles of wood, etc.	68	Articles of stone, plaster, etc.	94	Furniture, bedding, etc.
45	Cork and articles of cork	69	Ceramic products	95	Toys, games, etc.
46	Manufactures of straw, of esparto, etc.	70	Glass and glassware	96	Miscellaneous manuf. articles
47	Pulp of wood or of other fibrous cellulosic material	71	Natural or cultured pearls, precious or semi-precious stones, precious metals, etc.	97	Works of art, antiques, etc.

Note: In the Uruguay Round negotiations, certain items in chapters 25 to 97 were classified as 'agricultural' products.

Fig. 11.1 Tariffs on manufactured products, EU12, 1995 and 2000

Source: WTO (1995*b*: 54).

Table 11.1. EU employment, production, and trade by sector, 1993

NACE code	Description	Employment (million)	Production	Value added[a]	Imports (Ecu bn.)		Exports		Production (1985 prices)	Import penetration (%)
					Total	Extra	Total	Extra		
2100	Extraction and preparation of metallurgical ores	n.a.	n.a.	n.a.	5.3	4.4	0.8	0.3	n.a.	n.a.
2200	Metals (preliminary processing)	0.7	106.9	32.2	58.6	27.3	55.5	22.4	123.6	24.4
2210	Iron and steel	0.3	51.6	16.4	17.5	4.1	24.5	10.3	58.5	9.0
2300	Non-metallic minerals	0.1	n.a.	n.a.	5.1	3.0	3.2	1.0	n.a.	n.a.
2400	Non-metallic mineral production	0.9	95.1	44.2	16.2	4.4	22.9	9.3	90.6	4.9
2500	Chemicals	1.6	276.9	107.9	114.4	34.9	131.1	58.1	283.1	13.8
2570	Pharmaceuticals	0.4	68.9	31.7	16.0	6.3	22.4	12.5	68.4	10.1
2600	Man-made fibres	0.0	7.0	2.4	5.3	1.3	4.2	1.2	7.6	18.0
3100	Metal articles	2.0	169.7	77.5	27.5	9.9	35.5	15.3	163.1	6.0
3200	Mechanical engineering	2.1	210.7	90.4	75.8	30.8	125.6	75.1	193.9	18.5
3300	Office & DP machinery	0.2	44.9	16.9	50.1	25.3	36.4	12.0	52.1	43.5
3400	Electrical engineering	2.4	252.0	113.7	108.9	53.7	109.9	49.9	255.3	21.0
3500	Motor vehicles and parts	1.7	245.2	79.1	99.2	21.9	113.2	36.7	223.5	9.5
3600	Other transport	0.7	70.3	28.5	42.1	20.6	47.0	24.5	66.8	31.0
3610	Shipbuilding	0.2	15.5	5.1	4.1	3.3	6.7	5.5	14.5	24.9

Code	Industry									
3700	Instrument engineering	0.3	25.1	13.2	23.9	12.9	22.0	10.8	23.2	47.4
4100	Food, drink, tobacco	2.4	457.8	144.6	82.7	21.9	93.6	30.8	437.9	4.9
4200	Sugar manufacture and refining	n.a.	n.a.	n.a.	2.1	1.2	2.6	1.4	n.a.	n.a.
4300	Textile industry	n.a.	n.a.	n.a.	44.4	19.7	45.1	17.1	n.a.	n.a.
4400	Leather and leather goods	0.1	9.1	3.0	6.0	3.7	6.1	3.5	9.6	40.0
4500	Footwear and clothing	1.1	67.4	24.1	42.1	24.9	32.1	12.7	65.6	31.3
4530	Clothing	0.8	45.4	16.9	27.7	18.0	18.2	7.1	43.9	32.0
4600	Timber and wooden industry	0.9	74.0	29.7	22.5	13.5	16.9	6.0	70.2	16.5
4700	Paper; printing and publishing	1.4	164.1	69.0	35.5	17.7	30.0	10.9	163.7	10.4
4800	Processing of rubber and plastics	1.1	104.2	44.5	31.9	9.3	36.7	12.3	101.3	9.2
4900	Other manufacturing industry	0.2	19.8	9.1	58.3	29.5	72.2	37.6	19.1	n.a.
5000	Building and civil engineering	3.4	320.5	147.6	n.a.	n.a.	n.a.	n.a.	312.4	n.a.
9001	Manufacturing industry	20.9	2,621.5	1,032.6	970.7	394.1	1,061.4	457.2	2,573.8	15.4

Note: n.a. = not available.
[a] At market prices.

Source: WTO (1995b: i. 197).

Table 11.2. **EU12 trade in manufactures, 1994**

Product groups	Exports				Imports ($ bn.)	Net exports ($ bn.)
	Percentage distribution					
	Total ($ bn.)	Intra–EU	Other Western Europe	Rest of the world		
Iron and Steel	49.77	60	11	29	42.07	7.70
Chemicals	198.04	57	11	31	162.09	35.95
Other semi-manufactures	136.83	58	16	30	135.86	.97
Machinery and Transport equipment	583.47	53	11	36	518.13	65.84
Power-generating equipment	22.87	35	8	57	19.41	3.46
Other non-electrical machinery	152.59	40	12	48	45.73	56.86
Office and telecommunications equipment	109.54	59	11	30	146.77	−37.32
Electrical machinery	66.95	52	12	35	66.95	5.26
Automotive products	173.96	66	10	24	145.43	28.53
Other transport equipment	58.06	46	8	46	58.06	8.95
Textiles	48.31	60	11	29	45.07	3.24
Clothing	39.50	63	16	22	61.80	−22.30
Other consumer goods	147.43	53	15	33	146.69	0.74
TOTAL MANUFACTURES	1,523.36	58	11	32	1,527.46	−4.1

Note: Product groups are defined according to Revision 3 of the Standard International Trade Classification (SITC Rev. 3).
Source: WTO (1995c).

paper products, furniture, selected toys, and soaps and detergents will be eliminated. The highest tariffs in 2000 will be on textiles and clothing, aluminium, and passenger cars (at 10 per cent), all of which are now regarded as the products of 'sensitive', i.e. declining, industries, but also those on radio and TV sets will be at 14 per cent (WTO, 1995*b*: i. 52, 94, 104).

Services were brought into the negotiations for the first time. However, the system of negotiation was different from that of goods, with countries making offers generally on condition that others did so also. Many of these negotiations—for example, telecommunications and maritime transport—were not completed as this book was being written (June 1996).

11.5. **EU's preferential agreements**

The EU has entered into a wide range of other preferential agreements. Generally, these have been signed bilaterally with individual countries. The benefits the countries get from them depends not only on the degree of preference available but also on whether the products they produce conform to the 'rules of origin'. The 'rules of origin' for preference schemes are that the product must be wholly produced or have undergone 'sufficient transformation' in the exporting beneficiary country. A product using imported inputs qualifies 'if the four-digit tariff heading of final products differs from that of the inputs' (GATT 1991: i. 119, 120). Sometimes the EU accepts cumulation between the output of the EU and the country, or between the output of several members of the same regional group. This makes it easier for a country, particularly a developing one, to meet the 'rules-of-origin' requirements.

Lomé Agreements

At the outset, the EC formed bilateral free trade areas with the 'Overseas Territories'—mainly former colonies and territories of the six original Member States. The membership of this scheme has been steadily increased by a succession of Lomé Agreements to seventy African (excluding South Africa), Carribean, and Pacific (ACP) countries. For cumulation purposes, the Overseas Countries and Territories (OCT) associated with the EU and the EU are regarded as one unit; this in effect gives preferences to EU inputs. Despite this preferential access to the EU market, the ACP's proportion of EU imports has fallen significantly since the 1980s (WTO 1995b: i. 27). To other members of GATT it represented a wider preferential scheme. The EC endeavoured to use the Trade and Development provision Article XXXVI, added to GATT in 1965, under which developed countries do not insist on reciprocity in trade negotiations with developing countries to justify the Lomé agreements. However, it was not regarded as in conformity with Article XXIV and GATT eventually gave the fourth Lomé convention a waiver (WTO 1995a).

Generalized system of preference

In response to the developing countries in UNCTAD, the EC also established in 1971 a Generalized System of Preference (GSP), by which they were permitted to export their manufactures tariff-free to the EC up to a certain limit (tariff quota), but this had to be renegotiated each year. At the beginning of January 1995 this was replaced by a *revised GSP scheme* covering 145 countries and the entire industrial sector except for armaments. Under the general regime of the new GSP, tariff quotas are scrapped to be replaced by a degree of tariff preference which depends on the 'sensitivity' of the product being imported and the 'development index' of exporting countries. There are four categories of sensitivity:

1. 'very sensitive' products (textiles, clothing and ferro-alloys), for which the preferential rate of duty is 85 per cent of the regular duty;

2. 'sensitive products', which include footwear, electronics, and motor vehicles, for which the preferential duty is 70 per cent of the regular duty;

3. 'semi-sensitive' products, for which the preferential duty is 35 per cent of the regular duty; and

4. 'non-sensitive' products, for which the preferential rate is zero.

However, the least developed countries and the Andean pact countries gain more favourable treatment.

Although this is not due to be reviewed before January 1999, under certain conditions a country can be 'graduated' through or out of the GSP. These conditions depend on, first, the beneficiary country's *development index*,[1] which is dependent on its per capita income as a percentage of that of the EU, and the value of all manufactured exports from the beneficiary country as a proportion of total EU manufactured exports. The second criterion is the *specialization index*[2] in the product category being considered. There are twenty-one separate product categories, including one each for textiles, clothing, footwear, steel products, consumer electronics, and motor vehicles. Export specialization for a beneficiary country then depends on its share of EU imports in that product category, and its overall share of EU imports—that is, the total value of EU imports from the beneficiary country as a proportion of global EU imports. As can be seen, both of these indexes will tend to be higher *ceteris paribus*, the more open and the larger the country. Country-product combinations that have incurred graduation are: Argentina, raw hides and skins; China, articles of leather and footwear; Hong Kong, clothing; India, raw hides and skins, articles of leather, and textiles; Indonesia, wood and articles of wood, and footwear; Malaysia, wood and articles of wood; Singapore, all electronic goods; South Korea, articles of leather and footwear; Thailand, footwear; and Pakistan, raw hides and skins, articles of leather, and textiles (WTO 1995b: i. 28–37).

Rules of origin for the GSP are generally based on the change in tariff classification. Regional accumulation is possible for the Asean and Andean Pact countries. Since 1995 new provisions allow all products of EU origin to be considered as 'originating' from the beneficiary country—the so-called 'donor-country' rule. The CEC expects this to encourage joint ventures to process EU materials and components (WTO 1995b: i. 30).

Least developed countries qualify for total exemption from customs duties on industrial products and some agricultural products and do not have to comply with the rules of origin. However, the EC reserves the right to employ safeguard measures. The CEC also intends to introduce a special incentive GSP regime to help beneficiary countries 'improve the quality of their development through the application of more advanced social and environmental policies' (ibid.).

'The CEC argues that the new GSP system, although conceptually complex . . . (has the advantages of) . . . transparency and stability, ease of implementation, reduced administrative costs and . . . the strengthening of the GSP as a Development tool' (ibid.). The author of this chapter considers these objectives are buried by the complexity of the scheme.

The EU's free trade agreement with EFTA

When the UK, Denmark, and Ireland joined in 1973, the EC formed a free trade area in manufactures with the remaining members of EFTA. There has, therefore, effectively been free trade in manufactures throughout most of Western Europe since 1973. But in forming the free trade area, EFTA changed its rules of origin to conform to those of the EC. These are the change in tariff heading, already mentioned, plus a large number of product-specific rules often based on value added. However, in considering whether a product from an EFTA country was eligible for free trade status, the EC did not allow cumulation of processing carried out in other EFTA countries. This became included only when the European Economic Area (EEA) Treaty come into effect at the beginning of 1994 (Hoekman and Leidy 1993). The EEA also removed barriers to trade in services.

Eastern Europe

The breakaway of the Eastern European countries from the Soviet bloc after 1989 faced the EU with a quandary. On the one hand, it was anxious to assist the rehabilitation of these newly democratic states into the free markets of the Western world. On the other hand, the industries in which the Central and Eastern European Countries (CEECs) appeared most competitive were the 'sensitive' ones—that is, the declining industries that the EU was doing its best to protect in many cases by the imposition of quotas. Horticulture and textiles and clothing were the most important, but so also were coal and iron and steel.

The EU moved tentatively at first, extending to the CEECs (Bulgaria, the Czech and Slovak Republics, Hungary, Poland, and Romania) the generalized system of preference provisions it had instituted for developing countries. Then, between 1991 and 1993, the EU negotiated with each of the six countries broadly similar agreements termed the Europe Agreements. The objective of these was the establishment of a free trade area in goods and services between the EU and these countries within ten years. Quotas and tariffs were removed on industrial products *except* for those listed in the annexes. Annex II comprises raw materials and primary products for which the removal of tariffs was slower. Annex III comprises an array of 'sensitive' products such as footwear and furniture, which account for a sizeable proportion of the CEECs' exports, for which quantitative restrictions were removed but tariff quotas remained. Textiles and Clothing are covered by a special protocol I by which EU tariffs are gradually removed over five years and quotas on imports from the CEECs are increased twice as fast as negotiated for the developing countries under the Uruguay Round and thus should disappear after five years. Protocol II covers coal and steel products for which EU tariffs are reduced or eliminated but on which some quotas are retained. There is very little liberalization of agriculture—this is a major problem and the Common

Agricultural Policy of the EU will have to be scrapped in its present form before the CEECs can become members; otherwise, the financial burden will become too great (Winters and Wang 1994).

In 1992 four of the six CEECs—the Czech Republic, the Slovak Republic, Hungary, and Poland—formed their own Central European Free Trade Association (CEFTA). The EU now allows a cumulation of value added throughout the EU and CEFTA to determine whether a product is allowed free-trade-area status.

The Baltic Republics—Latvia, Lithuania, and Estonia—signed free trade agreements with the EU in July 1994. The agreements provided for free trade in industrial goods and the EU granted limited concessions in agricultural trade (Enders and Wonnacott 1996).

Mediterranean countries

The CEC considers that the Mediterranean countries need to obtain 'comparable accords', similar but not identical to the Europe Agreements. In 1995 it approved a plan progressively to establish a free trade area in manufactures by 2010, and to liberalize trade in agriculture and services, and capital (WTO 1995*b*: ii. 23).

Preferential agreements of the EU in 1996

At the beginning of 1996 the EU entered into a customs union with Turkey. Turkey becomes part of the Single European Market (SEM) and adopts EU trade legislation and its common external tariff. However, there appear to be qualifications with respect to textiles, and free trade in agricultural products is not anticipated to be achievable until 2005 (Barham and Southey 1995).

Now that agriculture is explicitly included within the domain of the WTO its requirement that a free trade area (FTA) should cover substantially all trade between the members forming it is likely to be more strictly enforced. This may curb the EU's willingness to establish FTAs as goodwill gestures, many apparently on the initiative of individual commissioners (Southey 1996*a*, 1996*b*, 1996*c*).

This has already caused problems in the EU's negotiations of a trade pact with South Africa; the exclusion list accounts for 38 per cent of South Africa's agricultural exports and it is not clear whether it will be agreed by either South Africa or the WTO (Southey 1996*b*).

We have discussed only a few of the twenty-six EU trade agreements which were in force in February 1996, many of which have been signed in the previous five years (Southey 1996*a*). It should be borne in mind that many of these overlap, so that, for instance, the Lomé countries do not get any additional benefits from the GSP.

There now exists what the WTO describes as a 'hub-and-spoke system'. The EU is the hub with all impediments on trade removed between Member States, and the spokes are the groups of countries which have preferential agreements with the EU but which may have no corresponding degree of liberalization between each other (WTO 1995a). A feature that may determine the ability of a spoke to trade is the *rules of origin* written into the preferential agreement. These lateral impediments to trade not only mean that resource allocation is inferior to that of free trade or even of a fully established free trade area but may also entail considerable costs of compliance. A study of the original EC EFTA agreement suggested that the cost of border formalities to determine the origin of products amounted to 3 per cent of the value of goods concerned, even though 75 per cent of EC EFTA trade benefited from the FTA (Herin 1986). The EC also found that only 21 per cent of eligible imports from GSP beneficiary countries into the EC benefited from the original GSP (Waer 1994).

Thus the protective ring around the EU consists of the common external tariff, which, for industrial products under the Uruguay Round, will be lowered to 3.7 per cent by 2000 (and under many preferential agreements has been removed entirely), together with a complex of preferential arrangements and other devices. As tariffs are lowered, other impediments to trade become more apparent. The EU retention of the use of 'contingent' protection—that is, safeguard and anti-dumping measures—in most preferential schemes adds an element of hazard to them. However, the Uruguay Round included an Agreement on Safeguards by which the parties agreed to the phasing-out of all existing VERs within four years of it coming into force. One exception was allowed, the duration of which should not extend beyond the end of 1999, and the EU opted for this to be the VER it had concluded with Japan on automobiles (Mattoo and Mavroidis 1995). The EU has also agreed to more stringent rules for ascertaining dumping.

None the less the EU gives the impression of entering into preferential schemes as a means of placating neighbouring countries or as a means of exerting political influence with others but then modifying a beneficiary country's access immediately it begins to show success in its exports. Nowhere is this better exemplified than in its provisions for 'graduating' countries out of the GSP. This contributes to the uncertainty of its trading partners and is likely to discourage marginal suppliers. Although intra-marginal exporters to the EU may benefit from preferences, it is not clear how much effect they have had on the overall pattern of trade. It is noticeable that, although Asia is the EU's largest export market, its share of that market is shrinking (Montagnon and Bardacke 1996).

The General Agreement on Trade in Services was negotiated in a different way with countries putting their offers on the table conditional, generally, on the offers of other countries. Negotiations have been delayed (June 1996) with respect to telecommunications and shipping largely because of the political difficulty the USA has in reaching agreement.

But the Commission itself paid much more attention to the internal barriers to intra-EC trade.

11.6. **Policy towards internal trade within the EU**

Article 3 of the Treaty of Rome, signed in 1957, included provisions for

(a) the elimination, as between Member States, of customs and of quantitative restrictions in regard to the import and export of goods as well as of all other measures having equivalent effect;

(b) the establishment of a common customs tariff and of a common commercial policy towards third countries.

These provisions were expanded in the following articles, but then in Article 36 it was stated that these 'shall not preclude prohibitions or restrictions on imports, exports, or goods in transit justified on the grounds of public morality; public policy; public security; the protection of health and life of humans, animals or plants . . . Provided always that such prohibitions or restrictions shall not be used as a means of arbitrary discrimination nor as a disguised restriction on trade between Member States'.[3] Articles 100–2 provided the legal framework for 'harmonizing' these national restrictions if they affect trade.

Thus not only were all tariffs and quotas to be abolished but so also was any national regulation that interfered with intra-EC trade. Thus was the EC Commission set upon the road to 'harmonization', which proved to be very slow and arduous.

Soon after the UK joined the EC in 1973 instances of 'harmonization' aroused the ire of the UK populace, as one consumer product after the other appeared to be under threat; one of these was, for instance, British chocolate—because UK manufacturers were not required, as on the Continent, to include cocoa butter and generally used a cheaper vegetable oil as a substitute. Eventually the UK, Denmark, and Ireland were allowed to use up to 5 per cent vegetable fat in their chocolate as an exemption from the 1973 directive (Maitland 1996). This process culminated in a case brought by a German company, Rewe-Zentral, which was trying to import the French blackcurrant liqueur 'cassis', which had a lower alcohol content than required by German law. The European Court ruled in 1978 that consumer protection could have been achieved by a label indicating the alcohol content: the German requirement was not essential. The 'Cassis de Dijon' principle, essentially one of mutual recognition of standards, has become of increasing importance ever since.

However, there are areas in which the process of harmonization has been more fruitful, in particular with regard to the safety requirements for motor vehicles; the harmonization of technical requirements for passenger cars was completed in 1992; the requirements were accepted in 1993, are due to become mandatory in 1996, and are also to be extended to other vehicles (WTO 1995b: ii. 44). There are other areas where agreements on standards have become very important and sometimes essential to communication—as, for instance, in the case of electronics—and they will be discussed later.

The Commission has also been engaged in removing other obstacles to trade. Some of these have been erected by firms to protect their markets. Under Articles 92–4 of the

Treaty, the Commission forbids national governments from subsidizing the direct costs of its domestic firms in a way which distorts competition between Member States. There are some escape clauses, but export aid is not allowed.

By the 1980s there were still in being a large number of non-tariff barriers to trade. They applied not only to goods but also to services. The Single European Act (SEA) of 1986 set the beginning of 1993 as the date by which these should be removed, establishing the Single European Market (SEM). Non-tariff barriers existed where Member States had retained their own individual non-tariff barriers on imports from third countries. With the SEM these should have disappeared. Those on imports of cars from Japan, and textiles and clothing, will be discussed later.

Recently this liberalization has been extended to trade in power. Trade already takes place; the UK, for instance, was a net importer of 16,883 gigawatt hours in 1994, largely taking advantage of the difference in the peak consumption times of France and Britain. But in 1996 it was agreed progressively to liberalize the EU market so that large users could shop around. Clearly this is easier and competition is greater if the power sector is privatized (Buckley and Holberton 1996).

Public procurement

One of the most important barriers to trade is that associated with public procurement. In 1987 public procurement accounted for 16 per cent of GDP (GATT 1991: i. 15), and in 1984 a third of these were manufactures (*European Economy*, Mar. 1988, p. 55). Traditionally, national firms considered they had a right to supply their own government and nationalized industries, and therefore the proportion of public procurement supplied by imports was very much less than in the private sector. This is inconsistent with the ethos of the EU. Under the SEA, public procurement orders have to be submitted for tenders which are open to suppliers in all Member States.

In tandem with the reduction in barriers to intra-EU trade, the negotiations that took place under first the Tokyo Round in 1973–9 and then the Uruguay Round in 1986–94 included the proposals for opening up public procurement to international competition. In this forum, the EU endeavoured to maintain some degree of protection, a 3 per cent tariff, on tenders from outside the EU to supply the EU markets. But this was not agreed by EU's trading partners and the area of public procurement subject to international competition agreed in the Tokyo Round was extended by the Uruguay Round. Under a new Agreement on Government Procurement which was to have come into effect at the beginning of 1996, there will be a tenfold increase in its coverage; for central government the threshold above which it comes into effect is about £100,000, for local authorities in the region of £150,000, for public utilities around £300,000 and for construction contracts £3 million. It has been drawn up on the basis of mutual reciprocity, which has included a major bilateral agreement between the USA and the EU (DTI 1994).

Next we turn to the sectoral provisions, where we consider EU policy towards the 'sensitive' sectors of textiles and clothing, motor vehicles, and the 'sunrise' industry of electronics.

11.7. **Textiles and clothing**

Protective measures

The most elaborate system of protection the EC engaged in was for the benefit of its textile and clothing industries. These are classic declining industries. The textile industry was in the forefront of European industrialization and its position was later reinforced by its uptake of man-made fibres, the production of which became particularly important in Germany from the 1930s onwards. The clothing industry developed later and in France and Italy it is best known for high fashion often set by its couture houses. Thus continental European countries have regarded themselves as exporters of these products, although it has become increasingly obvious that the costs of production in developing countries were much lower.

When the EC was formed, most of its six members maintained their severe restrictions on imports of textiles and clothing from Japan and developing countries. However, developing countries were increasing their exports of cotton textiles to the more liberal countries such as the USA, Denmark, and the UK, which, however, eventually responded by introducing quotas on them. (At the same time the UK removed all restrictions on imports from members of EFTA when it was formed in 1959.) In an endeavour to halt this proliferation of quotas, GATT introduced, in 1961, a Short Term Arrangement and then, in 1962, a Long Term Arrangement (LTA) for cotton textiles. The LTA permitted the bilateral negotiation of quotas but stated that they should not be less than the actual imports of the previous year and were normally to be increased by 5 per cent a year. Although the LTA violated the main principle of non-discrimination, GATT hoped that its provisions would restrict unbridled protectionism. Under the LTA the EC agreed to increase its import quotas by 88 per cent, a development dourly dismissed by a Lancashire millowner as '88 per cent of nowt is nowt'.

The entry of the UK, Denmark, and Ireland into the EC in 1973 brought in two of the most open economies with respect to cotton textiles. However, textile producers in the UK were looking forward to entry, anticipating a much greater degree of protection from developing countries.

Developing countries had increased their export earnings, in spite of the LTA, by increasing their exports of items with higher value added such as clothing. They had also increased their exports of textiles with less than 50 per cent cotton which were not covered by the LTA. The USA responded in 1971 by negotiating quotas on imports of man-made fibre textiles and clothing. Once more GATT endeavoured to control their proliferation, in this case by agreeing to extend the LTA to include most fibres. The Arrangement Regarding International Trade in Textiles—the Multi-Fibre Arrangement (MFA)—came into operation in 1974. It embraced textiles and clothing of most textile fibres (excluding hard fibres and initially ramie and silk). Bilateral agreements were negotiable under it but were to be expanded by 6 per cent a year. The MFA was subsequently renewed three times, with new versions coming into operation in 1978, 1982, and 1986, and was then extended until the completion of the Uruguay Round. In 1986 the scope of the Agreement was expanded to cover goods made from silk blends and vegetable fibres.

The development of trade under the MFA

As can be seen from Tables 11.3 and 11.4, in value terms imports of textiles appear to have quadrupled and imports of clothing increased by 8.5 times between 1974 and 1993. But the EU expanded by three countries—Greece, Spain, and Portugal—during the period, although they were initially only minor importers, and in the absence of a

Table 11.3. **Textile imports of the EC/EU during the MFAs, by major suppliers, 1974, 1981, and 1993**

Origin	1974 (MFA 1) EC9		1981 (MFA 3) EC10		1993 (MFA 4) EU12	
	Value ($US bn.)	Share (%)	Value ($US bn.)	Share (%)	Value ($US bn.)	Share (%)
World	10.62	100.0	19.20	100.0	40.53	100.0
EC/EU	7.18	67.6	12.30	64.1	26.36	65.0
Western Europe	8.42	79.3	14.81	77.2	30.35	74.9
Turkey	0.11	1.0	0.31	1.6	0.82	2.0
USA	0.50	4.7	0.83	4.3	1.20	3.0
Japan	0.13	1.2	0.39	2.0	0.71	1.7
CEECs and former USSR	0.2	1.9	0.32	1.7	0.85	2.1
South Korea	0.06	0.6	0.20	1.1	0.39	1.0
Taiwan	0.13	1.2	0.14	0.7	0.36	0.9
Hong Kong	0.12	1.2	0.16	0.8	0.05[a]	0.1
China	0.12	1.1	0.38	2.0	1.13	2.8
India	0.16	1.5	0.40	2.1	1.24	3.1
Pakistan	0.12	1.2	0.23	1.2	0.77	1.9
Indonesia	n.a.	n.a.	n.a.	n.a.	0.62	1.5
Thailand	n.a.	n.a.	0.09	0.5	0.31	0.8

Note: n.a. = not available.

[a] Domestic exports.

Source: WTO (1995c).

Table 11.4. **Clothing imports of the EC/EU during the MFAs, by major suppliers, 1974, 1981, and 1993**

Origin	1974 (MFA 1) EC9		1981 (MFA 3) EC10		1993 (MFA 4) EU12	
	Value ($US bn.)	Share (%)	Value ($US bn.)	Share (%)	Value ($US bn.)	Share (%)
World	7.05	100.0	17.94	100.0	59.82	100.0
EC/EU	3.75	53.2	8.47	47.2	24.62	41.2
Western Europe	4.86	68.9	10.53	58.7	30.98	51.8
Turkey	0.08	1.1	n.a.	n.a.	3.56	6.0
USA	0.07	1.0	0.35	2.0	0.69	1.2
CEECs and former USSR	0.44	6.2	0.81	4.5	4.13	6.9
Hong Kong	0.82	11.6	1.89	10.5	4.11	6.9
South Korea	0.22	3.1	1.10	6.2	0.96	1.6
Taiwan	0.18	2.5	0.43	2.4	n.a.	n.a.
China	n.a.	n.a.	0.31	1.7	4.40	7.4
India	0.07	1.0	0.42	2.3	1.80	3.0
Indonesia	n.a.	n.a.	n.a.	n.a.	1.20	2.0
Thailand	n.a.	n.a.	n.a.	n.a.	0.85	1.4
Bangladesh	n.a.	n.a.	n.a.	n.a.	0.79	1.3
Pakistan	n.a.	n.a.	n.a.	n.a.	0.75	1.3
Malaysia	n.a.	n.a.	n.a.	n.a.	0.69	1.2

Note: n.a. = not available.

Source: WTO (1995c).

price index it is difficult to ascertain the quantitative increase. The EU's position is strongest in textiles, where in 1994 it was still a net exporter and, indeed, accounted for 23 per cent of US imports; two-thirds of its imports of textiles still comes from other Member States. By contrast, the EU share of EU clothing imports has fallen considerably. The EU is now a large net importer of clothing and imports now account for 32 per cent of consumption (see Tables 11.1 and 11.2). In spite of the MFA, there has been a considerable increase in imports from developing countries. However, the influence of the MFA is shown particularly in the clothing market—see Table 11.4—in the way in which the shares of the most restricted countries, Hong Kong, South Korea, and Taiwan, have fallen, whereas there has been a clear increase in those of India and China. Indonesia, Thailand, Pakistan, Malaysia, and Bangladesh have now begun to emerge as significant suppliers to the EU market. Bangladesh, as the poorest country, faces no quota restrictions.

Present trade arrangements

The EU uses four instruments to restrict and monitor trade. First, with respect to monitoring, for those countries not facing quotas there is a system of surveillance so that importers have to obtain export licences in their applications for import licences. Certificates of origin are required for all countries except Turkey (Majmudar 1996: 42, 43). However, consumers are not provided with this information and therefore cannot benefit from it. These are just administrative barriers to trade.

In respect of protection, tariffs are relatively high compared with other manufactures—that is, 0–25 per cent for non-preferential sources of supply. Tariffs on textiles and clothing are also to be reduced. But they will still remain relatively high in the USA and Australia, areas to which EU countries export these products. But it is the MFA quotas which represent the greatest restriction on trade.

The categorization of products to which the quotas are applied differs between industrialized countries, and has varied over time; in 1996 the EU had 163 categories.[4] These products are then placed into groups, IB, IIB, or IIIB, for clothing according to their 'sensitivity', or level of import penetration. The most sensitive clothing products—that is, those in Group IB—are, with the category number given in brackets, T-shirts (4), pullovers (5), trousers (6), blouses (7), and shirts (8). The quotas for individual countries in 1996 are shown in Table 11.5. For the dominant supplying countries (Hong Kong, South Korea, Taiwan, and China), product categories are also classified by fibre blends, with separate quantity restraints sometimes being applied to each type. Some flexibility is introduced into this system by a 'swing' provision, whereby an exporting country can transfer a quota between product categories in the same year, a provision by which part of the unused portion of its previous year's quota can be 'carried over', and a 'carry-forward' provision by which it can utilize some of the following year's quota (Majmudar 1996).

In addition, there are special provisions for outward processing traffic (OPT). This generally involves continental EU countries contracting out their more labour-intensive processes to Eastern Europe. When an EU country exports textiles or clothing for further processing in another country and then reimports it, the only tariff imposed is on the value added. In 1993 OPT accounted for 10 per cent of extra-EU's imports of clothing, with Germany importing 60 per cent of it (WTO 1995b: i. 101).

Under the WTO Agreement on Textiles and Clothing negotiated as part of the Uruguay Round, these MFA quotas are due to be phased out gradually from 1 January 1995 and eliminated by 2005. This is to be carried out in three stages, based on the quantity of imports in 1990. An importing country can choose the categories to be integrated subject to the proviso that they must be selected from each of the following groups:

- tops and yarns;

Table 11.5. **EU quotas for Clothing imports in Group IB, 1996 (1,000 pieces)**

Country	T–shirts Cat. (4)	Pullovers Cat. (5)	Trousers Cat. (6)	Blouses Cat. (7)	Shirts Cat. (8)
Belarus	671	570	298	400	297
Brazil	36,792	n.a.	3,827	n.a.	n.a.
Bulgaria	n.a.	5,185	2,500	1,909	5,662
China	75,243	23,586	24,787	11,888	16,705
Czech Rep.	8,106	4,362	4,392	1,740	5,641
Hong Kong	45,793	35,729	63,015	36,861	53,767
				6a 52,898	
Hungary	12,252	6,341	4,984	2,898	3,416
India	55,221	29,000	7,343	57,268	41,048
Indonesia	36,332	28,538	10,351	7,624	11,995
Macao	13,257	12,383	13,355	5,204	7,288
Malaysia	11,911	5,530	7,006	30,374	7,275
Pakistan	23,757	6,281	25,596	15,390	5,027
Philippines	19,044	9,114	7,935	5,042	6,061
Poland	25,199	9,395	6,848	n.a.	4,820
Romania	29,568	19,212	8,919	2,332	11,404
Russia	2,505	1,588	2,788	785	2,392
Singapore	21,606	12,273	12,483	10,583	7,173
Slovak Rep.	3,497	3,767	3,396	1,309	3,668
South Korea	14,721	33,869	5,729	9,639	31,808
Sri Lanka	n.a.	n.a.	7,379	11,429	9,346
Taiwan	10,701	20,876	5,450	3,353	8,879
Thailand	29,956	21,132	7,616	7,129	4,396
Ukraine	1,500	1,200	1,100	500	800
Vietnam	4,345	1,680	2,749	140	8,339

Note: n.a. = not available.
Source: CEC, DGI, 10 June 1996.

- fabrics;
- made-up textile products; and
- clothing.

Let us assume that the growth rate for the non-liberalized products is G. The timetable comprises:

stage 1, beginning 1 January 1995, 16 per cent of textiles and clothing trade in volume terms came under normal world trade rules, and the quotas of the remaining products are to increase by 16 per cent a year for the next three successive years—that is, by ($G \times 1.16$) per cent p.a.

stage 2, beginning 1 January 1998, an additional 17 per cent of trade must be completely liberalized and the remaining quotas must be increased by 25 per cent in each of the next four successive years—that is, by ($G \times 1.16 \times 1.25$ per cent) p.a.

stage 3, beginning 1 January 2002, an additional 18 per cent of 1990 trade must be completely liberalized. Remaining quotas must be increased at a rate at least 27 per cent higher than under stage 2 in each of the following three years—that is, by (G 1.16 $\times$ 1.25 $\times$ 1.27) per cent p.a.

stage 4, end of transition, all quotas abolished (Khanna 1994).

However, the industrialized countries are dragging their feet; the USA, EU and Canada have started with products not currently subject to import restraints (which at the moment account for a third of imports). Therefore, it will be some time before the Uruguay round has any effect. The EU continues to restrain more products from the dominant suppliers, Taiwan, China, Hong Kong, and South Korea, and restrict the growth of the quotas on them to around 0–2 per cent p.a., whereas it is more liberal with respect to its imports of clothing from India, Thailand, and the Philippines, allowing quotas to grow by 6–7 per cent. It has no quotas on imports of clothing from Bangladesh.

The conflicting interests involved in the Agreement on Textiles and Clothing (ATM) to liberalize the MFA were aired at a conference in March 1996 of the major importing and exporting countries organized by the Foreign Trade Association (FTA) representing the interests of the importing retail trade in Europe, and the International Textiles and Clothing Bureau (ITCB) representing the interests of developing countries. The CEC and European producers adduced as need for protection, the 2.5 million workers in the EU textile and clothing industries and the loss of 800,000 jobs in these industries over the previous ten years. They wanted greater access for their up-market products in developing countries in exchange for further liberalization of the EU market for developing country producers. India's representatives firmly rebuffed suggestions for such a linkage, and were very disappointed at the lack of liberalization so far. Textiles (and clothing) account for 20 per cent of India's industrial output, employ 50 million people, and provide 35 per cent of its foreign-exchange earnings. China's representative said that it was due to its net exports of textiles and clothing of US$22.1 billion that it could buy airbus aircraft and other Western high-tech products. But China was facing increasing barriers to its trade; in 1996 the full m.f.n. tariff was imposed on its clothing exports to the EU rather than the previous GSP one. In addition, it had had thirty-four new quotas imposed by the EU under the bilateral Silk Agreement. In China, textiles and clothing account for 16.1 per cent of industrial output, employ 15 million people, and account for 25.5 per cent of industrial output. Thus it was argued that the developing countries were much more dependent on textiles and clothing than the EU (de Coster 1996).

They were also concerned about the special preferential agreements negotiated with the CEECs, including Bulgaria, the Czech Republic, Hungary, Poland, Romania, and Slovakia, whereby, 'For textiles and clothing, import duties on CEEC output will be abolished over six years and those on outward processing trade—whereby CEEC producers receive materials from a EC firm, process them and return them to the same firm—immediately. Quantitative restrictions will be removed in not less than five years and not more than half the time agreed in the Uruguay Round for the abolition of the MFA' (Winters and Wang 1994: 35). This means that the CEECs receive preferential treatment in comparison to the MFA developing countries.

Furthermore the CEC responded to the pleas of Eurocoton, the trade body, concerning unfair competition by proposing in September 1996 anti-dumping duties of between 3 per cent and 36 per cent on imports of undyed cotton fabric from India, Pakistan, Indonesia, China, Taiwan, and Egypt, which are said to be undercutting German, French, and Italian weavers by between 28 and 36 per cent. Little cotton fabric is now produced in Europe, it is just over a fifth of the amount imported. The UK producers who dye, print, and finish the fabric, most of which goes into home furnishings, were furious and very anxious that their costs should not be raised, as they are already facing increasing competition from finished imports (Luesby 1996).

However, the EU industry was angry at the list of textiles and clothing products the CEC proposed to free from quotas on 1 January 1998, published on 2 October 1996. It covered 17.84 per cent of EU imports in 1990, thus slightly above the minimum required, and included twenty-four products, nineteen of which were subject to quota. But the quotas were underutilized, apart from that for knitted gloves and mittens, of which very few are supplied by the EU (Anson 1996).

11.8. Motor vehicles

The car industry, previously viewed as an 'engine of growth' in the EU, is now regarded as a 'sensitive' sector. The larger European countries used to support their 'champions', their indigenous manufacturers of mass-produced cars, which were generally heavily dependent on their domestic markets. But the attitude of member governments is changing now that they are faced with increasing air pollution in cities because of the use of passenger cars. Furthermore, in the UK, even though motorways are overcrowded, there is increasing public resistance to the sacrifice of the countryside to yet more roads.

The CEC has endeavoured to restrict the amount of assistance that governments give to domestic producers. At the end of 1995 it eventually agreed to the Spanish government giving £240 million aid to SEAT, owned by VW, as part of a restructuring plan that would involve job cuts and plant closures, and reduce SEAT's capacity by 29 per cent, which would involve a 5 per cent reduction in VW's output in the EEA (Tucker and White 1995). But in 1990 Renault had to pay back FF6 billion to the French government for not following proper procedures.

The CEC has also endeavoured to remove obstacles to the functioning of the internal market. Technical requirements have now been harmonized, as described earlier. The CEC has also tried to improve competition in distribution. The problem is the tying of distributors to certain manufacturers. This is inconsistent with the requirement that practices should be prohibited which may affect trade between Member States and which have as their object or effect the prevention, restriction, or distortion of competition within the EU. But this may be declared inapplicable if it improves the production or distribution of goods, or promotes technical or economic progress, while allowing consumers a fair share of resulting benefit. This is termed Block Exemption.

Motor-vehicle dealers have argued that cars are technically complex and that restricting competition benefits consumers. Because motor vehicles are expensive, technically complex, and require expert maintenance and repair, it is necessary to maintain a network of qualified dealers who can stock parts and have the technical knowledge, expertise, and equipment necessary to specialize in particular brands of vehicles. In 1985 a regulation was introduced allowing 'block exemption' for ten years, and this was renewed in 1995 with qualifications for another ten years. In 1996 independent car dealers won their case in the European Court of Justice (ECJ) to buy vehicles in the cheapest EU market for resale in their own countries (Tucker 1996).

The variation in the list price of the same or corresponding motor vehicle is taken by the CEC as an indication of the degree to which impediments to trade between Member States still exist; they should not differ by more that 12 per cent over a period of less than a year, nor by more than 18 per cent between Member States.

The CEC regarded the car industry as the manufacturing industry likely to provide some of the greatest benefits from the creation of the SEM (*European Economy*, Mar. 1988, p. 186). The market for cars is regarded as an example of an imperfectly competitive market. Consumers can distinguish the products of each firm and firms compete as much in the provision of new models as by price. In the econometric model used by Smith and Venables (see Chapter 3), each firm is regarded as producing in its home country and in selling abroad it is 'invading' the territory of another. It reduces prices in its export market partly by reducing the monopoly power of the firms already there. Consumption increases. As the firm expands its output it can exploit further its economies of scale and thus costs also fall. This is an attractive picture of consumers benefiting without producers losing as a result of international trade. Furthermore this enables producers to expand not only to reduce imports but also to increase exports.

This kind of calculation can be criticized on a number of counts. Most of the data used relating to economies of scale were drawn from the 1960s (Pratten 1988), and the greater use of computers, particularly in changing from one specification to another, must have changed these considerably.

However, the most important omission from the Commission's analysis was to ignore the importance of multinationals, in particular foreign multinationals. In the exercise, foreign subsidiaries operating in the EC were treated like domestic firms.

Before discussing further the activities of the multinationals let us take note of the ring of protection around the EC. By July 1968, when the CET first become effective, it was at a level of 22 per cent for assembled cars and of 14 per cent for components. The level of protection has been very slowly reduced over time. Under the Uruguay Round the duty on cars is unchanged at 10 per cent and on trucks at 22 per cent, but by 2000 the duty on light commercial vehicles will be reduced to 10 per cent, and the duties on parts and components will be cut by a third on average (WTO 1995b: ii. 32, 44).

However, in addition to these tariffs, individual Members States of the EC had widely different restraints on vehicle imports from Japan; in the UK they were limited to 11 per cent of the market and in France to 3 per cent, whilst in Italy they were limited to 2,500 cars and 750 light commercial vehicles (CVs) per annum and in Spain even fewer (GATT 1991: i). Under the SEM these national quotas were no longer valid. Under an agreement reached with Japan in July 1991, these national quotas are due to be phased out and replaced by an overall quota of 1.23 million units of cars and light commercial vehicles and trucks (up to 5 tonnes) in 1999, calculated on the basis of a forecast 15.1 million vehicle market for the EU as a whole. All restraints are due to be removed by 2000. During the transitional period, EU and Japanese officials will meet twice a year to monitor the past and forecast future level of imports both in total and to each restricted market, in relation to the size of the market as a whole. There are to be 'no restrictions on Japanese investment or on the free circulation of its products in the Community' i.e. on motor vehicles produced by Japanese 'transplants' (*Financial Times*, 5 Aug. 1991).

The US multinationals Ford, General Motors, and Chrysler had established subsidiaries in European countries before the second World War. The formation and expansion of the EC, by reducing the costs of sending products across national boundaries, made it easier for them to locate production in the lowest cost source within the EC. The harmonization, based on the agreement on safety standards for cars in 1993,[5] which is due to be extended to other vehicles, has made it even easier to do so (WTO 1995b: ii. 44).

The US multinationals were attracted to Belgium in the 1960s by a plentiful supply of male labour willing to work shifts (owing to the closure of the coal mines). Thus, although it had no indigenous producers, Belgium emerged as a significant producer and exporter of cars in the 1970s.

Then, in the 1970s, the multinationals were attracted to Spain, which, at that time, was not yet a member of the EC. This was partly due to the low wage rates in the country but also to make it easier to supply the rapidly expanding, but highly protected, Spanish home market. Ford succeeded in persuading the Spanish government to lower its tariffs on imported components to 5 per cent, to allow it 100 per cent ownership (previously foreign firms had been limited to 50 per cent), and to reduce its national content requirement from 95 per cent to 50 per cent, provided two-thirds of production was exported. Thus began the integration of Spanish vehicle production into the European market and a very rapid increase in Spanish exports (Dicken 1992). Also, over the succeeding period, VW eventually took over one of Spain's largest vehicle assembly plants, SEAT, as the manufacturing base for its small car, the Polo.

Meanwhile, in the 1970s, Japan had emerged as the lowest cost and most efficient producer of small and medium-sized cars. Exports had increased but, as detailed above, their entry into the EC was restricted. Then, in the 1980s, the Japanese producers

Nissan, Toyota, and Honda began to invest in the EC, particularly in the UK. Rather than setting up in the traditional areas of volume car production, which had acquired a reputation for being strike prone, they invested in greenfield sites. From the outset, production was intended not only for the UK domestic market but also for export to the rest of Europe. Having declined, after entry into the EC, the UK's car production began to increase and so did its exports.

The French regarded this establishment of Japanese 'transplant' factories in the UK with dislike and suspicion. Peugeot's chairman has described them as a 'Japanese air-craft carrier' off the coast of Europe (*Independent*, Jan. 1993). At first France threatened to include imports from Nissan's UK plant within their overall Japanese quota unless it had an EC content of 80 per cent. However, this would have been inconsistent with the EC definition of non-preferential production whereby 'origin is assigned to the country where a product has been wholly obtained or where it has undergone its "*last substantial working or processing*"' (GATT 1991a: 118–19). Eventually, the EC Commission persuaded France to accept these cars as being of UK origin and, in any case, the local content very soon reached 80 per cent.

However, this raises the question of what is meant by car manufacturing. Assembly itself accounts for about 10 per cent of the value of a car; prior to that the main activities are the production of engines and transmission, the production of bodies, and the manufacture of a wide range of components ranging from spark plugs to windscreen wipers. About 60 per cent of a car's value is comprised of components bought from outside (Simonian 1996). Thus, the transfer of the final stage of production from one country to another tends to affect the trade in intermediate products. The extent of the type of trade has also been affected by the just-in-time (JIT) production methods introduced by the Japanese. These require the component suppliers to be able to deliver their products within a certain time to the final producers. As a result, although the establishment of Japanese production in the UK initially led to increased imports of components, this tailed off as more components came to be purchased from domestic suppliers—and, in some cases, the Japanese component manufacturers also invested in production facilities within the UK.

A somewhat different strategy has been pursued by Ford and VW—namely, that of 'globalization' whereby standardization has been aimed for throughout the world. VW has had a particularly difficult task in so far as it has had to integrate VW and Audi in Germany with SEAT in Spain and Skoda in the Czech Republic. The aim of Ferdinand Piech, its chairman, is to reduce VW's sixteen platforms (chassis) to four to be the foundation of all the future models of VW, Audi, SEAT, and Skoda (Simonian 1996).

All firms are under pressure to reduce the development costs of bringing out a new car, sometimes by sharing it, and also to reduce production costs. Germany has the highest labour costs per hour and its industry has said that there is likely to be a reduction of 100,000 workers in the car and component industry before the end of the decade (Münchau 1996). The UK has the lowest wage costs in the developed world, but this advantage appears to be partly eroded by her low productivity in car manufacture

Lynden Moore

(Done and Griffiths 1995). But Britain's producers of motor components appear relatively profitable; she has three out of the top ten performing companies, whereas Germany has none (Griffiths 1996).

Thus the response of firms manufacturing cars and components has been to transfer production to areas where wages are low and labour flexible—that is, to the poorer parts of Europe. Fiat has opened a new factory in southern Italy with a capacity of 450,000 cars and Ford and VW have set up a new plant in Portugal (Simonian 1995). Most of the Japanese direct investment in cars has gone to the UK but some to Spain. Eastern Europe, in particular Poland, may soon become another such area of development; VW's acquisition of a stake in Skoda, Czechslovakia, was just the beginning of this trend. In 1995 VW continued to transfer its production of labour-intensive niche products from Wolfsburg in Germany to Bratislava in Slovakia, where the wages of the highly educated workforce are a tenth of those in Germany (Done 1995).

European producers are now facing stagnant replacement domestic markets. The removal of non-tariff barriers to trade between member countries while still maintaining restrictions on imports from Japan has led to a relocation of production within Europe. Britain's output, which fell from 1.7 million units when she entered the EC to 887,679 units in 1982, is now rising because of the investment of foreign firms—the US Ford and GM, the Japanese firms Nissan, Toyota, and Honda, and now BMW, which took over Rover in 1994; in 1995 UK production was almost 1.6 million units.

As can be seen from Table 11.2, 66 per cent of the exports of Member States go to other members and another 10 per cent go to other countries in Western Europe. Table 11.6 shows the change in the value of exports between 1980 and 1994 and the distribution of exports of the EU as a whole and the major producing Member States in 1994 between the major regions. The heavy dependence of EU producers on the European

Table 11.6. **Exports of Automotive Products, 1980, 1993, and 1994**

Origin	Total exports ($USbn.)			1994 distribution of exports (%)			
	1980	1993	1994	EU(12)	Western Europe	North America	Asia
EU12	65.1	147.0	173.96	65.7	75.5	7.6	7.2
Western Europe	70.4	159.7	190.0	65.4	75.1	7.9	7.2
Germany	27.7	60.5	70.46	51.3	64.7	12.3	12.3
France	13.1	24.2	28.35	73.8	82.3	3.4	2.2
Belgium	6.4	18.1	21.70	n.a.	n.a.	n.a.	n.a.
Spain	2.4	13.9	17.81	n.a.	n.a.	n.a.	n.a.
UK	7.6	13.5	15.51	67.9	74.5	9.8	9.4
Italy	5.9	11.0	13.59	n.a.	n.a.	n.a.	n.a.

Note: n.a. = not available.

Source: WTO (1995c).

316

market is clear, with two-thirds of their exports going to other members of the EU12 and three-quarters going to Western Europe. Imports are increasing. The EU still has a positive trade balance in automotive products of $28.5 billion. But overcapacity in the industry is 25–30 per cent. Cars still cost more in Europe than in the USA or Japan (Simonian 1995). The hopes of the CEC have not materialized. Far from the EU becoming a more successful exporter it is facing a world in which all the major developing countries want to establish their own car manufacturing plants and in many cases hope to export to the EU. South Korea is already supplying four brands, the best known of which are Hyundai and Daewoo, whilst Proton of Malaysia and Tata of India entered the European market in the 1990s and are increasing their sales (Simonian 1995). EU firms are increasingly investing abroad or forming joint ventures rather that endeavouring to export from the EU.

11.9. High–technology industries

The OECD definition of a high-technology industry is one that is 'based not on a once and for all dose of technology but for which a continuous stream of new products and processes is necessary in order to keep in the market' (OECD 1970: 123, 135). However, for practical purposes such industries are defined in terms of input rather than output—that is, those industries for which expenditure on research and development (R&D) is more than 4 per cent of value added are regarded as high tech. This group of industries, which includes aerospace, electronic and electrical equipment, and pharmaceuticals, has remained the same for the past thirty years. That is not to deny the importance of innovations to other industries.

Why should EU governments be concerned by their high-technology industries? Why do they not leave them to market forces? One reason is that some countries, in particular France, dislike being dependent on other countries—that is, the USA and Japan—for their technology. National aspirations to be at the forefront, at the leading edge of technology, also appear to have been transferred to the EU level. There is also the fear of European countries being pushed down the skills ladder, becoming a low-skill, low-income, environment.

The recent position

The CEC has investigated the overall trade balance of the EU both in high-technology manufactures, and also in receipts for the use of technology. As can be seen from Table 11.7, although in the early 1980s the EC ratio of exports of high-technology products to imports for the EFTA countries and the most competitive developing countries[6] was greater than 1 (although it was less than this for the USA and Japan), by 1991 imports

Table 11.7. **EC trade in high-tech products: export/import ratio by selected trade part-ners, 1982–1991**

Partner	1982	1984	1986	1987	1988	1989	1990	1991
Extra-EC	1.1	1.0	1.0	0.9	0.8	0.8	0.8	0.8
USA	0.4	0.5	0.6	0.6	0.5	0.5	0.5	0.5
Japan	0.2	0.1	0.1	0.1	0.1	0.1	0.1	0.1
EFTA	1.2	1.2	1.2	1.1	1.1	1.1	1.1	0.9
MC15[a]	2.0	1.2	1.2	0.9	0.7	0.8	0.8	0.7

[a] Most competitive developing countries (see n. 6).

Source: CEC (1993: 214).

of high-technology products were greater than exports from these four areas. The EU's slight overall surplus on high-technology products had given way to a deficit (CEC 1993: 214).

In 1988, as can be seen from Table 11.8, all the larger countries of the EC had negative balances for technology transfer; the USA was the only large country with a positive balance.

This suggests that the international position of the EU in high-technology products is not strong and is deteriorating.

Table 11.8. **Receipts, payments, and balance of payments on technology trade, 1988; growth in receipts and payments, 1984–1988**

Country	Receipts ($USm.)	Payments ($USm.)	Balance	Growth in receipts (%)	Growth in payments (%)
Belgium	1,300	1,862	−562	121.1	163.4
Denmark (1985)[a]	217	190	27	102.8	167.6
Germany	3,924	4,687	−763	648.9	366.4
Greece	n.a.	12	n.a.	n.a.	9.1
Spain	187	1,416	−1,229	55.8	189.6
France	1,522	1,914	−392	84.5	108.8
Ireland (1983)	717	328	389	n.a.	n.a.
Italy	654	1,207	−553	336.0	136.2
Netherlands	518	951	−433	156.4	142.0
Portugal (1985)[a]	4	36	−32	−20.0	2.8
UK	1,896	2,068	−172	114.0	144.7
USA	10,858	2,054	8,804	106.1	184.1
Japan	1,956	2.480	−524	77.0	121.2

Note: n.a. = not applicable.

Source: CEC (1993: 166).

In trade policy the EU has shown least concern with respect to pharmaceuticals, in which Europe traditionally has had a strong position as a net exporter and for which import penetration is only 10 per cent (see Table 11.1). As already mentioned, under the Uruguay Round, the EU has agreed to abolish import tariffs on pharmaceuticals.

Electronics

The CEC has appeared most concerned about EU firms being at the leading edge of technology with respect to the electrical and electronics industry. Most government assistance to this industry in the UK and France, as in the USA, went initially for defence purposes. This was not permitted in Germany and Japan, and as a result their firms appear to have developed a more commercial orientation. Japan purchased the right to use US innovations and was very adept at developing them for consumer products.

In the 1980s Japan became the leading producer of 'active' electronic components—that is, semiconductors, integrated circuits, and microprocessors. In 1989 it accounted for 42 per cent of the total world production, with the USA accounting for 26 per cent, and Europe only 12 per cent. Of the European total, West Germany accounted for 31 per cent, France 19 per cent and the UK 16 per cent (Dicken 1992: 311). Recently the USA appears to have reclaimed its position as the largest producer (*Financial Times*, 11 Dec. 1992). As far as can be ascertained, the EU is a net importer of most types of electronic products.

The EU has sought to strengthen its position in these industries by the direct subsidisation of research. It has, in particular, encouraged intercountry research projects.

France has been allowed to subsidize its computer firm Groupe Bull in spite of strong objections from other EU firms. Between 1989 and 1994 it lost FF20 billion and then requested FF11.1 billion (£1.33 billion) for restructuring and eventual privatization. Private companies are very critical of the EU competition commissioner, Mr Karel Van Miert, for allowing it (*Financial Times*, 4 Oct. 1994, 7 Oct. 1994, 13 Oct. 1994). But it is now making a profit.

EU's encouragement of European mergers

The EC encouraged the growth of large European firms—regarded as more capable of R&D. But in the USA, innovation is often carried out by smaller firms. In November 1992 the French and Italian governments announced an investment of $2 billion over five years in SGS-Thomson (France and Italy each own 45 per cent), the world's twelfth largest microchip-maker. However, Siemens and Philips refused to participate in this venture. Heinz Hagmaster, head of the semiconductor division at Philips, said: 'The same (semiconductor) plant, of the same size, making the same product in the same production volumes will have 10 to 20 per cent higher costs in Europe than its identical sisters in the US and Japan, and more than 30 per cent higher costs than an identical plant in a newly industrialised country.' As a result there has been a consistent tendency for the European firms to transfer operations to the South-East Asia region (*Financial Times*, 16 Nov. 1992). But at the time of writing (1996) SGS-Thomson is very profitable. In terms of market share it is thirteenth and it has annual sales of $1 billion and is the world's largest player in the analogue semiconductor market (telecommunications, automotive, and audio industries). It is investing in a new semiconductor plant costing $800 million (Ridding 1995*a*). The French government is now (1996) endeavouring to privatize Thompson.

Siemens is also investing £1.1 billion in a semiconductor chip plant in Tyneside, and 2.5 billion DM in a microelectronics centre in Dresden to produce memory chips (Tighe 1995).

The CEC likes alliances and mergers of EU firms such as GEC and Siemens with respect to Plessey. However, each is a large cautious firm, with large cash balances (in 1995 GEC had a cashpile of £2.9 billion (Wighton 1995: 5) and no good record of innovation).

The natural tendency of firms has been to seek alliances outside with US and Japanese firms such as the recent agreement of IBM (US), Motorola (US), Siemens (Germany), and Toshiba (Japan) to produce high-powered memory chips—a gigabyte dynamic random access memory (D-Ram).

Protection

The French would like to increase the protection of what they claim are 'infant' or rather 'sunrise' industries. The UK and Germany do not, because in many cases protection of the producers of intermediates raises the costs of other consuming firms. It may also raise the price of investment as well as of consumer goods.

The EU has a relatively high CET of 14 per cent on integrated circuits, radios, television receivers, and video recorders. Telecommunication devices have a tariff of 7.5 per cent and computer equipment 3.5 per cent. There has been a series of cases where the EU has been criticized for reclassifying a product into a higher tariff category. At the beginning of 1996 the EU, under pressure from Japan, agreed to drop its plan to reclassify CD-Rom drives as consumer electronic products facing a tariff of 14 per cent rather than a computer peripheral. The USA complained that Ireland had reclassified computer networking devices as telecom devices bearing a CET of 7.5 per cent rather than computer equipment of 3.5 per cent. The UK has reclassified personal computers that can be used as televisions as consumer electronic products with a tariff of 14 per cent (Williams 1996). With such easily transportable products, these decisions have implications for the location of production and direct investment. Is it any wonder that there is now a proposal to scrap all EU tariffs on IT products including computers, semiconductors, and software by the year 2000 (Dunne 1995)? However, the CEC appears to be trying to gain more access to the Japanese silicon chip market in exchange for doing so. The USA and Japan had a five-year trade accord by which the Japanese agreed to open 20 per cent of their semiconductor market to foreign producers. So far US firms have gained 19 per cent of it and the EU 1.5 per cent. The EU, feeling squeezed out, would like it replaced by a three-way accord, but the Japanese do not want any extension of the agreement and the managed trade that it implies (Dawkins and Clark 1996; Kehoe 1996; Nakamoto 1996).

In the 1980s many EC Member States had imposed VERs on electronic goods imported from Japan. In mid-1990 the following Japanese products were subject to bilateral quotas: radio and TV sets (France, Italy, Spain), colour TV sets, transistors, and integrated circuits (France and Italy), TV cameras, TV tubes, car radios, hi-fi radios, radio recorders, and antennae (Italy) (GATT: i. 213–14). Faced with these limitations the Japanese firms began to invest in other parts of South East Asia to supply the EC market. These EC Member States then extended the VERs to include these countries as well. But these had to be phased out with the introduction of the SEM in 1993 and now the CEC claims that there are none (WTO 1995b: i. 57).

Many of these electrical consumer products might not be regarded as representing the leading edge of technology. Indeed, many of them are produced in developing countries with very little R&D expenditure. However, the argument appears to be that the EU firms must be profitable in these in order to remain in the high-technology sector of the industry. There are now only two indigenous producers of consumer electronic products left, Philips (Netherlands) and SGS-Thomson (France).

In the 1980s the EC started using anti-dumping procedures as a form of protective policy. The situation for electronic goods at the end of April 1996 is shown in Table 11.9. The countries shown have producers on whose exports to the EU anti-dumping duties are imposed, or who have agreed to supply products at a certain minimum price. In May 1994 the EU imposed anti-dumping duties of as much as 96.8 per cent on imports of broadcasting cameras made by five Japanese electronics companies as a response to complaints by Philips (Netherlands) and Thomson (France). The Japanese market share had risen from 52 per cent in 1989 to 70 per cent in 1992. The duties on cameras from the individual firms were 62.6 per cent on Sony, 82.9 on Ikegami Tsushinki, 52.7 per cent on Denshi, and 96.8 per cent on Matsushita and JVC, which the Commission said did not cooperate in its investigation. They are also very high for large aluminium electrolytic capacitors. The highest anti-dumping duty on floppy discs is for Malaysia, and then for Mexico and the USA at 44 per cent with some exceptions.

In addition, after an anti-dumping investigation, in 1990, the CEC negotiated a minimum import price with eleven Japanese semiconductor producers of dynamic random access memory (DRAM) chips; an anti-dumping duty of 60 per cent was imposed on exporters who did not participate in the undertaking (GATT 1991: i. 214). The EC also imposed a provisional anti-dumping duty of 10.1 per cent on imports of memory chips from South Korea as it began an investigation into dumping (*Financial Times*, 18 Sept. 1992). This has buttressed the position of European electronic firms already

Table 11.9. **Definitive anti-dumping duties and undertakings in force, 30 April 1996**

Product	Country	Duty or range (%)	Date of expiry
Audio tapes	Japan	25.5–15.2	5 May 1996
	South Korea	9.2–0	
Car radios	South Korea	34.4–3.4	8 Aug. 1997
Colour TVs (small)	South Korea	19.6–10.4	In force until outcome of
	China	15.3–7.5	review, 20 July 1996
	Hong Kong	4.8–2.1	
Colour TVs (all sizes)	Malaysia	23.4–7.5	1 Apr. 2000
	Singapore	23.6–0	1 Apr. 2000
	Thailand	29.8–3	1 Apr. 2000
Colour TVs (large)	South Korea	17.9–0	In force until outcome of
	China	25.6	review
Electronic weighing scales	South Korea	26.7–9.3	22 Oct. 1998
	Singapore	31–15.4	22 Oct. 1998
	Japan	31.6–15.3	28 Apr. 1998
Floppy discs	China	39.4–35.6	21 Oct. 1998
	Japan	40.9–6.1	21 Oct. 1998
	Taiwan	32.7–19.8	21 Oct. 1998
	Hong Kong	27.4–6.7	10 Sept. 1999
	South Korea	8.1	10 Sept. 1999
	Malaysia	46.4–12.8	13 Apr. 2201
	Mexico	44–0	13 Apr. 1996
	USA	44–0	13 Apr. 1996
Large aluminium electrolytic capacitors	Japan	75–11.6	4 Dec. 1997
	South Korea	70.6	18 June 1999
	Taiwan	75.8–10.7	18 June 1999
TV broadcast cameras	Japan	96.8–52.7	30 Apr. 1999
Microwave ovens	China	20.8	4 Jan. 2001
	Malaysia	31.7	4 Jan. 2001
	Thailand	31.8–20.3	4 Jan. 2001
	South Korea	32.8–4.8	4 Jan. 2001
Video cassettes and cassette reels	South Korea	3.8–1.9	In force until outcome of
	Hong Kong	21.9–0	review, 25 Oct. 1996
	China	Ecu 2.22–0.92	
Photocopiers	Japan	20–10	11 Oct. 1997

Source: Information supplied by the Department of Trade and Industry, UK.

established in Europe (often to supply the defence industries), and induced US and Japanese firms to establish subsidiaries. In 1988 five of the ten leading semiconductor firms in Europe were American. In addition, there was IBM (US), which produces its own semiconductors and which for a long time has dominated the world market in mainframe computers. Since Fujitsu took over ICL(UK) in the 1980s, there has been no European producer of mainframe computers (Dicken 1992). However, there are a number of European producers in the personal-computer market, the largest being Olivetti, with 6.4 per cent of the market (*Financial Times*, 19 Feb. 1993).

In September 1995 the CEC reimposed anti-dumping duties of 20 per cent on Japanese photocopiers and extended them to larger models, arguing that the Japanese companies concerned—Canon Copier, Ricoh, Matsushita, Minolta, Konica, Sharp, and Toshiba—were continuing to dump their products at artificially low prices on the European market to the detriment of the European photocopying industry. This was in response to complainants Rank Xerox, Oce Nederalan, and Olivetti-Canon, for whom the duties provide a breathing space. Duties were initially imposed in 1987 and since then *imports* of Japanese photocopiers have fallen sharply. But their market share has increased, as the Japanese companies have moved production to locations inside the EU (*Financial Times*, 15 Sept. 1995, p. 5; 18 Sept. 1995, p. 3).

In 1995 the CEC imposed provisional anti-dumping duties on microwave ovens from China, South Korea, Thailand, and Malaysia after investigating complaints from the domestic industry that 'dumped' imports had increased from 2.17 million units accounting for 30.4 per cent of the market in 1989 to 3.05 million units accounting for 42 per cent of the market, and that the EU industry had suffered substantial injury as a result (*Financial Times*, 11 July 1995).

There has been strong criticism of the EU for introducing these measures. The GATT's anti-dumping provision was meant to prevent a firm from selling in a particular market below its price in other markets, or below the cost of production, as a temporary competitive strategy to bankrupt competitors, after which prices would be raised again. It was not meant to be used to exclude external competitors whose long-term costs were lower. The EU's method of calculation and its use of statistics have been severely criticized. The anti-dumping duties imposed have often been very high and have varied greatly between firms exporting from the same country. The lowest cost and most efficient firms appear to have been the most penalized. Sometimes, in order to avoid their imposition, the Japanese firms have agreed not to sell below a certain price.

These non-tariff barriers have similar effects to a tariff in raising the price of the products on the EU market. The national Consumer Council of the UK calculated that the annual cost to EC consumers of anti-dumping duties on video cassette recorders was Ecu 272.5 million (1989), on compact disc players Ecu 146.1 million (1989), on video cassettes Ecu 48 million (1987), on dot matrix printers Ecu 512.6 million (1988), on electronic typewriters Ecu 104.5 million (1987), and on photocopiers Ecu 339.5 million (1988) (quoted in GATT 1991: i. 213).

Direct investment

The high prices in the EU protected market have encouraged investment though not necessarily by European firms. Colour television production in the UK was ceded first to the European firms Philips (Netherlands) and Thomson[7] (France) and then to inward-investing Japanese firms. Now virtually all colour televisions and video recorders produced in the UK are made by foreign firms (Eltis and Fraser 1992). The UK also imports more than it exports, although it would be necessary to know the imported inputs in order to calculate the effect on the balance of payments.

The EU is very concerned that such inward investment should not be of 'screw-driver' plants, mere assemblers of imported components. In order to prevent this, it has sometimes tried to impose duties on the imported components. In many cases it has treated the foreign subsidiary more harshly than its indigenous firm, which may be importing a relatively higher proportion of its components.

But the UK has benefited not only from direct investment in products using silicon chips but now also from investment in the production of semiconductors themselves. This production is capital- rather than labour-intensive with a plant costing $1 billion or more, but it also requires clean air, copious water supplies, an adequate labour force, and reliable utilities (Kehoe and Taylor 1995). Well-provided with these, Scotland is the most popular location and 'Silicon Glen' provides 35 per cent of the personal computers and 1 in 10 of the microchips made in Europe. Electronic products account for more than 40 per cent of Scotland's exports (Buxton 1995b). Thus the UK's electronic industry is largely the result of foreign direct investment and output is about twice the level it was in the early 1970s. Furthermore there are many plans to expand output: Fujitsu (Japan) is planning an £816 million expansion of its semiconductor plant in Durham, QPL (Korea) will open a £230 million semiconductor in South Wales (Cane and Tighe 1996), Shinho Electronic Telecommunications (Korea) is planning an £8.2 million assembly plant of computer monitors in Fife (Burton and Buxton 1996), Siemens (Germany) is building a £1.1 billion chip plant in north Tyneside (Tighe 1995), and LG (South Korea) is reported to be planning a combined semiconductor and consumer electronics plant in South Wales (Parker and Buxton 1996). In 1994, the UK was the fourth largest exporter of office machines and telecom equipment, with 5.9 per cent of the world market. Thus it was the largest European exporter. It was the fifth largest importer and its net balance was −$1.48 billion. The only large developed country with positive net exports is Japan.

The importance of foreign-owned companies reflects the position in UK manufacturing as a whole. The UK's stock of foreign investment has risen from £52 billion in 1986 to £131 billion in 1994 and the UK has 40 per cent of the stock of UK and Japanese investment in the enlarged EU. Foreign-owned companies provide 18 per cent of the UK manufacturing jobs, 24 per cent of its net output, 32 per cent of manufacturing investment, and about 40 per cent of its manufactured exports (Buxton 1995a). But it is unlikely that this is what the EU Commission means by a strong industry.

Standards

Another area of operation has been in the establishment of standards. In the Tokyo Round the EC agreed not to use its establishment of standards as a form of protection for its domestic industry. None the less, at the 1986 meeting of the International Radio Consultative Committee (CCIR) it refused to agree to a Japanese–US standard for a high definition television (HDTV) system because it wanted to insulate the European market from competition from US and Japanese producers. The EC adopted a rival 1,250-line system and proposed an evolutionary MAC system, claiming that this would minimize the transition costs for EC consumers, although EC consumer organizations complained that they had not been consulted. After the EC taxpayer had invested Ecu 625 million (£516 million) in R&D with additional funds by Philips (Netherlands) and Thomson (France), the UK blocked any further expenditure, which it said would serve no good purpose. Then at the beginning of 1993 Philips announced that, although it had carried out the development work, it would not produce any HDTVs because there were no programmes to transmit on it. Meanwhile the Japanese had begun broadcasting eight hours a day on their HDTV system and US firms had developed a digital technology which appeared likely to sweep the board (*Financial Times*, 17 Nov. 1992; 9 Feb. 1993; 11 Feb. 1993). At the beginning of 1993 the programme was cancelled and the incoming EU commissioner, Mr Martin Bangemann, said that the EU would have to adopt the US standard (*Financial Times*, 19 Feb. 1993). Since then the EU has been more cooperative at an international level with respect to the establishment of standards, which are becoming increasingly important in telecommunications and data transmission.

11.10. Conclusion

The CEC was originally just concerned with removing impediments to trade between member countries. The CETs on imports of manufactures from third countries were being gradually reduced in the course of GATT negotiations. But individual Member States were surreptitiously introducing VERs and other non-tariff barriers to protect their industries against imports from Japan and developing, mainly Asian, countries. Their individual VERs had to be removed with the introduction of the SEM at the beginning of 1993.

Meanwhile, the CEC had begun to use anti-dumping duties generally at the behest of EU firms and without consultation with consumers as an additional non-tariff barrier. These have been used not only to protect declining industries but also against imports of consumer electronic products. The effect has been to encourage the growth of a foreign-owned electronics industry in the UK.

The EU also concluded a whole series of preferential or free trade area agreements, partly, it appears, as a means of extending its political influence or placating countries who were not able to join the EU as full members. In the international arena fears have been expressed that this 'regionalization' of international trade might undermine the multilateralism of the WTO. However, with respect to services and power, the liberalization that the EU has achieved between its Member States has shown the way to agreements at an international level.

Under the Uruguay Round the scope of negotiations was broadened by GATT to include the products of the 'sensitive' industries—namely, agriculture and textiles and clothing. These remain areas in which the EU is very slow to put liberalization into effect, and this also applies to government procurement. Services have been brought under the domain of GATT, now replaced by the WTO, although most of the arrangements concerning them have yet to be concluded.

Discussion questions

1. Why did GATT, and now the WTO, which are devoted to the principle of non-discrimination, permit the formation of customs unions and free trade areas and what conditions did they attach to these? To what extent has the EU complied with these provisions?

2. How do the provisions of the Uruguay Round affect the trade policy of the EU with respect to trade in manufactures?

3. What trade barriers has the EU imposed in order to foster its 'high-tech' industries? What effect have they had?

NOTES

1. Mathematically, the development index is equal to half the sum of the logarithm of relative income plus the logarithm of relative manufactured exports.
2. Algebraically, the specialization index is equal to the ratio of the sectoral share in EU imports to the global share in EU imports.
3. The ban on exports of beef is not discussed here.
4. But the textile agreement includes products which were not included in the original MFA agreement; thus the importing countries have been able to water down the initial stages of liberalization by proffering products which had not been restricted.
5. Optional in 1993, and mandatory in 1996 (WTO 1995*b*: ii. 44).
6. Argentina, Brazil, Hong Kong, India, Indonesia, Israel, Macau, Malaysia, Mexico, Philippines, Singapore, South Korea, Taiwan, Thailand, and the former Yugoslavia.
7. Ferguson was acquired by Thomson in 1987.

REFERENCES

Anderson, K., and Blackhurst, R. (1993) (eds.), *Regional Integration and the Global Trading System* (London: Harvester Wheatsheaf for GATT).

Anson, R. (1996), Editorial, *Textile Outlook International* (Sept.).

Balassa, B. (1974), 'Trade Creation and Trade Diversion in the European Common Market', *Manchester School*, 62/2: 93–135.

Barham, J., and Southey, C. (1995), 'Turkish–EU Customs Union Wins Backing from MEPs', *Financial Times* (14 Dec.).

Buckley, N., and Holberton, S. (1996), 'Plug for the Generation Gap', *Financial Times* (26 June).

Burton, J., and Buxton, J., (1996), 'Koreans to Invest £8m in Scotland', *Financial Times* (30 May).

—— Cane, A., and Tighe, C. (1994), *Financial Times* (18 Oct.), 12.

Buxton, J. (1995a), 'London is Voted the Best City again', *Financial Times* (24 Oct.), 4.

—— (1995b), 'New Monarchs of the Glen', *Financial Times* (15 Nov.), 21.

Cane, A., and Tighe, C. (1996), 'Fujitsu Delays Semiconductor Plan', *Financial Times* (2–3 Mar.).

—— and Ridding, J. (1993), 'Bull Pleads for FFr9.2bn Aid', *Financial Times* (4 Oct.).

CEC (1993): Commission of the European Communities, *European Economy No. 52: The European Community as a World Trade Partner* (Brussels: CEC).

Cline, W. R. (1983) (ed.), *Trade Policy in the 1980s* (Washington: Institute for International Economics).

Dawkins, W., and Clark, B. (1996), 'Tokyo Faces Brussels Pressure on Chips', *Financial Times* (29 Apr.).

de Coster, Jozef (1996), 'Liberalisation of World Trade in Textiles and Clothing: The Views of Exporting and Importing Countries', *Textile Outlook International* (July).

Dicken, P. (1992), *Global Shift*, 2nd edn. (London: Paul Chapman).

Done, K. (1995), 'Volkswagen Switches Work to Low-Cost Unit in Slovakia', *Financial Times* (19 Dec.).

—— and Griffiths, J. (1995), 'Quantity, But Not Enough Quality', *Financial Times* (16 Mar.).

DTI (1994): Department of Trade and Industry, *The Uruguay Round of Multilateral Trade Negotiations 1986–94*, Cm 2579 (London: HMSO).

Dunne, N. (1995), 'US and EU to Discuss Ending IT Tariffs', *Financial Times* (1 Dec.).

Eltis, W., and Fraser, D. (1992), 'The Contribution of Japanese Industrial Success to Britain and to Europe', *National Westminster Bank Quarterly Review* (Nov.), 2–19.

Enders, A., and Wonnacott R. J. (1996), 'Liberalization of East–West European Trade', *The World Economy* 19/3 (May).

Fazey, I. H. (1994), 'Merseyside to Gain 259 Sony Jobs', *Financial Times* (8 Nov.).

GATT (1986a), General Agreement of Tariffs and Trade, *The Text of the General Agreement on Tariffs and Trade* (Geneva: GATT).

—— (1986b), *The Texts of the Tokyo Round Agreements* (Geneva: GATT).

—— (1991a), *Trade Policy Review The European Communities 1991*, 2 vols. (Geneva: GATT).

—— (1992), *International Trade 90–91*, ii (Geneva: GATT).

Greenaway, D., Hyclak, T., and Thornton, R., (1989) (eds.), *Economic Aspects of Regional Trading Arrangements* (London: Harvester).

Griffiths, J. (1996a), 'Growth Runs into a Jam', *Financial Times, World Motor Industry* (5 Mar.).

—— (1996b), 'Germans Slip in Motor Parts Profits League', *Financial Times* (25 May).

Hamilton, C. B. (1990), *Textiles Trade and the Developing Countries; Eliminating the Multi-Fibre Arrangement in the 1990s* (Washington: World Bank).

Herin, J. (1986), 'Rules of Origin and Differences between Tariff Levels in EFTA and in the EC', Occasional paper No. 13, EFTA, quoted in Waer (1994).

Hill, A., and Ridding, J., (1993), 'Brussels Probes State Aid to Bull Computer Group', *Financial Times* (7 Oct.).

Hine, R. C. (1985), *The Political Economy of European Trade* (Brighton: Harvester).

Hoekman, B., and Leidy, M. (1993), 'Holes and Loopholes in Integration Agreements: History and Prospects', in Anderson and Blackhurst (1993).

Jonquieres, G. de (1994), 'High Duties against Japan', *Financial Times* (4 May).

Keesing, D. B., and Wolf, M. (1980), *Textile Quotas against Developing Countries* (Thames Essay No. 23; London: Trade Policy Research Centre).

Kehoe, L. (1996), 'Japanese "Split on Chip Pact Demand" ', *Financial Times* (13 June).

—— and Taylor, P. (1995), 'The Chips are Down as the Stakes Rise', *Financial Times* (3 Aug.), 17.

Khanna, Sri Ram (1994), 'The New Gatt Agreement: Implications for the World's Textile and Clothing Industries', *Textile Outlook International* (Mar.).

Luesby, J. (1996), 'Textile Makers Warn on Anti-Dumping Move', *Financial Times* (17 Sept.).

Maitland, A. (1996), 'European Commission Grapples with the Content of Chocolate', *Financial Times* (20 Mar.).

Majmudar, M. (1996), 'The MFA Phase-Out and EU Clothing Sourcing: Forecasts to 2005', *Textile Outlook International* (Mar.).

Mattoo, A., and Mavroidis, P. C. (1995), 'The EC–Japan Consensus on Cars: Interaction between Trade and Competition Policy', *The World Economy*, 18/3.

Maxcy, G. (1981), *The Multinational Motor Industry* (London: Croom Helm).

Montagnon, P., and Bardacke, T. (1996), 'Door Open to Wider Europe–Asia Links', *Financial Times* (26 Feb.).

Moore, L. (1991), 'International Trade in Textiles and Clothing', *Journal of the Textile Institute*, 82/2.

Münchau, W. (1996), 'German Carmakers Warn on Jobs', *Financial Times* (1 Feb.).

Nakamoto, M. (1996), 'Tokyo Rejects Three-Way Semiconductor Accord', *Financial Times* (24 Apr.).

NCC (1990a), National Consumer Council, *International Trade and the Consumer*, Working Paper 1. *Consumer Electronics and the EC's anti-dumping policy* (London: NCC).

—— (1990b), *International Trade and the Consumer*, Working Paper 2: *Textiles and Clothes* (London: NCC).

OECD (1970), Organization for Economic Cooperation and Development, *Gaps in Technology: Analytical Report* (Paris: OECD).

—— (1983), *Long Term Outlook for the World Automobile Industry* (Paris: OECD).

—— (1995), *Regional Integration and the Multilateral Trading System—Synergy and Divergence* (Paris: OECD).

Parker, G., and Buxton, J. (1996), 'Welsh Fear Move to Poach Korean Plant', *Financial Times* (22 June).

Pratten, C. (1988), 'A Survey of the Economies of Scale', Study No. 17 undertaken for the 'Costs of Non-Europe' Project, *Documents*, ii (Brussels–Luxembourg: CEC).

Ridding, J. (1995a), 'Thomson may be Privatised next Spring', *Financial Times* (18 Oct.).

—— (1995b), 'Contender Power Up for Semiconductor Wars', *Financial Times* (18 Oct.).

Silberston, Z. A. (1984), *The Multi-fibre Arrangement and the UK Economy* (London: HMSO).

—— (1989), *The Future of the Multi-Fibre Arrangement: Implications for the UK Economy* (London: HMSO).

Simonian, H., (1995), 'Hard Road to Higher Sales', *Financial Times* (15 Dec.).

—— (1996), 'Going Global is Nothing New', *Financial Times, World Motor Industry* (5 Mar.), p. IV.

Southey, C. (1996*a*), 'EU under fire for trade pact proliferation', *Financial Times.*

—— (1996*b*), 'EU Settles Rift over Trade Pact with South Africa', *Financial Times* (26 Mar.).

—— (1996*c*), 'Issue of Free Trade Divides EU's Farm Ministers', *Financial Times* (6 May).

Swann, D. (1988), *The Economics of the Common Market*, 6th edn. (Harmondsworth: Penguin).

Taylor, P. (1995), 'Germans Hope to take Revenge on Rivals from Far East', *Financial Times* (15 Dec.).

Tharakan, P. K. M., and Kol, J. (1989), *Intra-Industry Trade* (London: Macmillan).

Tighe, C. (1995), 'Siemens Wastes No Time on Tyneside', *Financial Times* (15 Dec.).

Tucker, E. (1996), 'Private Car Dealers Win Cross-Border Sales Ruling', *Financial Times* (16 Feb.).

—— and Ridding, J. (1994*a*), 'French Aid for Groupe Bull seems Likely to be Approved', *Financial Times* (7 Oct.).

—— —— (1994*b*), 'Brussels Approves £1.33bn Rescue for Bull', *Financial Times* (13 Oct.).

—— and White, D. (1995), 'Seat Agrees to Cut Capacity by 30%', *Financial Times* (5 Oct.).

Waer, P. (1994), 'European Community Rules of Origin', in Edwin Vermulst, Paul Waer, and Jacques Bourgeois (eds.), *Rules of Origin in International Trade* (Ann Arbor, Mich.: University of Michigan Press).

Walter, I. (1983), 'Structural Adjustment and Trade Policy in the International Steel Industry', in William R. Cline (ed.), *Trade Policy in the 1980s* (Washington: Institute for International Economics).

Williams, F. (1995), 'WTO Chief Tries to Avoid Confrontation', *Financial Times* (14 Dec.).

—— (1996), 'US Attacks EU Tariffs on Computers', *Financial Times* (23 May).

Wighton, D. (1995), 'A Record that was Easy to Break', *Financial Times* (8–9 July).

Winters, L. A., and Wang, Z. K. (1994), *Eastern Europe's International Trade* (Manchester: Manchester University Press).

Wonnacott, R. J. (1996), 'Hub-and-Spoke System versus a Free Trade Area', *World Economy*, 19/3 (May).

—— and Enders, A. (1996), 'Liberalization of East–West European Trade', *World Economy*, 19/3 (May).

WTO (1995*a*): World Trade Organization, *Regionalism and the World Trading System* (Geneva: WTO).

—— (1995*b*), *Trade Policy Review European Union*, 2 vols. (Geneva: WTO).

—— (1995*c*), *International Trade 1995 Trends and Statistics* (Geneva: WTO).

CHAPTER 12

The European Monetary System

ROBIN BLADEN-HOVELL

12.1. Introduction

Prior to the crises of 1992 and 1993 in the European foreign-exchange markets, the Exchange Rate Mechanism (ERM) of the European Monetary System (EMS) represented the cornerstone of international monetary arrangements within Europe and looked set to provide the operational framework that would lead eventually to complete monetary union among EC Member States. Bilateral exchange rates between the EC countries had remained remarkably stable for an extended period within the ERM framework and appeared to exhibit lower levels of variability than other, non-ERM, rates. The last major adjustment of European exchange rates had occurred in 1987 and, since that date, the system had successfully incorporated three additional currencies: the Spanish peseta in June 1989, UK sterling in October 1990, and the Portuguese escudo in April 1992; and had witnessed German monetary unification in 1990. The success of the system seemed further underlined by the decisions of some non-EC countries (Sweden, Norway, and Finland) unilaterally to tie their currencies to the ERM. By the end of the period of turbulence, however, the framework appeared to be in crisis. Two major currencies, the Italian lira and UK sterling, had suspended their membership; the Spanish peseta and Portuguese escudo had devalued within the system; the permissible band of fluctuation around central parity rates had been substantially widened to 15 per cent; the non-ERM adherents to the system (in the Swedish case, after a spectacular but unsuccessful defence) had severed their links with the system, and upon the enlargement of the EU in 1995 only one of the three new members (Austria) chose to join the system.

The purpose of the current chapter is to survey the performance and achievements of the system and to highlight the factors that led up to the events of September 1992 when the lira and pound sterling suspended their membership of the system, and the effects of the subsequent crisis of 1993. The chapter contains five sections. The key provisions of the system are outlined in Section 12.2 of the paper; this is followed by a discussion of the system's performance from its inception to 1995. The issue of whether the ERM is simply a Deutschmark-zone is considered in Section 12.4, whilst the question of whether capital controls are necessary for the system to function is tackled in Section 12.5. Of course, the turbulence experienced in the foreign-exchange markets during 1992 and 1993 is not entirely independent of these two issues. The virtual freedom of movement for international capital together with the dominant position of Germany and its unwillingness to operate monetary policy from a European (rather than a German) perspective is frequently blamed for the crisis in the system. These questions are considered in detail in Section 12.6 of the paper. A brief summary of the main points and conclusions completes the chapter.

12.2. **Provisions of the mechanism**

The EMS was established in March 1979 with the intention of creating a 'zone of monetary stability' within Europe. The origins of the system may be traced to the 1970 Werner Report, which proposed the achievement of complete monetary union within the EC by 1980. Although circumstances at the time led to the original timetable for this proposal being abandoned almost immediately, a further attempt to relaunch the idea of a European zone of exchange-rate stability was made in the aftermath of the breakdown of the Bretton Woods system and the Smithsonian Agreement of December 1971. In the March of the following year the EC countries embarked on an experiment to restrict the range of fluctuation between their currencies to a band of ±2.25 per cent. Anticipating imminent accession to the EC, the UK, Norway, Denmark, and Ireland also participated in this scheme, which became known as the Snake. The Snake was unable to withstand the considerable turbulence in the currency markets; some countries left the system quite soon after joining (the UK, Ireland), whilst others left and rejoined only to leave again (France). By 1977 only a core group of five countries (Germany, Denmark, the Netherlands, Belgium, and Luxembourg) remained. Nevertheless, the desire to stabilize exchange rates between the EC member countries remained strong, and agreement on a more effective means for achieving this was finally achieved at the Council of Ministers meeting held in Brussels in December 1978.[1] The European Monetary System began operation from the following March.

The EMS is formally organized around a basket of EU currencies that comprise the European Currency Unit (Ecu), which acts as the numeraire for the ERM and the unit of account for all EU transactions. The Ecu is a composite currency that contains specific amounts of the currencies of all member states, including those which do not participate in the ERM. Thus, at the beginning of 1996, the Ecu contained the Greek drachma, the Italian lira, and the UK pound sterling, even though Greece has never participated in the ERM, whilst Italy and the UK both suspended their membership in September 1992.[2] The composition of the Ecu has been subject to periodic review, the review period being set initially as every five years.

The composition of the Ecu set at each of the reviews, together with the weight of each currency in the Ecu is shown in Table 12.1. From this we can see that the Ecu consists literally of so many Deutschmarks, so many French francs, so many pounds sterling, and so on. However, the actual weight of each currency in the basket will change because of exchange-rate movements and the weights shown in column five of the table are those prevailing on 6 March 1995 following the most recent realignment of the system.

The centrepiece of the EMS is its ERM. This provides for the 'currency grid', a set of all bilateral exchange rates between participating countries with a nominated central rate for each and a permissible band of fluctuation. As a matter of arithmetic, a currency's central rate is re-expressed in terms of the Ecu; but the essence of the ERM is the obligation to maintain bilateral exchange rates within the permitted bands of fluctuation. Prior to the decision taken by European finance ministers in August 1992, to allow ERM currencies to float within a margin of ± 15 per cent, the size of this band was set at ± 2.25 per cent for the majority of participating countries. Italy, however, had negotiated a transitional arrangement which initially allowed it to operate within a wider, ± 6 per cent, band of fluctuation. Italy eventually adopted the narrower ± 2.25 per cent band in January, 1990, but the transitional arrangement involving the use of the wider band was extended to three new participants: Spain (June 1989), the UK (October 1990), and Portugal (April 1992) upon their joining the mechanism.

Table 12.1. **Composition and weighting of the Ecu, 1979–1995**

Country (currency)	Composition of the Ecu			
	13 Mar. 1979– 14 Sept. 1984	17 Sept. 1984– 20 Sept. 1989	20 Sept. 1989–	Weight as of 6 Mar. 1995
Belgium/Luxembourg (franc)	3.800	3.850	3.431	8.71
Denmark (krone)	0.217	0.219	0.1976	2.71
France (franc)	1.150	1.310	1.332	20.79
Germany (mark)	0.828	0.719	0.6242	32.68
Greece (drachma)	n.a.	1.150	1.440	0.49
Ireland (punt)	0.00759	0.00871	0.008552	1.08
Italy (lira)	100.000	140.000	151.8	7.21
Netherlands (guilder)	0.286	0.256	0.2198	10.21
Portugal (escudo)	n.a.	n.a.	1.393	0.71
Spain (peseta)	n.a.	n.a.	6.885	4.24
UK (sterling)	0.0885	0.0878	0.08784	11.17
				100.0

Note: n.a. = not applicable.

Central rates are not irrevocably fixed within the system, but may be adjusted, or realigned, after consultation among EMS members. One of the principal objectives of the ERM, however, has been to keep such realignments to a minimum and especially to prevent devaluation being used as an competitive instrument of policy within Europe. To this end, central banks are obliged to intervene in the foreign-exchange market in order to keep their currencies within the permitted margins of fluctuation. The intervention rules themselves are relatively straightforward and designed to impose symmetry of adjustment on the system.[3] When a currency diverges from its central rate by the amount permitted by its band of fluctuation, currently ±15 per cent, the central banks of the strongest and the weakest currency within the system are equally obliged to intervene in order to stabilize the currency. Since any of the bilateral exchange rates can trigger an intervention, measuring the maximum appreciation and depreciation against the weakest and strongest currency respectively means that the effective band of fluctuation is narrower in practice than the 15 per cent margin would suggest.

The parity grid and permissible band of fluctuation operating in the ERM since 6 March 1995, following the most recent realignment within the system, is shown in Table 12.2. For participating countries, column 1 of the table shows the central parity value of a currency expressed in terms of the Ecu; for non-participating countries, such as the UK and Italy, the Ecu value shown in column 1 is the one used in EU transactions. The bilateral central rates calculated as the ratio of the Ecu par values, together with the upper and lower limits at which intervention must occur, may be read from the three entries in the remainder of the Table 12.2. Hence the bilateral German–French central rate is given as 335.386 FF per 100 DM with an upper and lower intervention limit of 389.48 FF and 288.81 FF respectively.

The innovation in the EMS of the divergence indicator, based upon the concept of the 'Maximum Divergence Spread' (MDS), provides a further example of the desire to promote symmetry of adjustment within the system. The MDS, expressed as a percentage, is calculated as $\pm 15 \, (1 - w_i)$, where w_i denotes the weight of currency i, and indicates the maximum percentage by which a currency's market Ecu rate may fluctuate[4] against its Ecu central rate before the currency reaches its bilateral margin against any other ERM currency. The divergence indicator is based on the notion of a divergence threshold, which is set at 75 per cent of the MDS.[5] By construction, a currency departing from its central rate should cross the divergence threshold and trigger the divergence indicator before it reaches any of the bilateral margins defined by the currency grid. The formal provision of the EMS provides that, when a currency triggers its divergence threshold, a presumption is created that the country in question should undertake appropriate adjustments, whether by intervention in the foreign-exchange market or by fiscal or monetary policy action perhaps including a realignment of its currency. Because the design of the divergence indicator was based on a currency's Ecu rate divergence, the device was thought of as singling out that particular currency which stood out against 'the rest of the pack'. It was by intention even-handed, applying equally to a currency standing out on the 'strong' as on the 'weak' side. This was the

Table 12.2. Central rates and intervention limit rates in force since 6 March 1995

	1 Ecu =	100 Belgian francs =	100 Danish krona =	100 German marks =	100 Spanish peseta =	100 French francs =	1 Irish pound =	100 Dutch guilders =	100 Austrian schillings =	100 Portuguese escudo =
Belgian franc	39.3960	—	627.880	2395.20	28.1525	714.030	57.7445	2125.60	340.420	23.3645
		—	540.723	2062.55	24.2447	614.977	49.7289	1830.54	293.163	20.1214
		—	465.665	1776.20	20.8795	529.660	42.8260	1576.45	252.470	17.3285
Danish krona	7.2858	21.4747	—	442.968	5.20640	132.066	10.6792	393.105	62.9561	4.32100
		18.4928	—	381.443	4.48376	113.732	9.19676	338.537	54.2170	3.72119
		15.9266	—	328.461	3.86140	97.9430	7.92014	291.544	46.6910	3.2046
German mark	1.91007	5.63000	30.4450	—	1.36500	34.6250	2.80000	103.058	16.5050	1.13280
		4.84837	26.2162	—	1.17548	29.8164	2.41105	88.7526	14.2136	0.975561
		4.17500	22.5750	—	1.01230	25.6750	2.07600	76.4326	12.2410	0.840100
Spanish peseta	162.493	478.944	2589.80	9878.50	—	2945.40	238.175	8767.30	1404.10	96.3670
		412.461	2230.27	8507.18	—	2536.54	205.113	7550.30	1209.18	82.9927
		355.206	1920.70	7326.00	—	2184.40	176.641	6502.20	1041.30	71.4690
French franc	6.40608	18.8800	102.100	389.480	4.57780	—	9.38950	345.650	55.3545	3.79920
		16.2608	87.9257	335.386	3.94237	—	8.08631	297.661	47.6706	3.27188
		14.0050	75.7200	288.810	3.39510	—	6.96400	256.350	41.0533	2.81770
Irish pound	0.792214	2.33503	12.6261	48.1696	0.566120	14.3599	—	42.7439	6.84544	0.469841
		2.01090	10.8734	41.4757	0.487537	12.3666	—	36.8105	5.89521	0.404620
		1.73176	9.36403	35.7143	0.419859	10.6500	—	31.7007	5.07688	0.348453
Dutch guilder	2.15214	6.34340	34.3002	130.834	1.53793	39.0091	3.15450	—	18.5963	1.27637
		5.46286	29.5389	112.673	1.32445	33.5953	2.71662	—	16.0149	1.09920
		4.70454	25.4385	97.0325	1.14060	28.9381	2.33952	—	13.7918	0.946611
Austrian schilling	13.4383	39.6089	214.174	816.927	9.60338	243.586	19.6971	725.065	—	7.97000
		34.1107	184.444	703.550	8.27008	209.773	16.9629	624.417	—	6.86356
		29.3757	158.841	605.877	7.12200	180.654	14.6082	537.740	—	5.91086
Portuguese escudo	195.792	577.090	3120.50	11903.3	139.540	3549.00	286.983	10564.0	1691.80	—
		496.984	2687.31	10250.5	120.493	3056.35	247.145	9097.55	1456.97	—
		428.000	2314.30	8827.70	103.770	2632.10	212.838	7834.70	1254.70	—
Greek drachma	292.867	n.a.	n.a.	n.a.	n.a.	n.a.	n.a.	n.a.	n.a.	n.a.
Italian lira	2106.15	n.a.	n.a.	n.a.	n.a.	n.a.	n.a.	n.a.	n.a.	n.a.
UK pound	0.786652	n.a.	n.a.	n.a.	n.a.	n.a.	n.a.	n.a.	n.a.	n.a.

Note: n.a. = not applicable.
Source: Eurostat, 12 (1995); ECU–EMS Information and Central Bank Interest Rates, ECSC–EC–EAEC, Brussels.

sense in which the divergence indicator construct appeared to underpin the desire for symmetry.

In order to finance their obligation to defend the bilateral currency bands, countries participating in the ERM may draw upon the credit facilities of the European Monetary Cooperation Fund (EMCF). The most important of these instruments is the Very Short Term Financing (VSTF) facility, which provides finance for intervention in the foreign-exchange markets, which is undertaken when the currency reaches its limit—so-called marginal intervention. This facility takes the form of a line of mutual credit which extends among the central banks of the system. Since marginal intervention is compulsory and must be conducted in unlimited quantities by the two central banks whose currencies have reached their bilateral margin, this credit line is automatic and unlimited.[6]

In principle, the design of the VSTF facility has important implications for monetary conditions in countries that are pushed to their bilateral margins. The use of the credit lines in these circumstances results in an increase in the liabilities of the central bank managing the stronger currency and an increase in the assets of the central bank managing the weaker currency. As a result, marginal intervention should produce a monetary expansion in the country with the stronger currency and a monetary contraction in the country with the weaker currency. In practice, however, the extent to which ERM members have allowed their domestic monetary policy to be dictated by the needs of the ERM has varied considerably, with Germany, in particular, typically acting to sterilize the monetary effects of ERM intervention. We discuss this asymmetry of the operation of the system in Section 12.3 of the current chapter.

12.3. The operation of the EMS in practice

Although the ERM was conceived of as providing a framework for monetary stability within Europe, exchange rates were not considered immutably fixed, at least not at first. Adjustments or realignments of the central parities were allowed, and the early years of the system, in particular, featured a number of realignments of these central rates.

In this respect, the design of the ERM benefited from the experience that policy-makers had gained previously in attempting to implement parity changes within otherwise fixed-rate systems. Under the institutional arrangements that characterized both the Bretton Woods system and the Snake, for example, countries generally resisted parity changes for as long as possible, with the result that, when adjustment did occur, it was typically brought about, or accompanied by, intense speculative pressure. Speculators were in effect able to benefit from what became known as a 'one-way bet' on the currency movement. With the direction of movement in the currency known with almost complete certainty, speculators could afford to adopt extreme positions in the foreign-exchange market by borrowing the weak currency in order to buy the strong one in anticipation of a devaluation. The potential gains from such speculative activity are enormous. The gross gains produced by correctly anticipating a 10 per cent devaluation on the day, for example, would be equivalent to an annual interest differential equal to (10×365) 3,650 per cent. By comparison, until the recent turbulence in the European foreign-exchange markets, realignments within the ERM have mostly been made without excessive speculative pressure developing. Realignments became less frequent within the system as time elapsed, and many exchange-rate adjustments occurred without disturbing the market rate, which remained within existing bands, thus eliminating the one-way speculative option that accompanies discrete exchange-rate movements.

Details of the realignments within the ERM, over the period 1979–95, are presented in Table 12.3. Inspection of the table reveals that three distinct sub-periods may be distinguished in the history of the ERM. The first period, from March 1979 until January 1987, was characterized by frequent and often sizeable realignments of the currencies within the system. This was followed by a five-year period of relative stability in which the system expanded to include the Spanish peseta, the Portugese escudo, and the British pound, and in which the only realignment was a technical adjustment that accompanied the Italian decision to adopt the narrower intervention limits. This golden age came to an end with the currency crisis of September 1992, which saw the Italian lira and British pound leave the system and initiated a prolonged period of volatility in which the intervention limits were widened (in August 1993) to a value of ± 15 per cent. Upon enlargement of the EU, only one of the three new Members decided to participate in the system, the Austrian schilling joining on 7 January 1995.

One important feature of the exchange-rate adjustments over the early period was the increasing tendency for such realignments not to accommodate fully the differences in inflation among the ERM countries, as the period progressed. During the first four years of operation, for example, the degree of inflation offset provided by the nominal realignments within the period amounted to just over 100 per cent in the case of countries participating in the narrow band of the ERM. From 1983 onwards, however, the degree of inflation compensation fell considerably with the offset to the inflation differential between Germany and other narrow-band currencies amounting to only 50 per cent during the latter period.

The apparent ability of the ERM to stabilize variations in exchange rates is typically accounted as one of the most successful aspects of the system. As indicated in Table 12.4, however, whilst this stabilizing effect seems clear for intra-EMS exchange rates, it is less clearly visible for movements in the exchange rates between ERM members and the rest of the world. Here, exchange-rate variability is measured as the standard deviation of the monthly percentage change of the nominal bilateral exchange rate—these standard deviations being aggregated into single values through the use of the Ecu currency weights in the case of the ERM and EU non-ERM groups respectively.

High-frequency measures of this nature can be used to adduce evidence concerning the short-run volatility of the exchange rate but do not illuminate the question whether

Table 12.3. Realignments in central parities, 1979–1995

Date of realignment

Currency	24 Sept. 1979	30 Nov. 1979	22 Feb. 1981	5 Oct. 1981	22 Feb. 1982	14 June 1982	21 Mar. 1983	20 July 1985	7 Apr. 1986	4 Aug. 1986	12 Jan. 1987	8 Jan. 1990	13 Sept. 1992	16 Sept. 1992	22 Nov. 1992	2 Feb. 1993	14 May 1993	2 Aug. 1993	6 Mar. 1995
Belgium franc	0.0	0.0	0.0	0.0	-8.5	0.0	+1.5	+2.0	+1.0	0.0	+2.0	0.0	+3.5	0.0	0.0	0.0	0.0	b	0.0
Danish krona	-3.0	-4.8	0.0	0.0	-3.0	0.0	+2.5	+2.0	+1.0	0.0	0.0	0.0	+3.5	0.0	0.0	0.0	0.0	b	0.0
German mark	+2.0	0.0	0.0	+5.5	0.0	+4.25	+5.5	+2.0	+3.0	0.0	+3.0	0.0	+3.5	0.0	0.0	0.0	0.0	b	0.0
French franc	0.0	0.0	0.0	-3.0	0.0	-5.75	-2.5	+2.0	-3.0	0.0	0.0	0.0	+3.5	0.0	0.0	0.0	0.0	b	0.0
Irish pound	0.0	0.0	0.0	0.0	0.0	0.0	-3.5	+2.0	0.0	-8.0	0.0	0.0	+3.5	0.0	0.0	-10.0	0.0	b	0.0
Italian lira	0.0	0.0	-6.0	-3.0	0.0	-2.75	-2.5	-6.0	0.0	0.0	0.0	-3.75	-3.5	a	-	-	-	-	-
Dutch guilder	0.0	0.0	0.0	+5.5	0.0	+4.25	+3.5	+2.0	+3.0	0.0	+3.0	0.0	+3.5	0.0	0.0	0.0	0.0	b	0.0
Spanish peseta			Entered ERM, 19 June 1989										+3.5	-5.0	-6.0	0.0	-8.0	b	-7.0
UK pound				Entered ERM, 8 October 1990									+3.5	a	-	-	-	-	-
Portuguese escudo						Entered ERM, 6 April 1992							+3.5	0.0	-6.0	0.0	-6.5	b	-3.5
Austrian schilling								Entered ERM, 7 January 1995											0

[a] Currency exited from ERM.
[b] Widening of the fluctuation band to ±15 per cent.

Source: CEC, General Report on the Activities of the EU, various issues.

Table 12.4. **Variability of bilateral nominal exchange rates for the ERM countries, the EC non-ERM, and the USA and Japan, 1979–1989**

Countries	1974–8	1979–83	1984–6	1987–9
Against 20 industrialized countries				
USA	2.1	2.3	2.6	2.4
Japan	2.4	2.9	2.7	2.4
ERM	1.8	1.6	1.3	1.1
Non-ERM countries	2.4	2.4	2.2	1.7
Against ERM countries				
USA	2.2	2.6	3.0	2.8
Japan	2.3	2.7	2.1	1.9
ERM	1.6	0.9	0.6	0.4
Non-ERM countries	2.2	2.3	1.8	1.4

Source: CEC (1990: tables 3.4–3.6).

exchange rates are misaligned or not. Misalignment in this context refers to the capacity for the real exchange rate, or competitiveness, to depart from its equilibrium value over lengthy periods of time.[7] Such departures, if left uncorrected, pose particular problems for the pattern of trade and, ultimately, for the spatial location of production among countries.

The welfare effects of a reduction in volatility, on the other hand, are probably not great; what counts is whether the volatility can be predicted and whether traders can hedge themselves with little cost against it. In conventional theory the forward markets afford hedging opportunities at low cost for short horizons. However, a finding that the EMS reduced short-run volatility in nominal exchange rates suggests that it may also have prevented misalignments from growing as quickly as they might otherwise have done, which might be recorded as a more substantial achievement. But it does seem clear that any such dampening effect was not enough to discourage some significant misalignment from eventually emerging. Indeed, some observers (see below) attribute the crash of the EMS in part to perceptions that some currencies had become seriously misaligned.

Despite the original intention of making adjustment within the ERM symmetric, considerable evidence has accumulated which suggests that substantial asymmetries remained within the system. Two factors in particular are commonly identified as being illustrative of these operational asymmetries. The first relates to the fact that the Deutschmark is now widely acknowledged as providing the *de facto* nominal anchor and reserve currency of the system, with dollar interventions dominated by the actions of the Bundesbank. Secondly, the burden of intervention to support parities within the ERM has been disproportionately borne by the weaker, and generally non-German, currencies.[8] In addition, as Mastropasqua *et al.* (1988) find, the Bundesbank typically tends to offset the domestic monetary consequences of German involvement in supporting activities by buying or selling interest-bearing debt to the private sector—so-called sterilization operations. As a result, monetary policy in Germany is determined by domestic considerations alone, whilst the remaining, non-German, ERM members essentially accommodate the stance of German monetary policy. Moreover, the relevance of this result has become increasingly important as ERM members have placed greater reliance on their currency value *vis-à-vis* the Deutschmark rather than their Ecu parity.[9] As a consequence of this, ERM members have typically found themselves constrained by their bilateral limits relative to the strongest currency rather than the divergence thresholds of the system. These factors, together with the adoption of the ERM as a disinflationary framework by the non-German members of the system, led investigators to propose that, to all practical intents and purposes, the operations of the ERM had come to conform to a 'greater Deutschmark-zone'. This proposition, usually ascribed to Giavazzi and Giovannini (1989) and Giavazzi and Pagano (1988), is considered in greater detail in the next section.

12.4. **The German leadership hypothesis**

Whilst the relative performance of the German economy and the historical strength of the German balance of payments obviously suggest that Germany merits an important role within the ERM, the willingness of other countries to accept Germany as the dominant partner implies that these countries must anticipate benefits accruing from the arrangement. For non-German members of the ERM, these gains have usually been expressed in terms of the benefits they achieve by 'importing' Germany's reputation for counter-inflationary policy.

This proposition is based upon the notion of a 'reputational policy' of the form described by Barro and Gordon (1983). Here the costs to a country, in terms of the loss of output, associated with a policy of inflation reduction, depend crucially upon the ability of the authorities to convince the private sector that they mean to pursue an effective counter-inflationary policy and will not renege on this commitment. Within this framework, credible governments may make announcements concerning future disinflationary strategy and, because these announcements are believed by the private sector, they have the immediate effect of reducing inflationary expectations within the economy. As a consequence, the desired effects of policy may be achieved at a lower unemployment cost than would have occurred had the reputation of the authorities been lower.

Within the ERM, the counter-inflationary stance of German monetary policy is generally well known. The decision of countries to pre-commit themselves to a fixed exchange rate with respect to Germany therefore constitutes a very visible commitment to low inflation which is relatively straightforward for the private sector to monitor. The alternative, assuming that the fixed exchange-rate system is maintained, is a gradual erosion of competitiveness for the higher inflation country.[10] Of course, the decision by countries to pre-commit to the German standard implies that the operation of the ERM will be asymmetric in the way described previously: the Bundesbank independently chooses its monetary policy, whilst all remaining EMS members 'tie their hands' on monetary policy and simply target their exchange rates to the Deutschmark. The EMS is *de facto* a Deutschmark zone.[11]

Although the intuitive argument in favour of the German leadership hypothesis is compelling, the empirical evidence that may be adduced in its favour is less than fully supportive. Evidence relating to the interaction of monetary policy among ERM members, for example, suggests a rich structure of cross-country interactions: German monetary policy influences the other ERM members, but is itself affected by monetary developments that originate elsewhere in the system, especially in France. French monetary policy also influences policy developments among the non-German ERM members.

Strictly interpreted, this evidence would appear to run counter to the notion of German leadership, but does favour a view of the EMS operating in a symmetric, or bipolar, manner with France and Germany representing the two poles of behaviour in the latter case. Weber (1991), in particular, argues that a bipolar interpretation of the EMS, with Germany offering members a hard currency option and France offering a soft currency option, provides a convenient framework for analysing developments within the system prior to 1987. He suggests, however, that the system has become increasingly dominated by the Deutschmark from 1987 onwards as the disinflationary stance of ERM members hardened.

Direct tests of whether the EMS has facilitated a convergence on the inflation performance of Germany have also produced conflicting evidence. A casual inspection of the data relating to the inflation performance of ERM and non-ERM countries, for example, suggests that, overall, ERM countries have performed little, if at all, better than non-ERM countries in reducing inflation. However, more sophisticated exercises that investigate whether German inflation 'affects' wage and price developments in other ERM countries (see, for example, Artis and Nachane 1990) find strong evidence of an 'EMS effect' in the sense that the predicted inflation in Germany was a significant determinant of price inflation in all EMS countries except the UK over the period Feb. 1979–Feb. 1985. This result is frequently interpreted in an expectational context—in effect, ERM membership disciplines the economy by raising the cost of inflation.

Although the evidence in favour of a special ERM disinflation effect appears compelling, it should not, however, be accepted too readily. Alternative arguments may be found which would account for the inflationary experience of ERM members. In particular, at the time of ERM formation, the policy stance among industrialized countries generally, and the ERM participants specifically, was predisposed towards a lower inflationary environment. Evidence of an 'ERM effect' may therefore reflect a selection bias rather than a performance effect arising as a result of the system's operation.

12.5. **Capital controls**

The maintenance of capital controls within a system of managed exchange rates is usually based upon two arguments. These arguments highlight the potential of capital controls to limit the extent of fluctuations in domestic interest rates in the period immediately prior to a discrete change of the exchange rate that is anticipated by the market, and suggest that, by adopting capital controls, the monetary authorities can avert speculative attacks against their foreign-exchange position. In each case, therefore, the role of the currency speculator is crucial.

The motivation behind speculative capital flows is one of making a capital gain from anticipated movements in spot rates or interest rates. A risk-neutral currency speculator would be indifferent between holding sterling or Deutschmark denominated assets, for example, if the interest rate on sterling assets equalled the interest rate on Deutschmarks plus the anticipated depreciation of sterling relative to the Deutschmark—the uncovered interest parity condition. If the anticipated sterling devaluation exceeds the sterling interest advantage, holders of sterling assets will switch their portfolio into Deutschmarks in the expectation of making a capital gain by repurchasing sterling at a lower value in the future. Moreover, irrespective of whether the interest differential offsets the expected currency movement or not, since the value of domestic currency falls with a devaluation, holders of domestic high-powered money have an incentive to avoid the loss by selling the domestic currency to the central bank in exchange for foreign currency prior to the devaluation, then buying domestic currency back once the devaluation has occurred. If foreign-exchange transactions were costless, the effect of such speculative activity would be to reduce the foreign-exchange reserves of the central bank to zero.

The difficulty is that, within a regime of controlled floating, the interest differential required to offset expected currency movements is typically very high. A simple example may be used to illustrate the point. Suppose that a discrete devaluation, equivalent to a fall of 5 per cent per annum, was expected next month within an otherwise fixed rate regime. The interest differential required to offset this would be 5 per cent on comparable one-year bonds. For interest-bearing instruments of shorter maturity, however, the required interest differential would be correspondingly higher: 20 per cent on three-month assets, 60 per cent on one-month assets, and well in excess of 100 per cent on overnight deposits.[12] Capital controls can protect domestic interest rates from the need to assume such levels when discrete changes in the currency value are expected by the market. They do so by prohibiting domestic and foreign residents from borrowing at the domestic rate of interest in order to lend abroad in the expectation of capital gains from the currency movement. Of course, such a prohibition on currency transactions would also have the advantage of preventing speculative attacks on the foreign reserve position of the central bank.

In investigating the effectiveness of capital controls, attention has focused on the size of the on-shore/off-shore interest differential. Indeed, the persistent differential between domestic and off-shore interest rates, which became huge every time realignments were expected, is generally taken as evidence that capital controls were binding. In the absence of capital controls, this differential should represent a pure arbitrage opportunity for agents operating in the foreign-exchange market. Evidence obtained by de Grauwe (1989) and Giavazzi and Giovannini (1990), however, suggests that capital controls enabled France and Italy in particular to violate the interest-parity condition and, as a result, allowed ERM members to maintain a considerable degree of monetary autonomy especially during the early days of the ERM. The importance of capital controls was progressively reduced within the ERM following the Capital Liberalization Directive of 1988.[13] Controls were removed entirely from capital movements in and out of France and Italy, and the two-tier foreign-exchange market that allowed discrimination between commercial and capital account transactions in Belgium was eliminated. By 1990 controls remained in effect for Greece, Ireland, Portugal, and Spain, and even in these countries the scope of control was very limited. Controls were finally removed just before the 1992 deadline.

As a consequence of this progressive reduction in capital controls, the potential for capital movements among the ERM countries has increased substantially and this feature has brought to the fore the need for much closer coordination of monetary policies. This policy dilemma lay at the heart of what Padoa-Schioppa (1988) termed the 'inconsistent quartet'—the inconsistent set of four characteristics of an international monetary system: free trade, free capital movements, national policy autonomy, and fixed exchange rates. The difficulty is in reconciling these four characteristics within one system. During the first phase of ERM, free movement of capital and fixity of the exchange rate was compromised by the presence of capital controls and the frequent realignments of the system. Together these factors allowed members to maintain some degree of policy autonomy. With the progressive removal of capital controls and the relative stabilization of exchange rates during the latter half of the 1980s, the only means of reconciling the otherwise inconsistent characteristics is by countries sacrificing policy autonomy. In practice this sacrifice was forced upon countries by the developing economic and financial conditions. Monetary autonomy was progressively eroded throughout the 1980s as nominal interest rates among ERM participants converged, with interest-rate differentials increasingly tending to reflect the markets' assessment of the expected depreciation for each currency.

One particular problem that may arise with the erosion of monetary autonomy and consequent convergence of nominal interest rates among ERM members is that the interest-rate convergence may not necessarily go hand in hand with the inflation convergence discussed previously. When it does not, real interest rates will fall, aggregate demand will increase, and further inflationary pressures and instability will develop within the system. This problem, referred to as the Walters critique (see Walters 1986), may result in the anti-inflation discipline of the system disappearing and being replaced instead by a mechanism which promotes the development of inflationary pressure within the system.

The heart of this problem lies in the potential discrepancy between the low inflation-stable exchange rate expectations of the financial market and the expectations held by agents in the goods and labour markets. Where the financial markets' expectations are not shared, the exchange-rate system may become 'excessively credible' and, because of the credibility of the exchange rate on foreign exchanges, the monetary authorities are unable to adopt a sufficiently tight monetary policy to fight inflation.

Problems of this sort highlight the potential difficulties that may arise in attempting to reconcile the four Padoa-Schioppa characteristics within the monetary system. The removal of obstacles to trade, and success in maintaining exchange-rate stability, may bring about nominal interest-rate convergence, but may fail to generate convergence in other indicators of economic performance unless supported by coordinated policy action elsewhere in the economy. More importantly, failure to achieve such convergence may ultimately place a question mark against the prospects of survival for the system itself.

12.6. Crisis in the ERM

The events in the foreign exchange and financial markets associated with the crisis in the ERM during September 1992 and July–August 1993 have been among the most important since the EC began. Strain on the system had been mounting for some time. Although the underlying causes of the events have still not been fully resolved, it is apparent that the decision not to revalue the Deutschmark following German unification in 1989 must feature strongly. The immediate consequence of this decision was that incipient inflationary pressure within Germany was met by the Bundesbank with higher interest rates, and the relative freedom with which capital could move among the ERM countries meant that little impediment prevented these rates being transmitted to other members of the system. As a result, severe deflationary pressure built up in the majority of countries. This pressure was further exacerbated by the decision of the UK government to use the ERM as the mainstay of its domestic disinflationary strategy and to join at a central parity that many commentators suggested was too high.[14]

In the event, the immediate trigger for the exchange-market crisis was the political uncertainty that surrounded the referenda on the Maastricht Treaty. Denmark had rejected the treaty in early June, and the resultant strengthening of the Deutschmark placed considerable pressure on the lira and sterling. For the lira, market concern over the country's high level of public debt and excessive budget deficit contributed to these pressures. In the UK the continued recession and weak current-account position influenced market perceptions that sterling might be devalued within the ERM given the apparent constraints on interest rates in that country. Tension was partially eased by intervention, particularly in support of the lira during the summer. By the end of the August, however, pressure again began to mount on the approach to the French referendum concerning the Maastricht Treaty, fed especially by opinion polls that suggested a significant risk of rejection.

Currency speculation reached a peak in September. Massive intervention was required by the middle of the month in order to prevent the lira falling below its ERM floor, despite a sharp increase in short-term interest rates. The lira was devalued by 7 per cent on 12 September but remained under considerable pressure in the week that followed. At the same time the Spanish peseta fell from the top of its ERM band to the bottom. Comparable levels of intervention were required to prevent sterling falling below its ERM floor on 16 September yet, despite this and a 2 per cent rise in official interest rates, sterling's membership of the ERM had to be suspended. Because intervention and higher interest rates had failed to keep the lira off its ERM floor, it, too, was suspended on 17 September. After the departure of the lira and sterling from the system, the French franc came under intense pressure, especially after the close (positive) result for the referendum. This was only beaten off by a combined defence operation mounted by the French and German central banks.

After the September crisis, significant pressure re-emerged among the ERM currencies in November. The Spanish peseta and Portuguese escudo were both devalued by 6 per cent on 22 November. By the end of the year sterling had depreciated by approximately 15 per cent, the Italian lira by 16 per cent, while the French franc and German mark were little changed.

Pressure on the ERM continued through much of 1993. The Irish pound was devalued by 10 per cent in February; the Spanish peseta and portugese escudo were devalued by 8 per cent and 6.5 per cent respectively in May and, on 30 July the French and Belgian francs, the Danish krone, the Spanish peseta, and the Portuguese escudo all fell close to their floors against the Deutschmark, despite substantial intervention by central banks. Only the Dutch guilder remained unscathed. As a consequence, finance ministers and central bankers decided on 2 August that operational changes were required to the structure of the ERM and announced that new margins of fluctuation, amounting to ±15 per cent either side of the central rate, would be permitted within the ERM. Only the Netherlands chose, by bilateral arrangement, to retain the original ±2.25 per cent band against the Deutschmark. The European Monetary System had all but collapsed.

Apart from its obvious impact in weakening a central component of the European drive towards greater economic integration, the currency turmoil of 1992–3 has also had important implications for economic conditions within Europe more generally. This is particularly apparent from the evidence regarding the effect of the currency crisis on cost competitiveness and growth. Commission estimates, for example, suggest that increased uncertainty associated with the currency crisis contributed to an overall slowdown in European economic growth in 1995 of between 0.25 and 0.5 of a percentage point. In those countries where the currency depreciated during the crisis, this slowdown in growth has been accompanied by an increase in both the nominal interest rate and inflation, a factor which has itself compounded household uncertainty. Conversely, in countries where the currency appreciated, the slowdown in growth has been accompanied by a general decline in inflationary pressure.[15] In terms of the effect that the crisis has had on cost competitiveness, measured in terms of unit labour costs, the outcome has been less clear cut and has largely been dominated by country-specific factors. In some cases, notably France and Austria, where cost competitiveness had improved appreciably over the period prior to 1992, the currency crisis served effectively to eliminate the earlier gains; in countries such as Italy and Germany, where the pre-crisis movement in competitiveness had been limited, the nominal changes that occurred between 1992 and 1995 led to a significant gain in competitiveness in the case of Italy (of some 24 per cent), but a significant loss (of some 20 per cent) in the case of Germany. In contrast, competitiveness in the UK appears to have been remarkably unchanged by the whole crisis experience.

Reforming the EMS in the light of these events is obviously of paramount importance, especially given the key role that the ERM has been given in the drive for European Monetary Union (EMU) (see Chapter 13 for details). Although the precise detail of these reforms remains uncertain, a number of candidates for reform have been identified in the literature. The most promising of these relates, in general terms, to the reimposition of capital controls within the EMS. Eichengreen, Tobin, and Wyplosz (1995), for example, propose that all institutions taking an open position in the foreign-exchange market be required to make non-interest bearing deposits with their central bank. Such measures were previously utilized by countries such as Spain and Italy in order to slow down adverse speculative pressure, the cost of the scheme being passed on to currency traders and thereby discouraging the 'one-way bet'. Of course, this type of policy would not provide permanent support for weak currencies, but would enable monetary authorities to pursue orderly intervention or realignment unconstrained by the threat of a speculative attack.

12.7. Conclusions

From its introduction in 1979, the ERM has provided a framework for nominal exchange-rate stability within Europe. In the early period the EMS acted very much like a crawling peg with a number of realignments, often involving a devaluation of the French franc against the Deutschmark. The system subsequently shifted away from this characterization and adopted the features of a semi-fixed regime. From 1987 onwards, as France pursued its *franc fort* policy, the franc maintained its position against the Deutschmark, and the counter-inflationary stance of the system was strengthened, with a consequent rise in disinflationary pressures throughout Europe.

In addition to its impact on nominal exchange rates, the ERM is often credited with stabilizing real exchange rates via its effect on the inflation rates of the ERM members. The precise mechanism for achieving this end, however, is unclear, though the role of Germany as the low-inflation, dominant partner of the system appears to be important in this respect. The evidence suggests, however, that lower inflation among the non-German ERM countries has been possible only by accepting a marked increase in unemployment.

In the light of the events of 1992–3, it is clear that the ERM is vunerable to speculative attack. Whilst relaxation of capital controls throughout Europe may have contributed to this situation, the failure of Member States to adopt a flexible attitude with respect to realignments within the EMS must also bear some part of the blame. As originally designed, the system would have required a realignment of the Deutschmark following reunification, and the subsequent events in European foreign-exchange markets might have been substantially different had this course of action been adopted.

Discussion questions

1. Explain what is meant by the terms:
   (a) maximum deviation spread,
   (b) parity grid,
   (c) divergence indicator, and
   (d) central parity.
   Outline the role that each of these plays in the operation of the ERM.
2. Outline the factors that you think were particularly important in contributing to the crisis in the ERM in 1992–3. In each case indicate the mechanism by which the stability of the system was affected.
3. What is the 'Walters critique'? To what extent does the critique provide a basis for believing that the role of the ERM as a disinflationary mechanism may be compromised?

FURTHER READING

The following references are recommended as supplementary reading to this chapter. Giavazzi and Giovannini (1989) provide an excellent discussion of the operation of the ERM during the 1980s and consider the issue of the ERM as a Deutschmark zone, together with the question of capital controls. The prospective development of EMU from the ERM is considered by Gros and Thygesen (1992), whilst the issue of ERM credibility is dealt with by Weber (1991).

NOTES

1. The original members of the EMS were Belgium, Denmark, France, Germany, Ireland, Italy, Netherlands, and the UK. The UK, however, initially chose not to participate in the ERM.
2. Formally, the behaviour of Italy and of the UK was different. Italy formally maintained the lira within the ERM but refrained from supporting the currency, whilst the UK withdrew from the mechanism altogether.

3. Asymmetric adjustment was characteristic of both the Bretton Woods system and the Snake. The loss of foreign-exchange reserves by deficit nations placed a greater obligation for countries with weaker currencies to adjust than reserve accumulation did for strong currencies.

4. The adjustment $(1 - w_i)$ recognizes the fact that when a currency moves away from its central rate it pulls the value of the Ecu with it. The extent of the movement in the Ecu depends upon the weight of the particular currency in the composition of the Ecu, and adjusts the divergence threshold to reflect deviations of a currency from other currencies in the Ecu basket.

5. An adjustment was made in calculating the divergence threshold to account for the non-participation of the drachma, and the wider margins adopted within the ERM by Italy, Portugal, Spain, and the UK.

6. The repayment period for the VSTF facility was initially set at forty-five days following the month in which intervention occurred. However, this period was subsequently extended to seventy-five days by the Basle–Nyborg agreement signed in September 1987. The Basle–Nyborg accord also made the VSTF facility available on a voluntary basis for financing *intra-marginal* intervention (that is, foreign exchange market intervention undertaken *before* a currency hits its ceiling or floor against any other).

7. The distinction between short-run volatility and long-run misalignment was drawn by Williamson (1983). For a discussion of the empirical evidence, see Artis and Taylor (1988).

8. An important point in this respect is that, 1992–3 aside, most of the intervention has been *intra marginal*, which, by its very nature, has operated in an asymmetric manner; Germany never initiated much intra-marginal intervention itself.

9. A clear example of such behaviour is reflected in the fact that when the UK joined the system, emphasis was placed almost entirely on the sterling–Deutschmark value rather than the central Ecu rate.

10. Of course, this erosion of competitiveness, itself, may be considered part of the adjustment mechanism. At the extreme, industries experiencing a loss of competitiveness will reduce output and thereby contribute to increased unemployment within the economy.

11. For an interesting comparison of the 'rules of the game' as contained in the statutes of the original EMS and those implied by the greater Deutschmark area model, see McKinnon (1993).

12. On 18 September 1992, for example, overnight interest rates in Ireland were set at 300 per cent; on 26 November the overnight rate was 100 per cent; on 3 August 1993 Danish overnight rates reached 250 per cent.

13. Capital controls in the UK were removed by the Conservative government in 1979.

14. On the question of whether Britain joined the ERM at the right rate, see, for example, Williamson (1991) and Wren-Lewis *et al.* (1991). Wren-Lewis, for example, estimated that sterling was overvalued by some 20 per cent.

15. Specifically, Germany, Denmark, France, the Netherlands, Austria, and Belgium recorded an appreciation of their nominal effective exchange rates between 1992 and 1995, while Italy, Spain, Greece, Portugal, and the UK saw their nominal effective rates depreciate.

REFERENCES

Artis, M. J. (1986), 'The European Monetary System: An Evaluation', *Journal of Policy Modeling*, 9/1: 175–98.

—— and Nachane, D. (1990), 'Wages and Prices in Europe: A Test of the German Leadership Hypothesis', *Weltwirtschaftliches Archiv*, 126 (Mar.), 59–77.

—— and Taylor, M. P. (1988), 'Exchange Rates, Interest Rates, Capital Controls and the European Monetary System: Assessing the Track Record', in F. Giavazzi, S. Micossi, and M. H. Miller (eds.), *The European Monetary System* (Cambridge: Cambridge University Press), 185–206.

Barro, R., and Gordon, D. (1983), 'Rules, Discretion and Reputation in a Model of Monetary Policy', *Journal of Monetary Economics*, 12: 589–610.

CEC (1990): Commission of the European Communities, 'One Market, One Money: An Evaluation of the Potential Benefits and Costs of Forming an Economic and Monetary Union', *European Economy*, 44: 1–351.

—— *General Report on the Activities of the EU*, various issues.

De Grauwe, P. (1989), *Is the European Monetary System a DM-zone?* (Discussion Paper No. 126; London: Centre of Economic Policy Research).

Eichengreen, B., Tobin J., and Wyplosz, C. (1995), 'Two Cases for Sand in the Wheels of International Finance', *Economic Journal*, 105/428: 162–72.

Giavazzi, F., and Giovannini, A. (1989), *Limiting Exchange Rate Flexibility* (Cambridge, Mass.: MIT Press).

—— and Pagano, M. (1988), 'The Advantage of Tying one's Hands: EMS Discipline and Central Bank Credibility', *European Economic Review*, 32: 1055–82.

Gros, G., and Tyghesen, N. (1992), *From the European Monetary System to European Monetary Union* (London: Longman).

McKinnon, R. I. (1993), 'The Rules of the Game: International Money in Historical Perspective', *Journal of Economic Literature*, 31 (Mar.), 1–44.

Mastropasqua, C., Micossi, S., and Rinaldi, R. (1988), 'Interventions, Sterilization and Monetary Policy in European Monetary System Countries 1979–87', in F. Giavazzi, S. Micossi, and M. Miller (eds.), *The European Monetary System* (Cambridge: Cambridge University Press), 252–87.

Padoa-Schioppa, T. (1988), 'The European Monetary System: A Long-Term View', in F. Giavazzi, S. Micossi, and M. Miller (eds.), *The European Monetary System* (Cambridge: Cambridge University Press), 369–84.

Walters, A. (1986), Britain's Economic Renaissance (Oxford: Oxford University Press).

Weber, A. A. (1991), 'Reputation and Credibility in the European Monetary System', *Economic Policy*, 12 (Apr.), 58–102.

Williamson, J. (1983), *The Exchange Rate System* (Policy Analyses in International Economics, 5; Washington: Institute for International Economics).

—— (1991), 'FEERs and the ERM', *National Institute Economic Review* (Aug.), 45–50.

Wren-Lewis, S., Westaway, P., Soteri, S., and Barrell, R. (1991), 'Evaluating the U.K.'s Choice of Entry Rate into the ERM', *Manchester School, Supplement*, 59: 1–22.

CHAPTER 13

European Monetary Union

MIKE ARTIS

13.1. Introduction

With the agreements reached at Maastricht at the end of 1991, the Member States of the European Community (EC) came to the end of an unparalleled effort to think through the implications of monetary union in Europe. The resultant Treaty on European Union (TEU) set out a constitution for the Central Bank of the Union, a timetable for the approach to full union, and a set of criteria or fitness conditions for membership which individual countries would have to satisfy. This was the culmination of a process of intergovernmental discussion and negotiation inaugurated by the setting-up of the Delors Committee in June 1988, which was charged with setting out the requirements for a move to full monetary union in Europe. Such a project had been mooted before (back in 1970, the Werner Committee (CEC 1970) had set a date for monetary union of 1980), but it had never before been so carefully analysed.

However, it soon became clear that the translation of the Maastricht Treaty into practical progress towards the ultimate target was fraught with difficulty. First, the Danish people failed to ratify the Treaty in a first referendum called for the purpose; then the French referendum of July 1992 produced only a small majority in favour (the so-called 'petit oui'); whilst the ratification process in the UK Parliament proved to be exceptionally long drawn out. But the tribulations attending the process which contributed to the confusion about the immediate prospects for monetary union also served to initiate the débâcle of the Exchange Rate Mechanism (ERM) of the European Monetary System (EMS) in 1992–3. In September 1992 the pound sterling and Italian lira were both forced to float against other European currencies; around the same time, the Spanish peseta and the Portuguese escudo were obliged to devalue. Later on the Irish pound was devalued. There were intermittent tensions and speculative raids throughout the following months, culminating in the crisis at the end of July 1993 which resulted in the decision early in August to widen the bands of the ERM to 15 per cent (for details, see Chapter 12). The abandonment of the narrow-bands ERM was a setback to the momentum towards achieving complete monetary union before the end of the century. Yet there remained in many countries an evident desire to realize this goal, and the Maastricht Treaty provides a formal framework for its realization. Within this framework, the decision was taken at the 1995 Madrid meeting of the Council of Ministers to aim to create a monetary union of eligible countries by 1 January 1999. In Section 5 of this chapter we provide a discussion of the prospects (as they appeared in June 1996) of success in this endeavour.

In the next section we turn to a discussion of the general principles of monetary union.[1] After that the discussion returns to an account of the specific promptings behind the process of negotiation which led to Maastricht and the TEU. This too illustrates some general principles, for it will be argued that there is an ineluctable tendency towards exchange rate and monetary union in Europe; whatever doubts there may be about the realization of European Monetary Union (EMU) in the near future, EMU in the long run is a more certain bet. Then we will examine the provisions of the TEU, before entering on the discussion, in the final section, of the immediate outlook for EMU.

13.2. **Monetary union: the general principles**

A monetary union between two or more countries means that those countries agree to maintain the same currency. In the European context, where before there were French and Belgian francs, Italian lire, Dutch guilders, German Deutschmarks, and so on, there would after monetary union be a single currency (which, it has now been determined, will be called the Euro). Thus the central point about a monetary union is that, when countries proceed to join one, they give up the possibility for their own currency to be separate from those in the other countries and *therefore give up the possibility of having an independent monetary policy and allowing the rate of exchange between their own currency and those of the other members of the union to vary.*

A cost-benefit analysis

The appraisal of the pros and cons of joining a monetary union can be thought of as a cost-benefit analysis.[2] Since the key feature of belonging to a monetary union is that it is no longer possible to allow the rate of exchange to vary between your own country's currency and those of the other members of the union, this cost-benefit analysis can be re-expressed as follows. The benefits of monetary union are the benefits of having a single currency to use over a wider area; the costs are the costs of not being able to let the exchange rate (against other member countries) vary.

The general view is that the costs and benefits so expressed fall and rise respectively with the degree of integration between the economies concerned. This is shown in Fig. 13.1 (taken from Krugman 1990). Costs and benefits are expressed as a percentage of GDP along the vertical axis, whilst integration—perhaps measured as the ratio of intra-union trade to GDP—is measured along the horizontal. The CC curve then shows the costs of union as falling with integration, whilst the BB curve shows the benefits of union as rising with integration. If this representation is correct (and the more detailed analysis below indicates that it may be subject to some qualification), and European integration is growing with time, then at some point in the future the representative European economy will have passed to the right of the point t^*, where benefits begin to exceed costs. Indeed some European economies are probably already in this position.

We need now to discuss more generally the nature of the costs and benefits of monetary union and to verify the slopes of the CC and BB curves shown in Fig. 13.1.

The benefits of a single currency

The most obvious and clear-cut benefit of a single currency is that it is no longer necessary to incur the costs of exchange from one currency to another. Any traveller will know that these costs are not negligible: first of all, there will be a commission charge (usually a fixed amount); secondly, the price at which the traveller can purchase foreign currency for domestic currency will differ from (specifically will be lower than) the price at which he can exchange back his surplus foreign currency. This pricing schedule reflects the fact that the provision of foreign-exchange services uses up real resources. There are large economies of scale in foreign-exchange transactions, so that the position for big traders is in fact much less costly than it is for the average tourist. Nevertheless, these foreign-exchange transactions costs are not negligible and their removal constitutes a gain from monetary union. A moment's reflection suggests that this gain will indeed rise with integration—since the larger the ratio of trade to GDP, the greater the benefit from *not* have to change from one currency to another. This motivates the upward slope of the BB schedule in Fig. 13.1. The gain will also be bigger the less efficient (and thus the more costly) the *existing* foreign-exchange-transactions system, so countries with backward banking systems will gain more from monetary union (on this score, anyway) than those with more advanced systems. The Commission, in its analysis of EMU (CEC 1990), quantified this transactions-cost gain from the move to a single currency, for the then-existing EC as a whole, at 0.2 per cent of EC GDP.

Other gains have also been claimed for a single currency; unlike the expected benefit from the reduction in transactions costs, these other benefits cannot readily be quantified—though this does *not* necessarily mean that they are small. In particular, it seems likely that the removal of exchange-rate variations between the economies of the EU would provide much more assurance to corporate location decisions. At present, a

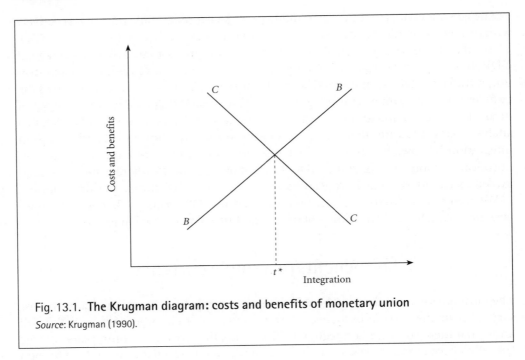

Fig. 13.1. The Krugman diagram: costs and benefits of monetary union

Source: Krugman (1990).

company contemplating the location of a new plant within the European economy has to take account of the risk of exchange-rate variation, and this may lead it at the margin to 'scatter' its plants across the various economies, as this would be a way of hedging the risk of exchange-rate variation. Removing this source of uncertainty, the argument goes, would allow investors to locate according to economies of scale and would lead to more plants of the optimum size, bringing about a reduction in unit costs of production and a clear increase in efficiency. (It should be clear that what is required here is a reduction in *real* exchange-rate uncertainty, and the argument assumes that, in the absence of nominal exchange-rate jumps, countries' international competitiveness would be much more stable.) Clearly, this source of gain would take time to realize; indeed, it would only be realized as new investment decisions take place.

At a more general level it has been argued (e.g. by the Commission (CEC 1990)) that removing exchange-rate uncertainty would reduce the risk premium in real interest rates; if so, it would encourage more investment and capital accumulation, leading to increases in output per head. However, it can be disputed how far removing one source of uncertainty will lead to a reduction in overall uncertainty in the economy: some economists argue that there is an irreducible 'lump of uncertainty' in an economy, which can only be shifted around, not reduced in size. On this argument, abolishing exchange-rate uncertainty will lead to greater uncertainty in some other respect: there might be more uncertainty about countries' tax regimes, for example, as national governments turn to fiscal devices to offset their inability to allow exchange-rate variations to cushion the effects of adverse shocks on the economy.

Another source of benefit from establishing a single currency could arise from a reduction in the market discrimination that currently exists (with the prices of motor cars of the same specification, for example, standing higher in the UK than they do in France), as the quotation of prices in common currency encourages arbitrage activity and reduces the market segmentation on which such discrimination relies. A move to a single currency would also allow economies to be made in the holding of non-European currencies; there are economies of scale to be had from the holding of any reserve (a commonplace conclusion to be drawn from inventory theory), so the required holdings of foreign-exchange reserves in the new European Central Bank would be less than the sum of the holdings of the present individual national central banks. How far such a gain would be realized would depend on the evolution of a European exchange-rate policy. Finally, it can be argued that, with a single common currency, Europe would be represented as a single member with a strong voice in a world economy dominated by the 'Group of Three' (G3)—Japan, the USA, and Europe. Europe might have a stronger voice in such a milieu than in the present set-up, where the annual 'Summit Seven' (G7) meetings, though including no less than four European powers—France, Italy, Germany, and the UK—as well as Japan, the USA, and Canada, do so on the basis that each country represents itself and the pan-European interest is not necessarily expressed.[3]

The costs of forgoing exchange-rate variability

The point of having separate currencies with an exchange rate between them is to be able to let that exchange rate change. In classical economic analysis, the purpose of letting the exchange rate change is to have it act as a shock absorber for disturbances that impact on the partner economies in different ways—in the jargon, the absorb *asymmetric* shocks. Since going to monetary union involves giving up this shock absorber, the following questions need to be examined:

- How good is the exchange rate as a shock absorber? Does increasing integration make it less or more useful?

- How likely are asymmetric shocks to occur? Can we say whether integration makes them less or more likely?

- Are there alternative shock absorbers which could be made to function in a monetary union?

We examine first the way in which the exchange rate is supposed to act as a shock absorber in the framework of AD/AS analysis.

Fig. 13.2 presents the analysis diagrammatically. Fig. 13.2*a* refers to, say, France; Fig.

13.2*b* to, say, Germany. The exchange rate is taken to be fixed but adjustable. On the assumption, initially, that nominal wages are fixed, the aggregate-supply (AS) schedule slopes up from left to right in price–output space for both countries, because, as prices rise, real wage costs fall, leading employers to take on more labour and produce more output. The aggregate-demand (AD) schedule slopes down from left to right, because, with a lower price, the economy will be more competitive, with a higher demand for exports and a lower demand for imports; and because, with lower prices, the value of real money balances will rise. An increase in government expenditure or a shift in demand independent of price will cause a shift of the schedule. Suppose now that the exchange rate is changed—specifically, that the French franc is devalued in terms of the German Deutschmark. French output becomes cheaper relative to German output. This will mean that the aggregate demand for French output will rise and that for German output will fall. The AD schedule in the left-hand diagram will move to the right and that in the right-hand diagram will move to the left.

Now suppose that, from an initial position indicated by the AD_0 and AS_0 schedules with the corresponding price and output levels, a shock occurs which—because of the structure of the economies—is asymmetric between them. For example—the suggestion is fanciful, but the point is general—suppose that consumers' tastes change. It becomes unfashionable to drink champagne, whereas the consumption of sausages becomes the acme of good taste. The French economy is relatively intensive in champagne, whilst the Germany economy is intensive in the production of sausages. So the 'taste change' implies a leftward shift in the AD curve in France to AD_1 and a rightward shift of the AD curve in Germany to AD_1. Output will fall below equilibrium in France and rise above it in Germany; prices will rise in Germany and fall in France. However, it appears that a devaluation of the French franc in terms of the Deutschmark could provide exactly the right offset. A devaluation will shift the AD curve in France to the right and the AD curve in Germany to the left, as shown by the broken arrows. In fact, a depreciation of the right amount will restore the original position. This is the classic argument for the exchange rate as shock absorber for asymmetric shocks.[4]

There is, however, a catch. The price indicated by P (P_F or P_G) in Fig. 13.2 is the 'domestic' price level, the value-added or GDP deflator. However, in terms of what their money wages can buy, workers will be concerned with the consumer price index—that is, the price of the basket of goods consumed by the representative worker. The consumption basket of French workers will undoubtedly contain sausages imported from Germany—along with many other imported items, of course. A devaluation of the French franc will raise the franc price of all these items: the consumer price index will rise, even if domestic price levels (both in France and in Germany) stay the same. Algebraically, we can write the consumer price index in France, P_{CF}, in terms of the domestic price indices P_F and P_G and the exchange rate e as $P_{CF} = aP_F + (1 - a)eP_G$. Here, a and $(1 - a)$ are the shares of domestic and imported (German) goods in the French consumption basket. Clearly a rise in e (a devaluation) will increase the value of P_{CF} for given values of P_F and P_G. This point is very important. If the French economy

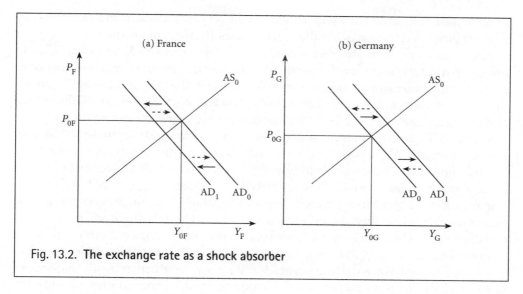

Fig. 13.2. The exchange rate as a shock absorber

is quite integrated with Germany and a is therefore quite small, a given rise in e will raise P_{CF} quite a lot. French workers' real wagers (W_F/P_{CF}) will fall noticeably. This is likely to lead to a demand by French workers for a rise in nominal wages sufficient to compensate them for the loss of real wages, due, as they see it, to the devaluation. If so, then the AS schedule will shift to the left in the left-hand part of the diagram and the offset provided by devaluation will be imperfect. Prices will rise and output will not be restored to its previous level. It is not hard to see that, if the French government were to respond by promoting a fresh devaluation, this would only produce a further rise in nominal wages and so prices. 'Real-wage resistance' (where workers attempt to protect real wages by nominal wage increases), if accompanied by repeated devaluations, will quickly produce a wage–price–devaluation spiral.

The qualification to the usefulness of the nominal exchange rate as a shock absorber, then, is a that wage–price reactions may undo the effect of the nominal exchange-rate adjustment. The classical theory assumes in essence that a nominal exchange-rate change *is* a real exchange-rate change. Yet a good deal of experience suggests that nominal exchange-rate changes can excite wage–price reactions that undo the effect of the change before very long. Experience to this effect in the 1970s and 1980s is one of the reasons why the EMU project seemed acceptable to many countries. It is also a reason why the *CC* curve in Fig. 13.1 slopes down from left to right—for, the more integrated economies become, the larger the portion of the consumption basket which is imported and the faster and the more pronounced the negative wage–price reactions to nominal exchange-rate change are likely to be.

Whilst the shock-absorber role of the exchange rate is subject to qualification, it is by no means true that the qualification is absolute. Whilst exchange-rate depreciation does tend to excite offsetting wage–price reactions, these reactions are not necessarily immediate or immutable to policy actions. At the very least an exchange-rate depreciation can give a breathing space while other policies are brought into play.

But, of course, a shock absorber is needed only if there are shocks to absorb. Clearly, unexpected developments are frequent, yet it is important to note that it is *differences* in economic structure which make shocks asymmetric: in the taste shock example above, the shock was asymmetric only because of the different specializations of the French and German economies. Is it likely that the process of integration among the European economies will produce 'more similar' economic structures and thus make asymmetric shocks less likely? The answer to this question is difficult to determine. If integration means 'convergence', then by definition the European economies are set to become more homogeneous—perhaps in tastes as well as production structures; but if integration means more specialization according to comparative advantage, as classical trade theory would suggest, then the answer is the opposite. The evidence from the USA suggests that there is likely to be more specialization between regions of a monetary union than between countries (albeit neighbouring) which still have their own independent currencies. Indeed, when the benefits of EMU were discussed earlier in this chapter, one of those identified was precisely the likelihood of greater concentration of output in large-scale units with less scattering of plant across the European production area.

It is also as well to recall that, despite the impression that had been growing of a Europe of ever-more convergent economies, the experience of German unification has been precisely one of an asymmetric shock of an almost textbook quality. This shock clearly put insupportable strain on many of the exchange rates in the ERM (see Chapter 12); had those exchange rates been 'irrevocably locked', as in a monetary union, there clearly would have been a very big price to pay. Fortunately, it does seem possible to describe this particular shock as unique and unrepeatable.

It is also fortunate that the exchange rate, itself imperfect in this role, is not the only possible absorber of asymmetric shocks. There are several other mechanisms worth discussing in this context. Community regional policy (see Chapter 7); community budgetary policy (see Chapter 14); national fiscal policy; factor migration; and wage–price flexibility.

Community regional policy clearly provides a mechanism for offsetting the repercussions of asymmetric shocks between countries; but it is not easy to see this mechanism playing a major role in monetary union—to date, its scale has simply been too small. What about *community budgetary policy*? US economists, viewing the proposal for monetary union in Europe, emphasize that in the USA the federal budget offers an automatic stabilizing function between the various states.[5] Because of the federal income tax, a state which falls on bad times (say, Texas when oil prices are low) automatically has to pay less income tax; and various federal expenditures, including federal support of unemployment compensation payments, would expand in such a context. The combined effect is that, through reduced federal tax requirements and higher federal expenditure entitlements, a temporarily disadvantaged state obtains a substantial offset to any primary income fall. (Whilst the precise figures are the subject of dispute, a commonly quoted estimate is that '30c in the $' of primary income decline is buffered in this way.) However, the EU does not have a budget of anything like the scale of the US federal budget. Nevertheless some observers argue that it should be possible to obtain a stabilizing effect without the huge scale of tax revenues and expenditures of the US budget, or, relative to GDP, of any of the national European budgets for that matter. The major expenditure items—defence, education, welfare payments, and so on—could continue to remain the property of national budgets. What is needed is a mechanism which defines when a member country is faring badly, relative to its usual average, in relation to the other countries, and a transfer system that will provide a degree of corrective support (see Goodhart 1994 for further explanation). However, whilst something like this may be feasible in principle, no such provisions were contained in the Maastricht Treaty, nor have they yet been articulated at a practical (policy) level.

Alternatively, it may be argued that *national fiscal policies* can be relied upon to perform a stabilizing function with some efficiency. Recall that in terms of Fig. 13.2 it was argued that government spending would shift the AD schedules; so an active national fiscal policy could be used to offset asymmetric shocks. Within a monetary union the resultant budget deficits would be comparatively easy to finance. For temporary shocks, indeed, the solution is ideal. In the case of permanent shocks, however, a real adjustment, not a demand adjustment, is what is called for; from this point of view it could be argued that the use of fiscal policy serves only to delay and hinder the adjustment that is, in the end, the only real solution. Unfortunately, it is not always easy to tell, in practice, whether a given shock is permanent or temporary.

The final two alternative mechanisms under consideration do provide such a real adjustment. *Factor migration* removes the problem of unemployed (and symmetrically overstrained) resources in an obvious way. In terms of the earlier fanciful example, unemployed French champagne workers could migrate to work in German sausage factories. This simultaneously relieves the labour shortage in Germany and resolves the unemployment problem in France. Within national boundaries unemployed resources tend to move more freely than between countries, and at present labour mobility between the Member States of the EU is quite limited. Over the longer run, with the aid of measures like the mutual recognition of professional qualifications, this position may of course change.

The final mechanism referred to is *wage–price flexibility*. For any permanent shock, an adjustment of real wages and relative prices is in fact what is required to provide a complete solution to the problem, rather than simply a temporary buffer. Paradoxically, some of the buffer mechanisms suggested can work against the long-run solution. For example, lavish support of a depressed region is unlikely to assist in bringing about the adjustment to lower relative real wages that is needed. Hence, it can be argued, the relative absence of credible alternative absorbers to the exchange rate in a European monetary union may not be such a bad thing: for it will hasten, not hinder, the development of *more flexible wage–price responses*. What this means can be represented quite simply in terms of the AD/AS analysis presented before: but this time we concentrate only on the left-hand part of the diagram—the case of the country (in our example, France) suffering a deflationary demand shock. Fig. 13.3 shows a case where, from the initial position (shown by AD_0, AS_0), a permanent adverse demand shock causes an initial deflation (shown by the distance $Y_{OF} - Y_F$). Underlying AS_0 is a particular nominal wage; should nominal wages fall, the AS schedule will move to the right. With wage–price flexibility the deflation in output (and accompanying unemployment) will produce precisely such a result. In the end AS moves to AS_1 and equilibrium output is restored. French wages and output prices will have fallen; French consumer prices will not have fallen as much (German prices will have stayed the same or risen, and the exchange rate is fixed), so French real wages will have fallen. But this is the nature of the shock: the swing of tastes against the product that France is 'good at' understandably reduces French living standards. Without devaluation, this adjustment has to be brought about by a deflationary response to the initial fall in output. Even with devaluation, this final result cannot be avoided if full employment is to be restored—but the path of adjustment will be different, involving some inflation as well as some unemployment. The first best adjustment, of course, would be for wages and prices to adjust instantly.

The analysis above covers the case for and against monetary union in Europe in general terms and provides an elaboration of the approach depicted by the Krugman diagram. The next question is to ask why the project of EMU became so important in the late 1980s. The general analysis can be drawn on to help us answer this question.

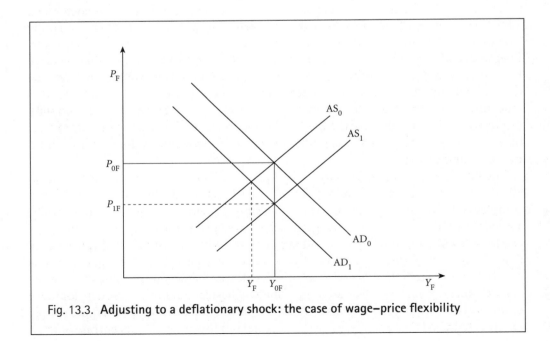

Fig. 13.3. **Adjusting to a deflationary shock: the case of wage–price flexibility**

13.3. **The background to the Maastricht negotiations**

One answer to the question posed in this section—why did the EMU project 'take off' in the late 1980s?—is that it was the success of the EMS which led countries to embrace the idea of full monetary union.

The operation and achievements of the EMS are discussed at length in Chapter 12 of this book and the reader is referred there for a detailed treatment. The central point for present purposes is that towards the end of the 1980s there was a widespread belief that the EMS had been successful beyond all expectations. It had not only been successful in its proximate objective—that of stabilizing nominal exchange rates between participating economies. It was also viewed as having provided a framework for counter-inflationary policies in Europe, through which other countries had, in effect, been able to import into their own systems the counter-inflationary success and reputation of the Bundesbank. By committing themselves to an exchange-rate peg against the Deutschmark, other countries were pledging to contain their own inflation to German levels. However, the dominance of Germany implied in such a description of the EMS was in practice diluted by the fact that countries could realign their central parities and could use the protection afforded by exchange controls over capital flows (so-called 'capital controls') to opt out of the requirement always to follow German policy in detail. This compromise was felt to have worked well, but by the late 1980s the continued maintenance of the compromise was undermined by the commitment, undertaken under the Single European ('1992') legislation, to phase out capital controls. This seemed liable to make realignments more difficult to engineer without inviting uncontrollable speculation. For this reason the dominance of Germany would be increased. Such a prospect was not welcome to the larger countries, like France, which began to press for a 'European' solution, with a European Central Bank (ECB) in which France might have a say and for which economic conditions in France would be as relevant as those in Germany.

This development can usefully be viewed in terms of Padoa-Schioppa's 'inconsistent quartet' (Padoa-Schioppa 1988), which comprises

- free trade
- free capital movements,
- fixed exchange rates, and
- national policy autonomy.

The Padoa-Schioppa proposition is that international monetary arrangements can never succeed in reconciling all four of these desirable conditions. Historically, all such arrangements have involved some compromise: thus, under the post-war Bretton Woods system there was a substantial compromise on the freedom of capital movements (at least to begin with); in the earlier stages of EMS there was a similar, though less drastic, compromise, together with some compromise on fixed exchange rates (which were changed through realignments), as well as some compromise of national policy autonomy to the extent implied by acceptance of German dominance in the interest of curbing inflation. With a desire to maintain fixed exchange rates and free trade, the commitment to phase out capital controls pointed to a loss of national policy autonomy. The EMU solution can be thought of as the only way to retrieve a degree of autonomy, in the context of sharing in the common decisions of a ECB.

Of course, an alternative compromise in these circumstances would have been to abandon fixed exchange rates as a goal and instead to embrace the floating-rate solution. However, not only would that have appeared to throw away the prime achievement of the EMS; it would also have been seen as fundamentally contrary to the need for a customs union like the EC to maintain fairly stable competitive conditions and as contrary to the requirements of common EC policies. The argument was that, if countries engage in periodic devaluations, this would be seen as an attempt to steal a competitive march on partner economies, and would lead to an unravelling of the counter-protectionist achievements of the EC. As for the second point, this is amply illustrated by the difficulties posed for the operation of the Common Agricultural Policy (CAP) by changing exchange rates. Since the basis of the CAP is the setting of common prices across Europe, producing a given pattern of competitiveness, changes in intra-European exchange rates require detailed intervention to maintain the intention of the originally agreed set of prices. The more common European policies there are, the more fixed exchange rates are needed (see Giavazzi and Giovannini 1989).

However, it was not only economic considerations of the type mentioned above that sparked the recent interest in EMU. The unification of Germany also provided an important stimulus. The prospect of this event promoted a desire to involve Germany in West European institutions and arrangements. The belief was that this would be a constructive way of containing the interests of an even larger and more powerful Germany—as against the alternative in which a new Germany would dominate the rest of Europe by virtue of its sheer economic size and influence. EMU is a leading example of just such an institution.

With these important factors in the background, the first fruit of the newly awakened interest was the formation of a committee in 1988 (the so-called Delors Committee) to study the way in which progress might be made towards monetary union in Europe (the committee was *not* asked to conduct a cost-benefit analysis of the proposal). Reporting just one year later, the Delors Committee established a number of important features that were subsequently to influence the shape of the Treaty on European Union (TEU). As our interest is in the provisions of the Treaty itself rather than in the detail of the Delors Report, we can be brief in summarizing its main contributions. First, the Delors Report was *gradualist*, in that it specified an approach through three stages to full monetary union. In Stage One, all countries should be in the narrow fluctuation band of the ERM, with realignment still a feature of the adjustment process and all capital controls phased out. In Stage Two it was expected that resort to realignment would take place 'only in exceptional circumstances' and that convergence of the economies would be substantially realized. The European System of Central Banks (ESCB) would be set up, and the margins of fluctuation might be narrowed in preparation for the final stage. In Stage Three exchange rates would become 'irrevocably locked', and this would lead to monetary union. An ECB, at the head of the ESCB, would be ready to conduct policy on its own initiative in Stage Three. Substantiating the 'gradualist' image of the Report, these proposals for transitional stages contained no dates, save for the initiation of Stage One, suggested for 1 July 1990. Despite being gradualist in this sense, however, the Delors Report dismissed the possibility of gradualism in another sense: it rejected the idea that a common currency should be created which could circulate in parallel with national moneys before being adopted as the *single* currency in Stage Three.[6] Perhaps the most controversial aspect of the Report was that it introduced the idea that participating countries would have to agree to some constraints on their *fiscal* positions, as well as forgoing independence in monetary policy. (As this is also a feature of the TEU, we postpone consideration of the rationale for fiscal constraints to the next section.) Finally, the Report indicated the necessity for a careful construction of the constitution of the ECB that it proposed and the need for an intergovernmental conference (IGC) to set out the amendments to the Treaty of Rome that would be required by a commitment to move to monetary union.

13.4. The provisions of the TEU

The Treaty that emerged from the IGC and was agreed upon in Maastricht in December 1991 substantially followed the lead given by the Delors Report. It put flesh on the bones of the Delors Report's 'stages', by giving dates; it elaborated on the meaning of convergence and on the meaning of fiscal discipline by spelling out precise 'convergence criteria'; and it spelt out in detail a constitution for the ECB. The Treaty reflected the outcome of intensive diplomacy spaced over several weeks, in which the interests of the participating countries were expressed. From what is known of the negotiating process it is possible to attribute some of the key features of the Treaty to the intervention or insistence of particular countries, although, as already indicated, most of these are already to be found in the Report of the Delors Committee.[7] Thus, the stringency of the fiscal criteria is commonly attributed to the insistence of Germany, as is the institutional character of Stage Two in the Treaty provisions. On the other hand, the comparatively early dates proposed and the provision for a 'two-tier' approach to EMU are commonly attributed to the influence of France. It must be borne in mind that, although the Treaty was signed and agreed to (with some waivers) by all participants, the interests of the different countries are diverse. (We return to this issue in the last section.)

The stages

The Treaty uses the same language of transitional stages as the Delors Report; but it assumed that Stage One had already been reached. Stage Two was defined to start on 1 January 1994 when the European Monetary Institute (EMI) would commence its work. The EMI was not envisaged as having executive power to conduct monetary policy or even to promote its coordination across the member countries, although it might make recommendations and form opinions in this regard; the EMI's main job was to study the requirements of the ECB, which would have executive power in Stage Three, when a single common currency would replace the individual national currencies of the participating countries. In terms of timing, the Treaty provides for Stage Three to commence at the earliest on 1 January 1997, on the basis of that majority of countries which satisfies the 'convergence criteria'. However, in the absence of such a majority, the Treaty provides for Stage Three to commence in any case not later than 1 January 1999 on the basis of that minority of countries which satisfies the criteria.

The convergence criteria

The Treaty spells out criteria which a country must satisfy in order to be eligible for membership of the EMU. The point of these criteria, in general, is to ensure that the constraints on policy implied by participation in the EMU are likely to prove acceptable within the country concerned. This calculation cannot simply be left to the judgement of the government of that country because of the consequences implied for other members of the union of a bad judgement: a political crisis arising in one member country could spill over to others. For example, if a particular country found it too difficult to accept the unemployment implied by the policies of the ECB, political pressure would arise to modify those policies, perhaps with the consequence that inflationary pressures would be created for other members of the union.[8]

The TEU criteria come under four heads and relate to: inflation convergence; interest-rate convergence (as explained below, these can be thought of as indirect inflation convergence criteria); a country's exchange-rate conduct; and, finally, the fiscal criteria.

According to the *inflation-convergence criterion*, a country's inflation rate (measured by consumer prices) should be observed, over a period of a year before the examination, not to have exceeded by more than 1.5 per cent that of the three best performing countries. The *interest-rate-convergence criterion* requires that a country's average long-term nominal interest rate over the same period should not have exceeded that of the three best price performers by more than 2 per cent. This criterion can be thought of as relying on the forward-lookingness of financial markets to provide an assurance that inflation convergence, if observed, is not simply a 'flash in the pan'. If it were, then the country would be likely to fail the interest-rate criterion, because the expected future inflation would be built into a high-interest differential against the good performers. The position of each of the EMS countries, with respect to the inflation and interest-rate criteria, is spelt out in detail in Chapter 2.

The *exchange-rate criterion* requires that a country's exchange rate should have been within the normal fluctuation margins of the EMS, 'without tension' and without a depreciation having been initiated, for at least two years. The two *fiscal criteria* specify reference values for the ratio of the budget deficit to GDP (at 3 per cent) and for the ratio of the stock of outstanding government debt to GDP (at 60 per cent) and require that a country should not exceed these reference values, although there are escape clauses. A country may still be deemed to qualify under the fiscal-convergence criteria if the excess of actual over reference value is 'exceptional and temporary' and 'declining continuously and substantially' (in the case of the deficit) and is 'sufficiently diminishing and approaching the reference value at a satisfactory pace' (in the case of the debt-to-GDP ratio). The position of each of the Member States with respect to the fiscal criteria is shown in Chapter 2.

The role of the fiscal criteria has been hotly debated. These criteria are designed to hold, not only as convergence criteria in the transition to EMU, but also after EMU has been established. The argument in their favour can take one of two (or both) forms. One argument is that what restrains a government of a country on a floating or adjustable-peg exchange rate from indulging in fiscal expansion is the apprehension that this would cause a depreciation leading to inflation. But inside a monetary union this restraint would be removed. The country's 'exchange rate' against other members is irrevocably fixed, and the country need fear no inflationary reprisal for its fiscal actions. But such actions could harm other countries—say, by inducing a depreciation of the exchange rate of the Euro against the dollar and the yen. But there is an obvious difficulty with the premiss of this argument, much theory and some recent experience suggesting that fiscal expansion leads to exchange-rate appreciation, not depreciation.

In any event, a more prominent argument in defence of the fiscal criteria is that connected with the idea that excessive public debts result in resort to the printing press ('monetization').[9] Despite the fact that its constitution (see below) forbids the ECB to lend to any national government, which might be thought to provide a safeguard against resort to the printing press in this case, the fear is that a country with an unmanageable public debt problem (Italy is the country which observers have most in mind in this context) could constitute a political crisis of an order that could create strong pressure on the ECB to pursue an expansionary monetary policy. This might occur, either directly through pressure from the country concerned and from other governments wishing to demonstrate 'solidarity', or indirectly through the pressures arising from the threatened collapse of European banks and financial institutions holding the bonds of the problem country in their portfolios. As the crisis looms, the value of these bonds would plummet, putting the safety of deposits in doubt and creating the potential for a 'sauve qui peut' run on the financial system. Once again, the fact that the ECB is not burdened with responsibility for the financial system in the Maastricht constitution is not necessarily felt to be a sufficient safeguard.

It is possible to question the force of these arguments. It can be argued that, if a government over-borrows and precipitates a debt crisis, then that is its own affair, at least as long as there is no presumption of a bail-out by other governments: that all that was needed was to make this clear was always the UK government's (unavailing) line of argument in the negotiations that led to the TEU. And indeed, as already mentioned, the constitution of the ECB specifically forbids it from lending to a national government and assigns it no bank supervision duty. Moreover, it must be pointed out that placing limits on governments' room for fiscal manœuvre emasculates one of the adjustment tools that governments might need when exchange rates are fixed. It is not surprising that the fiscal criteria in the TEU turned out to be one of the most controversial parts of that Treaty. Countries expect participation in monetary union to involve the resignation of national monetary autonomy—this is what it is all about, after all; resigning a considerable degree of autonomy over fiscal policy both in the run-up to EMU and thereafter is a different matter. A partial resolution of this difficulty lies in the escape clauses that accompany the fiscal criteria and in the fact that the criteria will inevitably bite more deeply in the transition than afterwards.

The ECB

None of the general analytical arguments concerning monetary unions which were reviewed earlier touched on the issue of inflation control. Yet, in the context of EMU this has been of the utmost importance, and a great deal of effort has been put into the design of a constitution for the ECB which, it is hoped, will secure the goal of price stability. The reasons for this emphasis are not far to seek. First of all, much of the success of the EMS (or, more strictly, the ERM) as it was perceived was identified with the fact that member countries used it as a counter-inflationary framework; in the move from ERM to EMU, countries necessarily lose the ability to use the Deutschmark as their counter-inflationary 'anchor', and a replacement is needed. Secondly, the dominant country involved—Germany—for good historical reasons places great store on a stable currency. EMU without Germany would be meaningless; but for Germany to participate in EMU requires that the ECB should be oriented towards producing a stable level of prices.

The attention paid to the design of the constitution of the ECB, as a means of ensuring low-inflation outcomes, conforms to a comparatively recent economic literature which is concerned with the analysis of credibility in economic policy. The analysis in question takes for granted that the technical means exist to control inflation and concentrates instead on the question whether policy-makers will always *wish* to control inflation. It is a standard proposition in macroeconomic analysis to say that, whilst it is possible to reduce unemployment below the 'natural' or equilibrium rate by raising inflation, this is only a temporary trade-off; once agents become accustomed to the inflation rate, the trade-off disappears. The contribution of the modern analysis of credibility in economic policy is to take this point one step further. If governments are prone to take advantage of this temporary trade-off, then agents will come to expect them to do so and consequently will predict a high level of inflation. This means that in the long run unemployment will be at its natural rate (which it would be anyway), while inflation will be much higher than socially desirable. The analysis goes on to suggest that a way round this problem is to find a means for making commitments on low inflation credible. If they are credible, then the long-run solution will provide low inflation, as desired. One means of bringing this state of affairs about, it has been suggested, is to make the ECB independent of electoral pressure and to invite it to pursue the objective of price stability with no, or little, qualification. Empirical analysis shows an inverse correlation between independence in central banks and the rate of inflation: the more independent the central bank, the lower the inflation rate (Grilli, Masciandaro, and Tabellini 1991).

Independence in this context has several dimensions: it is not just that the ECB should be formally independent in the constitutional sense. It is necessary that the terms of office of the Governor and the Board of Directors should protect these individuals from pressure to deviate from the objective of price stability. The ECB should not be burdened with other duties and obligations that might oblige it to engage in an expensive monetary policy incompatible with the control of inflation. The Deutsche Bundesbank has many of these features and in the Maastricht constitution for the ECB we can see many of the same features—typically somewhat strengthened—repeated. To begin with, the ECB is independent of national governments and of the Commission. It is at the centre of the ESCB, a system comprised of central banks which are themselves required to be independent. The ESCB is given one principal goal of monetary policy—that of price stability. The Treaty says that 'the primary objective of the ESCB shall be to maintain price stability'. It goes on to add, 'Without prejudice to the objective of price stability, it shall support the general economic policies in the Community . . .' (Article 2). This qualification has not generally been seen as providing a significant dilution of the primary objective of the ESCB. The ECB is forbidden from lending to national governments or to Commission organizations; the responsibility for the supervision of banks and financial institutions is placed elsewhere. This is so, in order that its pursuit of price stability will not be compromised by actions taken in pursuit of these other possible obligations. Similarly, whilst exchange-rate policy is not the ECB's direct prerogative, it is afforded considerable influence over any such policy. In addition, the terms of office of the Governor and members of the Board are drawn up in such a way as to reduce the possibility that ECB officials might act as if they were 'representatives' of their country under the influence of their country's government.

On the face of it, then, the statutes of the ECB seem to guarantee a very high degree of independence to that institution. Indeed, some observers have queried whether the provisions do not go too far in this direction. Thus, it is common (though not universal) practice for central banks to be assigned the duty of supervision of the banking and financial system. A central bank will almost certainly acquire relevant information for this task in the course of carrying out monetary policy operations and this information is wasted if the task of supervision is assigned to another institution. Another disadvantage of an 'excessively' independent central bank is that it makes difficult, if not impossible, the task of coordinating fiscal and monetary policy and, still more, of promoting such a coordination within the context of an international (G3) agreement to coordinate economic policy. Efforts towards concluding such agreements are a recurrent feature of international economic policy, the latest episode being the one inaugurated by the USA in 1985—the so-called 'Plaza Agreement'—an effort which foundered only some three years later. One of the reasons for its eventual demise is said to be the failure to coordinate fiscal with monetary actions.

One reason why the proposed constitution of the ESCB–ECB is so 'hard' is probably that there is an apprehension that a new institution with no accumulated reputation needs extra advantages to compensate for its lack of history. But this suggestion reveals a point of difficulty with the constitutional approach. Transplanting a constitution—even a strengthened one—is not the same as transplanting history: it may be that, in countries with low inflation and independent central banks, it is history that makes the actions of the central bank, which must often be harsh ones, acceptable to the public. Thus, the Bundesbank has latitude to make temporarily 'unpopular' decisions; similar actions undertaken by the ECB might not be well received in some of the countries in the EMU—say, in the inflation-prone economies of Italy, the UK, or Spain. This is another reason, of course, for the insistence on convergence criteria.

13.5. Prospects for EMU

At the 1995 Madrid Summit meeting, the participating countries decided to aim to form a monetary union by 1 January 1999. It was clear that there would not be a majority of countries eligible to form a monetary union at the earlier date of 1997 suggested by the Treaty. But a 'small-core' monetary union seemed a possible prospect for 1999. It was agreed that a decision should be taken by June 1998, on the basis of data then available up to 1997 as to the composition of the EMU which could start on 1 January 1999. The transition path did not appear easy—as discussed below, a number of the convergence criteria looked difficult in prospect to fulfil—but by mid-1996 it appeared more likely than not that a small group of countries would be able to initiate monetary union on the due date. Lending force to this assessment, a decision had been taken (at the Madrid Summit) to call the new currency the Euro, and a technical assessment had been made that the physical introduction of Euro notes and coins would take place in 2002. In the interim, whilst governments would make all new issues of debt in Euros, national currencies would still exist and the EMU would serve to lock together the exchange rates of those currencies selected, with zero fluctuation margins.

The position with respect to the convergence criteria involved a number of problems, however. First of all, the crises of 1992 and 1993 had resulted in the pound sterling and the Italian lira leaving the ERM altogether and in a widening of the bands of fluctuation to ±15 per cent, a move described at the time as 'temporary and expedient'. Yet the Treaty required that a currency should have been maintained within the 'normal' bands of fluctuation for at least two years, without severe tension and without any devaluation having been initiated by the country concerned. No decisions had been taken by the beginning of June 1996 as to how the exchange-rate criterion has to be interpreted in the new circumstances. Would ±15 per cent take the place of the ±2.25 per cent intended by the Treaty? Or would it be necessary to maintain a currency within ±2¼ per cent *de facto*? And, in the latter interpretation, would it then be necessary for a currency to participate in the ERM as such? The only decision that had been taken was to defer judgement on these issues until the middle of 1998. Possibly one reason why no decision had been made was a fear of giving the currency markets 'something to shoot at'. The wide-band ERM had been successful in deterring speculation: suggesting a renarrowing of the band would invite a renewal of speculative flows which could only be managed if the EMI were to start to act a the European Central Bank even before 1 January 1999.[10]

If the exchange-rate criterion posed some problems, it was the fiscal-policy criterion which was widely acknowledged as the most difficult. In 1995, none of the countries (save Luxembourg) satisfied a strict interpretation of the two criteria—a budget deficit/GDP ratio of less than 3 per cent and a debt/GDP ratio of less than 60 per cent. Indeed all countries, except Luxembourg and Ireland, had been found to be in 'excessive deficit'. The Irish case was an interesting exception in that the Commission, and subsequently the Council of Ministers, had used the qualifying words in the Maastricht Treaty to 'overlook' Ireland's debt/GDP ratio, which, whilst over 60 per cent, was clearly falling. The prospects for 1997, as viewed by the Commission in its May 1996 forecast, are set out in Chapter 2 (see pp. 54–7). They acknowledge the substantial corrective actions promised by many governments and suggest that, at least by 1997, Germany and France will satisfy a strict interpretation of the criteria.

However, it is easy to be sceptical that this result will come about. The commitment of countries to fiscal consolidation is certainly real but the context in which it is taking place—with falling rates of GDP growth—is hostile to the achievement of the reference values. In fact, of course, the Treaty does not require this: the reference values are just that—and the protocol to the fiscal deficit procedure makes it clear that exceptions are allowable (as in the case of Ireland). The reason why the 'strict interpretation' has taken hold is primarily a political one, since in Germany the public's nervousness about the commitment to EMU was answered, both by a Constitutional Court decision and by numerous politicians' statements, to the effect that the criteria should be interpreted 'strictly', before German participation could be contemplated.

In these circumstances, if some accommodation is to be made for countries whose fiscal ratios exceed the reference values, it seems likely that reference will be made to a 'stability pact'. Such a pact, first promoted by the German Minister of Finance, would provide for a discipline of fiscal behaviour in countries *after* the monetary union is formed. This could go some way to providing the reassurance that Germany needs and is preferable to insisting on a 'strict interpretation' in a situation of slow growth and recession where such insistence may have needlessly damaging effects on output and employment.[11]

Few countries seem likely to offend against the inflation or interest-rate criteria by 1997 (see Chapter 2, pp. 57–8, for an assessment).

The problem of the 'ins' and the 'outs'

With the possible benefit of some leeway in the interpretation of the fiscal criteria, perhaps accommodated by agreement on a stability pact, the stage seemed set (as of mid-1996) for a core of countries to form an initial monetary union as on 1 January, 1999. That core would certainly need to include France and Germany, without either of which monetary union makes little sense. Then Austria and the Netherlands could both qualify. Some observers would then add Luxembourg, Belgium, Ireland, Finland, and Denmark. Luxembourg would formally qualify, yet Belgium's debt/GDP ratio might exclude its participation in the initial union, setting at risk the monetary union which already exists between Belgium and Luxembourg. Ireland, similarly, is likely formally to qualify but it is arguable that its close links with the UK would make participation in a European monetary union more sensible if the UK were also participating. Denmark has a formal opt-out but might reverse this by referendum. Spain, Portugal, Italy, Sweden, Greece, and the UK seem less likely to be among the countries forming the initial 'small-core' monetary union, whether because of an inability to satisfy the criteria, because of a close relationship with an excluded country, or because of reservations about the enterprise.

Clearly there is some doubt about the size of the initial group and the identity of the countries joining it. But it looks as though that group could comprise up to one-half of the potential membership, with some larger countries outside the core to begin with. This raises the question of the relationship between the 'Ins' and the 'Outs'. To promote the early formation of a complete monetary union seems to be indicated by the need to preserve the single market. The 'Ins' could suspect that those countries which stay 'Out' are doing so in order to exploit a competitive advantage by devaluing their currency against the Euro. They would like some agreement to exclude this. The 'Outs' could equally suspect that the 'Ins' are arranging matters to advantage themselves from their early participation in the monetary union. To take care of those problems it seems important that the period of waiting before the 'Outs' also qualify for membership should be short and that there should be arrangements in the meanwhile which provide the assurances that both the 'Ins' and the 'Outs' require. Some kind of 'ERM II', with limited intervention commitments from the ECB, has been suggested. Given the heterogeneity of the 'Outs' group, this may prove a difficult arrangement to operate. The relationship between the 'Ins' and the 'Outs' constitutes, unfortunately, a 'danger area' in EU affairs.

Discussion questions

1. Describe the nature of the costs and benefits of EMU.
2. What are the key features of the statutes of the ECB? What is their economic significance?
3. Why do the Maastricht criteria for membership of an EMU specify conditions pertaining to fiscal policy? How compelling do you find these arguments?

FURTHER READING

An accessible and comprehensive treatment of the theory of monetary integration is to be found in Paul de Grauwe's book on the subject (de Grauwe 1992), whilst the historical dimension of monetary integration in Europe is well covered in Gros and Thygesen (1992). For an authoritative account of the provisions in the TEU pertaining to EMU, Kenen's (1995) book is indispensable. Discussion Papers of the Centre for Economic Policy Research provide a constant stream of high-level academic analysis of the EMU project, while day-to-day developments are best followed through the pages of the *Financial Times*.

NOTES

1. Accessible book-length treatments appear in de Grauwe (1992), Gros and Thygesen (1992), and Kenen (1995). Emerson and Huhne (1990) provide a shorter, highly readable, account.
2. More precisely, this is the economist's way of appraising such an option. It may be that the overriding imperatives are political, in which case the cost-benefit analysis tells us something about the economic cost (or possibly, additional benefit) of taking up an option which is overwhelmingly attractive on political grounds: Goodhart (1994) provides an account which explicitly confronts the issues of political economy as they arise in this context.
3. The President of the Commission has 'observer' status at G7 meetings.
4. Note that, if the shock were symmetric, the exchange rate would not be a helpful shock absorber. For example, if the taste change had been from champagne *and* sausages to (say) Stilton cheese, then it would be helpful for the sterling–French franc and sterling–Deutschmark exchange rates both to appreciate, but it would not be helpful for the French franc–Deutschmark rate to change.
5. The pioneering contribution in this vein was by Sala-i-Martin and Sachs (1992).

6. The Delors Report viewed a parallel currency as bringing with it the danger of inflation. During the negotiations in the intergovernmental conference which led to the TEU the UK government proposed a parallel currency—the so-called 'hard Ecu'—the chief feature of which was its counter-inflationary characteristic. However, the proposal was widely viewed as a diversionary tactic by a government not really committed to monetary union, and, perhaps for this reason, was not pursued beyond the stage of discussion.

7. The membership of the Delors Committee was not directly representative of governments. The core of the committee membership was constituted by the Governors of the central banks of the EMS; in addition, there were three independent persons, and two Commission members, including the Chairman, M. Delors.

8. Given Germany's dominant position in the negotiations leading to the Treaty, this rationale for the convergence criteria must be held to emanate from Germany's concern to see that all prospective members of the monetary union should share her own attachment to 'stability-oriented policies'. See Winkler (1996) for an account of the criteria from this point of view.

9. For a technical treatment of this issue, see e.g. Leslie (1993).

10. See Artis and Lewis (1993).

11. This is discussed further in Artis (1996).

REFERENCES

Artis, M. J. (1996), 'Alternative Transitions to EMU', *Economic Journal*, 106 (July), 1005–15.

—— and Lewis, M. K. (1993), 'Après le déluge: Exchange Rate and Monetary Policy in Britain and Europe', *Oxford Review of Economic Policy* (Sept.), 36–61.

CEC (1970): Commission for the European Communities, *Report to the Council and the Commission on the Realization by Stages of Economic and Monetary Union in the Community* (the Werner Report), Supplement to Bulletin II–1970 of the European Communities (Brussels: CEC).

—— (1989), *Report on Economic and Monetary Union in the European Community* (the Delors Report) (Luxembourg: Office for Official Publications of the European Communities).

—— (1990), 'One Market, One Money: An Evaluation of the Potential Benefits and Costs of Forming an Economic and Monetary Union', *European Economy* (Oct.), 44: 1–351.

De Grauwe, P. (1992), *The Economics of Monetary Integration* (Oxford: Oxford University Press).

Emerson, M., and Huhne, C. (1990), *The ECU Report* (London: Pan Books).

Giavazzi, F., and Giovannini, A. (1989), *Limiting Exchange Rate Flexibility: The European Monetary System* (Cambridge, Mass.: MIT Press).

Goodhart, C. A. E. (1994), 'The Political Economy of Monetary Union', in Peter B. Kenen (ed.), *Understanding Interdependence: The Macroeconomics of the Open Economy*, papers presented at a conference honouring the fiftieth anniversary of *Essays in International Finance* (Princeton: Princeton University Press).

Grilli, V., Masciandaro, D., and Tabellini, G. (1991), 'Political and Monetary Institutions and Public Financial Policies in the Industrial Countries', *Economic Policy*, 13 (Oct.), 341–92.

Gros, D., and Thygesen, N. (1992), *European Monetary Integration* (Harlow: Longman).

Kenen, P. B. (1995), *Economic and Monetary Union in Europe* (Cambridge: Cambridge University Press).

Krugman, P. (1990), 'Policy Problems of a Monetary Union', in P. de Grauwe and L. Papademos (eds.), *The European Monetary System in the 1990s* (Harlow: Longman).

Leslie, D. G. (1993), *Advanced Macroeconomics* (Maidenhead: McGraw-Hill).

Padoa-Schioppa, T. (1988), 'The European Monetary System: A Long Term View', in F. Giavazzi, S. Micossi, and M. Miller (eds.), *The European Monetary System* (Cambridge: Cambridge University Press), 369–84.

Sala-i-Martin, X., and Sachs, J. (1992), 'Fiscal Federalism and Optimum Currency Areas: Evidence for Europe from the United States', in M. B. Canzoneri, V. Grilli, and P. R. Masson (eds.), *Establishing a Central Bank: Issues in Europe and Lessons from the United States* (Cambridge: Cambridge University Press), 195–219.

Winkler, B. (1996), 'Towards a Strategic View on EMU: A Critical Survey', *Journal of Public Policy*, 16/1 (Jan.–Apr.), 1–28.

CHAPTER 14

The EU Budget

ROBIN BLADEN-HOVELL and ELIZABETH SYMONS

14.1. Introduction

Budgetary considerations have dominated the proceedings of the European Community (EC)—and later the European Union—for much of its forty-year history. Disputes about whether the EC should have its own financial resources, rivalry among the EC institutions over which of them—the Commission, the Council of Ministers, or the European Parliament (EP)—should exercise control over the budget, together with the problem of budgetary imbalance, particularly with respect to the UK, all contributed to periods of budgetary crisis. Moreover, unlike the budgets of national governments, the EU budget is circumscribed by a strict prohibition on borrowing. Budget balance was written into the Treaty of Rome, and subsequent amendments only served to relax the restriction on borrowing for a limited range of specific purposes—to support the balance of payments and to promote investment within the EU. As a result, the financial resources available to the EC or the EU at any time have been of central importance in determining the scale of activities, and have effectively dictated the timing and pace at which policies have developed. The purpose of this chapter is to describe the current structure and provisions of the EU budget and to review the major developments that gave rise to these budgetary arrangements.

A number of important changes have taken place in the EU budget since the publication of the last edition. These changes were largely contained within the Inter-Institutional Agreement which was eventually signed at Edinburgh in 1992. This agreement, known as the Delors II package, continued the reforms initiated in 1988 and established financial perspectives for the period until 1999. The key elements of the reform were a gradual relaxation of the ceiling on own resources and the prioritization of structural operations which provide assistance to the least favoured regions of the EU. These developments are discussed in detail below.

The chapter contains seven sections. The broad structure and the procedural arrangements for the budget are presented in Section 14.2. A detailed analysis of the general budget is undertaken in subsequent sections of the chapter: revenue and the issue of 'own resources', together with the question of budgetary imbalance for the UK, are covered in Section 14.3; expenditure is discussed in Section 14.4. The income and expenditure components of the budget are brought together in Section 14.5, where we outline the problems of trying to define the net budgetary balance for EU members, whilst policy options relating to possible future developments for the budget are presented in Section 14.6. A summary of the main issues and conclusions completes the chapter.

14.2. Background

EU policies provided for by the 1957 Treaties of Rome (the European Economic Community (EEC) and the European Atomic Energy Community (Euratom)) and the administrative expenditures of Union institutions are financed by the general budget of the EU. Operations provided for by the 1951 Treaty of Paris, and the promotion of trade with associated developing countries, are financed by separate specific budgets—the European Coal and Steel Community (ECSC) budget, and the European Development Fund (EDF), respectively.

The general budget of the EU is small in relation to the national budgets of the Member States, accounting for some 1.1 per cent of EU GDP in 1995 compared with more than 40 per cent, on average, for the budgets of Member States' national governments. Many areas of EU policy are regulatory in nature and have little requirement for spending, except for administration. Thus, for example, the EU's role in policing the customs union, or in implementing competition policy, requires limited financial resources. As indicated by Fig. 14.1, the main area of expenditure is on agricultural policy and, in particular, on the agricultural guarantee that aims to maintain stable prices for farm output above the world level through intervention in the market for agricultural produce.[1] Appropriations for the agricultural guarantee contained in the 1995 budget, for example, accounted for some 50 per cent of total EU spending—a proportion that has fallen significantly from the peak values obtained in the early and mid-1980s, when agricultural spending frequently represented over 70 per cent of EC expenditure.

The Commission, the Council of Ministers, and the EP are all involved, to varying degrees, in the adoption and execution of the general budget. The budgetary procedure begins with the Commission preparing a 'preliminary draft budget' for the EU based upon estimates of expenditure proposed by the EU institutions.[2] The preliminary draft budget is initially submitted to the Council of Ministers, who establish, by means of a qualified majority, the form of the draft budget to be placed before the EP.

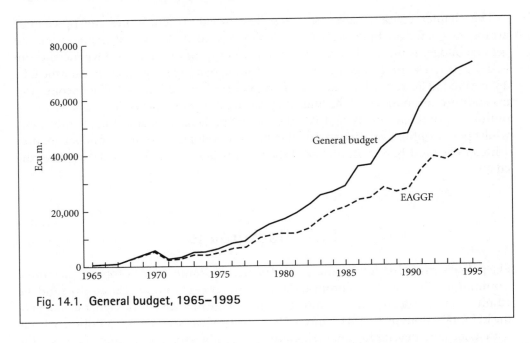

Fig. 14.1. **General budget, 1965–1995**

Since 1975 the EP has had the right to propose amendments to the draft budget and, following the first reading of the document in the EP, the modified draft is returned to the Council for a second reading by that body. On its second reading, the Council must secure a qualified majority in order either to accept any of the modifications proposed by the EP that increase expenditure, or to reject amendments that do not. Unless the entire budget is subsequently rejected by the EP, the level of compulsory expenditure—spending that relates to commitments derived from the internal and external obligations of the EU which are established by the Treaties, or by secondary legislation adopted in accordance with the Treaties—is determined at this stage of the budgetary procedure.[3] The second reading of the budget by the EP is mainly concerned with the level of non-compulsory expenditure for which the EP may reject or accept the Council's proposals. Unless the EP rejects the budget entirely, the Parliamentary President then declares the budget to be adopted.

This balance of power between the Council and the EP in the budgetary decision-making process was very slow to emerge, the period between 1975 and 1987, in particular, being especially difficult in this respect. Granting the EP the power to amend the draft budget proposed by Council effectively split the legislative and budgetary functions of the EC. Legislative power in the EU now rests solely with the Council, while, since 1975, budgetary power has been shared by the EP and the Council.

Disagreement between the institutions led to a series of incidents during the early 1980s that effectively paralysed the budgetary procedures of the EC. In December 1979, for example, the EP rejected the draft budget for 1980, with the result that the budgetary procedure was delayed by six months.[4] During this six-month period, the financing of the budget had to proceed month by month on the basis of the previously agreed budget—the so-called provisional-twelfths arrangement. This facility was utilized again in 1982 and 1985, when the EP once more rejected the draft budget, and yet again in 1988, when the Council was unable to establish a draft of the budget for that year because of the lack of political agreement concerning a new limit for EC resources.

Various attempts at improving the budgetary procedure were made throughout the period from 1975 onwards and these met with varying degrees of success. One of the more successful reforms was the Inter-Institutional Agreement signed in 1988. This settlement, whilst not seeking to alter the respective budgetary powers of the various institutions, set out the basis upon which the EP and the Council could achieve a joint agreement concerning the overall size of the budget and redirected budgetary discussion to the question of allocating resources within each of the ceilings of the financial perspective. Collaboration between the institutions was strengthened further by the Inter-Institutional Agreement signed in October 1992. This established a pre-budget meeting between the various institutions at which priorities for the budget for the coming year could be discussed ahead of the Commission's decision on the preliminary draft. This is supplemented by *ad hoc* conciliation meetings on the amount of compulsory expenditure, held at the Council's first reading.

14.3. **Revenue and own resources**

During the first twelve years of the EC's existence, the budget was funded entirely by members' direct contributions. After 1970, however, the budget was financed from the 'own resources' of the EC—that is, by revenues that the Member States agreed should be the resources of the Community by right. As shown in Table 14.1, the own-resources system established in 1970 had three elements: customs duties on goods imported from outside the EC, agricultural levies, and a contribution based on the hypothetical yield of a harmonized-base VAT. Because the range of goods subject to VAT in different countries varied, the VAT base adopted by the EC for this purpose was standardized, with the EC being entitled to, at most, the revenue generated from a notional 1 per cent VAT rate applied to this 'harmonized' base.

As the 1970s progressed, it became apparent that the original system of own resources was inadequate in a number of important respects, the essential problem being twofold. First, the yield from traditional own resources, such as customs duties and agricultural levies, fell gradually during the 1970s as progress was made worldwide in dismantling tariffs by means of the General Agreement on Trade and Tariffs (GATT) negotiations, and the EC itself became increasingly self-sufficient in the production of agricultural products.[5] Secondly, VAT revenue effectively stagnated over the period as the share of GNP accounted for by consumer expenditure declined throughout the EC.

Table 14.1. **The development of financial resources for the budget**

Agreement	Dates in force	Details of resources	UK rebate details
EEC and Euratom established by the Treaties of Rome, March 1957.	1958–70	1. Revenue consists entirely of contributions by the Member States.	n.a.
Original 'own-resources' system of funding EC general budget established by the Luxembourg agreement, April 1970.	1970–84	1. Customs levies and duties on imports from outside EC; 2. agricultural levies; 3. VAT-based contribution, calculated on a harmonised (i.e. hypothetical) base, subject to a maximum rate of 1%.	'Financial mechanism' to reduce VAT contribution of Member States meeting certain criteria: available 1976–80, but never triggered. From 1979 UK 'compensation' agreed in form of expenditure measures agreed at various dates.
Fontainebleau summit, June 1984.	1984–7	1. As above; 2. as above; 3. maximum VAT rate raised to 1.4%.	UK rebate as reduction in VAT rate applied to UK (two-thirds of difference between UK % share of VAT and UK's share of allocable spending; German contribution to financing of UK rebate limited to two-thirds of full amount).
Brussels (Delors I) agreement, February, 1988	1988–92	1. As above; 2. as above; 3. maximum VAT rate retained at 1.4%, but VAT base capped at 55% of GNP in all Member States; 4. 'fourth resource', calculated in relation to GNP of Member States; 5. aggregate revenues limited to 1.2% of EC GNP.	As under Fontainbleau system, adjusted to reflect capped VAT base and additional GNP-based resource.
Edinburgh (Delors II) agreement, December 1992	1993–99	1. As above; 2. as above; 3. as above until 1995, with maximum rate progressively reduced to 1% between 1995 and 1999; 4. as above; 5. aggregate revenues to rise to 1.27% of EU GNP by 1999 and system of revenue-raising slightly modified to take account of 'contributive capacity'.	As above.

Note: n.a. = not applicable.

Source: Adapted from Smith (1992).

The combined effect of these two factors was to place considerable pressure on the own-resource system at precisely the time when the spending needs of the EC increased both because of new policies being adopted and the accession of new EC members.

An initial attempt at resolving the budgetary crisis was made at the European Council meeting at Fontainebleau in June 1984. The new system, based on the principle of raising the notional VAT ceiling to 1.4 per cent, took effect from January 1986, with transitional financing arrangements being applied to the budgets of 1984 and 1985. These temporary arrangements involved intergovernmental advances which were repayable in the case of the 1984 budget, but were non-repayable for the 1985 budget. In 1986, however, the budget outturn was virtually at the limit of the 1.4 per cent VAT ceiling, with budget balance being obtained only by means of deferring certain items of agricultural expenditure until 1987.[6] The Fontainebleau reform had effectively failed.

A solution to the EC's budgetary difficulties was eventually found in 1988. By then, the third enlargement of the EC to include Spain and Portugal on 1 January 1986, together with the successful conclusion of the Single European Act (SEA) in February 1986 setting out the medium-term goals of the EC, had established a sounder political base for a thorough reform of EC finances. In February 1987 the Commission presented comprehensive reform proposals (see CEC 1987a, 1987b), which together became known as the 'Delors I package'. The broad outline of this package was subsequently adopted at the Brussels European Council meeting held on 11–12 February 1988, the proposal being finally accepted in June 1988.

The main thrust of the Delors I package was to ensure that the EC be given suitable resources that would be sufficient to enable it to operate throughout the period 1988–92. The reform maintained the traditional own resources derived from customs duties and agricultural levies and, subject to minor modifications to the VAT base described in Table 14.1, proposed that the VAT resource continue with a ceiling of 1.4 per cent. To these traditional own resources, however, the Delors I package proposed adding a new, 'fourth resource'. This new source of finance was to be a variable, 'topping-up' resource which would provide the revenue required to cover expenditure in excess of the traditional own resources and VAT receipts, subject to an overall ceiling for the total of all own resources of 1.2 per cent of EC GNP.

The overall effect of introducing the GNP-based fourth resource was to make the EC tax system more progressive by tying each Member State's contribution more closely to actual levels of prosperity within the EC. The uniform rate of the fourth resource was determined by reference to the additional revenue needed during each budgetary procedure to cover the EC's requirements.

Further reform of the budget was introduced in the Inter-Institutional Agreement signed at Edinburgh in December 1992. These measures, which were collectively known as Delors II, were designed to give shape to the policies arising from the European Council's Maastricht agreements and support the second stage of economic and monetary union (see CEC 1992b). The reforms contained a new set of financial perspectives covering the period 1993–9 which prioritized three main areas: external action, economic and social cohesion, and creating a favourable environment for European competitiveness. In order to fund initiatives in these areas, the Agreement proposed that the ceiling on own resources be gradually increased: from 1.2 per cent of EU GNP in 1993 to 1.27 per cent in 1999. Although the Delors II package contained no major change in the method of raising these resources for the EU, it did propose rebalancing the third and fourth resources in order to strengthen the link between contributions to the budget and capacity to pay. The proposals entail a gradual shift in favour of financing the budget from the fourth resource, based on GNP, the current maximum VAT rate of 1.4 per cent being retained until 1995 then progressively reduced to 1 per cent between 1995 and 1999, the size of the uniform base being reduced to 50 per cent over the same period.

The 1994 budget was the last to come under the financial perspectives adopted at Edinburgh for EU12. The 1995 budget procedure was governed by the revised financial perspectives adjusted in accordance with the Inter-Institutional Agreement to take account of the new requirements and resources of the enlarged EU incorporating Austria, Finland, and Sweden. In this respect the Commission took the view that the additional own resources resulting from enlargement should be assigned to three types of objective: raising expenditure ceilings over the entire period to cover new requirements resulting from enlargement, notably structural funds and agri-budgetary compensation for acceding countries; raising expenditures on various operations for which requirements had been updated (internal policy expenditure was increased by 7 per cent in line with the relative size of acceding countries, external policy expenditure was increased by 6.3 per cent); and, finally, the margin between the expenditure ceiling and own resources was restored and enlarged to cope with cyclical variations in resources or unforeseen expenditures.

Complete details of the own resources of the EU in 1996, disaggregated by Member State, are shown in Table 14.2. In this year, 48.9 per cent of the total EU budget was derived from VAT receipts, a further 47.2 per cent coming from customs duties and the GNP-based fourth resource with agricultural levies, including those from sugar and isoglucose, together contributing only 2.4 per cent of EU finance. In terms of the contributions from the individual Member States in 1996, Germany accounted for 30 per cent of the total own-resources received by the EU, whilst four countries— Germany, France, Italy, and the UK, together accounted for almost 71 per cent of the total funding.

The VAT own resource and compensation for the UK

The issue of budgetary imbalance was central to the financial difficulties experienced by the EC during the 1970s and early 1980s. The issue had two dimensions: a UK problem that dates from as early as 1974 and which underlay the renegotiation of the UK's terms of entry to the EC in that year; a German problem, first expressed at the European

Table 14.2. **Own resources in 1996, by Member State (Ecu m.)**

Member State	Type of resource							
	Agricultural levies	Sugar and isoglucose	Customs duties	Total traditional own resources	VAT own resources at uniform rate	GNP own resources	Compensation for UK VAT rebate	Total financing
Austria	11.2	33.2	361.9	406.3	1086.7	727.7	128.1	2,348.8
Belgium	42.4	75.4	855.8	973.6	1,136.0	848.1	149.3	3,107.0
Denmark	4.3	40.9	219.6	264.8	677.7	528.8	93.1	1,564.4
Finland	15.6	8.3	235.0	258.9	521.1	390.4	68.7	1,239.1
France	44.9	320.0	1,203.0	1,567.9	7,126.1	4,799.4	845.0	14,338.4
Germany	133.7	339.0	3,591.0	4,063.7	12,106.0	7,493.6	757.5	24,420.8
Greece	7.2	19.3	135.0	161.5	599.1	370.7	65.3	1,196.5
Ireland	2.6	8.4	229.5	240.5	315.9	179.5	31.6	767.6
Italy	75.3	119.2	953.6	1,148.2	4,460.4	3,622.4	637.8	9,868.8
Luxembourg	0.09	—	15.1	15.2	100.6	57.2	10.1	183.1
Netherlands	67.3	81.7	1,325.8	1,474.8	1,824.8	1,215.4	214.0	4,729.0
Portugal	95.4	0.5	134.6	230.5	588.4	334.4	58.9	1,212.3
Spain	56.7	48.7	546.1	651.5	2,508.6	1,724.7	303.7	5,188.3
Sweden	41.0	21.9	580.9	643.7	875.3	698.4	123.0	2,340.4
UK	180.0	69.2	2,466.0	2,715.2	5,865.8	3,721.0	−3,486.0	8,816.1
TOTAL	777.6 (0.9)	1,185.8 (1.5)	12,852.9 (15.8)	14,816.3 (18.2)	39,792.3 (48.9)	26,711.7 (32.8)	0	81,320.3 (100)

Source: CEC (1996: 153).

Council meeting held in London in 1981, which highlighted the German position as main contributor to the EC and proposed a reduction in that country's share of financing the compensation for the UK.

For the UK, the problem of budgetary imbalance arose essentially as a result of two features characteristic of the UK economy. On the one hand, the UK represented a country with a small agricultural sector, importing a large proportion of farm produce from outside the EC, and as such it benefited very little from the EC's agricultural spending. On the other hand, the UK found itself a large contributor to the financing of the EC, because a very large proportion of the country's GNP was accounted for by the EC's VAT base. After 1974, the EC budget contained various provisions for correcting the contribution made by the UK, bringing the UK's contribution more closely in line with the expenditures of the EC within the UK.

The first correcting mechanism was agreed at the European Council meeting held in Dublin in March 1975. Under this arrangement, compensation, in the form of partial repayment of VAT contributions, was to be provided from the EC budget to any country that found itself satisfying three conditions: a per capita GDP less than 85 per cent of the EC average; a rate of growth less than 120 per cent of the EC average, and with a share in EC revenue at least 10 per cent higher than its share in EC GDP. At the time of the agreement it was expected that this arrangement would benefit Ireland and Italy in addition to the UK. In practice, however, the conditions governing the repayment of VAT contributions were never triggered by any of these countries during the period 1976–80 that the arrangement was in force. As a result, a second correcting mechanism, that took the form of increased Regional Fund expenditures in the UK, was agreed at the Dublin European Council meeting of November 1979. However, the criteria determining the size of these expenditures were never made clear, and the administration of these funds was marked by continual dispute. This situation continued until 1984, when the Fontainebleau agreement established a more systematic basis of compensation for the UK.

Under the Fontainebleau agreement, the UK received an abatement to its contribution to the EC budget, calculated as two-thirds of the difference between the UK's percentage share of VAT payments to the EC, and the UK's percentage share of those parts of EC expenditure that can be allocated to Member States.[8] This reduction in the UK contribution was financed by additional payments made by all other Member States, except Germany, in accordance with their respective percentage share of VAT payments. For Germany, however, allowance was made, in recognition of that country's position as main contributor to the EC. Accordingly it was required to pay only two-thirds of its normal share of the compensation, the balance being divided among the remaining Members on the same scale.

The effect of incorporating compensatory payments to the UK in the determination of the VAT own resource in 1996 is shown in Table 14.3. Here the amount of VAT own resource, calculated at a uniform rate of 1.25 per cent, is shown for each country in column 1. The effect of capping the VAT base at 55 per cent of GNP at market prices benefits Ireland, Luxembourg, and Portugal in this stage of the process. The gross amount of compensation for the UK is deducted from the total obtained and shared among the other members of the EC in accordance with the procedure described above; this is shown in column 2. New totals for each country, obtained by summing columns 1 and 2, are given in column 3. The maximum VAT contribution made by any country, set at 1.4 per cent by the 1992 Edinburgh agreement, is shown in column 4 of the table, the actual own-resource contribution for any country (shown in column 6) being the lesser of the amounts shown in columns 3 and 4. Where a country's potential contribution to the VAT own resource in any year exceeds the 1.4 per cent upper limit, as was the case for Belgium, Denmark, Finland, Italy, and Sweden in 1996, the difference is carried across and paid by the Member under the heading of the GNP-based, 'fourth resource'.

The determination of the fourth resource is shown on the right-hand side of the table. The uniform rate for the fourth-resource is calculated as the ratio of the fourth resource requirement in any particular year and the value of 1 per cent of EU GNP. In 1996 the rate was equal to 0.39 per cent, application of which yields the additional resource at a uniform rate for each Member State. Adding the difference between a

Table 14.3. Determination of the VAT and fourth own resource, 1996 (Ecu m.)

Member State	VAT own resource						Fourth resource		
	VAT own resource at uniform rate	Compensation for the UK	Total	VAT at 1.4%	Compensation for the UK to be added to the fourth resource	VAT own resources	Fourth resource at a uniform rate	Compensation for the UK not covered by VAT	Total fourth resource
Austria	1,086.7	128.1	1,214.8	1,219.0	–	1,214.8	727.7	–	727.7
Belgium	1,136.0	149.3	1,285.3	1,274.3	11.0	1,274.3	848.0	11.0	859.0
Denmark	677.7	93.1	770.8	760.2	10.6	760.2	528.8	10.6	539.4
Finland	521.1	68.7	589.8	584.5	5.3	584.5	390.4	5.3	395.7
France	7,126.1	845.0	7,971.1	7,993.7	–	7,971.1	4,799.3	–	4,799.3
Germany	12,106.0	757.5	12,863.5	13,580.0	–	12,863.5	7,493.6	–	7,493.6
Greece	599.1	65.3	664.3	672.0	–	664.3	370.7	–	370.7
Ireland[a]	315.9	31.6	347.5	354.4	–	347.5	179.6	–	179.6
Italy	4,460.4	637.8	5,098.2	5,003.5	94.7	5,003.5	3,622.4	94.7	3,717.1
Luxembourg[a]	100.6	10.1	110.7	112.9	–	110.7	57.2	–	57.2
Netherlands	1,824.8	214.0	2,038.8	2,046.9	–	2,038.8	1,215.4	–	1,215.4
Portugal[a]	588.4	58.9	647.3	660.0	–	647.3	334.5	–	334.5
Spain	2,508.6	303.7	2,812.2	2,814.0	–	2,812.2	1,724.4	–	1,724.4
Sweden	875.3	123.0	998.2	981.8	16.4	981.8	698.4	16.4	714.8
UK	5,865.8	–3,486.0	2,379.8	6,580.0	–	2,379.8	3,721.0	–	3,721.0
TOTAL	39,792.3	0	39,792.3	44,637.2	138.0	39,654.3	26,711.8	138.0	26,849.8

a VAT base capped at 55%.

Source: CEC (1996: 150, 151).

country's potential VAT contribution and the maximum VAT contribution at the 1.4 per cent rate then yields the total value of the fourth resource.

14.4. Expenditure

Expenditure by the EU may be broadly classified under two headings: compulsory expenditure and non-compulsory expenditure. The distinction is largely political and is closely tied to the division of budgetary power between the EP and the Council of Ministers, which together constitute the budgetary authority for the Community. Generally speaking, the division places expenditure made under the European Agricultural Guidance and Guarantee Fund (EAGGF) Guarantee Section and repayments and aid to Member States in the compulsory category, whilst classifying expenditure under the headings of structural funds and cohesion policies, appropriations for operations in the energy sector, and virtually all administrative expenditure as noncompulsory.

The importance of the distinction between these two categories of expenditure lies in the fact that, subject to certain constraints, the EP has the final say on non-compulsory spending. The limit to the EP's power in this respect was originally specified in Article 203(9) of the Treaty of Rome, as amended at Luxembourg in 1970. This agreement stated that the rate of increase of non-compulsory expenditure was limited to a 'statistical maximum rate' derived from a formula based upon three factors: the rate of growth in the EC, the rate of inflation, and the size of Member States' budgets. There was, however, a provision for this ceiling to be exceeded by agreement between the Council of Ministers and the EP. If the Council approved a draft budget which increased non-compulsory expenditure by more than half the 'maximum' rate of increase, the EP had the power to add further expenditure of up to one-half of the 'maximum' rate. The real maximum is therefore up to 50 per cent greater than the 'maximum' determined by the formula and, in effect, the Council of Ministers could restrain aggregate expenditure only by allowing the EP a significant say in deciding priorities for non-compulsory expenditure.[9]

Thus the budgetary system established by the Treaty of Rome had a strong bias towards increased spending. Between 1980 and 1989, for example, non-compulsory expenditure rose faster than the statistical maximum rate in every financial year except 1985.

In June 1988 the EC adopted the broad outlines of a financial reform—the Delors I package—in order to ensure a more orderly increase in expenditure and a better balance of spending across the various expenditure categories. The essence of the reform was to promote budgetary discipline by placing the objectives of the general budget within the context of a medium-term programme. The perspective was subsequently updated annually by the Commission at the beginning of the budgetary process,

Table 14.4. Financial perspective for 1993–1999, as agreed at the Edinburgh Summit (appropriations for commitments, Ecu m., 1992 prices)

Year	Common Agricultural Policy	Structural operations			Internal policy	External action	Reserves			Total appropriations			Own-resource ceiling (as % of GNP)
		Structural Funds	Cohesion Fund	Total			Monetary Reserve	Guarantee Reserve	Total reserves	for commitment	for payment	for payment as % of GNP	
1993	35,230	19,777	1,500	21,277	3,940	4,150	1,000	300	1,300	69,177	65,908	1.20	1.20
1994	35,095	20,135	1,750	21,855	4,084	4,200	1,000	300	1,300	69,944	67,036	1.19	1.20
1995	35,722	21,480	2,000	23,480	4,323	4,580	500	300	800	74,485	69,150	1.20	1.21
1996	36,364	22,740	2,250	24,990	4,520	4,860	500	300	800	75,224	71,290	1.21	1.22
1997	37,023	24,026	2,500	26,526	4,710	5,130	500	300	800	77,987	74,491	1.23	1.24
1998	37,697	25,690	2,550	28,240	4,910	5,580	500	300	800	80,977	77,249	1.25	1.26
1999	38,389	27,400	2,600	30,000	5,100	5,900	500	300	800	84,089	80,114	1.26	1.27

Source: CEC (1993: 382).

ceilings being adjusted in line with movements in GNP and prices, adjusted to take account of the actual conditions of implementation in the previous year, or revised on the basis of a proposal by the Commission.

The financial perspectives introduced by the Edinburgh agreement in 1992 continued the process of structural reform. Under the new perspectives, outlined in Table 14.4, expenditure was classified under five broad headings, with each being subject to specific annual expansion limits. The first heading, relating to agriculture, extended the principle of an agricultural guideline originally introduced in the Delors I package and which limited the annual rate of increase in agricultural expenditure to 74 per cent of the rate of growth of EU GNP in any period, to cover all expenditure under the reformed CAP. In contrast, increased expenditure was assigned to prioritized measures designed to assist the least-favoured regions of the EU and external action. Structural expenditure on cohesion measures, for example, was increased by 75 per cent from Ecu 21 billion in 1993 to Ecu 30 billion in 1999. This expenditure is organized under two main headings: Structural Funds, which are directed at Objective I regions where GNP is less than or equal to 75 per cent of the EU average; and a Cohesion Fund, which is specifically designed to help four Member States (Spain, Greece, Ireland, and Portugal) whose GNP is less than 90 per cent of the EU average and who have drawn up a programme for meeting the convergence criteria of the Treaty on European Union (TEU).

The Edinburgh agreement also increased the resources assigned to internal policies, largely covering expenditure on research and development and the encouragement and development of trans-European networks (TENs) in the areas of transport, energy, telecommunications, and environmental infrastructure, by around 30 per cent by 1999.[11] The TENs measures were aimed principally at promoting the interconnection and inter-operability of national infrastructure networks and at facilitating access to such networks. The measures recognize the fact that the provision of infrastructure on a purely national basis has resulted in insufficient cross-border connections, technical incompatibilities among national networks, and a failure to exploit systems economies. Action at the EU level is therefore desirable, since the volume of cross-border transport is expected to increase with developments in the single market and infrastructure bottlenecks would otherwise counter the benefits of increasing integration.

The fourth heading prioritized under the Edinburgh agreement was external action. Resources under this heading were set to increase by more than 40 per cent to Ecu 5.9 billion by 1999. Part of this increase, amounting to some Ecu 0.2 billion in 1993, rising to Ecu 0.3 billion in 1999, was designated as a new emergency aid reserve to cover the cost of unforeseen emergency relief over the period. Two other reserves were listed under the fifth heading: a Monetary Reserve which was designed to meet unforeseen budgetary overshoots, and a Guarantee Reserve which was created to finance an insurance fund against the risk of third-country default on loans guaranteed by the EU.

Summing across these headings and taking into account expenditure on administration yields the total level of appropriation for the EU. In any year these expenditures may be considered on an appropriations-for-commitment basis or, alternatively, be expressed in cash-flow terms as appropriations for payment. The payment figures, expressed as a percentage of GNP, may then be compared with the own-resource ceiling imposed by the Edinburgh agreement.

Details of payments made by the EU in 1994, classified by sector and recipient, are shown in Table 14.5.[12] Spending under each heading is assigned to Member States on the basis of the location of the relevant EU expenditure. The total allocated in this way accounts for some 85 per cent of the total budget, the remaining 15 per cent relating mainly to expenditure on overseas aid and administration.

Table 14.5. **Payments made in 1994, by sector and recipient Member State (Ecu m.)**

Member State	EAGGF Guarantee	EAGGF Guidance	ERDF	ESF	Admin.	Other	Total
Belgium	1,174.4	42.8	77.9	87.3	600.6	529.8	2,512.8
Denmark	1,287.9	66.6	14.8	38.7	3.7	85.4	1,495.1
France	8,048.8	384.1	460.8	453.3	23.0	554.6	9,924.5
Germany	5,271.6	476.0	726.8	611.9	24.0	619.0	7,729.2
Greece	2,723.5	332.4	912.0	444.6	3.1	428.7	4,844.2
Ireland	1,527.1	128.9	213.3	339.8	2.6	179.1	2,390.0
Italy	3,481.4	328.3	665.1	385.8	17.7	341.0	5,219.2
Luxembourg	12.7	6.6	3.0	4.0	303.6	89.2	419.1
Netherlands	1,935.9	31.3	60.0	173.1	17.1	198.6	2,416.0
Portugal	713.3	450.0	1,120.7	260.8	2.4	496.4	3,042.6
Spain	4,426.9	527.4	1,361.2	660.2	5.3	853.7	7,834.7
UK	3,001.9	121.4	788.6	685.4	46.7	614.7	5,258.6
Misc.	–	–	6.6	–	2,515.9	4,695.1	7,217.7
TOTAL	33,605.4	2,893.9	6,410.8	4,144.8	3,565.6	9,684.3	60,304.8

Source: CEC (1995: 17).

The largest category of expenditure is listed under the heading of the EAGGF Guarantee, which occurs as a result of the operation of the Common Agricultural Policy (CAP). This item of expenditure was introduced into the budget in April 1962 and is associated with the various types of intervention expenditure on agricultural markets, refunds on exports of agricultural products to non-member countries, and half of the expenditure connected with the set-aside programme. The next three columns reflect expenditure on structural operations conducted by the EU. These comprise the Guidance Section of the EAGGF (introduced in 1964), the European Regional Development Fund (ERDF) (introduced in 1975), and the European Social Fund (ESF) (introduced in 1958). Together they accounted for 22 per cent of the total budget in 1994. The essential purpose of all three funds is to promote better economic and social cohesion within the EU. In each case the EU contribution must be accompanied by national funding and so involves cooperation between the Commission and the Member States' authorities. Use of the Structural Funds is determined by five objectives

Robin Bladen-Hovell and Elizabeth Symons

which were set out in 1986 under the SEA. These objectives state that the Funds should contribute to: the promotion of the development and structural adjustment of the regions whose development is lagging behind; the conversion of regions seriously affected by industrial decline; the fight against long-term unemployment; the occupational integration of young people; and, finally, the adjustment of agricultural structures and development of rural areas.

Alongside these Funds, the EU also finances a series of other structural operations which have far smaller budgets. These include, for example, the Cohesion Fund which was established by the TEU and which began operation in 1993. Its objective is to strengthen economic and social cohesion by improving transport infrastructure and environmental protection in Ireland, Spain, Portugal, and Greece. In 1994 it financed a total of fifty-one projects in the four countries at a cost of Ecu 1,852 billion. These expenditures, together with spending on the common transport policy, the common fisheries policy, energy, technology, cooperation with developing countries, and administration, are collected together in column 7 of the table. A breakdown, by country, of expenditure under the Cohesion Fund is given in Table 14.6.

Table 14.6. **Commitment appropriations in 1993–1994, the Cohesion Fund**

Member State	Environment		Transport		Total breakdown	
	Ecu m.	%	Ecu m.	%	Ecu m.	%
Greece	198.1	59.7	134.0	40.3	332.1	17.9
Spain	519.3	51.0	498.9	49.0	1,081.2	55.0
Ireland	71.8	43.0	96.0	57.0	167.8	9.1
Portugal	134.2	40.0	200.1	60.0	334.3	18.0
Total	923.4	40.0	929.0	60.0	1,852.4	100.0

Source: CEC (1994: 26).

14.5. **The net balance**

Information similar to that contained in Sections 14.3 and 14.4 provides a basis for calculating the 'net contributions' of the individual Member States and can thereby be used to identify, at least at one level, the cross-country distributional incidence of the EU's budget. Official estimates of the net contribution begin by identifying those items of EU expenditure which may be allocated to the individual Member States. As indicated by Table 14.5, these comprise some 85 per cent of the total budget. On the revenue side, member states are assumed to contribute to this spending in proportion to their own-resource contributions that they make to the EU budget as a whole (see Table 14.2). The difference between the two values, expressed as a proportion of per capita

386

GDP for the individual Member States, then corresponds to a notion of formal incidence commonly adopted in the public-finance literature. The effect of using this calculation to rank EU members by their 'net contribution' in 1994 is shown in Fig. 14.2:
on this basis Luxembourg, Ireland, Portugal, and Greece appear as the main beneficiaries of the EU budget; Germany and the Netherlands were the main contributors. These
relative net contributions were similar to the figures reported for 1991 in the first edition.

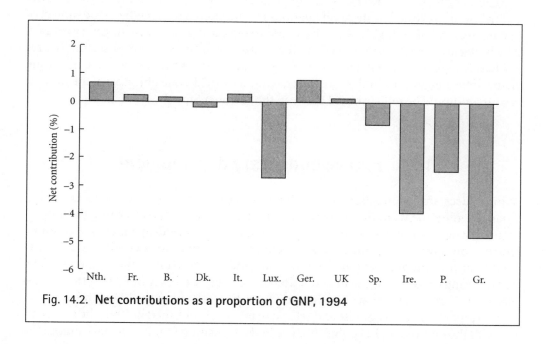

Fig. 14.2. **Net contributions as a proportion of GNP, 1994**

As is well known, however, calculations of cross-country distributive incidence of
this form are subject to a variety of theoretical and practical problems (see Ardy 1988).
At a practical level, for example, the assignment of EU revenue or expenditure may not
be a particularly good guide to the location of where either the benefits of spending or
the burden of taxes will be felt. This argument is most commonly made in the context
of the 'Rotterdam effect' in recording revenues received from customs duties. Goods
imported through major ports in the EU will pay duties at the point of entry, even if
they are subsequently consumed elsewhere in the EU. Similarly, agricultural export
subsidies may be recorded in a different Member State from the residence of the farmer
who produced the goods being exported.

The second objection is, in many respects, even more fundamental. A number of EU
measures have economic effects which are more far-reaching than simply the impact of
expenditure. EU intervention purchases of agricultural goods, for example, reduce

supply generally and hence increase prices throughout the EU, irrespective of where the intervention takes place. Where these EU-produced goods are traded between Member States, at prices higher than would otherwise prevail, real income transfers take place. Resource transfers arising through unbalanced agricultural trade within the EU, for instance, represent a significant component of the overall economic gains and losses to Member States of the CAP, and should, therefore, be considered at the same time as the resource flows associated with the formal incidence of the budget.

Whether the finances of the EU should take any formal account of the pattern of net contributions revealed by these calculations is a question which has been the subject of exhaustive, and often highly politicized, discussion during previous budgetary rounds. The budgetary problems of the UK in the 1980s may be considered to exemplify precisely this type of disagreement. As has been made clear in the discussion concerning many of the items of the budget, however, it may be a deliberate objective of the EU that resources should be redistributed between the Member States.

14.6. **Future budgetary developments**

Whilst successful completion of the Delors II agreement addressed the EU public-finance requirements in the short to medium term, questions concerning the longer-term role and structure of the budget remain. Both the deepening of economic integration across the EU and a reassessment of the functions to be conducted at the EU level require a reappraisal of the attendant size and composition of the EU budget. The approaching deadline for the introduction of the single currency in 1999 at the latest is also likely to move budgetary considerations to the forefront of the EU agenda.

Two reports addressing these and related issues were published in 1993, the first dealing with the question of EU public finance in the transition to full monetary union; the second dealing with the question of fiscal federalism and the appropriate use of the EU budget to further the successful operation of the emerging economic, social, and political union (see CEC 1993a, 1993b). The question of the potential use of the budget for EU-wide or regional stabilization within a prospective monetary union is central to both sets of discussions.

The *prima facie* case for increasing EU involvement in the management of economic activity is based upon the increasing interdependence of national economies through increasing trade, capital flows, and internationally transmitted inflationary impulses. The more closely integrated the EU becomes, the less effective will be national instruments of demand management. This problem is compounded by the fact that, within a monetary union, a single currency necessarily implies a single monetary policy, with consequent loss of national monetary autonomy to respond to country-specific conditions. Monetary union also carries implications for national fiscal policy. Linkages between the public-sector deficit and its financing, on the one hand, and the external balance, on the other, implies that budgetary policy across Europe will need to be harmonized.

The remedy typically proposed in these circumstances is to internalize the spillover effects between countries by pursuing the objectives of policy at a higher level of government, either through policy coordination, or by means of direct policy action. The latter would, of course, require that the EU budget assume an explicit stabilizing role.

The conventional wisdom in this respect as, for example, detailed in the MacDougall Report (CEC 1977), was that a successful transition to monetary union would require a substantial increase in the size of the budget—the MacDougall Report itself advocating a budget of between 5 and 7 per cent of EC GDP, with the larger budget being assigned to regional and counter-cyclical policies. Traditionally, the current budget has usually been considered too small to be effective for stabilization at the EU-wide level, a problem compounded by the prohibition on the EU running deficits. The multi-annual nature of budgetary programming within the EU also implies that the budget lacks the necessary flexibility to be used in a counter-cyclical manner. Indeed, because budget spending limits are expressed as ratios of EU GNP, the budget currently has a pro-cyclical bias at the aggregate level. Similarly, with the exception of specific-purpose significance in the case, for example, of Ireland, Portugal, and Greece, the budget's general redistributive capacity is weak. In the absence of auto-stabilizers or other shock-absorbing capabilities, the intra-EU redistributive capacity is largely determined by three factors: a country's contribution to EU VAT receipts; the share of agriculture in national GDP; and the intervention of Structural Funds. It is these three factors which effectively drive the net contributions for Member States shown in Fig. 14.2.

More recent consideration of this issue, however, has suggested that EU-wide stabilization would best be achieved through the coordination of national fiscal policies and that effective regional stabilization would be available at far smaller budgetary cost than considered in the MacDougall Report. Italianer and Vanheukelen (1993), for example, propose an automatic stabilization scheme based upon fluctuations in unemployment across Europe which would provide approximately the same degree of inter-regional stabilization as currently available in the USA at a budgetary cost of only 0.2 per cent of EU GDP.

The absence of an EU-wide role for the budget and an application of the subsidiarity principle would suggest that a budget of around 2 per cent of EU GDP would be compatible with economic and monetary union, even after allowing for the introduction of a small specific stabilizing element. However, some adjustment to the structure of EU expenditure would be required, particularly in the area of agriculture support, in order for this size of budget to be effective and able to respond to the challenge of a social union and the prospective enlargement of the EU to the east.

One important candidate for possible reform is CAP. Assistance under the CAP has until now primarily taken the form of price support, as distinct from direct income support unrelated to production. Although price support is cheaper to operate, it is well recognized as having a more damaging effect on economic welfare than income support, because it induces larger distortions to resource allocation on account of the fact that it influences consumption as well as production. Moreover, because it is linked to production, the benefits of CAP are narrowly based, with some 80 per cent of the current support accruing to only 20 per cent of farmers. Agricultural support would, therefore, become more effective in the future if CAP were switched to become a direct income support mechanism.

The principal disadvantage of such a change is the fact that, for any given level of assistance to the agricultural sector, the visible budgetary cost will be higher under an income support scheme. This is because the main mechanism operating in a price support mechanism is an income transfer from consumers to producers via the price mechanism. Recent evidence from the OECD, for example, estimates that 75 per cent of the cost of current agricultural assistance delivered under the CAP is borne by the consumer, with only 25 per cent appearing in the EU budget. Greater efficiency in agricultural support may, therefore, be possible only if agriculture expenditure were allowed to rise, at least in the short to medium term. In the longer term, of course, part of these higher budgetary outlays may be offset by the ability to target income support schemes more effectively.

In the longer term, the main determinants of the size of the budget are likely to be the requirements of social union and enlargement to the east. The main budgetary implications in the case of broadening EU membership to include countries in Eastern Europe, for example, derive from the Structural Funds. Quantifying the prospective size of these budgetary requirements is, however, fraught with difficulty in that it depends upon how economically backward such countries are at the time of accession, which in turn depends on the amount of assistance provided to them prior to that date. Calculations based upon the present per capita levels of cohesion assistance of some Ecu 200 per year to Greece and Portugal would suggest that an East European population of, say, 50 million would require assistance of approximately Ecu 10 billion, or 0.2 per cent of EU GDP. The magnitude of this prospective expenditure naturally implies that the size of future spending in favour of East European economies prior to these countries acceding to the Union is particularly important.

Funding these and other expenditures will, of course, require developments on the own-resource side of the budget. In this respect it is important to note that the original EC aspiration to be funded autonomously has largely failed, with the current system of funding carrying an additional defect arising from the regressive impact in relation to GDP that it imposes on poorer Member States.[13] The main cause of this regressivity is VAT. This is currently collected from Member States by means of a notional harmonized base which is relatively larger in countries with a high consumption ratio, which in practice turn out to be the poorer Member States. Whilst capping the VAT base at 55 per cent of a country's GDP effectively severs the indirect tax link in a number of countries since it implies a shift from VAT to GNP funding, advocates of the development of new own resources typically argue that any such development should take the process further and move in the direction of progressivity with respect to Member States' shares of financing the EU budget.

Candidates for new forms of own resources in this respect include the profits of the European Central Bank, the revenue from the application of a CO_2 emissions tax, and corporate taxes. Various criteria are used to determining the assignment of these resources to the EU level. In the case of the central bank profits,[14] for example, it is usually argued that the revenues would be difficult if not impossible to allocate between Member States except in an arbitrary manner; in the case of corporate taxes, the tax base is highly mobile, implying that a low tax rate in one country will erode the tax base in another country; or, in the case of a CO_2 emissions tax, the tax is the most effective means of achieving a collective EU policy objective of reducing CO_2 emissions.

The potential revenue generated from these new own resources would, of course, depend in part upon the rate at which the taxes were levied. Commission estimates, for example, suggest that a \$US10 per barrel CO_2 tax would generate revenue in excess of 1 per cent of EU GNP; corresponding calculations by the Bank of International Settlements suggests that Central Bank profits could give rise to further revenues of around 0.5 per cent of GNP. If implemented, such funding accruing at the EU level would prove to be more than adequate to meet the demands placed on the EU budget as the EU undertakes its next stage of development.

14.7. Conclusions

Despite its relatively small size, the budget has dominated debate within the EC and the EU for much of their forty-year history. Dispute over the control of expenditure and rivalry between the various institutions has frequently resulted in budgetary negotiations being conducted in an atmosphere of political crisis. Financial reforms which establish budgetary procedures that avoid such difficulties have therefore been a characteristic feature of EC and EU development for much of the period.

Existing budgetary arrangements were first established in 1988 and revised in 1992 as a means of overcoming many of these problems. By establishing a medium-term framework of financial perspectives and adding the fourth resource, the Delors I reform was able to stabilize expenditure and guarantee adequate finance for the budget. The Delors II package has extended these reforms and has relaxed the budgetary constraint still further in the run up to monetary union.

However, many budgetary issues remain unresolved. In particular, the role of the EU budget in promoting EU-wide and interregional stabilization is still far from clear. Current opinion appears to favour the idea that the former should be achieved by means of coordinated national budgetary policy action, whilst the prospective cost of providing the latter is sufficiently low as to make it possible within even a modestly expanded budget. Funding this budget will of course require the EU to be equipped with additional own resources. Estimates suggest that the prime candidates in this respect—notably a European CO_2 emissions tax and the profits of the European Central Bank—should provide more than adequate funds for this purpose.

Discussion questions

1. Explain briefly why a carbon tax, corporate taxes, and an ECB profits tax might sensibly form part of a new 'own resource' for the EU.

2. Outline the reasons for and against the use of the EU budget for counter-cyclical policy.

3. In 1988 the EC introduced a series of budgetary reforms. What was the central feature of these reforms and how were they intended to operate? How were these reforms modified by the Edinburgh Agreement of 1992?

FURTHER READING

The following references are recommended as supplementary reading to this chapter. A comprehensive discussion of prospective developments to the EU budget is provided in CEC (1993*b*). This comprises surveys, case-studies, and analysis relating to EU public finance, including a discussion of the issues surrounding fiscal federalism and what it might contribute to European development. For a review of existing EU policies and their budgetary consequences, see Wallace and Wallace (1996).

NOTES

1. Details of the agricultural policies followed by the EU are detailed in Chapter 4.
2. The preliminary draft budget is also subject to the limits set by the financial perspectives. These limits are discussed in Section 14.4.
3. Conversely, all other expenditure is non-compulsory. This definition was agreed in the joint declaration signed on behalf of the EC on 30 June 1982.
4. The EP rejected the draft budget on just three occasions. These rejections relate to the budgets of 1980, 1982, and 1985.
5. Agricultural levies in this context actually cover three sources of revenue. Agricultural levies in the strict sense relate to variable taxes charged within the framework of the Common Agricultural Policy (CAP) on imports of agricultural products from non-member countries. In addition, however, sugar levies are imposed on sugar companies which pay them either to cover expenditure on market support (production levies) or to regulate disposal (storage levies). A final category, isoglucose production levies, was introduced in May 1977 and serves the same purpose as the sugar levy, even though isoglucose is not an agricultural product.
6. In practice, the effective VAT rate was less than 1.4 per cent, owing to the UK refund.
7. In the Commission's original proposals, relaxation on the own resource ceiling would have increased the budget to 1.37 per cent of EU GNP by 1997.

8. Obviously the formula meant that the scale of the UK's abatement would vary from year to year as the pattern of revenue and expenditure varied across the EC.

9. Even the 'real maximum' is not a figure that the Treaty makes binding on the budgetary authority. By agreement, the Council and the EP (acting by a supermajority) may agree whatever rate of increase they wish, though this ability is now subject to an 'Inter-Institutional Agreement on budgetary discipline'.

10. The financial perspective for 1991, for example, was revised in 1990 in order to provide aid to Central and Eastern Europe and to take account of the financial consequences of German unification and the Gulf crisis. Details of the financial perspectives for the period 1988–92 were given in the first edition of this book.

11. Community financing of TENs is controversial. Three types of aid are available: feasibility studies, loan guarantees, interest rate subsidies and, by way of exception, cofinancing of certain projects. The largest element of this expenditure is allocated to transport TENs.

12. 1994 is the most recent year for which information about expenditure, classified in this way, is available.

13. That is, poorer Member States tend to pay more than their 'fair' GDP share.

14. These profits arise as a result of the European Central Bank's position as monopoly issuer of liabilities which carry low, or no, rate of interest. These liabilities make up the monetary base. The Central Bank's profits stem from the return on interest-bearing assets which form the counterpart to the monetary base.

REFERENCES

Ardy, B. (1988), 'The National Incidence of the European Community Budget', *Journal of Common Market Studies*, 26 (June) 401–29.

CEC (1977): Commission of the European Communities, *Report of the Study Group on the Role of Public Finance in European Integration*, i. General Report, ii. *Individual Contributions and Working Papers* (the MacDougall Report) (Economic and Financial Series, Nos. A13 and B13; Brussels: CEC).

—— (1987*a*), *The Single Act: A New Frontier for Europe*, COM (87) 100 (Brussels: CEC).

—— (1987*b*), *Report on the Financing of the European Communities Budget*, COM (87) 101 (Brussels: CEC).

—— (1992*a*), *Community Public Finance: The European Budget after the 1988 Reform* (Brussels: CEC).

—— (1992*b*), *From the Single Act to Maastricht and Beyond: The Means to Match our Ambitions*, COM(92)2000 (Brussels: CEC).

—— (1993*a*), *Stable Money—Sound Finances: Community Public Finance in the Perspective of EMU* (European Economy: Report and Studies No. 53; Brussels: CEC).

—— (1993*b*), *The Economics of Community Public Finance* (European Economy: Report and Studies, No. 5; Brussels: CEC).

—— (1994), *Financial Report of the European Community* (Brussels: CEC).

—— (1995), *Financial Report for the European Community* (Brussels: CEC).

—— (1996), *Official Journal of the European Communities*, L22, vol. 39 (Brussels: CEC).

Eichengreen, B. (1993), 'European Monetary Unification', *Journal of Economic Literature*, 31 (Sept.), 1321–57.

Italianer, A., and M. Vanheukelen (1993), 'Proposals for Community Stabilization Mechanisms: Some Historical Applications', in CEC (1993*a*).

Smith, S. (1992), 'The European Budget after 1992', Working Paper (London: Institute for Fiscal Studies).

Strasser, D. (1992), *The Finances of Europe: The Budgetary and Financial Law of the European Communities*, 7th edn. (Luxembourg: CEC).

Wallace, H., and Wallace, W. (1996), *Policy-Making in the European Union* (Oxford: Oxford University Press).

CHAPTER 15

Foreign Aid and External Assistance

FREDERICK NIXSON

15.1. Introduction

Foreign aid or economic assistance consists of transfers of real resources to less-developed countries (LDCs) on concessional terms. It excludes, by definition, purely commercial transactions, and should also exclude military aid, which, although it is non-commercial and concessional, does not have as its main objective the promotion of economic development. Aid raises a number of fundamental questions about development and underdevelopment and the relationship between rich and poor countries (although not all donor countries are rich: China has made substantial sums of aid available in the past to countries such as Tanzania). These include the following:

- Why do donors give aid?
- Why do poor countries accept aid?
- How should aid be given?
      loans versus grants
      tied aid versus untied aid
      bilateral versus multilateral aid
      project versus programme aid
- Which countries should be given aid?
- What is the impact of aid on the process of growth and development?
- What is the nature of the aid relationship?

Clearly, simple and straightforward answers cannot be given to these questions, and, even after fifty years of experience of aid, the debate continues (recent contributions to the debate include Cassen *et al.* 1986; Mosley 1987; Riddell 1987). Donors give aid for a number of reasons. Humanitarian motives may dominate, but more usually there are economic, political, and strategic factors that determine the amounts given and the countries selected by donors for assistance.

Equally, poor countries may accept aid for a variety of reasons—the urgency of the problems facing them, the domestic absence or shortage of the resources that aid can provide, the building-up of a relationship with a donor or group of donor countries for political reasons, and the role that aid can play in maintaining a particular regime in power and/or consolidating and extending its power.

Aid can be given in various forms—as grants or loans, technical assistance, or commodity (largely food) aid—and with various forms of conditionality attached. Aid may be given for a project (to build a road, for example) or be made available for a programme (e.g. in the transport sector). Bilateral aid is given by the aid agency of one country (the UK Overseas Development Administration, for example) to recipients in another. Multilateral aid (through the EU, the World Bank, or various UN agencies, for example) is usually considered to be superior to bilateral aid, as it avoids the problems that can arise in bilateral one-to-one relationships. Bilateral aid is normally tied (either to a particular project or programme and must be spent in the donor country); multilateral aid may be project- or programme-tied, but, by definition, it cannot be tied to a particular country.

Aid can be tied in various ways (Bhagwati 1967) through formal and informal restrictions, the use of export and import credits, and aid provided in the form of technical services and goods. There is general agreement that tied aid reduces its value to the recipient (lower-cost sources of supply in non-donor countries will not be allowed to bid for aid projects). Tied aid benefits donor-country enterprises and its extensive use has led in the past to allegations that aid policy is subservient to a donor country's commercial interests.

When we consider the effectiveness of aid, it is useful to refer to what Mosley (1987: ch. 5) has called the 'macro-micro paradox'. This refers to the apparent paradox that, whereas the microeconomic evaluation of aid projects is usually positive, there appears to be no statistically significant correlation, either positive or negative, between inflows of aid and the rate of growth of the recipient economy. Mosley (1987: 139–40) and White (1992) suggest various reasons why this situation exists—inaccurate measurement and fungibility within the public sector (that is, if certain conditions are satisfied, aid can never be completely tied to a specific project (see Singer 1965)), and backwash effects from aid-financed activities that affect adversely the private sector.

Our knowledge of the impact of aid on development—so defined as to include economic growth, structural change, and the move towards certain socio-economic goods (less poverty, more employment, greater life expectancy, etc.)—is thus piecemeal and incomplete. We cannot prove that aid is either necessary or sufficient for economic and social development or that the relationship between donor and recipient countries is either advantageous or disadvantageous to the latter. Despite their policy statements, the aid programmes of most bilateral donors are dominated by political and geo-strategic considerations. If humanitarian factors are not of the highest priority, it should not surprise us if we find it difficult to establish a positive causal connection between aid and development.[1]

15.2. EU development policy

The development policy of the EU has a number of distinct components which have evolved separately over time. The Lomé Conventions represent the oldest and most fully developed area and are the main focus of attention of this chapter (see Section 15.5). But the EU has also developed (i) a Mediterranean policy, based on a series of bilateral agreements,[2] (ii) a series of cooperation instruments linked to common policies (generalized trade preferences, participation in commodity agreements, food aid), and (iii) an aid system set up by the EU on a unilateral basis. This includes emergency aid given in the event of natural or other disasters, aid to non-governmental organizations (NGOs) working on development projects in the Third World, financial and technical contributions to development projects, and industrial cooperation by means of financial aid to enterprises.

The EU emphasizes the 'fundamental characteristics' of its development policy (Frisch 1992). These include

- contractual arrangements freely negotiated by the EU and African, Caribbean, and Pacific (ACP) economies;
- the creation of joint institutions to allow continuing dialogue; and
- the global approach to cooperation involving a wide range of instruments in the fields of both trade and aid.

In 1989 EC Development Cooperation commitments and payments accounted for less than 3 per cent of the EC budget (a fall of almost 50 per cent over the 1980s) (CEC 1990), and, as has been noted by a number of observers, development aid is only one, and perhaps not the most important, way in which the EU influences the development of both ACP economies in particular and Third World economies in general. The EU's commercial policy (the generalized system of preferences) and its Common Agricultural Policy (CAP), as well as the bilateral aid programmes of individual Member States, all exert powerful influences, and, even though we focus on aid in this chapter, these other influences should not be forgotten.

Although, as noted above, the focus of this chapter is on the Lomé Conventions, it should be noted that the EU gives significant amounts of aid to a number of non-ACP states, a point we return to in the discussion of Table 15.8 below.

With respect to the Lomé Conventions, the EU emphasizes the notions of equality and partnership (Lister 1992), although the notion of 'partnership' has been challenged by a number of commentators, and the aid relationship is a complex one, more in the realm of political economy than economics more narrowly defined. We note here the historical, cultural, commercial, and strategic factors which underlie relationships between rich and poor countries in general and the EU and ACP states in particular, and focus on only one aspect of those relationships: aid.

15.3. **A note on aid statistics: terms and definitions**

All members of the EU are members of the Organization for Economic Cooperation and Development (OECD). One of the specialized committees of the OECD is the Development Assistance Committee (DAC), the members of which have agreed 'to secure an expansion of aggregate volume of resources made available to developing countries and to improve their effectiveness'.

The Commission of the European Communities (CEC) takes part in the work of the OECD and is a member of the DAC. Greece is not a member of the DAC and it is therefore not included in the DAC aid tables. Greece does contribute, however, to EU aid programmes and multilateral institutions.

'Aid' or 'assistance' refers only to items which qualify as 'Official Development Assistance' (ODA)—that is, grants or loans

- undertaken by the official sector;
- with promotion of economic development or welfare as main objectives;
- at concessional financial terms (if a loan, at least 25 per cent grant element).

Technical cooperation is included in aid. It consists almost entirely of grants to nationals of developing countries receiving education or training at home or abroad and payments to defray the costs of teachers, administrators, advisers, and so on, serving in developing countries.

15.4. **The ODA record of EU Member States**

Total ODA from DAC countries to developing countries and multilateral organizations increased in 1994 to $US59 billion from $US56.5 billion in 1993. Allowing for price changes and changes in exchange rates *vis-à-vis* the US dollar, this represented an increase in real terms of 0.5 per cent.

Of the total of $US59 billion, the USA and Japan accounted for $US9.9 billion and $US13.2 billion respectively (all figures rounded). The fourteen EU members of the DAC accounted for $US30.4 billion—that is, approximately 51 per cent of the total (see Table 15.1).

Table 15.1. Net ODA from EU countries to developing countries and multilateral organizations, 1983–4 to 1994

Member State	Net disbursements at current prices and exchange rates $ million			Per cent of GNP			Change in percentage 1993/4			Annual average % change in volume[a] 1988/9–1993/4
	1983–4 average	1990	1994	1983–4 average	1990	1994	In national currency	In $	In volume terms[a]	
Austria	169	394	655	0.26	0.25	0.33	18.3	20.4	14.8	9.2
Belgium	463	889	726	0.58	0.46	0.32	–13.2	–10.4	–15.1	–2.0
Denmark	422	1,171	1,446	0.79	0.94	1.03	5.9	7.9	2.2	3.9
Finland	166	846	290	0.34	0.65	0.31	–25.4	–18.3	–27.2	–11.4
France	2,967	7,163	8,466	0.59	0.60	0.64	4.9	7.0	3.4	3.0
Germany	2,979	6,320	6,818	0.47	0.42	0.34	–3.8	–2.0	–6.0	1.5
Ireland	34	57	109	0.21	0.16	0.25	31.5	34.2	29.3	11.0
Italy	983	3,395	2,705	0.24	0.31	0.27	–8.8	–11.1	–11.7	–5.2
Luxembourg	6	25	59	0.12	0.21	0.40	16.1	19.9	13.4	19.4
Netherlands	1,232	2,538	2,517	0.96	0.92	0.76	–2.4	–0.3	–4.2	–1.2
Portugal	10	148	308	0.05	0.25	0.35	28.6	24.5	22.9	12.4
Spain	102	965	1,305	0.06	0.20	0.28	5.4	0.1	0.9	22.4
Sweden	747	2,007	1,819	0.82	0.91	0.96	1.9	2.9	–0.9	0.7
UK	1,520	2,638	3,197	0.34	0.27	0.31	7.4	9.5	5.2	0.6
Total EU	11,800	28,557	30,420	0.44	0.44	0.42	0.7	1.9	–1.6	1.3
Total DAC	27,450	52,961	59,152	0.34	0.33	0.30	2.1	4.7	0.5	0.5

a At 1993 exchange rates and prices.

Source: OECD (1995, A7–A8, table 4; A11–A12, table 6a).

Frederick Nixson

For DAC members as a whole, ODA as a proportion of GNP was 0.30 per cent in 1994. For the fourteen EU members, the equivalent figure was 0.42 per cent, ranging from 1.03 per cent for Denmark to 0.25 per cent for Ireland. This ratio has remained remarkably stable over recent years, although Austria, Denmark, France, Ireland, Luxembourg, Portugal, Spain, and Sweden have registered increases from the mid-1980s to the mid-1990s and Belgium, Finland, Germany, Italy, the Netherlands, and the UK have registered falls.

The accession to the EU of Austria, Sweden, and Finland in 1995 was seen as a positive move as far as development cooperation was concerned. In 1994 their total ODA amounted to $US2.8 billion (Table 15.1), with Sweden alone contributing $US1.8 billion. The Finnish aid programme suffered massive cutbacks in the 1990s, although Finland has made efforts to improve the quality and the impact of its aid (OECD 1995: 108).

The annual average change in the real value (at 1993 prices) of ODA over the period 1988/9–1993/4 was 0.5 per cent for all DAC members and 1.3 per cent for the fourteen EU members. Belgium, Finland, Italy, and Portugal registered negative growth over this period. The real value of the UK's ODA fell over the 1980/1–1990/1 period but grew slightly in the 1990s. The EU average annual growth rate was higher than that for all DAC countries, in part because of the zero and negative growth in ODA of Japan and the USA respectively over the 1988/9–1993/4 period (OECD 1995: A11–A12, table 6a). The countries with the highest growth rates—Austria, Ireland, Luxembourg, Portugal, and Spain—started from low bases, and, with the exception of Spain in 1994, were relatively small donors.

A variety of burden-sharing indicators is given in Tables 15.1 and 15.2. Table 15.1 includes data on ODA as a share of GNP, and we can note that in 1994 only Denmark, the Netherlands, and Sweden exceeded the UN target of a 0.7 per cent ODA/GNP ratio. Of the three largest donors in absolute terms, only the French ratio of ODA to GNP has risen over the 1980s and 1990s. In the case of Germany and the UK, the ratio has fallen, although there has been some rise in the ratio for the UK in the 1990s. That the EU average is above that of the DAC as a whole is largely owing to the very poor burden-sharing indicators of the two largest global donors—Japan (an ODA/GNP ratio of 0.29 in 1994) and the USA (an ODA/GNP ratio of 0.15 in 1994).

Table 15.2 gives details of two further burden-sharing indicators—the grant equivalent of ODA as a percentage of GNP and ODA per capita of the donor country. The latter set of figures allows us to make some interesting comparisons. France is the largest EU donor, both in absolute and per capita terms. But Germany, the second largest donor in absolute terms, is behind Luxembourg, Denmark, and Sweden in per capita terms. The UK and Italy, the third and fourth largest EU donors in absolute terms, are amongst the lowest donors in per capita terms, ahead only of Spain and Portugal.

Another burden-sharing indicator is aid appropriations as a percentage of the central government budget. In a period of general budgetary constraint, aid budgets are

Table 15.2. **Burden-sharing indicators, net disbursements, various years**

Member State	Grant equivalent of total ODA[a] as % GNP (1993–4 average)	ODA per capita of donor country (1993 $)		Multilateral ODA as % of GNP[b] (1993–4 average)
		1983/4	1993/4	
Austria	0.31	50	73	–
Belgium	0.36	102	75	0.15
Denmark	n.a.	171	260	0.45
Finland	0.38	52	60	–
France	0.63	110	279	0.14
Germany	0.36	81	166	0.13
Ireland	0.23	16	52	0.11
Italy	0.30	34	50	0.10
Luxembourg	0.38	n.a.	272	0.13
Netherlands	0.86	160	162	0.24
Portugal	n.a.	n.a.	28	0.09
Spain	0.25	n.a.	33	0.09
Sweden	0.97	159	201	–
UK	0.32	46	52	0.14
DAC average	0.31	69	77	0.09

Note: n.a. = not available.

  [a] Calculated on a gross disbursement basis.

  [b] Including CEC. Capital subscriptions are on a deposit basis.

Source: OECD (1995: A13–A14, table 7).

often vulnerable and aid expenditures are amongst the first items to be cut. The unweighted average for all DAC countries in 1990 was 1.8 per cent. For twelve DAC members only this figure fell to 1.45 per cent as an average for 1992–3 (OECD 1994: B3–B4, table 7). Over the period 1980–90, ODA as a proportion of the central government budget fell in Belgium, Germany, the Netherlands, and the UK. Only in the case of France and Italy was there a slight rise over the whole decade, and even that masked a fall between 1985 and 1990 (OECD 1992: 90, table V-4).

Finland is a dramatic example of a country undergoing large cuts in its aid budget. Finland's bilateral ODA fell from $US586 million in 1991 to $US214 in 1994, representing a fall from 0.8 per cent of GNP to 0.31 per cent over the period. What the OECD (1995: 108) has called an 'unprecedented' fall was in large part the result of new funding obligations arising from Finland's accession to the EU, claims made for and by the Central and Eastern European Countries (CEECs) and the New Independent States of the former Soviet Union (NIS) and the severe economic difficulties in Finland following the break-up of the USSR.

Although it is recognized that multilateral institutions have a key role to play in the development process, most donor countries, for the reasons outlined above, prefer to maintain direct control over their aid programmes through bilateral relationships. The early to mid-1970s saw a significant expansion in the role of multilateral aid, including a major expansion of aid from EC members through EC programmes. In the later half of the 1970s, the proportion of ODA channelled through multilateral institutions levelled off, and in the 1980s the proportion, expressed as a percentage of GNP, actually declined (OECD 1992: 42, table V-5). Multilateral ODA as a percentage of GNP is detailed in the last column of Table 15.2 and further details of EU Member States' contributions to multilateral organizations in 1994 are given in Table 15.3.

Table 15.3. **ODA from EU countries to multilateral organizations, 1994**

Member State	Total		CEC ($m.)		CEC as % total multilateral aid	CEC as % total net ODA
	$m.	% of total net ODA	Total	of which EDF		
Austria	120	18.3	—	—	—	—
Belgium	291	40.1	197	84	67.7	27.1
Denmark	643	44.5	95	44	14.8	6.6
Finland	76	26.2	—	—	—	—
France	1,855	21.9	915	512	49.3	10.8
Germany	2,674	39.2	1,413	554	52.8	20.7
Ireland	53	48.6	37	12	69.8	33.9
Italy	870	32.2	613	278	70.5	22.7
Luxembourg	19	32.2	10	—	—	—
Netherlands	816	32.4	279	119	34.2	11.1
Portugal	93	30.2	69	19	74.2	22.4
Spain	450	34.5	334	131	74.2	25.6
Sweden	446	24.5	—	—	—	—
UK	1,435	44.9	746	352	52.0	23.3
TOTAL EU	9,841	32.3	4,708	2,105	47.8	15.6
TOTAL DAC	17,864	30.2	—	—		

Note: A dash indicates a nil or negligible amount.

Source: OECD (1995: A39–A40, table 23; A7–A8, table 4).

Column 2 of Table 15.3 gives the percentage of total net ODA going to multilateral organizations. In 1994, the EU average was 32.3 per cent, with Ireland channelling nearly 49 per cent of its ODA through multilateral organizations and France 22 per cent. The UK's figure of approximately 45 per cent is the highest for the larger EU donors.

The middle two columns of Table 15.3 give details of ODA which is channelled through the Commission of the European Communities (CEC) and the European Development Fund (EDF) in particular. As is to be expected, Germany, France, the UK, and Italy are the largest absolute contributors both to the CEC and the EDF.

The fifth column shows the CEC's share of the multilateral aid of EU donors. For the smaller donors, it is perhaps not surprising that they choose to channel a significant proportion of their multilateral aid through the CEC. Ireland, Spain, Portugal, and Belgium are notable in this respect. But Italy too channels just over 70 per cent of its multilateral aid through the CEC, as compared to a figure for the UK of 52 per cent.

A slightly different picture emerges when we consider the final column of Table 15.3. France, the largest absolute EU donor, not only channels the smallest proportion of its total net ODA through multilateral bodies (Column 2), but also devotes the smallest proportion of total net ODA to the CEC. The UK, on the other hand, devotes approximately 45 per cent of its total net ODA to multilateral bodies, compared to the EU average of 32.3 per cent[3] with over 23 per cent of net ODA going to the CEC. It is clear from these figures that France exercises greater bilateral control over its aid programme than does the UK, and that only three relatively small donors—Spain, Ireland, and Belgium—contribute a larger share of total net ODA to the CEC than does the UK (Italy is roughly similar to the UK in this respect). Of the other EU members, Denmark and the Netherlands are relatively small donors in percentage terms to the CEC, and Ireland and Luxembourg are relatively small donors in absolute terms.

Table 15.4 gives an indication as to the relative global importance of the EU as a multilateral institution. In 1994 it provided $US4.3 billion of concessional finance, an increase of $US694 million over 1993. As a proportion of total concessional finance available, the EU accounted in 1994 for 22.8 per cent, representing a small increase over 1993 but a fall compared to 1992. Given that the EU on average supplies over 20 per cent of global multilateral concessional finance, it is a multilateral institution of some importance.

Table 15.4. **Net disbursements of concessional and non-concessional flows by CEC (at current prices and exchange rates)**

Year	Net disbursements				
	$ million			As % of total flows of multilateral organisations	
	Concessional	Non-concessional		Concessional	Non-concessional
1970–1	203	34		17.2	4.1
1975–6	591	42		15.4	1.6
1980	1,043	257		13.4	5.3
1988	2,508	56		22.5	0.9
1989	2,420	121		19.5	1.7
1990	2,563	264		19.0	2.6
1991	3,478	154		21.5	2.3
1992	4,170	582		23.8	15.5
1993	3,637	3		22.0	0.04
1994	4,331	7		22.8	0.19

Source: OECD (1995: A41–A42, table 25).

Frederick Nixson

Non-concessional lending tended to stagnate in the late 1980s and has since fluctu-ated dramatically from year-to-year—see, for example, the huge increase in 1992 and the even greater decrease in 1993. In part this stagnation and instability has been the consequence of recipient countries with severe economic problems cutting back on investment projects as a result of the implementation of structural adjustment pro-grammes (OECD 1991: 119).

As noted above, aid can be either tied or untied. The tying of aid has always been a controversial topic, with critics arguing that tying reduces the value of aid and lowers its 'quality'. The other determinant of the 'quality' of aid is its grant element. This reflects the financial terms of a commitment: interest rate, maturity (interval to final repay-ment), and grace period (interval to first repayment of capital). The grant element measures the concessionality—that is, the softness—of a loan. The market rate of inter-est is conventionally taken to be 10 per cent. The grant element of a loan is thus nil for a loan with an interest rate of 10 per cent or higher and, by definition, the grant element of a grant is 100 per cent. The grant element will lie in between these two limits for a soft loan. Although maturity and grace periods are important, it is the interest rate that is the major determinant of the softness of a loan (OECD 1992: A-99–100).

The data in Table 15.5 show that EU Member States in general score highly with respect to the concessionality of their aid, with high grant elements in all cases,

Table 15.5. **Financial terms of ODA commitments, 1981–2 and 1993–4 averages**

Member State	Grant element of total ODA (norm 86%)		% bilateral ODA untied[a]
	1981–2 average	1993–4 average	1993
Austria	57.1	87.6	36.3
Belgium	98.0	(83.9)	n.a.
Denmark	95.4	—	n.a.
Finland	95.8	98.9	46.5
France	85.0	88.4	23.5
Germany	86.2	92.2	33.0
Ireland	100.0	100.0	—
Italy	90.1	97.4	19.6
Luxembourg	100.0	100.0	—
Netherlands	94.3	99.9	n.a.
Portugal	—	—	42.6
Spain	—	(83.9)	n.a.
Sweden	99.4	99.9	22.4
United Kingdom	98.4	98.2	18.8
TOTAL DAC	89.2	90.8	38.4

Notes: Parentheses indicate a secretarial estimate in whole or in part. A dash indicates a nil or negligible amount.

n.a. = not available.

[a] Fully and freely available for essentially worldwide procurement.

Source: OECD (1995: A47, table 28; A50, table 31).

although the estimates for Belgium and Spain are below the OECD norm of 86 per cent. They do less well, however, with respect to the tying of aid. In 1993 only three small donors—Austria, Finland, and Portugal—and Germany had one-third or more of their bilateral aid untied (multilateral aid, by definition, cannot be tied to individual donor countries). In 1990 both France and the Netherlands had more than one-third of aid untied, but the proportion had fallen dramatically by 1993 (OECD 1992: A-15, table 6).[4] Changes in policy and performance over time in individual donor countries are a reflection of changes in political administration, changing budgetary priorities, and the result of policy reviews and changing priorities.

The major uses of EU ODA are shown in Table 15.6. Social and administrative infrastructure is the largest sector receiving aid, taking 30 per cent of the total in 1992/3, above the average for the DAC as a whole. The directly productive sectors of the economy—agriculture and industry and other production—received less than 20 per cent of total commitments in 1992/3, slightly above the DAC average. Programme assistance has increased in relative importance in recent years, in part reflecting changed EU priorities (see section on structural adjustment below).

As far as variations between EU members are concerned, of the largest donors, France devotes the largest proportion of its aid budget to social and administrative infrastructure and is more committed to programme assistance. In the case of the UK, it is clear that there has been a shift in sectoral priorities, over the period covered in Table 15.6, from industry and other productive activities to social and administrative infrastructure.

The final point to be considered in this general overview relates to the geographical distribution of EU aid. The regional distribution is given in Table 15.7; Sub-Saharan Africa remains the major recipient of EU aid, although its share has fallen since the early 1970s. It is important to note the difference between gross disbursement (the total amount disbursed or spent over a given accounting period) and net disbursements (gross disbursements less any repayments of loan principal during the same period). In general, gross disbursements for Sub-Saharan Africa (Table 15.8 gives details for individual countries on a gross basis) are greater than net disbursements (Table 15.7).

Concern has been expressed in the Third World that the changes that have occurred in Eastern Europe and the former Soviet Union will cause a diversion of aid from developing countries conventionally defined. Some of the countries of the former Soviet Union, such as the Central Asian Republics, have similar characteristics to developing countries. A small number of countries have been added to the list of aid recipients, including Albania, Kazakstan, Kyrgyzstan (now the Kyrgyz Republic), Tajikistan, Turkmanistan, Uzbekistan, Armenia, Georgia, and Azerbaijan. From 1993, Central and Eastern European Countries/New Independent States of the former Soviet Union (CEEC/NIS) countries in transition have been included in Part II of a new list of aid recipients (excluding those countries listed above;) (OECD 1995: 126–7, A101).[5] In general, DAC members have argued that so far there has been very limited aid diversion and it is difficult to predict how important an issue this will become in the future.

Table 15.6. Major aid uses by individual EU members, 1975–6 to 1992–3 (% of total commitments)

Member States	Social and administrative		Economic infrastructure		Agriculture		Industry and other production		Food aid		Programme assistance		Other	
	1975–6	1992–3	1975–6	1992–3	1975–6	1992–3	1975–6	1992–3	1975–6	1992–3	1975–6	1992–3	1975–6	1992–3
Austria	7.0	15.9	0.7	15.9	3.3	1.6	25.2	6.1	–	0.6	–	0.3	63.7	59.6
Belgium	3.8	34.6	0.9	4.4	2.1	11.6	1.3	9.4	2.2	2.9	0.9	1.0	88.9	36.1
Denmark	14.0	41.8	–	7.2	11.4	6.7	24.4	2.0	3.4	–	8.2	4.5	38.6	37.7
Finland	10.9	17.1	8.8	10.0	3.5	13.5	11.0	12.7	7.3	0.4	–	1.8	58.5	44.5
France	53.7	36.1	13.0	12.1	7.0	8.1	16.6	5.3	1.1	0.5	5.1	13.8	3.6	24.2
Germany	23.4	24.5	17.7	16.9	7.6	6.6	17.7	6.8	3.1	2.4	2.6	4.6	28.0	38.3
Ireland	–	47.9	–	8.3	–	5.9	–	5.9	–	2.9	–	–	100.0	29.0
Italy	14.0	14.4	2.0	17.2	2.9	7.0	28.4	7.4	–	5.4	–	3.1	52.6	45.5
Luxembourg	–	19.4	–	6.9	–	15.1	–	3.3	–	7.6	–	–	–	47.7
Netherlands	36.4	25.1	10.7	6.0	20.9	17.1	10.7	1.8	3.0	3.7	0.6	5.8	17.7	40.6
Portugal	–	15.0	–	2.7	–	0.5	–	1.1	–	–	–	3.1	–	77.5
Spain	–	24.3	–	44.4	–	1.5	–	18.4	–	0.8	–	–	–	10.8
Sweden	22.2	29.0	2.5	12.0	9.0	11.8	14.7	2.9	8.4	0.1	0.9	5.8	42.2	38.4
UK	4.8	30.1	3.4	15.8	4.3	11.0	54.4	7.2	1.8	2.9	5.0	11.9	26.3	21.1
TOTAL DAC	20.1	24.6	10.2	17.6	8.1	8.2	13.7	6.3	13.1	3.0	5.9	12.0	28.9	28.4

Note: A dash indicates a nil or negligible amount.

Source: OECD (1995: A43–A44, table 26).

Table 15.7. Regional distribution of ODA, 1983–4 to 1993–4 (% of net disbursements, two-year average)

Region	1983/4	1993/4
Sub-Saharan Africa	36.3 (24.3)	47.4 (37.8)
South and Central Asia	24.5 (24.8)	10.7 (13.6)
Other Asia and Oceania	15.6 (18.4)	16.9 (22.4)
Middle East and North Africa	13.3 (20.2)	12.4 (14.5)
Latin America and Caribbean	10.3 (12.3)	12.7 (11.8)

Notes: Includes imputed multilateral flows. Excludes Europe and unspecified. Figures in brackets are for all DAC ODA.

Source: OECD (1995: A68, table 41).

Table 15.8 gives details of the major EC/EU aid recipients over the period of the 1970s to 1990s. Two points deserve special mention. First the percentage of total ODA accounted for by the fifteen largest recipients has fallen dramatically, from almost 67 per cent of the total in 1970/1 to 35.5 per cent in 1993/4. Secondly, there have been significant changes in the country composition of the 'top' fifteen recipients. Three 'new' recipients appear in the list—the States of Ex-Yugoslavia, South Africa (previously the Black Communities of South Africa), and Palestinian Administered Areas, reflecting political changes that have occurred over the past few years. Five of the recipients in the 'top' fifteen (The States of Ex-Yugoslavia, Morocco, Egypt, Palestinian Administered Areas, and Bangladesh) are not ACP member states, yet together they accounted in 1993/4 for over 16 per cent of EU gross disbursements. This emphasizes the point made above (Section 15.2) that, although most attention is given to ACP member states, the EU has wider interests which encompass South Asia, the Middle East, and, to a more limited extent, Latin America.

Egypt, the largest recipient of EU aid in 1990/1, had dropped to fourth place in 1993/4. Egypt remains, however, the largest individual recipient of total DAC aid (5.0 per cent of the total in 1993/4) and the second largest recipient, after Israel, of US aid (OECD 1995: A82–A83, table 42). Another notable change is the disappearance of India from the 'top' fifteen, even though it remains the fourth largest recipient of total DAC aid (1993/4).

The geographical distribution of aid thus reflects a mixture of historical relationships, contemporary geo-political realities, commercial interests, and humanitarian concerns. The EU, as a major multilateral donor, is perhaps less partisan than major bilateral donors (the USA and France, for example), but the geographical distribution of its aid nevertheless reflects its perceptions of regional and global interests.

Table 15.8. **Major recipients of EC/EU aid, 1970–1 to 1993–4 (% of total ODA, gross disbursements)**

1970–1		1980–1		1993–4	
Country	Aid	Country	Aid	Country	Aid
Cameroon	9.0	India	9.6	Sts. of Ex-Yugoslavia	6.5
Zaire	8.4	Sudan	4.1	Morocco	4.5
Senegal	8.2	Egypt	3.6	Ethiopia	3.4
Madagascar	6.1	Bangladesh	3.5	Egypt	2.3
Côte d'Ivoire	4.9	Senegal	3.4	Zambia	2.1
Burkina Faso	4.2	Somalia	3.1	Mozambique	2.0
India	3.7	Ethiopia	3.0	Côte d'Ivoire	1.9
Niger	3.5	Zaire	2.8	Tanzania	1.8
Mali	3.3	Mali	2.7	Zimbabwe	1.7
Gabon	3.0	Tanzania	2.6	Nigeria	1.7
Chad	3.0	Kenya	2.4	South Africa	1.7
Turkey	2.8	Zambia	1.9	Palestinian adm. areas	1.6
Togo	2.7	Madagascar	1.9	Burkina Faso	1.5
Algeria	2.2	Guinea	1.7	Cameroon	1.4
Benin	2.2	Rwanda	1.6	Bangladesh	1.4
Total above	66.9	Total above	47.9	Total above	35.5
Multilateral ODA	0.0	Multilateral ODA	0.0	Multilateral ODA	9.0
Unallocated	3.6	Unallocated	10.3	Unallocated	12.4
TOTAL ODA ($US m.)	203	TOTAL ODA ($US m.)	1,244	TOTAL ODA ($US m.)	4,550

Source: OEDC (1995: A84, table 42).

15.5. **The Lomé Conventions**

Historical background

The Lomé Convention between the fifteen Member States of the EU and the seventy ACP states represents the main framework within which cooperation between the EU and the Third World takes place.

Of the seventy ACP states (sixty-eight original members with Namibia joining at independence in April 1990 and Eritrea after it achieved independence from Ethiopia in 1993), forty-seven are from Africa, fifteen are from the Caribbean, and eight are from the Pacific. A number of overseas countries and territories (OCTs) (particularly those of the UK and France) remain a part of the system.

When the Treaty of Rome was signed in 1957, most of the countries that now constitute the ACP were still colonies. The Treaty of Rome provided for an element of aid to these colonies, however, in the form of an implementing Convention added to the

Treaty. It provided for a form of unilateral association between the EC and its Member States and OCTs through which trade and aid links could be maintained.

The first EDF was established in 1958 and gave grants for economic and social infra-structure projects largely in French-speaking OCTs. The 1960s was a decade of decolonization, and in 1963 the Yaounde (Cameroon) Convention was signed between the EC6 and eighteen now-independent African countries (including Madagascar). A second EDF was established to give loans as well as grants, and the Convention included provisions for preferential trade arrangements and for the provision of financial and technical assistance. The Second Yaounde Convention was signed in 1969, with a third EDF.

In January 1973 the UK joined the EC and some twenty Commonwealth countries were included in the protocol to the Act of Accession, opening the way to the negotiation of some form of special relationship with the EC—an opportunity also offered to those independent states in Africa that were neither members of the Commonwealth nor members of the AASM grouping (Association of African States and Madagascar) which had negotiated the Yaounde Conventions).

After a period of some uncertainty as to how newly independent ACP countries would view their position *vis-à-vis* Europe, the first Lomé Convention was signed in February 1975 in Togo, and, in June 1975, forty-six ACP countries institutionalized themselves as a group with a permanent structure.

Lomé I has been described as a 'partnership of equals' and a number of joint institutions were created to administer the Convention. It introduced Stabex—a system designed to stabilize commodity earnings (see below)—and, at a time of stalemate in the global negotiations aimed at the creation of a New International Economic Order (NIEO), it 'appeared to offer an opportunity for a group of industrialised and developing countries to break out of the impasse . . . to establish a regional arrangement that would incorporate a number of items on the NIEO agenda' (Stevens 1990: 77).

The optimism that characterized Lomé I was shown to be premature by events that followed the first oil-price shock of 1973–4. A brief boom in some primary commodity prices was followed by the second oil-price shock of 1979–80. The Sub-Saharan economies in particular were hard hit by global economic instability and began a period of stagnant or falling per capita incomes from which the majority of African economies have not yet recovered.

Lomé II was signed in 1980, with a larger EDF and a Sysmin facility (see below), but was regarded as disappointing by the ACP. Lomé III was signed in 1985, as the 'decade of structural adjustment' (see below) was beginning to emerge. Lomé III made a commitment to 'self-reliant development' on the basis of food security and self-sufficiency, enhanced by a broad-ranging 'policy dialogue' between EC Member States and the ACP states. Stabex conditionality was tightened up (see below), however, and policy dialogue increasingly encompassed involvement in macroeconomic policy-making through the provision of resources through programmes of structural adjustment.

Stevens (1990: 84) argues that the first three Lomé Conventions did not lead to a radical transformation in the economies of the ACP. Lomé aid has been widely criticized on two counts: (i) it has been poorly used, financing projects either poorly designed or whose possibilities of success have been weakened by a hostile policy environment, and (ii) aid has been badly administered by the donor, with slow rates of disbursement. Donor procedures are allegedly slow and cumbersome, with duplicated appraisal procedures, over-centralization, and 'meddling' by Member States (Stevens 1990: 85).

In addition, it was argued that the 'aid relationship' had changed over time, with the EC attempting to impose a more orthodox donor recipient relationship than was initially felt either necessary or desirable. 'Policy dialogue' had increasingly come to mean a shift in the balance of power for aid decision-making towards the EC to give it a greater voice in the selection of aid-financed projects and sectoral policies relevant to the success of those projects (Stevens 1990: 84).

Lomé IV

The Fourth Lomé Convention was signed in December 1989. For the first time it covered a period of ten years, although the Financial Protocol covered the first five years only with mandatory renewal provided for at the end of that time.

The negotiations in 1989 anticipated the possibility of reviewing the actual text of the Convention midway through its term. This was not to be a global renegotiation and the emphasis was to be on a few essential points of mutual concern to the treaty partners. The mid-term review negotiations opened in May 1994 and were completed in June 1995. The results were formalized in the agreement signed in Mauritius in November 1995. The full text of the revised Lomé IV Convention is published in the *Courier* (1966).

The 1990 Convention highlighted new areas of development aid policy which had been somewhat neglected in the previous conventions:

(a) protection of the environment: the control of desertification and a commitment to ensure that economic and social development was based on a sustainable balance between economic objectives, management of natural resources, and improvement of human resources;

(b) agricultural cooperation and food security: the emphasis was on the regional dimension of food security policies and the role of women in rural development;

(c) industry and services: industrial cooperation and the promotion of services that support economic development were given new prominence. Such services included support for external trade, promotion of tourism, and development of transport and communications and information technology.

(d) cultural and social cooperation: this was extended to new issues such as population, nutrition, and women in development;

(e) other provisions in Lomé IV included a special programme of aid to the countries of Sub-Saharan Africa which had low incomes and large debts and specific measures to assist the least-developed landlocked and island ACP states. As in previous conventions, there were provisions for emergency aid for the victims of natural disasters, refugees, and repatriated persons.

The review of the Lomé IV provisions was classified under four headings: institutional and political; thematic and sectoral; commercial; and financial (*Courier* 1996: 8).

With respect to institutional and political issues, a statement was incorporated into Article 5 referring to the recognition and application of democratic principles, the consolidation of the rule of law and good governance. Observance of human rights and respect for democracy and the rule of law are now regarded as essential elements of the Convention and if one of these principles is violated, procedures exist with a view to remedying the situation.

Thematic and sectoral issues covered a range of activities including cultural cooperation, industrial cooperation, decentralized cooperation, maritime transport, and Stabex (considered below).

Finance

With respect to finance, a new Financial Protocol covering the period 1995–2000 was agreed (Table 15.9). An overall amount of Ecu 14.6 billion was negotiated, an increase of 22 per cent in Ecu terms *vis-à-vis* the first period (Ecu 12 billion) and an increase of 49 per cent expressed in dollar terms. Apart from the funds managed by the European Investment Bank (EIB), all financing is in the form of grants.

Programmable aid remains the central feature of ACP–EU cooperation, representing the largest single component of the EU's financial contribution to the ACP member states. The attempt is made to make it available on a reasonably predictable basis, within the context of an on-going dialogue between the EU and the recipient ACP member state. The EU defines its own development objectives in Annex IIIa (Community declaration on Article 4 (*Courier* 1996: 179). Reference is made to sustainable economic and social development in developing countries, poverty alleviation, the smooth and gradual integration into the world economy of ACP states, the promotion of the private sector, and the development and consolidation of democracy and respect for human rights and fundamental liberties. These objectives are combined with the development strategy of each ACP member state. The latter will draw up a draft indicative programme and will then reach agreement with the EU on the actual indicative programme, taking into account the total programmable resources made available by the EU. The indicative programme agreed by the two parties had to be adopted within twelve months of the signing of the second financial protocol (October 1996 at the latest).

Table 15.9. Lomé IV Conventions: Financial Protocol, 1995–2000 (Ecu m.)

EDF funding			12,967
of which			
* Stabex		1,800	
* Sysmin		575	
* Grants		9,592	
of which			
Structural adjustment[1]	1,400		
Emergency/refugee assistance	260		
Interest–rate subsidies	370		
Regional cooperation	1,300		
Other grants	6,262		
* Risk Capital		1,000	
EIB funding			1,658
Total funding			14,625

Resources specifically allocated to structural adjustment. Part of the national programme monies may also be allocated for this purpose.

Note: In addition to the Ecu 14,625 allocated to ACP states, a sum of Ecu 200 m. has been earmarked for overseas countries and territories.

Source: Courier (1996: 12).

Structural adjustment

In very broad terms, structural adjustment is a set of policies designed to reduce internal and external imbalances in an economy. Whereas stabilization policies are largely concerned with the reduction in aggregate demand, structural adjustment focuses on the increase in aggregate supply. Both sets of policies complement each other and both share many common elements—more liberal trade policy (removal of quantitative restrictions, reduction in tariffs), improved resource mobilization and allocation (through fiscal and monetary reform, removal of subsidies, reform of public enterprises, reform of agricultural sector pricing policies), and institutional reforms.

The Lomé IV provisions that cover structural adjustment (Articles 243–50) emphasize that these policies are intended to promote long-term development in the ACP states, accelerate the growth of output and employment, and be consistent with the political and economic model of the ACP state in question. Adjustment has to be economically viable and socially and politically bearable. These are ambitious objectives, the achievement of which cannot be taken for granted. The record of structural adjustment programmes is mixed, to say the least, and, although the EU argues that it will be pragmatic and realistic in its approach, only time will tell whether this will ensure success.

The revised Lomé IV Convention makes reference to the use of structural adjustment resources to encourage regional integration efforts and to support reforms leading to intra-regional economic liberalization. Support will be given to the harmonization and coordination of macroeconomic and sectoral policies to fulfil the dual aim of regional integration and structural reform at the national level (Article 243).

Trade and commodities

It is important to keep in mind that trade policy, though not of direct concern in this chapter, probably has a greater economic impact on the ACP states than development cooperation policy *per se* ('Trade not Aid' has been a slogan popular in the Third World for many years). The ACP states enjoy free access to the EU market for the majority of their agricultural and manufactured products. These agreements were extended and strengthened in Lomé IV and there was also increased support for processing, marketing, distribution, and transport activities.

The revised Lomé IV Convention signals an important change of emphasis, however, with two new Articles (6a and 15a). Article 6a emphasizes the importance of trade in the development process and states that adequate resources should be devoted to the expansion of ACP trade. Article 15a states that trade development shall be aimed at 'developing, diversifying and increasing the ACP States' trade and improving their competitiveness in their domestic markets, the regional and intra-ACP market, and in the Community and international markets'. In other words, although concessionality remains important as far as EU–ACP trade is concerned, in future the focus is on the development of competitiveness of ACP exports.

Stabex

An important element in the Lomé Conventions has been Stabex (System for the Stabilization of Export Earnings). The basic aim of Stabex has not changed over the four Conventions. That aim is to remedy: 'the harmful effects of the instability of export earnings and to help the ACP states overcome one of the main obstacles to the stability, profitability and to enable them in this way to ensure economic and social progress for their peoples by helping to safeguard their purchasing power' (Article 186(1)). When it was introduced in 1975, the Stabex system was welcomed for its innovatory approach, its simplicity of operation, and the relatively rapid transfers that it provided. The ACP states supported Stabex, seeing it as providing them with soft (untied) aid inflows which were less troublesome than project aid and which, for the smaller ACP states, often provided quite significant amounts of foreign exchange.

Stabex under Lomé I and II was virtually unique as a scheme of development assistance. It had no specifically prescribed end-use, there was no formal conditionality, and it was not procurement-tied. Hewitt (1983) evaluated a sample of Stabex transfers over its first five-year period of operation (Lomé I) and during the first two years of Lomé II.

Frederick Nixson

His conclusions were in general positive, although only a relatively small proportion of the $US200 million disbursed had been used directly in favour of the export crop or commodity that had triggered the claim.

Lomé III saw a change with respect to conditionality and specified that transfers were to be devoted to maintaining financial flows in affected sectors or 'for the purpose of promoting diversification, directed towards other appropriate sectors and used for economic and social development' (Article 147(2)). These changes were in part a reflection of the EU's concern with policy dialogue and structural adjustment referred to above. Lomé IV has seen a further tightening of conditionality, with respect to the uses to which transfers can be put, although it has been extended to include new products, and there are a number of other changes to make it more flexible and fairer to recipients.

Stabex can be drawn upon by any ACP states. It applies to the earnings from an ACP state's exports of the products covered by Stabex if, during the year preceding the year of application, earnings from the export of each product to all destinations represent at least 5 per cent of total export earnings (this is the so-called 'dependency threshold'). For the least developed, landlocked, and island states, the figure is 1 per cent. The reference level against which the shortfall in export earnings is measured is taken to be the average of export earnings during the previous six years (less the two years with the highest and lowest figures). The transfer basis (that is the amount to be reimbursed to the ACP state) is the difference between the reference level and the actual earnings in the year of application, minus an amount corresponding to 4.5 per cent of the reference level (in the case of the least-developed ACP states, this figure is 1 per cent).

There were other changes in the technical details of Stabex under Lomé IV as compared to Lomé III, but for the purposes of the present discussion what is important are the changes in conditionality. The sector that records the loss of export earnings must be given priority, although the concept of 'sector' is a wide one and includes production, processing, marketing, distribution, and transport activities within it. Diversification into other productive activities within the agricultural sector is permitted once difficulties in the sector that triggered the claim are overcome.

However, the revised Lomé IV Convention makes one important change in this respect. Article 209(4) states that, where there is a structural adjustment programme in place, including operations designed to restructure production and export activities or to achieve diversification, Stabex monies may be used in conformity with these efforts and in order to support any consistent reform policy.

Stabex transfers by product are detailed in Table 15.10. It can be clearly seen that coffee has been the majority beneficiary of the system, taking 34 per cent of Stabex transfers over Lomé I–III. For the first time since 1975, there were no Stabex transfers in 1992. Although thirty-two countries should have had transfers, only Ecu 33 million left over from 1992 payments were in fact paid out. It was anticipated that 'catching up' would require large Stabex transfers in 1994 and subsequent years.

Table 15.10. Stabex transfers by product, 1975–1989

Product/group products	Lomé III (1985–9)		Lomé I–III 1975–89	
	Allocated amounts (Ecu)	% of the total	Allocated amounts (Ecu)	% of the total
Coffee	589,494,410	40.40	850,571,356	33.78
Groundnuts	168,023,123	11.52	440,641,445	17.50
Cocoa/cocoa products	203,908,818	13.92	353,456,761	14.04
Cotton	84,611,974	5.80	164,505,748	6.53
Timber	107,111,119	7.34	147,493,817	5.86
Coco–copra products	101,336,328	6.95	143,532,914	5.70
Palm–oil products	77,727,124	5.33	92,239,282	3.66
Iron ore			61,789,536	2.45
Tea	45,905,104	3.15	56,531,537	2.24
Oil cakes	20,848,292	1.43	52,434,242	2.08
Others	60,894,295	4.16	156,927,537	6.16
TOTAL	1,459,050,587	100.00	2,518,224,175	100.00

Source: Courier (1992a).

Sysmin

This is a special facility set up for those ACP states whose mining sectors occupy an important place in their economies and which are facing difficulties—technical, economic, or political—beyond the control of the state or the undertaking concerned. When such difficulties threaten the viability of the undertaking, leading to a significant fall in revenue for the ACP state, financial assistance will be made available, either to re-establish or to rationalize, at a viable level, production and export capacity, or to be used to encourage conversion or diversification of projects or programmes (full details are given in Lomé IV, Title II, chapter 3, Articles 214–19, reprinted in *Courier* (1996)).

It covers copper, phosphates, manganese, bauxite and alumina, tin iron ore, and uranium (and, in certain circumstances, gold). The record of Sysmin under Lomé III was disappointing, and steps have been taken in Lomé IV to simplify and improve its functioning. Its key concerns are viability and diversification. Sysmin operations will also be possible where an ACP state's export earnings suffer as a result of disruption but without the viability of the mining sector necessarily being affected.

Sysmin activities have expanded in the early-1990s, with eighty-six payments worth Ecu 64 million made in 1993. With persistent crises in the mining sector of many ACP member states, it is felt that Sysmin is bound to go on growing (*Courier* 1994: 9).

The European Development Fund (EDF)

The financial resources which the EU makes available for development projects in the ACP states are channelled through the EDF. As can be seen in Table 15.9, the EDF has Ecu 12,927 million to disburse over the period 1995–2000.

All EDF financial transfers are now in the form of grants so as not to add to their burden of debt. Table 15.11 gives details of the sectoral distribution of EDF aid for Lomé II and III. It can be seen that high priority has been attached to rural development under Lomé III, with an almost doubling of the absolute amount of aid made available, and an increase in its share of total aid from just under 25 per cent to approximately 30 per cent. The aid share allocated to transport and communications has fallen, explained in part by a deliberate shift away from this sector (especially aid assistance for roads and bridges). The decline in the share of the industrial sector is in part a reflection of earlier difficulties experienced with Sysmin.

Table 15.11. **Sectoral breakdown of EDF aid approved up to 30 June 1991**

Sectors	Lomé II		Lomé III	
	Ecu m.	%	Ecu m.	%
Rural production	1,133	24.7	2,092	29.8
Transport and communication	833	18.2	1,092	15.4
Industry	916	20.0	798	11.4
Health, social development, and water engineering	677	14.8	521	7.5
Stabex	630	13.7	1,436	20.5
Others[a]	393	8.6	1,089	15.5
TOTAL	4,582	100.00	7,028	100.0

[a] Includes emergency aid, aid to refugees, trade promotion, and various smaller sectors.

Source: Courier (1992a).

Health, social development, and water engineering have also experienced both an absolute fall and a fall in their share of total aid. In health, there has been greater emphasis on operational expenditure (technical assistance, training, and operational costs) and on health campaigns, and less on the financing of infrastructure (construction and equipment). The social sector and water engineering have in part received less because large multi-component programmes in the rural sector now include both the social dimension and water-engineering sector expenditures.

The EDF programming and implementation cycle is longer than the standard five-year Lomé Convention period. The Commission thus has to manage various Funds, at different stages of development, at the same time. Operations set up under the 5th EDF

(Lomé II, 1979) and the 6th EDF (Lomé III, 1984) were still in the course of financing in 1992. Lomé IV has been in operation since 1990, but it was only in 1993 that the 7th EDF payments exceeded those of the 6th EDF.

Data on the sectoral breakdown of Lomé IV aid are not yet available. The available evidence however suggests a move away from the agricultural sector to the benefit of the social sector, especially health and education, and the modernization of administration. A breakdown of aid focusing on technical sector rather than sectoral distribution shows transport and communications infrastructure, water supplies and drainage, the environment and institutional support in the lead (*Courier* 1994: 9). The change is not in the target sectors themselves but in the technical means used to reach those targets, a shift which serves to highlight the support offered for the ACPs' structural adjustment process.

Stabex transfers have increased as a proportion of the total (from 14 to 21 per cent approximately) and there are a number of new instruments classified under 'others'. These include quick disbursing import programmes, so-called 'thematic actions'—especially against desertification, drought, and national disasters, aid to refugees, and increased support for trade promotion.

The financial provisions for development aid assistance by the EIB are shown separately in Table 15.9. The EIB's contribution to aid takes the form of loans at market rates, which are reduced by means of EDF aid (amounting to Ecu 1,200 million under Lomé IV) to between 3 and 6 per cent per annum. EIB lending has gone mainly to help in financing infrastructure development, although there has been a decline in that sector's share, with a corresponding increase in lending to the energy sector. In the industrial sector, there has been a shift in lending away from large industrial projects towards support for small and medium-sized projects, reflecting the EIB's commitment to promoting the small and medium-sized private enterprise sector, through local financial intermediaries (investment corporations, development banks and so on).

The geographical distribution of EU aid

Tables 15.12 and 15.13 give an indication of which ACP states receive the most European aid through the EDF and Stabex.

With respect to the distribution of payments by the EDF, it can be seen that the 'top ten' recipients, all from Sub-Saharan Africa, received over 41 per cent of the total over the period 1960–88. Francophone countries received approximately three-quarters of the total funding accounted for by the 'top ten'.

The EU agrees upon a 'National Indicative Programme' with each ACP state, but the allocation of aid between the ACP states is decided upon by the EU unilaterally and according to its own, unpublished criteria. Statistical analysis (Anyadike-Danes and Anyadike-Danes 1992) suggested that, although population and per capita income were important criteria, as too was the special status accorded to the 'least developed'

Frederick Nixson

Table 15.12. **Total European development funds: breakdown of cumulative payments by beneficiary country, 1960–1986**

Country	Total (Ecu m.)	% of total
Senegal	471.7	6.0
Zaire	401.6	5.1
Côte d'Ivoire	342.5	4.4
Madagascar	337.8	4.3
Sudan	322.1	4.1
Cameroon	309.8	3.9
Ethiopia	300.7	3.8
Mali	283.9	3.6
Niger	278.2	3.5
Tanzania	224.8	2.9
Sub-total	3,273.1	41.7
TOTAL ACP	7,850.9	100.0

Source: Eurostat (1988: 208).

Table 15.13. **Geographical distribution of Stabex transfers, 1975–1985**

Country	Total (Ecu m.)	% of total
Senegal	237.8	16.0
Côte d'Ivoire	158.3	10.6
Sudan	142.5	9.6
Papua New Guinea	97.1	6.5
Ghana	90.6	6.1
Ethiopia	60.2	4.0
Tanzania	50.5	3.4
Kenya	44.9	3.0
Togo	42.2	2.8
Mauritania	37.0	2.5
Sub-total	961.1	64.5
TOTAL Transfers	1,487.8	100.0

Source: Eurostat (1988: 210).

ACP states, African ACP states on average benefited more than non-African members, and Lomé aid allocations were influenced by pre-Lomé associations with the EC (the AASM members).

The geographical distribution of Stabex transfers, shown in Table 15.13, is 'easier' to explain, depending as it does on the export performance of the commodities covered by the scheme. However, African economies are the major beneficiaries (Senegal and Côte d'Ivoire accounted for over one-quarter of total transfers over the period 1975–85) and Papua New Guinea is the only non-African recipient in the 'top ten'.

The French commitment to Africa, in particular, is very strong, and reflects the notion of 'Eurafricanism'—the idea that Europe and Africa are organic complements for one another (Lister 1992). Others might interpret the relationship as one of dependency and domination.

15.6. Conclusions

As Panic (1992) has noted, few countries have had as much experience with foreign aid as the Member States of the EU. They were large recipients of aid during and after the Second World War (both relief aid and assistance under the Marshall Plan). With post-war reconstruction complete, they have become the most important donors of ODA, along with the USA and Japan.

As we have argued above, all aid, and the aid relationship itself, is open to criticism, and EU aid is no exception in this respect. The size, nature, and the effectiveness of EU ODA have been subject to criticism, not least because of the long lags between commitment and actual disbursement.[6] The EU aid programme, in addition, has been attacked 'for its failure to carry out adequate preliminary studies and to adapt projects to local conditions' (Panic 1992: 12).

The EU itself (*Courier* 1994: 10) notes the contradictions between political trends in some ACPs and the demands of Lomé IV, where Article 5 emphasizes the importance of respect for human rights, democratic principles, and the rule of law. At the end of 1993, seven countries—Haiti, Liberia, Somalia, Zaire, Sudan, Togo, and Equatorial Guinea—faced aid sanctions, and a number of other countries suffered provisional suspension or slowing down of aid.

Credit has also been suspended when countries eligible for structural adjustment support were forced to drop reform policies because of economic difficulties. As of 1993, only fourteen of a potential thirty-eight recipients managed to obtain EU structural adjustment finance (*Courier* 1994: 10).

These criticisms are not unique to EU ODA and by international standards the EU is not a 'bad' donor. In the Lomé IV Convention, there are provisions for the more systematic and independent assessment of projects and for greater preference to be given to local enterprises in carrying out those projects. There is a desire to increase aid coordination between Member States (see below) and to give greater attention to the longer-term viability of EU ODA-funded projects.

Frederick Nixson

The impact of 1992 on development cooperation

The Single European Market (SEM) is likely to have a profound impact on Third World countries in general and the ACP states in particular. LDCs will be affected by growth and trade policy changes implied by the EU's internal-market programme, and there are implications too for issues such as direct foreign investment and international migration (Koekkoek, Kuyvenhoven, and Molle 1990).

There are, however, no direct references to development aid in the plan to complete the SEM. Stevens (1992) nevertheless outlines four main reasons why '1992' could have an effect both on the absolute amount of aid and its distribution.

1. Procurement: it would be logical to extend current moves to open government procurement so that all Member States can tender for aid contracts from any individual Member State (that is, the abolition of tying aid by source within the EU). Greater competition between Member States for aid contracts would, other things being equal, increase the value of aid.

2. Aid volume: if procurement-tying was abolished, aid volumes might fall (Member States could no longer use aid programmes to support domestic industries, for example).

3. Aid channels: more open procurement could lead to a greater proportion of Member States' ODA being channelled through multilateral institutions, including EU institutions (although there is no guarantee that multilateral aid will always avoid the drawbacks of bilateral ODA (Panic 1992: 17)).

4. Aid diversion: this has both intra- and extra-EU dimensions; intra-EU in that there may be a diversion of budgetary expenditures towards Member States adversely affected by the creation of the SEM (that is, away from ODA); extra-EU in that there may be a tendency to offer additional ODA to those LDCs most adversely affected by other consequences of the SEM (towards the Caribbean and the Mediterranean states, for example).

As yet, there has not been a significant diversion of aid from the LDCs towards Central and Eastern Europe and Russia, and financial aid to those areas is additional to conventional development aid (Stevens 1992: 30). In the medium term, however, Stevens suggests that the boundary between middle-income LDCs and Eastern Europe states may become blurred, and there is certainly concern amongst Third World aid recipients that such diversion may occur increasingly in the future.

Panic (1992) concludes that only if the SEM succeeds in raising and in equalizing the efficiency and income levels of Member States will it have a significant effect on ODA, but that 'whether individual Governments like it or not, the successful creation of the SEM would represent the first step towards much greater political as well as economic unification in Western Europe; and this would bring about a major shift in the Community's ODA in favour of centralised development assistance policies' (1992: 16).

Towards the year 2000

The Commission itself has highlighted some of these issues in its own development policy statements (see *Courier* 1992*b*).

It points to the lack of coordination between national and EU development cooperation policies, the lack of consistency between the latter and other EU policies, and the lack of a 'European expression and stimulus' in international bodies.

Article 130X (Title XVII) of the Treaty on European Union (TEU), provides for the coordination of development cooperation policies and for consultation between Member States and the EU on aid programmes. The objectives of development cooperation policy are to 'encourage the consolidation of democracy within the developing countries, within the framework of a return to political stability'. The aims of Article 130U(1) of the TEU are to ensure that

- the developing countries, especially the least developed, have lasting economic and social development;
- the developing countries gradually and harmoniously fit into the international economy; and
- poverty in the developing countries is combated.

With respect to regional variations in policy:

- Sub-Saharan Africa: EU priority support will go to policies aimed at economic restructuring and the democratic reform of the administration of those countries.
- The Mediterranean: emphasis will be placed on technical assistance to strengthen institutional reform and regional and economic cooperation.
- Latin America: emphasis will be on policy dialogue and the promotion of investment and the private sector.
- Asia: emphasis will be on boosting the EU's presence in the region (through trade and investment) and on increasing awareness of environmental issues. The least developed countries will continue to receive conventional development aid.

Pious exhortation and vague policy statements do not, of course, make for good development cooperation policies. The creation of the SEM and the coming into force of the TEU have brought about changes which will affect the different regions and countries of the Third World in different, and unpredictable, ways. The move to more aid being made available through multilateral channels is not unambiguously beneficial to recipients if at the same time it is accompanied by greater (and perhaps inappropriate or unacceptable) conditionality. The bilateral aid programmes of EU Member States will continue to be of importance, and it would be foolish to predict likely future changes in those programmes. Much will continue to depend on the quality of the aid relationship between donors and recipients and, more widely, on the overall development relationship, which will include issues of trade policy, market access, non-concessional resource transfers, and broader questions such as environmental concerns and international migration.

Discussion questions

1. Compare and contrast the record of the major EU aid donors during the 1990s.
2. What are the main factors which influence the 'aid relationship' between EU donors and ACP recipients?
3. Discuss the main changes that have occurred over time in the four Lomé Conventions. In what ways do the provisions of Lomé IV reflect changes in development policy in the 1980s?

FURTHER READING

DAC aid statistics are presented in the OECD *Development Co-operation Report*, published annually. This is the standard reference and also includes discussions of current aid and development issues. Cassen *et al.* (1986) and Mosley (1987) contain excellent general discussions of aid and its relation to development. Hewitt (1983) is an invaluable reference on the first years of Stabex. The full text of the Lomé IV Convention is to be found in the *Courier* (1996).

NOTES

1. More recent work carried out by Mosley and Hudson (forthcoming) for the Overseas Development Administration reaches more positive conclusions. In a test of aid impact based on time series rather than cross-section techniques, aid effectiveness emerges as having a positive and 'just significant' influence in the nineteen aid recipient countries sampled. The measured effectiveness of aid appears to have improved significantly since the early 1980s. Aid achieves a significant influence on investment and under-fives mortality. Also noted are the importance of the long term stock of aid, the higher levels of effectiveness of aid in poorer LDCs and the major negative influence of war and conflict on aid effectiveness.
2. Arguably, the EU's relations with non-members Mediterranean states now have a higher priority than those with ACP states. During the last round of negotiations revising Lomé IV in 1995, most EU Member States would only agree the aid package for ACP once they were satisfied that the aid allocations to Eastern Europe and the Mediterranean were adequate (Pariff 1996).
3. The comparable figures for the USA and Japan are 26.6% and 29.2% respectively.
4. The comparable figure for Japan in 1993 was 69%; the figure for the USA (1992) was 25.9%. Clearly there are significant differences in donor tying practices.
5. In 1994, the European Commission disbursed $US1.235 million of official aid for Part II countries, of which $US870 million went to CEECs and $US365 million to NIS (OECD 1995: 107).

6. There are 20–30 months between the submission of a project and the financing decision and even more between the financial decision and disbursement. In 1992 the Commission agreed on a new method of project cycle management and started using it in 1993 (the 'integrated approach').

REFERENCES

Anyadike-Danes, M. K., and Anyadike-Danes, M. N. (1992), 'The Geographic Allocation of the European Development Fund under the Lomé Conventions', *World Development*, 20/11 (Nov.), 1647–61.

Bhagwati, J. (1967), 'The Tying of Aid', UNCTAD Secretariat, TD/7/Supp. 4, United Nations; repr. in J. Bhagwati and R. S. Eckaus (eds.) *Foreign Aid* (Harmondsworth: Penguin, 1970), 235–93.

Cassen, R. *et al.* (1986), *Does Aid Work?* (Oxford: Clarendon Press).

CEC (1990): Commission of the European Communities, *The Community Budget: The Facts in Figures*, 3rd edn. (Luxembourg: CEC).

—— Directorate-General for Development (1992), *The Role of the Commission in Supporting Structural Adjustment in ACP States* (Luxembourg: SEC).

Courier (1990), 120 (Mar.–Apr., Brussels).

—— (1992*a*), 132 (Mar.–Apr., Brussels).

—— (1992*b*), 134 (July–Aug., Brussels).

—— (1994), 145 (May–June, Brussels).

—— (1996), 155 (Jan.–Feb., Brussels).

Eurostat (1988), *ACP Basic Statistics* (Luxembourg).

Frisch, D. (1992), 'The European Community's Development Policy in a Changing World', the Second Bradford Development Lecture, Oct., mimeo.

Glaser, T. (1990), 'EEC–ACP Cooperation: The Historical Perspective', *Courier*, 120 (Mar.–Apr.), 24–8.

Hewitt, A. (1983), 'Stabex: An Evaluation of the Economic Impact over the First Five Years', *World Development*, 11/2 (Dec.), 1005–27.

Koekkoek, A., Kuyvenhoven, A., and Molle, W. (1990), 'Europe 1992 and the Developing Countries: An Overview', *Journal of Common Market Studies*, 29/2 (Dec.), 111–31.

Lister, M. R. P. (1992), 'The European Community and Africa: A Development Regime', paper presented to Annual Conference, Development Studies Association, Nottingham, mimeo.

Mosley, P. (1987), *Overseas Aid: Its Defence and Reform* (Brighton: Wheatsheaf).

—— (1991), 'Structural Adjustment: A General Overview, 1980–9', in V. N. Balasubramanyam and S. Lall (eds.), *Current Issues in Development Economics* (Basingstoke: Macmillan), 223–42.

—— and Hudson, J. (forthcoming), *Aid Effectiveness: A Study of the Effectiveness of Overseas Aid in the Main Countries Receiving ODA Assistance* (University of Reading).

OECD (1991): Organization for Economic Cooperation and Development, *Development Cooperation: 1991 Report* (Paris: OECD).

—— (1992), *Development Cooperation: 1992 Report* (Paris: OECD).

—— (1995): *Development Cooperation: 1995 Report* (Paris: OECD).

Panic, M. (1992), 'The Single Market and Official Development Assistance: The Potential for Multilateralizing and Raising EU Assistance', *Journal of Development Planning*, 22 (New York: United Nations), 3–17.

Parfitt, T. (1996), 'An Analysis of the Euromed Relationship with Special Reference to Egypt', paper presented to Conference on Restructuring Egypt: Policies, Implications and Strategies, University of Manchester, May, mimeo.

Riddell, R. (1987), *Foreign Aid Reconsidered* (London: James Curry).

Singer, H. (1965), 'External Aid: For Plans or Projects?', *Economic Journal*, 75: 539–45; repr. in J. Bhagwati and R. S. Eckaus (eds.), *Foreign Aid* (Harmondsworth: Penguin, 1970), 294–302.

Stevens, C. (1990), 'The Lomé Convention', in K. Kiljunen (ed.), *Region-to-Region Cooperation between Developed and Developing Countries: The Potential for Mini NIEO* (Aldershot: Avebury, Gower Publishing Co.), 77–88.

—— (1992), 'The Single Market, All-European Integration and the Developing Countries: The Potential for Aid Diversion', *Journal of Development Planning*, 22: 19–35.

White, H. (1992), 'The Macroeconomic Impact of Development Aid: A Critical Survey', *Journal of Development Studies*, 28/2 (Jan.), 163–240.

INDEX

Index

Index

Index

430

Index

432

Index

Index

Index